Index
to
Loudoun County, Virginia
Land Deed Books
3N-3V
1826-1831

Patricia B. Duncan

WILLOW BEND BOOKS
2006

WILLOW BEND BOOKS
AN IMPRINT OF HERITAGE BOOKS, INC.

Books, CDs, and more—Worldwide

For our listing of thousands of titles see our website
at
www.HeritageBooks.com

Published 2006 by
HERITAGE BOOKS, INC.
Publishing Division
65 East Main Street
Westminster, Maryland 21157-5026

International Standard Book Number: 978-0-7884-4003-9

Introduction

The following is an extended index to Loudoun County, Virginia Deed Books 3N-3V. In addition to providing the basic information of book:page number, the date of the document, the date received in court, parties involved, and type of document, I have also included a brief description of the item, including adjoining neighbors, and witnesses.

Microfilms of these records are currently available from the Library of Virginia Interlibrary Loan Service. Copies of the documents may be obtained from the Office of Clerk of Circuit Court County of Loudoun, Box 550, Leesburg, VA 20178-0550.

Abbreviations:
 Admr - Administrator
 A/L – Assignment of lease
 AlexDC – Alexandria, District of Columbia
 B/S – Bargain and sale
 BaltMd – Baltimore, Maryland
 beq. - bequeathed
 BerkVa – Berkeley County, Virginia
 BoS - Bill of sale
 br/o – brother of
 CamP – Cameron Parish in Loudoun
 ChstrPa – Chester County, Pennsylvania
 CoE - Certificate of examination [of wife]
 CoI – certificate of importation [for slaves]
 Commr - commissioner
 cnvy/b – conveyed by (to person now selling the land)
 dau – daughter
 DBk letter(s):numbers - deed book:page
 delv. – examined and delivered to
 dev. – devised to
 div. – division (of estate of)
 d/o - daughter of
 DoE – Deed of Emancipation [for slaves]
 Exor – Executor
 Ffx – Fairfax County, Virginia
 Fqr – Fauquier County, Virginia
 FrdkMd – Frederick County, Maryland
 FrdkVa – Frederick County, Virginia
 Gent. – gentleman
 h/o - husband of
 HdnNJ – Hunterdon County, New Jersey
 Hllb - Hillsborough
 int. - interest

KingG – King George County, Virginia
L/L – Lease for life
L/R – Lease/release
Ldn – Loudoun County, Virginia
Lsbg - Leesburg
Mdbg – Middleburg
MontMd – Montgomery County, Maryland
[number]a = number of acres
PhilPa – Philadelphia County, Pa
PoA – Power of attorney
PrG – Prince George County, Maryland
PrWm – Prince William County, Virginia
prch/o – purchased of
RichVa – Richmond County, Virginia
RtCt – returned to court and ordered to be recorded
S/L – Surrender of lease
s/o - son of
ShelP – Shelburne Parish in Loudoun
StafVa – Stafford County, Virginia
und. - undivided
w/o - wife of
WashDC – Washington, D. C.
WashMd – Washington County, Maryland
wd/o – widow of
WstmVa – Westmoreland County, Virginia

Loudoun Co Deed Books 3N-3V

3N:001 Date: 7 Oct 1826 RtCt: 7 Oct 1826
Craven OSBURNE (trustee of Lewis ELLZEY for benefit of Joshua OSBURNE, Nov 1825) to Joshua OSBURNE. B/S of 300a 'Locust Thicket' and 'White Oak Bottom' occupied by Mahlon MORRIS under LS. Delv. to Joshua OSBURN 6 Jul 1833.

3N:002 Date: 28 Sep 1826 RtCt: 7 Oct 1826
James McDANIEL & wife Ann of Ldn to Townshend McVEIGH. Trust for debt to Edwin C. BROWN using Lot #15 in Mdbg. Wit: Burr POWELL, A. GIBSON. Delv. to BROWN 17 Jul 1827.

3N:003 Date: 13 Sep 1824 RtCt: 7 Oct 1826
Herod OSBURN of Ldn to Norval OSBURNE of Ldn. B/S of 5/9ths of 147a and 110 formerly owned and occupied by Nathan POTTS dec'd. Delv. to Norval 12 Nov 1836.

3N:005 Date: 14 Sep 1826 RtCt: 9 Oct 1826
Thomas J. NOLAND of Ldn to William NOLAND of Independence Co, Arkansas Territory. B/S of four ½a lots on Mercer St. in Aldie (conveyed in trust by Thomas H. KIRBY in Apr 1820).

3N:006 Date: 28 Sep 1826 RtCt: 9 Oct 1826
David McMULLEN & wife Barbara of Ldn to William HOGE of Ldn. B/S of 7a (devised from father Alexander McMULLEN dec'd). Wit: John SIMPSON, Thomas ROGERS. Delv. to B. F. TAYLOR pr order of Exor 22 Dec 1849.

3N:008 Date: 30 Sep 1826 RtCt: 9 Oct 1826
William HOGUE & wife Mary of Ldn to Daniel McMULLEN of Ldn. B/S of 5a (John WYNN prch/o Joseph HAINS) adj William WILKINSON and another lot of 2 roods. Wit: John SIMPSON, Thomas ROGERS.

3N:010 Date: 15 Sep 1826 RtCt: 9 Oct 1826
Enoch, Mahlon, Ephraim, Eli L., John and Daniel SCHOOLEY of Ldn to Thomas SCHOOLEY of Ldn. B/S of 65a (from tract of Reuben SCHOOLEY dec'd). Delv. to Thomas SCHOOLEY 27 Apr 1827.

3N:011 Date: 15 Sep 1826 RtCt: 9 Oct 1826
Enoch, Ephraim, Eli L., Thomas, John and Daniel SCHOOLEY of Ldn to Mahlon SCHOOLEY of Ldn. B/S of 2½a and 60½a (from tract of Reuben SCHOOLEY dec'd).

3N:013 Date: 15 Sep 1826 RtCt: 9 Oct 1826
Mahlon, Ephraim, Eli L., Thomas, John and Daniel SCHOOLEY of Ldn to Enoch SCHOOLEY of Ldn. B/S of 25½a on road from Lsbg to Wtfd and 7a adj __ MASON, __ GASSAWAY. (from tract of Reuben SCHOOLEY dec'd)

3N:015   Date: 15 Sep 1826   RtCt: 9 Oct 1826
Enoch, Mahlon, Eli L., Thomas, John and Daniel SCHOOLEY of Ldn to Ephraim SCHOOLEY of Ldn. B/S of 73¾a on road from Lsbg to Wtfd (from tract of Reuben SCHOOLEY dec'd) adj __ SANDFORD, __ PEUSEY. Delv. 22 Sep 1834.

3N:017   Date: 15 Sep 1826   RtCt: 9 Oct 1826
Enoch, Ephraim, Mahlon, Thomas, John and Daniel SCHOOLEY of Ldn to Eli L. SCHOOLEY of Ldn. B/S of 26a (from tract of Reuben SCHOOLEY dec'd). Delv. to Eli SCHOOLEY 27 Apr 1827.

3N:018   Date: 15 Sep 1826   RtCt: 9 Oct 1826
Enoch, Ephraim, Eli L., Thomas, Mahlon and Daniel SCHOOLEY of Ldn to John SCHOOLEY of Ldn. B/S of 58a (from tract of Reuben SCHOOLEY dec'd). Delv. to John SCHOOLEY 25 Sep 1834.

3N:019   Date: 15 Sep 1826   RtCt: 9 Oct 1826
Enoch, Ephraim, Eli L., Thomas, John and Mahlon SCHOOLEY of Ldn to Daniel SCHOOLEY of Ldn. B/S of 55a (from tract of Reuben SCHOOLEY dec'd). Delv. to Eli L. SCHOOLEY 28 Sep 1838.

3N:021   Date: 9 Oct 1826   RtCt: __ Oct 1826
Levi CARTER& wife Elizabeth of Ldn to George W. SAGAR of Ldn. B/S of interest in tract from James CARTER dec'd (purchased in 1826 from SAGAR). Wit: Thomas ROGERS, John SIMPSON. Delv. to SAGERS 13 Oct 1827.

3N:022   Date: 14 Oct 1826   RtCt: 16 Oct 1826
Richard H. HENDERSON (trustee of Robert BRADEN, Oct 1822) of Ldn to of Bank of Alexandria. B/S of 150a adj Sandford RAMEY, __ McGARRICK.

3N:023   Date: 28 Sep 1826   RtCt: 16 Oct 1826
Edwin C. BROWN & wife Elizabeth of Ldn to James McDANIEL of Ldn. B/S of ½a Lot #15 in Mdbg. Wit: Burr POWELL, A. GIBSON.

3N:024   Date: 28 Sep 1826   RtCt: 19 Oct 1826
James CARRUTHERS & wife Nancy of Ldn to Levi WHITE of Ldn. B/S of 76a adj William HOLMES. Wit: Samuel M. EDWARDS, John J. MATHIAS. Delv. 29 Jan 1827.

3N:026   Date: 20 Oct 1826   RtCt: 20 Oct 1826
Westwood A. LACEY of Ldn to Charles H. HAMILTON of Ldn. B/S of interest in lot at King and Royal Sts in Lsbg (from father Israel LACEY dec'd) now occupied by Mrs. WHEERY. Delv. to HAMILTON 6 Apr 1832.

3N:027   Date: 28 Aug 1826   RtCt: 20 Oct 1826
George SAUNDERS & wife Elizabeth of Ldn to Joshua PEUSEY and Simon SHOEMAKER Sr. of Ldn. Trust for debt to Thomas WHITE using 72a and land SAUNDERS prch/o John SAUNDERS. Wit: M. JANNEY, Joseph MORRISON, Mortimore McILHANY, George W. SHAWEN. Delv. to WHITE 9 Oct 1827.

3N:031 Date: 23 Aug 1826 RtCt: 21 Oct 1826
John BAYLEY of Ldn to Sampson HUTCHISON of Ldn. B/S of 137a adj George BAYLEY, Reuben HUTCHISON. Delv. to HUTCHISON 4 Jun 1827. Gives plat.

3N:033 Date: __ Oct 1826 RtCt: 24 Oct 1826
Westwood A. LACEY of Ldn to Charles H. [B.] HAMILTON of Ldn. B/S of interest (1/5th from brother John LACEY dec'd who is entitled to 1/7th from Israel LACEY dec'd) in lot at Royal and King Sts in Lsbg. Delv. to Charles B. HAMILTON, Charles H. being mistake 31 Aug 1830.

3N:034 Date: 16 Oct 1826 RtCt: 30 Oct 1826
Joshua PEUSEY of Ldn to Ephraim SCHOOLEY of Ldn. B/S of 2a on Kittocton mt. now occupied by PEUSEY. Delv. to SCHOOLEY 19 Mar 1830.

3N:035 Date: 6 Apr 1826 RtCt: 2 Nov 1826
Joseph SIMPSON blacksmith of Union to Samuel DUNKIN of Union. B/S of ¼a (town lot #1 in division of James REED dec'd allotted to his dau Mary BROWN).

3N:036 Date: 16 Oct 1826 RtCt: 6 Nov 1826
Thomas SWICK & wife Priscilla of Ldn to James BROWN of Ldn. B/S of 38a (conveyed by commrs. of John VANHORNE dec'd to his dau Ann VANHORN). Wit: Edward HALL, Thomas ROGERS. Delv. to BROWN 16 Mar 1831.

3N:038 Date: 1 May 1826 RtCt: 6 Nov 1826
Norval CHAMBLIN of Ldn to William JACOBS of FredVa. BoS for slave male Stephen abt 10y old and interest in negro slaves allotted to his mother by commrs. as her dower as wd/o William CHAMBLIN dec'd.

3N:039 Date: 16 Oct 1826 RtCt: 6 Nov 1826
Ephraim SCHOOLEY of Ldn to Joshua PEUSEY of Ldn. B/S of 1a on Kittocton mt formerly belonging to Reuben SCHOOLEY dec'd and allotted to Ephraim. Delv. 20 Feb 1834.

3N:040 Date: 13 Nov 1826 RtCt: 14 Nov 1826
Fayette BALL to James McILHANY. PoA – Agrees to be security with James McILHANY for Richard H. HENDERSON as Exor of Thomas R. MOTT dec'd.

3N:041 Date: 10 Nov 1826 RtCt: 10 Nov 1826
Norval CHAMBLIN of Ldn to Elijah PEACOCK of Ldn. B/S of house and lot in Wtfd (derived by m. to late Sarah VANDEVANTER).

3N:042 Date: 9 Jun 1826 RtCt: 10 Nov 1826
John WILLIAMS (trustee with Jacob MENDENHALL of John LIVINGSTON, May 1818) to Mahlon SCHOOLEY. B/S of ½a lot with house and shop on Second St in Wtfd. Delv. pr order 28 Dec 1827.

3N:043 Date: 13 Nov 1826 RtCt: 13 Nov 1826
Peter C. RUST, William GILMORE and John WILKERSON. Bond on RUST as constable.

3N:044 Date: 13 Nov 1826 RtCt: 13 Nov 1826
Peyton POWELL and William GILLMORE. Bond on POWELL as constable.

3N:044 Date: 13 Nov 1826 RtCt: 13 Nov 1826
Charles DUNCAN, Benjamin BRIDGES and Lewellen HUTCHISON. Bond on DUNCAN as constable.

3N:045 Date: 13 Nov 1826 RtCt: 13 Nov 1826
George RICHARDS and John ROSE to Pres. and Directors of Literary Fund. Bond on RICHARDS as treasurer.

3N:046 Date: 11 Nov 1826 RtCt: 11 Nov 1826
Norval CHAMBLIN & wife Sarah of Ldn to Israel T. GRIFFITH of Ldn. B/S of 24a and 3a (conveyed by Henry PLAISTER Jun 1826 and by CHAMBLIN in trust to Price JACOBS) adj Jonah TAVENER, James BROWN. Delv. to GRIFFITH 8 Sep 1828.

3N:047 Date: 22 Mar 1826 RtCt: 13 Nov 1826
John AXLINE Jr. & wife Christina of Ldn to Charles SACHMON of Ldn. B/S of 4a (prch/o Henry AXLINE). Wit: John HAMILTON, George W. SHAWEN.

3N:048 Date: 10 Nov 1826 RtCt: 13 Nov 1826
William TOMLINSON wife Caroline of Ldn to Samuel HOGUE of Ldn. B/S of interest in land nr North Fork Meeting House of William TOMLINSON Sr. dec'd. Wit: William CARR, John SIMPSON. Delv. pr order 28 Mar 1836.

3N:049 Date: 13 Nov 1826 RtCt: 13 Nov 1826
Dpty James H. McVEIGH for Shff Ludwell LEE (from insolvent debtor John WINN) to William HOGUE. B/S of farm animals, household and personal items at sale of 8 Sep 1826.

3N:050 Date: 7 Aug 1826 RtCt: 13 Nov 1826
Robert A. LACEY of Warren Co Ky to Neoima LACEY, Huldah LACEY and Ruth LACEY of Ldn. B/S of interest in estate of Tracey [Tacey?] LACEY dec'd and interest he had from John LACEY dec'd in estate of Tracey LACEY.

3N:052 Date: 11 Sep 1826 RtCt: 13 Nov 1826
Dpty James H. McVEIGH for Shff Ludwell LEE (from insolvent debtor John WINN) to William HOGUE. B/S of 109a adj Stephen McPHERSON, Enoch FRANCIS. Delv. to HOGE 6 Jan 1831.

3N:053 Date: 1 Nov 1826 RtCt: 14 Nov 1826
William A. BINNS of Ldn to John A BINNS of Ldn. Trust for debt to Catharine A. DURHAM using 200a (devised by father Charles BINNS).

3N:054 Date: 27 Sep 1826 RtCt: 16 Nov 1826
Noble BEVERIDGE of Ldn to Ann C. HERRIFORD wd/o Francis
HERRIFORD dec'd, Mary A. B. HERRIFORD, Margaret A.
HERRIFORD and John B. HERRIFORD (ch/o Francis dec'd) of Fqr.
B/S of 250a nr Bull Run mt. late in occupancy of Rawleigh GREEN.

3N:056 Date: 16 Oct 1826 RtCt: 16 Nov 1826
Ann C. HERRIFORD, Mary A. B. HERRIFORD, Margaret A.
HERRIFORD & John B. HERRIFORD of Fqr to Benjamin R. LACEY
of Ldn. B/S of 150a adj Major POWELL, __ TALBOTT. Delv. to
LACEY 3 Nov 1828.

3N:057 Date: 18 Nov 1826 RtCt: 18 Nov 1826
Henry Moore DAVIS and dau Jane H. DAVIS of Hardy Co Va to
Henry SAUNDERS (Capt. of U.S. Army). B/S of lot and house in
Lsbg at present occupied by John LYON and the widow DYKES.
Delv. to SAUNDERS 5 Oct 1846?.

3N:059 Date: 9 Oct 1826 RtCt: 16 Oct 1826
George SAGARS of Ldn to John HOLMES of Ldn. Trust for debt to
Valentine HIBBS using interest in land of James CARTER dec'd late
of Ldn.

3N:059 Date: 5 Jul 1826 RtCt: 23 Mar 1826
Betty LEWIS wd/o John LEWIS dec'd of Ldn to Rebecca LEWIS.
Relinquishes right of dower to land conveyed by husband.

3N:060 Date: 22 Nov 1826 RtCt: 23 Nov 1826
Thomas H. LUCKETT to Lloyd NOLAND and Henry Fenton
LUCKETT. Trust for Thomas as Exor of Elizabeth NOLAND dec'd
(bonds by Elizabeth to Samuel CLAPHAM) using slaves Jim & wife
Sarah, Rosetta & her 3 children Sarah Ann, Frank & infant child,
farm and household items.

3N:062 Date: 3 Sep 1826 RtCt: 1 Dec 1826
Aaron MILLER & wife Mary of Ldn to George GRIMES of Ldn. B/S
of 1½a adj Archibald MORRISON. Wit: George W. SHAWEN,
Mortimore McILHANY.

3N:063 Date: 4 Apr 1826 RtCt: 2 Dec 1826
Jonathan EWERS & wife Mary of Ldn to Andrew HESSER of Ldn.
B/S of 1a adj Isaac NICHOLS, Thomas EWERS. Wit: Notley C.
WILLIAMS, Thomas NICHOLS. Delv. to HESSER 29 Dec 1835.

3N:065 Date: 3 Oct 1826 RtCt: 3 Dec 1826
Joseph WOOD & wife Lydia of Ldn to Thomas WHITE and Robert
MOFFETT of Ldn. Trust for debt to Joshua PEUSEY using 80a with
several exceptions (prch/o Exors of Mahlon JANNEY dec'd, Mar
1817) adj Joseph TALBOT, Jonas POTTS, M. SULLIVAN, Stephen
BALL, Benjamin STEER, new addition to Wtfd. Wit: Noble S.
BRADEN, Presley CORDELL. Delv. to PUSEY 20 May 1828.

3N:068   Date: 5 Dec 1826   RtCt: 5 Dec 1826
John UNDERWOOD to Everitt SAUNDERS. Trust for W. C. SELDON Jr. as security using negro man Peter aged abt 45y, boy Truman aged abt 14y, farm items.

3N:070   Date: 7 Jun 1826   RtCt: 5 Dec 1826
Thomas CHINN & wife Ann to Elias CHINN. B/S of interest in land allotted to Frances CHINN now dec'd (died intestate) adj Town'd McVEIGH, Sythy ATWELL, Silas BEATTY (see deed of Thomas CHINN to Nancy, Catherine, Patty, Francis & Elias CHINN). Wit: Burr POWELL, A. GIBSON.

3N:071   Date: 16 Jul 1819   RtCt: 6 Dec 1826
A. G. MONROE. Receipt for last payment due from Capt. John ROSE for guardianship acct for his wife Mrs. Bithiny MONROE.

3N:071   Date: 2 Nov 1826   RtCt: 8 Dec 1826
George COOPER, Jacob COOPER & wife Mary, John COOPER & wife Mary/Magdalena and William COOPER of Ldn to John COMFER of Ldn. B/S of 58a adj Anthony SOUDER. Wit: Alex CORDELL, George VINSELL, George SMITH, George W. SHAWEN, Presley CORDELL. Delv. to COMPHER 25 May 1827.

3N:073   Date: 19 Aug 1826   RtCt: 11 Dec 1826
John WILDMAN dec'd. Renouncement of will by widow Eleanor WILDMAN on 18 Mar 1826. Dower laid out 19 Aug 1826 for 20a of wood land out of tract purchased by late John from Ignatius ELGIN, all the home farm except 2 fields totaling 40a. Divisors: Jno. J. MATHIAS, William THRIFT, Isaac W. HAWLING.

3N:074   Date: 18 Nov 1826   RtCt: 18 Nov 1826
L. P. W. BALCH Esqr & wife Eliza E. W. of FredMd to Jesse TIMMS, B. W. HARRISON and Charles G. ESKRIDGE of Ldn. Trust for debt to George CARTER of Oatlands using 128a (conveyed by Nicholas OSBURNE, May 1823). Wit: Thomas SAUNDERS, John McCORMICK. Delv. to Jesse TIMMS 5 Jun 1827.

3N:077   Date: 15 Nov 1826   RtCt: 18 Nov 1826
William A. BINNS of Ldn to Charles G. ESKRIDGE. Trust for debt to John GRAY using land where BINNS lives devised by his father Charles BINNS dec'd.

3N:079   Date: 11 Dec 1826   RtCt: 12 Dec 1826
Thomas J. JOHNSON dec'd. Division – court order dated 13 Dec 1825; Lot # 1 (584a) & Lot #2 (157a) to widow Rebecca JOHNSON; Lot #3 (186a) to Thomas James JOHNSON; Lot #4 (189a) to Margaret JOHNSON; Lot #5 (183a) to Ann Jennings JOHNSON. Divisors: Samuel DAWSON, William CHILTON, Jno. J. MATHIAS. Gives detailed plat.

3N:082   Date: 4 Dec 1826   RtCt: 11 Dec 1826
John HULLS of Ldn to Roberdeau ANNIN of Ldn. Trust for debt to John NIXON of Ldn using farm animals and items.

3N:083   Date: 13 Dec 1826   RtCt: 13 Dec 1826
George HEAD of Ldn to George RICHARDS of Ldn. Trust for debt to
Samuel M. BOSS of Ldn using lot on Liberty St in Lsbg occupied by
HEAD (prch/o SURGHENOR and DOWE and ROSSELL). Delv. pr
order from BOSS 8 Oct 1827.

3N:085   Date: 13 Dec 1826   RtCt: 14 Dec 1826
Jeremiah W. BRONAUGH Jr. of Ldn to Francis W. LUCKETT of
Ldn. B/S of interest in estate of father William BRONAUGH dec'd in
trust for him and for future support and then enjoyed by his mother,
brothers and sisters. Delv. to LUCKETT 28 Sep 1832.

3N:086   Date: 16 Dec 1826   RtCt: 16 Dec 1826
John A. BINNS of Ldn (trustee of Daniel GREENWALL, Oct 1825) to
John GRAY of Ldn. B/S of lot on King St in Lsbg.

3N:087   Date: 21 Dec 1826   RtCt: 21 Dec 1826
Septimus TUSTON of Lsbg to Lewis KLEIN of Wtfd. BoS for slave
John HAWKINS for 12 years today. Wit: Charles G. ESKRIDGE.
Delv. to KLEIN 15 May 1827.

3N:087   Date: 5 Dec 1826   RtCt: 21 Dec 1826
William PAXON & wife Jane of Ldn to Thomas WHITE and William
CLENDENING of Ldn. Trust for debt to Sarah NIXON of Ldn using
218a where PAXON lives (prch/o heirs of William HOUGH, Samuel
HOUGH & Mahlon HOUGH Exors of John HOUGH dec'd, Apr 1806)
adj Anthony WRIGHT, Patterson WRIGHT. Wit: George W.
SHAWEN, Presley CORDELL. Delv. to Ab'm SMITH pr order 13 Oct
1828.

3N:090   Date: 22 Dec 1826   RtCt: 22 Dec 1826
Jacob DAMEWOOD/DAYMOOD and Elenor MARSTELLER.
Marriage contract – neither subject to others debts and Jacob to be
paid for improvements to Elenor lots.

3N:091   Date: 17 Jan 1826   RtCt: 22 Dec 1826
Eliza WILLIAMS and Joseph WILLIAMS of Mercer Co Ky (2 of 5
ch/o John WILLIAMS dec'd of Mercer Co Ky, s/o John dec'd
mentioned below, br/o Mary and Daniel WILLIAMS) to Ellis
WILLIAMS of Ldn. B/S of interest in estates of Mary WILLIAMS
dec'd and Daniel WILLIAMS dec'd as 2 of the 7 ch/o John
WILLIAMS dec'd late of Ldn, now in possession of widow Martha
WILLIAMS. Wit: Henery FERGURSON, Christopher BLAGROVE.
Delv. to Ellis WILLIAMS 13 Jul 1834.

3N:093   Date: 22 Dec 1821   RtCt: 23 Dec 1826
Henry PEERS of Ldn to Henry CLAGGETT of Ldn. Trust for debt to
Eleanor PEERS of Ldn using house and lot on Market St in Lsbg.

3N:094   Date: 2 Dec 1826   RtCt: 26 Dec 1826
John LONG & wife Catherine and John MULL of Ldn to John
BOOTH of Ldn. B/S of Lot #1 (to Catherine MULL now LONG) and

Lot #2 (to John) in division of __ MULL's estate. Wit: Ebenezer GRUBB, George W. SHAWEN.

3N:096 Date: 26 Dec 1826 RtCt: 28 Dec 1826
Richard H. HENDERSON and Samuel M. EDWARDS of Ldn to Elijah VIOLETT of Ldn. Release of trust for debt to Sandford RAMEY on house and lot.

3N:098 Date: 29 Nov 1826 RtCt: 5 Jan 1827
Charles BURR of WashDC and wife Mary A. BURR (dau of Elizabeth TIPPETT) of WashDC. Charles and Mary agreed to live separately and Mary will not be under Charles' control or molestation and she entitled to half of the property they shared. Trust to mother Elizabeth using Mary's interest in lot on Horsepen Run from her father Cartwright dec'd late of Washington (described in deed from Alexander YOUNG to Thomas YOUNG Sep 1817). Delv. pr order Jan 1831.

3N:105 Date: 4 Jan 1827 RtCt: 5 Jan 1827
George HEAD of Ldn to John JANNEY of Ldn. Trust for debt to Hannah J. GOVER of Ldn using house and lot on Liberty St in Lsbg.

3N:107 Date: 23 Dec 1826 RtCt: 6 Jan 1827
John ROSE & wife Anna to Charles G. ESKRIDGE. Trust for debt to Martha S. BLINCOE (Exor. of Sampson BLINCOE dec'd) using lot on King St in Lsbg adj __ CLINE and __a tract ROSE prch/o Henery STEPHENS. Wit: Alfred A. ESKRIDGE, Roberdeau ANNIN, William J. JONES.

3N:110 Date: 8 Jul 1826 RtCt: 11 Jul 1826/6 Jan 1827
James McILHANY and Richard H. HENDERSON of Ldn to Charles BINNS of Ldn. Bond on conveyance of lot in Lsbg. Delv. to BINNS 29 Oct 1836.

3N:111 Date: 12 Nov 1826 RtCt: 6 Jan 1827
Ludwell E. POWELL of Shelby Co Ky to William BENTON of Ldn. B/S of 4a (from tract of Elisha POWELL dec'd, full relinquishment by BENTON & wife on interest BENTON prch/o Robert POWELL on dower of mother Ann LILLY late Ann POWELL wd/o Elisha POWELL dec'd) adj BENTON's purchase from heirs of William MARTIN dec'd, John KILE Sr. (including undivided 2a from another prch/o BENTON from Robert POWELL). Delv. to BENTON 11 Jan 1828.

3N:112 Date: 6 Jan 1827 RtCt: 6 Jan 1827
William SEEDERS of Lsbg to John SURGHNOR of Lsbg. Mortgage using household items.

3N:113 Date: 2 Dec 1826 RtCt: 7 Jan 1827
George W. HENERY [HENRY] of Ldn to Charles G. ESKRIDGE of Ldn. Trust for debt to John GRAY using 103a (conveyed by Jozabed WHITE). Wit: Alfred A. ESKRIDGE, Thomas RUSSELL, Robert MOFFETT.

3N:114 Date: 13 Mar 1824 RtCt: ___
Daniel VERNON & Jonah TURNER (commrs. in Chanc. Ct decree of 11 Jun 1823) and John WALKER to Jonathan EWERS. B/S of sold 13¾ (allotted to Letititia WALKER, since dec'd, w/o John WALKER) in division of her father Jesse HUMPHREY dec'd).

3N:116 Date: 8 Feb 1827 RtCt: 13 Feb 1827
Sarah ROZZELL of Ldn. DoE for negro man Isaac abt 22y old. Wit: Sandford J. RAMEY, Robt. R. HOUGH, Stephen C. DONOHOE.

3N:117 Date: 24 Mar 1826 RtCt: 9 Jan 1827
Report on division of real estate of Thomas LACEY dec'd. 4a and house nr Wtfd on Lsbg Road and 1/8a lot in Wtfd nr Mrs. Mary FOX, Edward DORSEY's carpenter shop on road to Friends Meeting House to Thomas LACEY; ¼a and brick house on Main St in Wtfd adj __ McGEATH, __ PAXON to Patience LACEY; leaving other land to be divided in the future between Ruanna, Rachael and Piaty? LACEY. Divisors: Jno. SCHOOLEY, Isaac WALKER, S. HOUGH.

3N:118 Date: 6 Sep 1826 RtCt: 8 Jan 1827
Samuel M. EDWARDS of Ldn to James RUST of Ldn. Trust for Richard H. HENDERSON of Ldn as endorser on note to Bank of Valley using 1/3 part of house & lot on N side of Market St in Lsbg (56a conveyed by John G. WATT) and land on Kittocton and slave men Adam, Charles, Jim, Voll, Ann & her 3 children Lana, William & female infant, Little Peg & her child, Helen, Mary, Harriet, Margaret, Charlotte, Milly and George children of Old Peggy.

3N:120 Date: 8 Jan 1827 RtCt: 8 Jan 1827
William MORROW to Richard H. HENDERSON. Trust for debt on property in Charles Town JeffVa to Charles F. MERCER using (house & lot in Wtfd assigned to William from dower of Jane MORROW wd/o John MORROW dec'd) (MORROW suing HENDERSON and Robert BRADEN and HENDERSON will pay MERCER).

3N:120 Date: 8 Jan 1827 RtCt: 8 Jan 1827
Edmond CARTER (now in jail) of Ldn to Isaac NICHOLS of Ldn. Trust for Bernard TAYLOR and Volentine V. PURCELL of Ldn as security to get out of jail using bond held on Thomas MARKS, Abdon DILLON and David LOVETT, credits in possession of William M. JENNERS, notes on James CAUGHOM? Jr., Eli McKNIGHT, farm animals, farm and household items, crops. Wit: Z. DULANEY, Samuel HAMMATT, William M. JENNERS.

3N:123 Date: 7 Jun 1826 RtCt: 24 Nov 1826/9 Jan 1827
Stephen SANDS and Noble S. BRADEN of Ldn to Lewis KLEIN of Ldn. B/S of 'stable lot' in Wtfd (prch/o John BALL) adj KLEIN. Wit: George W. HOUGH, R. BRADEN, D. SHAWEN, Thomas J. MARLOWE. Delv. to KLEIN 15 May 1827. Includes doc. to Noble S.

BRADEN to convey to Lewis KLEIN 'stable lot' conveyed to him in trust by SANDS in Jun 1826.

3N:125 Date: __ Jan 1827 RtCt: 9 Jan 1827
William MISKELL of Ldn to John MARTIN of Ldn. Trust for debt to Samuel M. BOSS of Ldn using household items.

3N:126 Date: 9 Dec 1826 RtCt: 9 Jan 1827
Presley WIGGINGTON & wife Sarah Ann to John SHRIVER and Jesse NEER. Trust for debt to Samuel NEER using 5¾a adj George MILLER, John CONRAD. Wit: Ebenezer GRUBB, John WHITE. Delv. to NEAR 6 May 1837.

3N:128 Date: 10 Nov 1826 RtCt: 10 Jan 1827
Cyrus BURSON & wife Phebe of Ldn to James HOGE of Ldn. Trust for debt to Samuel PEUGH using 134a (cnvy/b Joseph BURSON & wife Mary). Wit: Francis W. LUCKETT, N. C. WILLIAMS. Delv. pr order 17 Apr 1832.

3N:130 Date: 22 Sep 1826 RtCt: 10 Jan 1827
Barbara NORTON of Ldn to Jonathan LOVETT of Ldn. B/S of interest in land devised by Nathaniel NORTON dec'd.

3N:131 Date: 7 Sep 1826 RtCt: 10 Jan 1827
Townshend McVEIGH & wife Keron of Mdbg to Hugh SMITH. Trust for debt to William BATTSON of Fqr (Exor of John BATTSON dec'd) using 157½a adj Fauquier Rd, James BATTSON. Wit: Burr POWELL, A. GIBSON. Delv. pr order 1 Sep 1829.

3N:134 Date: 9 Nov 1826 RtCt: 10 Jan 1827
Samuel PEUGH & wife Mary of Ldn to Cyrus BURSON of Ldn. B/S of 29¾a. Wit: Francis W. LUCKETT, N. C. WILLIAMS. Delv. pr order 14 Jan 1828.

3N:135 Date: 2 Jan 1827 RtCt: 14 Jan 1827
Arthur GARNER of Ldn to John MARTIN of Ldn. Trust for debt to John SURGHNOR of Ldn using farm animals, farm and household items. Wit: Jno. A. BINNS, John SHAW. Delv. to MARTIN 5 Jun 1827.

3N:136 Date: 22 Jul 1826 RtCt: 13 Jan 1827
Hugh ROGERS & wife Mary and Moses WILSON and wife Tamar of Ldn to James B. WILSON of Ldn. B/S of 24a on Goose Creek adj Dennis McCARTY, Hugh SMITH, Miller HOGUE (previous deed of trust from Moses WILSON to John SINCLAIR and Jonathan CARTER which was sold to Hugh ROGERS and by him to James B. WILSON, but Tamar had not agreed). Wit: Burr SMITH, Abner GIBSON. Delv. to James B. WILSON 14 Nov 1827.

3N:138 Date: 26 Oct 1826 RtCt: 15 Jan 1827
Foushee TEBBS to Willoughby W. TEBBS. Trust for debt to John SPENCE using negro girl Anna abt 15y old. Wit: A. MILLAN, Jno. WILLIAMS, Jos. D. BELL.

3N:139 Date: 16 Nov 1826 RtCt: 15 Jan 1827
Foushee F. TEBBS to John W. TYLER. Debt to Sally LINTON (Admr of John LINTON dec'd) using negro boy Lige abt 18y old. Wit: A. MILLAN, Jno. WILLIAMS, Joseph A. [D.?] BELL.

3N:140 Date: 16 Nov 1826 RtCt: 15 Jan 1827
Foushee F. TEBBS to John W. TYLER. Trust for debt to Henry B. TYLER using household items. Wit: A. MILLAN, Jno. WILLIAMS, Jos. D. BELL.

3N:142 Date: __ Dec 1826 RtCt: 15 Jan 1827
Foushee TEBBS of Ldn to John W. TYLER of PrWm. Trust for debt to Charles HUNTON and Eppa HUNTON joint merchants in Firm of C & E HUNTON using slaves Peter, Anthony, sheep and horses.

3N:143 Date: 12 Dec 1826 RtCt: 15 Jan 1827
Thomas GASSAWAY & wife Henerietta of Ldn to George M. CHICHESTER of Ldn. B/S of lot in Lsbg adj James WOODS, Jotham WRIGHT, __ WILDMAN, __ McCABE. Wit: Samuel DAWSON, Jno. J. MATHIAS. Delv. pr order 7 Jun 1828.

3N:145 Date: 13 Jan 1827 RtCt: 16 Jan 1827
Samuel M. EDWARDS & wife Ann of Ldn to Presley SAUNDERS and Everitt SAUNDERS of Ldn. Trust for George MARKS, John ROSE, George RHODES, Edw'd HAMMATT, Richard H. HENDERSON and George RUST Jr. as endorsers on note of Jan 1827 to Bank of the Valley using personal property mentioned in trust to James RUST of Sep 1826. Delv. to Presley SAUNDERS 4 Oct 1842.

3N:149 Date: 13 Dec 1825 RtCt: 16 Jan 1827
Samuel M. EDWARDS & wife Ann of Ldn to Presley SAUNDERS of Ldn. Trust for Everett SAUNDERS and James RUST of Ldn as securities for EDWARDS as committee of idiot Susanah ANSELL using lot on S side of Royal St in Lsbg (conveyed by Joshua RILEY Sep 1823). Wit: John H. McCABE, Thomas SANDERS. Delv. to Presley SAUNDERS 25 Jun 1834.

3N:151 Date: 16 Jan 1827 RtCt: 16 Jan 1827
William H. HOUGH and Bernard TAYLOR of Ldn (trustee of Charles TURNER & wife Matilda) to Yardley TAYLOR of Ldn. B/S of 61a on N fork of Goose Creek. Delv. to Yardley TAYLOR 20 Jan 1829.

3N:153 Date: 16 Oct 1826 RtCt: 19 Jan 1827
John COOPER & wife Eve of Ldn to James MERCHANT of Ldn. B/S of 31a nr Short Hill and James NIXON, Daniel COOPER, Jacob RUSE. Wit: Samuel HOUGH, George W. SHAWEN.

3N:154 Date: 13 Jul 1826 RtCt: 20 Jan 1827
George MULL & wife Abigail of Ldn to John ROOF of Ldn. B/S of 1a at foot of Short Hill adj Mrs. GOWER, MULL, ___ MOORE. Wit: Presley CORDELL, George W. SHAWEN. Delv. to ROOF 18 Aug 1838.

3N:156   Date: 22 Jul 1826   RtCt: 22 Jan 1827
Isaac EATON & wife Malinda of Mt. Gilead to Ezra BOLEN of Ldn.
B/S of ½a in Mt. Gilead adj George TAVENER, old road from Coe's
Mill to North Fork. Wit: John SIMPSON, Thomas ROGERS. Delv. to
BOLEN 15 Oct 1827.

3N:158   Date: 23 Oct 1824   RtCt: 25 Jan 1827
George PELTER & wife Catherine of FredVa to Lewis BERKLEY of
Ldn. B/S of 2½a adj Lot #20 in Aldie. Delv. to BERKLY 11 Sep 1834.

3N:160   Date: 1 Dec 1826   RtCt: 25 Jan 1827
John MARKS & wife Lydia of Perry Co Ohio to Thomas DRAKE of
Ldn. B/S of 53a (from trust of Samuel SINCLAIR to Edward B.
GRADY for use of John MARKS) adj Isaiah MARKS, Samuel
DUNCAN.

3N:163   Date: 18 Sep 1826   RtCt: 26 Jan 1827
Craven WALKER & wife Alice of Union to Jesse HOGE of Ldn. Trust
for debt to James HOGE using ¼a lot in Union (cnvy/b William
GALLAHER May 1826) adj Seth SMITH; and two cording machines.
Wit: Francis W. LUCKETT, Edward HALL. Delv. to William HOGE pr
order of James HOGE 14 Mar 1829.

3N:165   Date: 30 Dec 1826   RtCt: 27 Jan 1827
Isaac E. STEER of Ldn to Mahlon SCHOOLEY of Ldn. B/S of 7a adj
Mahlon SCHOOLEY.

3N:166   Date: 8 Jan 1827   RtCt: 27 Jan 1827
James HOGE (trustee of Jesse BURSON & wife Martha, May 1819
to Sampson BLINCOE since dec'd) of Ldn to John PANCOAST Jr.
of Ldn. B/S of 139a (conveyed to BURSON by Jacob
STONEBURNER) adj __ McMULLEN, __ FIELDING, __ LYNN.
Delv. to PANCOAST 9 May 1828.

3N:168   Date: 1 Feb 1827   RtCt: 1 Feb 1827
David SHAWEN of Ldn to Richard H. HENDERSON of Ldn. Trust for
debt to Lewis WALKER of Ohio using 103½a (91a prch/o Noah
HIXON Feb 1821 and 13½a from Thomas SWAYNE Apr 1821).
Delv. to HENDERSON 2 Jan 1828.

3N:170   Date: 6 Jan 1827   RtCt: Feb 1827
Jacob MARSHALL of Ldn to Humphrey B. POWELL of Ldn. Trust
for William REED to join MARSHALL in bond to Cuthb't OWENS
using negro boy Jennings 16y old next August left to him by his
father in law Joshua BUCKLEY and farm animals.

3N:171   Date: 13 May 1826   RtCt: 5 Feb 1827
Meshack LACEY of Mdbg to Dr. Elias LACEY & son Joseph of Ldn.
Trust for debt to Benjamin R. LACEY using ½a Lot #27 at
Washington and Madison Sts where Meshack now lives. Wit:
Anthony McCRADY, T. W. DORMON, James H. HALLEY. Delv. to
B. W. HARRISON it being for his use as pr assignment on bond 2
May 1827.

3N:173   Date: 29 Jan 1827   RtCt: 12 Feb 1827
Craven BROWN. Oath as 2nd Lt of a Co of Artillery in 2nd Reg 2nd Div of Militia.

3N:174   Date: 12 Feb 1827   RtCt: 12 Feb 1827
James McDANIEL, Lloyd NOLAND and William KING. Bond on McDANIEL as constable.

3N:174   Date: 3 Feb 1827   RtCt: 13 Feb 1827
William T. T. MASON (as commr) of Ldn to William M. McCARTY & wife Emily of Ldn. B/S of 1/3 of Ohio lands and Ky lands of Stevens T. MASON dec'd (suit of Dec 1822 in Winchester of McCARTY agst John T. MASON & Mary MASON trustees of will of Stevens T. MASON dec'd, both John and Mary now dec'd).

3N:176   Date: 18 Oct 1826   RtCt: 20 Dec 1826
Thomas JONES of Ldn to John SMARR of Ldn. BoS for black man Samuel. Wit William SMARR.

3N:176   Date: 31 Jan 1827   RtCt: 11 Feb 1827
Price JACOBS of Ldn to Benjamin MITCHELL of Ldn. Trust for debt to George MARKS using negro man George and girl Kitty.

3N:177   Date: 8 Feb 1827   RtCt: 11 Feb 1827
James BRADY of Ldn to James BRADY Jr. of Ldn. B/S of lot with buildings in Lsbg (prch/o John LITTLEJOHN). Wit: Jno. A. BINNS, Charles G. ESKRIDGE, William J. JONES. Delv. to James BRADY 28 Feb 1837.

3N:178   Date: 3 Feb 1827   RtCt: 11 Feb 1827
James BRADY of Lsbg to John A. BINNS of Lsbg. Trust for debt to James BRADY Jr. using household items.

3N:180   Date: 4 Apr 1823   RtCt: 12 Feb 1827
William NOLAND & wife Catherine of Ldn to Matthew ADAM of Ldn. B/S of 1a on N side of Ashby's Gap Turnpike Road adj Thomas J. NOLAND, opposite the Aldie Mill. Wit: Leven LUCKETT, Abner GIBSON. Delv. to William F. ADAM 24 Oct 1833.

3N:182   Date: 2 Nov 1826   RtCt: 12 Feb 1827
Hugh ROGERS & wife Mary of Ldn to Jesse McVEIGH of Ldn. B/S of 48a taken from NW end of Rogers' farm adj Silas BEATTY, Edwin C. BROWN. Wit: Burr POWELL, A. GIBSON. Delv. to McVEIGH 3 Aug 1833.

3N:184   Date: 15 May 1826   RtCt: 12 Feb 1827
William GALLEHER & wife Margery of Ldn to Craven WALKER of Ldn. B/S of ¼a lot in Union adj Seth SMITH. Wit: William BRONAUGH, Francis W. LUCKETT.

3N:185   Date: 12 Feb 1827   RtCt: 13 Feb 1827
Peter COOPER of Ldn to Thomas WHITE of Ldn. Trust for debt to Simon SHOEMAKER of Ldn (paid judgments agst COOPER by L. P. W. BALCH and Thomas GASSAWAY ass'ees of Robert

MOFFETT) using 80a of grain on land of Mary FOX, farm animals and items.

3N:187   Date: 13 Mar 1826   RtCt: 13 Feb 1827

Dpty Horrace LUCKETT for Shff Ludwell LEE to Joseph TULEY of Ldn. B/S of 80-100a (cnvy/b insolvent debtor Hiland CROWE Mar 1826)

3N:188   Date: 13 Mar 1826   RtCt: 13 Feb 1827

Dpty Horrace LUCKETT for Shff Ludwell LEE to Joseph TULEY. B/S of 513a and adj 43a (cnvy/b insolvent debtor Hiland CROWE Mar 1826).

3N:190   Date: 24 Jan 1827   RtCt: 13 Feb 1827

John BEATTY of Ldn to Fayette BALL and William D. DRISH of Ldn. Trust for George M. CHICHESTER with Joseph BROWN and Samuel C. BOSS as security for BEATTY as guardian of Amanda, Malvinia and Elizabeth Harriet BEATY infant children of David BEATTY dec'd on bond of Feb 1825 using 167a (cnvy/b John Elliott Jan 1792).

3N:191   Date: 13 Jan 1827   RtCt: 13 Feb 1827

John BOYD & wife Elizabeth of Ldn to H. B. POWELL of Ldn. Trust for debt to L. W. STOCKTON for contract to carry the mail on route from Alex to Winchester using interest in lot in Mdbg where BOYD lives. Wit: Burr POWELL, A. GIBSON.

3N:194   Date: 13 Feb 1827   RtCt: 24 Feb 1827

Thomson MASON of Ldn to John H. CANBY of Ldn. Trust for debt to Richard Barnes MASON of St. Mary's Co Md and William T. T. MASON of Ldn using interest in crops on Samuel LUCKETT's farm now in occupation of Michael WHITMAN and crops of late Westwood T. MASON and negro man Jerry and horses. Wit: Peyton R. PAGE, Charles FEAGAN, William H. BRYAN, Addison H. CLARKE. Delv. to William T. T. MASON 19 May 1827.

3N:196   Date: 16 Feb 1827   RtCt: 16 Feb 1827

Samuel MURRAY (insolvent debtor) to Shff Ludwell LEE. B/S of __a (cnvy/b MURRAY to George RICHARDS Sep 1825, DBk LLL:121, for benefit of Simon A. BINNS and William BINNS Jr.)

3N:197   Date: 1 Jan 1827   RtCt: 13 Feb 1827

Edward SANDERS of Ldn to Norval OSBURNE of Ldn. Trust for debt to John A. MARMADUKE and John & Silas MARMADUKE of Ldn using negro boys Billy or Bill and Mandeville.

3N:199   Date: 17 Feb 1827   RtCt: 18 Feb 1827

Edward SANDERS of Ldn to William CLENDENING of Ldn. Trust for debt to Samuel CLENDENING of Ldn using negroes William and Mandeville and farm animals, household items. Delv. to Samuel CLENDENING 26 Oct 1846.

3N:201 Date: 17 Feb 1827 RtCt: 19 Feb 1827
John DRISH nr Lsbg and William D. DRISH of Lsbg. Agreement –
terms for John's sale to William of house and lot on King St known
as the tavern stand now occupied by Mrs. FOLEY. Delv. to William
D. DRISH 18 Apr 1829.

3N:203 Date: 17 Feb 1827 RtCt: 19 Feb 1827
John DRISH of Ldn to William D. DRISH of Ldn. B/S of house and
lot on King St. in Lsbg know as the tavern stand now occupied by
Mrs. FOLEY adj Market house and courthouse. Delv. to William D.
DRISH 18 __ 1829.

3N:204 Date: 1 Apr 1826 RtCt: 21 Feb 1827
James CURRELL of Ldn to Notley C. WILLIAMS and John J.
CURRELL. BoS of negro male slave Kendal and farm animals, farm
and household items. Wit: Thomas G. HUMPHREY, William L.
ADAMS. Delv. to N. C. WILLIAMS 25 Feb 1830.

3N:205 Date: 3 Feb 1827 RtCt: 21 Feb 1827
Mary MULL of Ldn to Cassandra BASFORD of Ldn. B/S of 2a (part
of Lot #4 in division of MULL's estate allotted to Mary).

3N:206 Date: 20 Feb 1827 RtCt: 21 Feb 1827
Joseph HOUGH & wife Lucy C. of Ldn to Henery CLAGGETT and
Samuel M. EDWARDS of Ldn. Trust for debt to Joshua PEUSEY
bond of Feb 1827 to Asa PECK assigned to PEUSEY) of Ldn using
47a where HOUGH now lives (cnvy/b Bernard HOUGH Mar 1821).
Wit: James RUST, John H. McCABE. Delv. to PUSY 6 Dec 1827.

3N:209 Date: 19 Feb 1827 RtCt: 22 Feb 1827
Benjamin WHITE of Ldn to Betsey CROSS (free woman of collor) of
Ldn. BoS of negro man Jess. Wit: Amos BEALE, James H.
SHIELDS.

3N:210 Date: 5 Jul 1826 RtCt: 24 Feb 1827
Joshua OSBURNE and Turner OSBURNE (trustees of Adam
WINEGARDNER for benefit of Thomas GREGG and Jehu
HOLLINGSWORTH) of Ldn to Thomas GREGG S. H. of Ldn. B/S of
land adj Enos POTTS. Delv. to Thomas GREGG Admrs 17 Jan
1828.

3N:211 Date: 26 Feb 1827 RtCt: 26 Feb 1827
John UMBAUGH of Ldn to John A. BINNS of Ldn. Trust for debt to
Philip HEATER of Ldn using 173a (prch/o Wm. GREGG May 1822,
DBk EEE:300). Delv. to HEATER 3 Mar 1834.

3N:213 Date: 21 Apr 1827 RtCt: 27 Feb 1827
George W. HENERY [HENRY] of Ldn to James McILHANY of Ldn.
Trust for debt to Richard H. HENDERSON of Ldn using slaves for
life Evelina & her 2 children Edmund and Amanda. Delv. to
HENDERSON 21 Jul 1828.

3N:214   Date: 22 Feb 1827   RtCt: 28 Feb 1827
Stephen SANDS and William STOCKS. Division of 125a (from
Jacob SANDS dec'd, by right of descent the prop. of Elizabeth
STOCKS w/o William STOCKS and Stephen SANDS). Gives 67½a
adj William PAXON, Eneas WILLIAMS, John ROBERTSON to
Stephen and he relinquishes claim to remaining 57½a. Wit: George
W. SHAWEN, Robt. BRADEN.

3N:216   Date: 31 Jan 1827   RtCt: 1 Mar 1827
Barbara NORTON (insolvent debtor) to Shff Ludwell LEE. B/S of
whole estate including interest in trust (DBk MMM:358).

3N:217   Date: 28 Nov 1827 [26]   RtCt: 1 Mar 1827
Thomson MASON of Ldn to John ROSE of Ldn. Trust for debt to
Thomson F. MASON of AlexDC using slaves Belcher, Moses,
Simon, Quitinia & Melvida. Delv. to Thomson F. MASON 5 Aug
1828.

3N:219   Date: 2 Mar 1827   RtCt: 2 Mar 1827
John KLINE of Ldn to George RICHARDS. Trust as gift to KLINE's
sister Katherine w/o John S. EDWARDS of Lsbg using household
items.

3N:220   Date: 2 Mar 1827   RtCt: 2 Mar 1827
John McCORMICK of Lsbg to Richard H. HENDERSON of Lsbg.
Trust for debt to Benjamin SHRIEVE Jr. using 64a. Delv. to
SHRIEVE 20 Sep 1827.

3N:222   Date: 3 Mar 1827   RtCt: 3 Mar 1827
William CRAVEN of Ldn to Samuel CRAVEN of Ldn. B/S of
undivided 25¾a share from land of father Abner CRAVEN dec'd,
reserving widow's dower. Delv. to CRAVEN 8 Jun 1828.

3N:223   Date: 3 Mar 1827   RtCt: 3 Mar 1827
John G. HILL and Enoch SHRIGLEY of Ldn to Noble S. BRADEN of
Ldn. Trust for debt to John BALL of Ldn using land conveyed by
BALL (see next entry). Delv. to BRADEN 15 Jul 1828.

3N:225   Date: 3 Mar 1827   RtCt: 3 Mar 1827
John BALL of Ldn to John G. HILL and Enoch SHRIGLEY of Ldn.
B/S of 1a (conveyed by Isaac BALL Oct 1826) adj schoolhouse lot.

3N:226   Date: 4 Jan 1823   RtCt: 3 Mar 1827
Burr POWELL as acting Exor of Leven POWELL dec'd & for himself.
Consents to sale by William CHILTON Esqr for negro Hannah to her
husband Moses BUTLER as payment of debt by CHILTON to
Samuel and Isaac NICHOLS in trust to Lloyd NOLAND. BoS of 3
Mar 1827 from William CHILTON to Moses.

3N:227   Date: 20 Oct 1826   RtCt: 3 Mar 1827
Isaac BALL of Ldn to John BALL of Ldn. B/S of 1a adj __ DAVIS,
schoolhouse lot, __ SHAWEN (cnvy/b Isaac HOUGH Sep 1813).

3N:229   Date: 2 Mar 1827   RtCt: 5 Mar 1827
Walter LANGLEY & wife Susanna of Ldn to John CHEW of Ldn. B/S
of 44a adj __ HUFFMAN, CHEW, __ URTON and 10a adj __
URTON (conveyed by John LUKE of FredVa). Wit: Notley C.
WILLIAMS, John W. GRAYSON. Delv. pr order 12 Feb 1828.

3N:232   Date: 9 May 1825   RtCt: 12 Sep 1826/6 Mar 1827
Elizabeth HARDEN to Townshend McVEIGH. Trust to secure note
from Thomas BISCOE (bound to Stephen GARRETT Admr. of
William HARDON dec'd) using negro girl Charlotte age 2y, farm
animals, household items. Delv. to BISCOE 16 Aug 1827. Wit:
Stephen GARRETT, Robert ROSE, Jesse McVEIGH.

3N:234   Date: 22 Feb 1827   RtCt: 7 Mar 1827
Thomas J. NOLAND of Ldn to H. B. POWELL of Ldn. Trust for debt
to Lewis BERKLEY of Ldn using slave Matilda a yellow woman with
her 3 children Albert, Oscar and Wallace, and boy William. Delv. to
BERKLEY 11 Sep 1834.

3N:235   Date: 1 Sep 1823   RtCt: 10 Mar 1827
Joshua RILEY of Ldn to Samuel M. EDWARDS of Ldn. B/S of lot
with tannery and building in Lsbg adj Lots #65 & #66 on Royal St.
Delv. to EDWARDS 25 Jun 1834.

3N:237   Date: 1 Sep 1823   RtCt: 10 Mar 1827
Samuel M. EDWARDS & wife Ann of Ldn to Joshua RILEY of Ldn.
B/S of lot in Lsbg at Church & Loudoun Sts. Wit: John H. McCABE,
Thomas SANDERS. Delv. to RILEY 20 Aug 1828.

3N:239   Date: 12 Dec 1826   RtCt: 10 Mar 1827
Leonard R. POSTON & wife Mary E. of Ldn to Richard K.
LITTLETON of Ldn. Trust for debt to John K. LITTLETON of Ldn
using 47a at foot of Blue Ridge adj Capt. George RUST (dev. by
father Wilsey POSTON dec'd who prch/o Stacey JANNEY Apr 1796)
and interest in adj 94a leased by Denny FAIRFAX to David
MORGAN Oct 1787 who A/L to John and Dawson BROWN in Jun
1792 who sold to Wilsey in Oct 1795. Wit: Benjamin GRAYSON,
Cuthbert POWELL. Delv. to William K. LITTLETON 11 Mar 1845.

3N:243   Date: 24 Dec 1826   RtCt: 10 Mar 1827
John AXLINE & wife Christina of Ldn to Frederick ROLLER of Ldn.
B/S of 20½a (conveyed by Henery AXLINE) adj Charles SACKMAN,
Jacob VIRTS. Wit: Robert BRADEN, Ebenezer GRUBB. Delv. to
ROLLER 7 Mar 1828.

3N:245   Date: 22 Mar 1826   RtCt: 10 Mar 1827
Henery AXLINE & wife Catherine of Ldn to John AXLINE of Ldn. B/S
of 130a (conveyed by John AXLINE Sr. Jan 1817) adj David
AXLINE, Jacob VIRTZ, Philip EVERHART. Wit: John HAMILTON,
George W. SHAWEN. Delv. to Jno. AXLINE 17 Aug 1827.

3N:247   Date: 9 Mar 1827   RtCt: 12 Mar 1827
Arriss BUCKNER to Rich'd H. HENDERSON. PoA to deliver bonds as security for Charles LEWIS as Sheriff. Wit: Samuel M. EDWARDS.

3N:247   Date: 31 Oct 1826   RtCt: 12 Mar 1827
Beniah WHITE. Appointment as Capt in 56th Reg 6th Brig 2nd Div of Militia. Delv. to White 6 Nov 1827.

3N:248   Date: 4 Jan 1827   RtCt: 12 Jan 1827
Charles LEWIS. Commissioned as Sheriff.

3N:248   Date: 4 Jan 1827   RtCt: 12 Mar 1827
Charles LEWIS, Aris BUCKNER, William ELLZEY, John BAYLY, Robert MOFFETT, Asa ROGERS, William THRIFT, Hugh SMITH & Thomas B. MERSHON. Bond on LEWIS as Sheriff to collect levies and poor rates.

3N:249   Date: 4 Jan 1827   RtCt: 12 Mar 1827
Charles LEWIS, Aris BUCKNER, William ELLZEY, John BAYLY, Robert MOFFETT, Asa ROGERS, William THRIFT, Hugh SMITH & Thomas B. MERSHON. Bond on LEWIS as Sheriff to collect taxes.

3N:250   Date: 4 Jan 1827   RtCt: 12 Mar 1827
Charles LEWIS, Aris BUCKNER, William ELLZEY, John BAYLY, Robert MOFFETT, Asa ROGERS, William THRIFT, Hugh SMITH & Thomas B. MERSHON. Bond on LEWIS as Sheriff to collect officers fees.

3N:251   Date: 14 Mar 1827   RtCt: 14 Mar 1827
Charles L. CLOWES, James BROWN and John BROWN. Bond on CLOWES as constable.

3N:252   Date: 27 Nov 1826   RtCt: 14 Mar 1827
Joseph and Samuel HATCHER. Division of lands held in partnership, from case of Hannah HATCHER Admr of Joseph HATCHER dec'd vs. Caleb RECTOR & wife Mary Ann & others – Lot #1 (80a) with mill to heirs of Samuel HATCHER dec'd; Lot #2 (120a) & 93a in Fqr (prch/o heirs of Ralph MURRAY dec'd) to heirs of Joseph HATCHER dec'd, widow Hannah HATCHER (also rent from house & 8a occupied by James HARLES). Gives detailed plat. Divisors: Daniel EACHES, John SINCLAIR, Samuel DUNCAN.

3N:255   Date: 6 Sep 1826   RtCt: ___
Isaac and Samuel NICHOLS Sr. Division – Isaac NICHOLS Jr., William HOGUE & William PIGGOTT (Exors of Samuel NICHOLS dec'd) agst Isaac NICHOLS Sr. - Lot #1 (1 share) remaining part of Cox & Gregg tract of 962a, tract prch/o David TAYLOR of 96a, tract where Mahlon CRAVEN now resides of 180a, tract where James HOGUE now resides of 112a, tract prch/o James COCHRANE Jr. nr Goose Creek Meeting House of 22a, 16a from tract laid off in survey of Samuel NICHOLS Jr.; Lot #2 – Griggsvile tract of 135a with

doubtful title and will be left undivided until later. Divisors: David SMITH, Daniel JANNEY, Joshua GORE, Notley C. WILLIAM.

3N:258 Date: 8 Oct 1826 RtCt: 9 Oct 1826
Barbary DERRY (Exor of Philip DERRY dec'd) to son Peter DERRY. PoA. Wit: Jno. A. BINNS.

3N:258 Date: 27 Feb 1827 RtCt: 12 Mar 1827
Casper JOHNSON & wife Martha of Ldn to Jacob ISH of Ldn. B/S of 159½a (conveyed by John WILLSON & wife Sarah Jan 1816) on Lsbg mountain road adj David DANIEL, John WILLSON, heirs of William SWART dec'd. Wit: Sampson HUTCHISON, Benjamin JOHNSON, John ISH, John SIMPSON, Thomas ROGERS.

3N:260 Date: 2 Nov 1826 RtCt: 12 Mar 1827
John EVANS of Ldn to Daniel COCKERILL of Ldn. Trust for debt to Asa WELLS using crops on premise of James BEANS, farm animals, farm and household items. Wit: Mahlon CRAVEN, James BOLEN, Sandford BIRDET.

3N:262 Date: 1 Feb 1827 RtCt: 12 Mar 1827
Joshua RILEY & wife Ann of Lsbg to John A. BINNS of Lsbg. Trust for debt to Mary HUNT of Ldn using lot in Lsbg prch/o BINNS in Jun 1822 (DBk EEE:230). Delv. to BINNS 11 Jun 1829.

3N:264 Date: 27 Jan 1827 RtCt: 12 Mar 1827
George SAUNDERS & wife Elizabeth of Ldn to John BOOTH of Ldn. B/S of 6a (allotted in div. of lands of James BOOTH dec'd) and 6a allotted to Aaron BOOTH. Wit: Mortimore McILHANY, George W. SHAWEN.

3N:267 Date: 18 Dec 1826 RtCt: 12 Mar 1827
Ludwell LEE of Ldn to John MIDDLEBURG of Ldn. B/S of 20a 'Bellmont' where LEE resides on road from Lsbg to Alexandria and another 15a. Delv. to John MIDDLEBURG 20 Nov 1827.

3N:268 Date: 5 Mar 1827 RtCt: 12 Mar 1827
William CLAYTON of Ldn to Timothy CARRINGTON of Ldn. B/S of ½a (allotted in div. of William CLATON dec'd). Delv. to CARRINGTON 4 Jun 1827.

3N:270 Date: 3 Aug 1826 RtCt: 12 Mar 1827
Charles CHAMBLIN and Joshua OSBURNE (acting trustees of Calvin THATCHER for benefit of Henson ELLIOTT Jun 1821 and for benefit of Joshua OSBURNE Nov 1822) of Ldn to Jacob COST of Ldn. B/S of 190a (formerly prop. of Richard THATCHER now dec'd) adj late John LOVE, James BEST, Dr. Jonathan HEATON. Delv. to COST 16 Aug 1829.

3N:272 Date: 20 Feb 1827 RtCt: 12 Mar 1827
Burr POWELL & wife Catherine of Ldn to Hugh ROGERS of Ldn. B/S of 49a on S side of Ashby Gap Turnpike opposite land of ROGERS, adj Townsend McVEIGH, Mrs. E. NOLAND. Wit: A. GIBSON, John ASHBY, H. SMITH, Francis W. LUCKETT.

3N:275   Date: 5 Mar 1827   RtCt: 12 Mar 1827
Hugh ROGERS & wife Polly of Ldn to Humphrey B. POWELL of Ldn. Trust for debt to Burr POWELL using 49a (deed from Burr POWELL Feb 1827). Wit: Francis W. LUCKETT, A. GIBSON.

3N:278   Date: 26 May 1826   RtCt: 12 Mar 1827
Joseph WOOD & wife Lydia of Ldn to George BUTLER of Ldn. B/S of ¼a adj Wtfd, Mahlon JANNEY.

3N:280   Date: 2 Mar 1827   RtCt: 12 Mar 1827
Stephen McPHERSON & wife Sarah of Ldn to Ruth TRAYHERN w/o Thomas of Ldn. B/S of 3a adj Samuel PEUGH, James BROWN. Wit: Peyton POWELL, Mahlon CRAVEN, Thomas ONEALE. Delv. pr order 10 Oct 1827.

3N:281   Date: 10 Mar 1827   RtCt: 12 Mar 1827
Stephen McPHERSON Sr. & wife Sarah of Ldn to Stephen McPHERSON Jr. of Ldn. B/S of 80a adj Mahlon EVANS, Joseph GARRETT, William WILKINSON, William HOGUE. Wit: Peyton POWELL, Mahlon CRAVEN, Thomas ONEALE. Delv. to Stephen Jr. 10 Oct 1827.

3N:283   Date: 4 Jul 1826   RtCt: 12 Mar 1827
Joshua HUTCHISON of Ffx to Thomas W. LEE of Ldn. B/S of 2 lots (part of JOHNSON survey). Delv. to LEE 9 Jan 1835.

3N:285   Date: 15 Jan 1827   RtCt: 12 Mar 1827
Seton W. NORRIS & wife Abbey W. of Ffx to Thomas DARNE of Ldn. B/S of 120a (part of several prch/o William LANE Sr. from John TURBERVILLE, the last dated Mar 1798, devised to dau Abbey now NORRISS and present wife of Turbert R. BETTON in div. of 1819) part in Ldn and part in Ffx. Wit: B. M. LANE, George N. BERKLEY, Alex WAUGH. Delv. to DARNE 18 Sep 1829.

3N:288   Date: 5 Mar 1827   RtCt: 12 Mar 1827
Mason MARKS of Ldn to John GRAHAM of Ldn. Trust for debt of Mary MARKS of Ldn using negro boy Stephen. Transfer of claim dated 5 Jan 1827 on trust to Joshua OSBURNE for benefit of her dau Margaret HUMPHREY from Mary MARKS. Delv. to GRAHAM 5 Oct 1837.

3N:290   Date: 12 Mar 1827   RtCt: 12 Mar 1827
Abel MARKS of Ldn to John GRAHAM of Ldn. Trust for debt to Joshua OSBURNE trustee for Mary Margaret HUMPHREY of Ldn using negro girl Emily abt 15 or 16y old.

3N:292   Date: 1 Mar 1827   RtCt: 12 Mar 1827
George WENNER & wife Mary of Ldn to John WENNER of Ldn. B/S of 15¾a (Lot #5 in division of lands of William WENNER dec'd) and 2½a wood lot and 1/12th interest in widow's dower. Wit: George W. SHAWEN, John J. MATHIAS.

3N:294   Date: 3 Mar 1827   RtCt: 12 Mar 1827
William WENNER & wife Elizabeth of Ldn to John WENNER of Ldn.
B/S of 14½a (Lot #10 in division of land of William WENNER dec'd)
and interest in widow's dower. Wit: Ebenezer GRUBB, George W.
SHAWEN.

3N:297   Date: 27 Mar 1822   RtCt: 10 Jan 1825/12 Mar 1827
Adam HOUSHOLDER & wife Sarah of Ldn to Jacob WALTMAN son
Samuel [? – son of Samuel] of Ldn. B/S of 115a (cnvy/b George
MANN Feb 1802, DBk BB:365) adj __ COMPHER, __ COOPER, __
WILLIAMS. Wit: Alex CORDELL, Ruth HOUSEHOLDER, Mary
HOUSEHOLDER, Robert MOFFETT, Abiel JENNERS, S. HOUGH.

3N:299   Date: 19 Dec 1826   RtCt: 13 Mar 1827
Richard S. JONES of Ldn to Hugh SMITH of Ldn. B/S of 7a (from
will of mother Sarah JONES) adj SMITH, Isaac HUGHES, late
Sampson BLINCOE. Wit: John JONES, Thomas JONES, Philip
JONES, James IDEN, Samuel CARTER. Delv. to SMITH 2 Aug
1836.

3N:300   Date: 14 Mar 1827   RtCt: 14 Mar 1827
James HAMILTON & wife Cassandra of Lsbg to Erasmus G.
HAMILTON of Lsbg. B/S of lot and house on Back St in Lsbg adj
HAMILTON. Wit: Samuel M. EDWARDS, John H. McCABE. Delv. to
HAMILTON 31 May 1827.

3N:302   Date: 29 Jan 1827   RtCt: 15 Mar 1827
Jacob WALTMAN the 3rd to Alex'r CORDELL. Trust for debt to
Emanuel WALTMAN using undivided interest in estate of Jacob
WALTMAN dec'd.

3N:304   Date: 24 Feb 1827   RtCt: 28 Mar 1827
Joshua OSBURNE. DoE for negro man Dennis BUCKNEY abt 33y
old. Wit: Samuel M. EDWARDS, John JANNEY.

3N:304   Date: 21 Mar 1827   RtCt: 21 Mar 1827
Ann DAILEY of Ldn to son Grafton DAILEY of Ldn. BoS for horse.

3N:305   Date: 21 Mar 1827   RtCt: 21 Mar 1827
Charles G. ESKRIDGE of Ldn to Simon A. BINNS of Ldn. Release
of trust for debt to Samuel M. BOSS using 220a adj Benjamin
SHRIEVE, Charles BINNS (DBk JJJ:381).

3N:306   Date: 1 Mar 1827   RtCt: 23 Mar 1827
Joshua LONG (f/o Durett) to son Benjamin LONG. B/S of tanyard nr
Hllb and personal estate of Durett LONG (late of Harpers Ferry now
dec'd intestate and without issue, estate belongs to his father). Delv.
to Benjamin LONG 13 Jun 1827.

3N:308   Date: 5 Feb 1827   RtCt: 24 Mar 1827
Peter R. BEVERLY of AlexDC to Robert BEVERLEY. B/S of 570¾a
Lot #6 in Shannondale (Ferdinando FAIRFAX gave deed of trust of
26 Jun 1820 to Peter R. BEVERLY of Blandfield attorney in fact of
Robert BEVERLY).

3N:310   Date: 22 Mar 1827   RtCt: 25 Mar 1827
Daniel COOPER & wife Elizabeth of Ldn to Frederick A. DAVISSON of Ldn. B/S of 134a where COOPER has lived for 12-13y (in exchange for discharge of 3 bonds from COOPER to DAVISSON) adj Mortimore McILHANY, James MERCHANT, John STATLER, heirs of Archibald MORRISON. Wit: Ebenezer GRUBB, Mortimer McILHANY. Delv. 8 Oct 1827.

3N:312   Date: 21 Mar 1827   RtCt: 26 Mar 1827
Simon A. BINNS & wife Sarah and Samuel MURRAY & wife Mary Ann of Ldn to Ignatius ELGIN of Ldn. B/S of 220a adj William HAWLING, Charles BINNS, Gust'a ELGIN. Wit: John F. McCABE, Samuel M. EDWARDS.

3N:315   Date: ___   RtCt: 27 Mar 1827
Joshua OSBURNE of Ldn to Anne Elizabeth ELLZEY, Mary Cecilia ELLZEY and Rosannah Mortimore ELLZEY (infants under the age of 21y, ch/o Lewis ELLZEY & Rosannah ELLZEY dec'd his wife formerly Rosannah McILHANY) of Ldn. B/S of 'Locust Thickett' and 'White Oak bottom' tracts nr end of Short Hill in occupation of Mahlon MORRIS (under LS to Lewis ELLZEY, were sold by trust of Nov 1825 by Lewis to Craven OSBURNE for benefit of Joshua OSBURNE).

3N:319   Date: 27 Mar 1827   RtCt: 27 Mar 1827
Thomas HEIR to John A. BINNS. Trust for debt to Michael MORRALLEE using horse and cart.

3N:320   Date: 21 Mar 1827   RtCt: 27 Mar 1827
John W. WOOD of Ldn to John SHAW of Ldn. B/S of lot on Back St in Lsbg (part of lot prch/o Jesse BAYLEY) adj SHAW, John SAUNDERS in occupation of his mother Patience SAUNDERS. Delv. to SHAW 6 Nov 1830.

3N:321   Date: 30 Mar 1827   RtCt: 31 Mar 1827
Shff Ludwell LEE by his late Dpty William THRIFT to Elizabeth HAINES of Ldn. B/S of lot of __a adj Edm'd J. LEE (committed to Shff from estate of Stacey HAINES dec'd).

3N:322   Date: 30 Mar 1827   RtCt: 31 Mar 1827
Elizabeth HAINES of Ldn to Charles W. D. BINNS of Ldn. Trust for debt to Shff Ludwell LEE using above land. Wit: William J. JONES, Enos WILDMAN, Roberdeau ANNIN.

3N:324   Date: 26 May 1826   RtCt: 31 Mar 1827
Zeneas REEDER & wife Martha late LEETH of Columbiana Co Ohio to Joseph JANNEY Sr. of Ldn. B/S of 25a (allotted to Martha and her brother James LEETH in div. of real estate of grandfather John VIOLETT dec'd). Wit: Israel REEDER, James MILLER. Delv. pr order 17 Sep 1827.

3N:326   Date: 6 Apr 1827   RtCt: 6 Apr 1827
Charles William Douglas BINNS of Ldn to Charles Douglas BINNS. Gift of negro girl Eliza STOTT. Delv. to Chs. BINNS Sr. 1 Oct 1836.

3N:327   Date: 23 Oct 1826   RtCt: 12 Mar 1827
Jared POTTS (son & heir of Nathan POTTS dec'd) & wife Lusinda of Botetourt Co Va to Norval OSBURNE of Ldn. B/S of 1/9th part of two adj tracts of 147a and 110a. Delv. to OSBURNE 12 Sep 1836.

3N:329   Date: 28 Mar 1827   RtCt: 7 Apr 1827
Joseph EIDSON & wife Elizabeth of Ldn to David GALLAHER of Ldn. B/S of 33a on Beaverdam adj Uriel GLASSCOCK, Reuben TRIPLETT dec'd. Wit: Burr POWELL, Abner GIBSON. Delv. to GALLAHER 29 Oct 1828.

3N:331   Date: 9 Apr 1827   RtCt: 9 Apr 1827
William H. HOUGH and Thomas PHILIPS of Ldn to John WOLFORD. Release of trust of Jul 1824 for debt to William STEER (Admr of John HOUGH dec'd).

3N:333   Date: 23 Mar 1827   RtCt: 9 Apr 1827
Jacob SLATER & wife Christena of Ldn to William SLATER of Ldn. B/S of 9½a Lot #6 with tanyard from division of estate of John SLATER dec'd. Wit: Mortimore McILHANY, George W. SHAWEN. Delv. 29 Jul 1831.

3N:335   Date: 4 Apr 1827   RtCt: 9 Apr 1827
Uriel GLASSCOCK & wife Nancy of Ldn to James RUST of Ldn. Trust for debt to James VERNON of Ldn using 98a adj __ WILKINSON, __ McGEATH, __ McMULLEN (conveyed by VERNON). Wit: John W. GRAYSON, Edward HALL.

3N:338   Date: 23 Mar 1827   RtCt: 9 Apr 1827
William BRADFIELD (trustee of Robert CHEW for benefit of Israel CLAYTON, Jul 1822) of Ldn to John CHEW of Ldn. B/S of 49¾a Lot #2 & 51¾a Lot #18 from division of William CLAYTON dec'd (reserving ½a on paved road nr Snickersville sold by Robert CHEW to Ruel MARSHALL). Delv. pr order 12 Feb 1828.

3N:340   Date: 9 Apr 1827   RtCt: 9 Apr 1827
Michael SOUDER of Ldn to Casper SPRING of Ldn. B/S of 20a Lot #7 allotted in division of lands of Philip SOUDER dec'd to dau Margaret SOUDER dec'd (directed to be sold by Exor Michael SOUDER). Delv. pr order 16 Apr 1828.

3N:342   Date: 9 Apr 1827   RtCt: 9 Apr 1827
Jacob SILCOTT of Ldn to Jesse SILCOTT of Ldn. Trust for debt to Conrad BITZER using 65a on Beaverdam adj Amos HIBBS, Isaac COGSILL, Samuel DUNCAN, Joseph GOURLEY. Delv. to BITZER 23 Sep 1833.

3N:345   Date: 28 Mar 1827   RtCt: 9 Apr 1827
French SIMPSON & wife Elizabeth of Ldn to John ISH of Ldn. Trust for debt to Jacob ISH and to John SIMPSON (Exor of Henson

SIMPSON dec'd with securities Hamilton ROGERS and William R. McCARTY and when ROGERS died SIMPSON became security) of Ldn using 100a and pers. prop of slaves Neale and Whorton. Delv. to ISH trustee 19 Dec 1832.

3N:349   Date: 21 Nov 1826   RtCt: 9 Apr 1827
Arthur ORRISON & wife Betsy of Ldn to Nathaniel S. ODEN and James McFARLAN. Trust for debt to Amos SKINNER using bond to Delia SMITH (Exor of George SMITH dec'd, who was assee of William NOLAND) with Amos SKINNER, Lewis GRIGSBY & William POLEN as security using 228a prch/o William NOLAND Jun 1818. Wit: Robert BAYLEY, Ariss BUCKNER.

3N:352   Date: 1 Dec 1825   RtCt: 9 Apr 1827
S. B. T. CALDWELL & wife Mary E. of Ldn to Joshua OSBURNE Esqr. Trust for debt to Timothy TAYLOR Esqr using 1a adj Marcus HUMPHREY, Thomas HUMPHREY, and also personal items. Wit: Craven OSBURNE, Thomas NICHOLS.

3N:356   Date: 8 Feb 1826   RtCt: 10 Apr 1827
Alexander CORDELL & wife Diana of Ldn to Sandford RAMEY of Ldn. B/S of lot in Lsbg (prch/o Martin CORDELL) on road from Lsbg to Nolands Ferry adj John MANSFIELD and a 1a lot (conveyed by John DAVIS) adj RAMEY. Wit: Presley CORDELL, John HAMILTON.

3N:358   Date: 9 Apr 1827   RtCt: 9 Apr 1827
Eli TAVENER & wife Nancy of Ldn to Charles B. HAMILTON of Ldn. B/S of 2a on great road adj Hannah JANNEY. Wit: Presley CORDELL, Thomas ROGERS. Delv. to Nancy HAMILTON pr order 4 Sep 1841.

3N:361   Date: 1 Mar 1827   RtCt: 10 Apr 1827
Stephen SANDS of Ldn to William STOCKS of Ldn. B/S of 45½a adj William PAXON, old road from Wtfd to Taylortown, Eneas WILLIAMS. Delv. to Nathan STOCKS pr order of William STOCKS 14 Aug 1847.

3N:363   Date: 20 Nov 1826   RtCt: 10 Apr 1827
William BENTON & wife Sarah of Ldn to Ludwell E. POWELL of Shelby Co Ky. B/S of interest in 7a of dower right of Ann LILLY late POWELL wd/o Elisha POWELL dec'd (prch/o Robert POWELL). Wit: Burr POWELL, A. GIBSON.

3N:365   Date: 25 Nov 1826   RtCt: 10 Apr 1827
James POWELL & wife Mary of Hampshire Co Va to Ludwell E. POWELL of Shelby Co Ky. B/S of 2a (share of brother William POWELL dec'd from undivided real estate of his father Elisha POWELL dec'd).

3N:367   Date: 24 Nov 1826   RtCt: 10 Apr 1827
John KILE Jr. & wife Winefred of Ldn to Ludwell E. POWELL of Shelby Co Ky. B/S of 18a on Bear branch of Goose Creek

(undivided share from estate of Elisha POWELL dec'd, including share of dower in right of Winnefred, her claim to share of brother William POWELL dec'd, and his claim by purchase of Pierce NOLAND). Wit: John SINCLAIR, Samson GUY, James L. POWELL, Francis W. LUCKETT, Edward HALL.

3N:369   Date: 2 Apr 1827   RtCt: 10 Apr 1827
Jesse HOGE of Ldn to James THOMPSON of Ldn. B/S of 135a (from trust by Isaiah POTTS Jan 1825) adj William WHITE, Levi WHITE, Isaac HUGHES. Delv. to THOMPSON 29 Oct 1827.

3N:371   Date: 26 Oct 1826   RtCt: 10 Apr 1827
Theoderick M. HERREFORD & wife Eliza of Ldn to Thomas A. HERREFORD of Ldn. B/S of land where Theo. now resides (conveyed in 1820 by Thomas A. HERREFORD) adj John TORBET, John HANN, Thomas FRED Jr. Wit: Notley C. WILLIAMS, John W. GRAYSON.

3N:373   Date: __ 1826   RtCt: 10 Apr 1827
Thomas DRAKE of Ldn to Joshua T. HOPE (also gives as Christian HOPE) of Ldn. B/S of ½a in Bloomfield adj DRAKE, John G. HUMPHREY, John L. GILL. Delv. to Joshua T. HOPE 6 Oct 1827.

3N:375   Date: 13 Jan 1827   RtCt: 10 Apr 1827
Morris OSBURNE & wife Jane of Ldn to son Richard OSBURNE Jr. of Ldn. B/S of 317a where Richard now lives (conveyed by trustees Stephen C. ROZELL, John LITTLEJOHN & Samuel BOGESS) nr Cotockton Creek, adj Peter WARNER. Wit: Craven OSBURNE, John WHITE. Delv. to Richard OSBURNE Jr. 29 Jul 1831.

3N:378   Date: __ 1827   RtCt: 9 Apr 1827
John P. DULANY and Daniel EACHES of Ldn to Hiram SEATON of Ldn. B/S of 82a (conveyed by William VICKERS Apr 1818 lately occupied by widow Mary LEITH) and 109a (conveyed by Jonathan CARTER with a lease by Agnes CARTER wd/o Richard CARTER dec'd).

3N:378   Date: 9 Apr 1827   RtCt: 10 Apr 1827
Luther FRANK to Martin L. FRANK (as agent of Mary Magdaline FRANK). BoS for numerous household items (for debt due to Mary).

3N:381   Date: 2 Apr 1827   RtCt: 11 Apr 1827
Jacob HOUSER & wife Abigail of Ldn to Samuel KALB of Ldn. B/S of 147a adj William WOLFORD, Margaret SAUNDERS, __ HAMILTON, Simon SHOEMAKER, Meeting House lot. Wit: George W. SHAWEN, Samuel HOUGH. Delv. to KALB 30 Jan 1828.

3N:383   Date: 7 Aug 1826   RtCt: 13 Apr 1827
Fielder BURCH & wife Sarah of Ldn to Ishmael VANHORNE of Ldn. B/S of Lot #6, #7 & #8 (¾a) in German Settlement (formerly owned by David LOVETT) adj Thomas STEPHENS. Wit: John W. GRAYSON, Edward HALL. Delv. pr order 1 Jan 1828.

3N:385 Date: 10 Apr 1827 RtCt: 14 Apr 1827
George W. HENERY [HENRY] of Ldn to Jacob BONCE of Ldn. B/S of 3a nr Wtfd (part of Lot #3 sold by Amos GIBSON to John E. PARMES) adj Benjamin JONSON, Asa MOORE dec'd.

3N:386 Date: 13 Apr 1827 RtCt: 14 Apr 1827
Jacob BONCE of Ldn to George W. HENERY [HENRY] of Ldn. Trust for debt to George W. HENERY using above land.

3N:389 Date: 22 Mar 1827 RtCt: 14 Apr 1827
Andrew CAMPBELL & wife Jane/Jean of Ldn to William CARR of Ldn. B/S of 150a adj __ WILKINSON. Wit: Samuel M. EDWARDS, Jno. J. MATHIAS.

3N:391 Date: 16 Jul 1824 RtCt: 16 Apr 1827
Christopher C. McINTYRE of Ldn to Isaac & Samuel NICHOLS of Ldn. B/S of 4a (by ct decree of Jun 1824, conveyed by commr S. M. EDWARDS on part of infant ch/o Pattrick McINTYRE dec'd).

3N:393 Date: 17 Nov 1826 RtCt: 16 Apr 1827
Charles Fenton MERCER of Ldn to Samuel M. EDWARDS and James McILHANY of Ldn. Trust for Richard H. HENDERSON as endorser on bank notes using 135a Aldie Mills, farm and dwelling house now in possession of Benjamin HIXON and Thomas MAUND and 127a adj wood lot and all interest in lands sold to Benjamin HAGERMAN and land prch/o Benjamin MOFFETT. Delv. to HENDERSON 13 Sep 1832.

3N:397 Date: 16 Jul 1824 RtCt: 16 Apr 1827
Samuel M. EDWARDS of Ldn to Isaac & Samuel NICHOLS of Ldn. B/S of 4¾a (from suit of Jun 1824 with EDWARDS as commr. for infant heirs of Pattrick McINTYRE dec'd) adj Henery BROWN, said NICHOLS.

3N:399 Date: 16 Apr 1827 RtCt: 17 Apr 1827
Samuel DAWSON of Ldn to Fayette BALL of Ldn. Trust for debt to Thomas GASSAWAY of Ldn using 300a (prch/o William NOLAND). Wit: Roberdeau ANNIN, John W. COE, William J. JONES.

3N:401 Date: 6 Dec 1826 RtCt: 19 Apr 1827
James STUBBLEFIELD & wife Mary of JeffVa to Jacob WATERS of Ldn. B/S of 59a adj John CONNARD, __ EVANS, __ DEMORY. Wit: Andrew HUNTER.

3N:404 Date: 9 Apr 1827 RtCt: 19 Apr 1827
George M. CHICHESTER & wife Mary of Ldn to William M. McCARTY of Ldn. B/S of 166a in German Settlement (prch/o Thomas GASSAWAY) adj M. MARLOW. Wit: William ELLZEY, Samuel M. EDWARDS. Delv. to McCARTY 14 Aug 1832.

3N:406 Date: 26 Apr 1823 RtCt: 20 Apr 1827
Aaron DAILEY & wife Polly of Ldn to Leesburg Turnpike Co. B/S of ½a nr Lsbg & road to Edwards Ferry (part of tract where DAILEY

resides). Wit: Thomas R. MOTT, H. H. HAMILTON, W. D. DRISH.
Release by John THOMAS for trust to Isaac WRIGHT.

3N:408 Date: 26 Mar 1827 RtCt: 20 Apr 1827
Stephen BEARD & wife Orpah of Ldn to Naomi LACEY, Huldah
LACEY & Ruth LACEY of Ldn. B/S of interest in estate of Tacey
LACEY dec'd and pers. estate of Joseph LACEY dec'd. Wit: John
BAYLY, Robt. BAYLY.

3N:410 Date: 3 Apr 1827 RtCt: 21 Apr 1827
Samuel KALB & wife Susannah of Ldn to William STEER and John
HAMILTON Jr. of Ldn. Trust for debt to Jacob HOUSER of Ldn
using land conveyed by HOUSER Apr 1827. Wit: George W.
SHAWEN, Samuel HOUGH.

3N:414 Date: 18 Apr 1827 RtCt: 23 Apr 1827
William M. McCARTY & wife Emily of Ldn to George M.
CHICHESTER of Ldn. B/S of 585a on Potomac adj William
GRAYSON, McCARTY. Wit: John McCORMICK, Samuel M.
EDWARDS. Delv. to CHICHESTER 15 Apr 1834.

3N:416 Date: 19 Apr 1827 RtCt: 23 Apr 1827
George M. CHICHESTER & wife Mary of Ldn to William T. T.
MASON of Ldn. Trust for debt to Thomas CRAMPKIM of MontMd
using above 585a. Wit: William ELLZEY, Samuel M. EDWARDS.
Delv. to John JANNEY Esq. pr order of CRAMPKIN Admr 19 Oct
1832.

3N:419 Date: 3 Feb 1827 RtCt: 30 Apr 1827
William CHILTON & wife Sarah of Ldn to George RHODES of Ldn.
B/S of 4a (in RHODES' possession since 9 Mar 1820 by exchange
of land) adj __ RUST. Wit: John McCORMICK, John J. MATHIAS.
Delv. to RHODES 9 Sep 1836.

3O:001 Date: 23 Apr 1827 RtCt: 1 May 1827
James HORSEMAN & wife Jemmima to John C. TIPPETT. B/S of
190a on Broad Run (from will of father William HORSEMAN dec'd,
prch/o John LYONS). Wit: Johnston CLEVELAND, James DARNE,
Elisha KITCHEN. Delv. to TIPPETT 13 Nov 1837.

3O:003 Date: 25 Apr 1827 RtCt: 2 May 1827
William M. McCARTY & wife Emily of Ldn to Benjamin SHRIEVE Jr.
of Ldn. B/S of 36a (cnvy/b Geo. RUST Jr. Jul 1823, DBk GGG:028)
nr Lsbg on Carolina Road adj __ MURRY, __ HARRIS, __
CLAGGETT. Wit: Hamilton ROGERS, John BAYLY. Delv. to
SHRIEVE 9 Aug 1827.

3O:005 Date: 2 May 1827 RtCt: 2 May 1827
Thomas KIDWELL (insolvent debtor - suit of 4 Apr 1827 by Admrs of
James HEATON) to Sheriff Charles LEWIS. B/S of rights to 84a
(cnvy/b John MATHIAS) where he now lives and adj 45a (cnvy/b
Edmund J. LEE) and 2a on E side of Blue Ridge (prch/o James
McBRIDE) adj William & Hiram McBRIDE.

3O:007   Date: 3 May 1827   RtCt: 4 May 1827
Sophia/Sophy MARTIN (wd/o Jacob MARTIN formerly of Lsbg) of
FredMd to Samuel STERRETT of Lsbg. B/S of her interest (during
her lifetime) in lot & house on King St in Lsbg (cnvy/b Charles
ELGIN) now occupied by STERRETT and Robert R. HOUGH
apothecary. Delv. to STERRETT 7 May.

3O:008   Date: 11 Jun 1825   RtCt: 5 May 1827
James COCHRAN(E) Jr. & wife Rachael of Ldn to Benjamin
BRADFIELD of Ldn. B/S of 18a adj ___ ZIMMERMAN. Delv. to
BRADFIELD 29 Aug 1827.

3O:010   Date: 10 Feb 1827   RtCt: 7 May 1827
John ALT & wife Mary of Ldn to William ALT of Ldn. B/S of 118a
(cnvy/b Robert CAMPBELL Dec 1818, DBk XX:260) and 77a
(cnvy/b John DULIN Mar 1816, DBk TT:356) less 20a sold to Bazzill
NEWMAN, and 47a cnvy/b William ALT to Newman and 5¼a cnvy/b
Wm. ALT to D. EVELAND and 4a sold to Saml. COX but not cnvy
(the 2 tracts sold by William to John on 17 Aug 1826, DBk
MMM:399). Wit: Noble S. BRADEN, Saml. HOUGH. Delv. to Wm.
ALT 5 Nov 1830.

3O:013   Date: 28 Apr 1827   RtCt: 8 May 1827
William H. HOUGH & wife Mary Ann of Ldn to Amasa HOUGH and
Joseph BOND of Ldn. Trust for debt to Thomas PHILLIPS of Ldn
using 278a adj Isaac STEER, widow HOUGH, Joseph POSTON,
Robert BRADEN, Jacob WINE. Wit: Noble S. BRADEN, Saml.
HOUGH.

3O:018   Date: 1 Mar 1827   RtCt: 8 May 1827
Ann WRIGHT of Lsbg to Samuel M. BOSS of Lsbg. B/S of lot on N
side of Loudoun St with wooden house now occupied by WRIGHT
(for her benefit during her lifetime). Delv. to BOSS 26 Aug 1827.

3O:020   Date: 9 May 1827   RtCt: 9 May 1827
George COOPER, Adam COOPER & wife Susan of Ldn and John
HEIRS & wife Catherine late COOPER of PhilPa by attornies Geo.
and Adam COOPER to Charles GULATT and Samuel M.
EDWARDS of Ldn. Britton SAUNDERS & wife Ann of Ldn. B/S of
6a for benefit of Ann SAUNDERS (late ECKHART). Wit: John
ROSE, Hamilton ROGERS. Delv. to EDWARDS 6 Oct 1827.

3O:023   Date: 22 Mar 1827   RtCt: 11 May 1827
Zachariah DULANEY of Ldn to Nathaniel MANNING & wife
Euphemia of Ldn. Release of trust of 21 Sep 1822 for debt to Amos
BEANS.

3O:025   Date: 23 Mar 1827   RtCt: 11 May 1827
Nathaniel MANNING & wife Euphamia of Ldn to John WHITE,
Ebenezer GRUBB and John WRIGHT of Ldn. Trust using 178a -
Zachariah DULANEY sold trust 22 Jun 1826 to John WRIGHT.
Names of creditors – Admr of John WHITE, Josiah WHITE, John

WRIGHT, Ebenezer GRUBB, J. SHOWATER, William TAYLOR, Morris OSBURNE, Pattrick McGAVICK, Walter WOODYARD, Isaac WALKER, Joshua OSBURNE, Amos BEANS, Nich. HATCHER, James LOVE, Archibald McDANIEL, James NIXON, Daniel EACHES, White & Clendening, Carver WILLIS, Presley CORDELL, Mary FOX, James McGAVICK, Paxton BEANS, Christian GROVER, David LOVETT, Saml. NEAR, M. PURCELL, Valentine PURCELL, Ashby & Stribling, James SHIRLY, Beverly WAUGH, Sarah NIXON, David POTTS, Thomas PHILLIPS, Robert BRADEN, William BROWN, James DILLON, Peter DEMORY, William GRAHAM, heirs of Dr. HEATON, Robert OGDEN, Andrew OGDEN. Wit: Noble S. BRADEN, Mortimore McILHANY. Delv. to WRIGHT 13 Mar 1828.

3O:031   Date: 13 Nov 1824   RtCt: 25 Apr 1825/11 May 1827
John SHAW of Lsbg to Peter FEICHTER of Lsbg. LS of lot on N side of Market St in Lsbg adj Benjamin MAULSBY. Delv. to FEICHTER Nov 1827.

3O:035   Date: 25 Apr 1827   RtCt: 12 May 1827
Henery AXLINE & wife Catherine of Muskingum Co Ohio to Peter WIRTZ of Ldn. B/S of 10¼a (Lot #3 cnvy/b Christopher BURNHOUSE 21 Sep 1816) on E side of Short Hill adj Edmund JENNINGS. Delv. pr order 9 Oct 1827.

3O:038   Date: 11 May 1827   RtCt: 12 May 1827
Richard H. HENDERSON & wife Orra M. of Ldn to Burr W. HARRISON of Ldn. B/S of house & lot on Market St opposite the back, adj Samuel CARR, William L. POWELL. Wit: Alfred A. ESKRIDGE, William J. JONES, Roberdeau ANNIN, John McCORMICK, Samuel M. EDWARDS.

3O:040   Date: 15 Sep 1826   RtCt: 14 Jun 1827
Sarah JONES dec'd. Division – decree of 10 May 1825: 7a Lot #1 to son Richard JONES (he sold 1/7th part to Hugh SMITH prior to her death); 27a Lot #2 to Hugh SMITH (entitled to by purchase of 2 shares and 1 share in right of wife Elizabeth); 40a Lot #3 to Thomas JONES (sold his interest to Hugh SMITH); and 34a Lot #4 to William JONES (his full share & 10a from mother's will). Gives plat. Divisors: James HIXON, John SINCLAIR, Jesse McVEIGH, John SIMPSON.

3O:042   Date: 16 Apr 1827   RtCt: 14 May 1827
William GALLIHER Sr. dec'd. Division of 134a nr house of Samuel DUNKIN, Bethesda Meeting House – 37a dower Lot #1 to widow Mary GALLIHER; 5a Lot #6 (by consent of Eli C. GALLIHER for whom it was drawn) and 3a wood Lot #5 to David GALLIHER; 6a Lot #4 and 3a wood Lot #3 to Leah McKENNEY heirs; 7a Lot #10 and 1a wood Lot #6 to John GALLIHER; 10a Lot #7 to William GALLIHER; 5a Lot #3 and 3a wood Lot #2 to Samuel GALLIHER; 6a Lot #5 and 3a wood Lot #4 to Caleb M. GALLIHER; 10a Lot #11 to Thomas GALLIHER;10a Lot #11 to Anna WERG; 9a Lot #9 to Mary VANDENVENTER; 6a Lot #2 and 3a wood Lot #1 to Eli C.

GALLIHER. Gives plat. Divisors: Gourley REEDER, Seth SMITH, Price JACOBS.

3O:048   Date: 14 May 1827   RtCt: 14 May 1827
John WEADON, Jacob SILCOTT, Benjamin MITCHELL and Henery HUTCHISON. Bond on WEADON as constable.

3O:049   Date: 28 Mar 1827   RtCt: 28 Mar 1827
Joseph HILLIARD & wife Ann Eliza of Lsbg to Rich'd. H. HENDERSON, Samuel M. EDWARDS and Burr W. HARRISON of Ldn. Trust for debt to George CARTER of Oatlands using lot on Back St in Lsbg adj Charles BINNS, blacksmith shop, John McCORMICK. Wit: John McCORMICK, John H. McCABE. Delv. to Jesse TIMMS by direction of Geo. CARTER 8 Nov 1827.

3O:053   Date: 14 May 1827   RtCt: 14 May 1827
Benjamin JACKSON of Ldn to Joshua PANCOAST of Ldn. Trust for debt to Joshua GREGG of Ldn using 102a adj Stephen McPHERSON, George MARKS.

3O:055   Date: 12 May 1827   RtCt: 14 May 1827
Israel WILLIAMS to John W. WILLIAMS. Trust for debt to Daniel POTTERFIELD using 93a. Delv. to POTTERFIELD 14 Apr 1829.

3O:058   Date: 8 May 1827   RtCt: 14 May 1827
Isaac NICHOLS Jr., William HOGE & William PIGGOTT (Exors of Samuel NICHOLS dec'd) of Ldn to Stacy TAVENER of Ldn. B/S of 46a on Beaverdam Creek adj Stephen George ROZELL, Joseph GARRETT, Levi TATE, David YOUNG, Edith HATCHER, Jonah TAVENER. Delv. to TAVENER 15 Apr 1828.

3O:059   Date: ___ 1827   RtCt: 14 May 1827
Isaac NICHOLS Jr., William HOGE & William PIGGOTT (Exors of Samuel NICHOLS dec'd) of Ldn to David YOUNG and Edith HATCHER of Ldn. B/S of 185a [or 155a?] on Beaverdam Creek adj Jonah TAVENER, Joshua PANCOAST, John GREGG, Levi TATE, Stacey TAVENER. Delv. to YOUNG 12 May 1841.

3O:061   Date: 14 May 1827   RtCt: 14 May 1827
Thomas HATCHER of Ldn to William PIGGOTT of Ldn. B/S of 144a on NW fork of Goose Creek adj John PANCOAST, Abdon DILLON, Isaac NICHOLS Sr., Abel JANNEY, Joshua PANCOAST. Delv. to PIGGOTT 16 Jul 1831.

3O:063   Date: 11 May 1827   RtCt: 14 May 1827
Isaac NICHOLS Jr., William HOGE & William PIGGOTT (Exors of Samuel NICHOLS dec'd) of Ldn to Thomas NICHOLS of Ldn. B/S of 97a on NW fork of Goose Creek adj __ EVANS, heirs of Charles JOHNSON, Abel JANNEY. Wit: Yardley TAYLOR, Jonah SANDS, Jonah TAVENER.

3O:065   Date: 11 May 1827   RtCt: 14 May 1827
Isaac NICHOLS Jr., William HOGE & William PIGGOTT (Exors of Samuel NICHOLS dec'd) of Ldn to Thomas HATCHER of Ldn. B/S

of 144a on NW fork of Goose Creek adj John PANCOAST, Abdon DILLON, Isaac NICHOLS Sr., __ EVANS, Abel JANNEY.

3O:067 Date: 11 May 1827 RtCt: 14 May 1827
Isaac NICHOLS Jr., William HOGE & William PIGGOTT (Exors of Samuel NICHOLS dec'd) of Ldn to Jonah TAVENER of Ldn. B/S of 96a on Beaverdam Creek adj Stephen G. ROZELL, David YOUNG, Edith HATCHER, Joshua PANCOAST, Abdon DILLON.

3O:069 Date: 10 May 1827 RtCt: 14 May 1827
Mary MARKS of Ldn to Samuel B. T. CALDWELL of Ldn. Trust for Joshua OSBURNE of Ldn as her security to Timothy TAYLOR Sr. and debts to Bennett MARKS of Ldn and her son Thomas MARKS late of Ldn for hire of negro boy Jim using negro man Jesse formerly the property of Thomas MARKS, farm and household items and right of dower to __a and slaves Ralph, Jim, Hannah and her children Tereny?, Eliza, Wesley, Madison, Smith, Squire, Mahlon and her sucking child, Dinah and her children Charlotte, Humphrey, Lewis and Massey. Delv. to CAL[D]WELL 10 Mar 1828.

3O:072 Date: 10 May 1827 RtCt: 14 May 1827
Johnston CLEVELAND (attorney for Esaias HORSMAN) to John C. TIPPETT. B/S of 190a (willed to Esaias by father William HORSEMAN, prch/o John LYONS). Delv. to TIPPETT 29 May 1841.

3O:074 Date: 11 Mar 1827 RtCt: 14 May 1827
Isaac NICHOLS Jr., William HOGE & William PIGGOTT (Exors of Samuel NICHOLS dec'd) of Ldn to Abdon DILLON of Ldn. B/S of 134a on NW fork of Goose Creek adj John PANCOAST, William PIGGOTT, Joshua PANCOAST, heirs of Samuel NICHOLS Jr., Jonah TAVENER. Delv. to DILLON 25 Jan 1830.

3O:076 Date: 14 May 1827 RtCt: 14 May 1827
William. C. CHILTON of Ldn to Humphrey B. POWELL of Ldn. Trust for debt to Burr POWELL, Cuthbert POWELL and Alfred H. POWELL (trustees of Sarah H. CHILTON) using interest in estate of Leven POWELL dec'd for use of his mother Sarah H. CHILTON.

3O:078 Date: 12 May 1827 RtCt: 14 May 1827
Samuel BRYERLY of FredVa and Elizabeth Telliferro HARRISON (wd/o Thomas HARRISON dec'd of Ldn). Marriage contract - Elizabeth has 300a, 1/3 of money in hands of John FITZHUGH from sale of 200a in PrWm, and negroes George age abt 53y, Nancy 58y, Bennet 33y, Robinson 26y, Lizzy 22y, Jeffrey 21y, James 12y, Edmond 11y, Sophy 10y, Freelove 8y, Daphney 6y, Mary raising? 15 months, Lucy 46y, Caroline 31y, Rosanna 22y, Lucinda 15y, Annice 11y, Matilda 9y, Joseph 8y, Henery nearly 3y, Carter 19 months, Horrace 18 months and Frank 2½y. Elizabeth to use 1/3 for support of new husband and joint family. Her daughters Ann and Francis [sic] shall have free boarding as long as they remain single. Superanuated slaves to be kept with Elizabeth at joint charge. At Samuel's death she will have no claim to his estate. Put in trust with

Wm. C. FITZHUGH and Cuthbert POWELL. Delv. pr order 15 Dec 1847.

3O:082   Date: 31 Mar 1827   RtCt: 14 May 1827

James LOVE & wife Susanna of Ldn to Henery SHAFFER of Ldn. B/S of 6a on S side of Kittockton Creek adj Samuel GREGG dec'd, Nathan GREGG, Robert BRADEN. Wit: Chas. B. HAMILTON, Presley CORDELL. Delv. to SHAFFER 4 Dec 1828.

3O:085   Date: 31 Oct 1826   RtCt: 14 May 1827

William MORAN of Washington Co Ky to John L. BERKLEY of Ldn. PoA for claims agst estate of father William MORAN dec'd with Admr D.S. William THRIFT. Wit: Chas. LEWIS, Wm. MERSHON.

3O:085   Date: 12 May 1827   RtCt: 14 May 1827

Jonah TAVENER & wife Miriam of Ldn to Isaac NICHOLS Jr., William HOGE and William PIGGOTT (Exors of Samuel NICHOLS dec'd) of Ldn. Trust for debt to Exors using 96a. Delv pr order 4 Sep 1837.

3O:089   Date: 12 Oct 1826   RtCt: 14 May 1827

James RUST & wife Sally of Ldn to Richard H. HENDERSON of Ldn. B/S of house & lot in Lsbg (cnvy/b HENDERSON) on Market St adj Presley CORDELL, HENDERSON, and Church St. (now occupied by Samuel CARR). Wit: John H. McCABE, Saml. M. EDWARDS.

3O:091   Date: 10 Sep 1827   RtCt: 10 Sep 1827

George HAY of Ldn to Richard H. HENDERSON as trustee for HAY's daughter Maria Antonetta RINGGOLD (w/o General RINGGOLD) of Washington Co Md. Gift of slave Sally (prch/o estate of Miles SELDEN dec'd) and 2 of her children (Geoffrey abt 7y and Nicholas not 1y old). Delv. to HAY 11 Oct 1827.

3O:092   Date: 11 Jun 1827   RtCt: 9 Jul 1827

James HAMILTON dec'd. Division – court order of 13 Feb 1827; 216a Lot #1 & 79a Lot #3 (¾ part of real estate in one lot to Charles B. HAMILTON and John HAMILTON together; Charles then purchased brother John's share); 55a Lot #2 and 12½a short hill Lot #5 (1/8 share to Enos WILDMAN & wife Jane, late Jane HAMILTON); 60a Lot #3 and 12a short hill Lot #4 to Ann B. HAMILTON. Divisors: Presley CORDELL, Joshua PUSEY, Thomas WHITE. Gives detailed plats.

3O:096   Date: 9 Jul 1827   RtCt: 9 Jul 1827

Edward HAMMATT, Samuel HAMMATT, John H. MONROE and Samuel M. BOSS. Bond on Edward HAMMATT as constable.

3O:097   Date: 9 Jul 1827   RtCt: 9 Jul 1827

Reed THOMPSON, Jacob G. POSTON and Elijah PEACOCK. Bond on THOMPSON as constable.

3O:098   Date: 6 Jul 1827   RtCt: 6 Jul 1827
Robert SANFORD of Ldn to son Augustine M. SANFORD of Ldn.
B/S of negro men Tom and Jack, boys Caleb and Frank and woman
Rachael, farm and household items – for support of Robert during
his lifetime.

3O:099   Date: 13 Jun 1827   RtCt: 6 Jul 1827
Rich'd H. HENDERSON (from trust of Aug 1822 from Thomas HEIR
& wife Jane late of Ldn) of Lsbg to Michael MORALLEE of Lsbg. B/S
of house & lot to E of Lsbg.

3O:100   Date: 16 Jun 1827   RtCt: 5 Jul 1827
Jane ROBERDEAU of FredVa to grandson Roberdeau ANNIN. Gift
of household items. Delv. to ANNIN 22 Nov 1827.

3O:102   Date: 3 Jul 1827   RtCt: 5 Jul 1827
Price JACOBS & wife Catherine of Ldn to Henly/Hendley H.
GREGG of Ldn. Trust for debt to Joshua GREGG using 120a
(prch/o Boston WOOSTER and William BRONAUGH), 60a (prch/o
Aaron BROWN) and 90a (prch/o Samuel DUNCAN). Wit: Edward
HALL, Notley C. WILLIAMS.

3O:104   Date: 2 Jul 1827   RtCt: 2 Jul 1827
John McCORMICK of Ldn to William GABBY of Washington Co Md.
Trust for debt to Helen? C. McCORMICK, Alexander LAWRENCE,
Hugh McCORMICK, Cornell & Nostrand of NY and Joseph
DURYEE of NY, James THOMAS of Georgetown, Bank of the
Valley, Margaret MARTIN using ¾a lot in Lsbg adj James GARNER,
64a on Catoctin Mt. adj Richard H. HENDERSON, Thomas TEBBS,
and life estate in house & lot at corner of King & Market St,
numerous farm and household items. Delv. to Roberdeau ANNIN 14
Mar 1828 per order.

3O:108   Date: 29 Mar 1827   RtCt: 15 May 1827
Charles SACKMAN & wife Sarah of Ldn to Conrad ROLLER and
John ROLLER of Ldn. B/S of 4a adj __ VERTS. Wit: Saml. HOUGH,
Mort. McILHANY. Delv. to ROLLER 30 Jan 1828.

3O:110   Date: 16 May 1827   RtCt: 16 May 1827
Samuel SIMPSON of Ldn to Jacob ISH of Ldn. B/S of 607¼a on
Goose Creek (part of tract cnvy to Mary SIMPSON in division of ___
dec'd by William THRELKELD).

3O:112   Date: 12 Apr 1827   RtCt: 14 May 1827
Thomas ROGERS and William HOLMES to Aquilla MEAD of Ldn.
Release of trust of 11 Jun 1823 on 7a.

3O:112   Date: 23 Apr 1827   RtCt: 17 May 1827
Hiram SEATON & wife Nancy of Ldn to Elijah ANDERSON of Ldn.
B/S of 82¼a (prch/o Robert M. POWELL by William VICKERS Apr
1818) on N side of Goose Creek adj James PLASTER, Wm. LEITH,
Elisha POWELL, James LEITH dec'd. Wit: Francis W. LUCKETT,
Edward HALL. Delv. per order 9 Jun 1830.

3O:115   Date: 10 Apr 1827   RtCt: 18 May 1827
Michael SPRING & wife Rachel of Ldn to Joshua PUSEY of Ldn.
B/S of 3a adj PUSEY. Wit: John H. McCABE, Saml. M. EDWARDS.
Delv. 20 Feb 1834.

3O:117   Date: 23 Mar 1827   RtCt: 19 May 1827
John E. PARMER (trustee of Charles G. EDWARDS) of Jeff Va to
Samuel E. TAYLOR of Ldn. Release of trust on 104a.

3O:119   Date: 3 May 1827   RtCt: 19 May 1827
James MERCHANT & wife Mary to Simon SHOEMAKER. Trust for
debt to John COOPER using 31a (cnvy/b Danl. COOPER to John
COOPER) adj James NIXON. Delv. to COOPER 10 Dec 1831.

3O:122   Date: 29 Dec 1826   RtCt: 14 May 1827
George BEATY of Ldn to Edmund TYLER of Ldn. Trust for debt to
Stephen GARRETT using ¼a (prch/o Andrew BEATY Dec 1822)
and negro woman Ann and girls Clarissa and Matilda. Wit: Jesse
McVEIGH, Balaam OSBURN, Jos. HOCKINGS. Delv. to GARRETT
5 Mar 1828.

3O:124   Date: 26 Feb 1827   RtCt: 21 May 1827
Walter LANGLEY & wife Susanna of Ldn to John VERNON,
Abraham VERNON, Elizabeth HARLOW, David GIBSON, Abner
GIBSON, Eli GIBSON, Levi GIBSON, Nancy HIXON and Rebeckah
HIXON (heirs of Daniel and Rebeckah VERNON dec'd) of Ldn. B/S
of 20a on S side of Blue Ridge adj __ CARRINGTON, __ LANGLEY.
Wit: Notley C. WILLIAMS, John W. GRAYSON. Delv. to Abner
GIBSON 15 Nov 1831.

3O:126   Date: 21 May 1827   RtCt: 22 May 1827
Rich'd. H. HENDERSON & wife Orra Moore of Ldn to Enoch
HARPER of Ldn. B/S of 7a (prch/o Henry CRAINE) adj HARPER,
Samuel M. EDWARDS. Wit: Samuel M. EDWARDS, James RUST.

3O:128   Date: 8 Sep 1826   RtCt: 28 May 1827
Elijah KENT of Lsbg to Robert R. HOUGH of Lsbg. Trust for benefit
of Elizabeth KENT (w/o Elijah) using household items. Wit: R. G.
SAUNDERS, Thos. RUSSELL, William D. LEWIS.

3O:129   Date: 29 May 1827   RtCt: 29 May 1827
Henry PEERS of Lsbg (insolvent debtor) to Sheriff Charles LEWIS
of Ldn. B/S of house & lot on Market St in Lsbg used by PEERS as
tavern, and another lot by alley formerly Fielding BROWN'; slaves
John Diggs, Monica, Louisa, Mary, Butler, household items (in trust
for benefit of Eleanor PEERS Dec 1826) (suits of capias ad
satisfaciendum by Giles TILLETT ass'ee of William DRISH &c, John
HAMERLY ass'ee of William DRISH and the Commonwealth).

3O:131   Date: 29 May 1827   RtCt: 29 May 1827
John JACKSON of Ldn (insolvent debtor) to Sheriff Charles LEWIS
of Ldn. B/S of 27a where JACKSON lives adj William H. HOUGH,

William E. STEER (suit of capias ad satisfaciendum by John HAMILTON).

3O:132 Date: __ Mar 1827 RtCt: 30 May 1827
William P. FOX & wife Catherine E. of Ldn to Elizabeth SULLIVAN of Ldn. B/S of 12a adj __ GRAYSON, 63a on E side of road from Wtfd to Mrs. LACEY's Tavern and 10a adj __ PUSEY (lots cnvy/b Josabed WHITE). Wit: John WHITE, Craven OSBURN. Delv. to SULLIVAN 2 Apr 1835.

3O:135 Date: 15 May 1827 RtCt: 31 May 1827
Stephen WILSON & wife Hannah of Ldn to William WILSON of Ldn. B/S of 111a on NW fork of Goose Creek adj Abdon DILLON, __ COPELAND. Wit: Craven OSBURN, Thomas NICHOLAS. Delv. to William WILSON 1 Jul 1837.

3O:138 Date: 15 May 1827 RtCt: 31 May 1827
William WILSON & wife Elizabeth of Ldn to Yardley TAYLOR of Ldn. Trust for debt to Stephen WILSON using 211a [not 111a] adj Thomas GREGG, Benj. DANIEL, __ DILLON. Wit: Thomas NICHOLAS, Craven OSBURN. Delv. to TAYLOR 4 Aug 1837.

3O:142 Date: 28 May 1827 RtCt: 2 Jun 1827
Seaton W. NORIS & wife Abby W. of Ffx to Johnston CLEVELAND of Ldn. B/S of 130a adj Aris BUCKNER, heirs of TU[R]BERVILLE. Wit: B. R. LANE. J. S. L. TRIPLETT, Jno. H. HALLEY. Delv. to CLEVELAND 9 Jun 1828.

3O:145 Date: 4 Apr 1827 RtCt: 4 Jun 1827
James VERNON & wife Nancy of Ldn to Uriel GLASSCOCK of Ldn. B/S of 98a (dev. to VERNON by James MARSH) adj __ McGETH, __ McMULLEN. Wit: John W. GRAYSON, Edward HALL. Delv. to GLASSCOCK 30 May 1831.

3O:148 Date: 5 Oct 1826 RtCt: 5 Jun 1827
George JANNEY and Elisha JANNEY of Ldn to Abel JANNEY of Ldn. B/S of adj tracts covered by the dam of Millville on big Goosecreek (cnvy/b Burr POWELL, Robert FULTON, William VICKERS, Mason FRENCH and Edward CARTER). Delv. to Abel JANNEY 21 Nov 1828.

3O:150 Date: 16 Jun 1826 RtCt: 6 Jun 1827
John NEAR & wife Eve of Ldn to Absalom VANVACTER of JeffVa. B/S of 8a adj John CONRAD, James STUBBLEFIELD, __ NICEWANGER. Wit: Rob. W. MIDDLETON, D. LONG, Jno. S. GALLAHER.

3O:153 Date: 26 May 1827 RtCt: 15 Jun 1827
David NEAR & wife Susannah of Ldn to James STUBBLEFIELD of JeffVa. B/S of 6½a on Potomac (part of Near's farm). Small drawing. Wit: Andrew HUNTER, George STUBBLEFIELD. Delv. per order 7 Jul 1831.

3O:157   Date: 20 Jun 1827   RtCt: 21 Jun 1827
John H. MORRIS of Lsbg to John A. BINNS of Lsbg. Trust for debt to William KING of Lsbg using household items.

3O:159   Date: 23 Jun 1827   RtCt: 23 Jun 1827
Charles P. TUTT of Ldn to George M. CHICHESTER of Ldn. Trust to CHICHESTER as security using farm animals, household items, mortgage by James H. HAMILTON for property in NY.

3O:161   Date: 30 May 1827   RtCt: 23 Jun 1827
George HARRIS & wife Sarah Ann of Wtfd to Isaac WALKER and Jesse GOVER of Wtfd. Trust for Thomas PHILLIPS, John WILLIAMS and Joseph BOND as security on Admr bond of estate of Ann MOORE dec'd (m/o wife Sarah Ann) using ¾a willed by Asa MOORE to wife Ann MOORE now occupied by Thomas PHILIPS. Wit: Noble S. BRADEN, Samuel HOUGH.

3O:166   Date: 6 Dec 1826   RtCt: 24 Jun 1827
Robert WHITE & wife Mary of Franklin Co Indiana to Samuel BEANS of Ldn. B/S of 12a (Lot #9 in div. of estate of Jasper POULSON dec'd). Wit: Stacy TAYLOR, Isaiah B. BEANS. Delv. to BEANS 12 May 1849.

3O:168   Date: 1 Nov 1826   RtCt: 24 Jun 1827
Mary WHITE (formerly Mary POULSON) of Franklin Co Indiana to Robert WHITE. PoA for transactions from estate of father Jasper POULSON who died intestate and rights to dower of mother Agnes POULSON.

3O:170   Date: 25 Jun 1827   RtCt: 25 Jun 1827
Margaret TILLETT of Ldn to Honor TILLETT and Samuel TILLETT of Ldn. Trust (Margaret about to marry Elias POOL of Ldn and wants protection against any of POOL's debts) of negro boy Jesse abt 9y old, cattle, household items, note for debt to Thomas SWANN, notes of Saml. CARR, Honor TILLETT, William SAUNDERS. Wit: Gunnell SAUNDERS, John HANSBOROUGH, C. C. McINTYRE.

3O:172   Date: 30 Jun 1826   RtCt: 27 Jun 1827
Richard H. HENDERSON of Ldn to John LLOYD of Ffx. B/S of 63a Millville tract and adj 124a (from trust of George JANNEY & wife Susannah and Elisha JANNEY & wife Lydia S., Jan 1823). Delv. to LLOYD 26 Mar 1828.

3O:174   Date: 27 Jun 1827   RtCt: 27 Jun 1827
Daniel JAMES of Ldn to John WHITE of Ldn. B/S of 87½a (dev. by Margaret McILHANY to Elias, Jonathan and Daniel JAMES May 1819).

3O:176   Date: 26 Dec 1826   RtCt: 28 Jun 1827
Samuel McPHERSON & wife Mary of Ldn to Rebecca McPHERSON of Ldn. B/S of 9a with stone mill house (cnvy/b L. P. W. BALCH May 1823). Wit: Wm. B. STEER, John McPHERSON, Joseph STEER,

Samuel HOUGH, Noble S. BRADEN. Delv. to Joshua PUSEY 28 Sep 1837.

3O:178 Date: 15 Jun 1827 RtCt: 29 Jun 1827
Benjamin HAGERMAN of Ldn to Asa ROGERS of Ldn. Trust for John BEVERIDGE Jr. of Ldn as security on bond to Jane WEATHERBY using slaves Travis, Mary and Esther. Delv. to ROGERS 14 Jun 1828. Wit: Jas. CRAIN, Wm. R. SWART.

3O:182 Date: 20 Jun 1827 RtCt: 30 Jun 1827
Andrew B. McMULLIN & wife Nancy of Ldn to Jonathan CARTER of Ldn. B/S of 10a on old turnpike road leading to Snickers Gap. Wit: Francis W. LUCKETT, A. GIBSON.

3O:185 Date: 7 Apr 1827 RtCt: 9 Apr/30 Jun 1827
Given HANDY to John FRANCIS and Edward WILSON. Trust for debt to Enoch FRANCIS using 147a (Lot #1 in div. of Enoch FRANCIS dec'd). Wit: James MOUNT, Robert CURRY.

3O:188 Date: 30 Jun 1827 RtCt: 30 Jun 1827
James MOUNT to Enoch FRANCIS. B/S of 90½a (from trust of Daniel BROWN & wife Rachel, Jun 1826, DBk WW:60, Wm. T. T. MASON bought, then sold to George RUST Jr., who sold to Enoch FRANCIS). Delv pr order 24 Nov 1830.

3O:191 Date: 15 May 1827 RtCt: 31 May 1827
Stephen WILSON & wife Hannah of Ldn to Jesse HOGE of Ldn. Trust for debt to William KENWORTHY of BaltMd using 183a on NW fork of Goose Creek adj John SPENCER, B. BRADFIELD. Wit: Craven OSBURN, Thomas NICHOLS. Delv. to WILSON 29 Jun 1829.

3O:195 Date: 30 May 1827 RtCt: 11 Jun 1827
Amos HARVEY to Samuel CLENDENING. Trust for debt to William THOMPSON and James THOMPSON using farm animals, household items, crops.

3O:199 Date: 4 Nov 1825 RtCt: 11 Jun 1827
Charles Fenton MERCER of Lsbg to Humphrey B. POWELL of Ldn. Trust to Burr POWELL of Chessnut hill in Ldn as endorser on bank note (bonds due MERCER from Hugh McGUIRE of Mason Co Va, Samuel LEWIS residing near Frankfort Ky, Benjamin HAGERMAN) using 140a with 2-story stone house abt 3m from Aldie and Mdbg now under lease to William GULICK.

3O:201 Date: 26 Sep 1826 RtCt: 11 Jun 1827
Elizabeth S. STONESTREET (wd/o Basil STONESTREET dec'd) and Joseph BLINCOE, Walter H. DORSETT, Augustus STONESTREET and John C. TRIPLETT (reps of Benjamin A. STONESTREET dec'd and Basil dec'd). Agreement that gives Elizabeth during her lifetime negro man Sam. Hockity late property of Benj. A. dec'd and at her death the reps. are given negroes Lucy,

Tildy and James (to be sold and profit divided). Wit: J. CLEVELAND, Jno. J. COLEMAN, R. H. COCKERILL.

3O:202   Date: 5 Apr 1827   RtCt: 11 Jun 1827
Eli PIERPOINT & wife Hannah of Ldn to Thomas B. LOVE of Ldn. B/S of Hannah's 1/7th (36a) of undivided 216a from John LOVE dec'd (prch/o John GREGG and Rich'd THATCHER Exors of Timothy HOWELL by John LOVE, Apr 1804 and part from Henry SMITH & wife Sarah Aug 1808). Wit: Craven OSBURN, John WHITE.

3O:205   Date: 28 Feb 1827   RtCt: 11 Jun 1827
Thomas DRAKE of Ldn to William SETTLE of Ldn. B/S of ¼a lot & house in Bloomfield adj Benjamin GRAYSON. Delv. pr order 17 Jul 1829.

3O:207   Date: 11 Jun 1827   RtCt: 11 Jun 1827
John MARTIN, Samuel M. BOSS and Robert R. HOUGH. Bond on MARTIN as constable.

3O:208   Date: 10 Nov 1826   RtCt: 11 Jun 1827
Asa ROGERS (Commr. for Henson SIMPSON in decree of 10 Jul 1826 for sale of interest of James SIMPSON dec'd in land) of Ldn to Daniel JANNEY of Ldn. B/S of 1/7th of 49a (purchased by James SIMPSON in his life from Adam ZIMMERMAN) where Eliza (wd/o Henry ZIMMERMAN) now lives as life estate, near Goose Creek meeting house, adj Bernard TAYLOR. Delv. to JANNEY 22 Mar 1828.

3O:210   Date: 11 Jun 1827   RtCt: 11 Jun 1827
William CLENDENING, William THOMPSON and Samuel CLENDENING. Bond on William CLENDENING as constable.

3O:211   Date: 19 May 1827   RtCt: 11 Jun 1827
Samuel PURCEL/PURSEL Jr. of Ldn to Samuel D. LASLIE of Ldn. B/S of ¼a (cnvy/b John HOUGH) E of Hllb adj D. LOVETT, B. LASLIE. Delv. to LESLIE 13 Jul 1829.

3O:213   Date: 11 Feb 1827   RtCt: 12 Jun 1827
Charles T. MAGILL & wife Mary D., William J. BRONAUGH & wife Mary C., Ludwell LUCKETT & wife Anna C., George Wm. BRONAUGH, Joseph W. BRONAUGH and Patrick H. W. BRONAUGH (heirs of Wm. BRONAUGH dec'd) to Francis W. LUCKETT & wife Sarah S. of Ldn. B/S of all rights to undivided tract on Great Kenhawa River. Wit: John McDOWELL, David GIBSON, A. GIBSON, Edward HALL. Delv. to LUCKETT 9 Jun 1830.

3O:217   Date: 25 May 1827   RtCt: 14 Jun 1827
John FITZHUGH & wife Marian of Ffx to Nathaniel TYLER of Ffx. Trust for debt to Benjamin R. LACEY & wife Julia Ann of Ffx using 200a 'Jacksons lot' in Ldn where Eleanor COOKSEY now resides (LS by Nathaniel FITZHUGH to Robert JACKSON) and additional 100a from tract where FITZHUGH now resides. Wit: A. TYLER, J. E.

DENEALE, R. H. HENDERSON. Delv. to Benj. R. LACEY 30 Oct 1828.

3O:221 Date: 6 Dec 1826 RtCt: 15 Jun 1827
Jacob WATERS of Ldn to Fontaine BECKHAM of JeffVa. Trust for debt to Andrew HUNTER of JeffVa using 59a (cnvy/b James STUBBLEFIELD) adj John CUNNARD, Adam EVANS.

3O:224 Date: 5 Jun 1827 RtCt: 11 Jun 1827
Richard W. STONESTREET & wife Eleanor of Lsbg to John ROSE of Ldn. Trust for debt to John G. WATT & wife Duanna of Lsbg using land conveyed this day by Watt. Wit: John H. McCABE, John McCORMICK.

3O:227 Date: 25 Jul 1827 RtCt: 30 Jul 1827
Enos W. NEWTON & wife Sarah of Ldn to Humphrey B. POWELL of Ldn. Trust for debt to Noble BEVERIDGE using ½ Lot #42 & #43 in Mdbg. Delv. to BEVERIDGE 17 Dec 1827. Wit: Burr POWELL, A. GIBSON.

3O:230 Date: 21 Jan 1826 RtCt: 27 Jun 1827
Joshua OVERFIELD to George H. ALLDER and Samuel LODGE. Trust for debt to Nathaniel NICHOLS and Thomas JAMES using 84a Lots #2 and 3 in div. of Martin OVERFIELD dec'd. Wit: H. ELLIOTT, Stephen JANNEY, George RICHARDSON, Henry TURNIPSEED. Delv. to ALDER 13 Jun 1828.

3O:232 Date: 6 Jul 1827 RtCt: 7 Aug 1827
Robert SANFORD of Ldn to Augustine M. SANFORD of Ldn. B/S of interest in land now in occupation of Robert on Catocton Mt. (cnvy/b James RATICOE).

3O:233 Date: 5 Jul 1827 RtCt: 9 Jul 1827
Mesheck LACEY of Mdbg to Asa ROGERS of Ldn. Trust for debt to Joshua OSBURN of Ldn using ½a Lot #27 in Mdbg.

3O:236 Date: 11 Sep 1826 RtCt: 9 Jul 1827
Asa ROGERS (trustee of James McCRAY, 16 Nov 1825) to Leven LUCKETT. B/S of 1¾a (prch/o David CARR) where McCRAY lives on Goose Creek, adj Andrew McMULLEN, Joseph CARR. Delv. to LUCKETT 11 Mar 1834.

3O:237 Date: 9 Jul 1827 RtCt: 9 Jul 1827
Charlotte SHORTZ/SHORTS to James McILHANY. Trust for debt to Philip HEATER using ¼ of 42a (derived from uncle Adam SHOVER dec'd) and slave William.

3O:239 Date: 9 Jul 1827 RtCt: 11 Jul 1827
Robert MOFFETT Jr. for Sheriff Charles LEWIS of Ldn to Eleanor PEERS of Ldn. B/S of interest of insolvent Henry PEERS in house and lot in Lsbg on Market St. and slaves John Diggs, Monica, Louisa, Nancy and Butler, household items. Wit: Giles TILLETT, John HAMMERLY, George W. HENRY, J. J. WOOD.

3O:240   Date: 28 May 1827   RtCt: 11 Jul 1827
James ALLEN & wife Martha of Ldn to David L. ALLEN of Ldn. B/S
of 100a (prch/o David SMALLY) adj __ BEAVERS, __ WARFORD.
Wit: Robert BAYLY, John BAYLY. Delv. to ALLEN 12 Jan 1829.

3O:242   Date: 9 Jul 1827   RtCt: 11 Jul 1827
Eleanor PEERS to Otho R. BEATTY. Trust for debt to William D.
DRISH, Robert BENTLEY and John GRAY using house and lot. Wit:
R. H. HENDERSON, Saml. M. EDWARDS, Joseph HILLIEA[R?]D.

3O:244   Date: 5 Jun 1827   RtCt: 16 Jul 1827
John G. WATT & wife Duanna/Dewanner of Ldn to Richard
STONESTREET of Ldn. B/S of 2a (cnvy/b Saml. M. EDWARDS Jan
1824, DBk JJJ:287). Wit: John McCORMICK, John H. McCABE.
Delv. to STONESTREET 27 Jun 1819.

3O:245   Date: 26 Aug 1824   RtCt: 11 Jul 1827
Foushee TEBBS & wife Margaret of PrWm to Betsey TEBBS of
PrWm. B/S of 540a (from will of William CARR Sr. dec'd – annuity
by children to mother Betsey). Delv. to James M. FARLING pr order
of Betsey TEBBS 22 Apr 1833.

3O:250   Date: 17 Feb 1827   RtCt: 17 Jul 1827
Andrew OGDEN & wife Elizabeth to Benjamin OGDEN. Trust for
debt to Robert OGDEN using tract adj John PAXSON, David
SHAWEN and tract adj Thos. SWAYNE. Wit: Noble S. BRADEN,
George W. SHAWEN. Delv. to Benj. OGDEN 27 Mar 1828.

3O:253   Date: 21 Jun 1827   RtCt: 19 Jul 1827
Sarah HUGHES (wd/o Thomas HUGHES dec'd late of Ldn), Samuel
HUGHES & wife Elizabeth, Hannah BROOKBANK late HUGHES,
Thomas BROOKBANK & wife Elizabeth late HUGHES, Elisha
HUGHES & wife Fanny, Thomas HUGHES & wife Ruth, Matthew
HUGHES & wife Jane, John HUGHES & wife Mary, Hezekiah
OGDEN & wife Lydia late HUGHES, and David LOGAN & wife Maria
late HUGHES (heirs of Thomas HUGHES dec'd) all of Franklin Co
Indiana (except Samuel HUGHES & wife, Elisha HUGHES & wife,
Thomas BROOKBANK & wife, Matthew HUGHES & wife and David
LOGAN who are of Union Co Indianna) to Elijah JAMES of Ldn. B/S
of 113a on Kittocton Creek adj William BROWN, James LOVE,
Joseph TAYLOR, __ TRIBBE. Wit: Alex'r HENDERSON, John
TEMPLETON, Daniel OGDEN.

3O:257   Date: 1 Aug 1827   RtCt: 1 Aug 1827
George NORWOOD of Lsbg to James GARRISON of Lsbg. BoS for
household items.

3O:258   Date: 1 Aug 1827   RtCt: 1 Aug 1827
James HOGE (trustee of Colen AULD) of Ldn to William CARR of
Ldn. B/S of 155a (from trust of widow and children of Richard
CARTER dec'd, Mar 1816, DBk TT:271).

3O:260 Date: 5 Apr 1827 RtCt: 1 Aug 1827
James LOVE & wife Susanna(h) of Ldn to Eli PIERPOINT of Ldn.
B/S of 2 equal thirds of tract prch/o James McILHANY by James
LOVE Sr. and cnvy/b his heirs to James LOVE May 1806; 1/24th
(1/8th of remainder) of tract inherited as heir of James LOVE Sr.; 1/8th
part of 1/3rd tract inherited by Samuel LOVE and sold to James;
1/168th part of tract inherited from John LOVE an heir of James
LOVE Sr.; 15/56ths of L/L in same 162a tract on S side of Kitocton
Creek adj Josiah WHITE, James COPELAND, William RUSSELL.
Wit: Presley CORDELL, Noble S. BRADEN. Delv. to PIERPOINT 15
Apr 1828.

3O:262 Date: 1 Aug 1827 RtCt: 1 Aug 1827
Charles P. TUTT (insolvent debtor) of Ldn to Sheriff Charles LEWIS
of Ldn. B/S of interest in trust of Jul 1823 conveyed to William T. T.
MASON, George M. CHICHESTER (suits of John H. CANBY and
Benj. EDWARDS).

3O:263 Date: 30 Jul 1827 RtCt: 1 Aug 1827
Edward HAMMATT of Lsbg to Thomas MORALLEE of Lsbg. B/S of
lot on S side of Market St and E side of Air St. (cnvy/b John
CRIDLER & wife Elizabeth Jan 1824, part in trust to Samuel
MULLIN – CRIDLER defaulted).

3O:264 Date: 31 Mar 1827 RtCt: 10 Aug 1827
Robert RUSSELL of Ldn to George SMITH of Ldn. B/S of 119a adj
Adam MILLER, Mrs. JACOB, E. GRUBB. Delv. to SMITH 5 Nov
1828.

3O:266 Date: 9 Aug 1827 RtCt: 10 Aug 1827
Adam EVANS to Sheriff Charles LEWIS. B/S of 60a adj John
CUNNARD, Jacob WATERS; and 2¾a where EVANS lives (writ of
capias ad satisfaciendum from James MOORE assi[g]nee of
Andrew HUNTER, appearance bail by Thomas METCALF). Wit:
Roberdeau ANNIN, Edw'd L. FANT, John W. COE.

3O:267 Date: 10 Aug 1827 RtCt: 4 Aug 1827
George SYPHERD of Ldn to Jacob EVERHART of Ldn. Trust for
debt to Peter DERRY of Ldn using household items, horses. Delv. to
DERRY 24 May 1831.

3O:269 Date: 17 Jul 1827 RtCt: 13 Aug 1827
Hamilton ROGERS. Oath as Major in 57th Reg 6th Brig 2nd Div of Va
Militia.

3O:269 Date: 18 Jun 1827 RtCt: 13 Aug 1827
Ramey G. SAUNDERS. Oath as Lt. Colonel in 57th Reg Va Militia.

3O:269 Date: 11 Jan 1827 RtCt: 13 Aug 1827
Benjamin MITCHELL, Stephen McPHERSON Jr. and Garrett
WALKER appointed commissioners to view Snickers Gap turnpike
road. Road built according to law.

3O:270   Date: 13 Aug 1827   RtCt: 13 Aug 1827
Wm. ROSE, R. H. HENDERSON and Johnston CLEVELAND. Bond on ROSE as constable.

3O:271   Date: 12 Mar 1827   RtCt: 14 Aug 1827
William REEDER dec'd. Division – court order dated 14 Feb 1827; (tract now occupied by Ammon EWER) 61a Lot #1 to heirs of dau. Sarah HATCHER dec'd; 54a Lot #2 to dau. Anna VICKERS; 55a Lot #4 to dau. Hannah HATCHER. Gives plat. Divisors: Samuel DUNCAN, John SINCLAIR, Ben. MITCHELL, Elijah ANDERSON.

3O:274   Date: 16 May 1827   RtCt: 13 Aug 1827
Patrick McGARVICK dec'd. Division – negro boy Henson abt 17 or 18y and 102a Lot #4 in Culpeper Co to Patrick McGARVICK; negro girl Ibby Ann age 1y and 24a Lot #2 in Culpeper to William McGARVICK; negro boy George aged 8 or 9y and 100a Lot #1 in Culpeper to William GRAYHAM & wife Tamar late McGARVICK; negro girl Mary aged 4y and house and Lot #2 and ½ of Lot #3 (lately occupied by John FENTON) in Janney's addition to Wtfd adj Robert and John BRADEN and Lot #59 opposite John WILLIAMS in addition to Wtfd to Amelia, Henry and John McGARVICK (heirs of James McGARVICK dec'd); negro woman Grace and 30a Lot #3 in Culpeper Co, ½ of lot with shop occupied by John MOUNT, Lot #6 and ½ of adj lot in Janney's addition to Wtfd to Pleasant McGARVICK (< 21y and not married). Divisors: Presley CORDELL, John BRADEN, Z. DULANEY. Gives plat.

3O:280   Date: 16 Apr 1827   RtCt: 14 Aug 1827
Jacob WALTMAN dec'd. Division – court order of 11 Apr 1827; 11a Lot #1 and 5a Lot #1 to Rachael WALTMAN; 21a Lot #2 and 6a Lot #2 to Joseph WALTMAN; 25a Lot #3 and 6a Lot #3 to Jacob WALTMAN; 26a Lot #4 and 6¼a Lot #4 to Mary Ann WALTMAN; 26a Lot #5 and 6a Lot #5 to Elias WALTMAN; 31a Lot #6 to Jonathan WENNER & wife Susanna; 38a Lot #7 to Emanuel WALTMAN; 39a Lot #8 to Margaret WALTMAN; 23a Lot #9 to Susannah WALTMAN. Gives plat. Divisors: John BOOTH, Geo. W. SHAWEN, Jacob EVERHART, Jno. J. MATHIAS.

3O:286   Date: 7 May 1826   RtCt: 11 Jul 1827
Zenus/Zenis READER & wife Martha late LEITH of Columbiana Co Ohio to William RHODES of Columbiana Co Ohio. PoA for monies from James VIOLET and William VICKERS dev. Martha from will of grandfather John VIOLET and grandmother Jemima VIOLETT, late of Ldn. Wit: Wm. BYE, George BROWN. Delv. 27 Feb 1830.

3O:289   Date: 17 May 1826   RtCt: 13 Aug 1827
John NYSWANGER/NISESWANER (s/o C[h]ristain) & wife Mary of Ldn to Catherine NYSWANGER (wd/o Henry NYSWANGER Sr. dec'd) of Ldn. B/S of 1/7th part of 2/3rd of 2 lots - 122½a on SE side of blue ridge between short hill and blue ridge nr harpers ferry, adj James RUSSELL; and 125a in JeffVa held by L/L of Henry Sr. dec'd

on NW side of blue ridge between ridge and Shanandoah River nr Harpers Ferry. Wit: Jno. J. MATHIAS, Peter DEMORY, Joshua OSBURN, John CONARD, Ebenezer GRUBB. Delv. pr order 9 Jun 1828.

3O:292 Date: 20 Jun 1827 RtCt: 13 Aug 1827
William KENWORTHY & wife Rebecca of BaltMd to Joseph GORE of Ldn. B/S of 60a adj George FAIRHURST, Aquila MEAD, Israel JANNEY, Blackstone JANNEY. Wit: Jesse HOGE, William HOGE, Howel DAVIS, John McCORMICK, John H. McCABE. Delv. to GORE 24 Jan 1831.

3O:296 Date: 19 Jul 1827 RtCt: 13 Aug 1827
Samuel WARD Jr. of NY (trustee of J. C. VandenHEVEAL) to William NOLAND & wife Catherine late of Ldn now of Territory of Arkansas. Release of trust of Nov 1820, DBk BBB:351.

3O:298 Date: 26 May 1827 RtCt: 13 Aug 1827
David SHAWEN of Ldn to Burr BRADEN of Ldn. Trust for note to Bank of the Valley using interest in life estate (½ of 207a) of William FOX dec'd.

3O:300 Date: 11 Jan 1827 RtCt: 13 Aug 1827
John RIMER of Bedford Co Va to Mathias PRINCE of Ldn. B/S of 6a on W side of short hill, adj PRINCE, John DEMORY. Wit: Ebenezer GRUBB, John CONARD, Peter DEMORY, John DEMORY, John NISESWANER Sr., William DERRY. Delv. to PRINCE 14 Mar 1837.

3O:302 Date: 30 May 1827 RtCt: 13 Aug 1827
William HOGE, Isaac NICKOLS and William PIGGOTT (Exors of Samuel NICKOLS Sr. dec'd) of Ldn to John NICKOLS of Ldn. B/S of 112a on Long Branch of Goose Creek adj heirs of John EWERS dec'd, Levi TATE, Joseph GARRETT. Delv. to John NICHOLS 27 Jun 1840.

3O:304 Date: 1 Nov 1826 RtCt: 13 Aug 1827
Joshua PUSEY & wife Mary of Ldn to Samuel SACKMON of Ldn. B/S of 1 rood lot former prop. of John SHAFFER (cnvy/b trustee William VERTS to PUSEY) adj George WINCEL, Lorrence RINKS. Wit: Noble S. BRADEN, Presley CORDELL.

3O:307 Date: 25 Jul 1827 RtCt: 13 Aug 1827
Dpty Thomas ROGERS for Sheriff Charles LEWIS to William H. HOUGH. B/S of 27a where John W. JACKSON now lives. Delv. to HOUGH 13 Apr 1829.

3O:309 Date: 17 May 1826 RtCt: 20 May/13 Aug 1827
Catherine NICEWANGER of Ldn to John NICEWANGER of Ldn. B/S of 78a in Shannondale adj John DEMORY. Wit: Jno. J. MATHIAS, Joshua OSBURN, Peter DEMORY, John CONARD. Delv. to John NICESWANGER 21 Nov 1828.

3O:310   Date: 6 Apr 1827   RtCt: 13 Aug 1827
James LOVE & Susanna of Ldn to Thomas B. LOVE of Ldn. B/S of 1/7th of 216a from John LOVE dec'd (prch/o Exors of Timothy HOWEL, Apr 1804 and of Henry SMITH Aug 1808). Wit: Presley CORDELL, Noble S. BRADEN.

3O:313   Date: 30 May 1827   RtCt: 13 Aug 1827
Isaac NICKOLS Jr., William HOGE and William PIGGOTT (Exors of Samuel NICKOLS dec'd) to Isaac NICKOL Sr. B/S of 22a (prch/b Isaac & Samuel NICKOLS of Yardley TAYLOR as trustee of James COCKRAN) adj __ ZIMMERMAN, Goose Creek Meeting.

3O:315   Date: 18 Oct 1810   RtCt: Nov 1810/13 Aug 1827
Philoporman R. LANE & wife Elizabeth of Ffx to David GALLEHER of Ldn. B/S of 103a (from div. of estate of father Col. Jos. LANE). Wit: Humph. PEAKE, Wm. LANE Jr., Wm. BRONAUGH, Wm. GALLEHER. Delv. to GALLEHER 29 Oct 1828.

3O:318   Date: 14 Aug 1827   RtCt: 14 Aug 1827
John MOORE and Jacob EVERHART (Commrs. for Maria WALTMAN dec'd) to Jacob WATERS. B/S of 40a Lot #4 from div. of John WALTMAN and ¼ of 48a widow's dower lot from div. Delv. to WATERS 14 Mar 1828.

3O:319   Date: 1 Aug 1827   RtCt: 14 Aug 1827
Foushee TEBBS & wife Margaret of Ldn and Elizabeth TEBBS of PrWm to John D. BELL of Ffx. Trust for debt to Samuel and John H. HALLY of Ldn using 200a on both sides of Bull Run in Ldn and PrWm. Wit: Ariss BUCKNER, Robert BAYLY. Delv. to John H. HALLEY 6 Feb 1829.

3O:323   Date: 1 Aug 1827   RtCt: 14 Aug 1827
William POLIN & wife Elizabeth of Ldn to Adrian SWART of Ldn. B/S of 145a on S side of old Alexandria Road adj James SWART, Sampson HUTCHISON. Wit: Robert BAYLY, John BAYLY. Delv. to Martin H. SWART Admr dbn of Adrian L. SWART dec'd, 30 Nov 1857.

3O:326   Date: 13 Aug 1826   RtCt: 14 Aug 1827
Hugh SMITH (Admr wwa of Samuel DAVIS dec'd) of Ldn to William DAVIS of Ldn. B/S of 124¾a (where Samuel died, prch/o George BAILEY, DBk NN:116) adj Samuel DISHMAN, Philip FRYE. Delv. to Wm. DAVIS 3 Feb 1832.

3O:328   Date: 28 Jul 1827   RtCt: 14 Aug 1827
John SIDEBOTTOM to Richard F. PAYTON/PEYTON. Trust for debt to Townsand D. PAYTON using household items distrained by Hugh SMITH.

3O:329   Date: 15 Aug 1827   RtCt: 15 Aug 1827
Joshua PUSEY & wife Mary of Ldn to Jacob SHOEMAKER of Ldn. B/S of 2a (prch/o trustees of John SHAFFER). Wit: James RUST, John SIMPSON. Delv. to SHOEMAKER 17 Mar 1830.

3O:331 Date: 16 Aug 1827 RtCt: 16 Aug 1827
Augustine M. SANFORD & wife Lydia of Ldn to Robert SANFORD. B/S of land and property during Robert's lifetime with agreement if Robert and his wife Sarah cannot live together in comfort (in Jul 1827 Robert cnvy to Augustine 160a plus slaves and personal property, Augustine agrees to reconvey to restore harmony with Robert's wife Sarah and his children Augustine and Mahala LACY) Stacy LACEY has slave Rachel and her child Frank. Delv. to Robert SANFORD 22 Sep 1831.

3O:333 Date: 15 Aug 1827 RtCt: 16 Aug 1827
Humphr. PEAKE and George WISE (Commrs of Alex. Ct. for Humphrey PEAKE) to James L. MARTIN of Ldn. B/S of 11a Lot #8 (of the late Ricketts & Newton) on S side of Lsbg Turnpike Road. Wit: Saml. HAMMETT, James GILMORE, James THOMAS. Delv. to MARTIN 2 May 1834.

3O:335 Date: 15 Aug 1827 RtCt: 16 Aug 1827
Humphr. PEAKE and George WISE (Commrs of Alex. Ct. for Humphrey PEAKE) to Samuel HAMMETT of Ldn. B/S of 12a Lot #7 and 10a Lot #9 (of the late Ricketts & Newton) n S. side of Lsbg Turnpike Road. Wit: Jas. L. MARTIN, James THOMAS, James GILMORE. Delv. to HAMMATT 16 Sep 1829.

3O:337 Date: 15 Aug 1827 RtCt: 16 Aug 1827
Humphr. PEAKE and George WISE (Commrs of Alex. Ct. for Humphrey PEAKE) to James THOMAS of Ldn. B/S of 118a Lot #1 (of the late Ricketts & Newton) adj __ SAUNDERS, __ AULT, __ EDWARDS. Wit: James GILMORE, James F. NEWTON, Rich. H. LOVE. Delv. to THOMAS 8 Sep 1828.

3O:339 Date: 17 Feb 1815 RtCt: 9 Oct 1815
Deborah McKNIGHT of Ldn to Thomas JAMES of Ldn. B/S of 10a adj Alex. HARRISON, __ WOODFORD. Wit: Edward CUNARD Jr., Charles CHAMBLIN, William CARTER. Delv. to JAMES 3 Oct 1828.

3O:341 Date: 22 Dec 1826 RtCt: 22 Aug 1827
John HUNT Jr. to John HUNT Sr. of Ldn. Bond – John Jr. sold to John Sr. 1/3 part of house & lot bequeathed to John Jr. by Major HUNT dec'd, adj William CARR. Wit: Samuel PURSEL Jr., Saml. CLENDENING.

3O:342 Date: 20 Aug 1827 RtCt: 23 Aug 1827
Eli McKNIGHT & wife Alley to James McILHANY. Trust for debt to Charles CHAMBLIN using 130a (from father William McKNIGHT dec'd) where McKNIGHT lives adj CHAMBLIN, D. LOVETT, Issachar BROWN, Robt. CARLISLE. Wit: Alfred A. ESKRIDGE, John W. COE, George W. HAMMETT, Craven OSBURN, Thomas NICKOLS. Delv. to McILHANY 16 Jun 1839.

3O:345   Date: 25 Aug 1827   RtCt: 25 Aug 1827
George SHOVER of Ldn (insolvent debtor) to Sheriff Charles
LEWIS. B/S of 48½a (part of tract of Adam SHOVER dec'd) and
interest in 21a derived by marriage from lands of John
SANDBOWER dec'd (writ of capias ad satisfaciendum from Robert
BRADEN use of Joseph WALTMAN).

3O:346   Date: 14 Mar 1827   RtCt: 29 Aug 1827
Charles Lewis GAINER and Matthew ORRISON of Ldn to Saml. M.
EDWARDS of Ldn. Trust to William GILMORE (and BOSS as
securities on notes to Rich'd H. HENDERSON as Exor of Thomas R.
MOTT dec'd) of Ldn using farm and household items, claims of
GAINER on Charles DUNKIN dec'd. Delv. to GILMORE 13 Feb
1828.

3O:350   Date: 15 Aug 1827   RtCt: 28 Aug 1827
Robert J. TAYLOR (trustee of Bank of Alexandria) of AlexVa to
Portia HODGSON of AlexVa. Release of trust of Jun 1826 on land
from father William LEE and brother William Ludwell LEE and
negroes. Delv. pr order filed DBk MMM:197.

3O:352   Date: 22 Aug 1827   RtCt: 28 Aug 1827
Benjamin HAGERMAN of Ldn to John BEVERIDGE of Ldn. Trust for
debt to Amos GULICK, estate of Dade POMEROY, Jonathan
BEARD, Lewis M. SMITH, Thomas ROBINSON, Masekeh YOUNG,
Lewis GRIGGSBY, Edmund TYLER, Thomas MAUND, David
HIXSON, John SKILLMAN, James SWART, Wm. BEATTY using
farm animals, household items. Delv. to BEVERIDGE 20 Aug 1828.

3O:354   Date: 21 May 1827   RtCt: 30 Aug 1827
James H. RUSSELL of Maysville, Mason Co Ky to Aaron RUSSELL
of Hllb. B/S of __a (dev. by will of William RUSSELL to James H.,
Aaron, etc.) adj Hannah PARKER, Benjamin LESLIE, Elisha
JANNEY.

3O:355   Date: 15 Aug 1827   RtCt: 31 Aug 1827
John T. PEARCE & wife Jane of Ldn to Gabriel VANDEVANTER of
Ldn. Trust for debt to John CARR of Ldn using house and lot on E
side of Back St in Lsbg (cnvy/b Edward HAMMET Sept 1824). Wit:
Wm. ELLZEY, John McCORMICK.

3O:358   Date: 5 Jun 1827   RtCt: 1 Sep 1827
William RICHARDS & wife Margaret of Ldn to William LEATH (s/o
William LEATH dec'd) of Ldn. B/S of 8a (part of tract allotted to
Robert M. POWELL in div. of Elisha POWELL dec'd, then
transferred to William VICKERS) adj Hiram SEATON. Wit: Edward
HALL, Francis W. LUCKETT.

3O:361   Date: 15 Aug 1827   RtCt: 3 Sep 1827
George SHOVER to Adam E. SHOVER. Trust for debt to Catherine
STONEBURNER using 21a interest from land of John SANBOWER

dec'd. Wit: Andrew BAUGHMAN, George SHOVER Jr., Adam HEFNER. Delv. pr order 18 Sep 1829.

3O:362   Date: 3 Sep 1827   RtCt: 4 Sep 1827
Dpty William THRIFT for late Sheriff James HAMILTON of Ldn to James A. PADGET of Ldn. B/S of 4/6th of land of Jacob JAMES father of William, Smith, Abigail and Anne (interest of insolvent Smith JAMES from brother William JAMES), and of Elisha FOX & wife Abigail, Joseph FOX & wife Anne (cnvy to William, DBk ZZ:103 and 114 and transferred to Smith). Interest was transferred to Burr POWELL, who transferred to Rich'd H. HENDERSON and now to James A. PADGET.

3O:364   Date: 4 Sep 1827   RtCt: 5 Sep 1827
Joshua B. OVERFIELD to Rich'd H. HENDERSON. Trust for debt to Catharine HANCOCK (assignee of Enos POTTS and J. B. OVERFIELD) and Thompson F. MASON using 200a adj Joseph RICHARDSON, William LODGE. Wit: Jas. SINCLAIR, Geo. L. BITZER, Saml. HAMMETT, John W. COE. Delv. to ?andy HENDERSON son of R. H. HENDERSON 8 Feb 1828.

3O:367   Date: 6 Sep 1827   RtCt: 8 Sep 1827
William TATE & wife Prescilla of Ldn to Yardley TAYLOR of Ldn. Trust for debt to Isaac NICHOLS Sr. using 53a adj Levi TATE, David YOUNG, Edith HATCHER. Wit: James HOGE, William PIGGOTT, Isaac NICKOLS, Samuel M. EDWARDS, John J. MATHIAS. Delv. to Thos. HATCHER pr order of Wm. HOGE Exor of Isaac NICKOLS Sr. 11 Mar 1828.

3O:370   Date: 11 May 1827   RtCt: 8 Sep 1827
Isaac NICHOLS Jr., William HOGE and William PIGGOTT (Exors of Samuel NICHOLS dec'd) to Andrew BIRDSALL of Ldn. B/S of 187a adj Samuel GREGG, __ SUDDITH, __ BROWN. Delv. to BIRDSALL 8 Feb 1834.

3O:373   Date: 5 Sep 1827   RtCt: 8 Sep 1827
Isaac NICHOLS Jr., William HOGE and William PIGGOTT (Exors of Samuel NICHOLS dec'd) to William TATE of Ldn. B/S of 53a on long branch of Beaverdam Creek, adj Levi TATE, William YOUNG. Delv. to TATE 12 May 1828.

3O:375   Date: 30 May 1827   RtCt: 8 Sep 1827
Andrew BIRDSALL & wife Lydia of Ldn to Yardley TAYLOR of Ldn. Trust for debt to Isaac NICHOLS Jr., William HOGE and William PIGGOTT (Exors of Samuel NICHOLS dec'd) using above 187a. Wit: Saml. M. EDWARDS, Jno. J. MATHIAS. Delv. to William PIGGOTT 25 Jul 1831.

3O:379   Date: 5 Sep 1827   RtCt: 8 Sep 1827
Isaac NICHOLS Jr., William HOGE and William PIGGOTT (Exors of Samuel NICHOLS dec'd) to Levi TATE of Ldn. B/S of 47a adj William TATE, Stacy TAVENER. Delv. to TATE 24 Mar 1828.

3O:381 Date: 17 Apr 1827 RtCt: 25 Apr 1827
Thomas O'NEAL of Ldn to Garrett WALKER of Ldn. Trust for debt to
Mahlon CRAVEN, Jonah TAVENNER Exor of James CARTER
dec'd with Stephen McPHERSON Jr. as security using farm animals.
Delv. to WALKER 25 Mar 1828.

3O:385 Date: 8 Sep 1826 RtCt: 8 Sep 1827
Isaac NICKOLS & wife Mary (d/o Joseph Gibson dec'd) of Ldn to
John GIBSON of Ldn. B/S of 4/7th of 272a from Joseph GIBSON
dec'd (shares from Mary NICKOLS, Esther SMITH w/o John,
Hannah BROOKE w/o Benjamin, Mirian GIBSON). Wit: Saml. M.
EDWARDS, Jno. J. MATHIAS.

3O:388 Date: 25 Feb 1827 RtCt: 10 Sep 1827
Adam VIRTZ to George W. FRENCH. Trust for debt to Charles
GULLATT and Saml. M. EDWARDS (trustees of Ann SANDERS)
using farm animals and wagon. Wit: Stacey LACEY.

[Pages 390-399 are missing, may have been misnumbered]

3O:400 Date: 10 Sep 1827 RtCt: 10 Sep 1827
Garrison B. FRENCH, John HOLMES, Samuel CROOKS and Hugh
BOGER Jr. Bond on FRENCH as constable.

3O:401 Date: 10 Sep 1827 RtCt: 10 Sep 1827
Jesse TIMMS and George CARTER. Bond on TIMMS as
Commissioner of Revenue in 1st district.

3O:402 Date: 16 Jun 1806 RtCt: 12 Jan 1807/8 Oct 1827
Ferdinando FAIRFAX of Jeff Va to William SMITH of Ldn. B/S of
136½a adj William WILDMAN, Jonathan LODGE, Thomas D.
STEPHENS. Wit: Edw'd McDANIEL, Wm. HOUGH 3rd, William
HICKMAN, Wm. H. HARDING. Delv. to SMITH 12 Mar 1828.

3O:404 Date: 8 Jun 1827 RtCt: 10 Sep 1827
Francis STRIBLING of FredVa to James McILHANY of Ldn. Trust for
debt to Bank of the Valley, Robert BENTLEY agent for Jane LOCK,
Sarah FOLEY Admr of Presley FOLEY, Taliaferro STRIBLING,
Richard H. HENDERSON, John J. HARDING, Camp BECKHAM
using 400a (occupied by James HILL, Amos WHITACRE, as
distributee of James McILHANY dec'd to wife Cecelia late
STRIBLING). Delv. to McILHANY 30 Aug 1836.

3O:407 Date: 12 May 1827 RtCt: 10 Sep 1827
Patrick B. MILHOLLIN of Hardy Co Va to Esther GRANT of Ldn. B/S
of 2a (dev. by his father, sold to GRANT 23 Jan 1823 but deed was
defective) adj Joshua PUSEY, John WILLIAMS, J. T. GRIFFITH.

3O:409 Date: 9 Sep 1827 RtCt: 10 Sep 1827
Jacob RAZOR & wife Dorcas of Ldn to Thomas J. MARLOW of Ldn.
Trust for debt to Peter COMPHER of Ldn using interest in land of
George RAZOR dec'd on S side of Catocton Mt. adj George M.
CHICHESTER, Truman GORE (now in possession of Mary RAZOR
wd/o George). Wit: Geo. W. SHAWEN, Noble S. BRADEN.

3O:413 Date: 10 Sep 1827 RtCt: 10 Sep 1827
John W. CROUSE & wife Margaret of Ldn to James STIDMAN of Ldn. B/S of undivided share in lot and house on E side of King St in Lsbg (from will of Elizabeth SMITH dec'd to daus Margaret and Eleanor). Wit: Saml. M. EDWARDS, John J. MATHIAS. Delv. to STIDMAN 24 Jun 1831.

3O:416 Date: 23 Aug 1827 RtCt: 10 Sep 1827
John AXLINE Jr. & wife Christena of Ldn to John CONARD Sr. of Ldn. B/S of 105a (cnvy/b Henry AXLINE Mar 1826) adj David AXLINE, Jacob WIRTS, Philip EVERHART, Jacob EMERY. Wit: Ebenezer GRUBB, Geo. W. SHAWEN. Delv. to John CONRAD 16 Jan 1829.

3O:419 Date: 15 Mar 1826 RtCt: 11 Sep 1827
William A. BINNS & wife Nancy of Ldn to Samuel MURRAY of Ldn. B/S of 1a on road from Lsbg to Carter's Mill. Wit: Jno. A. BINNS, A. A. ESKRIDGE, James McCLAIN, John McCORMICK, Presley CORDELL.

3O:421 Date: 11 Sep 1827 RtCt: 11 Sep 1827
William JENKINS to Philip HEATER. B/S of 113a (L. P. W. BALCH as Commr of Ct for heirs of Job JENKINS dec'd – land formerly belonged to William JENKINS dec'd subject to dower of widow Mary; Mary died Feb 1826). Delv. to HEATER 29 Apr 1836.

3O:423 Date: 10 Sep 1827 RtCt: 10 Sep 1827
Emanuel WALTMAN, Jacob WALTMAN and Jacob WATERS. Bond on Emanual WALTMAN as constable.

3O:424 Date: 28 Jun 1828 [27] RtCt: 28 Jun 1828 [27]
Rich'd H. HENDERSON to Joshua B. OVERFIELD. Release of trust. Delv. to OVERFIELD 26 May 1832.

3P:001 Date: 21 Apr 1827 RtCt: 14 Sep 1827
Thomas RUSSELL of Ldn to Edward DOWLING of Ldn. Trust for debt to Robert BRADEN Guardian for Jos. Lewis POTTS, Joshua PUSEY Exor of James NIXON, Jonas POTTS using 40a of grain belonging to heirs of David POTTS dec'd subject to rent, cows, household items. Wit: Jas. McILHANY, Noble S. BRADEN, John BRADEN.

3P:004 Date: 9 Jul 1826 RtCt: 18 Sep 1827
John DRISH of Ldn to Wilson J. DRISH of Ldn. B/S of 8-9a lot and house where DRISH resides on Turnpike Road adj Lsbg, John J. MATHIAS.

3P:005 Date: 18 Sep 1827 RtCt; 22 Sep 1827
Benjamin BRADFIELD to Thomas NICHOLS and James BRADFIELD. Trust for Stephen WILSON, Yardley TAYLOR, Daniel COCKRELL, William M. JENNERS as security in ct suit using 190a where James BRADFIELD resides adj David LOVETT, Rufus UPDIKE.

3P:008   Date: 18 Sep 1827   RtCt: 22 Sep 1827
Benjamin BRADFIELD & wife Rachael (with James BRADFIELD as Admr of Jonathan BRADFIELD dec'd) to James McILHANY and William M. JENNERS. Trust for debt to 18½a (prch/o James COCKRAN) adj Stephen WILSON. Wit: G. W. JENNERS, J. L. WILSON, D. COCKEREL, James P. BRADFIELD, Yardley TAYLOR. List of notes on Benjamin and Andrew BIRDSALL, Lee THOMPSON & Amos WHITACRE, David BROWN and Jonathan HIRST, Charles RITE & Yardley TAYLOR, Giles CRAVEN & Thomas GREGG, William SMITH, Daniel BROWN & Thomas EMER[S]ON, Henry G. TAYLOR & Yardley TAYLOR, Andrew & Benjn. BIRDSALL, Thomas GREGG & Amos WHITACRE, Bernard TAYLOR, Benj. & Timothy TAYLOR, William WILKINSON & John WRIGHT, Lee THOMPSON & John WHITACRE, Lee & Abraham SILCOTT, Stephen WILSON, Mary HOWELL, Anthony STONE? & D. COCKERELL.

3P:013   Date: 2 May 1827   RtCt: 27 Sep 1827
Samuel J. TEBBS & wife Hannah S. to John SPENCE & wife Mary, John P. DUVAL & wife Ann, Thomas F. TEBBS, Foushee TEBBS, and Samuel John TEBBS. B/S of lands of William CARR Sr. dec'd. Will of William CARR Sr. dec'd states on death any children of dau Betsey TEBBS in her lifetime would pass to other children (Samuel J. TEBBS, Willoughby W. TEBBS, Mary F. SPENCE, Ann F. DUVAL, Thomas F. TEBBS (certification from AlexDC), Foushee TEBBS and Margaret C. TRIPLETT. Deeds amongst children confirming partition. Deeds from Betsey in PrWm. Delv. to TEBBS 22 Mar 1828.

3P:019   Date: 12 Sep 1827   RtCt: 27 Sep 1827
Sarah DONOHOE of Ldn to Jesse HOGUE of Ldn. Trust for William HOGUE as security on note to Isaac NICHOLS Sr. using 66a Lot #3 of father Stephen ROSZEL, adj Shelburn Parrish Glebe. Delv. to Wm. HOGE 4 Aug 1829.

3P:021   Date: 26 Sep 1827   RtCt: 27 Sep 1827
Enos POTTS (now in jail from suit of Thomas GREGG) to Townsend McVEIGH. Trust for William REED as bail using crops.

3P:023   Date: 7 Aug 1826   RtCt: 28 Sep 1827
John A. BINNS & wife Mary M. of Ldn to James BROWN of Ldn. B/S of Lot #61 in Lsbg (cnvy/b Andrew JAMESON Aug 1819). Wit: William CARR, Saml. M. EDWARDS. Delv. to BROWN 22 Mar 1828.

3P:025   Date: 17 Sep 1827   RtCt: 28 Sep 1827
Benjamin BRADFIELD & wife Rachel, John BRADFIELD & wife Emily and Jonathan BRADFIELD & wife Sarah of Ldn to Stephen WILSON of Ldn. B/S of 289a adj Bernard TAYLOR, Jesse JANNEY, David SMITH, __ HOWELL, __ EMARSON, __ COCKRILL, __ TAYLOR. Wit: Presley CORDELL, Thomas NICHOLS.

3P:028   Date: 13 Sep 1827   RtCt: 29 Sep 1827
Evelyn B. DOUGLAS and George LEE of Ldn to Philip HOWSER. DOUGLAS and LEE lease to HOWSER the tenement where he lives – agreements on fencing, orchard, repair during lifetime of Ephraim CARTER now of Ky who is on original lease made by Thomas L. LEE to Peter CARTER. Wit: William LEFEVER. Delv. to HOWSER 18 Mar 1828.

3P:029   Date: 28 Sep 1827   RtCt: 29 Sep 1827
Horatio BALL of FredMd and John B. BALL of Ldn to Saml. M. EDWARDS of Ldn. Trust for debt to William CLINE of Ldn using 100a with merchant, grist and saw mill. Wit: W. ELLZEY, S. HOUGH, Jno. STEPHENSON. Delv. to CLINE 22 Oct 1835.

3P:032   Date: 28 Sep 1827   RtCt: 29 Sep 1827
William CLINE & wife Margaret of Ldn to Horatio BALL of FredMd and John B. BALL of Ldn. B/S of 100a (2/3 to Horatio and 1/3 to John B.) with merchant, grist and saw mill (cnvy/b Philip RAHN of Adam Co Pa May 1825). Wit: Wm. ELLZEY, Saml. HOUGH. Delv. to Horatio & John B. BALL 23 Sep 1835.

3P:035   Date: 22 Sep 1827   RtCt: 4 Oct 1827
John DRISH & wife Eleanor of Ldn to Thomas MORALLEE of Ldn. B/S of remaining ½ of lot prch/o Samuel MULLEN on W side of King St in Lsbg. Wit: John ROSE, Saml. M. EDWARDS.

3P:037   Date: 6 Oct 1827   RtCt: 8 Oct 1827
Elias POOL of Ldn to Samuel HAMMETT of Ldn. Trust for debt to Samuel CARR, Honor TILLETT trustees for Margaret POOL w/o Elias, James L. MARTIN, John GRAY, David OGDEN, William KING, Dr. Charles LEWIS of FredVa using crops on farm of Honor TILLETT, farm animals and items.

3P:039   Date: 10 Sep 1827   RtCt: 6 Oct 1827
William LITTLETON & wife Elizabeth of Ldn to Daniel POTTERFIELD of Ldn. B/S of undivided 1/9th of 155a and 1/9th of house & lot in Lsbg from Elizabeth's father Henry POTTERFIELD dec'd. Wit: Saml. DAWSON, Geo. W. SHAWEN. Delv. to POTTERFIELD 3 Mar 1834.

3P:042   Date: 3 Oct 1827   RtCt: 8 Oct 1827
Robert BRADEN of Wtfd. DoE for negro woman Alle aged 39y and her infant dau. Susan aged 4y (payment by her husband). Wit: Jesse GOVER, Flem. G. W. P. HIXSON, Noble S. BRADEN, David SHAWEN.

3P:043   Date: 9 Oct 1827   RtCt: 9 Oct 1827
Martin BRONAUGH to Sampson HUTCHISON. B/S (for support of Martin's wife Sally during her lifetime) of mulatto slave Alice, farm animals, note of William B. TYLER of PrWm, note of estate of William BRONAUGH dec'd father of wife, ½ interest in property of Sarah TYLOR of PrWm.

3P:045   Date: 11 Jun 1827   RtCt: 8 Nov 1827
William SUMMERS & wife Albina of Ldn to Elijah JAMES of Ldn. B/S of interest in land (Sep 1825 ruling in case of Mary PERREY an infant agst John and Sarah HUGHES infants – Commr. Stacy TAYLOR to sell 1/10th part of land of Thomas HUGHS dec'd which belonged to children of his son Hugh HUGHES dec'd – cnvy to SUMMERS). Wit: John WHITE, Craven OSBURN.

3P:047   Date: 11 Aug 1827   RtCt: 8 Oct 1827
Joseph B. FOX & wife Amanda O. of Ldn to Craven OSBURN of Ldn. B/S of 108a on E side at foot of Blue Ridge where FOX now lives adj Nancy WILLIAMS, __ POTTS, Joseph BEAL, James THOMPSON and ½ of 112½a where James THOMPSON now lives and claims under L/L and 248a adj __ HOUGH, __ THOMPSON; and 67a (tracts willed by Thos. LASLIE to dau. Amanda or allotted by Commrs). Wit: John WHITE, Mortimer McILHANY. Delv. to OSBURN 22 Sep 1828.

3P:051   Date: 1 Oct 1827   RtCt: 8 Oct 1827
Presley CORDELL & wife Amelia of Ldn to William L. Powell of Ldn. B/S of lot on S side of Market St. in Lsbg occupied by Col. Wm. ELLZEY, adj Samuel CARR. Wit: John H. McCABE, Samuel M. EDWARDS.

3P:053   Date: 11 Aug 1827   RtCt: 8 Oct 1827
Craven OSBURN of Ldn to Joseph B. FOX & wife Amanda O. of Ldn. B/S of 281a farm where OSBURN now lives on E side at foot of Blue Ridge adj Jane POTTS, Jesse HOWELL, Thos. OSBURN. Delv. to C. OSBURN pr Jos. B. FOX's order 19 Nov 1828.

3P:055   Date: 13 Aug 1827   RtCt: 8 Oct 1827
Joseph B. FOX & wife Amanda O. of Ldn to Joshua OSBURN of Ldn. Trust for debt to Craven OSBURN using above 188a (title may not be perfect). Wit: John WHITE, Mortimer McILHANY. Delv. to Craven OSBURN 22 Sep 1828.

3P:059   Date: 23 Aug 1827   RtCt: 9 Oct 1827
John AXLINE Jr. & wife Christina of Ldn to Phillip EVERHART of Ldn. B/S of 106a (cnvy/b father and mother Jan 1817) adj heirs of Jacob EMERY dec'd, David AXLINE. Wit: Ebenezer GRUBB, Geo. W. SHAWEN. Delv. to EVERHEART 22 Oct 1838.

3P:061   Date: 26 May 1827   RtCt: 9 Oct 1827
Philip EVERHART of Ldn to John H. BOGER of Ldn. B/S of 61a adj George COOPER, Peter WIRTS and 5a adj __ WINCEL. Wit: J. GRUBB, John BUMCROTS. Delv. to BOGER 7 Aug 1829.

3P:063   Date: 21 Sep 1827   RtCt: 9 Oct 1827
John BITTZER to Townsend McVEIGH. Trust for Silas BEATY for bonds to Conrad BITTZER, Admr of Joseph DONNEL dec'd, Admr of William BRONAUGH dec'd using 38a where BITTZER now lives, farm animals, farm and household items.

3P:066   Date: 27 Oct 1827   RtCt: 9 Nov 1827
John McCORMICK of Lsbg to Helen C. McCORMICK of Lsbg. B/S of lot at King and Market St. in Lsbg adj Dr. H. CLAGETT, John H. HARDING; and 2/3 of ½a lot and house formerly owned by Joseph KNOX on Market St. in Lsbg adj heirs of Henry McCABE, Samuel HAMILTON; and lot on Market St. adj heirs of POTTERFIELD, Chs. BINNS, S. B. T. CALDWELL; and lot on W end of Market St adj heirs of Stephen COOKE dec'd, James L. MARTIN, James GARNER; and 64a on road from Lsbg to J. VANDEVA[N]TER adj A. MAINS, C. G. ESKRIDGE, Thos. SWANN; and 1a on E end of Market St. by Fayette St. adj John J. MATHI[A]S, James GARNER, William JOHNSON. Delv. to Roberdeau ANNIN 25 Feb 1828.

3P:068   Date: 9 Oct 1827   RtCt: 9 Oct 1827
L. P. W. BALCH of Frederick, Md to David OGDEN of Lsbg. BoS for negro girl Harriet now in possession of OGDEN for 15y then freed, with any children to be freed at age 21y.

3P:069   Date: 22 Sep 1827   RtCt: 10 Oct 1827
Sheriff Charles LEWIS to Joseph WALTMAN. B/S of undivided 1/7th of 51a of Simon SHOVER dec'd (from insolvent George SHOVER on 25 Aug 1827; part of tract which Adam SHOVER died seized not listed in George's schedule); and 48a (Henry SHOVER inherited from Adam SHOVER dec'd and sold to George); and 21a (from John SANBOWER through George's marriage to his daughter Susannah SANBOWER). Wit: Philip EVERHART, William BAGLEY, Casper EVERHART.

3P:071   Date: 11 Apr 1826   RtCt: 10 Oct 1827
William ALEXANDER, C. POWELL and Wm. A. POWELL (Exors. of Cuthbert POWELL Jr. dec'd), John Leven POWELL and Alfred H. POWELL children of Leven POWELL Jr. to Burr POWELL. B/S of 10 1/6a adj Mdbg (cnvy/b Leven POWELL to Leven POWELL Jr. Oct 1806).

3P:073   Date: 11 Oct 1827   RtCt: 11 Oct 1827
Samuel MURRAY & wife Mary Ann of Ldn abt. to remove from the state to Simon A. BINNS. B/S (to discharge debts) of 1a with brick house where MURRAY lives prch/o William A. BINNS Sr. (given in trust of Sept 1825 to George RICHARDS of Ldn) and Mary Ann's interest in 30a (dev. by John A. BINNS dec'd subject to dower of widow Dewanner; and personal items). Long list of debts.

3P:077   Date: 10 Nov 1827   RtCt: 10 Nov 1827
Jesse McVEIGH and Hugh SMITH. Bond on McVEIGH as Commissioner of Revenue in 2nd District.

3P:078   Date: 10 Nov 1827   RtCt: ___
John BROWN dec'd. Division - 43a to Nimrod BROWN; 21a to Sarah BROWN. Ct. case of Sarah BROWN wd/o John BROWN dec'd and Nimrod BROWN vs Sarah BROWN infant of John

BROWN. Divisors: Charles CHAMBLIN, Jacob COST, David LOVETT.

3P:080   Date: 13 Nov 1827   RtCt: 13 Nov 1827
George RICHARDS and John ROSE. Bond on RICHARDS as Treasurer of the School Commissioners.

3P:081   Date: 16 Oct 1827   RtCt: 3 Nov 1827
John WILDMAN. Oath as Captain in 57th Reg 6th Brig 2nd Div of Militia.

3P:082   Date: 2 Nov 1827   RtCt: 12 Nov 1827
Dean JAMES. Oath as Captain in 57th Reg Va Militia.

3P:082   Date: 11 Oct 1827   RtCt: 12 Oct 1827
John McCoRMICK & wife Mary of Ldn to Rich'd H. HENDERSON and Jas. McILHANY. Trust for debt to Helen C. McCORMICK and Nostrand & White of NY using 64a W of Lsbg adj Chas. BINNS, Tho. F. TEBBS, Archibald MEANS, Thomas SWANN; and brick house and lot on N side of Market St now occupied by James BRADY; and wooden house and lot adj to the W. Wit: Saml. M. EDWARDS, James RUST. Delv. to R. ANNIN pr HENDERSON 20 Mar 1829.

3P:085   Date: 29 Oct 1827   RtCt: 10 Nov 1827
Robert BRADEN & wife Elizabeth of Ldn to Diademia PAXSON of Ldn. B/S of 10a (prch/o Samuel & Abigail GARRET Feb 1809). Wit: Presley CORDELL, Noble S. BRADEN. Delv. to Jas. PUSEY pr order 8 Apr 1831.

3P:087   Date: 29 Oct 1827   RtCt: 10 Nov 1827
William ROGERS & wife Elizabeth to James HOGE and William HOGE. Trust for debt to Isaac NICHOLS using 212a where ROGERS resides (prch/o James HIXSON) adj Richard F. PEYTON, James HIXSON, John COCKRAN. Wit: Burr POWELL, A. GIBSON. Delv. to Wm. HOGE 24 Nov 1829.

3P:090   Date: 10 Nov 1827   RtCt: 10 Nov 1827
Samuel CARR of Ldn to Henry CLAGETT of Ldn. Trust for William T. T. MASON as endorser on bank notes using lot and house in Lsbg where CARR resides. Delv. to MASON 29 Apr 1831.

3P:094   Date: 24 Oct 1827   RtCt: 10 Nov 1827
Joseph KNOX & wife Jannet of Ldn to John McCORMICK of Ldn. B/S of 2/3 of ½a on W end of Market St in Lsbg with brick and log house adj heirs of Henry McCABE, Samuel HAMILTON. Wit: John H. McCABE, Jno. J. MATHIAS.

3P:096   Date: 9 Nov 1827   RtCt: 9 Nov 1827
Aaron DAILY (insolvent debtor in jail) of Ldn to Sheriff Charles LEWIS. B/S of __a (prch/o Isaac WRIGHT) on E side of turnpike road below Lsbg adj Benjamin SHREVE Jr., Dr. SELDON, Edwards Ferry road (executions by Anne ROZELL Admr of Stephen ROZELL and Commonwealth of Va).

3P:098   Date: 16 Oct 1824   RtCt: 5 Nov 1827
Mahlon MORRIS & wife Catherine, Amos HARVEY & wife Elizabeth, Robert RUSSEL, William CLENDENING & wife Ruth, William RUSSEL & wife Nancy, Thomas RUSSEL & wife Mary of Ldn to Samuel TURNER of Ldn. B/S of 87a. Wit: Craven OSBURN, John WHITE.

3P:101   Date: 31 Oct 1827   RtCt: 30 Oct 1827
Alexander CORDELL (insolvent debtor in jail) to Sheriff Charles LEWIS. B/S of two ¼a lots in Lovettsville (cnvy/b David LOVETT) (writ of capias ad satisfacundum by Daniel BOLAND).

3P:102   Date: 21 Apr 1827   RtCt: 30 Oct 1827
Bernard SWART of Ldn to Harrison CROSS of Ldn. B/S of 1a (part of Goshen) adj William POLIN, Sudley Mills road, Mrs. HODGSON. Wit: John SINCLAIR, Wm. McNAB, Jesse ELGIN.

3P:104   Date: 24 Oct 1827   RtCt: 30 Oct 1827
Peyton R. PAGE of Ldn to Everit SAUNDERS of Ldn. Trust for debt to Saml. M. EDWARDS using crops, farm and household items.

3P:106   Date: 25 Oct 1827   RtCt: 30 Oct 1827
Peyton R. PAGE to Everit SAUNDERS. Trust for debt to Thomas SWANN, Richard H. HENDERSON, Robert MOFFETT, Temple MASON, David CARR using farm animals, household items.

3P:108   Date: 3 Mar 1827   RtCt: 30 Oct 1827
William POLIN & wife Elizabeth of Ldn to Harrison CROSS of Ldn. B/S of 7½a where POLIN lives adj road from old turnpike road to Sudley Mills by Aris BUCKNER's farm. Wit: John SINCLAIR, Barnet SWART, Alexander SWART, John SIMPSON, Wm. McNAB, Wm. B. HARRISON, Robert BAYLY.

3P:111   Date: 25 Sep 1827   RtCt: 29 Oct 1827
Zachariah ELLIS of Ldn to dau Mary ELLIS. Gift of household items, farm animals. Wit: Andrew T. HOSKINSON, Ann W. HOSKINSON. Delv. to Timothy McFADEN husband of Mary ELLIS 8 Oct 1832.

3P:112   Date: 6 Oct 1827   RtCt: 12 Oct 1827
Peyton R. PAGE to James GILMORE. Trust for debt to Everitt SAUNDERS using crops. Wit: R. G. SAUNDERS, J. L. DREAN, Thos. RUSSELL. Delv. to P. SAUNDERS on ___.

3P:113   Date: 14 May 1827   RtCt: 13 Oct 1827
Landon F. CARTER by attorney Alfred G. CARTER and Hebe S. G. CARTER now of Fqr to George HANCOCK of Ldn. B/S of 650a 'Heath, Hawley and Foley lots' adj the Sudley tract, Loghouse or Tecumseh tract.

3P:115   Date: 5 Oct 1827   RtCt: 15 Oct 1827
Peyton R. PAGE. Estate held by Mrs. Eliza PAGE when he married her was property of William H. BRYAN descending from her father – household items. Never claimed and gives his rights to William H.

BRYAN. Wit: Jno. SWANN, Addison H. CLARK, Everett SAUNDERS.

3P:116   Date: 15 Oct 1827   RtCt: 15 Oct 1827
Joseph T. NEWTON & wife Nelley S. of Ldn to Edmond J. LEE of Ldn. B/S of 24a on Lsbg turnpike road abt 2 miles below Lsbg. Wit: William CARR, Saml. M. EDWARDS.

3P:118   Date: 10 Oct 1827   RtCt: 15 Oct 1827
Frederick A. DAVISSON of Ldn to Yardley TAYLOR of Ldn. Trust for debt to Isaac NICKOLS Sr. using 134a (cnvy/b Daniel COOPER Mar 1827) adj Mortimer McILHANY, James MERCHANT, John STATLER, Rachael MORRISON. Wit: Isaac HOGE, Samuel LUMM, George BARTEN.

3P:120   Date: 14 Oct 1827   RtCt: 15 Oct 1827
William CARR & wife Mary of Ldn to George SHEAD of Ldn. B/S of lot in Lsbg adj John FEICHSTER on Loudoun St.

3P:120   Date: 5 Oct 1827   RtCt: 16 Oct 1827
John WILLIAMS & wife Eliza of Ldn to John BRADEN and George W. HENRY of Ldn. Trust for debt to John WORSLEY of Ldn using 183a (allotted to sons John & Sydnah in div. of Enos WILLIAMS dec'd, part cnvy/b Sydnah Mar 1826) on Kittoctin Creek adj Adam HOUSEHOLDER, __ BAKER, __ RAMY. Wit: Presley CORDELL, Noble S. BRADEN. Delv. to Jno. WORSLEY 4 Dec 1828.

3P:124   Date: 16 Oct 1827   RtCt: 17 Oct 1827
John FLOWERS of Ldn to John A. BINNS of Ldn. Trust for debt to John SHAW using household items. Wit: Washington JARVIS, George W. HAMMETT.

3P:126   Date: 28 Jul 1827   RtCt: 18 Oct 1827
John UMBAUGH & wife Catherine of Ldn to Thomas J. HARPER of Ldn. B/S of 2a (prch/o William GREGG) adj Collin AULD. Wit: Samuel DAWSON, George W. SHAWEN.

3P:128   Date: 17 Oct 1827   RtCt: 18 Oct 1827
Edward B. GRADY (trustee of Thomas CLOWES & wife Ann, May 1822, DBk EEE:407) to George MARKS. B/S of 204a (CLOWES transferred to MARKS).

3P:129   Date: 23 May 1827   RtCt: 19 Oct 1827
John SAUNDERS & wife Mary B. of Ldn to Capt. Henry SAUNDERS of Ldn. B/S of lot on N side of Loudoun St in Lsbg adj Mrs. WOODY with house occupied by Mrs. Patience SAUNDERS (cnvy/b James L. MARTIN Sep 1826, DBk MMM:393). Wit: Samuel M. EDWARDS, Thomas SAUNDERS.

3P:131   Date: 20 Oct 1827   RtCt: ___
Deed from John GRUBB to John HAMMILTON Jr. in trust for Elijah PEACOCK is acknowledged and admitted. Original Deed DBk LLL:344.

3P:131   Date: 5 Oct 1827   RtCt: 20 Oct 1827
John JONES to Richard S. JONES. Trust for debt to Richard S. JONES using crops, farm animals. Wit: John W. RACE, Charles CARTER. Delv. to Thos. JONES pr order 18 Jul 1828.

3P:132   Date: 20 Oct 1827   RtCt: 20 Oct 1827
Simon A. BINNS of Ldn to son William A. BINNS. Gift of horses, farm and household items.

3P:132   Date: 20 Sep 1827   RtCt: 20 Oct 1827
John COST & wife Rachel of Green Co Ohio to John SOUDER of Ldn. B/S of 28a Lot #8 in div. of Philip SOUDER and 4a Lot #2 on Catoctin Mt. Wit: Samuel DAWSON, George W. SHAWEN. Delv. to SOUDER 14 Feb 1831.

3P:135   Date: 15 Oct 1827   RtCt: 20 Oct 1827
John HAMILTON & wife Winifred of Ldn to Enos WILDMAN of Ldn. B/S of lot in Lsbg (prch/o Fleet SMITH) adj brewhouse lot, Market St, Thomas GASSAWAY, ashhouse, __ McCABE. Wit: George W. SHAWEN, Noble S. BRADEN. Delv. to Jane WILDMAN 2 Nov 1829.

3P:137   Date: 23 Oct 1827   RtCt: 24 Oct 1827
Elias POOL of Ldn to John A. BINNS of Ldn. Trust for Samuel CARR as security on purchased at sale on 'Liberia' farm of Thompson MASON using sideboard and clock.

3P:138   Date: 15 Oct 1827   RtCt: 25 Oct 1827
Philip MORGAN & wife Eliza of Ldn to Priscilla SHOEMAKER of Ldn. B/S of 1/6th of 2/3 of 200a of Daniel SHOEMAKER dec'd (other 1/3 is dower of Priscilla). Wit: Mortimer McILHANY, Saml. HOUGH. Delv pr order 26 Aug 1830.

3P:140   Date: 17 Sep 1827   RtCt: 25 Oct 1827
Emanuel WALTMAN to Alex'r CORDELL. Trust for debt to Maria SHOEMAKER using 1/9th of 37a allotted from father Jacob WALTMAN dec'd land. Wit: Michael VIRTS, Josiah SHOEMAKER, Jeremiah TITUS.

3P:143   Date: 27 Feb 1828 [27]   RtCt: 26 Oct 1827
Walter LANGLEY & wife Susanna of Ldn to Ruel MARSHALL and Miner REED of Ldn. B/S of 5a on Blue Ridge Mt. adj Amos CLATON, __ BRADFIELD, __ URTON. Wit: Notley C. WILLIAMS, John W. GRAYSON. Delv. pr order 1 Nov 1844.

3P:145   Date: 13 Sep 1827   RtCt: 12 Nov 1827
Philip GROVE & wife Eve of Ldn to Absalon VANVACTOR of JeffVa. B/S of 15a on W side of Short Hill adj James NEAR, William DERRY. Wit: David KEPHART, George W. MOLER. CoE in JeffVa.

3P:147   Date: 20 Feb 1827   RtCt: 13 Nov 1827
John BOYD of Mdbg to H. B. POWELL of Ldn. Trust for Edward SUMMERS of Fqr as security to Edward McGUIRE of Frederick using negro woman Sukey with her children Matilda, Mary, Frank and Maria.

3P:149   Date: 10 Nov 1827   RtCt: 12 Nov 1827
Thomas WHITE of Ldn to Robert WHITE of Georgetown DC. B/S of 88a adj William WILSON, Bernard TAYLOR, Richard MILTON and 56¼a (cnvy/b Lewis ELLZEY to Josiah WHITE 3rd Oct 1816 and by Joshua OSBURN to WHITE Aug 1827) on both sides of Blue Ridge part. in FredVa adj __ JANNEY. Delv. to Robert WHITE in DC 28 __ 1827.

3P:151   Date: 1 Nov 1827   RtCt: 13 Nov 1827
David SHAWEN to Mary FOX. B/S of lot (entitled to SHAWEN by marriage with Frances FOX dau of William FOX dec'd and by birth of a child now living to a life estate on portion of land).

3P:152   Date: 5 Sep 1827   RtCt: 12 Nov 1827
Henry FRAZIER & wife Ann of FredMd to James STUBBLEFIELD of JeffVa. B/S of __a (cnvy/b Frederick HENDSLY to FRAZIER and Erasmus WEST) adj STUBBLEFIELD, Potomac, __ WALTMAN. Wit: Jacob PROBASCO, Mary Ann DAVIS. Delv. pr order 7 Jul 1831, see DBk 3O:157 [?]

3P:154   Date: 12 Nov 1827   RtCt: 12 Nov 1827
James JOHNSON and John G. HUMPHREY (Exors of Abner G. HUMPHREY who was trustee of Abner HUMPHREY dec'd) and John G. HUMPHREY Exor of Thomas HUMPHREY dec'd) to Edward B. GRADY of Ldn. Release of trust of Jan 1823 on 58½a. Delv. pr DBk 2T:058 on 4 Feb 1830.

3P:156   Date: 10 Nov 1827   RtCt: 12 Nov 1827
Samuel DAWSON of Ldn to Thomas GASSAWAY of Ldn. Trust for debt to Casper MANTZ and Jacob NICHOLS of FredMd, John J. HARDING, Wm. D. DRISH and Elizabeth DAWSON of Ldn using 303a (cnvy/b Wm. NOLAND Jun 1816) and slaves Nat, Moses, William, Johnson, Nelson, Lloyd, Delia, Mariah, Charles, and Let and farm animals, household items.

3P:158   Date: 18 Oct 1827   RtCt: 12 Nov 1827
John BROWN & wife Margaret of Ldn to John CONARD of Ldn. B/S of 74a adj Wm. GRUBB, CONARD. Wit: Craven OSBURN, John WHITE. Delv. to John CONRAD 16 Jan 1829.

3P:161   Date: 25 Apr 1827   RtCt: 12 Nov 1827
Henry AXLINE & wife Catherine of Muskingum Co Ohio to John SORBOUGH of Ldn. B/S of 11a in Piedmont Manor (Lot #3 on plat by Robt. BRADEN, cnvy/b Philip EVERHEART Sept 1815) adj __ MULL. Wit: J. M. KEITH, Saml. THOMPSON, A. REED. Delv. to SARBAUGH 10 Nov 1834.

3P:163   Date: 14 Aug 1827   RtCt: 12 Nov 1827
Joshua OSBURN (trustee of Joshua WHITE, Oct 1816) of Ldn to Thomas WHITE of Ldn. B/S of 88a adj Abden DILLON, Stephen WILSON, Solomon DAVIS, Francis STRIBLING; and 56a on both

sides of the blue Ridge part in FredVa adj __ JANNEY. Delv. to WHITE 16 Aug 1830.

3P:165   Date: 12 Nov 1827   RtCt: 12 Nov 1827
Nimrod BROWN of Ldn to Hiram BROWN of Ldn. B/S of 39a (subject to dower of widow Sarah BROWN) adj Morris OSBURN, James COCKRAN, Betty SPENCE. Delv. to Hiram BROWN 14 Apr 1828.

3P:166   Date: 17 Oct 1827   RtCt: 13 Nov 1827
Daniel SETTLE & wife Jane of Ldn to Dean JAMES of Ldn. B/S of 219a (Thomas LYNE dec'd died seized of) adj Newman SETTLE, __ FOX, __ McGRAW, Timothy PAGIT; and 12a (devised to Newman SETTLE by father) adj SETTLE, Abigail JAMES. Wit: Nathaniel S. ODEN, Rufus BERKLEY, Fenton M. HANCOCK, William B. HARRISON, John BAYLEY. Delv. to Dean JAMES 27 Feb 1830.

3P:169   Date: 22 Nov 1827   RtCt: 22 Nov 1827
Samuel HOUGH of Ldn to Charles G. ESKRIDGE of Ldn. Trust for debt to John GREY using 184a (cnvy/b Lydia HOUGH) on Beaverdam Creek adj Wm. HOUGH, Michael COOPER, Margaret SAUNDERS, Joseph POSTON, __ BRADEN. Delv. to John GRAY 29 Sep 1832.

3P:171   Date: 20 Oct 1827   RtCt: 14 Nov 1827
Thomas TRAHORN/TRAYHERN & wife Ruth of Ldn to George MARKS of Ldn. B/S of 53¼a where TRAYHERN lives on road from Union nr Notley C. WILLIAMS, John DUNKIN, __ PUGH. Wit: Benjamin GRAYSON, John W. GRAYSON. Delv. to Col. Geo. MARKS 26 Nov 1830.

3P:174   Date: 15 Jan 1827   RtCt: 14 Nov 1827
Thomas KIDWELL & wife Elizabeth of Ldn to Henry SAGLE of Ldn. B/S of 5a on E side of blue Ridge adj Thomas HALL. Wit: Ebenezer GRUBB, John WHITE. Delv. to SAGLE 9 Sep 1839.

3P:176   Date: 20 Oct 1827   RtCt: 14 Nov 1827
George MARKS & wife Mahala of Ldn to David YOUNG and Saml. M. EDWARDS of Ldn. Trust for debt to John PANCOAST Jr. of Ldn using 204a (cnvy/b Thomas CLEWES). Wit: Benj. GRAYSON, John W. GRAYSON. Delv. to PANCOAST 26 Aug 1829.

3P:179   Date: 15 Nov 1827   RtCt: 15 Nov 1827
George SHEID of Ldn to John MARTIN of Ldn. Trust for debt to Samuel M. BOSS and Thomas ETHEL (on behalf of his wife, dau of SHEID, and delegate under will of her grandfather George KILGORE dec'd) of Ldn using interest on farm where SHEID lives, farm and household items, farm animals. Delv. to MARTIN 29 Jul 1829.

3P:181   Date: 16 Nov 1827   RtCt: 16 Nov 1827
D. ANNIN. Receipt for household items received 28 Jul 1825 of Roberdeau ANNIN which belonged to Wm. C. ANNIN of NY. Bond

to Roberdeau for yearly payment for use of items. Delv. to Roberdeau ANNIN 19 Apr 1828.

3P:182   Date: 6 Nov 1827   RtCt: 15 Nov 1827
Zachariah DULANY & wife Mary E. of Ldn to Joshua PUSEY of Ldn. B/S of 20a Lot #2 in div. of land of Joseph CAVENS dec'd (prch/o Joseph CAVENS) adj Joz. WHITE. Wit: Presley CORDELL, Noble S. BRADEN. Delv. 20 Feb 1834.

3P:184   Date: __ 1827   RtCt: 16 Nov 1827
William MISKILL of Ldn to John MARTIN of Ldn. Trust for debt to Saml. M. BOSS of Ldn using farm animals, household items.

3P:185   Date: 8 Nov 1827   RtCt: 17 Nov 1827
Charles Fenton MERCER of Aldie to Benjamin HAGERMAN of Ldn. B/S of 128a on Bullrun Mt. adj __ MOORE, __ MERCER, __ SIMPSON.

3P:186   Date: 8 Nov 1827   RtCt: 17 Nov 1827
Benjamin HAGERMAN & wife Velinda of Ldn to Humphrey B. POWELL of Ldn. Trust for debt to Charles Fenton MERCER of Ldn using 128a. Wit: Burr POWELL, Abner GIBSON. Delv. to POWELL 14 Mar 1828

3P:190   Date: 17 Nov 1827   RtCt: 20 Nov 1827
Moses BUTLER of Lsbg to George RICHARDS of Lsbg. Trust for debt to John A. BINNS using land prch/o John LITTLEJOHN (decree of Sup. Ct. in Winchester) and household items. Delv. to BINNS 14 Jul 1828.

3P:191   Date: 23 Nov 1827   RtCt: 23 Nov 1827
Joseph MORRISON of Ldn to Elijah PEACOCK of Ldn. B/S of 3¼a (formerly of Francis McKEMIE dec'd sold to MORRISON under decree of Ct in Winchester) adj MORRISON. Delv. to E. PEACOCK 29 Aug 1831.

3P:192   Date: 14 Sep 1827   RtCt: 24 Nov 1827
John AULT & wife Mary of Ldn to John COMPHER of Ldn. B/S of 29a Lot #1 and 21a Lot #2 allotted Elizabeth COMPHER and Wm. AULT from estate of Wm. AULT dec'd. Wit: George W. SHAWEN, Saml. HOUGH. Delv. to Wm. SLATER 24 Jul 1847.

3P:195   Date: 24 Nov 1827   RtCt: 24 Nov 1827
Edward DORSEY of Ldn to John JANNEY of Ldn. Trust for debt to George DORSEY of BaltMd using brick house and lot in Wtfd where Edward now resides (cnvy/b Conrad BITZER). Delv. to John JANNEY 24 Jul 1832.

3P:197   Date: 24 Nov 1827   RtCt: 24 Nov 1827
Conrad BITZER & wife Catherine of Ldn to Edward DORSEY of Ldn. B/S of brick house and lot in Wtfd occupied by DORSEY (cnvy/b Richard H. HENDERSON, DBk GGG:444). Wit: Presley CORDELL, Noble S. BRADEN. Delv. to DORSEY 20 Jun 1831.

3P:199   Date: 31 May 1827   RtCt: 25 Nov 1827
Jonathan LOVETT & wife Matilda, Elvira NORTON, Hiram
NORTON, John B. PATTERSON & wife Mahala and Barbara
NORTON of Ldn to Jacob GOUPHENOR of Ldn. B/S of interest in
75a late prop. of Nathaniel NORTON, adj John KILE. Wit: Burr
POWELL, A. GIBSON. Delv. to GOPHNER 4 Nov 1828.

3P:201   Date: 17 Aug 1827   RtCt: 27 Nov 1827
Robert BRADEN & wife Eliza of Ldn to John KALB of Ldn. B/S of
24a adj KALB, __ POTTERFIELD. Wit: George W. SHAWEN,
Presley CORDELL. Delv. to Saml. KALB Exor of John KALB 11 Apr
1831.

3P:203   Date: 20 Nov 1827   RtCt: 27 Nov 1827
William LYNE & wife Margaret of Ldn to Peter OATYER. B/S of 1a
(prch/o Charles LEWIS). Wit: Robert BAYLEY, William B.
HARRISON. Delv. to OYTER [OATYER] 12 Dec 1828.

3P:205   Date: 11 Dec 1827   RtCt: 11 Dec 1827
James L. MARTIN of Ldn. DoE for negro man Sim aged abt 25y.

3P:206   Date: 19 Nov 1827   RtCt: 20 Nov 1827
Samuel CARR of Lsbg to James SINCLAIR. Trust for Samuel
STERRETT as endorser on bank note using lot in Lsbg occupied as
store house by CARR and other lot CARR prch/o John DRISH,
household items, pieces of cloth. Wit: C. C. McINTYRE, L. BEARD,
C. G. ESKRIDGE. Delv. pr order 21 Jan 1831.

3P:207   Date: 19 Nov 1827   RtCt: 20 Nov 1827
Samuel CARR of Lsbg to Robert MOFFETT of Lsbg. Trust for
James SINCLAIR and Saml. STERRETT of Lsbg as security in bond
to Aldridge & Higdon using land and items listed above. Wit: C. C.
McINTYRE, L. BEARD, C. G. ESKRIDGE. Delv. pr order 21 Jan
1831.

3P:209   Date: 19 Nov 1827   RtCt: 20 Nov 1827
Samuel CARR to Wm. T. T. MASON. Trust for debt to John and
James POGUE Merchants of BaltMD using house & lot in Lsbg
where he resides. Wit: C. C. McINTYRE, Enos WILDMAN, William
M. JENNERS.

3P:210   Date: 26 Feb 1827   RtCt: 3 Dec 1827
Bernard HOUGH of Ldn to son Joseph HOUGH of Ldn. B/S of lot
where Joseph has lived for many years (part of tract Bernard gave
to Joseph Mar 1821).

3P:212   Date: 17 Apr 1826   RtCt: 4 Dec 1827
John W. ROSE of Lsbg to Elizabeth WOODY of Lsbg. Trust for debt
to Elizabeth WOODY using negro girl Jane aged abt 16y.

3P:213   Date: 15 Oct 1827   RtCt: 4 Dec 1827
Elijah JAMES & wife Sarah of Ldn to Samuel M. EDWARDS of Ldn.
Trust for debt to Philip OTTERBACK of WashDC using 113a (cnvy/b
Sarah HUGHES wd/o Thomas HUGHES dec'd and other heirs Jun

1827). Wit: John ROSE, William CARR. Delv. to EDWARDS 12 Nov 1833.

3P:217   Date: 13 Nov 1824   RtCt: 25 Apr 1825/6 Dec 1827
John SHAW of Lsbg to Peter FICHTER of Lsbg. LS of lot on lower end of Market St in Lsbg adj Benj. MAULSBY. On 3 Dec 1827 Rebecca SHAW as guardian for Susan Bayly SHAW agreed to transfer of lease from FICHTER to Edward HAINES. Delv. to HAINES 3 Nov 1828.

3P:221   Date: 10 Dec 1827   RtCt: 10 Dec 1827
Everett SAUNDERS, Isaac VANDEVENTER, Benj. SHRIEVE. Bond on SAUNDERS as constable.

3P:221   Date: 5 Dec 1827   RtCt: 11 Dec 1827
John W. ROSE of Ldn to Alfred A. ESKRIDGE of Ldn. Trust for debt to Elizabeth WOODY using negro girl Jane, household items. Wit: Joshua REILEY.

3P:223   Date: 11 Sep 1827   RtCt: 31 Oct/12 Dec 1827
Elizabeth HARDEN of Ldn to Edmund TYLER of Ldn. Trust for debt to Stephen GARRETT of Ldn using undivided ½ of 124a (prch/o Mary TAYLOR by Elizabeth and William HARDEN dec'd Apr 1807) adj Christopher ROSE. Wit: Jos. Hockings, Nicholas KLINE, Jonas POTTS. Delv. to GARRETT 12 May 1828.

3P:226   Date: 17 Sep 1827   RtCt: 14 Nov 1827
Stephen WILSON & wife Hannah P. of Ldn to Joshua PANCOAST and David YOUNG of Ldn. Trust for debt to John PANCOAST Sr. using 289a adj WILSON, Bernard TAYLOR, Jesse JANNEY, Wm. SMITH, Mary HOWELL, __ EMERSON, __ COCKRILL, __ ZIMMERMAN. Wit: Presley CORDELL, Thomas NICHOLS. Delv. pr order 26 Aug 1829.

3P:229   Date: 12 Nov 1827   RtCt: 10 Dec 1827
Sarah BROWN and Nimrod BROWN of Ldn to James COCKRAN of Ldn. B/S of 4a adj COCKRAN. Wit: H. ELLIOTT, David LOVETT, Craven OSBURN. Delv. to COCKRAN 13 Aug 1829.

3P:231   Date: 10 Nov 1827   RtCt: 10 Dec 1827
Daniel COCKERILLE (as Commr. in suit of Hiram DANIEL agst Elizabeth POTTS) to James THOMPSON. B/S of 24a (of Isa[i?]ah POTTS dec'd). Delv. to THOMPSON 14 Aug 1828.

3P:233   Date: 8 Dec 1827   RtCt: 10 Dec 1827
Elisha W. JACKSON & wife Rebecca of Mdbg to Burr WEEKS of Lsbg. Trust for debt to Waterman & Campbell using household items. Delv. to A. G. WATERMAN 27 Jun 1828.

3P:235   Date: 27 Sep 1827   RtCt: 10 Dec 1827
Benjamin C. RUSSEL of Wtfd to Susana SHIPMAN (dau of his wife Ethelus RUSSEL). Gift of household items. Delv. to S. SHIPMAN 11 Aug 1829.

3P:236 Date: 9 Nov 1827 RtCt: 10 Dec 1827
Ludwell LUCKETT & wife Ann C. of Ldn to William HOGE of Ldn. Trust for note to Isaac NICHOLS Sr. with Francis W. LUCKETT as security using interest in real estate of Wm. BRONAUGH dec'd and interest in estate of Jeremiah W. BRONAUGH dec'd (s/o Wm. dec'd and br/o Ann C.). Wit: Francis W. LUCKETT, Edward HALL. Delv. to Ludwell LUCKETT of Wm. HOGE an Exor 12 Aug 1833.

3P:239 Date: 29 Nov 1827 RtCt: 10 Dec 1827
Ammon EWERS of Ldn to William BENTON of Ldn. Trust for debt to Elijah ANDERSON of Ldn using farm animals.

3P:241 Date: 20 Oct 1827 RtCt: 14 Jan 1828
Members of Friendship Fire Co of Lsbg: David OGDON, John GRAY, Thomas BIRKBY, James THOMAS, O. R. BEATTY, Jno. J. MATHIAS, Saml. GILPIN, George K. FOX, John MARTIN, Thomas MORRALLEE, Enos WILDMAN, John H. McCABE, C. W. D. BINNS, Saml. M. EDWARDS, Wm. W. HAMMONTREE, Benjamin MAULSBY, Henry PEERS, John J. HARDING, John THOMAS, John S. MANLEY, David M. WALLACE, Jno. Nicholas KLINE, John C. LYON, R. G. SAUNDERS, Jacob FADLEY, Benjamin W. PERRY, Thomas FLOWERS, R. J. FLEMING, Presley SAUNDERS, Simon SMALE, William P. KNOX, William SEEDERS, John NEWTON, John LAMBAUGH, Richard Henry LEE, Rich'd H. HENDERSON, A. P. BRACKENRIDGE, A. JOHNSON, Saml. HAMMETT, Edward HUGHES, James Hervey CARSON, James STIDMAN, Benj'n F. OGDON, Edward HAMMETT, Benj'n SHREVE Jr., John PARROTT, Josiah L. DREAN, Robert BENTLEY, Geo. RICHARDS.

3P:242 Date: 7 Dec 1827 RtCt: 11 Dec 1827
Foushee TEBBS of Ldn to John W. TYLER of PrWm. Trust for debt to Willoughby W. TEBBS, Foushee C. TEBBS, Betsey TEBBS and John SPENCE Admr of __ CARR using 540 'Tecumseh' tract in Ldn and PrWm; and interest in 42a in Fqr (cnvy to William CARR and allotted to TEBBS and siblings) and 101a in PrWm on Broad Run; and 12 lots in Carrborough; and 1/7th interest in 240a of Dr. Wm. CARR dec'd in Fqr; and 1/11th of 269a 'Mount Horab' in StafVa; and 1/7th interest in 112a (purchased by Thomas CHAPMAN Exor of Wm. CARR); and 1/7th interest in land in Ohio & Ky inherited from father. Delv. to W. W. TEBBS 12 Aug 1828.

3P:246 Date: 11 Dec 1827 RtCt: 11 Dec 1827
Emanuel WALTMAN of Ldn to Jacob EVERHEART of Ldn. Trust for debt to William THOMPSON of Ldn using undivided interest in land of his brother Elias WALTMAN dec'd (formerly belonged to father of Emanuel, Elias and Jacob WALTMAN)

3P:247 Date: 27 Dec 1820 RtCt: 11 Dec 1827
Levi GIBSON of Fqr to Humph[re]y B. POWELL. Trust for debt to Burr POWELL using farm animals and items from division between

GIBSON and POWELL and crops. Wit: A. GIBSON. Delv. to B.
POWELL 12 Dec 1828. RtCt in Fqr 22 Jan 1821.

3P:249   Date: 7 Dec 1827   RtCt: 11 Dec 1827
George CARTER of Oatlands to William CARR, James CARR,
Robert FULTON, Gustavus ELGIN and David FULTON. B/S of ½a
(part of land prch/o Loveless CORNWELL) on W side of road from
Oatland Mills to Lsbg for public subscription for building a neighbor
public school and church or meeting house, and burial ground.

3P:252   Date: 1 Dec 1827   RtCt: 11 Dec 1827
Isaac NICHOLS & wife Mary of Ldn to Abraham and John VERNON,
Elizabeth HARLEN, and David, Abner, Eli and Levi GIBSON, Nancy
ROGERS and Rebecca HIXSON (heirs of Daniel & Rebecca
VERNON dec'd). B/S of 3 lots on NW fork of Beaverdam Creek –
10a, 19½a and 2 roods. Wit: Notley C. WILLIAMS, Burr POWELL.
Delv. to Abner GIBSON 15 Nov 1831.

3P:257   Date: 1 Nov 1827   RtCt: 11 Dec 1827
Andrew OGDON/OGDEN & wife Elizabeth of Ldn to James
McILHANY of Ldn. Trust for debt to Thomas WHITE of Ldn using 2
tracts cnvy/b John JANNEY Mar 1822. Wit: Noble S. BRADEN, Geo.
W. SHAWEN. Delv. to WHITE 14 Oct 1828.

3P:261   Date: 12 Dec 1827   RtCt: 12 Dec 1827
Joseph HOUGH & wife Lucy C. of Ldn to Samuel M. EDWARDS
and Robert MOFFETT of Ldn. Trust for debt to Thomas WHITE and
Joshua PUESEY of Ldn using land where HOUGH now lives (cnvy/b
Bernard HOUGH Mar 1821 and Feb 1827). Wit: John H. McCABE,
John J. MATHIAS. Delv. to PEWSEY 9 May 1828.

3P:264   Date: 14 May 1825   RtCt: 12 Dec 1827
Levi GIBSON of Fqr to Humphrey B. POWELL. Trust for debt to Burr
POWELL using farm animals and items, undivided estate as dist. of
sister Rebecca VERNON late of Ldn (and Hugh SMITH Exor of
Daniel VERNON). Delv. to Burr POWELL 12 Dec 1828.

3P:267   Date: 12 Dec 1827   RtCt: 12 Dec 1827
Samuel CARR of Lsbg to Burr William HARRISON of Lsbg. Trust for
debt to John and James POGUE merchants of BaltMd using lot on
King St in Lsbg, carriage and horses, subject to trust for William T.
T. MASON. Delv. to HARRISON 1 Jul 1828.

3P:270   Date: 10 Nov 1827   RtCt: 12 Dec 1827
Daniel P. CONRAD & wife Mary Ann of FredVa to Pres. & Directors
of Snickers Gap Turnpike Co. B/S of 1a with log house in Aldie
(prch/o Samuel M. EDWARDS attorney for Evan LLOYD dec'd Oct
1822, DBk FFF:031). Delv. to N. C. WILLIAMS 25 Feb 1830.

3P:273   Date: 7 Sep 1827   RtCt: 15 Dec 1827
Samuel HIXSON & wife Ruth of Ldn to Andrew S. ANDERSON and
Daniel STONE of Ldn. Trust for debt to Exor of William GREGG
dec'd using 86a where HIXSON resides (from will of father Timothy

HIXSON dec'd) adj Philip C. JONES, heirs of Jacob SANDS dec'd. Wit: William THRIFT, Elijah JAMES, George COPELAND. Delv pr order 19 Oct 1829.

3P:275 Date: 13 Mar 1826 RtCt: 14 Dec 1827
Dpty Wm. MERSHON for Sheriff Ludwell LEE to Horace LUCKETT. B/S of brick house and lot in Aldie now occupied by insolvent debtor Abraham M. FULTON. Delv. to LUCKETT 16 Dec 1828.

3P:277 Date: 16 Nov 1827 RtCt: 15 Dec 1827
Samuel CARR to Burr W. HARRISON. Trust for debt to Jno. & James POGUE using negro woman Delpha, woman Pleasant, girl Mary now in possession of CARR. Wit: H. B. POWELL, Chas. G. ESKRIDGE, H. SMITH. Delv. to HARRISON 1 Jul 1828.

3P:279 Date: 14 Dec 1827 RtCt: 17 Dec 1827
Samuel CARR of Ldn to David CARR of Ldn. Trust for John CARR and Joseph T. NEWTON of Ldn as endorsers on bank notes using 22a on Lsbg turnpike road adj Benj'n SHRIEVE, William GILMORE; and 11a adj James F. NEWTON; and lot in Lsbg with CARR's stable. Delv. to David CARR 3 Jan 1831.

3P:281 Date: 17 Dec 1827 RtCt: 17 Dec 1827
Samuel CARR of Lsbg to Richard H. HENDERSON of Lsbg. Trust for debt to William NORRIS & son, John L. HAMMOND, the Powhatan Manufacturing Co and Samuel HARELEN merchants of BaltMd using lot of leasehold land on King St in Lsbg with store house adj his present dwelling; and household items. Delv. to HENDERSON 14 May 1829.

3P:285 Date: 5 Jun 1827 RtCt: 16 Dec 1827
Mary PURDIM, Tunis TITUS, Prescilla SHOEMAKER, Elizabeth FITZGERALD, Wm. BUMCROTS (h/o Permelia PURDEM), Arey PERDEM (heirs of Jeremiah PURDEM dec'd late of Ldn) to Simon SHOEMAKER of Ldn. PoA for sale of real estate. Wit: R. H. HENDERSON, B. W. WHITE, Michael VERTS. Agreement of 5 Jul 1827 between Simon SHOEMAKER and John H. LEWIS – at time of death Jeremiah had 140a leased lot, LEWIS to rent, now rented to Aaron MILLER.

3P:288 Date: 22 Apr 1826 RtCt: 17 Dec 1827
Andrew HESSER & wife Mary of Ldn to Joshua PANCOAST of Ldn. Trust for debt to Jonathan EWERS using 1a (prch/o EWERS Apr 1826) adj Thomas EWERS, Isaac NICHOLS, EWERS. Wit: Notley C. WILLIAMS, Thomas NICHOLS.

3P:290 Date: 18 Oct 1827 RtCt: 18 Dec 1827
James SPENCE & wife Nancy of Ldn to Michael SAGLE of Ldn. B/S of 6a on W side of short hill adj __ CONARD, __ KIDWELL. Wit: Mortimer McILHANY, Craven OSBURN. Delv. pr order filed in another place 4 Apr 1849.

3P:293   Date: 20 Dec 1827   RtCt: 20 Dec 1827
Tasker C. QUINLAN of Ldn to John J. MATHIAS of Ldn. Trust for judgment by John THOMAS of Ldn using __a adj __ POTTS, Col. MERCER, Saml. TILLETT, Goose Creek.

3P:296   Date: 1 Sep 1827   RtCt: 21 Dec 1827
Jacob WALTMAN to Alex'r CORDELL and Jacob EVERHART. Trust for debt to Jacob WALTERS using 115a (transferred from Adam HOUSEHOLDER) adj Catocton Creek, John COMPHER, John W. WILLIAMS. Wit: John W. WILLIAMS, Geo. W. SHAWEN, Danl. MOOR.

3P:300   Date: 2 Nov 1827   RtCt: 24 Dec 1827
Henry PEYTON of Fqr to Richard O. GRAYSON of Ldn. BoS for undivided 1/7th of personal estate of Col. William BRONAUGH dec'd (from marriage with his dau. Elizabeth BRONAUGH). Delv. to GRAYSON 11 Feb 1831.

3P:301   Date: 14 Dec 1827   RtCt: 24 Dec 1827
Andrew S. ANDERSON and Samuel HIXSON (trustee of Samuel CLAPHAM, Apr 1824) of Ldn to Elizabeth CLAPHAM of Ldn. B/S of 300a (where HIXSON resides, from father Josias CLAPHAM dec'd) adj Mrs. JOHNSON, Moses DOWDLE, Joseph CRAVEN. Wit: D. SHAWEN, A. C. WILKINSON, David JACKSON, Thompson T. MASON, Timothy HIXSON, Rebecca HIXSON.

3P:305   Date: 24 Dec 1827   RtCt: 29 Dec 1827
Mahlon SCHOOLEY of Ldn to Eli L. SCHOOLEY of Ldn. B/S of ¼a Lot #6 in new addition to Wtfd on E side of High St.

3P:306   Date: 19 Jul 1827   RtCt: 31 Dec 1827
Sarah COX and Sarah BROWN of Ldn to Joseph BROWN of Ldn. B/S of interest in life estate to Sarah COX and Sarah BROWN in land willed to Joseph BROWN by Joseph COX.

3P:309   Date: 3 Oct 1827   RtCt: 1 Jan 1828
Solomon RUSE & wife Tabitha to Eli JANNEY and Charles B. HAMILTON. Trust for debt to Joseph TAVENNER using 15a adj John IREY, Joseph HOLMES, Hamilton ROGERS. Wit: John SIMPSON, Presley CORDELL.

3P:313   Date: 26 Dec 1827   RtCt: 7 Jan 1828
John J. MATHIAS (trustee of Betsey CLIFFORD of Lsbg) of Ldn to Samuel CARR of Ldn. B/S of interest in lot on SE corner of Loudoun & Back Sts. in Lsbg. Delv. to CARR 9 Sep 1830.

3P:314   Date: 16 Feb 1827   RtCt: 7 Jan 1828
Morris HUMPHREY & wife Mary Ann of Ross Co Ohio to brother Thomas HUMPHREY of Ldn. B/S of 13¼a (from father Jesse HUMPHREY dec'd). Wit: Hiram N. MEAD, Arthur McGEE.

3P:317   Date: 1 Jan 1828   RtCt: 7 Jan 1828
Joseph WOOD of Ldn to Rich'd H. HENDERSON of Ldn. Trust for debt to Joseph JANNEY of AlexDC using 83a on which Joshua

PUSEY has a lien; and 150a on which John WORSLEY has a lien; and farm animals and items.

3P:319   Date: 24 Dec 1827   RtCt: 7 Jan 1828
Philip FRY of Ldn to John FRY of Ldn. B/S of 184a on E side of short hill adj Thomas WHITE, __ MORRISON. Delv. 15 Feb 1875.

3P:320   Date: 26 Dec 1827   RtCt: 9 Jul 1828
Saml. TILLETT of Ldn to Samuel M. EDWARDS of Ldn. Trust for debt to John C. LYON of Ldn using 100a (part of tract cnvy/b Saml. CONNER Apr 1800) adj Thos. MOSS, Mrs. ROSZELL, Peter WEATHERLY. Delv. to BOSS 3 Feb 1830 pr note from S. M. EDWARDS.

3P:323   Date: 1 May 1827   RtCt: 11 Jan 1828
Hugh SMITH to William BENTON. Release of trust of Oct 1821 for debt to John, Edward and Andrew MARTIN.

3P:325   Date: 18 Jan 1828   RtCt: 7 Feb 1828
Sanford RAMEY of Ldn to Zachariah DULANEY of Ldn. Trust for debt to Lydia RAMEY (w/o Sanford) using 178a (prch/o Michael BOGER, Oct 1810) adj Thomas DAVIS, John BINNS less 14a purchased by BALL, DAVIS and FULTON; and 148a (prch/o William H. HARDING Aug 1807) adj Broad Run, James CAMPBELL, Michael BOGER, house where John SHORTS formerly lived; and 300a (prch/o Ferdinando FAIRFAX, Nov 1799 and Apr 1803) adj Anthony WRIGHT, Edward CONNER; and 17a (prch/o Susan P. B. HARDING dev. of John A. BINNS dec'd Jun 1822); and 33½a (prch/o Elizabeth A. B. HARDING dev. of John A. BINNS dec'd Jun 1822); and 4a (prch/o George FULTON Oct 1816) on S side of Broad Run; and lot in Lsbg (prch/o Alexander CORDELL) adj road from Lsbg to Nolands ferry; and slaves old Jack, Nan, Dick, Kitty (alias Matilda), Rachel, Emily, Rodney, Burr, Isaac & wife Matilda, Nancy, Eliza, Judah, Pleas (alias Pleasant), Nelson, Jack, Peg, Bill, Tish (alias Letitia), Amanda, Gus (alias Gustine), Daniel & wife Milly, Ross, Winefred, Milley the cook, Limas, Fenton, Austin, Nace, Tenor, George, Henry, Ann, Sam, Charlott, Pinky (alias Maria) and Bob; and farm animals, farm and household items. Wit: Geo. W. HENRY, John TORREYSON, Charles G. EDWARDS.

3P:331   Date: 10 Jan 1828   RtCt: 12 Jan 1828
Richard H. LOVE & wife Eliza Matilda of Ldn to Presley SAUNDERS of Ldn. Trust for William T. T. MASON and James SINCLAIR as endorsers on bank note using slaves Sally, Fich?, and her child Ellen. Wit: Wilson C. Selden Jr., John J. Mathias.

3P:333   Date: 27 Oct 1827   RtCt: 14 Jan 1828
Bayley KIMBLER of Ohio to Daniel KIMBLER of Ldn. B/S of interest in land of father John KIMBLER dec'd of Ldn.

3P:334 Date: 10 Dec 1827 RtCt: 14 Jan 1828
Lewis GRIGSBY of Ldn to Daniel COCKRELL of Ldn. Trust for debt to Giles CRAVEN using slaves Sally, Chana and George. Wit: James COCKRAN Jr., Joel CRAVEN, William McKNIGHT.

3P:336 Date: 10 Jan 1828 RtCt: 15 Jul 1828
Thomas BIRKBY & wife Sarah of Ldn to Joshua RILEY of Ldn. B/S of house and lot on Back St in Lsbg (cnvy/b Wm. AUSTIN, DBk WW:388) and part of lot (cnvy/b Wm. WOODY, DBk WW:403). Wit: Hamilton ROGERS, John H. McCABE.

3P:338 Date: 3 Dec 1827 RtCt: 15 Jan 1828
Joshua RILEY & wife Ann of Ldn to Thomas BIRKBY of Ldn. B/S of lot in Lsbg (cnvy/b Samuel BUCK Dec 1820, DBk BBB:372). Wit: Hamilton ROGERS, John H. McCABE.

3P:340 Date: 16 Jan 1828 RtCt: 16 Jan 1828
Thomas TAYLOR of Lsbg to George RICHARDS of Lsbg. Trust for debt to Samuel M. BOSS of Lsbg for goods using farm and household items. Delv. to BOSS 20 Jan 1839.

3P:341 Date: 6 Aug 1824 RtCt: 16 Jan 1828
David SHAWEN of Ldn to John PAXSON of Ldn. B/S of 6 lots (first 4 prch/b Cornelius SHAWEN dec'd) on or near Cotocton Creek – 19a mill lot (prch/o Enoch FRANCIS Aug 1803); 41a (prch/o Conrad FRITIPAUGH Apr 1803); 12a (prch/o John A. BINNS Apr 1811); 19¼a (prch/o Asa MOORE May 1812); 5a and 33½a (prch/o Stephenson HIXSON by George M. & David SHAWEN Jan 1821). Delv. to Sanford J. RAMEY pr order 12 Oct 1832.

3P:345 Date: 18 Jan 1828 RtCt: 18 Jan 1828
Charles SMITH of Ldn to John W. COE (Guardian of Ann SMITH) of Ldn. B/S of undivided half (other half owned by Ann SMITH d/o Charles) of 10a (formerly owned by Edward COE dec'd) nr Coe's Mill adj Edward M. COE dec'd, William COE.

3P:346 Date: 17 Jan 1828 RtCt: 17 Jan 1828
David SHAWEN of Ldn and John PAXSON of Ldn. Agreement – PAXSON purchased land, mill and distillery from SHAWEN late prop. of Cornelius SHAWEN dec'd (f/o David). PAXSON owes SHAWEN bonds. Cornelius' estate has several debts and legacies, including to Catherine his infant daughter, widow Mary, dau. Anne w/o PAXSON. Value of land was suppose to cover debts but has dropped. David released John from six bonds. Wit: Rich'd H. HENDERSON, Sm. PAXSON.

3P:349 Date: 18 Jan 1828 RtCt: 18 Jan 1828
David SHAWEN of Ldn to Sheriff Charles LEWIS. B/S (surrendered for suit of Thomas George & Thomas) of 4a (prch/o Jacob WINE); 90a (prch/o Noah HIXSON); 13½a (prch/o Thomas SWAYNE) with last 2 in trust to Richard H. HENDERSON for debt to Lewis WALKER assignee of Isaac WALKER.

3P:350   Date: 14 Jan 1828   RtCt: 19 Jan 1828
Francis DULIN of Ldn to Thomas SAUNDERS of Lsbg. Trust (to settle on his wife Margaret H. DULIN & children her interest in estate of her grandfather Presley SA(U)NDERS) of undivided personal property.

3P:352   Date: 24 Jan 1828   RtCt: 24 Jan 1828
Matthew ORRISON of Ldn to Wesley S. McPHERSON of Ldn. Trust for debt to William GILMORE of Ldn using 30a prch/o Benedick DARNELL, farm animals, farm and household items.

3P:355   Date: 30 Jul 1825   RtCt: 1 F[eb] 1828
Peter RUST Sr. of Ldn to son Peter RUST Jr. of Ldn. Gift of interest in land formerly of ch/o Charles LEWIS being undivided shares of Stephen and Catherine LEWIS except their interest in surplus of 19½a that Peter Sr. prch/o Rich'd H. HENDERSON and life estate prch/o Sheriff of Ldn; and slaves Jane & her children Maria (for grandchild Benjamin Franklin RUST) and Hannah (for grandchild Elizabeth F. RUST), Moses, James, Davy, Susan, Sarah, Moses the younger, Tim, Jack, Henry, Isaac, Leonard, Cordelia and her infant child now at the breast, farm animals, household items. Wit: John W. GRAYSON, Wm. H. DORSEY.

3P:357   Date: 5 Feb 1828 [?]   RtCt: 1 Feb 1828
Bernard HOUGH of Ldn to George RICHARDS of Ldn. Trust for debt to Michael MORALLEE, Samuel M. BOSS, Asa PECK and John MARTIN of Ldn using land on Loudoun St in Lsbg with 2 story frame house used partly as a shop and frame counting house adj Dr. George LEE, wd/o Dr. Charles BALL dec'd.

3P:359   Date: 12 Jul 1825   RtCt: 1 Feb 1828
Commr R. H. HENDERSON (1816 case of William BROWN agst LEWIS reps) of Ldn to Peter RUST Jr. of Ldn. B/S of 19½a cnvy/b Sheriff Stacey TAYLOR to Peter Jr. than bought by Peter Sr. – no deed was made before.

3P:361   Date: 12 Jul 1825   RtCt: 1 Feb 1828
Former Sheriff Stacy TAYLOR to Peter RUST Jr. of Ldn. B/S of 200a (in Sept 1813, from life estate of Charles LEWIS to Peter RUST Sr.) adj Joanna LEWIS, John VIOLETT, Hiram SEATON – conveying interest with no warantee of title.

3P:363   Date: 18 Mar 1826   RtCt: 2 Feb 1828
Richard H. LEE of Ldn to John FRANCIS and John M. WILSON of Ldn. Trust for debt to Enoch FRANCIS of Ldn using lot on SE corner of Market and Back Sts. in Lsbg now occupied by Dr. POWELL.

3P:365   Date: 9 Jan 1828   RtCt: 4 Feb 1828
Jacob WALTMAN and wife Martha of Albemarle Co Va to Emanuel WALTMAN of Ldn. B/S of 25a in German Settlement adj __ FRAZIER; and 6a adj __ EVERHEART (from div. of estate of father Jacob WALTMAN dec'd); and rights in undivided 1/6th of 26a and 6a

assigned to brother Elias WALTMAN (now dec'd). Wit: John IRVIN, Garret WHITE.

3P:369   Date: 5 Sep 1827   RtCt: 5 Feb 1828
Siblings Stephen George ROSZELL, Sarah DONOHOE late ROSZELL, Stephen Wesley ROSZELL, Phebe ROSZELL and Nancy ROSZELL. Partition of 387a adj Glebe of Shelburne Parish (willed by father Stephen ROSZELL to brother Stephen Chilton ROSZELL who died in 1823). Divisors: Sydnor BAILEY, John J. MATHIAS, Seth SMITH. Gives plat. 82¼a Lot #1 to Nancy; 86a Lot #2 to Stephen George ROSZELL; 66a Lot #3 to Sarah; 71a Lot #4 to Phebe; 81a Lot #5 to Stephen Wesley.

3P:372   Date: 13 Feb 1826   RtCt: 6 Feb 1828
Dpty Sheriff Lewis BEARD to Samuel HAMMETT of Ldn. B/S of undivided interest of Christopher C. McINTYRE in real estate of father Patrick McINTYRE dec'd (cnvy Dec 1825 DBk LLL:183, subject to lien in DBk LLL:179).

3P:374   Date: 4 Feb 1828   RtCt: 7 Feb 1828
Thomas MARKS & wife Keziah of Ldn to Isaac CAMP of Ldn. B/S of 150a (cnvy/b Mahlon JANNEY to father John MARKS in Nov 1763 and dev. to Thomas) adj Noah HATCHER, Wm. RAMSEY. Wit: John WHITE, Craven OSBURN. Delv. to CAMP 12 Aug 1829.

3P:376   Date: 21 Jan 1828   RtCt: 8 Feb 1828
Humphrey RICHARDS to Capt. Jno. BYRNE. Trust for debt to Caldwell CARR and Bushrod RUST (Admrs of Jos. CARR dec'd) using wagon and horses. Wit: J. M. CLARK, Thos. T. D. BROWN, Peter CARR.

3P:377   Date: 7 Feb 1828   RtCt: 8 Feb 1828
Sanford RAMEY & wife Lydia of Ldn to Zachariah DULANEY of Ld. Trust for benefit of Diana CORDELL w/o Alexander CORDELL of Ldn using 101a (3 tracts cnvy/b heirs of Thomas DAVIS dec'd, John JANNEY and Alex'r CORDELL). Wit: George W. SHAWEN, Noble S. BRADEN. Delv. pr order 15 Dec 1828.

3P:379   Date: 8 Feb 1828   RtCt: 8 Feb 1828
Richard H. HENDERSON & wife Orra Moore of Ldn to son Alexander HENDERSON of Ldn. Gift of lot with houses and meadow lot in Wtfd formerly the property of ___ MORROW dec'd now occupied by Thomas DARNALDSON.

3P:380   Date: ___ 1818   RtCt: 8 Feb 1828
Charles SCOTT (h/o Elizabeth DAVIS wd/o Thomas DAVIS), John DAVIS & wife Margaret, Joseph DAVIS & wife Sarah, Daniel DAVIS & wife Malinda, and Jacob DAVIS & wife Susannah (ch/o Thomas DAVIS dec'd) to Sanford RAMEY. B/S of undivided interest in 90a of Thomas dec'd, adj RAMEY, Cornelious SHAWEN, Adam HOUSEHOLDER. Wit: Alex'r CORDELL, John FAWLEY, Adam

HOUSEHOLDER. CoE for Joseph DAVIS & wife Sarah in Bedford Co Pa.

3P:384 Date: 22 Jan 1828 RtCt: 11 Feb 1828
Elizabeth CROSS. DoE for Jesse BESICKS (held as slave by bill of sale from Benjamin WHITE). Wit: Joel NIXSON, James RUSK.

3P:385 Date: 8 Feb 1828 RtCt: 8 Feb 1828
Prison Bounds. 10a lot in Lsbg. Gives detailed plat.

3P:387 Date: 11 Feb 1828 RtCt: 11 Feb 1828
Augustine M. SANFORD, Robert SANFORD, Daniel STONE and Wm. SLATER. Bond on Augustine as constable.

3P:388 Date: 2 Jul 1827 RtCt: 11 Feb 1828
Saml. M. EDWARDS. Oath as Colonel of 57th Reg 6th Brig 2nd Div of Va Militia.

3P:388 Date: 5 Nov 1827 RtCt: 11 Feb 1828
William SHREVE. Oath as Lt. in 57th Reg 6th Brig 2nd Div of Va Militia.

3P:388 Date: 24 Jan 1828 RtCt: 11 Feb 1828
Elizabeth LOVE of Ldn. DoE for negro man Moses WILLIAMS, aged abt 44y. Wit: David SMITH, William NICHOLS, Jonah SANDS.

3P:389 Date: 15 Jan 1828 RtCt: 11 Feb 1828
Charles LEWIS of Ldn. DoE for negro man Peter BIGBY.

3P:390 Date: 25 Dec 1827 RtCt: 8 Feb 1828
John HAMILTON of Ldn to Conrad R. DOWELL and James McILHANY. Trust for debt to Conrad BITZER using 3/7th of 200a 'Taylor Town Farm' former prop. of Henry TAYLOR. Wit: Th. ROGERS. Delv. to DOWELL 18 Feb 1830.

3P:392 Date: 17 Jan 1828 RtCt: 11 Feb 1828
John ANKERS of Ldn to John M. WILSON. Trust for debt to Newton KEENE of Ldn using farm animals, crops.

3P:393 Date: 11 Feb 1828 RtCt: 11 Feb 1828
Mrs. Elizabeth CLAPHAM to John C. SHELTON. Trust for debt to Bazil GORDON using 121a, 148a, 118a, 200a and 50a with mill (cnvy/b James W. FORD trustee Feb 1828).

3P:397 Date: 14 Sep 1827 RtCt: 11 Feb 1828
John AULT & wife Mary late Spring of Ldn to David WIRE of Ldn. B/S of undivided 1/12th of real estate of Andrew SPRING dec'd. Wit: Geo. W. SHAWEN, Saml. HOUGH. Delv. to WIRE 28 Apr 1829.

3P:399 Date: 14 Jan 1828 RtCt: 11 Feb 1828
Josiah GREGG, David SIMPSON, and Peter GREGG & late firm of Simpson & Gregg of Ldn to Benjamin MITCHELL of Ldn. Release of trust of Apr 1826 on 80a, DBk MMM:249.

3P:400 Date: 11 Feb 1828 RtCt: 11 Feb 1828
Noble S. BRADEN (Exor of Robert BRADEN dec'd of Wtfd) to Abijah JANNEY of AlexDC. Trust for benefit Ann HARPER late ELLICOTT

w/o Washington T. HARPER using 131a and 146a farmed by Zachariah DULANEY, adj John BRADEN.

3P:403   Date: 11 Feb 1828   RtCt: 11 Feb 1828
James W. FORD of StafVa (trustee of Samuel CLAPHAM, Jan 1823) to Elizabeth CLAPHAM of Ldn. B/S of 21a (cnvy/b William NOLAND Mar 1804); 148a (cnvy/b William NOLAND Nov 1809); 118a (cnvy/b Robert BENTLY Admr wwa of P. McINTYRE Aug 1821); 200a (cnvy/b Thomas GEORGE Oct 1779 to Josais CLAPHAM, then to Samuel); and 50a with mill (cnvy/ Fanny LEE Exor of Thomas L. LEE Dec 1818).

3P:405   Date: 10 Feb 1828   RtCt: 11 Feb 1828
Nathan GREGG of Ldn to George McPHERSON of Ldn. B/S of 3a (prch/o Nathaniel MANNING Feb 1824).

3P:407   Date: 8 Feb 1828   RtCt: 11 Feb 1828
John WRIGHT and Burr BRADEN of Ldn to Noble S. BRADEN (Exor of Robert BRADEN dec'd) of Ldn. B/S of land in trust from Robert BRADEN (DBk KKK:213 of May 1825) equally to John BRADEN, Joshua PUSEY (Exors of James NIXSON dec'd) and Noble S. BRADEN in his own right and as Exor of Joseph BRADEN dec'd.

3P:408   Date: 14 Jan 1828   RtCt: 11 Feb 1828
Benjamin MITCHELL & wife Martha C. of Ldn to Daniel HYDE of Ldn. B/S of 80a (4/5th of land allotted to Flavious J. LANE by Ct) adj Jeremiah W. BRONAUGH, heirs of Joseph HATCHER, John CRANE. Wit: Benjamin GRAYSON, John W. GRAYSON. Delv. to Wm. BENTON 12 Jan 1836 the said land being devised to him by will recorded in Spottsylvania Co.

3P:410   Date: 12 Jan 1828   RtCt: 11 Feb 1828
Nicholas KOONCE & wife Elizabeth of JeffVa to Jonathan PAINTER. B/S of 1a (cnvy/b Joseph BURRELL Dec 1820, DBk BBB:274) adj Elizabeth JACOBS; and 1a (cnvy/b Joseph BURRELL Dec 1822, DBk FFF:206) adj other lot. Wit: John FRAME, James SIMMS?

3P:413   Date: 21 Jan 1828   RtCt: 11 Feb 1828
Henry PLAISTER Sr. & wife Nancy of Ldn to Henry HUTCHESON (h/o Susan, d/o PLAISTER) of Ldn. Gift of 5a adj __ BRONAUGH, __ COXE, __ JONES, __ HANLY, Michael PLASTER. Wit: Francis W. LUCKETT, Edward HALL.

3P:415   Date: 9 Feb 1828   RtCt: 11 Feb 1828
Elizabeth BRADEN (wd/o Robert BRADEN dec'd) of Wtfd to trustees of Abijah JANNEY of AlexDC as trustee of Ann HARPER w/o Washington T. HARPER. B/S for interest in 2 tracts from sale agreement of 9 Feb 1828 by Noble S. BRADEN (Exor of Robert BRADEN dec'd).

3P:416   Date: 23 Oct 1827   RtCt: 11 Feb 1828
John HEIS & wife Catharine late COOPER of PhilPa and Adam COOPER & wife Susannah and George COOPER of Ldn to Charles GULLATT and Saml. M. EDWARDS. Trust of 2a with grist mill and machinery adj Mrs. SANDERS late EKART, heirs (COOPERS and HEIS) from div. of Casper EKART lands for benefit of Ann SAUNDERS w/o Britton SAUNDERS of Ldn. Wit: William ELLZEY, John J. MATHIAS. Delv. to Ann SANDERS for Presly? EKHART 22 Feb 1829.

3P:420   Date: 28 Jan 1828   RtCt: 11 Feb 1828
Eli C. GALLEHER & wife Susan of Ldn to Henry PLASTER Sr. of Ldn. B/S of interest (1 child part) in farm of William GALLIHER dec'd in Union; and 4 shares in widow's dower. CoE by John B. ARMSTEAD, French GLASCOCK in Fqr. Forwarded to Exor pr order 23 Dec 1852.

3Q:001   Date: 24 Dec 1827   RtCt: 10 Mar 1828
John FRY & wife Elizabeth of Ldn to Edward MORRISON of Ldn. B/S of 23a on E side of short hill (cnvy/b Philip FRY Dec 1827) adj MORRISON. Wit: Mortimer McILHANEY, George W. SHAWEN. Delv. to MORRISON 20 Sep 1828.

3Q:003   Date: 11 Feb 1828   RtCt: 12 Feb 1828
Thomas SAUNDERS of Ldn to Jacob ISH of Ldn. B/S of 82½a (from trust of 153a from John JONES Jun 1825, DBk KKK:302) adj George CARTER, John SIMPSON, Casper JOHNSON, Hugh SMITH.

3Q:004   Date: 7 Feb 1828   RtCt: 12 Feb 1828
William McMULLEN of Ldn to Humphrey B. POWELL of Ldn. Trust for debt to A. G. TEBBETTS using 80a adj Fielding LYNN, Jonathan CARTER now occupied by McMULLEN.

3Q:007   Date: 4 Feb 1828   RtCt: 12 Feb 1828
Ruel MARSHALL & wife Eleanor of Ldn to Samuel PALMER Jr. of Ldn. Trust for debt to John CHEW of Ldn using ½a on S side of paved road below Snickersville adj CHEW. Wit: Notley C. WILLIAMS, Craven OSBURN. Delv. to PALMER 24 Dec 1830.

3Q:009   Date: 6 Feb 1828   RtCt: 14 Feb 1828
George W. HENRY of Ldn to Robert MOFFETT of Ldn. Trust for debt to Rich'd. H. HENDERSON (case of John JANNEY ass'ee against Jozabed WHITE and HENRY) using negro Evelina and her children Edmund, Amanda and infant in arms Jackson. Delv. to HENDERSON 19 Jul 1828.

3Q:010   Date: 15 Feb 1828   RtCt: 15 Feb 1828
Samuel G. HAMILTON & wife Anna of Ldn to Richard H. HENDERSON, Burr W. HARRISON and Charles G. ESKRIDGE of Ldn. Trust for debt to George CARTER of Oatlands using 1a (Lot #1 & #2) on S side of Cornwall St in W addition of Lsbg adj Charles

BINNS, __ McCORMICK, Mrs. DOWLING. Wit: John J. MATHIAS, Saml. M. EDWARDS. Delv. to Jesse TIMMS by verbal order 17 Dec 1829. Second notation on different page of Delv. to A. A. ESKRIDGE 17 Dec 1829.

3Q:014 Date: 28 May 1827 RtCt: 23 Feb 1828
Elizabeth SULIVAN to Jos. H. Wright. Loan of household items and cows. Wit: Elizabeth B. SULIVAN. Delv. to Eliz. SULLIVAN 16 Aug 1829.

3Q:015 Date: 7 Jan 1828 RtCt: 22 Feb 1828
Samuel TURNER & wife Amanda M. of Ldn to Peter COMPHOR of Ldn. B/S of 87a adj __ PURCEL, __ ARNOLD, __McILHANY. Wit: John WHITE, Craven OSBURN. Delv. to Peter COMPHER 1 Jan 1829.

3Q:017 Date: 21 Feb 1828 RtCt: 21 Feb 1828
Samuel M. BOSS & wife Elizabeth F. of Ldn to George RICHARDS of Ldn. B/S of undivided interest in lot (see DBk GGG:112) in Lsbg (from estate of Thomas JACOBS dec'd of Lsbg). Wit: Wilson C. SELDEN Jr., Hamilton ROGERS.

3Q:019 Date: 12 Oct 1826 RtCt: 21 Feb 1828
Rich'd. H. HENDERSON & wife Orra Moore of Ldn to James RUST of Ldn. B/S of 147a (cnvy/b Samuel M. EDWARDS as trustee for HENDERSON). Wit: Saml. M. EDWARDS, John J. MATHIAS. Delv. to RUST 26 Sep 1834.

3Q:020 Date: 12 Sep 1827 RtCt: 20 Feb 1828
John DEMORY & wife Eve of Ldn to Christian NYSWANGER of Ldn. B/S of 139a adj __ RUSSELL, __ WRIGHT, __ DERRY. Wit: George LIT[T]LE, Absalom VANVACTER. CoE from JeffVa. Delv. to Ch'n NIESWANGER 30 Jul 1828.

3Q:023 Date: 20 Feb 1828 RtCt: 20 Feb 1828
James RUST & wife Sally of Ldn to Richard H. HENDERSON, Burr W. HARRISON, Charles G. ESKRIDGE and Jesse TIMMS of Ldn. Trust for debt to George CARTER of Oatlands using 361a (cnvy/b T. W. POWELL Sept 1817, DBk VV:211) adj John RICHARDS, Henry CARTER, Burr POWELL Jr., John RICHARDS, George NOBLE; and 160a (cnvy/b George RUST Jr. Jul 1817, DBk YY:379). Delv. to TIMMS pr order ___.

3Q:027 Date: 10 Sep 1827 RtCt: 26 Feb 1828
Thomas HUGHES & wife Martha of Ldn to William PIGGOTT of Ldn. B/S of 7a adj Samuel IDON; and 3a adj Stephen WILSON, Benjamin BRADFIELD, Bernard TAYLOR (lots prch jointly by Samuel HATCHER, William PIGGOTT and Thomas HUGHES of Walter KERRICK, May 1824). Wit: John SIMPSON, Thomas NICHOLS.

3Q:029 Date: 23 Feb 1828 RtCt: 26 Feb 1828
George COOPER (s/o Catherine HEIS) of Ldn to Charles GULLATT and Samuel M. EDWARDS of Ldn. Trust (for benefit of Ann

SANDERS late ECKART w/o Britton SANDERS agst possible claim on mill sold to Ann by George and Adam COOPER) using 120a late property of Casper ECKHART dec'd. Delv. to Ann SANDERS 22 Feb 1829.

3Q:031   Date: 31 Jan 1828   RtCt: 25 Feb 1828
William BALL & wife Pamelia of Ldn to Roger CHEW of Ldn. Trust for debt to Timothy CARRINGTON of Ldn using 1a (prch/o Joseph THOMAS and Phinehas THOMAS) in Snickersville adj William BRADFIELD, Amos CLAYTON, Minor REED; and farm animals, farm and household items. Wit: Notley C. WILLIAMS, Craven OSBURN.

3Q:033   Date: 1 Jan 1828   RtCt: 25 Feb 1828
Elijah KENT of Ldn to Edward HAMMETT of Lsbg. Trust for debt to Robert R. HOUGH of Lsbg using hog, farm and household items. Wit: Saml. GILPIN.

3Q:035   Date: 16 Oct 1827   RtCt: 25 Feb 1828
Joseph JANNEY of Ldn to Hiram SEATON of Ldn. B/S of 25a (allotted to Martha REEDER late LEATH in div. of lots allotted to her and her brother James LEATH from estate of grandfather John VOILET dec'd) adj __ LEWIS.

3Q:037   Date: 5 Feb 1828   RtCt: 23 Feb 1828
Jacob EVERHART of Ldn to Jacob MOCK and Henry RUSSELL of Ldn. B/S of 2a (from trust of Leonard THOMAS Apr 1826) adj William WRIGHT, main road from Wtfd to Nolands Ferry. Delv. to MOCK and RUSSELL 3 Feb 1831.

3Q:039   Date: 22 Feb 1828   RtCt: 1 Mar 1828
Samuel CARR & wife Lucy D. of Ldn to Samuel M. EDWARDS of Ldn B/S of ½a lot on S side of Market St in Lsbg (in trust for benefit of Elizabeth SERVICK w/o Christian SERWICK). Wit: Josiah L. DREAN, Thomas SANDERS, John J. MATHIAS.

3Q:041   Date: 3 Mar 1828   RtCt: 3 Mar 1828
Annanias ORRISON of Ldn to John PYOTT of Ldn. Trust for debt to James THOMPSON of Ldn using farm animals, farm and household items.

3Q:043   Date: 15 Dec 1827   RtCt: 4 Mar 1828
Bernard TAYLOR & wife Sarah of Ldn to Yardley TAYLOR of Ldn. B/S of 50a (cnvy/b Thomas HATCHER) on NW fork of Goose Creek adj William SMITH, Rebecca HATCHER, Stephen WILSON. Wit: Stephen GREGG, Smith GREGG, Susan GREGG, Presley CORDELL, Thomas NICHOLS. Delv. to Yardly TAYLOR 20 Jan 1829.

3Q:045   Date: 6 Mar 1828   RtCt: 7 Mar 1828
William EVERHART & wife Susannah of Ldn to John GEORGE of Ldn. B/S of 96a (prch/o Commrs. Jacob VIRTZ and David AXLINE Feb 1811) adj Peter DERRY, Michael EVERHART, Jacob SMITH,

John GEORGE; and 11a (cnvy/b Joseph LEWIS Jr.) adj __ MULL. Wit: Noble S. BRADEN, Mortimer McILHANY. Delv. to Jno. GEORGE 1 Feb 1833.

3Q:048   Date: 1 Sep 1823   RtCt: 30 Sep 1823/6 Mar 1828
Celia WALDRON of Aldie to Richard VANPELT of Aldie. B/S of 1a last lot in E extremity of Aldie on N side of Main St (prch/o Charles Fenton MERCER Feb 1822) adj Thomas GHEEN. Wit: J. BAYLY, William FOX, Jonathan EWERS, John HAMILTON.

3Q:049   Date: 8 Mar 1828   RtCt: 7 [?] Mar 1828
John VERNON of Ldn to Jonah TAVENER of Ldn. PoA for interest in estate of brother Daniel VERNON dec'd. Wit: Wm. CHILTON, Abner VERNON.

3Q:050   Date: 6 Jan 1821   RtCt: 10 Mar 1828
Joseph POSTON of Ldn. DoE for negro man James or Jim, aged abt 40y. Wit: Thomas PHILIPS, Rich'd TUNIS, Asa M. BOND, Daniel STONE.

3Q:051   Date: 16 Mar 1828   RtCt: 18 Mar 1828
Joseph HAWKINS, John SIMPSON, Jesse McVEIGH and Jno. A BINNS. Bond on HAWKINS as constable.

3Q:052   Date: 7 Mar 1828   RtCt: 6 [?] Mar 1828
Gerrard WYNKOOP of Ldn to Josiah L. DREAN of Ldn. Trust for debt to Saml. CARR of Ldn using farm animals and items.

3Q:053   Date: 1 Sep 1827   RtCt: 10 Mar 1828
Thomas CHAPPELL of Ldn to son James CHAPPELL. Gift of leased lot where Thomas now lives, farm animals, farm and household items. Wit: Walter LANHAM, Jesse FLEMING. Delv. pr order 14 Sep 1829.

3Q:054   Date: 8 Mar 1828   RtCt: 10 Mar 1828
Jefferson C. THOMAS and Elizabeth U. THOMAS (legatees of Philip THOMAS dec'd). Satisfied with settlement made by Thomas JAMES the Exor and release him. Wit: Nathan NICKOLS, Joseph THOMAS, Samuel LODGE.

3Q:054   Date: 20 Apr 1827   RtCt: 10 Mar 1828
Bernard SWART and Alexander SWART & wife Stella/Stilly of Ldn (sons of James SWART Sr.) to Matilda SIMPSON (w/o John SIMPSON and d/o James Sr.) of Ldn. B/S of their interest (all 4 agreed to div. 'Goshen' tract) in 85a on Broad Run adj John HUTCHESON, Ish BAILY, Reuben HUTCHESON, old Gum Spring road; and 30a wood lot. Wit: John SINCLAIR, Wm. McNAB, Jesse ELGIN, Robt. BAYLY, John BAYLY. Delv. to Jno. SIMPSON 24 Sep 1834.

3Q:057   Date: 9 Feb 1828   RtCt: 10 Mar 1828
Mason MARKS & wife Hannah of Ldn to John GRAHAM of Ldn. B/S of 30a Lot #6 in div. of Abel MARKS dec'd adj __ COCKRAN, __ HUMPHREYS. Wit: John WHITE, Craven OSBURN.

3Q:059 Date: 19 Feb 1828 RtCt: 10 Mar 1828
Daniel GLASSCOCK of Fqr to William BENTON of Ldn. B/S of 50a leased lot (prch under trust at sale of Andrew MARTIN).

3Q:060 Date: 21 Feb 1828 RtCt: 10 Mar 1828
Burr BRADEN & wife Mary D. of Ldn to Thomas WHITE of Ldn. B/S of 180a (prch/o Robert BRADEN Jul 1825) adj Jno. WRIGHT, Jonah THOMPSON, __ McCARTY, William SMITH, John CUMMINGS, John NICKLIN. Wit: Noble S. BRADEN, Saml. HOUGH. Delv. to WHITE 14 Oct 1828.

3Q:062 Date: 6 Sep 1827 RtCt: 12 Feb 1828
Abel MARKS (trustee of Mary MARKS dec'd) of Ldn to Joshua OSBURN of Ldn. Trust for debt to Samuel B. T. CALDWELL as Admr of Mary MARKS dec'd using undivided interest in negroes allotted Mary from estate of husband Abel MARKS dec'd and undivided interest in Mary's dower land. Wit: Thomas JAMES, James COCKRAN Sr., Nicholas OSBURN, Timothy CARRINGTON.

3Q:064 Date: 26 Feb 1828 RtCt: 10 Mar 1828
Caleb MARTIN of Ohio to James BOWLES of Ldn. B/S of 10½a (1/4th interest in 42a dower land of his mother Elizabeth MARTIN) adj Hiram SEATON, farm where BOWLES resides. Delv. to BOWLES 19 Aug 1831.

3Q:065 Date: 10 Oct 1823 RtCt: 10 Mar 1828
Epaminondas M. LANE of Ldn to Benjamin MITCHELL Jr. of Ldn. B/S of Lot #4 and wood Lot #4 allotted E. M.; Lot #5 and wood Lot #5 allotted to Elizabeth CRANE; and Lot #3 and wood Lot #5 allotted to Mrs. Catherine LANE (all from div. of Flavius J. LANE dec'd and cnvy to E. M. LANE).

3Q:067 Date: 11 Feb 1828 RtCt: 10 Mar 1828
Reuben MURRAY of Fqr to William BENTON of Ldn. Release of trust of Dec 1823 for debt to Alley SEATON of Ldn.

3Q:069 Date: 15 Dec 1827 RtCt: 10 Mar 1828
Mary HOWELL of Ldn to Joshua REED of Ldn. B/S of 17a (to heir Mary from estate of John SMITH dec'd) adj Thomas MARKS' still house lot, REED, Greggs Road. Wit: Bernard TAYLOR, Stephen GREGG, Smith GREGG, Susan GREGG.

3Q:070 Date: 22 Feb 1828 RtCt: 10 Mar 1828
Elizabeth BRADEN (wd/o Robert dec'd) of Ldn to Thomas WHITE of Ldn. Relinquishment of dower rights to 178a cnvy to Burr BRADEN in Jul 1825 and by Burr to WHITE in Feb 1828.

3Q:072 Date: 2 Jan 1828 RtCt: 10 Mar 1828
John HANN of Ldn to Eli McVEIGH of Ldn. B/S of 151a (less 6a to Mary PUGH wd/o Spencer PUGH dec'd from sale Feb 1817) occupied by HANN adj __ HERIFORD, Thomas TRAYHORN, John BAWLDWIN, Abel PALMER, John CHAMBLAIN. Delv. pr order 26 Aug 1829.

3Q:074 Date: 29 Feb 1828 RtCt: 10 Mar 1828
John IREY & wife Sarah of Ldn to George GRIMES of Ldn. B/S of
115a on Crooked Run adj George FAIRHERST, Eli JANNEY,
Joseph CLEWES, Solomon RUSE, William NICKOLS, James
HATCHER. Wit: William ELLZEY, Wilson C. SELDON. Delv. to
GRIMES 28 Aug 1828.

3Q:076 Date: 1 Mar 1828 RtCt: 10 Mar 1828
Adam SANBOWER & wife Christenah of Ldn to George BEAMER of
Ldn. B/S of 27¼a Lot #6 (Christenah's from div. of Peter HICKMAN
dec'd) and 2½a. Wit: Mortimer McILHANY, Geo. W. SHAWEN.
Delv. to Exor ?? POWELL 20 Feb 1879.

3Q:078 Date: 8 Mar 1828 RtCt: 10 Mar 1828
John BRADEN to Thomas WHITE. Release of trust to Burr BRADEN
in Jul 1825 for debt to Jonah TAVENER & Joseph TAVENER (Exor
of George TAVENER dec'd) and cnvy to WHITE Feb 1828 on
178¼a.

3Q:080 Date: 8 Sep 1827 RtCt: 10 Mar 1828
James HOGE of Ldn to John NIXON of Ldn. B/S of 20¼a (from trust
of Mar 1816 from William, George, Thos., Richard and John
CARTER and Catherine CARTER ch/o and wd/o Richard CARTER
dec'd, see DBk TT:271) adj Wm. HOLMES. Wit: John HOLMES,
French SIMPSON, Joseph FRED.

3Q:082 Date: 190 Mar 1828 RtCt: 10 Mar 1828
Thomas WHITE of Ldn to John BRADEN of Ldn. Trust for debt to
Jonah and Joseph TAVENER (Exors of George TAVENER dec'd)
using 180a.

3Q:084 Date: 3 Jan 1828 RtCt: 10 Mar 1828
Aaron MILLER & wife Mary of Ldn to Edward MORRISON of Ldn.
B/S of 7a adj heirs of Peter MILLER dec'd, __ BOLAND, __
GRIMES. Wit: Mortimer McILHANY, Geo. W. SHAWEN. Delv. to
MORRISON 20 Sep 1828.

3Q:086 Date: 19 Dec 1827 RtCt: 10 Mar 1828
John HAMILTON Jr. of Ldn to Edward MORRISON of Ldn. B/S of 7a
(trust of Aug 1825 from John GRUBB for benefit of Elijah PEACOCK
& John BROWN). Delv. to MORRISON 20 Sep 1828.

3Q:087 Date: 24 Dec 1827 RtCt: 10 Mar 1828
John GRUBB & wife Elizabeth of Ldn to Edward MORRISON of Ldn.
B/S of interest in above lot with use of spring on land of Simon
SHOEMAKER. Wit: Mortimer McILHANY, Geo. W. SHAWEN. Delv.
to MORRISON 20 Sep 1828.

3Q:089 Date: 21 Feb 1828 RtCt: 11 Mar 1828
Daniel EACHES of Fqr to H. B. POWELL. Trust for Joseph GORE
as endorser on bank note using negro boy Landon abt 12y old,
household items, note on Nathaniel MANNING, profits from mill

formerly owned by John GIBSON. Delv. to Thos. ROGERS by order of H. B. POWELL 13 Oct 1829.

3Q:092 Date: 11 Mar 1828 RtCt: 11 Mar 1828
Thomas HALL & wife Elizabeth of Ldn to David CARR and John J. MATHIAS of Ldn. Trust for debt to William CARR of Ldn using 100a where HALL lives, adj Peter COST, Anthony CUMMINGS, John NIXSON, Walter ELGIN. Wit: John MARTIN, Josiah L. DREAN. Delv. to David CARR 14 Mar 1831.

3Q:093 Date: 18 Mar 1826 RtCt: 12 Jun 1826
Sadler John WILLIAMS of Ldn to Sidnor WILLIAMS of Ldn. B/S of 1/6th part of 131a from father Enos WILLIAMS dec'd including interest in mother's dower Delv. to WILLIAMS 23 May 1833.

3Q:095 Date: 3 Aug 1827 RtCt: 12 Mar 1828
John TRIBBE/TRIBBY & wife Lydia of Holmes Co Ohio to Agness POULSON of Ldn. B/S of 12a Lot #2 in div. of Jasper POULSON dec'd. Delv. to POULSON 8 Dec 1828.

3Q:097 Date: 3 Aug 1827 RtCt: 12 Mar 1828
William POULSON & wife Elizabeth of Holmes Co Ohio to Thomas MARKS of Ldn. B/S of 12a Lot #10 in div. of Jasper POULSON dec'd. Wit: Jesse MORGAN, Thomas POULSON.

3Q:099 Date: 21 Feb 1828 RtCt: 14 Mar 1828
Elisha W. JACKSON of Ldn to H. B. POWELL of Ldn. Trust for debt to Hiram and Towns'd. McVEIGH using personal property cnvy/t Burr WEEKS in trust some time ago. Wit: John HITAFFER, H. SMITH, Joseph D. TAYLOR. Delv. to POWELL Jr. pr order McVEIGH 22 Jan 1828.

3Q:101 Date: 30 Jan 1828 RtCt: 14 Mar 1828
Nathan GREGG and Stephen GREGG (Exors of Thomas GREGG dec'd) to Washington WHITE, Richard WHITE and Elizabeth WHITE of Ldn. B/S of 130a (lately owned by Adam WINEGARDNER) adj Rufus UPDIKE, Gidney CLARK, Geo. LEWIS. Delv. pr order filed in bundle 3U:117, 1 Jun 1847.

3Q:102 Date: 15 Jan 1828 RtCt: 17 Mar 1828
Leonard R. POSTON & wife Mary E. of Ldn to John K. LITTLETON of Ldn. B/S of 47a on side of blue ridge adj George RUST, LITTLETON. Wit: Benjamin GRAYSON, John W. GRAYSON. Delv. to LITTLETON 3 Nov 1828.

3Q:105 Date: 17 Mar 1828 RtCt: 17 Mar 1828
William D. DRISH & wife __ of Ldn to James MARTIN and Presley CORDELL of Ldn. Trust for debt to Jacob FADELY of Ldn using lot on King St in Lsbg.

3Q:106 Date: 1 Sep 1828 RtCt: 17 Mar 1828
Samuel PURCEL 2nd of Ldn to John P. LOVE of Ldn. Trust for debt to Benjamin OGDEN using ¼a (Lot #16 and #17) on main road in

HIlb (cnvy/b Henry GRIFFIN and by trustees of town). Delv. to OGDON 12 Jun 1830.

3Q:108   Date: 17 Mar 1828   RtCt: 17 Mar 1828
Elisha M. P(E)UGH of Ldn to Nicholas OSBURN of Ldn. B/S of 40a Lot #5 in div. of Abel MARKS dec'd.

3Q:110   Date: 17 Mar 1828   RtCt: 17 Mar 1828
Jacob FADELEY & wife Polly of Ldn to William D. DRISH of Ldn. B/S of lot on King St in Lsbg adj DRISH, Dr. Henry CLAGETT. Wit: John H. McCABE, John J. MATHIAS. Delv. to DRISH 16 Aug 1838.

3Q:112   Date: 6 Mar 1828   RtCt: 10 Mar 1828
John McCORMICK & wife Mary of WashDC to James GARRISON. B/S of house and lot at King and Market Sts. in Lsbg. (formerly under trust of Jul 1827 to William GABBY for Hugh McCORMICK, Alexander LAWRENCE, Helen C. McCORMICK now w/o Roberdeau ANNIN). Wit: Chas. W. WHARTON, Jno. CHALMER. Delv. to GARRISON 17 Apr 1829.

3Q:116   Date: 28 Mar 1828   RtCt: 15 Apr 1828
Commission of Charles LEWIS to remain Sheriff.

3Q:116   Date: 14 Apr 1828   RtCt: 14 Apr 1828
Charles LEWIS, Wm. ELLZEY, Robert MOFFETT, Wm. THRIFT, Asa ROGERS, H. SMITH, Towns'd McVEIGH, Jacob SUMMERS, Aris BUCKNER. Bond on LEWIS as Sheriff to collect levies.

3Q:117   Date: 14 Apr 1828   RtCt: 14 Apr 1828
Charles LEWIS, Wm. ELLZEY, Robert MOFFETT, Wm. THRIFT, Asa ROGERS, H. SMITH, Towns'd McVEIGH, Jacob SUMMERS, Aris BUCKNER. Bond on LEWIS as Sheriff to collect Officers fees.

3Q:119   Date: 14 Apr 1828   RtCt: 14 Apr 1828
Charles LEWIS, Wm. ELLZEY, Robert MOFFETT, Wm. THRIFT, Asa ROGERS, H. SMITH, Towns'd McVEIGH, Jacob SUMMERS, Aris BUCKNER. Bond on LEWIS as Sheriff to collect taxes.

3Q:120   Date: 18 Mar 1828   RtCt: 18 Mar 1828
James GARRISON & wife Elizabeth of Lsbg to Richard H. HENDERSON of Lsbg. Trust for debt to Roberdeau ANNIN of WashDC using lot at King and Market Sts occupied by John H. HARDING and William ELLZEY. Wit: John H. McCABE, Geo. W. SHAWEN. Delv. to ANNIN 26 Jul 1828.

3Q:122   Date: 18 Mar 1828   RtCt: 18 Mar 1828
Richard KEENE (insolvent debtor) of Ldn to Sheriff Charles LEWIS. B/S of 220a where he lives cnvy/b him in trust to James LEWIS Sr., John BAILEY as Chas. LEWIS' trustees (debts to Thomas LATIMORE, Wm. SAFFER, Admr of Charles POWELL).

3Q:124   Date: 15 Mar 1828   RtCt: 22 Mar 1828
Samuel CARR of Ldn to Josiah L. DREAN of Ldn. Trust for debt to Samuel STERRETT, Joseph T. NEWTON and John CARR using numerous yard goods and household items.

3Q:126   Date: 21 Mar 1828   RtCt: 21 Mar 1828
William CHAMBLIN. Now 21 years old and acknowledges B/S of 22 Mar 1826 by Price JACOBS & wife Catherine, William JACOBS & wife Maria and William CHAMBLIN to Joseph HUMPHREY, DBk MMM:267.

3Q:126   Date: 5 Feb 1828   RtCt: 27 Mar 1828
Martin HARTMAN of JeffVA to Philip HOFFMAN of JeffVa. Trust for debt to Michael GARRY of Washington Co Md using 15½a from div. of Henry NICEWANNER dec'd. Wit: Sam BREITENBAUGH, William HACY, Geo. W. ROWLES, Charles CANVEY.

3Q:129   Date: 27 Mar 1828   RtCt: 27 Mar 1828
William HAMMETT of Ldn to Geo. RICHARDS of Ldn. Trust for debt to Samuel M. BOSS of Ldn using undivided interest in estate of brother George HAMMETT dec'd of Ldn. Delv. to BOSS 15 Jul 1828.

3Q:131   Date: 28 Mar 1828   RtCt: 28 Mar 1828
George W. HENRY of Ldn to William M. JENNERS of Ldn. Trust for debt to Charles B. HAMILTON using 103a (prch/o Jozabed WHITE, details in trust to JENNERS Nov 1825).

3Q:133   Date: 26 Oct 1827   RtCt: 2 Apr 1828
Turbutt R. BETTON & wife Eliza (d/o William LANE dec'd of Ffx, s/o Abby) of AlexDC late of Ffx to Johnston CLEVELAND of Ldn. B/S of 288a in Ldn and Ffx on Horsepen Run adj __ LEE, Francis AUBREY. Wit: N. KEENE, Adam LYNN. Delv. to CLEVELAND 4 Nov 1868.

3Q:136   Date: 20 Mar 1828   RtCt: 3 Apr 1828
Jacob ISH to John ISH. LS of 303a (in trust for benefit of dau. Lucinda ADAMS and children) nr Little River Meeting house adj John HUTCHESON, Chas. F. MERCER where John R. ADAMS & wife Lucinda now reside.

3Q:138   Date: 17 Mar 1828   RtCt: 7 Apr 1828
Samuel DUNKIN & wife Anna of Ldn to Craven SILCOTT of Ldn. B/S of ¼a town Lot #1 in div. of James REED dec'd allotted to dau. Mary then w/o Moses BROWN, adj Isaac BROWN, William GALLEHER, Elizabeth WILKINSON. Wit: Francis W. LUCKETT, John W. GRAYSON.

3Q:140   Date: 25 Feb 1828   RtCt: 7 Apr 1828
Thomas TRIBBE/TRIBBY Jr. & wife Deborah of Ldn to Stacy TAYLOR of Ldn. Trust for debt to Absalom BEANS using 12a Lot #1 in div. of Jasper POULSON dec'd, adj David GOODIN, James LOVE. Wit: John WHITE, Craven OSBURN.

3Q:143   Date: 10 Apr 1828   RtCt: 10 Apr 1828
Joshua RILEY & wife Nancy of Ldn to Simon SMALE of Ldn. B/S of lot on Back St in Lsbg adj SMALE, James FRENCH. Wit: John H. McCABE, Presley CORDELL. Delv. 27 Jun 1828.

3Q:145   Date: 20 Apr 1827   RtCt: 11 Aug 1827/17 Mar 1828
John SIMPSON & wife Matilda and Bernard & Alexander SWART & wife Stella. Partition of 234a Lot #3 in Goshen tract prch/o George B. WHITING by James SWART Sr. and made joint with children Bernard and Alexander SWART and Matilda SIMPSON w/o John SIMPSON. Wit: Wm. McNABB, Jesse ELGIN, Robt. BAYLY, John BAYLY.

3Q:148   Date: 30 Jan 1828   RtCt: 11 Apr 1828
Jehue HOLLINGSWORTH & wife Senior of Ldn to Isaac NICKOLS (s/o Wm.) of Ldn. Trust for debt to Wm. NICHOLS (Admr of Isaiah NICHOLS dec'd), Thomas GREGG using 55a where HOLLINGSWORTH resides adj. Samuel PURSELL, Jonath. HEATON. Wit: Towns'd McVEIGH, Samuel NICKOLS, Stacy NICKOLS, Hannah NICKOLS, Sarah NICKOLS. Delv. pr order of Isaac NICKOLS to Dr. Jonothan HEATON 3 Sep 1829.

3Q:149   Date: 13 Apr 1828   RtCt: 13 Apr 1828
William SMITH of Ldn to Amos BEANS of Ldn. B/S of 150a on Kittocton Creek adj John B. STEPHENS, __ McDANIEL, __ BRADEN, George HENRY.

3Q:151   Date: 25 Mar 1820   RtCt: 14 Apr 1828
Noah HATCHER & wife Rachel of Ldn to Thomas MORRIS of Ldn. B/S of 1a (from tract where HATCHER now resides) adj Stacy TAYLOR, Whitson BIRDSALL. Wit: Stacy TAYLOR, Joseph TAYLOR, Amor S. NICKOLS, John WHITE, Craven OSBURN. Delv. to MORRIS 19 Sep 1829.

3Q:154   Date: 27 Feb 1828   RtCt: 14 Apr 1828
Ct. Commr. Edmund TYLER of Ldn to Thomas GHEENE of Ldn. B/S of 17¼a (except ¼a for buying ground) nr Aldie (title from William EVANS for bond of 20 Oct 1802, case defendants Henry EVANS, Benjamin SWART & wife Polly, Jos. MELLON & wife Jane).

3Q:155   Date: 14 Mar 1828   RtCt: 14 Apr 1828
Ct. Commrs William CHILTON and Joel NIXSON (in div. of Jonathan HALL dec'd) to Walter ELGIN of Ldn. B/S of 110a (dev. to late Jonathan HALL dec'd by William HALL dec'd). Delv. to ELGIN 28 Oct 1828.

3Q:157   Date: 15 Mar 1828   RtCt: 14 Apr 1828
Deborah McKNIGHT of Ldn to Thomas JAMES of Ldn. B/S of 25a adj JAMES, Charles CHAMBLIN, John McKNIGHT. Wit: John CHAMBLIN, H. ELLIOTT, Charles CHAMBLIN. Delv. to JAMES 3 Oct 1828.

3Q:158   Date: 11 Apr 1823   RtCt: 5 May 1822/14 Apr 1828
Joseph CARR of Upperville to John L. DAGG of Upperville. LS ½a in Upperville adj Dr. T. W. SMITH. Wit: Peter C. RUSE, Caldwell CARR, John McPHERSON, James DAGG, Sydnor BAILEY. Delv. pr order filed DBk XXX:322, 25 Jun 1834.

3Q:159   Date: 11 Dec 1827   RtCt: 14 Apr 1828
Sydnor BAILEY of Ldn to William BENTON of Ldn. Release of trust of Feb 1822 for debt to John MARTIN formerly of Ldn.

3Q:161   Date: 19 Mar 1828   RtCt: 25 Mar/14 Apr 1828
Robert FULTON of Ldn to John H. MONROE and James L. MARTEN of Lsbg. B/S of ½ of Lot #8 in Lsbg (former prop of Jacob JACOBS dec'd sold by Commrs.) and also the adj lot (prch/o William MOXLEY, former prop of John WILDMAN & wife Eleanor) with house that Benjamin THORNTON formerly owned. Wit: William FULTON, Jacob FADLEY, David FULTON. Delv. to MONROE & MARTIN 25 Feb 1831.

3Q:163   Date: 17 Mar 1828   RtCt: 14 Apr 1828
Joseph LOVETT dec'd. Division for children Hannah LOVETT, John LOVETT & wife Naomi, Jonas LOVETT & wife Nancy to Jonathan LOVETT of Ldn. Died intestate but desired sons to have real estate and dau Hannah to have money. Samuel RICHARDS, Gourley REEDER and Robert FULTON of David to fix interest owed Hannah. 121a to Jonathan. Wit: Francis W. LUCKETT, John W. GRAYSON. Delv. pr order of Jonathan LOVETT 18 Oct 1837.

3Q:166   Date: 17 Mar 1828   RtCt: 14 Apr 1828
John LOVETT, Jonathan LOVETT and Jonas LOVETT to William GALLEHER. Trust for debt to Hannah LOVETT using land from div. of father Joseph LOVETT dec'd. Delv. to GALLEHER 11 Oct 1833.

3Q:168   Date: 17 Mar 1828   RtCt: 14 Apr 1828
Hannah LOVETT, Jonathan LOVETT & wife Matilda, Jonas LOVETT & wife Nancy to John LOVETT. From division of father Joseph LOVETT dec'd – two lots in Union to be rented or sold and John given 130a. John pays Hannah her interest and others give John their share of land in trust. Wit: Francis W. LUCKETT, John W. GRAYSON. Delv. to Jas. B. DUNKIN pr order 12 Aug 1833.

3Q:170   Date: 17 Mar 1828   RtCt: 14 Apr 1828
Hannah LOVETT, John LOVETT & wife Naomi, Jonathan LOVETT & wife Matilda of Ldn to Jonas LOVETT of Ldn. From div. of father Joseph LOVETT dec'd – 108a and 6a. Wit: Francis W. LUCKETT, John W. GRAYSON. Delv. to Jonas LOVETT 24 Aug 1832.

3Q:173   Date: 1 Mar 1828   RtCt: 16 Apr 1828
Frederick RUSE of Ldn to Henry RUSE of Ldn. B/S of 1/3rd of 185a (willed to Fred. {1/3rd} & Henry from Christian RUSE dec'd, cnvy/b Joseph LEWIS Jr. Sep 1803) adj Michael BOGER, Isaac RITCHIE. Delv. 25 Jun 1829.

3Q:175   Date: 14 Apr 1828   RtCt: 16 Apr 1828
William GABBY of Washington Co Md to John McCORMICK of WashDC. Release of trust of Jul 1827, DBk OOO:104, for debt to Alexander LAWRENCE, Helen C. McCORMICK. Wit: Christ'r

BURCKHARTT, Wm. WEBB. Delv. to R. ANNIN agent of M. McMORMICK 16 Mar 1836.

3Q:177   Date: 16 Apr 1828   RtCt: 16 Apr 1828
John G. HUMPHREY (Exor of Jane HUMPHREY dec'd) of Ldn to Issachar BROWN of Ldn. B/S of 60a adj Richard THATCHER, John GREGG.

3Q:179   Date: 26 Mar 1828   RtCt: 16 Apr 1828
Benj'n BARTON of Ldn to Nimrod NEWLON of Ldn. B/S of house & 1¼a (sold by Stephen McPHERSON to Benj'n GRAYSON Jr. dec'd) adj Col. George MARKS. Delv. pr order 12 Dec 1829.

3Q:180   Date: 11 Feb 1828   RtCt: 16 Apr 1828
James McILHANY of Ldn to Thomas J. MARLOW of Ldn. B/S of 48½a (trust of George SHOVER for debt to Valentine F. SHOVER derived from div. of Adam SHOVER dec'd). Delv. to MARLOW 23 Mar 1829.

3Q:182   Date: 18 Feb 1828   RtCt: 15 Apr 1828
Burr POWELL & wife Catherine of Ldn to Cuthbert POWELL and Abner GIBSON of Ldn. Trust for debt to Charles BENNETT of AlexDC for use of son George C. POWELL using 300a adj Hump. B. POWELL, Wm. BEVERIDGE, Hugh ROGERS, Wm. HANNAH's shop, heirs of Elizabeth BEATY, A. GIBSON, Marshall street. Wit: Asa ROGERS, James H. McVEIGH, Ths. W. GIBSON. Delv. R. H. H. per order of Chs. BENNETT 24 Sep 1828.

3Q:184   Date: 2 Apr 1828   RtCt: 16 Apr 1828
Adam CORDELL & wife Susan of Ldn to Jacob SLATER Sr. of Ldn. B/S of 11¾a Lot #6 from div. of Adam CORDELL dec'd, on Catoctin Creek. Wit: Mortimer McILHANY, Geo. W. SHAWEN. Delv. to William SLATER pr order 8 May 1837.

3Q:186   Date: 19 Dec 1827   RtCt: 15 Apr 1828
Barton EWERS & wife Rachel of Ldn to David LOVETT and Stephen JANNEY of Ldn. Trust for debt to Swithen NICHOLS using 120a adj school house, Thomas JONES, Joshua GREGG, John MARKS, Jonathan EWERS; and 112a adj other lot. Wit: Thomas NICHOLS, Notley C. WILLIAMS. Delv. to Swithen NICHOLS 25 May 1829.

3Q:190   Date: 1 Apr 1828   RtCt: 15 Apr 1828
John CASE & wife Christena of Ldn to Benjamin GRUBB of Ldn. B/S of 10a on E side of short hill (allotted to CASE in div. of Charles CRIM Sr. dec'd), adj GRUBB, Jacob CRIM. Wit: Mortimer McILHANY, Saml. HOUGH. Delv. to GRUBB 27 Jul 1829.

3Q:192   Date: 7 Nov 1827   RtCt: 15 Apr 1828
John VERNON & wife Phebe of Ldn to Uriel GLASSCOCK of Ldn. B/S of 102a (cnvy/b James MARSH Dec 1800) on Beaverdam adj Jonathan CARTER, __ FULTON. Wit: Francis W. LUCKETT, James RUST. Delv. to GLASSCOCK 30 May 1831.

3Q:194   Date: 19 May 1827   RtCt: 15 Apr 1828
John Leven POWELL of Ldn to Humphrey B. POWELL of Ldn. Trust
for debt to Burr POWELL, Cuth't POWELL and Alfred H. POWELL
(trustees of Sarah H. CHELTON) using 'blackoak thicket' allotted
John L. in div. of Leven POWELL dec'd. Wit: Cuthbert POWELL,
Henry T. HARRISON.

3Q:196   Date: 3 Jan 1827   RtCt: 15 Apr 1828
James ALLEN of Ldn to John BAYLY, James ALLEN, James
McFARLAND, Joshua LEE & Jacob SUMMERS (trustee of Hill
Seminary). B/S of ¼a to build school. Wit: M. C. SHOEMATE,
George KINGSMARK, James TILLETT, John BAYLY Jr. Delv. to
Jno. BAILY 30 Sep 1829.

3Q:198   Date: 11 Jan 1828   RtCt: 15 Apr 1828
Eli McVEIGH to Hugh SMITH. Trust for debt to John HANN using
151a (with 6a reserved to widow Mary PUGH dev. by Spencer
PUGH) occupied by HANN adj John TALBURT, Aaron BURSON,
Thomas TRAYHERN, John BALDWIN, Able PALMER, John
CHAMBLIN.

3Q:200   Date: 23 Apr 1828   RtCt: 23 Apr 1828
Rich'd. H. HENDERSON & wife Orra Moore of Ldn to Burr Wm.
HARRISON of Ldn. B/S of house at corner of Market & Church Sts
in Lsbg occupied by HENDERSON as an office. Wit: William
ELLZEY, Saml. M. EDWARDS.

3Q:201   Date: 29 Jan 1828   RtCt: 22 Apr 1828
James WARFORD & wife Elizabeth late MARKS of Livingston Co Ky
to brother Thomas MARKS. PoA for business as rep. of father Abel
MARKS dec'd who departed intestate.

3Q:204   Date: 22 Apr 1828   RtCt: 22 Apr 1828
Daniel ANNIN (insolvent debtor) of Ldn to Sheriff Charles LEWIS.
B/S of interest in 750a in Onchita Co Louisiana and interest in house
and lots in AlexDC in right of wife (dau. of Daniel ROBERDEAU)
now in possession of widow (cnvy/b heirs of Gen. ROBERDEAU,
debt to Wm. MILLER).

3Q:205   Date: 31 Mar 1828   RtCt: 12 Apr 1828
Samuel G. HAMILTON & wife Ann W. of Lsbg to Geo. RICHARDS
of Lsbg. Trust for debt to Samuel M. BOSS of Lsbg using lot at
corner of Cornwall & __ Sts in Lsbg (see trust from HAMILTON to
George CARTER, 15 Feb 1828). Wit: S. S. BOSS, Jas. L.
HAMILTON, Math'w HAMILTON, John H. McCABE, Saml. M.
EDWARDS. Delv. to BOSS 15 Jul 1828.

3Q:207   Date: 22 Apr 1828   RtCt: 22 Apr 1828
Commrs Richard H. HENDERSON and John JANNEY of Ldn (Ct.
decree of 13 Mar 1828 Mason MARKS & others agst Bennett
MARKS) to Morris OSBURN of Ldn. B/S of 140a at fork of road from

Lsbg to Snickers and Wormley Gap (assigned to dower of Mary MARKS wd/o Abel MARKS). Delv. to OSBURN 4 Jan 1830.

3Q:209   Date: 20 Feb 1828   RtCt: 26 Apr 1828
George W. SEEVERS (Marshall of Sup. Ct of Winchester) to Daniel GOLD of Corp. of Winchester. B/S of lot in Lsbg on W addition on Market St opposite the Presbyterian Meeting (Dec 1827 case of Bank of the Valley agst Phebe GOLD late SCOTT w/o Daniel GOLD)

3Q:211   Date: 28 Apr 1828   RtCt: 28 Apr 1828
Thomas POULTON & wife Lucinda of Ldn to John HESSAR of Ldn. B/S of undivided interest in 156a of her father Andrew HESSAR Sr. dec'd. Wit: Saml. M. EDWARDS, Presley CORDELL.

3Q:212   Date: 28 Apr 1828   RtCt: 28 Apr 1828
Andrew HESSAR Jr. & wife Mary of Ldn to John HESSAR of Ldn. B/S of undivided interest in 156a of his father Andrew HESSAR the elder dec'd (prch/o John W. DAVIS & wife Elizabeth Feb 1823, DBk FFF:402). Wit: Saml. M. EDWARDS, Presley CORDELL.

3Q:213   Date: 29 Apr 1828   RtCt: 29 Apr 1828
James COCKRAN Jr. & wife Rachel of Ldn to Jesse HOGE of Ldn. Trust for debt to Isaac NICHOLS Sr. using 24½a (allotted from estate of Jonathan BRADFIELD dec'd) where COCKRAN resides, adj Stephen WILSON, Bernard TAYLOR. Wit: Wilson C. SELDEN, Presley CORDELL. Delv. to Thos. HATCHER Exor. of NICKOLS 15 Aug 1829.

3Q:216   Date: 28 Apr 1828   RtCt: 29 Apr 1828
Berry CREBS to Samuel CAMPBELL of Ldn. B/S (in trust for benefit of CREB's wife and children) of interest in land dev. by Rawleigh CHINN to dau Elizabeth WILSON for her life and at her death sold and div. between her heirs, one of whom is Lucy J. his wife; and 1a in Mdbg (prch/o John UNDERWOOD), household items, cow and horse, bonds by Saml. CHINN, Francis O'BANION, Wm. UTTERBACK, Jas. TILLETT, Peyton SILCOTT, Thornton PARKER, accounts outstanding in his books for work done.

3Q:218   Date: 29 Apr 1828   RtCt: 29 Apr 1828
Charles CUNNINGHAM of Fred Md to George SNOUFFER of FredMd. B/S of interest and privilege of a ferry landing and road to and from Ldn Co (cnvy/b Thomas JOHNSON late of Ldn Dec 1814). Delv. to Young SNOUFFER by order of his Guardian filed 1 Aug 1832.

3Q:219   Date: 21 Apr 1828   RtCt: 29 Apr 1828
Boot and shoemaker Thomas N. JONES & wife Hannah of Union to Jesse HOGE of Ldn. Trust for debt to Isaac NICHOLS Sr. using frame house and ¼a Lot #5 in Union (from div. of James REED dec'd) occupied by JONES, adj late William GALLEHER, Isaac BROWN, Daniel LOVETT, __ PLAISTER, Thornton WALKER. Wit:

John W. GRAYSON, Benj'n GRAYSON. Delv. 8 Feb 1830 to W. HOGE.

3Q:222   Date: 7 Apr 1828   RtCt: 29 Apr 1828
Thomas MARKS & wife Keziah of Ldn to John P. LOVE of Ldn. B/S of 21a adj Isaac CAMP, Joshua REED, Jesse SILCOTT. Wit: Craven OSBURN, John WHITE. Delv. to LOVE 12 Jan 1828 [?].

3Q:224   Date: 16 Apr 1828   RtCt: 30 Apr 1828
George SAGERS & wife Delila of Ldn to James P. BRADFIELD of Ldn. B/S of 6a on NW fork of Goose Creek adj James BRADFIELD. Wit: Presley CORDELL, Saml. M. EDWARDS. Delv. to BRADFIELD 4 Apr 1836.

3Q:226   Date: 26 Feb 1828   RtCt: 3 May 1828
Robert COE & wife Elizabeth of Ldn to Joab EVELAND of Ldn. B/S of 7½a adj __ SANDERS. Wit: John SIMPSON, Thomas SANDERS.

3Q:229   Date: 24 Apr 1828   RtCt: 2 May 1828
Peter H. RUST of Ldn to H. B. POWELL of Ldn. Trust for debt to William SEATON of Ldn using 197¾a where RUST now resides (cnvy/b father Peter RUST dec'd) adj Hiram SEATON.

3Q:230   Date: 2 May 1828   RtCt: 2 May 1828
John ALDER of Ldn to Rich'd H. HENDERSON of Ldn. Trust for debt to Lewis WALKER of Jefferson Co Ohio using 3 lots cnvy/b HENDERSON this day. Delv. to HENDERSON 2 Jan 1833.

3Q:231   Date: 2 May 1828   RtCt: 2 May 1828
Rich'd. H. HENDERSON & wife Orra Moore of Ldn to John ALDER of Ldn. B/S of 90a and 13½a (cnvy/b Lewis WALKER in trust Feb 1827, DBk NNN:168); and 4a adj lot with logged house (cnvy/b David SHAWEN to Sheriff Charles LEWIS). Wit: Presley CORDELL, John H. McCABE. Delv. to ALDER 12 Oct 1829.

3Q:233   Date: 6 May 1828   RtCt: 6 May 1828
Geo. PURSEL and Enos POTTS (now in jail on capias ad satisfaciendum) to James McILHANY. Trust for debt to John WHITE using crops, horse and cow.

3Q:235   Date: 26 Feb 1828   RtCt: 1 May 1828
Robert R. HOUGH & wife Sarah C. of Ldn to Richard H. HENDERSON of Ldn. Trust for debt to Otho M. LINTHECUM of Georgetown using house & ½a on Royal St in Lsbg in occupation of HOUGH adj P. BOSS, James THOMAS. Wit: Presley CORDELL, John H. McCABE. Delv. to HENDERSON 21 Mar 1829.

3Q:237   Date: __ May 1828   RtCt: 5 May 1828
Daniel EVELAND (insolvent debtor in jail) to Sheriff Charles LEWIS. B/S of 5¼a near Goose Creek (cnvy/b William AULT Jun 1823, DBk FFF:478).

3Q:238   Date: 5 May 1828   RtCt: 7 May 1828
Mesheck LACEY of Ldn to Hugh SMITH of Ldn. Trust for Samuel CHINN as security in executions to Joshua PANCOAST, Conrad

BITZER, James TILLETT, John GREGG, James RUST ass'ee of William RUST (all agst LACEY & CHINN) using 2 lots (1a) in Mdbg occupied by LACEY as dwelling and hatters shop and negro woman Rachel, man Peter with wife Charlotte & 4 children Emily, Francis and two others. Delv. to CHINN 30 Aug 1836.

3Q:240 Date: 10 May 1828 RtCt: 10 May 1828
John TORBERT & wife Nancy of Ldn to Samuel M. EDWARDS and Henry S. TAYLOR of Ldn. Trust for debt to John PANCOAST of Ldn using 100a (cnvy/b Samuel BUTCHER to Samuel TORBERT and left to brothers & sister, John purchasing all shares but one) adj Thomas DRAKE, Meeting house, Samuel BUTCHER. Wit: Wilson C. SELDEN, Presley CORDELL. Delv. to PANCOAST 9 Nov 1829.

3Q:243 Date: 25 Feb 1828 RtCt: 12 May 1828
Elias JENKINS of Ldn to William M. JENNERS of Ldn. Trust for debt to Manderick YOUNG of DC using lot prch/o Henry JENKINS Jun 1816, DBk FFF:330. Wit: Alfred A. ESKRIDGE, Jas. L. HAMILTON, Edward L. FANT.

3Q:245 Date: 10 May 1828 RtCt: 10 May 1828
John PANCOAST Jr. of Ldn to John TORBERT of Ldn. Release of trust of Mar 1817 for debt to John PANCOAST Jr. (trustee Sampson BLINCOE has died without executing trust).

3Q:246 Date: 23 Apr 1828 RtCt: 12 May 1828
Joshua GORE. Oath as Captain in 56th Reg 6th Brig 2nd Div Va Militia. Delv. to GORE 28 Aug 1828.

3Q:247 Date: __ May 1828 RtCt: 18 May 1828
Presley CORDELL, John BRADEN & John M. WILSON (Commrs. in div. of estate of William MAINS dec'd) to Archibald MAINS (Exor of Mary MAINS dec'd). BoS for negro Moses or Moses HARRISON.

3Q:248 Date: __ May 1828 RtCt: 12 May 1828
Archibald MAINS (Exor of Mary MAINS dec'd) of Ldn. DoE for negro man Moses or Moses HARRISON aged abt 28y held as dower from estate of William MAINS dec'd to widow Mary MAINS dec'd.

3Q:249 Date: ___ 1828 RtCt: 14 May 1828
William HAWLING Sr. dec'd. Division – court order of 11 Feb 1828, 105a Lots #2 & Lot #6 to Hamilton ROGERS in right of wife Mary late Mary HAWLING; 109a Lot #1 & Lot #5 to William HAWLING; 116¼a Lot #3 to Jesse P. HATCH in right of wife Jane late HAWLING; 127a Lot #4 to Martha HAWLING (lots are on Potomac River); 136a Lot #8 to John HAWLING; 90a Lot #7 to Joseph L. HAWLING (these 2 lots are the home farm adj Charles BINNS, Joseph Mead). Divisors: Presley CORDELL, James RUST, Alfred BELT. Gives plat.

3Q:255 Date: __ May 1828 RtCt: 14 May 1828
Ct. Commrs. Presley CORDELL, John M. WILSON, John BRADEN to Archibald MAINS (Exor of Mary MAINS dec'd). BoS for negro

Moses, divided proceeds and lots between Archibald MAINS, 31¾a
Lot #2 with mill to William MAINS, 54¼a Lot #3 to Elizabeth
VANDEVANTER, 57¼a Lot #4 to children of Anna VANDEVANTER
dec'd (Mason CHAMBLIN & wife Dewanner, James SINCLAIR &
wife Leanah, John VANDEVA[N]TER, William VANDEVENTER,
Joseph VANDEVENTER, and Charles VANDEVENTER), 31¾a Lot
#1 to Washington M. CARR s/o Jane CARR. Support of negro
James to be from estate of Wm. MAINS dec'd. Gives plat.

3Q:261 Date: __ Jan 1828 RtCt: 15 May 1828
Capt. Thomas CHILTON dec'd. Division – court order dated 10 Dec
1827. 43a Lot #1 to Griffin TAYLOR & wife Susan; 46a Lot #2& 20a
Lot #3 to William MULLIKIN; 157½a Lot #4 to Manly T. RUST & wife
Sarah. Gives plat. Divisors: Saml. DAWSON, Saml. B. HARRIS,
John HAMILTON, Jno. J. MATHIAS.

3Q:264 Date: 14 May 1828 RtCt: 14 May 1828
Commrs. Rich'd H. HENDERSON and John JANNEY. Report on
payment arrangement with purchaser Morris OSBURN on sale of
dower land of Mary MARKS dec'd. Payments to Moses HUMPHREY
in right of wife Margaret, Thomas MARKS to trustee Joshua
OSBURN, Samuel MARKS, Watts MARKS, James WARFORD,
John HESSER, Elisha PEUGH, Abel MARKS, Mason MARKS.

3Q:266 Date: 15 Apr 1828 RtCt: 30 Apr 1828
James P. BRADFIELD & wife Elizabeth of Ldn to Elwood B. JAMES
and Thomas T. NICHOLS of Ldn. Trust for debt to George SAGERS
using 6a (prch/o SAGERS this date). Wit: Notley C. WILLIAMS,
Thomas NICHOLS. Delv. to Thomas T. NICHOLS pr order of Geo.
SAGER 8 Dec 1828.

3Q:269 Date: 15 Mar 1828 RtCt: 12 May 1828
George W. SEEVERS (Marshall of Sup. Ct. Winchester in case of
George THOMAS agst Henry ASHTON) to George THOMAS of
WashDC. B/S of mortgaged lots - 591a Lot #2 adj William B.
HARRISON, Charles LEWIS; 175a Lot #3 adj Wm. B. HARRISON;
157a Lot #4 adj Broad Run; 245a Lot #5; 284a Lot #6; 270a Lot #7
adj Mrs. PEYTON, Miss ELLZEY; 440¾a Lot #8; 215a Lot #9; 202a
Lot #10. Delv. to Johnston CLEVELAND agent of THOMAS 28 Sep
1831.

3Q:274 Date: 15 Apr 1828 RtCt: 12 May 1828
George W. SEEVERS (Marshall of Sup. Ct. Winchester in case of
Margaret UNDERWOOD agst heirs of Francis McKEMMIE) to
Joseph MORRISON. B/S of 20a adj Archibald MORRISON, John
SAUNDERS, Thomas WHITE, McKEMIE. Delv. to MORRISON 29
Jul 1828.

3Q:276 Date: 1 Apr 1828 RtCt: 12 May 1828
John CASE & wife Christena of Ldn to Jacob CRIM of Ldn. B/S of
10a on E side of Short Hill (allotted CASE in div. of Charles CRIM

Sr. dec'd) adj John CRIM. Wit: Mortimer McILHANY, Saml. HOUGH. Delv. to CRIM 24 Nov 1829.

3Q:279   Date: 18 Jun 1827   RtCt: 12 May 1828
Joseph LEWIS & wife Elizabeth O. of Ldn to Michael EVERHEART of Ldn. B/S of 3a (prch/o Ferdinando FAIRFAX 1803) on E side of Short Hill in Piedmont where EVERHEART resides. Wit: Benjamin GRAYSON, John W. GRAYSON.

3Q:281   Date: 16 Oct 1827   RtCt: 12 May 1828
Isaac HOUGH of Cincinnati Ohio to Simon SHOEMAKER, Saml. HOUGH, John HAMILTON Jr. and Samuel KALB (trustees of public school). B/S of lot nr Rehoboth Meeting house adj Samuel KALB, heirs of Michael COOPER.

3Q:282   Date: 19 Apr 1828   RtCt: 13 May 1828
George COOPER & wife Anna Mary of Ldn to John ROOF of Ldn. B/S of 9a on E side of Short Hill. Wit: Ebenezer GRUBB, Geo. W. SHAWEN. Delv. to ROOF 18 Aug 1838.

3Q:285   Date: 28 __ 1828   RtCt: 13 May 1828
Stephen SANDS of Ldn to Jonathan POTTERFIELD of Ldn. B/S of 12¾a adj __ WILLIAMS. Delv. to POTTERFIELD 3 Aug 1829.

3Q:286   Date: 11 Apr 1828   RtCt: 14 May 1828
Jacob COOPER & wife Mary, John COOPER & wife Mary and William COOPER & wife Elizabeth of Ldn to George COOPER of Ldn. B/S of 36a Lot #1 on Cotocton Mt. (interchanging of deeds as legatees of Frederick COOPER dec'd). Wit: Noble S. BRADEN, Geo. W. SHAWEN. Delv. pr order 19 May 1831.

3Q:289   Date: 12 May 1828   RtCt: 14 May 1828
Richard H. HENDERSON, Humphrey POWELL and Jesse TIMMS to Joseph DANIEL. Release of trust of Jul 1824 for debt to George CARTER of Oatlands.

3Q:290   Date: 11 Apr 1828   RtCt: 15 May 1828
George COOPER, Jacob COOPER & wife Mary, and John COOPER & wife Mary of Ldn to William COOPER of Ldn. B/S of 36a Lot #3 on Cococton Mt. (interchanging of deeds as legatees of Frederick COOPER dec'd). Wit: Noble S. BRADEN, George W. SHAWEN. Delv. to John COOPER pr order of Wm. COOPER 30 Mar 1835.

3Q:293   Date: 11 Apr 1828   RtCt: 15 May 1828
George COOPER, Jacob COOPER & wife Mary and William COOPER & wife Elizabeth of Ldn to John COOPER of Ldn. B/S of 48a Lot #4 on Cococton Mt. (interchanging of deeds as legatees of Frederick COOPER dec'd). Wit: Noble S. BRADEN, Geo. W. SHAWEN. Delv. pr order 12 Nov 1829.

3Q:296 Date: 17 May 1828 RtCt: 17 May 1828
Patience SA(U)NDERS (wd/o Henry SANDERS dec'd) of Ldn to
Thomas SANDERS (s/o Henry dec'd) of Ldn. B/S of dower rights.
Wit: Crayton SAUNDERS, John MARTIN, E. HAMMET.

3Q:297 Date: 17 May 1828 RtCt: 17 May 1828
Crayton SANDERS (s/o Henry SANDERS dec'd) of Ldn to Thomas
SANDERS of Ldn. B/S of his share in father's estate to cover
expenses paid by Thomas.

3Q:300 Date: 13 May 1828 RtCt: 17 May 1828
Thomas SANDERS of Ldn to John SANDERS of Ldn. B/S of house
and lot on King St in Lsbg (cnvy/b Thomas SWANN as trustee of
Henry CLAGET & Samuel HOUGH dec'd).

3Q:301 Date: 20 Nov 1827 RtCt: 19 May 1828
William LYNE of Ldn to Narcissa GHEEN of Ldn. B/S of interest in
land dev. to Narcissa GHEEN and her children by William
SUDDITH. Delv. to GHEEN 4 Dec 1828.

3Q:302 Date: 16 May 1828 RtCt: 19 May 1828
Daniel GOLD & wife Phebe of FredVa to George M. CHICHESTER
of Ldn. B/S of house and lot on N side of Market St opposite
Presbyterian Meeting house (cnvy/b George W. SEEVERS).

3Q:305 Date: 16 May 1828 RtCt: 21 May 1828
William HAMMERLY to James McILHANY. Trust for debt to Lewis
BEARD as Admr of Joseph BEARD dec'd, Pheneas JANNEY ass'ee
of Saml. CARR, Rich'd H. HENDERSON, William THRIFT using
house and ½a lot in Lsbg occupied by HAMMERLY.

3Q:307 Date: 18 May 1828 RtCt: 24 May 1828
John CRUMBAKER & wife Catherine of Ldn to David WIRE of Ldn.
B/S of 21¾a adj John SAGERS, John WINSEL, Peter FRY, __
SOUDERS. Wit: Samuel DAWSON, Geo. W. SHAWEN. Delv. to
WIRE 28 Apr 1829.

3Q:309 Date: 12 Apr 1827 RtCt: 24 May 1828
Alexander SWART and John SIMPSON & wife Matilda of Ldn and
Bernard SWART of Ldn (sons of James SWART Sr. and brothers of
Matilda). Partition of 143½a Lot #2 in Goshen tract (prch/o George
B. WHITING by James SWART Sr. made joint with his children) adj
Old Gum Spring road, John BAILY, Reuben HUTCHESON. Wit:
John SINCLAIR, Wm. McKNAB, Jesse ELGIN, Robert BAYLY, John
BAYLY.

3Q:312 Date: 6 May 1828 RtCt: 23 May 1828
William CARR and Bernard HOUGH of Ldn to Charles B.
ALEXANDER of Breckenridge Co Ky. Release of trust of Mar 1812
for debt to William CARR. Trustee Sampson BLINCOE now dec'd.

3Q:314 Date: 23 Nov 1827 RtCt: 23 May 1828
Thomas BISCOE to Ludwell LUCKETT. Trust for debt (with James
B. BISCOE & Horace LUCKETT) to Francis W. LUCKETT Exor. of

Wm. BRONAUGH dec'd. using 130a on N side of Goose Creek adj Jonathan CARTER, A. B. McMULLEN.

3Q:317   Date: 27 May 1828   RtCt: 28 May 1828
Thos. MARKS as attorney for James WARFORD & wife Elizabeth of Livingston Co Ky to Samuel MARKS of Ldn. B/S of 35a from div. of estate of Abel MARKS dec'd, adj Morris OSBURN, __ DANIELS. Wit: S. B. T. CALDWELL, Wm. D. DANIEL, T. S. STONE.

3Q: 319   Date: 23 Oct 1827   RtCt: 26 May 1828
John HEIS & wife Catherine late COOPER of PhilPa and Adam COOPER & wife Susanna and George COOPER of Ldn to Charles GULLATT & Samuel M. EDWARDS (trustees of Ann SAUNDERS w/o Britton). B/S of 2a with water grist mill and machinery. Wit: Valentine BURKART, T. M. RUSH, Wm. ELLZEY, Jno. J. MATHIAS. Delv. to Ann ECKART 23 Feb 1829.

3Q:323   Date: 26 Dec 1825   RtCt: 30 May 1828
Ludwell LEE of Ldn to Wilson C. SELDON Sr. of Ldn. B/S of use of Eden Island in Potomack (sold by Lee to SELDEN) along a road established by Thomas L. LEE (extended over dividing line).

3Q:324   Date: 1 May 1828   RtCt: 30 May 1828
Ludwell LEE of Ldn to Charles ESKRIDGE of Ldn. Trust for Eliza A. LEE of Ldn as security on note to Robert BENTLEY using slaves Reuben a blacksmith and Jesse a cooper.

3Q:326   Date: 31 May 1828   RtCt: 31 May 1828
Stephen W. ROSZELL (in jail under writ of capias ad satisfaciendum of John & James POGUE merchants) to Sheriff Charles LEWIS. B/S of 81a (willed by father Stephen ROSZELL in event brother Stephen C. ROSZELL died without issue) on North fork Creek and interest in land in possession of mother Sarah ROSZELL.

3Q:327   Date: 9 Jun 1828   RtCt: 9 Jun 1828
George H. ALLDER, Nathan NICHOLS and Mason CHAMBLIN. Bond on ALLDER as constable.

3Q:328   Date: 2 Jun 1828   RtCt: 2 Jun 1828
Philip VINCELL of Ldn to George VINCELL Jr. of Ldn. BoS for farm animals and crops on land of John VINCELL.

3Q:329   Date: 3 Jun 1828   RtCt: 3 Jun 1828
Richard H. LEE of Lsbg to Samuel M. EDWARDS and John JANNEY of Lsbg. Trust to cover debts before he leaves the state using all real and personal property including house and lot in Staunton in Augusta Co formerly owned by Erasmus STRIBLING Esqr, house & lot at corner of Market St occupied by Mrs. Fanny LEE, 33a nr Lsbg (part prch/o Dr. H. CLAGGETT), legacy to late wife due over 10-12y in hands of Mr. Alexander MAHON of Casline in Cumberland Co Pa, money due in hands of Mr. J. D. MAHON of Casline from late wife's father estate, interest from will of Miss Polly DUNCAN, interest in present wife's estate in hands of Mr. Wm. D.

MERRICK of Chas. Co Md, rent from Mrs. Fanny LEE subject to order on her in favour of B. W. HARRISON Admr Jno. T. WILSON, household items, books in library.

3Q:333 Date: 3 Jun 1828 RtCt: 3 Jun 1828
Eleanor PEERS and Ann H. PEERS of Ldn to Robert J. TAYLOR of AlexDC. Trust for debt to Charles BENNETT of AlexDC using house and lot on Market St in Lsbg occupied by Eleanor as a tavern. Delv. to R. H. HENDERSON pr order 8 Oct 1828.

3Q:335 Date: 24 Apr 1828 RtCt: 6 Jun 1828
Stephen McPHERSON & wife Mary and Sarah McPHERSON of Ldn to Benjamin BIRDSALL of Ldn. B/S of 80a on Beaverdam Creek adj Mahlon CRAVEN, John WYNN, Joseph GARRETT, John NICHOLS, William WILKINSON. Wit: John SIMPSON, Thomas NICHOLS. Delv. to BIRDSALL 23 Feb 1829.

3Q:338 Date: 9 Jun 1828 RtCt: 9 Jun 1828
Lott BARR, Joseph EIDSON and Henry HUTCHISON. Bond on BARR as constable.

3Q:339 Date: 28 May 1828 RtCt: 9 Jun 1828
Theodore DAVIDSON. Qualified as Lt. in 57th Reg 6th Brig 2nd Div of Va Militia.

3Q:340 Date: 9 Jun 1828 RtCt: 9 Jun 1828
Lewis GRIGSBY, Jacob SUMMERS, Elijah HUTCHISON. Bond on GRIGSBY as constable.

3Q:341 Date: 4 Jun 1828 RtCt: 7 Jun 1828
Ludwell LEE of Ldn to Charles G. ESKRIDGE of Ldn. Trust for Eliza A. LEE (d/o Ludwell) as security on judgments from Richard H. LEE using negro Rippin & his son Tom, Jim, Harry, John, Sampson, Kingston, Burwell, Bossy, Mille and Stephen.

3Q:342 Date: 24 Mar 1828 RtCt: 13 Jun 1828
Wilson C. SELDON of Ldn. DoE of negro Frank ($300 paid by Presley SAUNDERS). Wit: John MARTIN, Presley SAUNDERS.

3Q:343 Date: 28 Apr 1828 RtCt: 9 Jun 1828
Elizabeth HOLMES (wd/o Joseph HOLMES) and Samuel HOGE & wife Mary, William HOLMES, Elijah HOLMES & wife Elizabeth, Isaac HOLMES & wife Hannah, Thomas NICHOLS & wife Emily and Lott HOLMES (reps. of Joseph HOLMES dec'd of Ldn) to William SMITH of Ldn. B/S of 144a (prch/o John WILKS 1771 by William HOLMES and demised to son Joseph HOLMES) on NW fork of Goose Creek adj Mary HUGHES, Thomas HUGHES, Joseph CLEWES, blacksmith shop, Eli JANNEY. Wit: Thomas NICHOLS, John SIMPSON. Delv. pr order 14 Aug 1834.

3Q:346 Date: 26 May 1828 RtCt: 9 Jun 1828
Catherine MILLER (wd/o Peter MILLER dec'd), Adam MILLER & wife Elizabeth and Jesse MILLER & wife Rebecca of Ldn to George COOPER of Ldn. B/S of 50a on E side of Short Hill adj Philip FRY,

__ MORRISON, __ ROLLER. Wit: Samuel HOUGH, George W. SHAWEN. Delv. to COOPER 14 Apr 1835.

3Q:349   Date: 17 May 1828   RtCt: 9 Jun 1828
Michael SPRING & wife Rachel, John SPRING & wife Mary, Joseph SPRING & wife Elizabeth, David SPRING & wife Martha of Ldn to Henry FAWLEY of Ldn. B/S of undivided 4/12th of 2 tracts in German Settlement - 102½a (cnvy Apr 1796 to Andrew SPRING, DBk W:459) and 14a (cnvy/b Peter S[T]UCK Mar 1812, DBk PP:126 [128]). Wit: Samuel DAWSON, Geo. W. SHAWEN.

3Q:352   Date: 6 Jun 1828   RtCt: 9 Jun 1828
Roberdeau ANNIN of WashDC to Jacob WATERS of Ldn. B/S of 2a (from trust of Aug 1826, DBk MMM:361, of Adam EVANS who defaulted). Delv. to WATERS 11 Oct 1831.

3Q:354   Date: 12 Sep 1827   RtCt: 9 Jun 1828
Sarah NICHOLS and Joshua OSBURN (Exors of Nathan NICHOLS dec'd) of Ldn to Sarah NIXON of Ldn. B/S of 157a on SE side of blue ridge adj Joseph THOMAS, Philip THOMAS, Edward CUNARD. Wit: S. B. T. CALDWELL, Nathan NICKOLS, Craven OSBURN, Geo. H. ALLDER. Delv. to Abr'm SMITH pr order 13 Oct 1828.

3Q:355   Date: 7 May 1828   RtCt: 9 Jun 1828
Benjamin HIXSON & wife Tacey of Ldn to Caldwell CARR and Bushrod RUST (Admr of Joseph CARR dec'd) of Fqr. Trust for debt to Henley BOGGESS the elder, Samuel BOGGESS, Henley BOGGESS, Nancy E. BOGGESS, Jane E. BOGGESS, and Mariah C. BOGGESS (orphans of Rebecca BOGGESS formerly CARR and ch/o Henley BOGGESS their guardian) of Fqr using 180¼a adj __ ROGERS, __ RUST, James HIXSON and 3a with brick house the residence of HIXSON and 4a factory lot with 4 houses and 9¾a on turnpike road adj Sarah JONES (1/10th of estate of Joseph CARR dec'd late of Fqr to dau. Rebecca BOGGESS and her interest in estate of her half brother Peter CARR dec'd). Wit: Burr POWELL, A. GIBSON. Delv. to Caldwell CARR 11 May 1829.

3Q:358   Date: 22 Mar 1828   RtCt: 9 Jun 1828
William CARR & wife Mary of Ldn to David CARR of Ldn. B/S of 140a (prch/o Andrew CAMPBELL, DBk LLL:389) adj __ WILKINSON, __ VANDEVANTER, __ GARRETT. Wit: Presley CORDELL, John H. McCABE. Delv. to CARR 31 Mar 1834.

3Q:360   Date: 16 Feb 1828   RtCt: 9 Jun 1828
Hugh SMITH & wife Elizabeth of Ldn to James B. WILSON of Ldn. B/S of 11a (prch/o Dennis McCARTY, DBk DDD:464) on Goose Creek adj Dennis McCARTY, Hugh ROGERS. Wit: Burr POWELL, A. GIBSON. Delv. to WILSON 30 May 1831.

3Q:363 Date: 6 Jun 1828 RtCt: 9 Jun 1828
John SAUNDERS of Ldn to Elijah PEACOCK of Ldn. B/S of 147a where Margaret SAUNDERS recently dec'd lived and dev. to John. Delv. to SAUNDERS pr order ___.

3Q:364 Date: 23 May 1828 RtCt: 9 Jun 1828
Horace LUCKETT of Ldn to Humphrey B. POWELL of Ldn. Trust for bond (with Burr WEEKS) to Gourley REEDER and Jonah TAVENTER as securities to Rebecca HATCHER using 172a (cnvy/b Leven LUCKETT and Town'd D. PEYTON) on NE side of Snickers Turnpike road adj T. D. PEYTON, Wm. GULICK, Andrew BEATTY, heirs of Moses GULICK dec'd.

3Q:366 Date: 11 May 1827 RtCt: 9 Jun 1828
Isaac NICHOLS Jr., William HOGE and William PIGGOT (Exor of Samuel NICHOLS dec'd) of Ldn to Joshua PANCOAST of Ldn. B/S of 240a on NW fork of Goose Creek adj PANCOAST, Jonas JANNEY, Abel JANNEY, Abdon DILLON; and 59a John GREGG, David YOUNG, Edith HATCHER, Abdon DILLON, John PANCOAST. Wit: Andrew BIRDSALL, Bernard WATKINS, Yardley TAYLOR. Delv. pr order 24 May 1853.

3Q:369 Date: 8 Apr 1828 RtCt: 9 Jun 1828
Elizabeth HOUGH of Ldn to John WOLFORD of Ldn. B/S of her dower rights to real estate of late husband John HOUGH dec'd, but not any real estate from the death of his sister Rebecca HOUGH.

3Q:371 Date: 6 Jun 1828 RtCt: 10 Jun 1828
Dennis McCARTY of Ldn to Hugh SMITH of Ldn. Trust for George McCARTY as security on bonds to Peter SKINNER Admr of Aaron MASSUTH dec'd, David SIMPSON, Peter GREGG, Townshend McVEIGH, Fanny ARMSTEAD using negro man Cyrus abt 75y old, woman Let abt 65y old, man Luke abt 40y old, woman Maria abt 35y old, boy Jackson abt 6y old, girl Rose abt 5y old, Margaret abt 3y old, woman Susan abt 34y old, boy Alfred abt 15y old, girl Mima abt 10y old, boy Joseph abt 5y old, boy Washington abt 4 months old, girl Ann abt 3y old, household items, farm animals. Delv. to G. W. McCARTY 20 Nov 1834.

3Q:374 Date: 10 Jun 1828 RtCt: 11 Jun 1828
Christopher FRYE & wife Margaret of Ldn to Robert ROBERTS of Ldn. LS of 7a adj ___ KITZMILLER, ROBERTS; and 1a adj ___ FEICHSTER, ___ ROBERTS (LS of 78 104/160a nr Lsbg by James HERRIFORD Aug 1798 to Patrick CAVANS for 999y). Delv. to ROBERTS 3 May 1830.

3Q:376 Date: 11 Jun 1828 RtCt: 12 Jun 1828
Dpty Asa ROGERS for Sheriff Charles LEWIS to William MILLER of FredVa. B/S of interest of insolvent Daniel ANNIN in 750a in Auchita Parish Louisiana and interest in house & lot in AlexDC.

3Q:378 Date: 11 Jun 1828 RtCt: 11 Jun 1828
Samuel M. EDWARDS of Ldn to Robert ROBERTS of Ldn. Release of trust of Sep 1824 for debt to Richard H. HENDERSON, DBk III:292, on 24a.

3Q:379 Date: 21 Mar 1827 RtCt: 13 Jun 1828
Asa ROGERS of Ldn to Simon A. BINNS of Ldn. Release of trust for debt to A. C. CAZENOVE, etc. of Jan 1826 on 220a.

3Q:381 Date: 14 Jun 1828 RtCt: 16 Jun 1828
Thomas J. BENNETT to Thomas L. HUMPHREY. Trust for debt to Palmer & Chamlin joint partners using interest in land bought by Charles BENNETT from David LACEY adj John WESLEY and interest in land on Little Kanhawa in Wood Co. Delv. pr order 8 Feb 1830.

3Q:382 Date: 15 Mar 1828 RtCt: 16 Jun 1828
John MANN & wife Mary of Ldn to Charles CROOK of Ldn. B/S of 102a (part of cnvy/b George MANN Apr 1809) adj road from duck's mill to Roaches. Wit: Craven OSBURN, John WHITE.

3Q:385 Date: 1 Apr 1828 RtCt: 18 Jun 1828
Samuel BROWN & wife Hannah of Winchester, FredVa to Thomas BISCOE of Ldn. B/S of 9½a (cnvy/b Isaac BROWN Jr.).

3Q:388 Date: 25 May 1828 RtCt: 18 Jun 1828
Thomas BISCOE to Silas BEATTY. Trust for debt to Elizabeth, Susan, Mary and Julia Ann BISCOE using 130a where Thomas resides on Goose Creek adj Jon'a CARTER, A. B. McMULLIN and farm animals, farm and household items.

3Q:391 Date: 15 Mar 1828 RtCt: 23 Jun 1828
Robert R. HOUGH of Lsbg to Joseph HILLIARD of Lsbg. Trust for debt to Edward S. HOUGH of BaltMd using apothecary shop & furniture, house & lot in Lsbg adj Jas. THOMAS, Peter BOSS, household items, 100a in Hamshier.

3Q:394 Date: 18 Jun 1828 RtCt: 23 Jun 1828
Edmund J. LEE Jr. late of Ohio Co Va now Jeff Va to Joseph HOUGH of Ldn. Release of trust of Jun 1826 for debt to Thomas LACEY using 4a. Delv. to HOUGH 4 Nov 1828.

3Q:395 Date: 15 May 1828 RtCt: 27 Jun 1828
Edward B. GRADY to Joshua B. OVERFIELD. Release of trust of Jan 1821 for debt to Joseph RICHARDSON

3Q:398 Date: 7 Jun 1828 RtCt: 27 Jun 1828
Samuel CARR & wife Lucy of Ldn to David CARR of Ldn. Conveyance of dower rights in trust for debt to John CARR & Joseph T. NEWTON of Ldn. Wit: Saml. HAMMETT, John HANSBOROUGH, J. L. DREAN, Thomas FOUCH, Presley CORDELL. Delv. to CARR 5 Jan 1831.

3Q:399 Date: 24 Apr 1828 RtCt: 26 Jun 1828
Benjamin BIRDSALL of Ldn to Yardley TAYLOR of Ldn. Trust for debt to Stephen McPHERSON using 80a (cnvy/b Stephen McPHERSON Jr.) adj heirs of Joseph GARRETT, Mahlon CRAVEN, John WYNN, John NICHOLS, William WILKINSON. Delv. to McPHERSON 22 Apr 1829.

3Q:402 Date: 28 Jun 1828 RtCt: 28 Jun 1828
Joshua B. OVERFIELD & wife Anna of Ldn to Saml. M. EDWARDS of Ldn. Trust for debt to Isaac NICHOLS Sr. of Ldn using 216a Lot #3 from div. of Martin & Elizabeth OVERFIELD dec'd, DBk TT:267 and Lot #1, DBk LLL:216. Wit: Presley CORDELL, Jas. RUST.

3Q:405 Date: 3 Jul 1828 RtCt: 3 Jul 1828
John A. BINNS and Charles G. ESKRIDGE to Charles B. ALEXANDER. B/S of 317a (trust of Oct 1817 of George JANNEY, DBk VV:354, trustees John T. WILSON and Sampson BLINCOE have both died). Delv. to ALEXANDER 26 Jun 1834.

3Q:407 Date: 3 Jul 1828 RtCt: 3 Jul 1828
Charles G. EDWARDS of Ldn to Dinah DORSEY of Annarundel Co Md. BoS for negro woman Milly, girl Mary Jane, girl Eleanor, man Adam, farm animals, household items, medical and shop furniture, medicines, medical books in tenement in Wtfd.

3Q:408 Date: 30 May 1828 RtCt: 5 Jul 1828
W. A. BINNS (f/o Chas. BINNS) to Samuel HALL of Ldn. Trust for Thomas HALL as security for bonds to Robert MOFFETT using crops. Wit: Simon BINNS, Loveless CONWELL, Martin WILDMAN.

3Q:410 Date: 28 Jun 1828 RtCt: 3 Jun 1828
John ROSE to John A. BINNS of Ldn. B/S (in trust for benefit of dau. Charlotte w/o Dr. Isaac WILSON) of negro woman Nancy & her children Ann now abt 5y old, John now abt 3y old and Kit abt 18 months old, household items, horse. Delv. to BINNS 4 Feb 1829.

3Q:412 Date: 16 Jun 1828 RtCt: 7 Jan 1828
William M. McCARTY & wife Emily R. of Leon Co Fl to Simon YAKEY of Ldn. B/S of 26¾a in German Settlement (cnvy/b George M. CHICHESTER – shares of Peter COMPHER Jr. & Levi COLLINS from Peter COMPHOR Sr. dec'd). Delv. to YEAKEY 35 Mar 1829.

3Q:414 Date: 7 Jul 1828 RtCt: 8 Jul 1828
Susan ROMINE to Lawson OSBURN. B/S of 15a allotted to Susan in div. of father John ROMINE dec'd after dower to widow Rebecca. Delv. to OSBURN 1 Jan 1830.

3Q:417 Date: 9 Jul 1828 RtCt: 9 Jul 1828
Barnet HOUGH of Ldn to Geo. RICHARDS of Ldn. Trust for debt to Michael MORALLEE, Samuel M. BOSS, Asa PECK & John MARTIN of Ldn using negro Abraham until 10 Sep 1828.

3Q:418   Date: 9 Jul 1828   RtCt: 9 Jul 1828
Jacob TOWNER of Ldn to John H. MONROE of Ldn. Trust for debt
to Thos. BIRKBY of Ldn using household items. Wit: Saml. M.
EDWARDS.

3Q:420   Date: 23 Jun 1828   RtCt: 23 Jun 1828
Simon T. TAYLOR for himself and as attorney for Martha L.
FRENCH, Alice T. TAYLOR and Thomas S. TAYLOR to Martha S.
BLINCOE. B/S of lot on Back St in Lsbg (prch/o John DRAIN).

3Q:422   Date: ___   RtCt: 17 Jul 1828
Thomas S. TAYLOR, Martha L. FRENCH and Alice S. TAYLOR to
Simon T. TAYLOR of StafVa. PoA for sale of house & lot in Lsbg,
negro woman Hannah, personal property. Wit: A. DUVAL, Jn.
FITZHUGH. Acknowledgement for Martha and Alice in PrWm.

3Q:423   Date: 12 May 1828   RtCt: 14 Jul 1828
Amos FURGERSON of Ldn to Amos FURGERSON. BoS for negro
man Jesse & wife Rachel, man Humphrey, and Hannah and infant
child, man Isaac, boy Solomon, boy Randal, boy Daniel, woman
Esther & her dau. Leah & infant son, girl Anna, girl Lucinda, girl
Cornelia – slaves unto Erasmus G. TILLETT. Wit: James E.
STONESTREET, Saml. TILLETT.

3Q:424   Date: 9 Jul 1828   RtCt: 14 Jul 1828
David SIMPSON & wife Elizabeth of Ldn to H. B. POWELL of Ldn.
Trust for debt to H. BOGGS, Charles CARROLL, Wm. F. & A.
MURDOCK, Jarvis & Brown, Abraham PYKE, Clagett & Page,
Martin SIMPSON, Shaw Tiffany & Co, Wm. NORRIS & Son, Keyser
& Shaffer, Chas. FISHER, Robert H. MILLER, Cusking & Jewett, J.
& J. Pogue using lot in Mdbg where SIMPSON resides (prch/of Felix
TRIPLETT, Sept 1826). Wit: Burr POWELL, Abner GIBSON. Delv. to
POWELL 11 May 1829.

3Q:427   Date: 15 Jul 1828   RtCt: 15 Jul 1828
John UNDERWOOD to William M. JENNERS. Trust for William
THRIFT as security using one moriety in case of William THRIFT
agst Samuel UNDERWOOD (prch by Samuel UNDERWOOD of
Ludwell LEE) where John now resides. Delv. to THRIFT 27 Mar
1833.

3Q:428   Date: 14 Jul 1828   RtCt: 15 Jul 1828
John B. PATTERSON of Ldn to John A. BINNS of Ldn. Trust for
debt to Knight G. SMITH of Ldn using printing press, type cases,
stand. Delv. to BINNS 24 Mar 1829.

3Q:428   Date: 3 Oct 1828   RtCt: 26 Jul 1828
Zepheniah DAVIS & wife Mary of Ldn to Solomon RUSE of Ldn. B/S
of 15a adj John IREY, Joseph HOLMES, Hamilton ROGERS. Wit:
John SIMPSON, Presley CORDELL. Delv. to RUSE 10 Feb 1834.

3Q:432   Date: 25 Jun 1828   RtCt: 16 Jul 1828
William GORE of FredVa to Joseph LEWIS. Release of trust of Feb 1820 for debt to Josiah LOCKHART of FredVa.

3Q:433   Date: 8 Jul 1828   RtCt: 21 Jul 1828
Richard OSBURN & wife Pleasant of Ldn to Jon'a HEATON of Ldn. B/S of 72a (prch/o John G. HUMPHREY, Jas. JOHNSON) adj Joel OSBURN, __ BEANS. Wit: John WHITE, Craven OSBURN.

3Q:435   Date: 15 Jul 1828   RtCt: 21 Jul 1828
John H. McCABE & wife Mary to James McILHANY. Trust for debt to Robert BENTLEY using 9a adj John DRISH dec'd, Dr. SELDEN, Mrs. BALL, E. STEADMAN, H. HAMMERLEY. Wit: Saml. M. EDWARDS, John J. MATHIAS.

3Q:438   Date: __ Jul 1828   RtCt: 21 Jul 1828
Abijah JANNEY (trustee of Ann HARPER of AlexDC) to Noble S. BRADEN (Exor of Robert BRADEN decd) of Ldn. B/S of use of water from plaster mill to merchant mill as now used by John BRADEN (deed of Feb last did not convey rights). Delv. to BRADEN 19 Nov 1866.

3Q:440   Date: 21 Jun 1828   RtCt: 21 Jul 1828
John G. HUMPHREY and James JOHNSTON (Exors. of Abner G. HUMPHREY dec'd as trustee for Exors.) of Ldn to Richard OSBURN of Ldn. B/S of 146a adj Thomas HUMPHREY, Mason MARKS, Joel OSBURN. Delv. to OSBURN 5 Jun 1851.

3Q:442   Date: 22 Jul 1828   RtCt: 22 Jul 1828
Simon T. TAYLOR in own right and as attorney for Martha L. FRENCH, Alice T. TAYLOR and Thomas G. TAYLOR of StafVa to Otho R. BEATTY of Ldn. B/S of lot in Lsbg adj Martha BLINCOE. Delv. to BEATTY 24 Jun 1829.

3Q:443   Date: 23 Jul 1828   RtCt: 23 Jul 1828
William MAYNE of Ldn to Geo. RICHARDS of Ldn. Trust for debt to Charles HARDY of FredVa using household items.

3Q:445   Date: 25 Jul 1828   RtCt: 28 Jul 1828
Joab OSBURN Jr. of Ldn to Richard OSBURN Jr. of Ldn. Trust for debt to Morris OSBURN using farm animals, farm and household items.

3Q:447   Date: 28 Jul 1828   RtCt: 28 Jul 1828
Charles G. EDWARDS of Ldn to Dinah DORSEY of Anarundale Co Md. B/S of 2 lot in Wtfd (see DBk YY:328 and YY:330) and interest in land on Potomack and Goose Creek from father Benjamin EDWARDS dec'd.

3Q:449   Date: 19 Jul 1828   RtCt: 15 Aug 1828
Joshua OSBURN of Ldn. DoE for negro Resin WILLIAMS, yellowish complexion, abt 26y old. Wit: Herod OSBURN.

3Q:449 Date: __ Feb 1828 RtCt: 28 Jul 1828
Samuel HAWLEY to Jacob SUMMERS. Release of trust of 14 Feb 1825 for debt to Charles LEWIS (trustee James LEWIS has died). Wit: A. McCRADY, Jos. D. BELL.

3Q:450 Date: 20 Jul 1828 RtCt: 28 Jul 1828
Roberdeau ANNIN & wife Helen Curtis of WashDC to Charles G. ESKRIDGE of Lsbg. B/S of land cnvy to Helen (DBk PPP:066, and also see DBk EE:166 and EE:172, EE:156, EE:396, EE: 162, MM:426, EE:154, GG:490). Delv. to ESKRIDGE ___.

3Q:453 Date: 1 Apr 1828 RtCt: 28 Jul 1828
Harvey COGSIL & wife Mary of FredVa to Ishmael VANHORN of Ldn. B/S of 1a (cnvy/b John MAN). Wit: Mortimer McILHANY, Geo. W. SHAWEN. Delv. to D. POTTERFIELD pr order Mar 1832.

3Q:455 Date: 1 Jul 1828 RtCt: 28 Jul 1828
Farmer Samuel CLAPHAM & wife Elizabeth of Ldn to James B. MURRAY of NY. Trust for debt to Chatham Fire Insurance Co. using 68a where Thomas AWBREY lately lived adj John SEMPLE. Thomas GEORGE, plantation where Frederick WYSELL lived; and 300a (cnvy/b John Beale HOWARD, Francis HOLLAND 1798 to Josias CLAPHAM); and 150a (cnvy/b Anthony HAYNES May 1772 to Josias CLAPHAM, DBk M:131) adj Elizabeth MORRIS, Mary RICHARDSON. Wit: Arth'r BRONSON, Saml. ROULSTON.

3Q:461 Date: 24 Jul 1828 RtCt: 29 Jul 1828
Burr POWELL (trustee of Sarah UPP by husband John UPP) to Asa ROGERS. Trust for debt to William R. SWART using 84a above Mdbg allotted Sarah from estate of Thomas CHINN dec'd, ½ of town lot in Mdbg (other ½ to Sarah C. MYERS) and personal property – to obtain a delay in sale of items in trust. Wit: Saml. CAMPBELL, John BRADY, Francis W. LUCKETT, A. GIBSON. Delv. to Asa ROGERS 13 Jul 1829.

3Q:465 Date: 24 May 1827 RtCt: 29 Jul 1828
Hannah BROWN, Isaac YOUNG & wife Margaret, Vincent BROWN, Elizabeth BROWN, Mason BROWN & wife Malinda and William BROWN of Muskingum Co Ohio to Charles CHAMBLIN of Ldn. B/S of interest in 111a tract (from William BROWN dec'd, rights to Hannah during her lifetime and 6/7 shares) nr Scotland Mills adj __ WOODFORD.

3Q:468 Date: 21 Jun 1828 RtCt: 29 Jul 1828
James JOHNSON and John G.HUMPHREY (Exors of Abner G. HUMPHREY dec'd as trustee for Exors of Col. Thomas HUMPHREY dec'd) to Isaiah B. BEANS. Release of trust of Jan 1823 for debt to Thomas HUMPHREY.

3Q:470 Date: 29 Jul 1828 RtCt: 29 Jul 1828
George SYPHARD & wife Sarah late SANBOWER of Ldn to Jacob EVERHEART of Ldn. Trust for debt to Adam SANBOWER of Ldn

using 21a from estate of John SANBOWER dec'd. Wit: Asa ROGERS, Saml. M. EDWARDS, Tasker C. QUINLAN.

3Q:472 Date: 13 May 1828 RtCt: 30 Jul 1828
Hiram BROWN and Sarah BROWN of Ldn to David LOVETT of Ldn. Trust for debt to Swithen NICKOLS of Ldn using 39a nr blue ridge mt. adj Morris OSBURN, James COCKRAN. Wit: Craven OSBURN, John WHITE. Delv. to NICHOLS 25 May 1829.

3Q:475 Date: 27 Jul 1828 RtCt: 30 Jul 1828
Adam MILLER & wife Elizabeth of Ldn to Jesse MILLER of Ldn. B/S of interest in land of Peter MILLER dec'd. Wit: Samuel HOUGH, Geo. W. SHAWEN.

3Q:477 Date: 26 May 1828 RtCt: 30 Jul 1828
Humphrey SHEPHERD & wife Catherine of FredVa to Daniel COCKRELL of Ldn. B/S of 15a (part of tract prch/o William CASTLEMAN) on NW fork of Goose Creek adj David SMITH, Joseph GORE, William SMITH. Delv. to COCKERELL 12 Oct 1829.

3Q:479 Date: 4 Apr 1810 RtCt: 30 Jul 1828
Barton LUCAS & wife __ of Ldn to John McCORMICK of Ldn. B/S of 10a on Catocton Mt nr Lsbg (Lot #2 in BRADEN's survey). Wit: Saml. M. EDWARDS, Isaac LAROWE, French S. GRAY. Delv. to Chs. G. ESKRIDGE 24 Oct 1836.

3Q:480 Date: 6 Jul 1826 RtCt: 4 Aug 1828
Alfred H. POWELL of Winchester to John R. COOKE of Winchester. Release of trust of 30 Aug 1815 for debt to Edward McGUIRE of Winchester.

3Q:482 Date: 17 Mar 1821 RtCt: 30 Aug 1828
Catherine Eston COOKE (wd/o Stephen COOKE dec'd) to John R. COOKE. Release of dower on 438a on Goose Creek. Acknowledgment in Berkeley Co.

3Q:483 Date: 3 Aug 1828 RtCt: 5 Aug 1828
James BEAVERS to Miss Mahala BEAVERS. Assignment (in trust for use of Mary BEVERIDGE w/o Jno. BEVERIDGE) of part of debt due from Amos FERGURSON for purchase of land dev. by William BEAVERS.

3Q:483 Date: 31 May 1827 RtCt: 5 Aug 1828
Rachel AULT to dau. Rachel SPRING w/o Michael SPRING. Gift of household items. Other household items listed for both Rachel and sister Betsey COMPHY w/o John COMPHY.

3Q:484 Date: 5 Aug 1828 RtCt: 5 Aug 1828
Rachel AULT and John COMPHER. Agreement – assignment of dower interest in 30a where Michael SPRING now lives in exchange for care and board of Rachel if future situation requires. Wit: Edward Lewis FANT, Alfred A. ESKRIDGE.

3Q:485 Date: 6 Aug 1828 RtCt: 6 Aug 1828
Elias POOL to Alfred G. ESKRIDGE. Trust for James GARNER as surety in note to Thos. WHEELER Admr. of __ WHEELER dec'd and Alfred BELT Exor of Chas. THORNTON dec'd using farm animals, note on Geo. W. HENRY.

3Q:486 Date: 21 Jan 1828 RtCt: 7 Aug 1828
Enoch TRIPLETT & wife Polly of Ldn to Enoch GLASSCOCK of Ldn. B/S of 3a on S side of Goose Creek adj GLASSCOCK. Wit: Francis W. LUCKETT, Edward HALL. Delv. to GLASSCOCK 28 Nov 1828.

3Q:488 Date: 12 Jun 1828 RtCt: 12 Aug 1828
Daniel STONEBURNER dec'd. Division – 7a Lot #1 and 3a mt. Lot #1 to Henry STONEBURNER; 10a Lot #2 and 3a mt. Lot #2 to Henry GOODHART; 10a Lot #3 and 3a mt Lot #3 to Daniel STONEBURNER; 10a Lot #4 and 2a mt. Lot #4 to Peter STONEBURNER; 12a Lot #5 to Margaret STONEBURNER; 11½a Lot #6 and 2a mt Lot #6 to John LONG & wife Susan; 11a Lot #7 and 2a mt. Lot #7 to Catherine STONEBURNER; 11a Lot #8 and 2a mt. Lot #8 to Sarah STONEBURNER; 13a Lot #9 to Christian STONEBURNER; 35a Lot #10 to widow. Gives plat. Divisors: Saml. DAWSON, Jacob FAWLEY, Jno. J. MATHIAS.

3Q:493 Date: 2 Aug 1828 RtCt: 8 Aug 1828
Francis DULIN & wife __ to Richard H. HENDERSON. Trust for debt to William L. CLARKE using interest in estate of Presley SAUNDERS dec'd and household items, farm animals.

3Q:495 Date: 13 Aug 1828 RtCt: 13 Aug 1828
Jonathan ROBERTS. Oath as Lt. in Va Militia.

3Q:496 Date: 29 Jul 1828 RtCt: 14 Aug 1828
Field Officer metes and bounds for new Regiment meeting held at tavern of Col. N. OSBURN in Lsbg. Present: Brig. Gen. Geo RUST, Col. Charles TAYLOR of 56th, Col. Saml. M. EDWARDS of 57th, Lt. Col. Benj. MITCHELL of 56th, Lt. Col. Ramey G. SAUNDERS of 57th, Major Timothy TAYLOR Jr. of 56th, Major Hamilton ROGERS of 57th. Gives new bounds for 131st Reg, 56th Reg, and 57th Reg. First muster of 1st Batt. will be held at Bloomfield and the 2nd Batt. at Mountsville Snickers Gap.

3R:001 Date: 9 Aug 1828 RtCt: 11 Aug 1828
Philip FRYE of Ldn to Michael FRYE & Elizabeth WELTY (2 of his children). Gift of land where they live (prch/o Peter STONE Sep 1811); also left to them in his will.

3R:002 Date: 11 Aug 1828 RtCt: 11 Aug 1828
Thomas WHITE of Ldn to John WRIGHT of Ldn. B/S of 3a (part of prch/o Burr BRADEN) at Wtfd road & Lsbg road adj WRIGHT, James COPELAND. Delv. to R. L. WRIGHT agent of grantee 26 Mar 1857.

3R:003   Date: 7 Aug 1828   RtCt: 11 Aug 1828
Aaron WRIGHT of Ldn to Nancy W(H)RIGHT of Ldn. B/S of
undivided 1/8th of 196a and 4 lots in Wtfd from father Patterson
WRIGHT dec'd. Wit: Jos. H. WRIGHT. Delv. to Wm. WRIGHT 24
Apr 1844.

3R:004   Date: 28 Apr 1828   RtCt: 11 Aug 1828
Elizabeth HOLMES, Samuel HOGUE & wife Mary, William HOLMES
Jr., Isaac HOLMES & wife Hannah, Thomas NICHOLS & wife Emily
and Lot HOLMES of Ldn to Elijah HOLMES of Ldn. B/S of 52a
(cnvy/b Hamilton ROGERS to Joseph HOLMES) adj Digg's Valley,
heirs of Hamilton ROGERS dec'd. Wit: John SIMPSON, Tho.
NICHOLS. Delv. to Elij'h HOLMES 14 Aug 1834.

3R:006   Date: 9 Aug 1828   RtCt: 11 Aug 1828
Elizabeth WELTY of Ldn to Michael FRYE of Ldn. B/S of her interest
in land cnvy/b Philip FRYE Aug 1828.

3R:007   Date: 31 Jul 1826   RtCt: 11 Aug 1828
Dennis McCARTY (s/o Thadeous McCARTY dec'd) & wife Margaret
of Ldn to Washington McCARTY of Ldn. B/S of ½ of land dev. by
father on Goosecreek above mill dam with mill house and machinery
erect for their mutual benefit. Wit: Giles HAMMAT, Richard C.
McCARTY, William T. McCARTY, Tasker C. QUINLAN, John
SIMPSON.

3R:009   Date: 16 May 1828   RtCt: 11 Aug 1828
William VIRTZ & wife Phebe of Ldn to Jesse TRIBBY of Ldn. B/S of
8a (prch/o Peter R. BEVERLEY) adj Thomas WHITE, __ COOPER.
Wit: Noble S. BRADEN, Saml. HOUGH.

3R:011   Date: 11 Aug 1828   RtCt: 11 Aug 1828
Dennis McCARTY & wife Margaret of Ldn to Richard H.
HENDERSON of Ldn. Trust for debt to Robert J. TAYLOR using
300a on both side of Snickers gap turnpike road where McCARTY
now resides, dev. by his father Thaddeus McCARTY dec'd. Wit: G.
W. McCARTY, Richard C. McCARTY, Margaret McCARTY, A.
GIBSON, Tasker C. QUINLAN. Delv. to TAYLOR 1 Aug 1829.

3R:013   Date: 26 Apr 1828   RtCt: 11 Aug 1828
Amos SKINNER & wife Margaret of Ldn to Daniel KIMBLER and
George HANCOCK (school trustees). B/S of small piece of land
around house in Skinner's 'still house field' to erect a new house
called the Liberty School and meeting house, nr road from Aldie to
Centerville.

3R:015   Date: 12 Jan 1828   RtCt: 12 Aug 1828
Leonard R. POSTON of Ldn to John K. LITTLETON of Ldn. BoS for
farm animals, farm and household items, small crop. Delv. to
LITTLETON 24 Sep 1845.

3R:016   Date: 8 Aug 1828   RtCt: 12 Aug 1828
Chas. BINNS 3rd (s/o Wm.) of Ldn to Ann A. BINNS of Ldn. BoS of farm animals, farm and household items, crops.

3R:017   Date: 11 Apr 1828   RtCt: 12 Aug 1828
George COOPER, John COOPER & wife Mary and William COOPER & wife Elizabeth of Ldn to Jacob COOPER. B/S of 40a Lot #2 on Cotocton mt. (interchanging of deeds as legatees of Frederick COOPER dec'd). Wit: Noble S. BRADEN, Geo. W. SHAWEN. Delv. to Jacob COOPER 3 Mar 1835.

3R:019   Date: 13 Aug 1828   RtCt: 13 Aug 1828
French GARRISON of Ldn to Craven SILCOTT of Ldn. Trust for Jacob SILCOTT as security to James MILLER using household items, crop on land of Sampson BLINCOE dec'd. Delv. to Jacob SILCOTT 7 Mar 1829.

3R:021   Date: 6 Mar 1828   RtCt: 13 Aug 1828
James H. BENNETT of AlexDC to John JANNEY of Lsbg. Trust for debt to John HOOF of AlexDC using interest in real estate of father Charles BENNETT dec'd of Ldn. Delv. to JANNEY 27 Jan 1831.

3R:022   Date: 26 May 1828   RtCt: 15 Aug 1828
Charles SMITH of Ldn to Josiah L. DREAN of Ldn. Trust for debt to Samuel CARR using household items, note in hands of Jonah TAVENER agst Henry O. CLEGET, Stephen Wesley ROSZELL. Delv. to DREAN 24 Nov 1828.

3R:024   Date: 8 Jan 1828   RtCt: 18 Aug 1828
Saml. M. EDWARDS of Ldn to Charles SHEPHERD of Ldn. Release of trust of Nov 1824, DBk KKK:153, for debt to Thomas R. MOTT. Delv. to SHEPHARD 11 May 1836.

3R:025   Date: 21 Aug 1828   RtCt: 20 [?] Aug 1828
Thomas B. BEATTY of Ldn to Rich'd H. HENDERSON of Ldn. Trust for debt to Robert J. TAYLOR of AlexDC using slaves for life Ally, Susan, Margaret, Fenton and Jane, besides Sampson to serve 13y from August last.

3R:026   Date: 21 Aug 1828   RtCt: 22 Aug 1828
William R. SWART & wife Elizabeth of Fqr to A. G. WATERMAN of Mdbg. Trust for debt to Conrad BITZER of Ldn using 3½a adj Dr. Richard COCKRAN, John UPP in occupancy of Isaac BROWN. Wit: Francis W. LUCKETT, Abner GIBSON.

3R:028   Date: 22 Aug 1828   RtCt: 23 Aug 1828
Commrs. Humphrey PEAKE and George WISE (case in AlexDC of John STUMP and David RICKETTS agst John T. NEWTON &c) to Everett SAUNDERS of Ldn. B/S of 327a Lot #2 being farm occupied by James STONE. Wit: Chs. G. ESKRIDGE, Enos WILDMAN, Alfred A. ESKRIDGE. Delv. to SAUNDERS 24 Mar 1829.

3R:029 Date: 22 Aug 1828 RtCt: 23 Aug 1828
Everett SAUNDERS of Ldn to Joseph T. NEWTON of Ldn. Trust for debt to Humph. PEAKE and George WISE using above 327a. Wit: Enos WILDMAN, Alfred A. ESKRIDGE, Chs. G. ESKRIDGE.

3R:030 Date: 22 Aug 1828 RtCt: 23 Aug 1828
Joshua RILEY of Ldn to Rich'd H. HENDERSON. Trust for debt to J. & J. Douglas of AlexDC using lot in Lsbg (cnvy/b Samuel M. EDWARDS Sep 1823) at Church & Loudoun Sts. Delv. to Henderson 13 Mar 1830.

3R:031 Date: 21 Jun 1828 RtCt: 23 Aug 1828
Daniel CRIM & wife Mary of Ldn to John CRIM of Ldn. B/S of 30a from div. of Charles CRIM dec'd. Wit: Saml. HOUGH, George W. SHAWEN.

3R:033 Date: 25 Aug 1828 RtCt: 25 Aug 1828
William BRADFIELD to John BRADFIELD. Trust for Joshua OSBURN as security for bond as Guardian of Julian K. BRADFIELD orphan of Joseph BRADFIELD dec'd using household items, contents of shoemakers shop.

3R:035 Date: 29 Aug 1829 [28] RtCt: 29 Aug 1828
George W. SHAWEN to Rich'd. H. HENDERSON. B/S (for benefit of James EAKIN) of 193a (with wood lot where SHAWEN lives). Delv. to HENDERSON 27 Feb 1830.

3R:036 Date: 29 Aug 1828 RtCt: 29 Aug 1828
James GHEEN and Leroy GHEEN (ch/o William GHEEN dec'd & wife Narcissa) to Narcissa GHEEN. B/S of their 1/6th share of land dev. to Narcissa by their grandfather William SUDDITH dec'd. Wit: Richard H. HENDERSON. Delv. to Narcissa 4 Dec 1828.

3R:037 Date: 27 Aug 1828 RtCt: 30 Aug 1828
Joseph COX & wife Hannah of Ldn to William HOUGH of Ldn. B/S of 6a (prch/o John BRADEN) adj Samuel HARRIS, Jos. JANNEY. Wit: Presley CORDELL, John J. MATHIAS.

3R:038 Date: 22 Aug 1828 RtCt: 4 Sep 1828
Zachariah DULANEY (trustee of Lydia Ramey) to Sanford Jacob RAMEY s/o Jacob RAMEY dec'd and nephew of Lydia RAMEY w/o Sanford RAMEY. B/S of 300a (prch/o Ferdinando FAIRFAX Apr 1803) where Sandford and Lydia reside adj Anthony WRIGHT, road from Wtfd to Thompson's mill, Edward CONNER; and 17a (prch of Susan P. B. HARDING Jun 1822) adj Cotocton creek, James MOORE.

3R:042 Date: 22 Apr 1828 RtCt: 4 Sep 1828
Zachariah DULANEY (trustee of Lydia RAMEY) to Sanford Jacob RAMEY s/o Jacob Ramey dec'd and nephew of Lydia RAMEY w/o Sanford RAMEY. B/S of 178a (prch/o Michael BOGER Oct 1810, 192a less 14a sold to BALL, DAVIS and FULTON) adj Thomas DAVIS; and 148a (prch/o William H. HARDING Aug 1807) adj

James CAMPBELL, Michael BOGER; 23½a (prch/o Elizabeth A. B. HARDING Jun 1822); 4a with fulling mill (prch/o George FULTON Oct 1816) on Broad Run; lot in Lsbg (prch/o Alexander CORDELL Feb 1826); and slaves old Jack, Nan, Dick, Kitty (alias Matilda) Rachel, Emily, Rodney, Isaac, Tilda, Nancy, Eliza, Judah, Pleas (alias Pleasant) Nelson, Jack, Peg, Bill, Tish (alias Letitia), Amanda, Gus (alias Gustine), Milly the cook, Limas, Fenton, Austin, Nace, Tenor, George, Henry, Ann, Daniel, Milly w/o Daniel, Ross, Winefred, Sam, Charlotte, Pinkey (alias Maria) and Bob. Wit: Wm. H. LANE, Charles B. HARDING.

3R:048   Date: 28 Aug 1828   RtCt: 5 Sep 1828
Simon W. RUST of Ldn to William K. ISH of Ldn. B/S of undivided 1/6th of land where father Mathew RUST dec'd resided.

3R:049   Date: 6 Sep 1828   RtCt: 6 Sep 1828
Alfred H. POWELL of Ldn to William Alexander POWELL of Ldn. B/S of ¼ interest in 200a (from div. of Leven POWELL Jr. to Elizabeth POWELL wd/o Leven POWELL Jr. dec'd during her lifetime) nr Handy's mill on Goose Creek. Delv. to Wm. POWELL 10 Oct 1836.

3R:050   Date: 8 Sep 1828   RtCt: 8 Sep 1828
Jesse TIMMS and Wm. MERSHON. Bond on TIMMS as Commissioner of Revenue in 1st District.

3R:051   Date: 8 Sep 1828   RtCt: 8 Sep 1828
Jesse McVEIGH and Hugh SMITH. Bond on McVEIGH as Commissioner of Revenue in 2nd District.

3R:052   Date: 8 Sep 1828   RtCt: 8 Sep 1828
Andrew S. ANDERSON and Isaac McGARVICK. Bond on ANDERSON as constable.

3R:052   Date: 23 Aug 1828   RtCt: 8 Sep 1828
Capt. William HUMMER dec'd. Division – ct decree of 15 Nov 1827; 16½a Lot #1 to David BRIDGES & wife Nancy late HUMMER; 57a Lot #2 to Levi HUMMER; 93a Lot #3 to Robert DARNE & wife Frances late HUMMER; 73a Lot #4 to William HUMMER's heirs; 79a Lot #5 to Sarah KIRBY and heirs; 86a Lot #6 to Washington HUMMER; 162a Lot #7 to Polly CARVER late HUMMER. Divisors: J. CLEVELAND, Hugh GRAHAM, Benjamin BRIDGES. Gives plats.

3R:056   Date: 5 Sep 1828   RtCt: 8 Sep 1828
J. P. LOVE, E. A. LOVE, J. P. LOVE Guardian of Thomas LOVE Jr. Receipt of full settlement with David SMITH and Eli PIERPOINT Exors of dec'd father Thomas LOVE's estate.

3R:056   Date: 19 Aug 1826   RtCt: 8 Sep 1828
John WHITE of Ldn to Frederick A. DAVISSON of Ldn. Assignment of 3 bonds to WHITE by Daniel COOPER of Apr 1814 to DAVISSON to discharge claims agst WHITE as Guardian of DAVISSON.

3R:057 Date: 30 Aug 1828 RtCt: 9 Sep 1828
Ludwell LUCKETT to Thomas ROGERS. B/S of 130a (from trust of
Thomas BISCOE of Nov 1827 for debt to Francis W. LUCKETT).
Delv. to ROGERS 19 Oct 1836.

3R:058 Date: 3 Aug 1828 RtCt: 11 Aug 1828
Daniel STONE and Noble S. BRADEN of Ldn to Joseph BOND of
Ldn. Release of trust of May 1823 for debt to Peyton HOUGH of
Fredericksburg, Spottsylvania Co. Wit: Thomas PHILLIPS, Moses
JANNEY, Jesse GOVER.

3R:060 Date: 15 Jul 1828 RtCt: 13 Sep 1828
Samuel GILPIN & wife Rachel of MontMd to John SAUNDERS of
Ldn. Trust for debt to Evritt SAUNDERS of Ldn using ¼ of 2 story
brick house and ¼a lot in Wtfd adj Jesse GOVER, Samuel
JACKSON. Wit: John CANDLER, Henry A. COLLIER.

3R:062 Date: 31 Dec 1827 RtCt: 12 Sep 1828
Yeoman Daniel GALLEHER & wife Elizabeth of Ldn to Seth SMITH
of Ldn. B/S of 3a (cleared Lot #6 in div. of William GALLEHER
dec'd). Wit: Francis W. LUCKETT, Ed. HALL. Delv. pr order 21 Apr
1835.

3R:064 Date: 1 Sep 1828 RtCt: 13 Sep 1828
Samuel BROWN & wife Nancy of Ldn to Mahlon CRAVEN of Ldn.
B/S of all property inherited by Nancy from father James CARTER
dec'd (giving annual use for benefit of Nancy during her lifetime).
Wit: Burr POWELL, A. GIBSON. Delv. pr order 25 Mar 1829.

3R:066 Date: 1 Sep 1828 RtCt: 13 Sep 1828
Samuel BROWN & wife Nancy of Ldn to brother David F. BROWN
of Ldn. B/S of Beaverdam Mill property and 10¾a attached (Samuel
feels he is only entitled to half, that brother and his sisters Phebe,
Rebecca H., Amanda C, Martha & Ellen BROWN are entitled to the
remainder on property that Wm. HOGUE holds lien, and Samuel has
debts to brother, Mahlon CRAVEN, Sarah ROZEL, Jno. FRANCIS,
Enoch FRANCIS, Wm. BOLON, Hiram McVEIGH, Jno. PANCUST,
James MOUNT & Jno. WYNN). Wit: Burr POWELL, A. GIBSON.
Delv. pr order 25 Mar 1829.

3R:068 Date: 12 Sep 1828 RtCt: 16 Sep 1828
Samuel MARKS of Ldn to Morris OSBURN of Ldn. B/S of 52½a adj
Thos. James KILGORE, George NICHOLS, dower of Mary MARKS
dec'd. Wit: Albert OSBURN, Jonah OSBURN, Addison OSBURN.

3R:069 Date: 19 Sep 1828 RtCt: 20 Sep 1828
Edward MORRISON & wife Flora of Ldn to Jane MORRISON of
Ldn. B/S of 31a nr E base of Short Hill adj John FREY, John
GRUBB, Thos. WHITE; and free use of spring on land of Simon
SHOEMAKER. Wit: Mortimer McILHANY, Saml. HOUGH.

3R:071 Date: 22 Sep 1828 RtCt: 22 Sep 1828
Tasker C. QUINLAN of Ldn to Burr W. HARRISON of Ldn. Trust for debt to Henry T. HARRISON of Fqr using __a on Goose Creek.

3R:073 Date: 15 Sep 1828 RtCt: 24 Sep 1828
Lloyd NOLAND of Fqr to Burr POWELL, Cuthbert POWELL and Alfred H. POWELL (trustees of Sarah CHILTON). B/S of lot in Lsbg (from trust of Sep 1828 of William CHILTON cnvy/b Philip H. LUCKETT). Wit: A. G. WATERMAN, Saml. CAMPBELL, James McDANIEL.

3R:075 Date: 7 Apr 1828 RtCt: 26 Sep 1828
Thomas MARKS & wife Keziah of Ldn to Benjamin BIRDSALL of Ldn. B/S of 12a (Lot 10 allotted to William POLSON in div. of Jesper POLSON dec'd). Wit: John WHITE, Craven OSBURN. Delv. to BIRDSALL 11 Mar 1836.

3R:077 Date: 29 Sep 1828 RtCt: 29 Sep 1828
Samuel CARR of Lsbg to John JANNEY of Lsbg. Trust for debt to John McPHERSON & partner John BRIEN of Fred Md using interest in 24 shares of stock of Bank of the Valley and 9 shares of stock of Lsbg Turnpike Co.

3R:079 Date: 29 Sep 1828 RtCt: 29 Sep 1828
Barnett HOUGH of Ldn to David CARR and John H. MONROE of Ldn. Trust for debt to William CARR of Ldn using lot on Loudoun St in Lsbg (DBk V:240 and Y:107). Delv. to John H. MONROE 11 Oct 1831.

3R:081 Date: 29 Sep 1828 RtCt: 30 Sep 1828
George RICHARDS to Barnett HOUGH. Release of trust of Feb 1828, DBk PPP:357 and QQQ:417, for debt to Michael MORALLEE, Samuel M. BOSS, Asa PECK & John MARTIN.

3R:082 Date: 1 Oct 1828 RtCt: 1 Oct 1828
John DREAN of Ldn to Thomas MORALLEE of Ldn. B/S (for benefit of Sarah S. Seeders late DREAN w/o William SEEDERS) of lot in Lsbg on S side of Market St. Geo. RICHARDS, Geo. K. FOX, James BRADY Jr.

3R:084 Date: 27 Sep 1828 RtCt: 2 Oct 1828
Samuel MARKS of Ldn to Samuel B. T. CALDWELL of Ldn. Trust for debt to Morris OSBURN of Ldn using 35a Lot #3 in div. of Abel MARKS dec'd formerly allotted to Betsey WARFORD. Delv. pr order 13 Oct 1829.

3R:086 Date: 2 Oct 1828 RtCt: 4 Oct 1828
Foushee TEBBS of Ldn to Richard H. HENDERSON of Ldn. Trust for debt to Caldwell CARR and Bushrod RUST (Admrs of Joseph CARR dec'd), William FAWLE & Co of AlexDC and Kerr & Fitzhugh of AlexDC using 540a in Ldn and PrWm (cnvy/b William RUST Feb 1823, DBk III:122) where TEBBS resides. Wit: John JANNEY, Edward L. FANT, Chs. G. ESKRIDGE.

3R:088   Date: 30 Sep 1828   RtCt: 7 Oct 1828
Jacob MANN & wife Sarah of Ldn to James WEEKS of Mdbg. B/S of
Lot #39 and #40 in Mdbg (cnvy/b James KINCHELOE). Wit: Burr
POWELL, A. GIBSON. Delv. to WEEKS 21 Dec 1829.

3R:091   Date: 23 Jul 1828   RtCt: 11 Oct 1828
Saml. B. T. CALDWELL of Ldn to Chauncey BROOKS of BaltMd.
B/S of __a (from trust of Apr 1825 of Thomas BROWN to BROOKS,
cnvy/b Abraham SKILLMAN in 18__ and cnvy/b George NIXON in
18__). Delv pr order 26 Dec 1829.

3R:092   Date: 18 Aug 1828   RtCt: 13 Oct 1828
Joseph HOUGH. Oath as 2nd Lt. of company of artillery in 2nd Reg
2nd Div Va Militia.

3R:093   Date: 7 Aug 1828   RtCt: 18 Aug 1828
Samuel Craven SINCLAIR to Samuel DAWSON. Trust for debt to
Alfred BELT (Exor of Charles THORNTON dec'd) using slaves for
life Sucky & her unnamed infant child, Amanda, Mariah, and Ann,
Tom and Joe. Wit: James PYOTT, Wilfred ALLISTON, Susan
ALLISTON. Delv. to BELT 30 May 1832.

3R:095   Date: 2 Oct 1828   RtCt: 2 Oct 1828
Stacy TAYLOR, Joshua PANCOAST and Joshua GREGG of Ldn to
Richard ADAMS of Ldn. Release of trust from Benjamin DANIEL
(ADAMS later purchased trust) for debt to Joshua GREGG.

3R:096   Date: __ Oct 1828   RtCt: 13 Oct 1828
Amos HARVEY & wife Elizabeth of Ldn to Samuel CLENDENING of
Ldn. Trust for debt to James & William THOMPSON of Ldn using
90a (prch/o heirs of Ebenezer WILSON dec'd) where HARVEY
resides adj heirs of Thomas HOUGH, Jacob SHUTT, John
CAMPBELL, Jesse EVANS. Wit: John WHITE, Craven OSBURN.
Delv. to James THOMPSON 12 Oct 1830.

3R:098   Date: __ 1828   RtCt: 13 Oct 1828
Elizabeth JACOBS of Ldn to Jacob STONEBURNER (as trustee of
John VARNES) of Ldn. B/S of 1½a on E side of Cotoctin Mt. (part of
lot inherited from her father).

3R:100   Date: 15 Oct 1828   RtCt: 15 Oct 1828
David CRUMBAKER of Ldn to Philip HEATER of Ldn. B/S of 107½a
(formerly owned by mother Eve SAGER dec'd) adj John VINCEL,
Jacob FAWLEY, Ann SANBOWER. Delv. to HEATER 25 Jul 1829.

3R:101   Date: 20 Aug 1828   RtCt: 18 Oct 1828
Rich'd. H. HENDERSON & wife Orra Moore of Ldn to Josiah
GREGG of Ldn. B/S of house and lot in Union former prop. of
William H. DORSEY dec'd now occupied by __ CLEWES. Wit: Saml.
M. EDWARDS, Presley CORDELL. Delv. to GREGG 21 Jun 1830.

3R:102   Date: 4 Sep 1828   RtCt: 18 Oct 1828
David REECE (Exor of Thomas TRIBBY Jr. dec'd) to Elijah JAMES
of Ldn. B/S of 1 rood (part of farm of late TRIBBY) adj that already

sold to Mahlon JANNEY and to land prch/o heirs of Thomas HUGHES by Elijah. Delv. to JAMES 8 Oct 1836.

3R:104 Date: 12 May 1828 RtCt: 20 Oct 1828
Charles SHEPHERD & wife Elizabeth of Lsbg to Saml. M. EDWARDS of Lsbg. Trust for debt to John C. LYON of Lsbg using house and lot in Lsbg on S side of Cornwall St, adj Jno. G. WATT, Ignatius ELGIN. Delv. to Benjamin WATERS pr order ___.

3R:105 Date: 12 Apr 1822 RtCt: 21 Oct 1828
Elizabeth ELLZEY and Mary ELLZEY of Ldn to William ELLZEY of Ldn. B/S of 18a (granted William ELLZEY dec'd 16 Mar 1792) adj __ ASHTON, __ RUSSELL, __ LEE. Wit: Sarah ELLZEY, Frances W. ELLZEY, Catherine HARRISON. Delv. to Col. Wm. ELLZEY 19 Jun 1830.

3R:106 Date: 18 Oct 1828 RtCt: 21 Oct 1828
George FAIRHURST of Ldn to George GRIMES of Ldn. B/S of 48a (prch/o Abel DAVIS and part from Jeremiah FAIRHIRST) on NW fork of Goose Creek adj Eli JANNEY, GRIMES.

3R:108 Date: 20 Sep 1828 RtCt: 22 Oct 1828
William DANIEL & wife Sarah to S. B. T. CALDWELL. Trust for debt to John CURRELL using 23a Lot #3 in div. of father Joseph DANIEL dec'd. Wit: John WHITE, Craven OSBURN.

3R:110 Date: 2 Oct 1828 RtCt: 24 Oct 1828
William HANNAH & wife Vicy of Ldn to Humphrey B. POWELL of Ldn. Trust for debt to Stephen RAWLINGS using interest in lot where he resides (cnvy/b Burr POWELL on ground rent). Wit: Burr POWELL, A. GIBSON.

3R:112 Date: 30 Sep 1828 RtCt: 24 Oct 1828
James WEEKS of Ldn to H. B. POWELL of Ldn. Trust for debt to Jacob MANN of Ldn using Lot #39 in Mdbg (cnvy/b MANN). Wit: Burr POWELL.

3R:113 Date: 25 Oct 1828 RtCt: 25 Oct 1828
Gustavus A. MORAN & wife Lydia late Lidia D. EDWARDS to Charles LEWIS. Trust for debt to Rebecca EDWARDS using interest in L/L of 297a below Goose Creek; and negro man James aged abt 47y dev. from his father and hired for present year to Dr. John C. GREEN; farm animals, farm and household items (injunction in Winchester Ct by MORAN agt. Jeremiah HUTCHISON and Henry MILTON). Delv. to EDWARDS 20 May 1831.

3R:115 Date: 27 Oct 1828 RtCt: 27 [Oct] 1828
Robert R. HOUGH & wife Sarah C. of Lsbg to George RICHARDS of Lsbg. Trust for debt to Christian, David & Samuel KEENER druggists of BaltMd using house & lot in Lsbg on Royal St adj James THOMAS, Peter BOSS; household items. Wit: Hamilton ROGERS, Presley CORDELL. Delv. to RICHARDS 28 Feb 1829.

3R:118   Date: 27 Oct 1828   RtCt: 27 Oct 1828
Joseph HILLIARD to Robert R. HOUGH. Release of trust of Mar 1828 for debt to Edward S. HOUGH. Delv. to RICHARDS 28 Feb 1829 [repeat of entry from previous deed.]

3R:120   Date: 2 Sep 1828   RtCt: 28 Oct 1828
James McILHANY & wife Margaret of Ldn to Mahlon MORRIS of Ldn. B/S of 42a, 16a and 99¼a on Goose Creek adj __ BRADFIELD. Gives plat. Wit: Saml. M. EDWARDS, Presley CORDELL. Delv. to Robt. W. MORRIS pr order in 4T:028.

3R:122   Date: 1 Jul 1828   RtCt: 29 Oct 1828
Penelope B. ALEXANDER, Charles B. ALEXANDER and Charles P. TUTT to Josiah L. DREAN. Trust for debt to Samuel CARR using 1/3 part of tract cnvy/b John ALEXANDER to Bertrand EWELL (title then in suit, 1/3 by deed of 18 Mar 1814 from EWELL to Chas. B. ALEXANDER and Charles P. TUTT trustees of Penelope B. ALEXANDER [in WashDC]). Wit: C. H. W. WHARTON, Jno. CHALMERS. Delv to DREAN 29 Jun 1829.

3R:123   Date: 1 Nov 1828   RtCt: 1 Nov 1828
John TORREYSON of Ldn to Sanford J. RAMEY of Ldn. Trust for debt to Lewis TORREYSON using household items.

3R:125   Date: 16 Sep 1828   RtCt: 3 Nov 1828
Edward CATING & wife Martha of Jackson Co Ohio to Thomas M. HUMPHREY of Ldn. B/S of 1/6th interest in 29¾a of dower allotted to Mary HUMPHREY wd/o Jesse HUMPHREY dec'd. Wit: Simon DIXON, James BROOKE.

3R:127   Date: 10 Apr 1828   RtCt: 3 Nov 1828
Francis W. LUCKETT, Miner FURR, John P. DULANY to William BENTON. Release of trust of Jan 1821 by John, Edward and Andrew MARTIN for debt to Hiram SEATON.

3R:129   Date: 19 Apr 1828   RtCt: 3 Nov 1828
Caleb MARTIN (s/o Edward) to Amos DENHAM of Ldn. B/S of lease lot previously held by Elijah VIOLETT.

3R:130   Date: 26 May 1828   RtCt: 4 Nov 1828
Humphrey SHEPHERD & wife Catherine of FredVa to David SMITH of Ldn. B/S of 9a (prch/o William CASTLEMAN) on NW fork of Goose Creek adj Joseph GORE, SMITH. Wit: William CASTLEMAN, Edw'd J. SMITH.

3R:132   Date: 24 Mar 1828   RtCt: 4 Nov 1828
James BRADFIELD of Ldn to James P. BRADFIELD of Ldn. Warranty bond for purchase of 100a on SE end of James BRADFIELD's farm adj David LOVETT, Rufus UPDIKE. Wit: Timothy TAYLOR Jr., Timothy TAYLOR, Elwood B. JAMES. Delv. to Jas. P. 23 Mar 1829.

3R:133 Date: 11 Aug 1828 RtCt: 11 Aug 1828
John WHITE, Ebenezer GRUBB and John WRIGHT of Ldn to
Thomas WHITE of Ldn. B/S of 50a 'Manning's lower lot' and 73a
'Manning's upper lot' (from trust of Mar 1827 from Nathaniel
MANNING). Delv. to WHITE 16 Aug 1830.

3R:134 Date: 15 Jun 1828 RtCt: 4 Nov 1828
Jacob FADELY of Lsbg to William W. HAMMONTREE of Lsbg. LS
lot on E side of King St in Lsbg (part of lot cnvy/b John REIGOR to
Jane R. DAVIS). Wit: Alfred A. ESKRIDGE, Geo. LEE.

3R:136 Date: 7 Jun 1828 RtCt: 5 Nov 1828
John CONARD of Ldn to Christopher REDENOWER of JeffVa. B/S
of 2a in gap of short hill near Hllb (from trust of Aug 1825 from
Durett LONG). Delv. pr order to CONARD 23 Feb 1830.

3R:137 Date: 16 Oct 1828 RtCt: 4 Nov 1828
Burr BRADEN. DoE for negro man Ned aged abt 39y, 5' 5½" high,
dev. by will of father Robert BRADEN dec'd.

3R:138 Date: 23 Sep 1828 RtCt: 5 Nov 1828
Rebecca JOHNSON of FredMd to Simon YEAKY of Ldn. B/S of
17½a on Cotocton Creek (part of 'furnace tract' from div. of Thomas
JOHNSON Jr. dec'd). Delv. to YEAKY 15 Mar 1829.

3R:140 Date: 23 Oct 1828 RtCt: 10 Nov 1828
Geo. W. HENRY. Qualified as Major in 56th Reg 6th Brig 2nd Div of
Va Militia.

3R:140 Date: 14 Oct 1828 RtCt: 10 Nov 1828
David CONARD. Qualified as Captain in 56th Reg 6th Brig 2nd Div of
Va Militia.

3R:140 Date: 10 Nov 1828 RtCt: 10 Nov 1828
Peyton POWELL, Wm. GILMORE and Evan WILKINSON. Bond on
POWELL as constable.

3R:141 Date: 10 Oct [Nov?] 1828 RtCt: 10 Nov 1828
Peter C. RUST, William GILMORE and Wm. THRIFT. Bond on
RUST as constable.

3R:142 Date: 9 Nov 1828 RtCt: 10 Nov 1828
George RICHARDS and Jno. ROSE to Pres. and directors of the
literacy fund. Bond on RICHARDS as treasurer.

3R:142 Date: 10 Nov 1828 RtCt: 10 Nov 1828
Charles B. HAMILTON. DoE for slaves Winny aged 28y and her
children (with husband Henson) Anna aged 9y, Rose aged 8y, Mary
aged 4y, Presley aged 1y.

3R:143 Date: 10 Nov 1828 RtCt: 10 Nov 1828
Charles B. HAMILTON and John HAMILTON. DoE for negro man
Henson aged 33y.

3R:143   Date: 23 Nov 1828   RtCt: 24 Oct 1828
Thomas J. HARPER & wife Margaret of Ldn to Cassandria
PEACOCK of Ldn. B/S of 2a (prch/o John UMBAUGH) adj
UMBAUGH, __ AULD. Wit: Samuel DAWSON, George W.
SHAWEN. Delv. pr order 4 May 1830.

3R:145   Date: 27 Sep 1828   RtCt: 5 Nov 1828
William D. DANIEL & wife Sarah of Ldn to Isaiah B. BEANS of Ldn.
B/S of 23a Lot #3 in div. of Joseph DANIEL dec'd. Wit: Mason
MARKS, Mason OSBURN, Albert OSBURN.

3R:146   Date: 8 Nov 1828   RtCt: 10 Nov 1828
Jacob SILCOTT of Ldn to Craven SILCOT of Ldn. B/S of 65a
(cnvy/b Benjamin BROOKE) on Beaverdam adj Amos HIBBS, Isaac
COWGIL, Samuel DUNCAN, Joseph GOURLEY.

3R:147   Date: 8 Nov 1828   RtCt: 10 Nov 1828
Jacob SILCOTT of Ldn to Craven SILCOTT of Ldn. Trust for debt to
Solimon GIBSON, Stephen McPHERSON, James JOHNSTON and
Elizabeth BOOLIN of Ldn using farm animals, farm and household
items, crops.

3R:149   Date: 27 Sep 1828   RtCt: 10 Nov 1828
Israel T. GRIFFITH of Ldn to Eli TAVENNER of Ldn. B/S of 24a
(cnvy/b Norval CHAMBLIN Nov 1826) now occupied by John
COLLINS, adj Jonah TAVENNER, James BROWN. Delv. to
TAVENER 3 Feb 1837.

3R:151   Date: 10 Nov 1828   RtCt: 10 Nov 1828
John HAMMERLY & wife Jane of Ldn to Stacy LACEY of Ldn. B/S
of 1¼a lot in Lsbg (cnvy/b SMALLWOOD, MIDDLETON's trustee,
John DRISH and John H. McCABE). Wit: Presley CORDELL, Saml.
M. EDWARDS. Delv. to TAYLOR 29 Mar 1831.

3R:152   Date: __ 1828   RtCt: 12 Nov 1828
Wm. W. TEBBS of PrWm to Charles Binns TEBBS (s/o Dr. Thomas
F. TEBBS dec'd and nephew of Wm.) of Ldn. Gift of negro boy
Joseph born Feb 1824 and dev. by Margaret DOUGLASS now dec'd
to her niece Margaret H. D. TEBBS m/o Charles B., until Joseph
arrives at 25y old. Delv. 29 Oct 1836.

3R:153   Date: 13 Nov 1828   RtCt: 13 Nov 1828
Tasker C. QUINLAN (in jail due to debts) of Ldn to Jesse TIMMS
and Burr W. HARRISON of Ldn. B/S of all his property including
1425a on S side of Goose Creek adj Cuthbert POWELL, James
MONROE, George Carter GARRETT, Charles F. MERCER, Samuel
TILLETT with tenement occupied by Christopher ROSE and divided
among Benjamin JOHNSON, Samuel TILLETT and J. PILES, one
occupied by Samuel A. TILLETT, 'lime kiln lot' occupied by John
WEATHEROW, tract in Ffx he may be entitled to dev. from Robert
CARTER, 474a 'Cole's Point' in WstmVA on Potomac; and all other
real estate he is entitled to; horses, crops, bank stock of Bank of

Georgetown derived from William HAMILTON and William J.
NICHOLLS; claims from estate of John C. PECK and Robert
MITCHEL as his guardian and Carter MITCHEL as his guardian;
funds from Thomas ROWAND Admr. of Hugh QUINLAN dec'd. Delv.
to HARRISON 10 Oct 1829.

3R:158   Date: 13 Nov 1828   RtCt: 14 Nov 1828
William MERCHANT of Ldn to William THRIFT of Ldn. Trust for debt
to John GRAY of Lsbg using crop on farm of Wilson C. SELDEN Sr.
which he rents and lives on, household items, farm animals. Wit:
Chs. G. ESKRIDGE, Edward L. FANT.

3R:159   Date: 13 Nov 1828   RtCt: 14 Nov 1828
Tasker C. QUINLAN (insolvent debtor in jail) to Sheriff Charles
LEWIS. B/S of 1400a on Goose Creek and Ketocton mt., 400a in
WstmVa, ___a in Ffx (writ of capias ad satisfaciendum from Evan
WILKINSON ass'ee of Richard H. HENDERSON ass'ee of Presley
FOLEY dec'd, David SIMPSON & Peter GREGG merchants
assignees, Andrew CAMPBELL assignee of David CARR, William
CLINE, S. M. BOSS assignee of Thomas SAUNDERS, Thomas
WHITTLE assignee of S. B. T. CALDWELL). Delv. to Burr W.
HARRISON 10 Oct 1829.

3R:160   Date: 18 Nov 1828   RtCt: 21 Nov 1828
John COPELAND of Ldn to Jacob COOPER of Ldn. Trust for debt to
George WINSEL of Ldn using farm and household items.

3R:163   Date: 16 Oct 1828   RtCt: 25 Nov 1828
Aaron SANDERS & wife Susanna(h) C. of Ldn to George M.
CHICHESTER of Ldn. B/S of 5a on N side of Potomac and opposite
the lower end of Bowies Island. Wit: Fayette BALL, John H.
McCABE. Delv. to CHICHESTER 19 Jul 1831.

3R:165   Date: 26 Nov 1828   RtCt: 26 Nov 1828
Rachel MADDISON of Fayette Co Pa to William NETTLE of Ldn.
B/S of 3a allotted in div. of father Hugh FULTON dec'd adj ___
UMBAUGH.

3R:166   Date: 31 Mar 1827   RtCt: 28 Nov 1828
Stephen SANDS of Ldn to Thomas G. DOWDELL, Elizabeth E.
DOWDELL, Isaac S. DOWDELL and Mary Ann DOWDELL by
guardian Moses DOWDELL of Ldn. B/S of 9¼a adj DOWDELLS,
William STOCKS.

3R:168   Date: 29 Nov 1828   RtCt: 29 Nov 1828
Henry MOON of Ldn to Isaac W. MOON. BoS for household items.
Wit: Jonathan E. DORSEY, Wm. J. HANLEY.

3R:168   Date: 13 Nov 1828   RtCt: 4 Dec 1828
Yeoman John WILKINSON of Ldn to yeoman George KEENE of
Ldn. B/S of 48a nr Union (cnvy/b Jeremiah SANFORD and by Isaac
BROWN and by ___ CRAWFORD) adj late John WILLIAMS, Thomas
L. HUMPHREY. Delv. to KEENE 27 Mar 1830.

3R:170   Date: 5 Dec 1828   RtCt: 5 Dec 1828
John JONES (insolvent debtor) to Sheriff Charles LEWIS. B/S of 82a (prch/o John SIMPSON, with title in suit in Winchester).

3R:171   Date: 6 Dec 1828   RtCt: 6 Dec 1828
Walter ELGIN Jr. & wife Sarah of Ldn to Isaac HARRIS Sr. of Ldn. B/S of 110a (see DBk QQQ:155) where ELGIN now resides adj __ BENNEDUM, __ COST, __ HAMILTON, __ SANDERS, __ CARR. Wit: James L. MARTIN, Wm. P. HARRIS, Saml. HARRIS, John H. McCABE, Presley CORDELL.

3R:173   Date: 29 Nov 1828   RtCt: 8 Dec 1828
Charles LEWIS, Johnson CLEVELAND and Thomas B. MERSHON (Commr. in div. of George HUTCHISON dec'd) to Joshua HUTCHISON. B/S of adj Samuel HUTCHISON, John HUTCHISON Sr.

3R:174   Date: 24 Jan 1827   RtCt: 9 Dec 1828
Cartwright TIPPETT dec'd. Division – court order of 8 Jan 1827; slave old man Stephen, 3 children named James, Letty, Betsey, house & 33a Lot #1 to Elizabeth TIPPET her 1/3 dower; slave Dick and 128a Lot #2 to Mary BURR and her infant children; slave Kitty and her child Richard Henry and 156a Lot #3 to John C. TIPPET. Divisors: Johnston CLEVELAND, Thomas DARNE, Jno. J. COLEMAN, R. H. COCKERILLE. Gives plat.

3R:177   Date: 2 Mar 1819   RtCt: 2 Dec 1828
William MAINS of Ross Co Ohio to brother Archibald MAINS of Ldn. PoA

3R:179   Date: 22 Dec 1828   RtCt: 6 Jan 1829
Isaac HARRIS & wife Sara(h) of Ldn to James L. MARTIN of Ldn. B/S of 13a 'Kirk's Meadow' nr Lsbg (cnvy/b Craven PAYTON to James KIRK to son Robert KIRK, then to James KIRK). Wit: Presley CORDELL, John H. McCABE. Delv. to Saml. M. EDWARDS who has a deed for land ___.

3R:180   Date: 25 Dec 1827   RtCt: 8 Dec 1828
Washington WHITE, Rachel WHITE and Elizabeth WHITE to William WHITE. B/S of land they derived from father Josiah WHITE dec'd). Wit: Nathan GREGG, Stephen GREGG, Craven OSBURN, Thomas B. LOVE. Delv. to Wm. WHITE 12 Nov 1829.

3R:181   Date: 5 Apr 1828   RtCt: 8 Dec 1828
Joz. WHITE to Wm. WHITE. B/S of interest in real estate of Josiah WHITE dec'd (dev. to 3 of his children, listed in above deed). Wit: James GETTYS, Henry WERTZ. Acknowledgement by Joz. in WashDC. Delv. to Wm. WHITE 12 Nov 1829.

3R:182   Date: 7 Jan 1828   RtCt: 8 Dec 1828
Thomas B. LOVE & wife Leah late WHITE to William WHITE. B/S of interest in real estate of Josiah WHITE dec'd (as above). Wit: John WHITE, Craven OSBURN. Delv. to Wm. WHITE 12 Nov 1829.

3R:183   Date: 27 Sep 1828   RtCt: 8 Dec 1828
John P. LOVE, Eli A. LOVE and Thomas LOVE (by Guardian John P. LOVE) of Ldn to Thomas B. LOVE of Ldn. B/S of 31a (undivided 1/7th of tract of John LOVE dec'd).

3R:185   Date: 2 Dec 1828   RtCt: 2 Dec 1828
Archibald MAINES attorney for William MAINES of Ohio, William CARR & wife Mary and John CARR of Ldn to Thomas SANDERS of Ldn. B/S of 5a, 3a and 2a on hogback mt. (part of lot prch/o Carlisle & Whiting by CARR and MAINES Apr 1801) and (part of tract cnvy/b William RHODES to Dr. Henry CLAGETT Apr 1809 then to Henry SANDERS dec'd, in Sup. Ct suit). Wit: Presley CORDELL, John H. McCABE.

3R:188   Date: 15 Nov 1828   RtCt: 9 Dec 1828
Jacob MANN & wife Sarah of Ldn to James McDANIEL of Ldn. B/S of ½a nr Mdbg described in deed of 19 Sep 1820 by Burr POWELL, Jacob MANN & John BOYD. Wit: Burr POWELL, Abner GIBSON.

3R:190   Date: 21 Sep 1816   RtCt: 9 Dec 1828
Elias ODEN & wife Sarah of Zaneville Township, Muskingum Co Ohio to William LYNE of Ldn. B/S of 1/9th of lands of Thomas ODEN dec'd now in possession of widow. Wit: Charles LEWIS, Wm. B. HARRISON, Philip PALMER, Lewis AMBLER, James McFARLAND, John TAYLOR, Nathan COOPER. Delv. to Cep't? SUMMERS by order from LYNE 2 Mary 1829.

3R:191   Date: 10 Dec 1828   RtCt: 10 Dec 1828
James McILHANY of Ldn to John CONRAD of Ldn. Release of trust of Sep 1823 from John BROWN to Craven OSBURN and John A. MARMADUKE, DBk GGG:191. CONRAD has purchased land from BROWN.

3R:191   Date: 11 Dec 1828   RtCt: 12 Dec 1828
Aaron DIVINE of Loudoun to Charles W. D. BINNS of Loudoun. Trust for debt to William KING, John SURGHNOR, Samuel M. BOSS, William HAYMAN and Robert J. TAYLOR of Ldn using household items and lease lot on King St. where DIVINE lives adj shoe shop of Wm. KING.

3R:193   Date: 9 Dec 1828   RtCt: 15 Dec 1828
Mary HIXSON (wd/o Reuben dec'd) and Catherine HIXSON of Ldn to Adam HOUSEHOLDER of Ldn. B/S of 153 pole lot (part of tract cnvy/b Henry DAY under a mistake of his boundaries, adj Sanford RAMEY.

3R:194   Date: 2 Oct 1828   RtCt: 15 Dec 1828
Jacob MANN & wife Sarah of Mdbg to William Butler HARRISON of Ldn. B/S of part of Lot #3 with house & #4 with tan yard in Mdbg (cnvy/b Burr POWELL Sep 1817, less ½ of Lot #3 cnvy to Bernard MANN). Wit: Burr POWELL, Francis W. LUCKETT. Delv. to HARRISON 11 Mar 1829.

3R:196   Date: 2 Nov 1828   RtCt: 23 Dec 1828
Henry SHOVER & wife Rosannah of Union Co Ohio to Thomas J. MARLOW of Ldn. B/S of Lot #3 in div. of Adam SHOVER dec'd (cnvy/b trustees to MARLOW 11 Feb 1828). Wit: James BUCK, Henry SAGER, Clark PROVIN.

3R:198   Date: 23 Aug 1828   RtCt: 23 Dec 1828
Charles DUNCAN & wife Abigal of Wood Co Va to Benjamin BRIDGES and Lewellen HUTCHISON of Ldn. B/S of interest in land of Charles DUNCAN dec'd (to cover loss of BRIDGES and HUTCHISON as security for DUNCAN as constable). Delv. to BRIDGES 11 Feb 1839.

3R:200   Date: 1 Nov 1828   RtCt: 25 Dec 1828
Ludwell LEE of Ldn to James L. McKENNA of Alex DC. Trust using negro Phil & wife Betsy, Mary, Richard, Betsey, Cordelia, Ellen Esther, Frank & Jane children of Phil & Betsy and Jenny. Wit: Richard H. LEE, W. C. SELDEN Jr. Delv. pr order 4 Sep 1829.

3R:201   Date: 1 Dec 1828   RtCt: 25 Dec 1828
Francis W. LUCKETT & wife Sarah S. and Joseph W. BRONAUGH of Ldn to Caldwell CARR of Fqr. Trust for debt (with George W. BRONAUGH and Ludwell LUCKETT) to Daniel KEERFORT (Guardian of Amanda CARR) of Fqr using 200a from William BRONAUGH dec'd. Acknowledgment for BRONAUGH in Frederick Co. Wit: Burr POWELL, Abner GIBSON.

3R:204   Date: 8 Oct 1828   RtCt: 14 Oct 1828
Zachariah DULANEY of Ldn to Noble S. BRADEN of Ldn. Trust for Samuel IREY of Ldn as endorser on bank note using negro man Robin, woman Winny and her 2 children. Wit: F. W. P. HIXON, J. WILSON, Jos. BRADEN.

3R:205   Date: 26 Nov 1828   RtCt: 28 Dec 1828
Isaac EATON & wife Matilda of Mt. Gilead to William HOGE of Ldn. Trust for debt to Isaac NICKOLS of Ldn using house and 1a Lot #1 where EATON resides in Mt. Gilead at Loudoun and Balm Sts adj John C. LICKEY, Wm. HANDY. Wit: Jonathan HOGE, John LOCKARD, Thomas SANDERS, John SIMPSON. Delv. to Wm. HOGE Admr. of Jas. HOGE dec'd. 14 Mar 1829.

3R:208   Date: 11 Dec 1828   RtCt: 29 Dec 1828
John W. HANES of Dorchester Co Md to Charles W. BINNS of Ldn. PoA. Wit: St. George E. ROBERTS, Joseph K. TRAVENS.

3R:210   Date: 14 May 1828   RtCt: 29 Dec 1828
Elizabeth HARLAN of East Fallowfield township, Chester Co Pa to Aaron HARLAN of Ldn. PoA. Wit: Jesse KERSEY, John GRAVES. Delv. to Aaron HARLAN 11 May 1828.

3R:211   Date: 17 Dec 1828   RtCt: 25 Dec 1828
Ludwell LEE of Ldn to Saml. M. EDWARDS of Ldn. Trust for Joseph
LEWIS as endorser on bank note using 1350a on Lsbg turnpike
were LEE resides.

3R:213   Date: 1 Jan 1829   RtCt: 1 Jan 1829
Presley CORDELL of Ldn and James McILHANY of Ldn. Agreement
– negro boy London sold to McILHANY who agrees to emancipate
at end of 17y.

3R:214   Date: 1 Jan 1829   RtCt: 7 Jan 1829
Jacob WALTMAN (of Saml.) to William PAXSON & wife Jane.
Release of trust of Jul 1822 for debt to John ROBERTSON
(assigned from John COPELAND to Philip HEATER to
ROBERTSON).

3R:216   Date: 2 Jan 1829   RtCt: 7 Jan 1829
William PAXSON & wife Jane of Ldn to John ROBERTSON of Ldn.
B/S of 123a (prch/o Exor. of Joshua DANIEL dec'd, Apr 1811) on E
side of Cotocton adj ROBERTSON, __ PHILIPS, __ JONES; and
45a on W side of Cotocton Mt nr Bald Hill adj Rich'd WILLIAMS (less
acres cnvy to Valentine PURCELL Mary 1824). Wit: Noble S.
BRADEN, S. HOUGH. Delv to Robinson 16 Jul 1829.

3R:218   Date: ___   RtCt: 12 Jan 1829
James HOEY. Report to become a citizen – born, Parish of King
Kings County, age 31 years, nation: Ireland, allegiance to King of G.
Brittain, migrated from Kings County, place of intended residence:
Loudoun Co Va.

3R:219   Date: 12 Jan 1829   RtCt: 12 Jan 1829
Lydia RAMEY and Sanford J. RAMEY (Exors of Sanford RAMEY
dec'd). Agreement – made Apr 1825, not admitting will can remain in
force as it is inconsistent with a deed made by RAMEY 18 Jan 1828
conveying part of estate to Z. DULANEY; deed made with
DULANEY in Feb 1828 may be invalid. Wit: Johnston J. COLEMAN,
James WHALEY, Eleanor MORGAN. Delv. to S. J. RAMEY 19 Jul
1845.

3R:219   Date: 30 Dec 1828   RtCt: 13 Jan 1829
Rich'd H. HENDERSON. DoE for Alse WILLIAMS. Wit: L. BEARD,
S. J. FOLEY.

3R:220   Date: 29 Aug 1828   RtCt: 13 Jan 1829
James NICHOLS dec'd. Division – mansion house with 43a to
widow for dower; 17a Lot #1 and 11a mt. Lot #11 to Nathaniel
NICHOLS; 17a Lot #2 and 11a mt. Lot #17 to Joel NICHOLS; 17a
Lot #3 and 11a mt. Lot #12 to Sarah NICHOLS; 21½a Lot #4 and
11a mt. Lot #14 to Hannor NICHOLS; 5a Lot #5 and 11a mt. Lot
#15 to Emily PRYOR; 21½a Lot #6 and 11½a mt. Lot #16 to
Pleasant NICHOLS; 22½a Lot #7 and 11½a mt. Lot #13 to Tamzer
LODGE; 26½a Lot #8 and 11½a mt. Lot #10 to Enos NICHOLS; 58a

Lot #9 and small 1a lot to Dolphin NICHOLS. Divisors: Joel OSBURN, Thomas JAMES.

3R:224   Date: 1 Sep 1828   RtCt: 3 Nov 1828
Everett TRACEY & wife Tamar of Ldn to Nathaniel NICHOLS, Enos NICHOLS, Sarah NICHOLS, Emily PRIOR late NICHOLS w/o Samuel PRIOR, Joel NICHOLS, Tamzen LODGE late NICHOLS w/o Abner LODGE, Dolphin NICHOLS, Harman NICHOLS and Pleasant NICHOLS (heirs of James NICHOLS dec'd). B/S of 11a Lot #6 in div. of George NICHOLS dec'd nr Blue Ridge mt. at NW fork of Goose Creek. Wit: John WHITE, Craven OSBURN.

3R:226   Date: 1 Sep 1828   RtCt: 3 Nov 1828
Samuel A. JACKSON & wife Sarah, Nathaniel NICHOLS & wife Rachel, Joel NICHOLS & wife Sarah, Sarah NICHOLS, Thomas NICHOLS & wife Barbary, Everitt TRACEY & wife Tamer of Ldn to Thomas JAMES of Ldn. B/S of 83a (formerly George NICHOLS) and interest in 40a dower of Ann NICHOLS. Wit: Craven OSBURN, John WHITE. Delv. to James 10 Mar 1829.

3R:229   Date: 27 Dec 1828   RtCt: 12 Jan 1829
Elias L. CHINN of Va to Lott BARR of Ldn. B/S of 96a (cnvy/b Dpty Hugh SMITH). Delv. pr order 26 Aug 1829.

3R:230   Date: 8 Jan 1829   RtCt: 12 Jan 1829
Isaac BROWN Jr. of Ldn to Johnathan TAVENNER of Ldn. B/S of interest in estate of Jonah TAVENNER dec'd and interest from estate of Elizabeth TAVENNER former w/o Jonah dec'd or from estate of Jesse JANNEY dec'd. Delv. to TAVENNER 20 Feb 1835.

3R:232   Date: 31 Dec 1827   RtCt: 12 Jan 1829
Joseph MOORE of Ldn to Edmund TYLER of Ldn. Trust for debt to James G. MOORE of Ldn using negro woman Milly & her child Delsa. Wit: William S. ELGIN, William SMITH, John MOORE.

3R:233   Date: 10 Aug 1828   RtCt: 12 Jan 1829
Richard H. HENDERSON (as Commr. in case of Thomas H. YOUNG, etc. vs. Henry CRAWFORD, etc) to Charles J. KILGOUR of MontMd. B/S of 108a (from estate of Archibald YOU[N]G dec'd) whereon Henson ELLIOTT lived adj Charles CHAMBLIN. Delv. to KILGORE 15 Jan 1835.

3R:234   Date: 12 Jan 1829   RtCt: 12 Jan 1829
Thomas MORALLEE & wife Mary of Ldn to John CRIDLER of Ldn. B/S of lot in Lsbg now occupied by CRIDLER, adj reps of James D. FRENCH, Cridler's slaughter house.

3R:235   Date: 27 Dec 1828   RtCt: 12 Jan 1829
Dpty Hugh SMITH for Sheriff Charles LEWIS to Elias L. CHINN. B/S of 96a (surrendered by Thomas CHINN in 1827) adj T. McVEIGH, E. C. BROWN.

3R:237 Date: 6 Jan 1829 RtCt: 12 Jan 1829
James McDANIEL & wife Ann of Ldn to H. B. POWELL. Trust for note to Jacob ISH endorsed by Lloyd NOLAND and Horace LUCKETT using ½a Lot #15 in Mdbg. Wit: Burr POWELL, Tasker C. QUINLAN.

3R:239 Date: 10 Jan 1829 RtCt: 12 Jan 1829
William D. TUCKER of Ldn to Alfred H. POWELL of Ldn. Trust for debt to Burr WEEKS using farm animals, farm and household items, crops. Delv. to WEEKS 3 Jul 1829.

3R:241 Date: 21 Jun 1828 RtCt: 13 Jan 1829
Edwin C. BROWN (trustee to pay legacies dev. by James BATTSON dec'd to Thomas BATTSON's children Nancy (of age), Mahaly, Elizabeth & James as they become of age) of Ldn to John MORAN (a cullerd freeman) of Ldn. B/S of 7a (from estate of George BARR dec'd) on Goose Creek adj Peter TAWPERMON, Edward WILSON. Delv. to MORAN 25 Aug 1830.

3R:242 Date: 21 Jun 1828 RtCt: 13 Jan 1829
Abner GIBSON (trustee to pay legacies dev. by James BATTSON dec'd to Thomas BATTSON's children Nancy (of age), Mahaly, Elizabeth & James as they become of age) of Ldn to John MORAN (a cullerd freeman) of Ldn. B/S of 4a adj Peter TAWPERMAN, Edward WILSON, road from Mdbg to Handy's Mill, John TAWPERMAN. Delv. to MORAN 25 Aug 1830.

3R:244 Date: 26 Dec 1828 RtCt: 29 Dec 1828
Mason MARKS & wife Hannah of Ldn to Thomas ROGERS of Ldn. Trust for debt to Saml. B. T. CALDWELL using 23a allotted Hannah in div. of Joseph DANIEL dec'd. Wit: Craven OSBURN, Thomas NICHOLS.

3R:247 Date: 18 Oct 1828 RtCt: 14 Nov 1828
Thomas CARR. Oath as Ensign in Va Militia.

3R:247 Date: 21 Oct 1828 RtCt: 14 Nov 1828
Gabril VANDENVA(N)TER. Oath as Lt. in Va Militia.

3R:248 Date: 27 Sep 1828 RtCt: 14 Nov 1828
William SHREVE. Oath as Captain of Infantry in Va Militia.

3R:248 Date: 4 Oct 1828 RtCt: 16 Nov 1828
Matthew ELGIN. Oath as Lt. in Va Militia.

3R:248 Date: 14 Oct 1828 RtCt: 9 Dec 1828
John MANN vs. John MOORE in chancery. Survey - MANN entitled to 27 4/7a in possession of MOORE. Gives plat. Divisors: Thomas J. MARLOW, Jacob EVERHART, John J. MATHIAS.

3R:250 Date: 12 Jan 1824 RtCt: 14 Jan 1824
Edmond LOVETT & wife Elizabeth of Ldn to Tow[n]shend McVEIGH of Ldn. Trust for debt to Stephen McPHERSON of Ldn using 156a (cnvy/b Benjamin BIRDSALL Mar 1805, DBk FF:242, less 1a cnvy to

George CARTER) on Goose Creek and Cotocton Mt. Wit: Saml. M. EDWARDS, E. G. HAMILTON, E. HAMMAT, John THOMAS.

3R:253 Date: 13 Jan 1829 RtCt: 15 Jan 1829
George W. HENRY & wife Dewaner B. of Ldn to Joshua PUSEY of Ldn. B/S of 103a (prch/o Jozabed WHITE May 1823) adj Mary FOX, Aaron BEANS, William SMITH, Matthew BEANS. Wit: Noble S. BRADEN, Saml. HOUGH. Delv. 26 Feb 1834.

3R:255 Date: 6 Dec 1828 RtCt: 16 Jan 1829
Yeoman Henry H. HUTCHISON & wife Susan of Ldn to Seth SMITH of Ldn. Trust for debt to William HOGE using 101a (cnvy/b Samuel DUNKIN May 1824). Wit: Francis W. LUCKETT, John W. GRAYSON. Delv. to Wm. HOGE Exor of his sister 9 Aug 1830.

3R:257 Date: 17 Jan 1829 RtCt: 17 Jan 1829
David WALTMAN of Ldn to Jacob WATERS of Ldn. B/S of 30a Lot #3 & 7a #5 in div. of John WALTMAN dec'd. adj Jacob WALTMAN, widow SMITH, Jacob EVERHART.

3R:259 Date: 20 Jan 1829 RtCt: 24 Jan 1829
Eli OFFUTT of Ffx to Samuel DAWSON of Ldn. Trust (for benefit of Sally RUST w/o Mandley T. and her children) using for old negro man Jacob and household items (prop. of Mandley T. RUST sold under execution on 11 Feb 1824, James SWARTS purchased negro man Jacob, William THRIFT purchased other articles and OFFUTT purchased from them).

3R:260 Date: 26 Jan 1829 RtCt: 29 Jan 1829
James McDANIEL & wife Anne of Ldn to H. B. POWELL of Ldn. Trust for debt to A. G. WATERMAN & Co. using ½a Lot #15 in Mdbg where McDANIEL resides; and household items, items in connection with boot & shoe establishment. Wit: J. B. BISCOE, Tasker C. QUINLAN, Abner GIBSON. Delv. to A. G. WATERMAN 20 Mar 1829.

3R:262 Date: 8 Jan 1829 RtCt: 29 Jan 1829
Charles DRISH & wife Susannah of Tuscallosa Co Alabama to John GRAY of Ldn. B/S of part of Lot #21 with 2 story brick house in Lsbg at Market & King Sts (cnvy/b John RIGOR Jul 1815), DBk SS:487) adj heirs of Wm. WRIGHT dec'd, James WOOD, Robt. MOFFETT, __ GLASSGOW. Wit: John R. DRISH, Joseph CALDWELL, George D. SHORTRIDGE.

3R:265 Date: 13 Mar 1824 RtCt: 29 Jan 1829
John DRISH & wife Eleanor of Ldn to Benjamin W. PERRY of Ldn. B/S of ¼a (½ of lot) on W side of King St in Lsbg (cnvy/b S. MULLEN Nov 1821, DBk EEE:344). Wit: Abiel JENNERS, Saml. M. EDWARDS.

3R:267 Date: 26 Jan 1829 RtCt: 28 Jan 1829
James McDANIEL of Ldn to H. B. POWELL of Ldn. Trust for debt to Oliver DENHAM using household items, cows and horse. Wit: Saml.

CAMPBELL, A. G. WATERMAN, J. B. BISCOE, William McDANIEL, Tasker C. QUINLAN. Delv. pr order 29 Dec 1829.

3R:268   Date: 28 Jan 1829   RtCt: 29 Jan 1829
James McDANIEL & wife Ann of Ldn to Alfred H. POWELL Jr. of Ldn. Trust for Burr WEEKS & Richard COCKRAN as endorsers on bank note, debt to Hiram McVEIGH using ½a Lot #15 in Mdbg. Wit: J. B. BISCOE, Tasker C. QUINLAN, Feilding LITTLETON.

3R:270   Date: 28 Jan 1829   RtCt: 29 Jan 1829
James McDANIEL & wife ___ of Ldn to George C. POWELL of Ldn. Trust for Lloyd NOLAND as endorser on bank note (for hire of negro girls Rose & Sidney for 1829) and as his security as constable using lot prch/o Edwin C. BROWN (already in trust to NOLAND and Horace LUCKETT).

3R:272   Date: 30 Jan 1829   RtCt: 2 Feb 1829
Ann McDANIEL (w/o James McDANIEL) by attorney A. H. POWELL Jr. of Ldn to Alfred H. POWELL Jr. of Ldn. Trust for above debts using her interest in house and lot in Mdbg in occupancy of her husband James.

3R:273   Date: 2 Feb 1829   RtCt: 2 Feb 1829
Thomas DORRELL of Ldn to James McILHANY. Trust for debt to John RAMSEY (for 12y hire as a laborer as wagganer on his farm), James DORRELL and William WRIGHT using farm animals, farm and household items.

3R:274   Date: 21 Jan 1829   RtCt: 2 Feb 1829
Thomas W. DORMAN & wife M. R. of Ldn to George C. POWELL. Trust for debt to Lloyd NOLAND using ½a Lot #59 in Mdbg and lot S of it. Wit: Burr POWELL, Tasker C. QUINLAN.

3R:276   Date: 24 Dec 1828   RtCt: 3 Feb 1829
Nicholas OSBURN of Ldn to Burr Wm. HARRISON of Ldn. Trust for debt to Lydia HEATON and Jonathan HEATON (Admrs of James HEATON dec'd) using negro men Dan, Uriah and Bill, girl Harriet some 16y old.

3R:278   Date: 4 Feb 1829   RtCt: 4 Feb 1829
Richard H. HENDERSON of Ldn (as Commr. in case of Armstead LONG Guardian of infant children of Thos. R. MOTT dec'd agst the children) to Samuel M. BOSS of Ldn. B/S of house and lot on Market St. in Lsbg adj BOSS. Delv. to BOSS 4 Jul 1830.

3R:278   Date: 5 Feb 1829   RtCt: 5 Feb 1829
Joel OSBURN Jr. to Mason OSBURN. B/S of interest in 18a of wheat on farm of Morris OSBURN occupied by Joel.

3R:279   Date: 23 Jan 1829   RtCt: 6 Feb 1829
Jacob WALTMAN of Ldn to John JANNEY of Ldn. Trust for debt to Nathan NEAR of Ldn using 109½a (cnvy/b John HAMILTON April 1819, DBk ZZ:263). Wit: Edward L. FANT, Alfred A. ESKRIDGE, Jas. HAMILTON.

3R:281   Date: 9 Feb 1829   RtCt: 9 Feb 1829
Wm. BEVERIDGE, Horace LUCKETT and Wm. K. ISH. Bond on BEVERIDGE as constable.

3R:282   Date: 10 Feb 1829   RtCt: 10 Feb 1829
Jas. B. BISCOE, Hamilton ROGERS, Asa ROGERS, Jas. SINCLAIR, Wm. K. ISH, Thomas ROGERS, Benj. MITCHELL, Wm. MERSHON. Bond on BISCOE as constable.

3R:282   Date: 2 Jun 1828   RtCt: 9 Feb 1829
Charles CRIM & wife Christiana of Harrison Co Ohio to Adam CRIM of Ldn. B/S of 1/12th share of dower of Catherine CRIM in estate of Charles CRIM dec'd. Wit: David RINGER, George ALLBAWGH.

3R:284   Date: 19 Jun 1828   RtCt: 9 Feb 1829
George LAFFERTY & wife Anna late BACCHUS of JeffVa and Jane POTTS of Ldn to David POTTS, Jonas POTTS and William POTTS of Ldn. Release of trust of Dec 1809. Delv. to David POTTS 13 Jul 1829.

3R:286   Date: 29 Dec 1828   RtCt: 9 Feb 1829
Yeoman Cyrus BURSON & wife Phebe of Ldn to carpenter Thomas M. HUMPHREY of Ldn. B/S of 29a (interest in dower land of Mary wd/o Jesse HUMPHREY dec'd, cnvy/b Mary and present husband Samuel PEUGH, DBk NNN:134). Wit: Benjamin GRAYSON, John W. GRAYSON.

3R:287   Date: __ Jan 1829   RtCt: 9 Feb 1829
Ludwell LEE Esqr. of Ldn to Wilson C. SELDON Jr. of Ldn. B/S of 2¼a on Potomac adj LEE's dau. Eliza. Wit: J. R. BUSSARD, Fountaine ALEXANDER, Edw'd. E. COOKE.

3R:289   Date: 29 Feb 1828   RtCt: 9 Feb 1829
George MARKS & wife Mahala of Ldn to Joshua GREGG & Joshua PANCOAST of Ldn. Trust for debt to Benj. JACKSON of Ldn using 142a adj __ McPHERSON, __ HAW. Wit: Notley C. WILLIAMS, Thomas NICHOLS.

3R:291   Date: 9 Oct 1828   RtCt: 9 Feb 1829
Nathan NEER & wife Eliza of Ldn to Ezekiel POTTS and Edward POTTS of Ldn. B/S of 1/5th interest in 185a of Eliza's father Jonas POTTS dec'd, adj David POTTS, Wm. POTTS. Wit: John WHITE, Craven OSBURN. Delv. to Ezekiel & Edward 3 Mar 1834.

3R:293   Date: 15 Mar 1827   RtCt: 9 Feb 1829
Alexander S. TIDBALL and Francis STRIBLING & wife Cecelia of FredVa to Alice WHITACRE of Ldn. B/S of 173a (from 672a inherited by Cecelia from father James McILHANY dec'd, in trust of Apr 1821 to TIDBALL from STRIBLING who failed to pay) adj __ BRADFIELD.

3R:295   Date: 1 Dec 1828   RtCt: 9 Feb 1829
George SYPHERD & wife Sarah of Ldn to Joseph WALTMAN of Ldn. B/S of 18a (Lot #6 in 'lower place' from estate of John

SANBOWER dec'd) in German Settlement adj John WENNER, Michael SANBOWER; and 3a timber Lot #1. Wit: Saml. HOUGH, Geo. W. SHAWEN.

3R:297   Date: 9 Feb 1829   RtCt: 9 Feb 1829
Carpenter Thomas M. HUMPHREY of Ldn to Timothy TAYLOR Jr. of Ldn. Trust for debt to William BOLEN (of Edward) of Ldn using interest in dower of widow Mary in estate of Jesse HUMPHREY dec'd (cnvy/b Mary and present husband Samuel PEUGH to Cyrus BURSON, DBk NNN:134, who cnvy/t HUMPHREY Dec 1828). Delv. to BOLEN 17 Oct 1829.

3R:298   Date: 29 Dec 1828   RtCt: 9 Feb 1829
Blacksmith Elijah FARR & wife Sarah of Ldn to carpenter Thomas M. HUMPHREY of Ldn. B/S of 4a Lot #3 in div. of Jesse HUMPHREY dec'd (allotted to Rachel, d/o Jesse now w/o William FARR who cnvy/t Elijah). Wit: Ben. GRAYSON, John W. GRAYSON.

3R:300   Date: 9 Mar 1829   RtCt: 9 Mar 1829
Enos NICHOLS. Oath as Lt. in troop of Cavelry of Va Militia.

3R:300   Date: 25 Feb 1829   RtCt: 9 Mar 1829
James H. McVEIGH. Oath as Captain in 132nd Reg 6th Brig 2nd Div of Va Militia.

3R:300   Date: 9 Mar 1829   RtCt: 9 Mar 1829
William B. HARRISON, Horace LUCKETT, Robert MOFFETT, Benj'a SHREVE Jr., William MERSHON, Asa ROGERS, Thomas B. MERSHON, Saml. HAMMETT, Feilding LITTLETON, Geo. M. CHICHESTER & Hugh ROGERS. Bond on HARRISON as sheriff to collect officers fees.

3R:302   Date: 9 Mar 1829   RtCt: 9 Mar 1829
William B. HARRISON, Horace LUCKETT, Robert MOFFETT, Benj'a SHREVE Jr., William MERSHON, Asa ROGERS, Thomas B. MERSHON, Saml. Hammett, Feilding LITTLETON, Geo. M. CHICHESTER & Hugh ROGERS. Bond on HARRISON as sheriff to collect levies and poor rate.

3R:303   Date: 9 Mar 1829   RtCt: 9 Mar 1829
William B. HARRISON, Horace LUCKETT, Robert MOFFETT, Benj'a SHREVE Jr., William MERSHON, Asa ROGERS, Thomas B. MERSHON, Saml. HAMMETT, Feilding LITTLETON, Geo. M. CHICHESTER & Hugh ROGERS. Bond on HARRISON as sheriff to collect taxes.

3R:304   Date: 4 Feb 1829   RtCt: 14 Feb 1829
Elizabeth CLAPHAM of Ldn to Thomas C. DUVALL of Ldn. B/S of several tracts totaling 169a on Goose Creek with water grist, merchant and saw mill (cnvy to Samuel CLAPHAM Aug 1821, DBk DDD:087). Wit: Saml. DAWSON, Saml. M. EDWARDS. Delv. to DUVALL 15 May 1829.

3R:306   Date: 13 Feb 1829   RtCt: 16 Feb 1829
Isaac NICHOLS Jr. and James HOGUE to Benjamin GRAYSON. Release of trust of Apr 1822 for debt to Isaac and Samuel NICHOLS on farm of 200a nr Bloomfield and 50a wood lot.

3R:308   Date: 16 Feb 1829   RtCt: 17 Feb 1829
Mesheck LACEY of Mdbg to A. G. WATERMAN of Mdbg. Trust for debt to Burr WEEKS & Co. using house & lot in Mdbg occupied by LACEY as dwelling and WEEKS as store house. Delv. pr order 2 May 1829.

3R:309   Date: 24 Feb 1829   RtCt: 24 Feb 1829
Thomas FOUCH (insolvent debtor) to Sheriff Charles LEWIS. B/S of 184a from will of Thomas FOUCH dec'd and 1/3 of crop on farm.

3R:310   Date: 24 Feb 1829   RtCt: 24 Feb 1829
Joseph CANBY of Ldn to Mary HUGHES of Ldn. Marriage contract – 150a nr Cotocton mt, farm animals, farm and household items, notes, bonds put in trust with Thomas HUGHES.

3R:313   Date: 5 Feb 1829   RtCt: 24 Feb 1829
Thomas J. HARRISON (officer in U.S. Army) & wife Rebecca T. of Ldn to Peter OYTCHER of Ldn. B/S of 200a (interest in estate of Matthew HARRISON dec'd) on Goose Creek adj OYTCHER, heirs of Thomas R. MOTT, John M. HARRISON, mill lot. Wit: John BAILEY, Wilson C. SELDEN. Delv. to Jno. WILSON Exor of Peter OATYER 24 Mar 1835.

3R:315   Date: 23 Feb 1829   RtCt: 24 Feb 1829
Joseph LUKE & wife Elizabeth of Ldn to Benjamin F. TAYLOR of Ldn. B/S of 2a (part of land inherited by Thomas CLOWES where LUKE now resides) adj Lsbg road, Constantine HUGHES, Joshua GORE, Thomas HUGHES. Wit: Saml. M. EDWARDS, Presley CORDELL.

3R:316   Date: 10 May 1827   RtCt: 2 Dec 1829
John DRISH & wife Nelly of Ldn to John GRAY of Ldn. B/S of 14a (cnvy/b Jas. H. HAMILTON Mar 1825, DBk JJJ:323). Wit: Jno. A. BINNS, Jno. STEPHENSON, Wilson J. DRISH.

3R:318   Date: 20 Sep 1828   RtCt: 27 Feb 1829
Thomas PHILIPS & wife Rachel and Thomas PHILIPS & Joseph BOND (Exors of Asa MOORE dec'd) of Ldn to Burr Washington McKIM of Ldn. B/S of 2a (2 moieties from suit of Thomas PHILIPS agst Wm. STEER, Jul 1824, DBk HHH:276) adj lots from div. of John HOUGH dec'd. Wit: Noble S. BRADEN, Saml. HOUGH. Delv. to McKIM 29 Jul 1831.

3R:320   Date: 21 Jan 1829   RtCt: 28 Feb 1829
Lloyd NOLAND of Fqr to Thomas W. DORMAN of Mdbg. B/S of ½a Lot #59 in Mdbg and lot S of Lot #59. Delv. to DORMAN 29 Sep 1831.

3R:321   Date: 2 Mar 1829   RtCt: 2 Mar 1829
Conrad BITZER and John A. BINNS to Enos GARRETT. Release of trust for debt to Conrad BITZER.

3R:321   Date: 1 Nov 1828   RtCt: 3 Mar 1829
Joseph WALTMAN of Ldn to Thomas BUCKINGHAM of Ldn. B/S of 1a in German Settlement adj road to Berlin ferry, Jonathan WENNER. Delv. to W. WENNER pr order 22 Mar 1839.

3R:324   Date: 4 Mar 1829   RtCt: 5 Mar 1829
Ann H. PEERS and Eleanor PEERS of Lsbg to Rich'd H. HENDERSON of Lsbg. Trust for debt to Charles BENNETT of AlexDC using house & lot on Market St in Lsbg now occupied by Eleanor.

3R:325   Date: 10 Dec 1828   RtCt: 6 Mar 1829
James McILHANY of Ldn to John HAMILTON of Ldn. B/S of 2 lots (from trust of Andrew OGDEN, Nov 1827, DBk PPP:257, OGDON prch/o John JANNEY, Mar 1822, DBk EEE:073)

3R:325   Date: 14 Feb 1829   RtCt: 6 Mar 1829
Samuel JACKSON & wife Lavinia/Levinia of Ldn to William H. STONE of Ldn. Trust for debt to Israel T. GRIFFITH of Ldn using of lot in Wtfd (prch/o Samuel GOVER Sep 1820) adj Samuel GOVER, __ BRADEN, __ WHITE. Wit: Noble S. BRADEN, Geo. W. SHAWEN. Delv. pr order 22 Apr 1835.

3R:328   Date: 7 Feb 1829   RtCt: __ Feb 1829
George COOPER of Ldn to Robert MOFFETT of Ldn. Trust for debt to Samuel M. EDWARDS using part of estate of Cooper ECKART dec'd nr New Valley Meeting house. Wit: Alfred A. ESKRIDGE, E. FANT.

3R:329   Date: 7 Mar 1829   RtCt: 7 Mar 1829
Robert WADE Sr. of Ldn to John WADE of Ldn. B/S of 60a adj Robert, reps of Thomas CARR dec'd, William CARR, John CARR, David MARTIN; and 15-20a wooded lot between 'Ink's? field' and 'schoolhouse field'. Delv. to Jno. WADE 8 Dec 1829.

3R:330   Date: 7 Mar 1829   RtCt: 7 Mar 1829
John WADE of Ldn to Robert WADE Sr. of Ldn. B/S of above lot.

3R:330   Date: 7 Mar 1829   RtCt: 7 Mar 1829
Charles L. GARDNER & wife Elizabeth of Ldn to William L. SIMPSON of Ldn. B/S of 110a (1/7th share of Elizabeth from prop. of father Josiah MOFFETT dec'd) on Secolin run adj John LITTLETON, Thomas R. MOTT dec'd, Peter OAYTER commonly called Peter ATCHER. Wit: Saml. M. EDWARDS, John H. McCABE. Delv. to SIMPSON 9 Oct 1829.

3R:332   Date: 6 Mar 1819   RtCt: 17 Feb 1829
Strother M. HELM & wife Mary Ann of AlexDC to George BAYLY of FredVa. B/S of 40a (cnvy/b Stephen BEARD Oct 1816) adj George LEWIS, Matthew HARRISON; and 200a adj James TURLEY. Wit:

Jonah THOMPSON, A. FAW. Suit in Winchester Dec 1828 of BAILEY vs. HELM, refers to 2nd deed of 14 Mar 1823. Delv. to Robt. BAILY pr order 7 Aug 1830.

3R:336 Date: 14 Mar 1819 RtCt: 17 Feb 1829
Strother M. HELM & wife Mary Ann of AlexDC to George BAYLY of FredVa. B/S of 20a (cnvy/b Nathaniel POLIN) adj Mrs. REDMAN. Wit: William DOOLEY, A. D. BAWCUTT. Delv. to Robt. BAILY 7 Aug 1830.

3R:338 Date: 4 Sep 1828 RtCt: 9 Mar 1829
Dean JAMES of Ldn to John JAMES of Ldn. B/S of 101½a on Elk Licking run (cnvy/b Henry ASBURY). Wit: Thos. B. MERSHON, Bailys S. FOLEY, Arthur ORRISON.

3R:339 Date: 4 Sep 1828 RtCt: 9 Mar 1829
John JAMES of Ldn to Dean JAMES of Ldn. B/S of interest from div. of Wm. JAMES dec'd to son Wm. JAMES who has since div. also died; and interest in dower of mother Abigail JAMES where she now lives; and 51a to John from div. of father Wm. JAMES dec'd; and by request of Nancy JAMES her interest in 61a (from father Wm. JAMES dec'd) cnvy in trust by her & Smith JAMES to Dean & John JAMES Feb 1825; and Nancy's interest from brother Wm. JAMES dec'd from div. of father and her interest in mother's dower. Wit: Bailess S. FOLEY, Arthur ORRISON, Thos. B. MURSHON.

3R:341 Date: 19 Aug 1828 RtCt: 9 Mar 1829
Cuthbert POWELL to Josiah MURRAY of Fqr. B/S of 230a in Manor of Leeds on Blue Ridge adj Danl. THOMPSON (from trust of Nov 1823 from Elijah GLASSCOCK for debt to Joseph CARR). Wit: Charles L. POWELL, William RUST, Alfred RUST.

3R:342 Date: 29 Jan 1829 RtCt: 9 Mar 1829
Thomas WOOD & wife Eliza late SULLIVAN of Md and John C. SULLIVAN & wife Catherine of Fqr to John J. CURRELL of Ldn (paid to Luther O. SULLIVAN of Fqr. B/S of 233a (cnvy to Owen SULLIVAN by Solomon BETTON Jun 1819, DBk MM:241). Wit: Jas. NAYLOR, Henry McPHERSON.

3R:345 Date: 1 Jan 1828 RtCt: 9 Mar 1829
Dpty Thomas ROGERS for Sheriff Charles LEWIS to John JANNEY. B/S of two ¼a lots in Lovettsville (from insolvent debtor Alexander CORDELL in 1827, cnvy/b David LOVETT). Wit: David MILLER.

3R:346 Date: 6 Mar 1829 RtCt: 9 Mar 1829
Enos GARROTT & wife Nelly of Ldn to John BRADEN and Isaac E. STEAR of Ldn. Trust for debt to John WORSLEY of Ldn using 135a adj James GREENLEASE, Richard TAVENOR; and adj 11a lot. Wit: John H. McCABE, Presley CORDELL. Delv. to WORSLEY 19 Mar 1830.

3R:348   Date: 30 Sep 1828   RtCt: 9 Mar 1829
Yardley TAYLOR & wife Hannah of Ldn to Harvey HAMILTON of
Ldn. B/S of 37a on NW fork of Goose Creek adj David F. BEALL,
Isaac NICHOLS. Wit: Notley C. WILLIAMS, Thomas NICHOLS.
Delv. to HAMILTON 27 Jul 1831.

3R:351   Date: 23 Oct 1827   RtCt: 9 Mar 1829
Isaac HOUGH of Cincinnati Ohio to Samuel HOUGH of Ldn. B/S of
25a (prch/o Peter SANDERS) on E side of short hill.

3R:352   Date: 24 Nov 1828   RtCt: 9 Mar 1829
Michael COOPER & wife Hannah of Ldn to Isaac E. STEER (trustee
of Joshua PUSEY, Thomas WHITE guardian for his children, Sarah
NIXON guardian for her son James William NIXON, Abraham
SMITH who married with Mary NIXON dau of Sarah NIXON and
Samuel NIXON – reps of James NIXON dec'd). Trust for debts to
Joshua PUSEY, Thomas WHITE guardian, Sarah NIXON guardian
and Abraham SMITH using 114½a (prch/o Abiel JENNERS) adj
John WILLIAMS, William VIRTZ, road to Manning's mill. Wit: Noble
S. BRADEN, Saml. HOUGH. Delv. to PUSEY pr order 14 Aug 1829.

3R:355   Date: 1 Jan 1829   RtCt: 9 Mar 1829
John G. HUMPHREY of Ldn. DoE for negro woman Winney age
39y, and her daughter Rebecca age abt 2y (allotted in div. of estate
of Abner HUMPHREY dec'd).

3R:356   Date: 24 Feb 1829   RtCt: 9 Mar 1829
Michael HICKMAN & wife Catherine of Ldn to Jacob SHUMAKER of
Ldn. B/S of 30a part of Lot #7 in div. of Peter HICKMAN allotted to
Catherine BEAMER and exchanged with HICKMAN for Lot #2. Wit:
Geo. W. SHAWEN, Mor. McILHANY. Delv. to SHOEMAKER 23 Sep
1839.

3R:359   Date: 7 Mar 1829   RtCt: 9 Mar 1829
Miller HOGUE & wife Tacy of Ldn to James B. WILSON of Ldn. B/S
of 26¼a adj Dennis McCARTY, Moses WILSON, John RUSSEL,
road to Handy's Mill. Wit: Abner GIBSON, Tasker C. QUINLAN.
Delv. to WILSON 30 May 1831.

3R:360   Date: 7 Mar 1829   RtCt: 9 Mar 1829
Joseph WALTMAN of Ldn to Joseph EVERHART (Admr of Jacob
EVERHART dec'd) of Ldn. B/S of 132a (sold to WALTMAN by Exors
of Emanuel WALTMAN dec'd, prch by EVERHART while alive but
no deed executed) adj Jacob WALTMAN, John EVERHART, Joseph
EVERHART. Delv. to Jos. EVERHEART 28 Jun 1829.

3R:362   Date: 7 Mar 1829   RtCt: 9 Mar 1829
Joseph WALTMAN of Ldn to Joseph EVERHART of Ldn. B/S of 41a
(part of tract cnvy/b Admrs of Emanuel WALTMAN dec'd) adj Jacob
WALTMAN, Jacob EVERHART, David WALTMAN. Delv. to
EVERHEART 25 Jun 1829.

3R:364   Date: 29 Nov 1828   RtCt: 9 Mar 1829
Abel JANNEY & wife Lydia of Ldn to Benjamin RUST of Ldn. B/S of
155a on Beaverdam adj __ GIBSON, __ CARR, __ VERNON, __
CARTER. Wit: Notley C. WILLIAMS, Thomas NICHOLS. Delv. pr
order 11 Mar 1850.

3R:366   Date: 1 Jul 1828   RtCt: 9 Mar 1829
Harvey HAMILTON & wife Lucina of Ldn to Abel JANNEY of Ldn.
Trust for debt to Bernard TAYLOR using 37a on NW fork of Goose
Creek adj David F. BEALL, John HOLMES, Isaac NICHOLS. Wit:
Tho. NICHOLS, Notley C. WILLIAMS. Delv. Jesse HIRST pr order
26 Mar 1831.

3R:369   Date: 23 Feb 1829   RtCt: 9 Mar 1829
William PAXSON & wife Jane of Ldn to Henry RUSSELL of Ldn. B/S
of 95a (prch/o heirs of Wm. HIXSON dec'd) adj Isaac WALKER, Jno.
JANNEY, Cotocton Creek, Jno. HOUGH dec'd, John SCHOOLEY;
except 2½a unclaimed by Matthew PAXSON s/o Wm. dec'd. Wit:
Noble S. BRADEN, S. HOUGH. Delv. to RUSSELL 23 May 1829.

3R:371   Date: 15 Oct 1828   RtCt: 9 Mar 1829
Yeoman William R. COMBS & wife Sarah of StafVa to Mahlon
FULTON of Ldn. B/S of 1¾a in Bloomfield adj John RALPH, David
THARP, William SUMMERS, Jacob DRAKE. Delv. pr order 11 May
1828.

3R:373   Date: 17 Feb 1829 RtCt: 10 Mar 1829
John J. CURRELL & wife Permealia/Pammelia of Ldn to Humphrey
B. POWELL. Trust for debt to Luther O. SULLIVAN using 233a
(cnvy/b reps. of Owen SULLIVAN dec'd Dec 1828). Wit: Burr
POWELL, A. GIBSON.

3R:375   Date: 17 Feb 1829   RtCt: 10 Mar 1829
Jesse P. HATCH & wife Jane of Windsor Co Vermont to Hamilton
ROGERS of Ldn. B/S of 116¼a allotted in div. of Wm. HAWLING
dec'd.

3R:377   Date: 27 Feb 1827   RtCt: 10 Mar 1829
John B. PATTERSON to Obid WAITE. Trust for debt to W. G.
SINGLETON using household items. Delv. to WAITE 16 Jun 1829.

3R:379   Date: 4 Aug 1828   RtCt: 11 Mar 1829
Casper EVERHART & wife Mary of Ldn to William WERTZ/WIRTZ
Jr. of Ldn. B/S of __a (prch/o John MATHIAS Apr 1818) adj __
EVANS, Michael EVERHART, __ STUBBLEFIELD. Wit: Ebenezer
GRUBB, John WHITE. Delv. to WERTS 4 Apr 1832.

3R:381   Date: 6 Jan 1828   RtCt: 11 Mar 1829
John HAMILTON of Ldn to dau Dewanner B. HENRY of Ldn. B/S of
3/7th of 210a Taylor Town farm and 3/7th of mill and other buildings.
Delv. to G. W. HENRY 6 Nov 1833.

3R:382   Date: 12 Feb 1829   RtCt: 11 Mar 1829
William H. HOUGH of Ldn to John HAMILTON of Ldn. Release of trust of Mar 1823 for debt to Mary TAYLOR.

3R:384   Date: 26 Nov 1829 [28]   RtCt: 11 Mar 1829
Samuel HIXSON of Ldn to Andrew S. ANDERSON. BoS for slaves for life Forester & Kitty and their 6 children Helen, Henry, Byas, Margaret, Harriet & Emma. Wit: D. SHAWEN, David JACKSON, Z. DULANEY.

3R:385   Date: 29 Jan 1829   RtCt: 11 Mar 1829
Burr POWELL of Ldn to Jeremiah W. BRONAUGH of Georgetown DC. Release of trust of Sep 1817 for debt to Jas. JOHNSTON & Hugh JOHNSTON (now dec'd).

3R:387   Date: 9 Apr 1821   RtCt: 12 Mar 1829
William LINE/LYNE of Ldn to Jacob SUMMERS of Ldn. B/S of interest in 196a of Thomas ODEN dec'd (also allotted to widow). Wit: R. H. HENDERSON, John DULIN, Wm. L. TIMMS.

3R:387   Date: 9 Mar 1829   RtCt: 13 Mar 1829
George W. HENRY & wife Dewanner B. of Ldn to William H. GRAY of Ldn. Trust for debt to John GRAY using 3/7th of 210a Taylor Town farm and 3/7th mill and other buildings. Wit: S. HOUGH, Noble S. BRADEN.

3R:390   Date: 9 Jan 1829   RtCt: 12 Jan 1829
Mesheck LACEY of Ldn to Hugh SMITH of Ldn. Trust for Samuel CHINN as security on bonds using two lots (1a) in Mdbg occupied by LACEY as dwelling and hatters shop and negro woman Rachel, man Peter with wife Charlotte & their 4 children Emily, Francis & 2 younger children. Wit: James TILLETT, Jas. McDANIEL, Benj. SMITH. Delv. to CHINN 30 Aug 1836.

3R:392   Date: 16 Feb 1829   RtCt: 14 Mar 1829
Moses BROWN & wife Nancy of Ldn to Price JACOBS of Ldn. B/S of 4a on Beaverdam where BROWN resides. Wit: Notley C. WILLIAMS, Edward HALL.

3R:393   Date: 16 Mar 1829   RtCt: 19 Mar 1829
George W. HENRY & wife Dewanna B. of Ldn to Alfred A. ESKRIDGE of Ldn. Trust for Charles B. HAMILTON as security on debt to Daniel WINE for bank note using undivided 3/7th of real estate of Henry TAYLOR dec'd on Kittocton Creek with mills. Wit: Saml. HOUGH, Noble S. BRADEN.

3R:395   Date: 16 Mar 1829   RtCt: 19 Mar 1829
Charles B. HAMILTON and John HAMILTON to George W. HENRY. Release of trust to William M. JENNERS for Charles B. & John HAMILTON as security on debt to Daniel WINE using 103a.

3R:397   Date: 19 Mar 1829   RtCt: 19 Mar 1829
Joseph TAYLOR & wife Lydia of Ldn to Elijah JAMES of Ldn. B/S of 93a (prch/o heirs of Thomas HUGHES) on Kittocton Creek adj

James LOVE, __ POULSON, Samuel BEAN, mill. Wit: W. C. SELDEN, Saml. M. EDWARDS.

3R:399   Date: 19 Mar 1829   RtCt: 19 Mar 1829
Fielding BROWN of Ldn to James L. HAMILTON of Ldn. Trust for debt to Benjamin BROWN using farm and household items, family bible. Delv. to HAMILTON 24 Feb 1832.

3R:400   Date: 20 Mar 1829   RtCt: 20 Mar 1829
Sarah CHAMBLIN w/o Norval CHAMBLIN. Relinquishment of dower [for deed of 11 Nov 1826, DBk 3M:239, to Israel Thompson GRIFFITH]. Delv. to HAMILTON 30 sep 1830, filed 3S:035.

3R:401   Date: 20 Mar 1829   RtCt: 20 Mar 1829
Sarah W. T. CHAMBLIN w/o Norval CHAMBLIN. Relinquishment of dower [for deed of 28 Jan 1825, DBk 3I:359, to Price JACOBS].

3R:402   Date: 18 Mar 1829   RtCt: 23 Mar 1829
Samuel CHINN & wife Emily of Ldn to Daniel JANNEY & Hugh SMITH of Ldn. Trust for debt to William HOGUE of Ldn using 355a where CHINN resides adj H. B. POWELL, Noble BEVERIDGE, Philip FREY, Phebe SKINNER, Elizabeth WILSON. Wit: Burr POWELL, A. GIBSON. Delv. to HOGE 4 Aug 1829.

3R:404   Date: 17 Dec 1828   RtCt: 26 Mar 1829
George MILLER & wife Elizabeth of Ldn to William HOEY and James HOEY of Ldn. B/S of four ¼a Lots #9, #10, #11 & #12 in German Settlement now Lovettsville on Lovetts farm. Wit: Samuel DAWSON, Geo. W. SHAWEN. Delv. to Wm. HOY 27 Sep 1832.

3R:407   Date: 10 Dec 1828   RtCt: 26 Mar 1829
James McILHANY to Wayne McKIMMIE, Mary McKIMMIE lately married with Geo. HAMMOND, Henry ADAMS & wife Priscilla. Release of trust of Dec 1824 for debt to Elijah PEACOCK.

3R:408   Date: 19 Mar 1829   RtCt: 27 Mar 1829
Philip FRY of Ldn to Michael FRYE of Ldn. B/S (with natural love) of 112½a where Michael lives (cnvy/b Joseph LEWIS Jr. Sept 1806, DBk GG:493) adj John JACKSON, George COOPER, __ JANNEY; and 30a (cnvy/b John JANNEY Exor of Jos. JANNEY dec'd and Amos JANNEY Admr. of Abel JANNEY dec'd Dec 1803, DBk RR:422) on E side of short hill adj Amos JANNEY.

3R:410   Date: 10 Dec 1828   RtCt: 27 Mar 1829
William PAXSON & wife Jane of Ldn to John SCHOOLEY of Ldn. B/S of 2a on Catocton Creek adj Henry RUSSEL, Andrew OGDEN. Gives small plat. Wit: Noble S. BRADEN, Saml. HOUGH. Delv. to SCHOOLEY 16 Mar 1837.

3R:412   Date: 17 Mar 1829   RtCt: 28 Mar 1829
Benedict PADGETT & wife Eleanor of Ldn to Richard H. HENDERSON of Ldn. Trust for debt to Thornton WALKER using lot in Union (cnvy Mar 1828). Wit: Edward HALL, Francis W. LUCKETT.

3R:414 Date: 16 Mar 1829 RtCt: 28 Mar 1829
Thornton WALKER & wife Fanny of Ldn to Benedict PADGETT of Ldn. B/S of house and lot in Union (cnvy/b Craven WALKER Apr 1824). Wit: Edward HALL, Francis W. LUCKETT.

3R:416 Date: 27 Mar 1829 RtCt: 30 Mar 1829
Noble S. BRADEN (Exor of Robert BRADEN dec'd) of Ldn to David CONARD of Ldn. B/S of brick store house and lot in Wtfd (prch/o trustees of Margaret HIXSON dec'd). Wit: Geo. W. HENRY, H. DORSEY, Wm. NETTLE. Delv. pr order filed DBk HHH:082, 25 Nov 1829.

3R:417 Date: 13 Mar 1829 RtCt: 1 Apr 1829
William CRUIT & wife Hannah of Ldn to Andrew S. ANDERSON of Ldn. B/S of 2a in Wtfd at Mahlon St adj Robert BRADEN. Wit: Noble S. BRADEN, Saml. HOUGH. Delv. to ANDERSON 21 Apr 1831.

3R:419 Date: 1 Apr 1829 RtCt: 2 Apr 1829
David YOUNG of Ldn and James HATCHER of Fqr (Exors of James HATCHER dec'd) to Swithin NICHOLS of Ldn. B/S of 212a on NW fork of Goose Creek adj Edith HATCHER, George GRIMES, William NICHOLS, heirs of Samuel HATCHER, Jesse HIRST. Wit: William GIBSON, Thomas S. NICHOLS, Edith HATCHER. Delv. to Geo. McMULLEN pr order filed DBk 4M:046, 22 Mar 1854.

3R:421 Date: 10 Feb 1829 RtCt: 2 Apr 1829
Joseph H. WRIGHT (s/o Patterson WRIGHT dec'd) & wife Mary of Ldn to William WRIGHT of Ldn. B/S of 1/8th of 196a where Patterson dec'd resided; and 1/8th of house & lot in Wtfd adj Israel T. GRIFFITH; and 1/8th of ¾a in Wtfd adj P. McGAVACK; all subject to life estate of widow Nancy WRIGHT. Wit: N. S. BRADEN, S. HOUGH. Delv. to Wm. WRIGHT 24 Sep 1844.

3R:423 Date: 3 Apr 1829 RtCt: 3 Apr 1829
Henry GOODH(E)ART (insolvent debtor) to Sheriff William B. HARRISON. B/S of interest in estate of Daniel STONEBURNER dec'd by marriage with heir Elizabeth (none since he surrendered it to Admr Henry STONEBURNER for debt to estate) (capias ad satisfaciendum by Jonathan WENNER ass'ee of Chas. G. EDWARDS).

3R:424 Date: 4 Apr 1829 RtCt: 6 Apr 1829
Nathan GREGG Sr. and Stephen GREGG (Exors of Thomas GREGG dec'd) of Ldn to James McILHANY of Ldn. B/S of 339a (prch/o James McILHANY Sr. dec'd by Stephen GREGG Sr. f/o Stephen, Nov 1795).

3R:426 Date: 15 Jan 1829 RtCt: 11 Apr 1829
Nathan GREGG of Ldn to George McPHERSON & wife Priscilla of Ldn. B/S of 3a (from tract prch/o Nathaniel MANNING Feb 1824, DBk HHH:019) adj Andrew THOMPSON. Wit: Saml. M. EDWARDS, Presley CORDELL. Delv. to McPHERSON 9 Aug 1830.

3R:428   Date: 31 Jan 1829   RtCt: 11 Apr 1829
Thomas PHILIPS & wife Rachel and Joseph BOND & Thomas
PHILLIPS (Exors of Asa MOORE dec'd) of Ldn to John WOLFORD
of Ldn. B/S of 52a adj __ McILHANY, Mrs. PARKER, John WINE.
Wit: Noble S. BRADEN, Saml. HOUGH. Delv. to WOLFORD 10 Jun
1844.

3R:430   Date: 14 Apr 1829   RtCt: 13 [?] Apr 1829
Thomas POULTON, Thomas MORRIS and Jas. McILHANY. Bond
on POULTON as constable.

3R:431   Date: 12 Mar 1829   RtCt: 12 Mar 1829
Daniel MAGINNIS of Ldn to Archibald MAINS of Ldn. Trust for debt
to Asa CAMPBELL of Ldn using farm animals. Delv. to CAMPBELL
24 Dec 1829.

3R:432   Date: 19 Mar 1829   RtCt: 19 Mar 1829
Elijah JAMES & wife Sarah of Ldn to Valentine V. PURCEL and
Townsend HEATON of Ldn. Trust for debt to Joseph TAYLOR using
93a (prch/o Joseph TAYLOR) on Kittocton Creek adj James LOVE,
__ POULSON, Samuel BEANS, mill. Wit: W. C. SELDEN, Saml. M.
EDWARDS. Delv. to TAYLOR 12 Sep 1831.

3R:436   Date: 26 Mar 1829   RtCt: 30 Mar 1829
John RYAN to John A. BINNS. Trust for debt to Michael
MORALLEE using household items. Delv. pr order 3 Dec 1834.

3R:438   Date: 1 Nov 1828   RtCt: ___
William McCOY of Ldn to John SHAW of Ldn. Trust for debt to Wm.
W. KITZMILLER of Ldn using household items.

3R:440   Date: 21 Apr 1829   RtCt: 6 May 1829
Joshua SINGLETON & wife Nancy W. of Ldn to Robert SINGLETON
of Ldn. B/S of 339a (cnvy/b Robert SCOTT to Samuel
SINGLETON); and __a (cnvy/b Thomas TRIPLETT to Samuel
SINGLETON); and __a (cnvy/b Enoch TRIPLETT to Samuel
SINGLETON; and 1/7th of personal prop. including slaves of Samuel
SINGLETON dec'd. Wit: Burr POWELL, Abner GIBSON. Delv. to
Noble BEVERIDGE by direction of Lloyd NOLAND per letter filed 7
Apr 1841.

3R:442   Date: 24 Mar 1829   RtCt: 13 Apr 1829
Thomas J. NOLAND & wife Sarah of Ldn to Elizabeth M. NOLAND
of Ldn. B/S of 76a Lot #2 allotted to Sarah then MYERS in div. of
estate of Thomas CHINN dec'd. Wit: Burr POWELL, Abner GIBSON.

3R:444   Date: 3 Mar 1829   RtCt: 13 Apr 1829
Jacob COMPHER of Ldn to Jonas P. SCHOOLEY of Ldn. Trust for
debt to Samuel STOUTSENBERGER using 1¾a (cnvy/b Jno.
STOUTSENBERGER) where George ROW resides adj John
STOUTSENBERGER, John HAMILTON. Wit: Asa ROGERS, John
STOUTSENBERGER, George ROW, Thomas MARLOW, Jacob
STOUTSENBERGER.

3R:447   Date: 28 Mar 1829   RtCt: 13 Apr 1829
Samuel BROWN & wife Nancy of Ldn to George W. SAGER of Ldn.
B/S of interest in land of James CARTER dec'd. Wit: Burr POWELL,
A. GIBSON.

3R:448   Date: 13 Apr 1829   RtCt: 13 Apr 1829
Alfred SHIELDS of Ldn to Charles B. HAMILTON of Ldn. BoS for
household items.

3R:449   Date: 28 Mar 1829   RtCt: 13 Apr 1829
Mahlon CRAVEN to Samuel BROWN. Release of trust of Sep 1828
using Sarah's interest in father James CARTER's estate.

3R:451   Date: 13 Mar 1829   RtCt: 13 Apr 1829
Yardley TAYLOR and William BROWN (Exors of Samuel BROWN
dec'd) of Ldn to Betsey BROWN of Ldn. B/S of 120a (from will of
Richard BROWN dec'd to son Samuel) and Nathan GREGG,
George WARNER, William BROWN Sr., heirs of Israel PANCOAST.
Delv. to Betsey BROWN 20 Oct 1836.

3R:453   Date: 1 Apr 1829   RtCt: 13 Apr 1829
Joseph BOND & Jesse GOVER of Ldn to Isaac WALKER of Ldn.
Release of trust of Apr 1826 for debt to Thomas PHILLIPS Exor of
James MOORE dec'd on 185a.

3R:456   Date: 7 Jan 1829   RtCt: 13 Apr 1829
Noble S. BRADEN (Exor of Robert BRADEN dec'd) of Ldn to
Joseph MILLER of Ldn. B/S of 90a with L/L adj David AXLINE; and
25a 'vacant land' adj Edward JENNINGS.

3R:458   Date: __ 1829   RtCt: 13 Apr 1829
Daniel WENNER of Ldn to John WENNER of Ldn. B/S of 2 lots
inherited from father William WENNER's dec'd and interest in
widow's dower (15a and 1½a).

3R:460   Date: 13 Apr 1829   RtCt: 13 Apr 1829
Adam SANBOWER & wife Christena/Christiana of Ldn to Benjamin
GRUBB of Ldn. B/S of 22a allotted Christena in div. of Peter
HICKMAN dec'd. Wit: John J. MATHIAS, Noble S. BRADEN. Delv.
to GRUBB 26 Jan 1831.

3R:463   Date: 30 Mar 1829   RtCt: 13 Apr 1829
Yardley TAYLOR and William BROWN (Exors of Samuel BROWN
dec'd) of Ldn to Richard BROWN of Ldn. B/S of 10a from estate of
Samuel dec'd adj William BROWN. Delv. to Rich'd BROWN 13 Sep
1830.

3R:465   Date: 4 Mar 1829   RtCt: 13 Apr 1829
John G. PAXSON & wife Mahalah and Joseph Lewis POTTS of Ldn
to Ebenezer GRUBB Sr. and Edward DOWLING of Ldn. B/S of 180a
on W side of short hill adj John POTTS dec'd. Wit: B. WHITE, David
COPELAND, Newton DOWLING, David POTTS, Jonas POTTS,
Saml. HOUGH, Noble S. BRADEN. Delv. to GRUBB pr order of
DOWLING 10 May 1830.

3R:468 Date: 23 Oct 1829 RtCt: 13 Apr 1829
Samuel PEACH & wife Rebecca of AlexDC to Thomas W. SMITH
M.D. of Upperville Fqr. B/S of Rebecca's interest in land of John
GIBSON dec'd allotted to widow's dower; and land allotted in div. to
Alice GIBSON now BROWN along with Alice's share of widow's
dower (cnvy/b by David E. BROWN Feb 1826); and 14½a (cnvy/b
Elizabeth GIBSON his mother-in-law Jan 1824, DBk HHH:396). Wit:
Adam LYNN. Delv. pr order 12 Oct 1829.

3R:470 Date: 26 Mar 1829 RtCt: 14 Apr 1829
John L. DAGG of PhilPa to Benjamin SMITH and George Cuthbert
POWELL of Mdbg. B/S of Lots #26 & #32 in Mdbg. Wit: W. S.
BRANTLY, Thos. WATTSON, Jno. DAVIS.

3R:473 Date: 4 Apr 1829 RtCt: 14 Apr 1829
James McILHANY to Samuel CLENDENING and Jonathan
HEATON. Trust for debt to Nathan GREGG Sr. and Stephen
GREGG using 339a (cnvy/b Nathan and Stephen).

3S:001 Date: 13 Apr 1829 RtCt: 16 Apr 1829
Betsey BROWN of Ldn to Henry S. TAYLOR of Ldn. Trust for debt
to Yardley TAYLOR and William BROWN (Exors of Samuel BROWN
dec'd) using 120a adj Nathan GREGG, George WARNER, William
BROWN Sr., heirs of Israel PANCOAST. Delv. to TAYLOR 2 Apr
1831.

3S:003 Date: 17 Apr 1829 RtCt: 17 Apr 1829
Joseph HOUGH & wife Lucy of Ldn to Joshua PUSEY of Ldn. B/S of
100a (2 tracts cnvy/b Barnet HOUGH) adj __ LOVE, __ GILMORE,
__ CLEGGETT. Wit: Saml. M. EDWARDS, John H. McCABE. Delv.
to PUSEY 21 Jul 1829.

3S:005 Date: 18 Apr 1829 RtCt: 20 Apr 1829
George W. SEEVERS (Marshall of Sup. Ct of Winchester in case of
John J. HARDING agst Edward DULIN, Nov 1827) to Rich'd. H.
HENDERSON. B/S of 220a.

3S:007 Date: 18 Apr 1829 RtCt: 23 Apr 1829
Commr. John JANNEY of Ldn to Emanuel WALTMAN of Ldn. B/S of
30a (2 lots - interest of Elias WALTMAN dec'd in real estate of Jacob
WALTMAN dec'd, see DBk OOO:281).

3S:008 Date: __ Apr 1829 RtCt: 2 Apr 1829
Henson BUTLER of Ldn to Otho R. BEATTY of Ldn. Trust for benefit
of wife using household items.

3S:009 Date: 18 Apr 1829 RtCt: 23 Apr 1829
Emanuel WALTMAN of Ldn to Samuel M. EDWARDS of Ldn. Trust
for debt to John JANNEY (Commr. for sale of estate of Elias
WALTMAN dec'd) using 2 lots as above. Delv. to EDWARDS 8 Sep
1831.

3S:011   Date: 1 Apr 1829   RtCt: 27 Apr 1829

David BOGER & wife Catherine of Warren Co Ohio to Daniel WINE of Ldn. B/S of Catherine's undivided 1/5th of 216a of father Jacob WINE dec'd adj William H. HOUGH, heirs of Patterson WRIGHT dec'd. Wit: Jacob PENCE Jr., Danl. CRANE. Delv. to WINE 2 Mar 1831.

3S:014   Date: 26 Mar 1829   RtCt: 27 Apr 1829

George WINE & wife Margaret of Warren Co Ohio to Daniel WINE of Ldn. B/S of Margaret's undivided 1/5th of 216a of father Jacob WINE dec'd (prch/o John HOUGH dec'd Jan 1794 and Ferdinando FAIRFAX Oct 1805) adj William HOUGH, Cotocton Creek, Anthony CONARD, Benj. STEER. Wit: Danl. CRANE, Jacob PENCE Jr. Delv. to WINE 2 Mar 1831.

3S:018   Date: 11 Apr 1829   RtCt: 27 Apr 1829

George HUFF & wife Elizabeth of Muskingum Co Ohio to Daniel WINE of Ldn. B/S of Elizabeth's undivided 1/5th of 216a of father Jacob WINE dec'd adj Wm. H. HOUGH, heirs of Patterson WRIGHT dec'd. Wit: Albert COLE, Saml. THOMPSON. Delv. to WINE 2 Mar 1831.

3S:021   Date: 10 Feb 1829   RtCt: 28 Apr 1829

Receipt for payment of Robt. B. CAMPBELL for purchase of negroes Hary, Sampson, Jim & Bossy who were the property of Ludwell LEE taken by Executions in favour of the Bank of the Valley vs. LEE & others and sold to Dpty Shff Robt. MOFFETT for Sheriff Charles LEWIS.

3S:021   Date: 27 Apr 1829   RtCt: 28 Apr 1829

John H. BENNETT of to Jas. HAMILTON of Lsbg. Trust for debt to Chas. B. HAMILTON using interest in real estate of Charles BENNETT dec'd. of Ldn.

3S:022   Date: 1 Jun 1818   RtCt: 29 Apr 1829

Rich'd. H. HENDERSON & wife Orra Moore of Lsbg to Bank of the Valley. B/S of lot in Lsbg on Market St. at not yet named street with alley sep. lot of reps. of William WRIGHT. Wit: Samuel CLAPHAM, Patrick McINTYRE.

3S:024   Date: 23 Apr 1829   RtCt: 29 Apr 1829

James B. MURRAY of NY to William D. DRISH of Lsbg. Release of trust to John DRISH & wife Eleanor late of Lsbg in Jun 1825, DBk KKK:251 (who sold to William D. DRISH, DBk NNN:203) for debt to Chatham Fire Insurance Co. Wit: J. HAMMOND. Delv. to DRISH 23 Jun 1829.

3S:027   Date: 23 Apr 1829   RtCt: 1 May 1829

James B. MURRAY of NY to James GARRISON of Lsbg. Release of trust for John McCORMICK & wife Mary in Jun 1825 (who cnvy to Garrison) for debt to Chatham Fire Insurance Co.

3S:031 Date: 23 Apr 1829 RtCt: 2 May 1829
James B. MURRAY of NY to William KING of Ldn. Release of trust of Jun 1825 for debt to Chatham Fire Insurance Co.

3S:034 Date: 14 Mar 1829 RtCt: 1 May 1829
William D. TUCKER of Ldn to Edwin C. BROWN of Ldn. Trust for debt to Henry Fenton LUCKETT using farm items, crops. Delv. pr order 29 Jul 1829.

3S:035 Date: 14 Feb 1828 RtCt: 1 May 1829
William WRIGHT & wife ___ of Ldn to Israel T. GRIFFITH of Ldn. Trust for debt to Joseph H. WRIGHT of Ldn using 1/8th of real estate of Patterson WRIGHT dec'd subject to life estate of widow Nancy WRIGHT. Delv. to GRIFFITH 30 Sep 1830.

3S:038 Date: 4 May 1829 RtCt: 4 May 1829
James MONROE to William CHILTON. Trust for debt to Michael MORALEE (for carrying his canal contract in Md) using equipment to be used on the Ohio & Ches'k. Canal. Wit: B. W. SOWER, W. W. KITZMILLER, Tho. BIRKBY.

3S:040 Date: 7 May 1829 RtCt: 7 May 1829
Gabriel VANDEVANTER of Ldn to John S. PEARCE of BaltMd. Release of trust of Aug 1827, DBk HHH:355, for debt to John CARR.

3S:041 Date: 29 Apr 1829 RtCt: 7 May 1829
John S. PEARCE & wife Jane of BaltMd to Josiah HALL of Ldn. B/S of leased lot with brick dwelling (leased by John SURGHNOR, DBk HHH:088) and adj lot (DBk HHH:408). Wit: Henry W. GRAY, W. W. WAITE.

3S:044 Date: 17 Apr 1829 RtCt: 11 May 1829
John MARTIN. Qualified as Ensign in the Infantry of 57th Reg Va Militia.

3S:044 Date: 19 Apr 1829 RtCt: 11 May 1829
Alfred WRIGHT. Qualified as Lt. of Infantry in 132nd Reg of Va Militia.

3S:044 Date: __ May 1829 RtCt: 11 May 1829
Thomas MORALLEE of Ldn. DoE for negro man Henry aged abt 22y, yellowish complexion, free after 6 May 1829. Wit: Jno. A. BINNS, W. W. KITZMILLER.

3S:045 Date: 9 May 1829 RtCt: 12 May 1829
Thomas W. GIBSON. Oath as Ensign in 132nd Reg 6th Brig 2nd Div of Va Militia.

3S:045 Date: 12 May 1829 RtCt: 12 May 1829
John WEADON, Benjamin MITCHELL, Jacob SILCOTT and Henry HUTCHISON. Bond on WEADON as constable.

3S:046   Date: 25 Apr 1829   11 May 1829
Samuel C. SINCLAIR. Oath as 1st Lt. in troop of Cavelry 57th Reg Va Militia.

3S:046   Date: 25 Apr 1829   RtCt: 11 May 1829
Samuel CRAVEN. Oath as Cornet in troop of Cavelry in 57th Reg Va Militia.

3S:046   Date: 23 Apr 1829   RtCt: 11 May 1829
Erasmus G. TILLETT. Oath as 2nd Lt. in troop of Cavelry in 57th Reg Va Militia.

3S:047   Date: 29 Dec 1828   RtCt: 11 May 1829
Thomas M. HUMPHREY of Ldn to Seth SMITH of Ldn. Trust for debt to Elijah FARR of Ldn using 13¾a Lot #5 allotted Morris HUMPHREY in div. of Jesse HUMPHREY dec'd and 4a wooded Lot #3 allotted to Rachel HUMPHREY (cnvy to FARR then to Thomas M.). Delv. to SMITH 17 Mar 1831.

3S:049   Date: 22 Apr 1829   RtCt: 11 May 1829
John W. JACKSON & wife Mary of Ldn to William STEER of Ldn. Trust for debt to Elizabeth STEER using 27a from div. of John HOUGH dec'd adj Wm. H. HOUGH. Wit: Noble S. BRADEN, Saml. HOUGH.

3S:052   Date: 31 Dec 1828   RtCt: 11 May 1829
William SLATER of Ldn to John COMPHER Sr. of Ldn. B/S of interest in 27a Lot #2 and 6½a mt. Lot #2 allotted him in div. of father's estate (DBk LLL:34). Delv. to SLATER 24 Jul 1847.

3S:054   Date: 6 Mar 1828   RtCt: 11 May 1829
Roberdeau ANNIN & wife Helen C. (d/o John McCORMICK) of WashDC to Richard H. HENDERSON (trustee for Mary McCORMICK w/o John McCORMICK of WashDC). B/S of lot on S side of Market St adj Presbyterian Church and a lot on Liberty St adj Samuel G. HAMILTON and a lot with house on Market St adj Joseph KNOX (Mary will relinquish her rights to house and lot on King and Market St). Wit: C. H. W. WHORTON, Jno. CHALMERS. Delv. to Mary McCORMICK 5 Jun 1831.

3S:057   Date: 20 Mar 1829   RtCt: 11 May 1829
Norval CHAMBLIN & wife Sarah W. T. of Ldn to Elijah PEACOCK of Ldn. B/S of house and lot in Wtfd adj Isaac HOUGH, dev. to wife Sarah late VANDEVANTER. Wit: Tasker C. QUINLAN, John J. MATHIAS. Delv. to PEACOCK 8 Feb 1830.

3S:059   Date: 17 Feb 1829   RtCt: 11 May 1829
Thomas JONES, James JONES, Alexander LEE & wife Alice late JONES (heirs of Sarah JONES dec'd) of Ldn to Lewis BIRKLEY/BERKELEY of Ldn. B/S of 85a (cnvy/b John SINCLAIR May 1822 to Sarah) adj BERKELEY, James HIXSON. Wit: William B. HARRISON, John BAYLY. Delv. to BERKLY 11 Sep 1834.

3S:062 Date: 11 May 1829 RtCt: 11 May 1829
Christian SANBOWER of Ldn to Adam SANBOWER of Ldn. B/S of
½ interest in Lot #8 and Lot #9 (81a) in div. of John SANBOWER
dec'd (allotted to Christian and Adam jointly). Delv. to Adam 19 Feb
1833.

3S:064 Date: 17 Apr 1829 RtCt: 11 May 1829
William H. HOUGH of Ldn to John W. JACKSON of Ldn. B/S of 27a
(cnvy/b Dpty Thos. ROGERS Jul 1827) adj Wm. STEER.

3S:065 Date: 18 Nov 1828 RtCt: 11 May 1829
Mary STONEBURNER, Henry STONEBURNER & wife Sarah, Peter
STONEBURNER, Catherine STONEBURNER, Margaret
STONEBURNER, Sarah STONEBURNER, Christina
STONEBURNER and John LONG (heirs of Daniel STONEBURNER
dec'd of Ldn) to Adam SPRING of Ldn. B/S of 1a on Cotocton Mt.
(Daniel contracted sale before his death) adj Jacob SMITH, Henry
GOODHEART, Henry STONEBURNER, Peter FRY, George
BEAMER. Wit: Saml. DAWSON, Geo. W. SHAWEN. Delv. to
SPRING 14 Sep 1830.

3S:068 Date: 16 Feb 1829 RtCt: 11 May 1829
Hannah LOVETT, John LOVETT & wife Naomi, Jonathan LOVETT
& wife Matilda, and Jonas LOVETT & wife Nancy (surviving ch/o
Joseph LOVETT dec'd of Ldn) to Henry PLAISTER of Ldn. B/S of lot
in Union (cnvy/b Benjamin KENT to Joseph) adj lot cnvy to Nancy
GRAVES now w/o PLAISTER, Joseph GARDNER, western
boundary of town. Wit: Edw'd. HALL, Notley C. WILLIAMS.

3S:071 Date: 11 May 1809 [29?] RtCt: 11 May 1829
Ludwell LEE of Ldn to John MIDDLEBURG of Ldn. B/S of 16a
(except 1a with house already sold) on paved road from Lsbg to
AlexVa. Delv. to Middleburg 4 Dec 1829.

3S:072 Date: 9 May 1829 RtCt: 11 May 1829
Henry GOODHART & wife Elizabeth of Ldn to Henry
STONEBURNER of Ldn. B/S of Elizabeth's 10a & 3a lots from
estate of father Daniel STONEBURNER dec'd. Noble S. BRADEN,
George W. SHAWEN. Delv. pr order 19 Sep 1829 [or 39].

3S:074 Date: 11 May 1829 RtCt: 11 May 1829
David YOUNG and Isaac NICKOLS Jr. of Ldn to John GREGG of
Ldn. Release of trust Mar 1818 for debt to Isaac & Samuel
NICKOLS. Delv. to Jno. GREGG 1 Apr 1831.

3S:076 Date: 11 May 1829 RtCt: 11 May 1829
James HOGE and Isaac NICKOLS Jr. of Ldn to Amos GIBSON of
Ldn. Release of trust of Feb 1821 for debt to Isaac & Samuel
NICKOLS on 307½a.

3S:078 Date: 24 Jan 1829 RtCt: 11 May 1829
Burr POWELL & Abner GIBSON to John SINCLAIR. Release of
trust of Dec 1820 for debt to Noble BEVERIDGE.

3S:080   Date: 24 Jan 1829   RtCt: 11 May 1829
Humphrey B. POWELL to John SINCLAIR. Release of trust for debt to Abner GIBSON.

3S:082   Date: 23 Feb 1829   RtCt: 11 May 1829
Seth SMITH of Ldn to Isaac FRY & wife Hannah of Ldn. Release of trust of Jul 1823 of 1a (cnvy/b Isaac COWGILL & wife Mary).

3S:083   Date: 11 Dec 1828   RtCt: 11 May 1829
Rebecca DULIN wd/o John DULIN. Children are dissatisfied with will, promises not to dispose of real estate or slaves. Wit: Enoch FRANCIS, Thos. FRANCIS, Benjamin BRIDGES.

3S:083   Date: 18 May 1829   RtCt: 8 Jun 1829
Theodore N. DAVIDSON. Oath as Captain in 56th Reg 6th Brig 2nd Div of Va Militia. Delv. to DAVIDSON 19 Jun 1829.

3S:084   Date: 12 May 1829   RtCt: 12 May 1829
Burr W. HARRISON of Ldn to William Butler HARRISON of Ldn. Release of trust of Jun 1825 using 300a where HARRISON resides and 317a adj lot called 'Mahoney's tract' now occupied by Tho. GHEEN (DBk KKK:277).

3S:086   Date: 13 May 1829   RtCt: 13 May 1829
Mortimer McILHANY and Erasmus G. HAMMILTON of Ldn to Burr W. HARRISON and Jesse TIMMS of Ldn. B/S of 2214a 'Daniels lot' (from trust of Nov 1824, DC JJJ:084 from Tasker C. QUINLAN, William HAMILTON has died).

3S:088   Date: 29 Dec 1828   RtCt: 14 May 1829
Allen SINGLETON of Harden Co Ky to Robert SINGLETON of Fqr. B/S of 339a (cnvy/b Robert SCOTT Aug 1790, less 100a sold Isaac NICHOLLS) adj Goose Creek, __ MONTHIETH, __ TRIPLETT, Leven POWELL. Wit: Burr POWELL.

3S:089   Date: 3 Apr 1829   RtCt: 19 May 1829
Mary SMITH, Seth SMITH & wife Mary and Samuel SMITH & wife Rachel (ch/o Samuel SMITH dec'd) of Ldn to Thomas LITTLETON (s/o Charles) of Ldn. B/S of 105a (cnvy/b Nathaniel CRAWFORD, DBk CC:178 [177], and Jacob SILCOTT) on Beaverdam (agreed upon before Samuel's death). Wit: Cuthbert POWELL, Francis W. LUCKETT. Delv. to LITTLETON 27 Sep 1833.

3S:092   Date: 4 Mar 1829   RtCt: 19 May 1829
Aaron HOLLOWAY & wife Rachel and James McPHERSON & wife Kezia of Belmont Co Ohio, John SMITH & wife Elizabeth of Gurnsey Co Ohio (ch/o Samuel SMITH dec'd) to Thomas LITTLETON (s/o Charles) of Ldn. B/S of above land. Delv. to LITTLETON 27 Sep 1833.

3S:095   Date: 16 Feb 1829   RtCt: 19 May 1829
Amos SMITH & wife Rebecca of Hartford Co Md (ch/o Samuel SMITH dec'd) to Thomas LITTLETON (of Charles) of Ldn. B/S of above land. Delv. to LITTLETON 27 Sep 1833.

3S:097 Date: 15 Apr 1829 RtCt: 21 May 1829
Absalom KALB & wife Susannah of Franklin Pa to Samuel KALB
and Jesse NEAR of Ldn. Trust for debt to John KALB using 167a
(cnvy/b Samuel KALB Apr 1829). Wit: Noble S. BRADEN, Mortimer
McILHANY.

3S:101 Date: 15 Apr 1829 RtCt: 21 May 1829
Samuel KALB & wife Susannah of Ldn to Absalom KALB of Franklin
Co Pa. B/S of 147a (formerly Jacob HOWSER dec'd) adj church lot,
Wm. WOLFORD, schoolhouse, Margaret SAUNDERS, ___
HAMILTON, Simon SHOEMAKER; and 20a on E side of short hill
(cnvy/b today by father). Wit: Noble S. BRADEN, Mortimer
MCILHANY. Delv. to Absalom 11 May 1830.

3S:104 Date: 15 Apr 1829 RtCt: 21 May 1829
Samuel KALB & wife Susannah of Ldn to Absalom KALB of Franklin
Co Pa and Jesse NEAR of Ldn. Trust for debt to John KALB using
273a (cnvy/b John KALB today). Wit: Noble S. BRADEN, Mortimer
McILHANY.

3S:107 Date: 19 May 1829 RtCt: 23 May 1829
Joseph GREGG of Ldn to Joshua PANCOAST of Ldn. Trust for debt
to Joshua GREGG of Ldn using 131a adj Barton EWERS, Josiah
GREGG, Notley C. WILLIAMS.

3S:109 Date: 22 May 1829 RtCt: 23 May 1829
Levi HUMMER & wife Martha of Ldn to Washington HUMMER of
Ldn. B/S of 57a (allotted Levi in div. of Wm. HUMMER dec'd) on
Church road to Alexandria road. Wit: Saml. M. EDWARDS, Hamilton
ROGERS.

3S:111 Date: 24 Nov 1828 RtCt: 23 May 1829
James McILHANY & wife Margaret of Ldn to Robert OGDON of Ldn.
B/S of 313a (from div. of father James McILHANY dec'd, DBk
JJJ:090) now occupied by OGDON adj heirs of Andrew REED dec'd,
farm of Thomas GREGG dec'd, farm occupied by Thomas
DORRELL, heirs of Josiah WHITE dec'd, heirs of Thomas LOVE
dec'd, ___ BEANS. Wit: Thomas GASSAWAY, Saml. M.
EDWARDS. Delv. to McILHANY 10 Apr 1835.

3S:114 Date: 28 May 1829 RtCt: 28 May 1829
Joseph WALTMAN of Ldn to Jonathan WENNER of Ldn. B/S of
household items, negro girl Sarah (for benefit of Martha WALTMAN
w/o Jacob WALTMAN using). Delv. to WENNER 26 Jun 1834.

3S:115 Date: 29 May 1829 RtCt: 29 may 1829
Chs. W. D. BINNS to Elizabeth HAINES. Release of trust of Mar
1827 for debt to Dpty William THRIFT (Admr. of Stacy HAINES
dec'd).

3S:116 Date: 29 May 1829 RtCt: 29 May 1829
Ct. Commr. Burr W. HARRISON of Ldn to Thomas W. LEE. B/S all
interest in 196a of Richard ODEN, Thomas ODEN, John ODEN,

Hezekiah ODEN, Alexander ODEN, Lewis ODEN, William COOKSEY & wife Betsey late ODEN in tracts of Thomas ODEN dec'd (dower of widow Martha ODEN).

3S:118 Date: 1 Jun 1829 RtCt: 1 Jun 1829
Joseph LAYCOCK & wife Emily (ch/o William WHITE dec'd) of Ldn to John WHITE and Daniel WHITE of Ldn. B/S of undivided 1/5th of estate of William WHITE dec'd (includes land dev. to William by father Daniel WHITE dec'd, 213a prch/o John EBLIN, Joseph WHITE & Levi WHITE. Wit: John J. MATHIAS, Presley CORDELL.

3S:120 Date: 2 Jun 1829 RtCt: 2 Jun 1829
Stephen SANDS of Ldn to Jesse OXLEY of Ldn. B/S of 2 lots in Wtfd (cnvy/b John BALL) – 1 with a tavern adj Noble S. BRADEN, Thomas R. SAUNDERS and the other with a stable adj Lewis KLEIN, Elizabeth GORE.

3S:122 Date: 1 Jun 1829 RtCt: 2 Jun 1829
Isaac NICKOLS (trustee James HOGE now dec'd) to Thomas JAMES (heir and Admr. of Robert RUSSELL dec'd). Release of trust of Feb 1825 for debt to William HOGE, William PIGGOT and Thomas HATCHERS (Exors. of Samuel & Isaac NICHOLS dec'd) on 194a.

3S:124 Date: 2 Jun 1829 RtCt: 2 Jun 1829
Rich'd H. HENDERSON of Ldn to Edward A. GIBBS of Berkley Co Va. B/S of 76a (from trust of Feb 1822 from Stephen HIXSON, DBk DDD:374) Delv. pr order 2 Apr 1831.

3S:126 Date: 13 Mar 1820 RtCt: 3 Jun 1829
Charles RUSSELL & wife Margaret of Ldn to Edward B. GRADY of Ldn. Trust for debt to Notley C. WILLIAMS using 167a (cnvy/b Stephen McPHERSON) adj GRADY, __ BLEAKLY, __ WINN. Wit: Lee W. DURHAM, A. O. POWELL, William TAYLOR, Benjamin GRAYSON, John W. GRAYSON.

3S:128 Date: 27 May 1829 RtCt: 3 Jun 1829
William H. HANDY of Ldn to John WYNN of Ldn. Release of trust of Jan 1818 for debt to Joseph HAINS.

3S:130 Date: 5 Jun 1829 RtCt: 5 Jun 1829
Elizabeth RUSSELL of Ldn to daughters Sarah Ann RUSSELL, Eliza, and Charle Ann Elizabeth Jane. Gift of slaves (late prop. of husband) Joe, Harrison, men, Amos & Armstead boys, Sylve a woman, Harriet a girl and Adeline an infant and George a boy; and slave (her own prop) Henny a woman, Hester a girl & Maria a girl; and household items.

3S:131 Date: 6 Jun 1829 RtCt: 6 Jun 1829
Saml. M. EDWARDS of Ldn to Martena B. HUMMER w/o Washington HUMMER of Ldn. B/S of 160a (from trust on 224a, DBk YY:187, of William SHEID & wife Martena B. now HUMMER, SHEID defaulted). Delv. to Washington HUMMER 28 Feb 1837.

3S:133   Date: 6 May 1829   RtCt: 6 Jun 1829
Sup. Ct. Marshall of Winchester John S. MAGILL to John RICHARDSON of FredVa. B/S of undivided ½ of 43a 'Big Spring Mill prop' with merchant mill adj Fayette BALL (from case of RICHARDSON vs. George M. CHICHESTER and heirs of William COOKE dec'd – Elizabeth A., Alexander, William and Ann Maria COOKE infants). Delv. to RICHARDSON 28 Jul 1829.

3S:135   Date: 1 Nov 1828   RtCt: 6 Jun 1829
Richard H. LOVE to Charles W. BINNS. Trust for debt to James GARRISON for rent of house and shop using household items.

3S:136   Date: 6 Sep 1824   RtCt: 14 Mar 1825/8 Jun 1829
Sarah THRASHER (wd/o Elias THRASHER dec'd) and Malinda ___, Elias THRASHER, John THRASHER, Thomas THRASHER and Archibald THRASHER (ch/o Elias dec'd) of Ldn to Thomas J. MARLOW of Ldn. B/S of their interest in 123a (prch/o George SAGER Sr. Apr 1806 by Elias dec'd); and 88a (cnvy/by George SAGER Sr.). Wit: Daniel MILLER, Samuel COOK, Harvey COGSIL. Delv. to MARLOW 19 Jan 1836.

3S:138   Date: 19 May 1829   RtCt: 8 Jun 1829
John RICHARDS Jr. Oath as Captain of a Co of Rifleman in 1st Batt of 132nd Reg 6th Brig 2nd Div of Va Militia.

3S:138   Date: 21 Apr 1829   RtCt: 8 Jun 1829
Ryland JACOBS. Oath as Lt. in 132nd Reg 6th Brig 2nd Div of Va Militia.

3S:139   Date: 8 May 1829   RtCt: 8 Jun 1829
Henry HUTCHESON. Oath as Lt in 132nd Reg 6th Brig 2nd Div of Va Militia.

3S:139   Date: 21 Mar 1829   RtCt: 8 Jun 1829
Amos GULICK. Oath as Captain in 132nd Reg 6th Brig 2nd Div of Va Militia.

3S:140   Date: 27 Apr 1829   RtCt: 8 Jun 1829
Asa ROGERS. Oath as Colonel of 132nd Reg 6th Brig 2nd Div of Va Militia.

3S:140   Date: 16 May 1829   RtCt: 8 Jun 1829
Milburn PALMER. Oath as Ensign of Co of Riflemen in 132nd Reg 6th Brig 2nd Div of Va Militia.

3S:141   Date: 7 Feb 1829   RtCt: 8 Jun 1829
Jonathan COST. Qualified as Ensign of a Co of Riflemen in 2nd Batt of 56th Reg 6th Brig 2nd Div of Va Militia.

3S:142   Date: 8 Jun 1829   RtCt: 8 Jun 1829
William CLENDENING, William THOMPSON and Edward DOWLING. Bond on CLENDENING as constable.

3S:143   Date: 9 Jun 1829   RtCt: 8 [?] Jun 1829
Edward HAMMATT, James L. MARTIN and Samuel HAMMATT.
Bond on Edward HAMMATT as constable.

3S:143   Date: 10 Jun 1829   RtCt: 10 Jun 1829
Jno. MARTIN, Saml. M. BOSS and James THOMAS. Bond on
MARTIN as constable.

3S:144   Date: 4 Jun 1829   RtCt: 9 Jun 1829
Isaac NICHOLS dec'd. Division – 207a Lot #1 to Isaac HOGE; 207a
Lot #2 to Phebe HOGE; 207a Lot #3 to Elizabeth HOGE; 208a Lot
#4 to Rachel HOGE. Gives plat. Divisors: David SMITH, Daniel
JANNEY, Yardley TAYLOR.

3S:148   Date: 4 Apr 1829   RtCt: 9 Jun 1829
Daniel ROLLER & wife Margaret of Ldn to Conrad ROLLER and
John ROLLER of Ldn. B/S of undivided 1/3 of land sold June 1824
to Conrod, John and Daniel ROLLER by William ELLZEY. Wit: John
J. MATHIAS, Saml. HOUGH.

3S:150   Date: 25 Mar 1829   RtCt: 8 Jun 1829
John BROWN & wife Ann of Ldn to Eden CARTER of Ldn. B/S of
23a on Beaverdam where BROWN now resides adj Isaac BROWN,
Poor house. Wit: Benjamin GRAYSON, Francis W. LUCKETT. Delv.
to CARTER 8 Jul 1850.

3S:152   Date: 4 Apr 1829   RtCt: 8 Jun 1829
George MILLER & wife Elizabeth (d/o Jno. WALTMAN dec'd) of Ldn
to Daniel ROLLER of Ldn. B/S of 24a (from div. of Jno. WALTMAN
dec'd, DBk LLL:028) nr dutchman run. Wit: Saml. HOUGH, John J.
MATHIAS. Delv. to ROLLER 16 Mar 1846.

3S:155   Date: 26 May 1828   RtCt: 8 Jun 1829
Jane JANNEY, Phineas JANNEY, Pleasant JANNEY, Jonathan
JANNEY and Israel JANNEY (devisees of Israel JANNEY dec'd of
Ldn) to Daniel JANNEY of Ldn. Agreement – Daniel owed money to
Israel dec'd, made trust in Aug 1818 with William HOGE and Jesse
HOGE using lot with mills. Agreed as to how remainder of debt to be
paid. Acknowledgment of Israel in PhilPa, for Jane, Phineas,
Pleasant and Jonathan in AlexDC. Delv. to Pheneas 20 Aug 1840.

3S:159   Date: 31 Mar 1829   RtCt: 8 Jun 1829
George W. SAGER & wife Delilah of Ldn to Abram SKILLMAN Sr.
and John HOLMES of Ldn. Trust for debt to Philip VANSICKLER Sr.
using 3/6th of land of James CARTER dec'd (1/6th cnvy/b Levi
CARTER Oct 1826, 1/6th is undivided share of Delilah formerly
CARTER, and 1/6th cnvy/b Samuel BROWN Mar 1829). Wit:
Thomas NICHOLS, John SIMPSON.

3S:161   Date: 11 Mar 1829   RtCt: 8 Jun 1829
Dpty Thomas ROGERS for Sheriff Charles LEWIS to Burr W.
HARRISON of Ldn. B/S of 1400a on Goose Creek at Ketocton Mt.,

474a in WstmVa; __a in Ffx (from insolvent Tasker C. QUINLAN). Delv. to HARRISON 12 Oct 1829.

3S:163   Date: 6 Jun 1829   RtCt: 8 Jun 1829
Emanuel WALTMAN to Jonathan WENNER. Trust for debt to Joseph WALTMAN using 28a on S side of Short hill adj Adam SANBOWER, __ BOGER. Wit: Jacob WATERS.

3S:165   Date: 30 Jan 1829   RtCt: 8 Jun 1829
Israel WILLIAMS of Ldn to Fleming W. P. HIXON of Ldn. Trust for debt to Andrew S. ANDERSON of Ldn using 93a where WILLIAMS resides adj John ROBERTSON, Wm. STALKS, Henry POTTERFIELD dec'd, F. W. P. HIXON. Wit: Wm. FITZSIMMONS, J. T. GRIFFITH, J. L. POTTS.

3S:167   Date: 10 Jun 1829   RtCt: 10 Jun 1829
Edward C. THOMPSON to Joseph MEAD. Trust for Wm. THRIFT as security using farm animals, farm and household items.

3S:170   Date: 15 Jan 1829   RtCt: 9 Jun 1829
Benjamin GRAYSON of Ldn to Nathan LUFBOROUGH of DC. Trust for debt to Richard ROSS of MontMD using 1700a 'Belmont tract' where GRAYSON resides adj George RUST, George NOBLE, Mannor of Leeds.

3S:173   Date: 13 Jan 1829   RtCt: 9 Jun 1829
John P. LOVE of Ldn to Joshua REED of Ldn. B/S of 21a adj Isaac CAMP, REED, Jesse SILCOTT.

3S:174   Date: 29 Dec 1827   RtCt: 10 Jun 1829.
Solomon HOUSEHOLDER of Ldn to Thomas J. MARLOW of Ldn. B/S of 4a on E side of Short Hill adj Mary HICKMAN, __ GRUBB. Wit: John GRUBB, James TILLETT. Delv. to MARLOW 5 May 1830.

3S:176   Date: 6 Jun 1827   RtCt: 10 Jun 1829
Philip COOPER & wife Elizabeth of Ldn to George WINSEL of Ldn. B/S of 51¼a adj Peter VERTS, George COOPER. Wit: Mortimer McILHANY, Geo. W. SHAWEN. Delv. to WINSEL 13 Sep 1830.

3S:179   Date: 9 Jun 1829   RtCt: 13 Jul 1829
Edward E. COOKE and John R. COOKE & wife Maria P. to Richard H. HENDERSON. Trust for debt to William A. POWELL using 197a on Goose Creek (former prop. of Henry S. COOKE dec'd, sold to COOKE Apr 1829 by Commr. William A. POWELL). Wit: Daniel GOLD, John HEISKILL.

3S:181   Date: 11 Jun 1829   RtCt: 12 Jun 1829
Jane MORRISON Jr. of Ldn to Edward MORRISON of Ldn. B/S of 23a on E side of Short hill (part of tract cnvy/b Philip FRY to John FRY Dec 1827) adj Thomas WHITE, John GRUBB, MORRISON; and 7a adj lot (cnvy/b Edward to Jane Sep 1828) adj heirs of Archibald MORRISON dec'd, Simon SHOEMAKER, Thomas WHITE.

3S:184 Date: 24 Dec 1828 RtCt: 9 Mar/11 Jun 1829
Luther O. SULLIVAN with consent of Thomas WOOD & wife Eliza late SULLIVAN of Md, Mary SULLIVAN wd/o Owen SULLIVAN dec'd, John C. SULLIVAN, James B. SULLIVAN, Warner SULLIVAN, Matilda R. SULLIVAN & Wade SULLIVAN of Fqr to John J. CURRILL of Ldn. B/S of their interest in 232a (cnvy/b Solomon BETTON Jun 1810, DBk MM:241). Wit: H. B. POWELL, Burr WEEKS, A. G. WATERMAN, Enos WILDMAN, John THOMAS, Edward L. FANT.

3S:186 Date: 15 Apr 1829 RtCt: 11 Jun 1829
Margaret SPENCER of Holmes Co Ohio to Samuel CARTER of Ldn. B/S of 15a Lot #7 in div. of Jasper POULSON dec'd. Wit: Jesse MORGAN, Thos. POULSON. Delv. to CARTER 20 Jun 1846.

3S:188 Date: 27 Apr 1829 RtCt: 30 May /12 Jun 1829
Mary VICKERS, Abraham VICKERS, William VICKERS and Thomas VICKERS to John CONARD and Edward DOWLING. Trust for debt to Ebenezer GRUBB using farm animals, crops. Wit: Wm. CLENDENING, Jonathan CONARD, Joseph CONARD, John CONARD.

3S:190 Date: 13 Jun 1829 RtCt: 13 Jun 1829
Joshua RILEY & wife __ of Ldn to Richard H. HENDERSON of Ldn. Trust for debt to J. & J. DOUGLAS of AlexDC using lot on Loudoun St in Lsbg cnvy/b John A. BINNS Jun 1822, DBk EEE:230; unimproved lot on Liberty St cnvy/b Samuel TUSTIN Oct 1820, DBk BBB:368; lots on Back St. and on Liberty St a smiths shop and stable cnvy/b Thomas BIRKBY Dec 1827, DBk PPP:336. Delv. to HENDERSON 13 Mar 1830.

3S:192 Date: 23 Feb 1829 RtCt: 13 Jun 1829
Benjamin BURSON & wife Mary of Preble Co Ohio to Thomas M. HUMPHREY of Ldn. B/S of 14½a Lot #4 in div. of Jesse HUMPHREY dec'd f/o Mary). Wit: Isaac STEPHENS, Robert RHEA.

3S:195 Date: 6 Jun 1829 RtCt: 19 Jun 1829
James CARROLL of Mdbg to James McDANIEL of Mdbg. Trust for James TILLETT as security on bond to Hugh SMITH using household items. Delv. pr order to Burr WEEKS. 1 Aug 1829.

3S:196 Date: 1 Apr 1829 RtCt: 10 Jun/22 Jun 1829
Isaac BROWN & wife Sarah of Ldn to John BROWN of Ldn. B/S of 178¾a on Beaverdam (cnvy/b Nathaniel CRAWFORD Jan 1803) adj Robert SMITH, Samuel SMITH, Dawson BROWN, Benjamin OVERFIELD; and 26a adj lot, adj John WILKINSON, William CARTER; another adj 46a (cnvy/b William SMITH Sep 1806) adj James BURSON, Henry PLASTER; and 9a (in exchange with John WILKINSON in 1811). Wit: Samuel DUNCAN, Chas. L. CLEWS, Jos. H. CLEWS, Reuben TRIPLETT.

3S:198   Date: 15 Apr 1829   RtCt: 23 Jun 1829
John HAMILTON & wife Winefred of Ldn to Charles Bennett HAMILTON of Ldn. B/S of undivided 1/3 of lot on N side of Market St between Clerks Office and bank (from Charles BENNETT dec'd of Lsbg div. between dau Dewanner Gill WATT, granddau Jane WILDMAN & dau Winefred). Wit: Noble S. BRADEN, George W. SHAWEN. Delv. to HAMILTON 223 Dec 1829.

3S:201   Date: 22 Jun 1829   RtCt: 25 Jun 1829
Otho R. BEATTY of Ldn to Richard W. STONESTREET of Ldn. B/S of lot in Lsbg adj Martha BLINCOE on Back St, __ BAKER. Delv. to STONESTREET 6 May 1831.

3S:202   Date: 15 Jun 1829   RtCt: 2 Jul 1829
Samuel M. EDWARDS of Ldn to Philip VANSICKLE of Ldn. B/S of 77a (from trust from Stephen W. ROSZELL Dec 1823 to EDWARDS for benefit of Anna ROSZEL Admr of Stephen C. ROSZELL dec'd) on road from North fork meeting house adj VANSICKLE; interest of Thornton WALKER in 20a also conveyed. Delv. to VANSICKLER 16 Jan 1838.

3S:205   Date: 2 Dec 1828   RtCt: 2 Jul 1829
Stephen W. ROSZELL & wife Kitty of Ldn to Thornton WALKER of Ldn. B/S of 81a Lot #5 from div. of Stephen ROSZEL dec'd adj Philip VANSICKLER. Wit: Geo. H. NORRIS, Treadwell SMITH.

3S:207   Date: 6 Jul 1829   RtCt: 8 Jul 1829
Isaac M. BROWN of Ldn to Alfred H. POWELL Jr. of Ldn. Trust for debt to Burr WEEK & Co using negro woman Maria, household items, farm animals. Delv. to WEEKS 5 Mar 1830.

3S:209   Date: 27 Jun 1829   RtCt: 9 Jul 1829
Jacob WATERS of Ldn to Augustine M. SANFORD of Ldn. Trust for debt to Ishmael VANHORN using lots in German Settlement formerly owned by David and Maria WALTMAN from death of father John WALTMAN.

3S:211   Date: 15 Apr 1829   RtCt: 17 Jul 1829
John KALB & wife Susannah of Ldn to Samuel KALB of Ldn. B/S of 273a (2 tracts prch/o William D. DIGGS Dec 1814 and Feb 1816 and 1 tract prch/o Robert BRADEN 1827) adj Edmond JENNINGS, Robert BRADEN. Wit: Noble S. BRADEN, Mortimer McILHANY. Delv. to Saml. KALB 24 Dec 1829.

3S:214   Date: 18 Jul 1829   RtCt: 18 Jul 1828
Presley SAUNDERS of Ldn to Joseph MEAD of Ldn. BoS for negro woman Harriett (to serve 7y 6m from date) & her 3 children Ellzey aged 7y the 24 Mar 1830 (to serve 23y from 25 Mar 1830), Ann aged 5y the 30th of Dec 1829 (to serve 25y from 30 Dec 1829), and Emily aged 1y the 15 Oct 1829 (to serve 29y from 15 Oct 1829), then all emancipated; if any other children born they to serve 30 years.

3S:215   Date: 21 Jul 1829   RtCt: 21 Jul 1829
Joseph GORE of Ldn to Rebecca H. PIGGOTT late HATCHER, Thomas HATCHER, William HATCHER, Jonah HATCHER and Joshua HATCHER (ch/o Samuel HATCHER dec'd), and Hannah HATCHER (wd/o Joseph HATCHER dec'd) and Mary Ann RECTOR late HATCHER, Emsey Frances GIBSON late HATCHER, Gourley Reeder HATCHER, Amanda Malvina HATCHER, Anna Vickers HATCHER (ch/o Joseph HATCHER dec'd). B/S of 210a which GORE on 2 May 1818 sold to Samuel HATCHER and Joseph HATCHER now dec'd, land formerly held in partnership by GORE and Daniel EACHES).

3S:217   Date: 7 Feb 1829   RtCt: 9 Feb 1829
Joseph LEWIS of Ldn to Caldwell CARR of Upperville Fqr. Trust for debt to Daniel S. KERFOOT Guardian of Amanda M. CARR using 310a (cnvy/b Ferdinando FAIRFAX) where Jonathan McCARTY now resides and part with Samuel THOMPSON as tenant, adj Mahlon JANNEY, heirs of Edward McDONALD. Delv. to Caldwell CARR 14 Dec 1829.

3S:219   Date: 15 Jan 1827   RtCt: 27 Jul 1829
Thomas KIDWELL & wife Elizabeth of Ldn to William McBRIDE and Hiram McBRIDE of JeffVa. B/S of 22a adj __ MILLER, KIDWELL, __ DERRY. Wit: Ebenezer GRUBB, John WHITE.

3S:221   Date: 27 Jun 1829   RtCt: 27 Jul 1829
Thomas PHILIPS & Joseph BOND (Exors of Asa MOORE dec'd) and Thomas PHILLIPS & wife Rachel of Ldn to Benjamin GRUBB of Ldn. B/S of 18a on short hill (part of prch/o Frederick HANDSLEY Dec 1817) adj __ VINCELL, __ POTTERFIELD. Wit: Noble S. BRADEN, Geo. W. SHAWEN. Delv. to GRUBB 26 Jan 1831.

3S:223   Date: 18 Jul 1829   RtCt: 28 Jul 1829
Barton EWERS to Joseph GREGG. Release of trust of Apr 1822 for debt to Swithen NICKOLS on 162a.

3S:225   Date: 22 Jun 1829   RtCt: 29 Jul 1829
Samuel DUNKIN Sr. of Ldn to Samuel TORREYSON of Ldn. B/S of ¼a adj Union adj lot of Lydia HUTCHISON now w/o TORREYSON.

3S:226   Date: 15 Jul 1829   RtCt: 29 Jul 1829
Benjamin GRAYSON of Ldn to William F. CLARKE of Ldn. B/S of 2 lots (¼a) with houses in Bloomfield (from trust of Feb 1822 from Stephen R. MOUNT for debt to John W. GRAYSON with trustee Benjamin GRAYSON Jr. who died before debt paid), adj Jesse McVEIGH. Delv. to Jno. G. HUMPHRY pr order of CLARK 16 Jan 1832 filed DBk VVV:344.

3S:228   Date: 12 Jul 1829   RtCt: 30 Jul 1829
Jacob SILCOTT of Ldn and Thomas F. MILLER h/o Lucinda (d/o SILCOTT) of Ldn. Agreement – loan of household items for Lucinda & children's use. Wit: Seth SMITH, Craven WALKER.

3S:229 Date: 20 Jul 1829 RtCt: 30 Jul 1829
Mortimer McILHANY, John DAVIS, John LESLIE & wife Rachel and
Frederick A. DAVISSON, all of Ldn. Agreement – settlement of
boundaries and corners. Wit: Craven OSBURN, John WHITE.

3S:231 Date: 10 Mar 1827 RtCt: 10 Aug 1829
Moses GULICK dec'd. Allotment of dower to widow Mrs.
Patty/Martha GULICK – court order of 8 Jan 1827, 80a (with ½ of
smith shop to George GULICK with other ½ to be disposed of by
Admrs). Divisors: Hugh ROGERS, Jesse McVEIGH. Gives plat.

3S:232 Date: 16 May 1829 RtCt: 1 Aug 1829
Nancy LUCAS of PrWm to granddau Delilah LUCAS of Ldn. Gift of
farm animals, household items. Delv. to Delilah 1 Nov 1837.

3S:233 Date: 16 May 1829 RtCt: 1 Aug 1829
Nancy LUCAS of PrWm to grandson Isaiah LUCAS of Ldn. Gift of
farm animals.

3S:234 Date: 25 Dec 1828 RtCt: 1 Aug 1829
Thomas W. SMITH & wife Ann of Upperville Fqr to Mahlon
BALDWIN of Union and William WILKINSON nr Upperville. Trust for
debt to Samuel PEACH of AlexVa using lots cnvy/b PEACH nr
Upperville – allotment of Rebecca GIBSON now w/o PEACH from
John GIBSON dec'd, allotment to Alice GIBSON now w/o David E.
BROWN, and interest in dower of widow Elizabeth GIBSON; and
14½a, DBk HHH:396). Wit: Edward HALL, John W. GRAYSON.

3S:238 Date: 28 Aug 1826 RtCt: 3 Aug 1829
Francis J. TYTUS of Ldn to Joseph McDONALD of Ldn. B/S of 1/9th
interest of 184a (cnvy/b Jenkin PHILIPS in Oct 1793 to Samuel
TORBE[R]T then to TYTUS as heir of Samuel dec'd) adj Peter
ROMINES, Benjamin OVERFIELD. Wit: M. P. CHAMBLIN, Charles
L. CLOWES.

3S:240 Date: 27 Jun 1826 RtCt: 2 Aug 1829
Tuenies TYTUS & wife Jane of Muskingum Co Oh to Francis J.
TYTUS of FredVa. B/S of 1/9th interest in 184a as above (Jane an
heir of Samuel TORBERT dec'd).

3S:243 Date: 25 May 1829 RtCt: 6 Aug 1829
Samuel CLENDENING of Ldn to Joseph HOUGH of Ldn. B/S of 55
pole lot in Hllb adj Samuel CLENDENING, heirs of Josiah WHITE.
Delv. to HOUGH 30 Sep 1830.

3S:244 Date: 5 Aug 1829 RtCt: 6 Aug 1829
Saml. M. EDWARDS of Ldn to Charles HARDY of Ldn. Release of
trust of Jul 1826, DBk MMM:350, for debt to Thomas PHILLIPS
(Exor of James MOORE) & John LLOYD using 50a. Delv. to HARDY
18 Nov 1829.

3S:245 Date: 23 Jul 1829 RtCt: 8 Aug 1829
Richard H. HENDERSON of Lsbg to Enoch FRANCIS of Lsbg. B/S of ½a lot and house on Royal St in Lsbg (from trust of Feb 1828 from Robert R. HOUGH, DBk QQQ:235).

3S:247 Date: 18 Nov 1818 RtCt: 10 Aug 1829
Decree of 27 Nov 1818 in Sup Ct at Winchester. James SCOTT & wife Phebe agst John MINES and others. SCOTT can make mortgage with approval of MINES and others.

3S:248 Date: 10 Aug 1829 RtCt: 10 Aug 1829
George W. SHAWEN. Qualified as Captain in 56th Reg 6th Brig 2nd Div of Va Militia.

3S:248 Date: 27 Jun 1829 RtCt: 10 Aug 1829
Noah HIXON. Oath as Ensign in 56th Reg 6th Brig 2nd Div of Va Militia.

3S:249 Date: 11 Aug 1829 RtCt:11 Aug 1829
Richard L. HARRIS. Oath as Ensign in 56th Reg 6th Brig 2nd Div of Va Militia.

3S:250 Date: 14 Sep 1829 RtCt: 14 Sep 1829
William PIGGOTT and Isaac NICHOLS. Bond on PIGGOTT as Committee for Lydia NICHOLLS a lunatic.

3S:250 Date: 26 Dec 1828 RtCt: 10 Aug 1829
Saml. HOUGH & wife Jane G. of Ldn to Enoch SHRIGLEY of Ldn. B/S of 25a on E side of Short hill adj Robert BRADEN (prch/o Peter SAUNDERS by Dr. Isaac HOUGH who sold to Saml). Geo. W. SHAWEN, Noble S. BRADEN. Delv. to SHRIGLEY 9 Aug 1830.

3S:252 Date: 7 Mar 1829 RtCt: 10 Aug 1829
John RUSE & wife Sarah of Ldn to Amasa HOUGH of Ldn. B/S of lot in Wtfd (cnvy/b HOUGH Oct 1820). Wit: Noble S. BRADEN, Samuel HOUGH.

3S:254 Date: 8 Aug 1829 RtCt: 10 Aug 1829
Newton KEENE & wife Elizabeth of Ldn to Charles OFFUTT of Ldn. B/S of 150a adj Washington HUMMER, reps of William LANE. Wit: Johnston CLEVELAND, Thomas DARNE. Delv. to OFFUTT 6 Jan 1831.

3S:257 Date: 10 Aug 1829 RtCt: 10 Aug 1829
John EVANS of St. Louis Missouri and William EVANS of Ldn by attorney John EVANS to Charles OFFUTT of Ldn. B/S of 29a (part of 'Camels lot') adj __ HUMMER. Delv. to OFFUTT 6 Jan 1831.

3S:258 Date: 10 Aug 1829 RtCt: 10 Aug 1829
Joseph HOUGH of Ldn to John JANNEY of Ldn. Trust for debt to Nathan NEER using lot in Hllb adj Samuel CLENDENING, Josiah WHITE.

3S:260 Date: 23 Mar 1828 RtCt: 10 Aug 1829
David BRIDGESS & wife Nancy late HUMMER of Wilson Co Tennessee to Robert DARNE of Ldn. B/S of 16½a Lot #1 from div. of William HUMMER dec'd f/o Nancy.

3S:262 Date: 10 Aug 1829 RtCt: 10 Aug 1829
Isaac NICKOLS (other trustee James HOGE is dec'd) to Abel JANNEY. Release of trust of Apr 1821 for debt to Samuel & Isaac NICHOLS Sr. of 110a.

3S:264 Date: 6 Aug 1829 RtCt: 10 Aug 1829
James P. BRADFIELD & wife Elizabeth of Ldn to William YOUNG and Thomas T. NICKOLS of Ldn. Trust for debt to Jacob NICKOLS using 100a (title bond of 24 Mar 1828 from James BRADFIELD). Wit: Tho. NICHOLS, N. C. WILLIAMS.

3S:267 Date: 18 Jun 1829 RtCt: 10 Aug 1829
William P. EATON of Shannandoah Co Va to David BEALL and Amos GULICK of Ldn. B/S of ½a Lot #28 with log house at Loudoun St & Hope alley in Mt. Gilead adj J. C. LICKEY, W. HANDY dec'd.

3S:269 Date: 17 Jun 1829 RtCt: 10 Aug 1829
Joseph HOUGH & wife Rachel S. of Ldn to Aaron RUSSEL and Mahlon RUSSEL of Ldn. B/S of 1/9th interest in land of William RUSSELL dec'd (Rachel is heir) adj Benjamin LESLIE, Hannah PARKER, Mortimer McILHANY, Peter COMPHER. Wit: Craven OSBURN, John WHITE.

3S:271 Date: 10 Aug 1829 RtCt: 11 Aug 1829
Joseph HOUGH to Geo. RICHARDS. Trust for Samuel M. BOSS as security on bonds to Joseph HILLIARD, Robert BENTLEY, Richard H. HENDERSON Admr of Thos. R. MOTT dec'd, __ SAUNDERS, Wm. MERSHON using farm animals and items. Wit: Josiah L. DREAN, John L. DIVINE, James BRAWNER. Delv. to BOSS 26 Apr 1840.

3S:273 Date: 20 Jul 1829 RtCt: 12 Aug 1829
Henry RUSSELL & wife Matilda of Ldn to Archibald McDANIEL of Ldn. B/S of undivided 1/7th of 176a and 1/7/th of 1/7th interest from sister Mary Ann McDANIEL dec'd (as heirs of James McDANIEL dec'd) adj Thomas WHITE. Wit: Noble S. BRADEN, Saml. HOUGH. Delv. to Archibald McDANIEL Exor of said Edw'd [?] 20 Jun 1831.

3S:275 Date: 1 Dec 1828 RtCt: 12 Aug 1829
David OGDEN & wife Eliza of Ldn to Thomas C. DUVALL. B/S of lot in Lsbg at King & Cornwall Sts. adj Mrs. SAUNDERS late EKART, Wm. CLINE. Wit: John H. McCABE, Presley CORDELL.

3S:277 Date: 1 Dec 1828 RtCt: 12 Aug 1829
Thomas C. DUVALL & wife Emma of Ldn to Saml. M. EDWARDS of Ldn. Trust for debt to David OGDEN using above lot. Wit: John H. McCABE, Presley CORDELL.

3S:280   Date: 26 Mar 1829   RtCt: 21 Aug 1829
Burr POWELL to Richard COCHRAN. B/S of land nr Federal and
Pendleton St. allowing COCHRAN to comply with previous
agreement to build on land.

3S:283   Date: 25 Mar 1829   RtCt: 21 Aug 1829
James McDANIEL of Mdbg to Richard COCHRAN of Mdbg. B/S of
½a at Pendleton & Federal St. (cnvy/b Jacob MANN, where Nelson
GREEN once erected tanyard).

3S:285   Date: 20 Aug 1829   RtCt: 21 Aug 1829
Bank of Alexandria to Joshua PUSEY of Ldn. B/S of 150a in
Piedmont adj John NICKLIN, John CUMMING, Sanford RAMEY, __
McGARVICK (see DBk NNN:022). Delv. 20 Feb 1834.

3S:287   Date: 31 Feb 1829   RtCt: 24 Aug 1829
Daniel McMULLIN of Ldn to Samuel BROWN of Ldn. BoS for farm
animals, household items. Wit: Cagby JONES, Thomas ADLEY.

3S:288   Date: 25 Aug 1829   RtCt: 25 Aug 1829
Joseph HOUGH of Ldn to George RICHARDS of Ldn. Trust for
Saml. M. BOSS as security on bonds using household items. Wit:
John MARTIN, William A. JACOBS. Delv. to BOSS 2 Apr 1840.

3S:290   Date: 8 Aug 1829   RtCt: 27 Aug 1829
William D. DRISH & wife Harriet to Ellen Ann WILDMAN, Charles
Bennett WILDMAN, John Hamilton WILDMAN, Elizabeth Ann
WILDMAN and Bennett Hamilton WILDMAN (ch/o Enos WILDMAN
dec'd). B/S of house & lot on Market St. in Lsbg (cnvy/b Presley
CORDELL Oct 1823, sale arranged before death of Enos). Wit:
Tasker C. QUINLAN, Presley CORDELL.

3S:292   Date: 8 Aug 1827   RtCt: 27 Aug 1829
William D. DRISH & wife Harriet of Ldn to William L. POWELL of
Ldn. B/S of lot on Market St. in Lsbg. Wit: Tasker C. QUINLAN,
Presley CORDELL.

3S:294   Date: 25 Aug 1829   RtCt: 28 Aug 1829
Peter FEICHTER & wife Susannah late STONEBURNER of Ldn to
Jacob STONEBURNER of Ldn. B/S of interest in dower of Barbara
DRISH from div. of Jacob STONEBURNER dec'd; and interest in lot
allotted Christiana STONEBURNER now dec'd in div. of Jacob
dec'd. Wit: John H. McCABE, Presley CORDELL.

3S:296   Date: 31 Aug 1829   RtCt: 31 Aug 1829
Joseph BURGOYNE of Ldn to son Lewis BURGOYNE. Gift of
household items, hogs, bible.

3S:297   Date: 31 Aug 1829   RtCt: 31 Aug 1829
Michael BOGER of Ldn to Peter DERRY of Ldn. B/S of 27¾a in
German Settlement adj __ SWANK, __ STUCK, __ FRY, __
FAWLEY; and 10a (both from div. of Michael BOGER dec'd, DBk
III:036) adj __ BOOTH; and interest in 134½a assigned widow
Elizabeth BOGER; and interest in 29a Lot #7 allotted Elizabeth

BOGER the younger since dec'd and 11¼a Lot #1 to mother. Delv. to DERRY 22 Jul 1835.

3S:300 Date: 22 Aug 1829 RtCt: 3 Sep 1829
William FULTON of FredVa to David CONARD of Ldn. B/S of 16¾a Lot #8 in div. of father Hugh FULTON dec'd. Delv. pr order filed DBk HHH:082, 25 Nov 1829.

3S:301 Date: 30 Jun 1829 RtCt: 3 Sep 1829
George MARLOW (Exor of Edward MARLOW dec'd) of Ldn to Robert RUSSELL of Ldn. B/S of land adj Col. CLAPHAM dec'd, Anthony AMOND, Conrad SHAVER, Peter COMPHOR, __ YEAKEY; and another tract on W side of Kittocton Mt. adj Peter FRY, totaling 211a. Delv. to RUSSELL 27 Jan 1824.

3S:304 Date: 5 Sep 1829 RtCt: 5 Sep 1829
Rich'd H. HENDERSON of Lsbg to James WOOD of Lsbg. Release of trust of Oct 1823 for debt to Mandeville & Lamour of AlexDC.

3S:306 Date: 31 Mar 1826 RtCt: 8 Sep 1829
John SCHOOLEY, Wm. H. HOUGH and Daniel STONE (Exors of William HOUGH dec'd) of Ldn to Nathan MINOR of Ldn. B/S of lot (#4 at sale) in Wtfd on road from Friends Meeting to Wtfd adj Elizabeth GOARE.

3S:308 Date: 19 Apr 1828 RtCt: 8 Sep 1829
John BOGER & wife Margaret of Ldn to Henry HICKMAN of Ldn. B/S of 1a (cnvy/b Amos JANNEY Mar 1820) adj Benjamin GRUBB. Wit: Ebenezer GRUBB, Geo. W. SHAWEN. Delv. to HICKMAN 11 Apr 1831.

3S:310 Date: 1 Apr 1829 RtCt: 11 Apr 1829
James GARRISON & wife Elizabeth of Ldn to Charles G. ESKRIDGE of Ldn. Trust for debt to David OGDEN using lot at King & Market Sts in Lsbg (cnvy/b John McCORMICK Mar 1828, DBk QQQ:112) occupied by Dr. Geo. LEE, Jno. J. HARDING & John SHAW. Wit: Wilson C. SELDEN, Presley CORDELL.

3S:312 Date: 11 Sep 1829 RtCt: 11 Sep 1829
Alfred H. POWELL Jr. of Ldn to Stephen RAWLINGS of Ldn. B/S of 133 12/160a Lot #3 in div. of Leven POWELL Jr. dec'd. Delv. to RAWLINGS 8 Oct 1829.

3S:314 Date: 19 May 1828 RtCt: 12 Sep 1829
Simon A. BINNS of Ldn to Saml. M. EDWARDS of Ldn (trustee of Sarah BINNS). B/S of house & 1a lot; and 30a dev. by John A. BINNS dec'd to Mary Ann MURRAY late BINNS d/o Simon subject to life estate of Dewanner WATT late BINNS, DBk PPP:073 (for trust to Sarah BINNS w/o Simon, in exchange for her dower rights to farm sold to Ignatius ELGIN). Delv. to EDWARDS 17 Oct 1829.

3S:316   Date: 15 Jun 1829   RtCt: 12 Sep 1829
Jane GREEN to Ann Lucy, Hugh, Mary, James W., Sarah Ann, Charles T. & Eliza Jane GREEN (heirs of Geo. GREEN dec'd). B/S of dower Lot #16 in Mdbg occupied by John BRADY.

3S:317   Date: 14 Sep 1829   RtCt: 14 Sep 1829
Jesse TIMMS and Gustavus ELGIN. Bond on TIMMS as Commissioner of Revenue in 1st District.

3S:318   Date: 14 Sep 1829   RtCt: 14 Sep 1829
Jesse McVEIGH and H. B. POWELL. Bond on McVEIGH as Commissioner of Revenue in 2nd District.

3S:318   Date: 7 Dec 1816   RtCt: 14 Sep 1829
Jane McCABE wd/o Henry McCABE dec'd, John H. McCABE & wife Mary, Catherine DOWLING, John NEWTON & wife Harriet of Ldn to John MINES of Ldn (trustee of Phebe SCOTT and James SCOTT of Lsbg). B/S of ½a on W addition of Lsbg on N side of Market St adj Mrs. DOWLING. Wit: Abiel JENNERS, Robert BRADEN. Chancery suit of 19 Apr 1828 – Bank of Valley, John MINES and James H. HAMILTON agst Daniel GOLD & wife Phebe late SCOTT, Fayette BALL, Mary Eleanor MOTT and Armstead MOTT infant by George W. SEEVERS their Guardian adlitum.

3S:323   Date: 5 Jun 1829   RtCt: 14 Sep 1829
Rich'd OSBURN. Qualified as Col. in 2nd Reg of Cavalry 2nd Div Va Militia.

3S:323   Date: 14 Sep 1829   RtCt: 15 Sep 1829
Garrison B. FRENCH, Jno. HOLMES and Geo. W. FRENCH. Bond on Garrison B. FRENCH as constable.

3S:324   Date: 5 Sep 1829   RtCt: 15 Sep 1829
William BEATTY. Oath as Lt. in 132nd Reg 6th Brig 2nd Div Va Militia.

3S:324   Date: 15 Sep 1829   RtCt: 15 Sep 1829
Charles BINNS and Richard H. HENDERSON. Bond on BINNS as Clerk of the Court.

3S:325   Date: 15 Sep 1829   RtCt: 19 Sep 1829
William FLETCHER Jr. & wife Harriet of Ldn to Gourley REEDER of Ldn. Trust for debt to Amos HIBBS using 165a cnvy/b HIBBS. Wit: Benjamin GRAYSON, John W. GRAYSON. Delv. pr order 19 Oct 1829.

3S:327   Date: 11 Sep 1829   RtCt: 14 Sep 1829
Christianna WRIGHT (wd/o Saml. WRIGHT dec'd), Anthony WRIGHT & wife Sarah, William STREAM & wife Pleasant, John WRIGHT & wife Sarah, Nancy HURDLE, Samuel WRIGHT and Lewis WRIGHT of Ldn to John CONARD of Ldn. B/S of 131a (cnvy/b David LOVETT to Samuel dec'd Mar 1811) adj Nicholas TUCKER, Robert WHITE, Thomas HUMPHREY, Ezekiel POTTS. Wit: Craven OSBURN, John WHITE. Delv. pr order 16 May 1833, see DBk 3X:167.

3S:330   Date: 15 Sep 1829   RtCt: 16 Sep 1829
Jehu HOLLINGSWORTH & wife Senior of Ldn to Enos PURSEL, Burnard PURSEL and Edwin PURSEL of Ldn. B/S of 52a (cnvy/b Thomas GREGG, S.H.) adj Kitocton Creek, Lewis ELZEY, Jonathan HEATON, Joshua GORE; and 2a adj other lot. Wit: Stacy TAYLOR Jr., John CHAMBLIN, Lee THOMPSON, John WHITE, Thomas NICHOLS. Delv. to Enos PURSELL 6 Sep 1830.

3S:332   Date: 28 Aug 1829   RtCt: 3 Sep 1829
Jehu HOLLINGSWORTH & wife Senior of Ldn to William SUMMERS of Ldn. Trust for debt to estate of James McDANIEL, James & Archibald McDANIEL dec'd using undivided 1/6th interest in estate of Edward McDANIEL dec'd. Wit: Stacy TAYLOR Jr., James TIPPETT, Henry RUSSELL, Noble S. BRADEN, Mortimer McILHANY.

3S:335   Date: 15 Sep 1829   RtCt: 18 Sep 1829
Yeoman Amos HIBBS of Ldn to William FLETCHER (of Robert) of Ldn. B/S of 156a on Beaverdam adj Henry SMITH, George KEENE, M. & R. FULTON, Samuel RICHARDS, Thomas LITTLETON, Isaac COWGILL. Wit: Benjamin GRAYSON, John W. GRAYSON. Delv. pr order 14 May 1830.

3S:338   Date: 18 Sep 1829   RtCt: 19 Sep 1829
John BEACH(E) of Ldn to wife Celinah BEACHE. Gift of household items, book notes and open accounts. Wit: Quintin BARKER, Henry STEVENS.

3S:338   Date: 19 Sep 1829   RtCt: 19 Sep 1829
Mahala LYDER of Ldn to Nancy MORRIS w/o Thomas MORRIS of Ldn. B/S of 31a Lot #9 from div. of Lewis LYDER dec'd, DBk LLL:263. Delv. to MORRIS 3 Oct 1836.

3S:340   Date: 19 Sep 1829   RtCt: 19 Sep 1829
Sarah HESSER of Ldn to David HESSER of Ldn. B/S of undivided interest in estate of Andrew HESSER dec'd in Ldn. Delv. to Daniel HESSER 20 Jun 1840.

3S:341   Date: 19 Sep 1829   RtCt: 19 Sep 1829
George W. GLASSGOW of AlexDC to Presley CORDELL of Lsbg. Trust for Michael MORALLEE of Lsbg as bail in suit of James GARRISON using interest in estate of father Henry GLASSGOW dec'd of Ldn.

3S:343   Date: 30 Aug 1829   RtCt: 19 Sep 1829
William McCLOSKY to Gunnell SAUNDERS. Trust for debt to Evritt SAUNDERS using household items. Wit: C. C. McINTYRE, J. SAUNDERS, Wm. DIVINE.

3S:345   Date: 19 Sep 1829   RtCt: 19 Sep 1829
Thomas MORRIS & wife Nancy of Ldn to John HESSER of Ldn. B/S of undivided interest in real estate of Andrew HESSER dec'd. Wit: Saml. M. EDWARDS, Jno. J. MATHIAS.

3S:347   Date: 21 Sep 1829   RtCt: 25 Sep 1829
Hugh SMITH to Townsend McVEIGH. Release of trust of Aug 1827 for debt to William BATTSON (Exor of John BATTSON dec'd).

3S:349   Date: 28 Sep 1829   RtCt: 28 Sep 1829
Gustavus A. MORAN to William MORAN. Trust for debt to Sophia M. PRIMM using negro men Phil (hired to Edward HALL) and Harry (hired to John PRIMM in Fqr), household items.

3S:351   Date: 1 May 1829   RtCt: 29 Sep 1829
James MONROE of Oakhill to Samuel M. EDWARDS of Ldn. Trust for debt to Bank of the Valley using 215a (cnvy/b John P. DUVAL Nov 1825, DBk MMM:386).

3S:352   Date: 15 Sep 1829   RtCt: 29 Sep 1829
John CRIM & Margaret of Ldn to Daniel BOLAND of Ldn. B/S of 30a Lot # 4, 8a #6 & 5a #14 in div. of Charles CRIM dec'd. Wit: Mortimer McILHANY, Geo. W. SHAWEN. Delv. to BOLAND 22 May 1831.

3S:355   Date: 11 Oct 1828   RtCt: 2 Oct 1829
Casper EVERHART & wife Mary of Ldn to Michael EVERHART of Ldn. B/S of __a lot on W side of short hill adj William WERTZ Jr., __ STUBBLEFIELD. Wit: Ebenezer GRUBB, John WHITE. Delv. to EVERHART 13 Sep 1847.

3S:357   Date: 31 Mar 1829   RtCt: 2 Oct 1829
John EXLINE/AXLINE & wife Christinia of Muskingum Co Ohio to Michael EVERHART of Ldn. B/S of 10a in Piedmont Mannor (cnvy/b Enos GARRET to Joseph LEWIS Jr.). Wit: A. WILKINS, Saml. THOMPSON.

3S:359   Date: 24 Sep 1829   RtCt: 2 Oct 1829
Isaiah B. BEANS & wife Elizabeth, Samuel B. T. CALDWELL and John J. CURRELL & wife Pamela of Ldn to James HIXSON of Ldn. B/S of 23a Lot #3 in div. of Joseph DANIEL dec'd allotted to William D. DANIEL, adj James HIXSON, dower of Tacey DANIEL. Wit: John WHITE, Craven OSBURN.

3S:362   Date: 15 Sep 1829   RtCt: 2 Oct 1829
John MARTIN of Ldn to Presley SAUNDERS of Ldn. B/S of lot on Loudoun St in Lsbg (from trust of Nov 1827 from George SHEID, DBk PPP:179).

3S:363   Date: 2 Oct 1829   RtCt: 2 Oct 1829
George CROUSE & wife Eleanor/Catherine E. of Stark Co Ohio to James STIDMAN of Ldn. B/S of interest in house & lot on E side of King St in Lsbg of Perenah SMITH dec'd. Delv. to STIDMAN 24 Jun 1831.

3S:365   Date: 7 Mar 1829   RtCt: 4 Oct 1829
Ishmael VANHORN & wife Everline of Ldn to James & William HOEY of Ldn. B/S of ¾a (Lot #6, #7 & #8) formerly owned by David LOVETT in German Settlement, adj Thomas H. STEPHENS. Wit:

Saml. DAWSON, John J. MATHIAS. Delv. to Wm. HOEY 27 Sep 1832.

3S:366   Date: 6 Aug 1829   RtCt: 5 Oct 1829
William WARFORD & wife Elizabeth to John W. DAVIS. B/S of 75a adj Abraham WARFORD, William ALLEN. Wit: Robt. BAYLY, Charles LEWIS. Delv. to DAVIS 18 Jan 1832.

3S:368   Date: 12 Sep 1829   RtCt: 7 Oct 1829
Amos FURGUSON of Ldn to Erasmus G. TILLETT of Ldn. B/S of 50a adj Mathew HARRISON dec'd, William BEAVERS Sr. and 150a.

3S:369   Date: 7 Oct 1829   RtCt: 7 Oct 1829
Samuel WILLIAMS of Ldn to Craven OSBURN of Ldn. Trust for debt to John JANNEY of Ldn using 14a on E side of short hill (cnvy/b Daniel COOPER Sep 1823, DBk GGG:178). Delv. to JANNEY 26 Apr 1831.

3S:371   Date: 11 Aug 1828   RtCt: 8 Oct 1829
Samuel M. EDWARDS of Ldn to Eli OFFUTT of Ffx. B/S of interest in real estate of Susanna CHILTON dec'd and Thomas CHILTON dec'd (from trust of Feb 1824 from Manly T. RUST, DBk HHH:151). Delv. to OFFUTT 6 Aug 1830.

3S:373   Date: 12 Oct 1829   RtCt: 12 Oct 1829
Emanuel WALTMAN, Jacob WATERS and Jacob WALTMAN. Bond on Emanuel WALTMAN was constable.

3S:374   Date: 12 Oct 1829   RtCt: 12 Oct 1829
William ROSE and Johnston CLEVELAND. Bond on ROSE as constable.

3S:375   Date: 15 Sep 1829   RtCt: 12 Oct 1829
George S. MARKS. Oath as Capt. in Va Militia.

3S:375   Date: 10 Aug 1829   RtCt: 12 Oct 1829
Thompson M. BENNETT & wife Susan G. of Ldn to William S. EACHES of Ldn. B/S of 200a. Wit: Saml. M. EDWARDS, Presley CORDELL.

3S:377   Date: 13 Jun 1829   RtCt: 12 Oct 1829
George M. CHICHESTER & wife Mary of Ldn to Enos WILDMAN of Ldn. B/S of lot in Lsbg adj WILDMAN, James WOODS, Jotham WRIGHT, __ JOHNSON, __ McCABE, __ SAUNDERS. Wit: Fayette BALL, Thomas GASSAWAY.

3S:379   Date: 3 Oct 1829   RtCt: 12 Oct 1829
William COAD & wife Barbary of Ldn to Harmon BITZER of Ldn. B/S of 1a where COAD lives adj Peter TOWPERMAN, Mahlon BALDWIN, road from Handy's Mill to Mdbg. Wit: Burr POWELL, Abner GIBSON.

3S:380   Date: __ 1829   RtCt: 12 Oct 1829
John L. POWELL of Ldn to Stephen RAWLINGS of Ldn. B/S of 133 12/160a adj __ GLASSCOCK. Delv. pr order 16 Dec 1829.

3S:382 Date: 12 Oct 1828 RtCt: 12 Oct 1829
Dpty Wm. H. CRAVEN for Sheriff William B. HARRISON to Henry STONEBURNER of Ldn. B/S of 13½a from estate of Danl. STONEBURNER dec'd turned in by insolvent debtor Henry GOODHEART.

3S:383 Date: 12 Oct 1829 RtCt: 12 Oct 1829
Jane D. WILDMAN (wd/o Enos WILDMAN dec'd) in her own right and as guardian ad litem to Eleanor Ann WILDMAN, Charles J. B. WILDMAN, John W. WILDMAN, Elizabeth A. WILDMAN, Bennett H. WILDMAN and Jane Dewanner WILDMAN (infant ch/o Enos dec'd) of Ldn to Geo. M. CHICHESTER of Ldn. B/S of 2/14th interest in Big Spring Mill property (which Enos possessed on 5 Mar 1824 in exchange for house & lot in Lsbg) and undivided interest in 40a on Potomac River (DBk 3E:381 and 3G:200).

3S:386 Date: 4 Aug 1829 RtCt: 12 Oct 1829
Johnston CLEVELAND of Ldn as attorney for Hardage LANE of St. Lewis Co Missouri to Newton KEENE of Ldn. B/S of undivided interest in 346a 'Sisters tract' adj Benjamin BRIDGES, William HUMMERS, heirs of William LANE. Wit: R. H. COCKERILLE, Thomas DARNE, Washington HUMMER. Delv. to KEENE 23 Jan 1830.

3S:387 Date: 14 Sep 1829 RtCt: 12 Oct 1829
Jacob WILTER & wife Catherine of Washington Co Md to John CRIM of Ldn. B/S of 104a (cnvy/b Philip COOPER Oct 1825) adj heirs of Daniel SHUMAKER dec'd, George COOPER, Jacob EMARY. Wit: Mortimere McILHANY, Geo. W. SHAWEN. Delv. to CRIM 2 May 1834.

3S:390 Date: 15 Sep 1829 RtCt: 12 Oct 1829
John CRIM & wife Margaret of Ldn to Thomas WHITE and John GRUBB of Ldn. Trust for debt to Jacob WILTER using above land. Wit: Mortimere McILHANY, Geo. W. SHAWEN. Delv. pr order from WHITE & GRUBB 22 Aug 1834.

3S:393 Date: 10 Oct 1829 RtCt: 12 Oct 1829
Johnston CLEVELAND attorney for Hardage LANE of Ldn to Benjamin BRIDGES of Ldn. B/S of 215a from div. of Hardage LANE dec'd. Delv. to grantee 14 Apr 1856.

3S:394 Date: 3 Oct 1829 RtCt: 12 Oct 1829
Elisha KITCHEN & wife Susan of Ldn to James LATIMER of Ffx. Trust for debt to John EVANS of St. Lewis Co Missouri using 104a on old road from Lanesville to AlexDC. Wit: Johnston CLEVELAND, Thomas DARNE. Delv. pr order 23 Sep 1830.

3S:397 Date: 4 Aug 1829 RtCt: 12 Oct 1829
John EVANS of St. Louis Co Missouri to Elijah KITCHEN of Ldn. B/S of 104a where KITCHEN resides, adj Benjamin BRIDGES, road from Lanesville to AlexDC.

3S:399   Date: 31 Aug 1829   RtCt: 12 Oct 1829
Aaron MILLER & wife Mary of Ldn and Noah HIXSON & wife Celia of Ldn. Partition – MILLER bought shares from Stephenson HIXSON, Presley WILLIAMS & wife Jane, Daniel MILLER & wife Mary (ch/o Reuben HIXSON dec'd) under belief HIXSON owned land when it was vested to Mary HIXSON (wd/o of Reuben dec'd and m/o Stephenson, Jane & Mary as well as Noah HIXSON, Rachel MILLER dec'd former w/o Aaron, and Catherine HIXSON). Mary perfected title to 3/6ths over to Aaron and she dev. undivided 1/6th to son Noah, 1/6th to Catherine and 1/6th to Emily Jane, Mary Catherine & Rachel infant ch/o dau. Rachel MILLER dec'd. Aaron and Noah divide 28a, 37a & 65a. Wit: Geo. W. SHAWEN, Mortimer McILHANY.

3S:402   Date: 30 Sep 1829   RtCt: 12 Oct 1829
William HANNA & wife Vicy of Ldn to Asa ROGERS of Ldn. B/S of 1a on Ashby's Gap Turnpike road below Mdbg, adj Hugh ROGERS, Burr POWELL. Wit: Burr POWELL, A. GIBSON. Delv. pr order 5 Jan 1843.

3S:404   Date: 1 Oct 1829   RtCt: 3 Oct 1829
Joseph RICHARDSON & wife Susanna of Ldn to Joshua NICKOLS of Ldn. Trust for debt to Isaac NICKOLS of Ldn using 108a adj Lewis P. W. BALCH where RICHARDSON resides. Wit: Notley C. WILLIAMS, Thomas NICHOLS. Delv. to NICHOLS 20 Sep 1837.

3S:407   Date: 21 Sep 1829   RtCt: 13 Oct 1829
William PIGGOTT & wife Mary and heirs of Samuel HATCHER dec'd (Isaac PIGGOTT & wife Rebeccah, Thomas HATCHER & wife Nancy, William HATCHER, Jonah HATCHER and Joshua HATCHER) of Ldn to Levi COOKSEY and Obed COOKSEY of Ldn. B/S of 7a on NW fork of Goose Creek adj Samuel IDEN; and 3a adj Stephen WILSON, Bernard TAYLOR (cnvy/b Walter KERRICK May 1824, DBk LLL:390 and 388). Wit: Notley C. WILLIAMS, Thos. NICHOLS. Delv. to Levi COOKSEY 8 Jul 1833.

3S:410   Date: 13 Oct 1829   RtCt: 13 Oct 1829
Obed COOKSEY & wife Susannah and Levi COOKSEY & wife Elizabeth of Ldn to William NICKOLS of Ldn. Trust for debt to William PIGGOTT using 11a. Wit: George W. SHAWEN, Noble S. BRADEN.

3S:413   Date: 13 Sep 1829   RtCt: 13 Oct 1829
Edward HUGHES of WashDC to Daniel BOLAND of Ldn. B/S of 30a (from trust of Jun 1825 from Samuel SAWYER, when BOLAND was not a citizen and could not own land) adj __ HICKMAN, __ COOPER. Wit: William EMACK, Henry WERTZ.

3S:415   Date: 13 Oct 1829   RtCt: 13 Oct 1829
Enoch SHRIGLEY of Ldn to James GRUBB of Ldn. B/S of undivided ½ of 25a on E side of short hill (cnvy/b Saml. HOUGH) adj Robert BRADEN.

3S:417   Date: 28 Sep 1829   RtCt: 14 Oct 1829
Thomas NICKOLS & Isaac NICKOLS (Exor of Isaac NICKOLS dec'd) to Joseph TAYLOR of Ldn. B/S of 145a adj Israel HOWELL, William HOUGH, Samuel PURSEL, Abdon DILLON, Noah HATCHER. Delv. to TAYLOR 25 Nov 1829.

3S:419   Date: 20 Oct 1829   RtCt: 21 Oct 1829
James BOWMAN of Beaufort, South Carolina to Tasker C. QUINLAN of Ldn. PoA.

3S:420   Date: 22 Oct 1829   RtCt: 22 Oct 1829
Stephen WILSON & wife Hannah of Ldn to Mary HOWELL of Ldn. B/S of 1 rood lot adj Mary HOWELL, Joseph GORE. Wit: James RUST, Presley CORDELL.

3S:422   Date: 21 Oct 1829   RtCt: 22 Oct 1829
Samuel HOUGH of Christian Co Kentucky to William H. HOUGH of Ldn. B/S of interest in estate of father Wm. HOUGH dec'd. Delv. to W. H. HOUGH 11 Sep 1833.

3S:424   Date: 5 Aug 1829   RtCt: 29 Oct 1829
Elijah FARR & wife Sarah of Ldn to Price JACOBS of Ldn. B/S of 14a on Beaverdam (cnvy/b William FARR Oct 1825, DBk LLL:058, Lot #2 in div. of Jesse HUMPHREY assigned to dau Rachel now w/o of Wm. FARR). Wit: Benjamin GRAYSON, John W. GRAYSON.

3S:426   Date: 28 Oct 1829   RtCt: 31 Oct 1829
Samuel WILLIAMS of Ldn to Craven OSBURN of Ldn. Trust for debt to Nathaniel TYLER using 14a on E side of short hill (cnvy/b Daniel COOPER Sep 1823, DBk GGG:178).

3S:428   Date: 31 Aug 1829   RtCt: 2 Nov 1829
Eli McKNIGHT & wife Ally of Ldn o Enos BEST and Mary LYDER of Ldn. B/S of 132a adj Joseph HOUGH, Deborah McKNIGHT, Isacher BROWN, Thos. JAMES, Robert CARLISLE. Wit: N. C. WILLIAMS, Thomas NICHOLS.

3S:430   Date: 1 No 1829   RtCt: 5 Nov 1829
Charles B. TIPPETT of Lsbg to Asa JACKSON of Ldn. BoS for negro John alias John BOWMAN abt 7y of age, for 19y then freed if American Colonization Society finds him fit for transportation to Colony at Liberia if he consents to go.

3S:431   Date: 13 Jun 1828   RtCt: 7 Nov 1829
Thomas SWANN and Enoch MASON to Enos GARROTT. Release of trust of May 1813 for debt to William Dudley DIGGS on 220a.

3S:433   Date: 31 Aug 1829   RtCt: 9 Nov 1829
Ryland P. JACOBS. Oath as Captain in Va Militia.

3S:433   Date: 8 Aug 1829   RtCt: 14 Sep 1829
John F. SINGLETON & wife Lucinda of Lewis Co Va to William RUST of Fqr. B/S of interest in estate of Samuel SINGLETON dec'd of Ldn (s/o William SINGLETON who was br/o of Samuel dec'd who died without issue).

3S:435 Date: 9 Feb 1829 RtCt: 13 Apr 1829
David L. ALLEN of Ldn to James ALLEN of Ldn. B/S of 100a (cnvy/b James ALLEN) adj __ WARFORD. Wit: J. BAYLY, M. C. SHUMATE, S. C. ALLEN, Wm. ROSE, Matthew P. LEE.

3S:436 Date: 9 Nov 1829 RtCt: 9 Nov 1829
Zachariah DULANY of Ldn to James GARRISON of Ldn. B/S of 17a (prch/o Joseph CAVENS heir of Joseph dec'd) adj __ GRAYSON, __ COLEMAN, __ CRUTHERS.

3S:437 Date: 12 Sep 1829 RtCt: 9 Nov 1829
Nathan NEER & wife Eliza of Ldn to Craven OSBURN of Ldn. B/S of 140a (prch/o heirs of James NICKOLS dec'd) adj Thomas JAMES, Dolphin NICKOLS, Morris OSBURN. Wit: Mortimer McILHANY, John WHITE. Delv. to OSBURN 11 Jul 1831.

3S:439 Date: 12 Oct 1829 RtCt: 9 Nov 1829
Nathan NEER & wife Eliza of Ldn to Joshua OSBURN of Ldn. Trust for debt to Craven OSBURN using 240a [140a?] as above. Wit: John WHITE, Mortimer McILHANY.

3S:441 Date: 6 Nov 1829 RtCt: 9 Nov 1829
Fleming W. P. HIXSON of Ldn to Joseph LEWIS of Ldn. B/S of 176a (part of allotment from Timothy HIXSON dec'd) adj Israel WILLIAMS, Benjamin HOUGH, John UMBAUGH, William BROWN. Wit: Z. DULANEY, Elijah PEACOCK. Delv. to W. BAKER pr order 20 Nov 1833.

3S:442 Date: 5 Oct 1829 RtCt: 5 Oct 1829
Benjamin BRADFIELD & wife Rachel of Tippacanoe Co Indiana to William SMITH of Ldn. B/S of 18½a on NW fork of Goose Creek adj Stephen WILSON, BRADFIELD, __ ZIMMERMAN.

3S:444 Date: 15 Jul 1829 RtCt: 9 Nov 1829
John GRAY & wife Harriet, Eleanor DRISH wd/o John DRISH dec'd of Ldn to Thomas SANDERS of Ldn. B/S of 14a (cnvy/b James HAMILTON to John DRISH, Mar 1825, DBk JJJ:323). Wit: John J. MATHIAS, Presley CORDELL. Delv. to SAUNDERS 4 Oct 1836.

3S:445 Date: 13 Jun 1829 RtCt: 9 Nov 1829
James THOMPSON & wife Nancy of Ldn to Amor NICKOLS of Ldn. B/S of 160a adj __ NIXON, Wm. & Levi WHITE, Isaac HUGHES, __ JONES (parts cnvy/b Jesse HOGE Apr 1827 and Daniel COCKRILL Nov 1827). Wit: David SMITH, Ann BROWN, John H. BROWN. Wit: John WHITE, Craven OSBURN. Delv. to NICKOLS 11 Jan 1830.

3S:447 Date: 27 Aug 1829 RtCt: 9 Nov 1829
Charles RUSSELL & wife Margaret of Ldn to David HANDLEY of Ldn. B/S of 167a adj 'Navel Corner' to Mary CHEW, __ BLEAKLEY, __ BUTCHER. Delv. to HANDLY 18 Feb 1830.

3S:449 Date: 10 Apr 1829 RtCt: 9 Nov 1829
Benjamin GRAYSON (Admr of Benjamin GRAYSON Jr. dec'd) of Ldn to Samuel McGWIGWIN of Ldn. B/S of ¼a lowest lot in

Bloomfield opposite of John L. GILL (was in trust by Benj. Jr. now dec'd to Stephen R. MOUNT) adj Joseph BARTON, Richard CLARK. Delv. to McGUIGWIN 8 Jun 1830.

3S:451 Date: 12 Sep 1829 RtCt: 9 Nov 1829
Craven OSBURN of Ldn to Nathan NEER of Ldn. B/S of 108a (prch/o Joseph B. FOX) on E side of foot of blue ridge adj Jonah PURCEL, Nancy WILLIAMS, __ POTTS, Joseph BEAL; and ½ of 112½a where James THOMPSON lives claimed under L/L; and 240a adj __ HOUGH, __ THOMPSON; and 67a adj __ BACKHOUSE (all tracts were willed by Thomas LESLIE or allotted to his dau Amanda O.). Delv pr order 29 Dec 1831.

3S:454 Date: 2 Jun 1829 RtCt: 25 Sep 1829
Samuel T. PRYOR & wife Emily of Pickaway Co, Abner LODGE & wife Tamzen, Joel NICHOLS & wife Sarah of Bellmont Co Ohio, Nathan NICHOLS & wife Rachel, Enos NICHOLS & wife Edna, Sarah NICHOLS, Dolphin NICHOLS, Harman NICHOLS and Archibald VICKERS & wife Pleasant of Ldn (heirs of James NICHOLS dec'd) to Nathan NEER of Ldn. B/S of 140a on SE side of blue ridge (dev. by James NICHOLS Sr. to son James now dec'd) adj Thomas JAMES, Dolphin NICHOLS, Morris OSBURN, Nathan NICHOLS. Wit: Joshua OSBURN, Nathan NICHOLS, Enos OSBURN, James WYCOFF, John WHITE, Craven OSBURN.

3S:457 Date: 25 Jul 1829 RtCt: 9 Nov 1829
H. B. POWELL of Ldn to Hiram & Townsend McVEIGH of Ldn. B/S of Lot #47 & #48 in Mdbg (from trust of Jun 1824 from Enos W. NEWTON). Delv. to Townshend McVEIGH 13 Jun 1831.

3S:458 Date: 21 Oct 1829 RtCt: 10 Nov 1829
Samuel HIXSON & wife Ruth of Ldn to Andrew S. ANDERSON of Ldn. B/S of 86a allotted from estate of father Timothy HIXSON dec'd; and undivided interest in widow's dower; and undivided interest in undivided real estate of father. Wit: Mort'r. McILHANY, Noble S. BRADEN.

3S:461 Date: 21 Oct 1829 RtCt: 10 Nov 1829
William H. HOUGH & wife Mary Ann of Ldn to Andrew ANDERSON of Ldn. B/S of 1a in new addition to Wtfd (prch/o Joseph WOOD and Robert BRADEN) adj R. HENDERSON. Wit: Saml. HOUGH, Noble S. BRADEN. Delv. to F. HIXSON Admr of A. S. HENDERSON 15 Oct 1836.

3S:462 Date: 16 Oct 1829 RtCt: 10 Nov 1829
William SETTLE & wife Margaret of Ldn to Mahlon FULTON of Ldn. B/S of ¼a lot and house in Bloomfield adj Benjamin GRAYSON. Wit: Benjamin GRAYSON, Notley C. WILLIAMS.

3S:464 Date: 20 Oct 1829 RtCt: 10 Nov 1829
Andrew S. ANDERSON and Daniel STONE of Ldn to Samuel
HIXSON of Ldn. Release of trust of Sep 1827, DBk PPP:273, for
debt to John SCHOOLEY Exor of William GREGG.

3S:466 Date: 11 Nov 1829 RtCt: 12 Nov 1820
Loveless CONWELL & wife Elizabeth of Ldn to day Sarah
CARNICLE w/o Jacob CARNICLE of Ldn. Gift of 2a (prch/o Peter
BENEDUM Dec 1822, DBk FFF:173); and household items, farm
tools, money due him from John MOSS, William HALL, __ GIBSON.

3S:468 Date: 24 Aug 1829 RtCt: 13 Nov 1829
Benjamin BROOKE & wife Hannah of Fqr to Jesse RICHARDS of
Ldn. B/S of 4a on both sides of Pantherskin (part of tract cnvy/b
heirs of James GIBSON dec'd Jan 1819) adj James GIBSON dec'd
and his brother Moses GIBSON dec'd; and ¾a on Pantherskin
Creek adj John GIBSON, Dr. Thomas W. SMITH. Wit: Edward
HALL, Frances W. LUCKETT.

3S:470 Date: 15 Aug 1829 RtCt: 14 Nov 1829
Daniel POTTERFIELD & wife Mary of Ldn to Elizabeth
POTTERFIELD of Ldn. B/S of undivided 2/9th of 166a (from father
Henry POTTERFIELD dec'd except dower) adj Sydney, Phineas &
Israel WILLIAMS; and house & lot in Lsbg. After Elizabeth's death
over to Prescilla SHOEMAKER, Catherine POTTERFIELD,
Jonathan POTTERFIELD, Joseph POTTERFIELD, Sarah
POTTERFIELD, Jonah POTTERFIELD & Israel POTTERFIELD with
Daniel reserving 2/9th rights to dower. Wit: Noble S. BRADEN, Geo.
W. SHAWEN.

3S:472 Date: 16 Nov 1829 RtCt: 16 Nov 1829
Rebecca SHAW (wd/o John SHAW dec'd) of Ldn to Edward HANES
of Ldn. B/S of lot in Lsbg (John SHAW leased to Peter FEISTER,
DBK OOO:031, FEISTER assigned lease to HANES who is now
buying the lot) adj Benj MAULSBY. Wit: Jacob FADLEY,
Washington JAVIS, John SHAW.

3S:474 Date: 18 Nov 1829 RtCt: 18 Nov 1829
Charles HARDY of FredVa to John WILLIAMS of Washington Co
Md. B/S of 50a with fulling mill (cnvy/b John WILLIAMS). Delv. to
WILLIAMS 23 Aug 1830.

3S:475 Date: 12 Nov 1829 RtCt: 18 Nov 1829
Jacob CARNICLE & wife Sarah of Ldn to Elizabeth CONWELL (w/o
Loveless CONWELL, m/o Sarah) of Ldn. Gift of 2a (cnvy/b Loveless
& Elizabeth to Sarah in Nov 1829); and household items. Wit: W. C.
SELDEN, Tasker C. QUINLAN.

3S:477 Date: 6 Oct 1829 RtCt: 19 Nov 1830
Susannah FAWLEY (d/o Andrew SPRING) of Muskingum Co Ohio
to Henry FAWLEY of Ldn. B/S of undivided 1/12th of 102½a in
German Settlement (cnvy/b Earl of Tankerville and Henry A.

BENNETT to Andrew SPRING Apr 1796, DBk W:459) and 14a (cnvy/b Peter STUCK Mar 1812, DBk PP:126). Delv. to Henry FAWLEY 11 Jun 1830.

3S:478   Date: 29 Oct 1829   RtCt: 19 Nov 1829
Jacob BAKER & wife Catherine, Andrew SPRING & wife Mary, Daniel HORN & wife Mary, George SPRING & wife Elizabeth, John RAMBO & wife Elizabeth, John SMITLEY & wife Catherine, James HAYS & wife Nancy and Susannah SPRING of Muskingum, Morgan & Perry Cos. in Ohio to Henry FAWLEY of Ldn. B/S of undivided 3/12th of above listed lots (with exception of 3 minor heirs of Jacob SPRING dec'd entitled to 3/9th of 1/12th – Jacob SPRING, Sarah SPRING & Andrew SPRING of Ldn). Wit: George FAWLEY, Samuel C. SCHOLFIELD. Delv. to Henry FAWLEY 11 Jun 1830.

3S:482   Date: 12 Nov 1829   RtCt: 26 Nov 1829
Samuel HOUGH & wife Jane of Ldn to John H. McCABE of Ldn. B/S of 20a adj Wtfd (part of tract cnvy/b David JANNEY to Hough and McCABE jointly) adj graveyard lot, mill race, __ SCHOOLEY. Wit: Geo. W. SHAWEN, Craven OSBURN. Delv. to McCABE 12 Jan 1832.

3T:001   Date: 12 Nov 1829   RtCt: 26 Nov 1829
John H. McCABE & wife Mary of Ldn to Samuel HOUGH of Ldn. B/S of 59a (cnvy/b as above) adj Wtfd, Fairfax Meeting house, __ TOLBOTT. Wit: Presley CORDELL, Saml. M. EDWARDS. Delv. to his son Hanson pr order 19 Jun 1833.

3T:003   Date: 1 Apr 1829   RtCt: 28 Nov 1829
Wilson J. DRISH (s/o John DRISH dec'd) & wife Martha of Ldn to Fayette BALL. B/S of house & 8a lot on E end of Lsbg adj turnpike road, __ HAMMETT, Dr. SELDEN, John J. MATHIAS, Rich'd. H. HENDERSON. Eleanor DRISH relinquishes right of dower. Wit: John H. McCABE, John J. MATHIAS. Delv. to BALL present owner & occup. 12 May 1852.

3T:005   Date: 12 Jun 1829   RtCt: 28 Nov 1829
Robert RUSSELL of Ldn to Thomas J. MARLOW of Ldn. Trust for debt to George MARLOW (Exor of father Edward MARLOW dec'd) using 215a.

3T:006   Date: 27 Oct 1829   RtCt: 29 Oct 1829
Charles BINNS 3rd of Ldn to John A. BINNS of Ldn. Trust for store accounts with Samuel M. BOSS using crops.

3T:007   Date: 28 Nov 1829   RtCt: 30 Nov 1829
William PAXSON & wife Jane of Ldn to Andrew S. ANDERSON of Ldn. B/S of part of lot prch/o Enos WILLIAMS adj Edward DORSEY. Wit: Geo. W. SHAWEN, N. S. BRADEN.

3T:009   Date: 30 Sep 1829   RtCt: 1 Dec 1829
Jehu HOLLINGSWORTH & wife Senior of JeffVa to Archibald McDANIEL and Stacy TAYLOR Jr. of Ldn. B/S of 1/6th interest in

estate of Edward McDANIEL dec'd and 1/7th interest in estate of Ann McDANIEL dec'd; and 1/7th interest in estate of Mary Ann McDANIEL dec'd.

3T:011   Date: 1 Jun 1829   RtCt: 1 Dec 1829
Jacob SMITH (ch/o Samuel SMITH dec'd of Ldn) & wife Martha of Preble Co Ohio to Thomas LITTLETON of Ldn. B/S of interest in 105a (cnvy/b Nathaniel CRAWFORD, DBk CC:178). Wit: Isaac STEPHENS, James JACKSON. Delv. to LITTLETON 27 Sep 1833.

3T:012   Date: 1 Aug 1829   RtCt: 3 Dec 1829
Uriah BROWN of Muskingum Co Ohio to Charles CHAMBLIN of Ldn. B/S of 1/7th interest in 111a of father William BROWN dec'd nr Scotland Mills. Wit: Geo. DOLMAY, Lewellen HOWELL.

3T:014   Date: 14 Nov 1829   RtCt: 14 Nov 1829
Zachariah DULANY of Ldn to Samuel HOUGH of Ldn. Trust for Sanford J. RAMEY as security on bond using slaves Robin, Charlotte, Winny, Cyrus and Maria.

3T:015   Date: 20 Nov 1829   RtCt: 21 Nov 1829
Martin HIEGER of Coshocton Co Ohio by PoA for John LODGE & wife Catherine, Jacob WAGGONER & wife Elizabeth and Jacob HIEGER to Daniel BOLAND of Ldn. B/S of 21a from div. of Charles CRIM dec'd. Delv. to BOLAND 22 May 1831.

3T:016   Date: 7 Nov 1829   RtCt: 14 Dec 1829
Humphrey B. POWELL. Oath as Capt. of Troop of Cavalry in 2nd Reg 2nd Div of Va Militia.

3T:017   Date: 14 Dec 1829   RtCt: 14 Dec 1829
Joseph McGEATH. Qualified as Cornet in Va Militia.

3T:017   Date: 4 Nov 1829   RtCt: 14 Dec 1829
John HOLMES. Qualified as Lt. in Troop of Cavalry in 2nd Reg 2nd Div of Va Militia.

3T:017   Date: 28 Nov 1829   RtCt: 14 Dec 1829
Jesse RICHARDS & wife Eleanor of Ldn to Thomas ROGERS of Ldn. Trust for debt to Joseph GORE using land on Pantherskin cnvy/b Daniel EACHES and interest prch/o Mahlon GIBSON in dower of Elizabeth GIBSON wd/o John GIBSON dec'd. Wit: Burr POWELL, Abner GIBSON.

3T:020   Date: 1 Aug 1829   RtCt: 14 Dec 1829
Isaac E. STEER of Ldn to Joshua PUSEY of Ldn. B/S of 114½a (from trust of Nov 1828 from Michael COOPER) on road to Mannings Mill adj John WILLIAMS, __ VERTZ, Mary FOX, Patrick McGAVACK. Delv. 20 Feb 1834.

3T:021   Date: 22 Aug 1829   RtCt: 14 Dec 1829
Burr BRADEN & wife Mary D. of Tippecanoe Co Indiana to Heston HIRST of Ldn. B/S of ¼a (cnvy/b Robert BRADEN) in Hllb adj Mrs. HOUGH, Mrs. WHITE. Wit: John BISHOP, Levi THORNTON. Delv. to HIRST 10 May 1833.

3T:023   Date: 6 Oct 1829   RtCt: 14 Dec 1829
Jacob RAZOR & wife Dorcas to Jacob SHAFER. Trust for debt to
James HOOPER using 1/11th interest in land of George RAZOR
dec'd, adj George M. CHICHESTER, R. H. HENDERSON, Truman
GORE, Elizabeth CLAPHAM; and household items. Wit: Samuel
DAWSON, Geo. W. SHAWEN. Delv. to SHAFER 15 Jun 1830.

3T:025   Date: 28 Aug 1829   RtCt: 14 Dec 1829
Aaron OXLEY & wife Elizabeth, Enoch OXLEY & wife Elizabeth,
Lewis OXLEY & wife Jamima, James SMALLEY & wife Cynthia late
OXLEY, Calvin STEARNS & wife Mary late OXLEY and Moses
BARCLAY & wife Frances late OXLEY (ch/o Henry OXLEY dec'd of
Ldn) of Clinton Co Ohio to Samuel STATLER of Clinton Co Ohio.
B/S of 2 tracts containing 134a adj Capt. John ROSE, estate of
Charles ELGIN, Philip HEATOR (part dev. to children by father and
part by grandfather John OXLEY dec'd of Ldn). Wit: Ephraim
TRIBBY, Jonathan VANDEVORT. Delv. to STATLER 2 Dec 1831.

3T:029   Date: 13 May 1829   RtCt: 14 Dec 1829
James McILHANY & wife Margaret of Ldn to Nathaniel TYLER of
Ldn. B/S of lot and house in Lsbg (prch/o Wm. D. DRISH) on S side
of Cornwall St adj Lot #35, __ GRAY. Wit: Saml. M. EDWARDS,
John J. MATHIAS.

3T:031   Date: 19 Oct 1829   RtCt: 14 Dec 1829
Ct. apptd. Commr. William H. CRAVEN of Ldn to Eleanor, George
and Samuel SINCLAIR of Ldn. B/S of 10a (from estate of Amos
SINCLAIR dec'd) adj heirs of William HAWLING, said SINCLAIRS.

3T:032   Date: 24 Nov 1829   RtCt: 15 Dec 1829
Commr John H. BUTCHER of Ldn (case of BUTCHER agst
PHILLIPS) to Edward B. GRADY of Ldn. B/S of 88a (formerly of
John BUTCHER the elder) adj Mordecai THROCKMORTON, Enoch
FURR and 50a (formerly of Elizabeth BURKIN) adj Thomas A.
HERRIFORD, Newton FURR. Delv. to Jno. L. POWELL pr order of
heirs filed TT:058, 4 Feb 1830.

3T:033   Date: 9 Sep 1829   RtCt: 17 Dec 1829
Charles McKNIGHT of Alex DC to Jonathan BUTCHER (surviving
partner of Paton & Butcher) of AlexDC. B/S of 220a (deed of Jan
1825 to McKNIGHT from Richard H. HENDERSON, cnvy/b Henly
BOGGESS Dec 1819, for 220a adj George NOBLE, George RUST,
Herod THOMAS – part supposed to have adverse title as trustee for
late firm of Paton & Butcher and of Thomas Janney & Co.
BUTCHER has deed from trustee George H. JOHNSON of AlexDC
and former trustee Joseph JANNEY for 1/3 of 140a). Delv. to Jno.
JANNY pr order 15 Jul 1831.

3T:035   Date: 15 Dec 1829   RtCt: 18 Dec 1829
George GREGG of Ldn to Benjamin SHREVE Jr. of Ldn. Trust for
John WARR and Nicholas MONEY as security on bonds for Jno.
SCHOOLEY Exor of Wm. GREGG dec'd, Patrick BOLAND, Wm. H.

HOUGH, John HAMILTON using 8a on W side of Catocton Mt. adj
Wm. GREGG dec'd where Gregg now resides with house, stone
distillery, farm animals, household items, negro woman Cloe, girl
Hannah. Wit: Richard DAWSON, Mahlon SCHOOLEY, Maria
BOD[I]NE. Delv. to SHREVE 17 Oct 1830.

3T:037 Date: 10 Nov 1829 RtCt: 19 Nov 1829
William HOLMES Jr. to Jno. M. HARRISON. Trust for debt to
Jennings BECKWITH, Burr W. HARRISON, Henry T. HARRISON &
Edward L. BLACKBURN (Commrs. for div. of Tomazin ELLZEY
dec'd) using lot 5m W of Lsbg on road to Hllb.

3T:040 Date: 1 Jan 1830 RtCt: 1 Jan 1830
Burr W. HARRISON to Samuel BUCK. Release of trust of Jul 1826
for debt to William GILMORE, Samuel BAYLY, Charles THORNTON
on negro Barnett, woman Hannah & her child.

3T:041 Date: 1 Jan 1830 RtCt: 2 Jan 1830
William THRIFT & wife Maria to John M. HARRISON and Samuel M.
EDWARDS. Trust for debt to Jesse TIMMS and Burr W. HARRISON
using lot on Goose Creek (cnvy/b TIMMS and HARRISON). Wit: W.
C. SELDEN, Presley CORDELL. Delv. pr order 3 Feb 1836.

3T:044 Date: 1 Jan 1830 RtCt: 2 Jan 1830
Thomas J. BENNETT of Ldn to Reubin TRIPLETT of Ldn. Trust for
debt to David E. BROWN of Ldn using undivided 1/9th interest in
100a in Wood Co Va from father's estate; debt due from William
HOLMES after deducting trust of Joseph WOOD; and funds from
John WORSLEY Exor. of father's estate.

3T:046 Date: 1 Jan 1830 RtCt: 2 Jan 1830
Jesse TIMMS and Burr W. HARRISON to William THRIFT. B/S of
tract on Goose Creek with new stone house (from trust of Nov 1828
from T. C. QUINLAN) adj __ POWELL, Joseph HOCKING.

3T:047 Date: 21 May 1829 RtCt: 2 Jan 1830
John CHAMBLIN & wife Lydia, Mary PURCEL and John PURCEL &
wife Mary of Ldn to Valentine V. PURCEL of Ldn. B/S of interest in
Lot #1 with grist mill nr Hllb allotted as widow's dower in div. of
Thomas PURCEL dec'd. Wit: Craven OSBURN, John WHITE. Delv.
to V. V. PURSELL 6 Sep 1830.

3T:050 Date: 28 Sep 1829 RtCt: 2 Jan 1830
Agreement - Henrietta WILLIAMS of Ffx sold to Edward FRANCIS
slave Lewis MILLS. MILLS to serve 11y from this date and to pay
FRANCIS each year until 11y is up.

3T:051 Date: 1 Jan 1830 RtCt: 2 Jan 1829 [30]
Thomas J. BENNETT of Ldn to Reubin TRIPLETT of Ldn. Trust for
debt to Thornton WALKER of Ldn using undivided 1/9th interest in
dec'd father's 1000a in Wood Co.; debt due from William HOLMES
after deducting trust of Joseph WOOD.

3T:052   Date: 1 Jan 1830   RtCt: 4 Jan 1830
Thomas J. BENNETT of Ldn to William C. PALMER of Ldn. Trust for debt to John CHAMBLIN of Ldn using undivided 1/9th interest in dec'd father's 1000a in Wood Co.; interest in personal estate of father Charles BENNETT dec'd.; debt due from William HOLMES after deducting trust of Joseph WOOD. Wit: J. B. BISCOE, John WEADON, Thos. ROGERS. Delv. to CHAMBLIN 22 Mar 1830

3T:054   Date: 4 Nov 1829   RtCt: 9 Nov 1829
Samuel B. T. CALDWELL of Ldn to Samuel MARKS of Ldn. Release of trust of Sep 1828 for debt to Morris OSBURN using 35a.

3T:055   Date: 1 Jan 1830   RtCt: 6 Jan 1830
Mahlon SCHOOLEY & wife Elizabeth of Ldn to Jesse GOVER of Ldn. B/S of Lot #52 & #53 in Wtfd (cnvy/b Exors of Mahlon JANNEY dec'd). Delv. to GOVER 24 Jan 1831.

3T:057   Date: 5 Jan 1830   RtCt: 7 Jan 1830
Mrs. M. H. D. TEBBS. DoE for Sarah RIVERS d/o Daniel RIVERS and Eliza RIVERS an infant abt 1y old last fall.

3T:057   Date: 3 Jan 1830   RtCt: 7 Jan 1830
Elias POOL of Lsbg to James L. HAMILTON of Lsbg. Trust for Thomas H. CLEGGETT of Lsbg as security on note to Michael MORALLEE using farm and household items. Delv. to 9 Jul 1832.

3T:059   Date: 4 Jun 1829   RtCt: 7 Jan 1830
Ezekiel MOUNT of Ldn to Snickers Gap Turnpike Co. B/S of ¼a on N side of Snickers Gap Turnpike road above his stone house. Wit: William SMITH, Charles CARPENTER. Delv. to N. C. WILLIAMS, treasurer of company, 25 Feb 1830.

3T:060   Date: 1 Jan 1830   RtCt: 6 Jan 1830
William CARR to Elijah KENT. LS of lot adj Samuel HARPER, James L. MARTIN, for life of Elijah and his wife Elizabeth.

3T:061   Date: 14 Jul 1829   RtCt: 5 Feb 1830
Wm. James HANLEY of Ldn to Noble S. BRADEN of Ldn. Trust for debt to Thomas PHILLIPS (Exor of James MOORE dec'd) and Phillips & Bond using household items. Delv. to Jos. BOND 3 Dec 1830.

3T:063   Date: 30 Oct 1829   RtCt: 11 Jan 1830
Gustavus STONESTREET of Ldn to wife Hester STONESTREET and her children by him. Gift of his interest in estate of father Bazil STONESTREET (will of 18 Nov 1810). Wit: Charles OFFUTT, Gerard L. W. HUNTT.

3T:064   Date: 11 Jan 1829 [30?]   RtCt: 11 Jan 1830
Daniel JANNEY (Commr. for heirs of Isaac NICHOLS dec'd) to William SMITH. B/S of 22a (ct. ordered 9 Jun 1829) adj Goose Creek Meeting House, 'meadow lot', __ ZIMMERMAN. Delv. to Exor of SMITH 31 Jan 1843.

3T:065   Date: __ 1829   RtCt: 11 Jan 1830
Ignatius ELGIN of Ldn to Robert ELGIN of Ldn. B/S of 220a (prch/o Simon A. BINNS, Samuel MURRAY, DBk NNN:312) adj Centerville road, Isaac & William HAWLING, Charles BINNS, William A. BINNS, Gustavus ELGIN.

3T:066   Date: 13 Jun 1829   RtCt: 11 Jan 1830
William CHAMBLIN & wife Asenath to Joshua GREGG. Trust for debt to John HESSER using 40a prch/o HESSER. Wit: Notley C. WILLIAMS, Thomas NICHOLS. Delv. to HESSER 3 Apr 1835.

3T:069   Date: 18 Nov 1829   RtCt: 11 Jan 1830
Thomas JAMES & wife Margaret of Ross Co Ohio to John HESSER of Ldn. B/S of undivided interest in 156a dower land of Margaret from estate of father Andrew HESSER dec'd, adj John WEST, Samuel MOOR[E]. Wit: Clement BROWN, John WEBB.

3T:070   Date: 24 Jun 1829   RtCt: 11 Jan 1830
Jane JOHNSON of Ldn to Levi G. EWERS. B/S of slave Malinda and her children Tasker abt 20y old, Sally 18y old, Bill 16y old, Elizabeth 11y old, Sampson 9y old, Martha 5y old, Ann 4y old and an unnamed female infant (for benefit of Jane during her life and at her death for sister Sarah WILSON w/o John WILSON until her death, then to Sarah's children). Wit: John HOLMES, Thomas POULTON, James CRAIG. Delv. to EWERS 16 Jul 1830.

3T:071   Date: 30 Dec 1829   RtCt: 14 Jan 1830
Joshua B. OVERFIELD & wife Anna of Ldn to Samuel M. EDWARDS of Ldn. Trust for debt to John PANCOAST Sr. of Ldn using 84a (DBk OOO:230); and 216a (DBk QQQ:402). Wit: Notley C. WILLIAMS, Thos. NICHOLS. Delv. to EDWARDS 26 Mar 1835.

3T:074   Date: 23 Oct 1829   RtCt: 15 Jan 1830
Jane POTTS of Ldn to David POTTS, Jonas POTTS and William POTTS of Ldn. Release of trust of Dec 1809 to Anna BACCHUS now LAFFERTY and Jane.

3T:076   Date: 10 Aug 1829   RtCt: 15 Jan 1830
Joshua PUSEY & wife Mary of Ldn to Henry CLEGETT of Ldn. B/S of 100a (2 lots cnvy/b Joseph HOUGH) adj __ LOVE, __ GILMORE. Wit: Erasmus G. HAMILTON, Henry CLEGGETT Jr., Jno. STEPHENSON, Samuel HOUGH, Noble S. BRADEN.

3T:077   Date: 1 Jan 1830   RtCt: 16 Jan 1830
Colin AULD of AlexDC to Presley CORDELL of Ldn. B/S of Lot #6 in Lsbg with stone house adj __ FADELEY, __ WILSON. Wit: John RAMSAY.

3T:079   Date: 15 Jan 1830   RtCt: 20 Jan 1830
Edmund F. CARTER of Ldn to Samuel PURSEL Jr. of Ldn. Trust for debt to Valentine V. PURCEL using farm animals, household items. Delv. to PURSELL 31 Jul 1830.

3T:081   Date: 6 Jan 1830   RtCt: 22 Jan 1830
John McCORMICK & wife Mary of WashDC to Josias HALL of Ldn.
B/S of lot on Market St in Lsbg adj Charles BINNS, heirs of
GLASSGOW (McCORMICK sold in May 1823 to Presley SANDERS
who sold to S. B. T. CALDWELL, who sold to HALL). Wit: Robt.
CLARKE, Jno. CHALMERS.

3T:083   Date: 13 Jun 1829   RtCt: 25 Jan 1830
John HESSER & wife Lydia of Ldn to William CHAMBLIN of Ldn.
B/S of 40a (allotted to Lydia in div. of father Abel MARKS dec'd), adj
__ HUMPHREY. Wit: Notley C. WILLIAMS, Thomas NICHOLS.

3T:085   Date: 26 Jan 1830   RtCt: 26 Jan 1830
John UMBAUGH wife Catherine of Ldn to John HAMILTON and son
Charles B. HAMILTON. Trust for debt to Philip HEATER using 173a
where UMBAUGH resides adj __ ANSEL, __ DOUGLAS. Wit: John
ROSE, Presley CORDELL. Delv. the Exors 3 Mar 1836.

3T:088   Date: 26 Jan 1830   RtCt: 26 Jan 1830
David REECE (Exor of Thomas TRIBBY dec'd) of Ldn to Mahlon
JANNEY of Ldn. B/S of 107a (21a subject to dower of widow Mary
TRIBBY) adj Joseph LEWIS, William BROWN, __ HUGHES. This
deed replaces deed of Apr 1825 which had an error). Delv. to
JANNEY 12 Nov 1833.

3T:090   Date: 14 Sep 1829   RtCt: 28 Oct 1829
Stacy TAYLOR and Amos BEANS of Ldn to Jehu
HOLLINGSWORTH. Release of trust of 1822 for debt to Amos
BEANS.

3T:090   Date: 28 Jan 1830   RtCt: 28 Jan 1830
Abraham CARRELL & wife Nancy of FredVa to Laban LODGE of
Ldn. B/S of 2a Lot #7 in div. of estate of Lewis LYDER dec'd. Wit:
Presley CORDELL, Tasker C. QUINLAN. Delv. to LODGE 19 Mar
1839.

3T:092   Date: 27 Jan 1830   RtCt: 3 Feb 1830
Josiah BEATTY & wife Martha of Ldn to Hugh SMITH of Ldn. B/S of
23a (from lands of Joseph DANIEL dec'd which fell to Martha) adj
Townshend D. PEYTON, Wallace DANIEL, James HIXSON. Wit:
Burr POWELL, A. GIBSON. Delv. to SMITH 2 Aug 1836.

3T:094   Date: 5 Sep 1829   RtCt: 5 Feb 1830
William H. HANDY and John SINCLAIR to David CARTER. Release
of trust of Jan 1819 for debt to David ALEXANDER on 65a.

3T:096   Date: 15 Nov 1817   RtCt: 10 Jun 1818/5 Feb 1830
William McMULLEN of Ldn to Jonathan CARTER of Ldn. B/S of 2a
(allotted by will of father Alexander McMULLEN dec'd) adj road from
Vernon's fulling mill, Presley SAUNDERS. Wit: David ALEXANDER,
Andrew McMULLEN, Aug'stn LOVE. Delv. pr order 9 Apr 1846.

3T:097   Date: 8 Jan [Feb?] 1830   RtCt: 8 Feb 1830
Wm. ROSE Jr., R. H. HENDERSON and Jas. SWART. Bond on
ROSE as constable.

3T:097   Date: 8 Feb 1830   RtCt: 8 Feb 1830
Thos. L. HUMPHREY, Wm. C. PALMER and Jno. RICHARDS. Bond
on HUMPHREY as constable in 2nd district.

3T:098   Date: 8 Feb 1830   RtCt: 8 Feb 1830
A. M. SANFORD, Robert SANFORD and Jacob WATERS. Bond on
SANFORD as constable.

3T:099   Date: 27 Jan 1830   RtCt: 8 Feb 1830
Leven POWELL Jr. dec'd. Division – court order dated 10 Nov 1829;
56a Lot #1 to Mary E. POWELL and Mary C. POWELL widow and
infant of Cuthbert POWELL Jr. dec'd; 50a Lot #2 to Stephen
RAWLINGS; 47a Lot #3 and 47a Lot #4 to William A. POWELL.
Gives plat. Divisors: Francis W. LUCKETT, William DAVIS, Gabriel
SKINNER. Ct. case of Stephen RAWLINGS vs. Wm. A. POWELL,
Mary C. POWELL infant ch/o Cuthbert POWELL Jr. dec'd, Mary
POWELL wd/o Cuthbert dec'd, Abner GIBSON & wife Elizabeth late
POWELL wd/o Leven POWELL Jr. dec'd.

3T:102   Date: 17 Aug 1829   RtCt: 8 Feb 1829
Jacob WIRTZ/WIRTS dec'd. Division – court order dated 13 Jul
1829; 20a Lot #1 to David CONARD & wife Elizabeth; 43a Lot #2 to
Susannah WIRTS; 50a Lot #3 & 10a Lot #12 on short hill to Jacob
WIRTS; 40a Lot #4 to John WERTS; 39a Lot #5 & 13a Lot #13 on
short hill to William WIRTS; 42a Lot #6 & 14a Lot #15 on short hill to
Ebenezer GRUBB Jr. & wife Leah; 59a Lot #7 to Peter WIRTS; 43a
Lot #8 & 5a Lot #11 on short hill to Loucinda WIRTS; 58a Lot #9 &
13a Lot #14 on short hill to Mary Ann WIRTS; Lot #10 in div. of
Jacob WERTS dec'd includes 10a Lots #3, 30 Lot #5, #6, & #7 in
div. of David MULL dec'd to Henry WIRTS. Divisors: John
GEORGE, John WENNER, A. M. SANFORD. Gives plat. Case of
David CONARD & wife Elizabeth late WIRTS, Jno. WIRTS, Jacob
WIRTS, Peter WIRTS, Wm. WIRTS & Lucinda WIRTS under the
age of 21y by David CONARD next friend vs. Ebenezer Jr. & wife
Leah late WIRTS.

3T:107   Date: 14 Jan 1830   RtCt: 8 Feb 1830
Henry TAYLOR dec'd. Division – court order dated 9 Feb 1829;
114a Lot #1 with house and barn and 10a Lot #2 to Joshua
RATLIFF & wife Nancy and Harriet & Sarah TAYLOR jointly; 51a Lot
#3 with mill, miller house, lime kiln and loghouse occupied by Levi
COLLINS to be removed to George W. HENRY for his 3/7th
purchase from __; 41a Lot #4 with schoolhouse to be moved to
Robt. MOFFETT for 1/7th right of his purchase from Sampson
RICHARDS & wife __ late TAYLOR. Gives plat. Divisors: Saml.
DAWSON, Jno. J. MATHIAS, Joshua PUSEY, Thomas PHILLIPS.

3T:110   Date: 28 Feb 1829   RtCt: 8 Feb 1830
Joseph DANIEL dec'd. Division of 224a – 63a Lot #1 including mansion house to widow Tacy as dower; 23a Lot #2 to Humphrey DANIEL; 23a Lot #3 to William D. DANIEL; 23a Lot #4 to Josiah BEATY & wife Martha; 13a Lot #5 to Mason MARKS & wife Hannah; 23a Lot #6 to Wallace DANIEL; 23a Lot #7 to William ALBRITTIAN & wife Mary; 10a Lot #5 [8?] to __. Divisors: Jesse McVEIGH, Hugh ROGERS, Sanford ROGERS. Gives plat. Case of Tacy DANIEL wd/o Joseph DANIEL dec'd, Wm. A. ALBRITIAN & wife Mary late DANIEL, Mason MARKS & wife Hannah late DANIEL, Wm. D. DANIEL, Josiah BEATY & wife Martha late DANIEL & Wallace DANIEL vs. Joseph Humphrey DANIEL and Tacy DANIEL infant children of Joseph DANIEL dec'd.

3T:113   Date: 1 Jan 1830   RtCt: 16 Jan 1830
Presley CORDELL & wife Amelia of Ldn to Samuel M. EDWARDS of Ldn. Trust for debt to Collin AULD of AlexDC using Lot #6 with stone house in Lsbg (cnvy/b AULD 1 Jan 1830). Wit: Tasker C. QUINLAN, Jno. J. MATHIAS. Delv. pr order 3 Jan 1834.

3T:115   Date: 6 Feb 1830   RtCt: 6 Feb 1830
Daniel JANNEY and William NICHOLS (heirs of Isaac NICHOLS dec'd) of Ldn to William RUSSELL of Ldn. B/S of 125a in NE Wtfd (cnvy/b John McGETH jointly to Isaac & Samuel NICHOLS and William NICHOLS); and 45a (cnvy/b Isaac LAROWE in 2 deeds). Wit: Samuel NICHOLS, Lot HOLMES. Delv. to RUSSELL 27 Oct 1835.

3T:116   Date: 22 Jan 1830   RtCt: 8 Feb 1830
Humphrey B. POWELL of Ldn to John C. HANDY of Ldn. Release of trust of May 1822, DBk EEE:151, to Noble BEVERIDGE on lot in Wtfd.

3T:118   Date: 8 Feb 1830   RtCt: 8 Feb 1830
John WAR of Ldn to William HOLMES of Ldn. B/S of 41a (cnvy/b Thos. J. BENNETT). Delv. to HOLMES 12 Jul 1830.

3T:119   Date: 6 Feb 1830   RtCt: 8 Feb 1830
Townsend McVEIGH to James McDANIEL. Release of trust of Sep 1826 for debt to Edwin C. BROWN on Lot #15 in Mdbg. Wit: James ROGERS, Thomas ROGERS, Asa ROGERS.

3T:120   Date: 19 Jan 1830   RtCt: 8 Feb 1830
John J. MATHIAS & wife Caroline F. of Ldn to John FRY of Ldn. B/S of 10a at foot of short hill adj Katocton Creek, Francis AWBURY patent. Wit: Saml. M. EDWARDS, Tasker C. QUINLAN.

3T:122   Date: 4 Feb 1830   RtCt: 8 Feb 1830
John BOYD of Mdbg to Samuel CAMPBELL. Trust for A. G. WATERMAN, H. B. POWELL as endorsers on bank note using Lot #53 in Mdbg where he now resides. Wit: Tho. ROGERS, Asa ROGERS, Jas. ROGERS. Delv. to WATERMAN 4 Feb 1831.

3T:123 Date: 12 Jan 1830 RtCt: 8 Feb 1830
Jacob SUMMERS & wife Elizabeth to Alexander D. LEE. B/S of
185a where SUMMERS now resides adj William LYNE, Joshua
LEE. Wit: Charles LEWIS, John BAYLY. Delv. to LEE 23 Jan 1832.

3T:125 Date: 17 Sep 1829 RtCt: 8 Feb 1830
James TILLETT & wife Uree of Ldn to James THOMPSON of Ldn.
B/S of undivided ½ of 14a (cnvy/b James COPELAND to Uree and
Mary Ann HUMPHREY infant ch/o Charles HUMPHREY dec'd) on
NE side of short hill adj Andrew COPELAND, William & James
THOMPSON, heirs of Josiah WHITE dec'd. Wit: Craven OSBURN,
John WHITE. Delv. to THOMPSON 12 Jan 1835.

3T:126 Date: 17 Sep 1829 RtCt: 8 Feb 1830
James TILLETT & wife Uree and Margaret HUMPHREY wd/o of
Charles HUMPHREY dec'd of Ldn to James THOMPSON of Ldn.
B/S of undivided ½ of 136a (from estate of Charles dec'd) between
short hill and blue ridge adj John CONARD, James THOMPSON,
Andrew COPELAND. Wit: Craven OSBURN, John WHITE. Delv. to
THOMPSON 12 Jan 1835.

3T:129 Date: 30 Jan 1830 RtCt: 10 Feb 1830
Josiah BROWN & wife Mary of Ldn to Robert MOFFETT and
Mahlon SCHOOLEY. Trust for debt to Eli L. SCHOOLEY using ½a
lot at High and Fairfax Sts in Wtfd (formerly of Reuben SCHOOLEY,
cnvy/b Eli to BROWN). Wit: Saml. HOUGH, Noble S. BRADEN.
Delv. to SCHOOLEY 21 Jun 1830.

3T:131 Date: 28 Jan 1830 RtCt: 11 Feb 1830
Henry O. CLAGETT & wife Eveline of Ldn to Evan WILKISON of
Ldn. B/S of undivided interest of 16a (from George NIXON the elder
dec'd) on Beaverdam adj James DEWAR, William Carr COE,
Thomas BROWN. Wit: Burr POWELL, A. GIBSON. Delv. to
WILKISON 6 Dec 1834

3T:133 Date: 19 Sep 1829 RtCt: 11 Feb 1830
John BOOTHE of Ldn to Joseph EVERHEART of Ldn. Trust for
John GEORGE of Ldn as security for BOOTHE as Admr of John
BOOTHE the elder's bond to John MOORE and Daniel
HOUSEHOLDER using 68a (late lands of Jacob VIRTZ dec'd)
where BOOTHE lives adj John GEORGE, Susanna SMITH, John
WENNER.

3T:135 Date: 1 Jan 1830 RtCt: 12 Feb 1830
Burr W. HARRISON and Jesse TIMMS to George CARTER of
Oatlands. B/S of 126a 'lime kiln tract' (from trust of Nov 1828 from
Tasker C. QUINLAN). Delv. to CARTER 3 May 1839.

3T:137 Date: 10 Feb 1829 RtCt: 13 Feb 1830
Ludwell LEE of Ldn to John R. BUSSARD of Ldn. B/S of 175a
(except road through rocky branch farm to Dr. SELDEN's Island, left
for his use) adj Potomac; and 5a on SW side of Leesburg turnpike.

3T:139 Date: 6 Feb 1830 RtCt: 16 Feb 1830
Margaret McCARTY of Ldn to children Richard C. McCARTY,
Dennis T. McCARTY and Billington McCARTY of Ldn. Gift of farm
animals, farm and household items. Wit: G. W. McCARTY, Stephen
McCARTY.

3T:140 Date: 17 Dec 1829 RtCt: 17 Feb 1830
Thomas WHITE, John HAMILTON Jr. and William H. HOUGH
(Commrs. for Rebecca HOUGH dec'd) of Ldn to Jane HOUGH of
Ldn. B/S of 20a Lot #2 from div. of Rebecca's father John HOUGH
dec'd.

3T:142 Date: 15 Apr 1829 RtCt: 17 Feb 1830
Charles B. HAMILTON of Ldn to mother Winifred HAMILTON of Ldn.
Agreement – he gives Winifred his 1/3 share (from deed of Apr 1829
from John HAMILTON & wife Winifred) of house & lot in Lsbg
subject to div. between reps of Mrs. Gill WATT and Mrs. Jane
WILDMAN; she will pay taxes.

3T:143 Date: 3 Feb 1830 RtCt: 18 Feb 1830
Alfred LUCKETT of Louisville, Jefferson Co Ky to Horace LUCKETT
of Ldn. B/S of 192a (father Leven LUCKET dec'd prch/o heirs of
JOHNSON) adj Horace, Moses GULICK, William GULICK. Delv. to
Horace LUCKETT 28 Apr 1830.

3T:144 Date: 15 Feb 1830 RtCt: 18 Feb 1830
Andrew B. McMULLEN & wife Nancy of Ldn to Jonathan CARTER
of Ldn. B/S of 85a adj CARTER, James HOGE, heirs of Thomas
BISCOE, old Turnpike road to Snickers Gap, Goose Creek. Wit:
Burr POWELL, A. GIBSON.

3T:146 Date: 17 Feb 1830 RtCt: 18 Feb 1830
Emanuel WALTMAN of Ldn to Jacob SMITH of Ldn. LS for 12y of
25a cleared and 6a wooded allotted Jacob WALTMAN 3rd in div. of
father's estate cnvy/t Emanuel; and 26a cleared and 6a wooded
allotted to Elias WALTMAN in div. of father Jacob WALTMAN dec'd
and prch/o Emanuel; and 38a allotted to Emanuel; and 4a with
house allotted Joseph WALTMAN and cnvy/t Emanuel.

3T:148 Date: 18 Feb 1830 RtCt: 18 Feb 1830
Enoch SHRIGLEY to Ebenezer GRUBB. Trust for debt to James
GRUBB using 1a with house occupied by SHRIGLEY's mother adj
Thomas SMITH; undivided moriety of 25a timber lot on E side of
short hill (cnvy/ Saml. HOUGH) adj Peter VIRTZ; farm animals and
items.

3T:150 Date: 19 Oct 1829 RtCt: 19 Feb 1830
Catherine NICEWANGER of Ldn to John NICEWANGER of Ldn.
B/S of 9½a Lot #6 in div. of Henry NICEWANGER dec'd; and 3a lot.
Wit: E. GRUBB, George MILLER, John CONARD, David NEER.
Delv. to John 12 Nov 1832.

3T:151   Date: 9 Feb 1830   RtCt: 19 Feb 1830
William DERRY & wife Barbara of Ldn to Catherine COLE of Ldn.
B/S of 2 rood lot adj Matthias PRINCE, __ NICEWANGER. Wit:
Ebenezer GRUBB, John J. MATHIAS. Delv. to Joseph COLE h/o
Catharine 6 Aug 1846.

3T:153   Date: 15 Feb 1830   RtCt: 19 Feb 1830
William DERRY & wife Barbara of Ldn to Nicholas ROPP of Ldn.
Surrender of LS on __a. Wit: Ebenezer GRUBB, John J. MATHIAS.

3T:155   Date: 19 Feb 1830   RtCt: 19 Feb 1830
Conrad LONG to Samuel CROOK. Release of trust of Apr 1825 for
Charles COOK on 22¼a.

3T:156   Date: 25 Jan 1830   RtCt: 19 Feb 1830
H. B. POWELL to Albert G. WATERMAN. B/S of house & Lot #15 in
Mdbg (from trust of Dec 1828 from James McDANIEL & wife Ann).
Wit: Burr POWELL, Abner GIBSON. Delv. to Saml. CAMPBELL pr
order 24 Dec 1831.

3T:159   Date: 18 Oct 1827   RtCt: 19 Feb 1830
Peter DEMORY & wife Mary and Ebenezer GRUBB & wife Mary of
Ldn to John CONARD of Ldn. B/S of 104a between short hill and
blue ridge adj William GRUBB, __ BROWN, __ POTTS, Richard
GRUBB; and 12a adj __ BROWN; and 36a 'Dawson's lot' adj __
MORRISON. Wit: Craven OSBURN, John WHITE. Delv. pr order 16
May 1833, see 3T?, p 167.

3T:162   Date: 28 Oct 1829   RtCt: 11 Nov 1829
John T. SMITH of Ldn to Mahlon BALDWIN. Trust for debt to
Samuel SMITH of Ldn now starting for Ohio using household items
purchased from SMITH. Wit: Seth SMITH, Craven WALKER. Delv.
to pr order 9 Aug 1830.

3T:163   Date: 13 Jan 1830   RtCt: 20 Feb 1830
Commr Stacy TAYLOR (case of Samuel HUGHES and Elisha
HUGHES Exors of Thomas HUGHES dec'd, Hannah BROOKBANK
and Jeremiah ADAIR & wife Emily vs. Thomas, Elizabeth and John
BROOKBANK) of Ldn to Charles TAYLOR of Ldn. B/S of 50a nr NW
branch of Goose Creek adj Timothy TAYLOR, David JAMES, Rufus
UPDIKE. Wit: Saml. PURSEL Jr., Leven VERMILLION.

3T:164   Date: 30 Jan 1830   RtCt: 20 Feb 1830
Charles TAYLOR of Ldn to Valentine V. PURCEL of Ldn. Trust for
debt to Commr. Stacy TAYLOR using on above 50a.

3T:166   Date: 16 Nov 1829   RtCt: 20 Feb 1830
Maria BROWN of Ldn to Jonathan TAVENNER of Ldn. B/S of
undivided child's interest in land of father Jonah TAVENNER dec'd
and in dower. Delv. to TAVENER 20 Feb 1835.

3T:168   Date: 18 Jul 1829   RtCt: 20 Feb 1830
James MOUNT & wife Hannah of Ldn to Enoch FRANCIS of Ldn.
B/S of 299a subject to annuity for life to Mrs. Given HANDY. Wit:
Burr POWELL, A. GIBSON. Delv. pr order 24 Nov 1830.

3T:170   Date: 29 Dec 1829   RtCt: 23 Feb 1830
William S. GRAY, John H. SANDERS & wife Polly late GRAY, John
W. TAYLOR & wife Jemima late GRAY, Robert B. GRAY and James
R. GRAY (ch/o Presley GRAY & wife Agnes dec'd, sister of Samuel
SINGLETON dec'd) and Presley GRAY by attorney William S.
GRAY to Enoch GLASCOCK of Ldn. B/S of 339a on Ashby Gap
turnpike below Goose Creek Bridge where Samuel SINGLETON
resided at his death the mansion house being in Fqr but most of
land in Ldn. Delv. to GLASSCOCK 5 May 1830.

3T:172   Date: 22 Feb 1830   RtCt: 26 Feb 1830
James WILLIAMS and Burgess FRENCH of Ldn to Burr WEEKS of
Ldn. Trust for debt (with Charles E. CHINN) to Alfred PERKINS of
Frederick using negro girl Mary abt 10y old, farm animals, waggon.

3T:173   Date: 1 Mar 1830   RtCt: 3 Mar 1830
William HAYS & wife Sarah of Ldn to Samuel DAWSON of Ldn.
Trust for debt to Thomson F. MASON using farm animals, farm and
household items, crops. Wit: Charles HAYS, John T. HAYS, Noble
S. BRADEN, George W. SHAWEN. Delv. to MASON 9 Aug 1830.

3T:175   Date: 8 Feb 1830   RtCt: 3 Mar 1830
Sanford J. RAMEY of Ldn to Lydia RAMEY (to better discharge
claims as Exor. of Sanford RAMEY dec'd) of Ldn. B/S of lot in Lsbg
(prch/o Alexander CORDELL by SANFORD dec'd Feb 1826, adj
road from Lsbg to Noland ferry, John MANSFIELD.

3T:176   Date: 4 Mar 1830   RtCt: 4 Mar 1830
Benjamin McPHERSON (free man of colour) of Ldn to Saml. M.
EDWARDS of Ldn. Trust for debt to George RHODES of Ldn using
household items. Delv. to RHODES 9 Sep 1836.

3T:177   Date: 18 Oct 1827   RtCt: 6 Mar 1830
John CONARD & wife Barbara and Ebenezer GRUBB & wife Mary
of Ldn to Peter DEMORY of Ldn. B/S of 141a between short hill and
blue ridge (lately sold by John BAKER) adj GRUBB, Richard
GRUBB, __ POTTS, __ CHAMBLIN; and 55a adj __ POTTS, __
BROWN; and 11a (formerly part of Wm. GRUBB's farm); and 5a adj
Wm. GRUBB, __ MORRISON. Wit: Craven OSBURN, John WHITE.
Delv. to E. HARDING 26 Feb 1844.

3T:180   Date: 8 Mar 1830   RtCt: 8 Mar 1830
John POPE of Arkansas now in Ldn (Exor of Christopher GREENUP
dec'd) to Rich'd. H. HENDERSON. PoA.

3T:180   Date: 8 Mar 1830   RtCt: 8 Mar 1830
Wm. B. HARRISON, Horace LUCKETT, Thomas ROGERS, B.
SHRIEVE Jr., James ROGERS, Fielding LITTLETON, Robert

MOFFETT, Wm. H. CRAVEN, Asa ROGERS, Edward HAMMATT, Wm. MERSHON and Thos. B. MERSHON. Bond on HARRISON as Sheriff to collect taxes.

3T:181   Date: 8 Mar 1830   RtCt: 8 Mar 1830
Wm. B. HARRISON, Horace LUCKETT, Thomas ROGERS, B. SHRIEVE Jr., James ROGERS, Fielding LITTLETON, Robert MOFFETT, Wm. H. CRAVEN, Asa ROGERS, Edward HAMMATT, Wm. MERSHON and Thos. B. MERSHON. Bond on HARRISON as Sheriff to collect levies and poor rate.

3T:182   Date: 8 Mar 1830   RtCt: 8 Mar 1830
Wm. B. HARRISON, Horace LUCKETT, Thomas ROGERS, B. SHRIEVE Jr., James ROGERS, Fielding LITTLETON, Robert MOFFETT, Wm. H. CRAVEN, Asa ROGERS, Edward HAMMATT, Wm. MERSHON and Thos. B. MERSHON. Bond on HARRISON as Sheriff to collect officers fees.

3T:184   Date: 8 Mar 1830   RtCt: 8 Mar 1830
Joseph HAWKINS, John SIMPSON, Jesse TIMMS and Thos. ROGERS. Bond on HAWKINS as constable.

3T:184   Date: 8 Mar 1830   RtCt: 8 Mar 1830
Jacob G. PAXON, G. W. HENRY and Wm. RUSSELL. Bond on PAXSON as constable.

3T:185   Date: 8 Mar 1830   RtCt: 8 Mar 1830
Jacob WATERS, John MOORE and Ishmael VANHORN. Bond on WATERS as constable.

3T:185   Date: 9 Mar 1830   RtCt: 9 Mar 1830
Alfred POULTON & wife Lydia late LYDER, Letitia LYDER and Cornelia LYDER of Ldn to Joseph LODGE of Ldn. B/S of interest in Lot #1 on upper farm and wood Lot #1 allotted Cornelia, Lot #3 allotted Letitia, Lot #4 with wood Lot #3 allotted to Lydia from estate of Lewis LYDER dec'd (DBk LLL:261).

3T:187   Date: 10 Mar 1830   RtCt: 23 Mar 1830
Jeremiah W. BRONAUGH of Georgetown to Richard SMITH Cashier of WashDC. Trust for note to Bank of Columbia endorsed by John W. BRONAUGH and John MASON using 150a rented to Uriel GLASSCOCK adj William SMITH, William BRONAUGH, Thomas OWSLEY. Wit: E. BROOKE. Delv. to SMITH 6 Apr 1830.

3T:189   Date: 24 Dec 1828   RtCt: 9 Mar 1830
Amos SKINNER. Received money of Chas. LEWIS Exor of Jos. LEWIS dec'd fully discharging judgment in Weadon SMITH assee (use) and Amos SKINNER vs. Jno. SPENCER, Wm. SPENCER and Joseph LEWIS Sr. Wit: Wm. MERSHON.

3T:190   Date: ___   RtCt: 9 Mar 1830
John HUTCHISON dec'd. Division – court case of 11 Dec 1825; 95¼a including land from her father as dower to widow Keron HUTCHISON; 54a Lot #1 to Wesley & John HUTCHISON infant ch/o

Betsy HUTCHISON dec'd; 88a Lot # 2 to Lewis AMBLER & wife Sally; 66¾a Lot #3 to Bersheba, John, William and Joshua HUTCHISON ch/o William HUTCHISON dec'd; __a Lot #4 to Andrew HUTCHISON; 68a Lot #5 to John BRAGG & wife Rebecca; 46¾a Lot #6 to Silas HUTCHISON; 72a Lot #7 to Mary HUTCHISON. Gives plat. Divisors: Chs. LEWIS, Thos. B. MERSHON, G. HANCOCK. Delv. to B. F. SAFFER 24 Sep '98.

3T:195   Date: 8 Mar 1830   RtCt: 11 Mar 1830
Patrick H. DOUGLAS dec'd. Division – 54a Lot #1 as dower to widow Mrs. Evelin B. DOUGLASS; 72a Lot #2 to Dr. Geo. LEE; 105a Lot #3 to Hugh DOUGLAS, Wm. B. DOUGLAS & Eveline B. DOUGLAS (ch/o Patrick dec'd). Gives plat. Divisors: Johnston CLEVELAND, Jno. J. MATHIAS, Benj'n. BRIDGES.

3T:197   Date: 24 Dec 1829   RtCt: 11 Mar 1830
Samuel SINCLAIR dec'd. Division of slaves old Rubin, Daniel, Minca, Isabella & child Catherine, Frances, Corline, Mary, Mareah, Menervy, Maria, Sabra & son James, Amanda, Edney, Mesheck, Martha, John, Alse, Charles & Laurinda – suit of 14 Dec 1829; to Robt. SINGLETON entitled to 1 of ¾ shares 1 share in right of his purchase of his uncle Joshua SINGLETON & ¼ of the 1/7 by purchase of Allin SINGLETON 1/6 of the 1/7 in his own right & 2/6 of the ¼ in right of his 2 sisters Agness SINGLETON & Hellen MILLER by PoA – Rubin, Alce, Charles, Laurinda, Manervy; to Benjamin SINGLETON entitled to 1 share for himself & ½ share in right of prch/o William FLETCHER since the decree - Mereah, Sabro & child, Amanda, and John; to Hugh SMITH for Vincent SINGLETON – money; to Presley GRAY in right of his wife Agnes – negro Maria, Edney, Mary, and in right of his prch/o ¼ of a share of Enoch GLASSCOCK since decree given money; to John YOUNG in right of his wife Elizabeth – negro Meshech, Martha, Mariah; to James B. ALLENSWORTH in right of wife – negro Daniel; to Coleman DUNCAN in right of wife Elizabeth – money; to Benj'n S. YOUNG in right of himself 1/5 share – Isabella & child Charles; to B. S. YOUNG in right of his wife Nancy 1/6 share – negro child Caroline; to Robt. WICKLIFFE in right of his wife Agness 1/5 share – negro Frances; to Vincent SINGLETON 1/6 of 1/7 – money; to Philip ALLENSWORTH in right of wife Elizabeth 1/6 share – money; Moses WICKLIFFE in right of wife Nancy – money. Divisors: Jesse McVEIGH, Hugh ROGERS, Wm. R. SWART, Lloyd NOLAND.

3T:200   Date: 8 Feb 1830   RtCt: 8 Feb 1830
Jacob WALTMAN & wife Mary of Ldn to Presley CORDELL of Ldn. Trust for debt to Elijah JAMES using 115a (prch/o Adam HOUSEHOLDER) adj John COMPHER, George COOPER, George BAKER, John WILLIAMS.

3T:202   Date: 6 Mar 1830   RtCt: 13 Mar 1830
William T. T. MASON & wife Ann of Ldn to Charles J. CATLETT of
Ldn. B/S of 562½a 'Liberia' late residence of Thomson MASON. Wit:
Saml. DAWSON, Hamilton ROGERS. Delv. to CATLETT 3 May
1832.

3T:204   Date: 8 Mar 1830   RtCt: 8 Mar 1830
Henry BENEDUM & wife Elizabeth of Ldn to John W. WOOD of Ldn.
B/S of lot adj WOOD in Lsbg. Delv. to WOOD 18 Dec 1839.

3T:205   Date: 6 Feb 1830   RtCt: 8 Mar 1830
William RUSSELL & wife Catherine of Ldn to Thomas PHILIPS and
Joseph BOND of Ldn. Trust for debt to Daniel JANNEY using 2 lots
of 171a former prop. of Isaac NICKOLS dec'd and William
NICKOLS. Wit: Saml. HOUGH, Noble S. BRADEN.

3T:208   Date: 13 Sep 1827   RtCt: 8 Mar 1830
George PURCEL & wife Martha of Ldn to Valentine V. PURCEL of
Ldn. B/S of interest in lot in Hllb as heir of Thomas PURCEL dec'd
now in possession of David LOVETT, Saml. CLENDENING, reps of
Joseph WHITE dec'd & Saml. PURCEL; and other lot now occupied
as a street. Wit: Thomas NICHOLS, Craven OSBURN. Delv. to V. V.
PURCELL 9 Jul 1834.

3T:210   Date: 8 Mar 1830   RtCt: 8 Mar 1830
Ephraim SCHOOLEY, Mahlon SCHOOLEY, Daniel SCHOOLEY,
Thomas SCHOOLEY and John SCHOOLEY of Ldn to Eli L.
SCHOOLEY of Ldn. B/S of 25½a on road from Lsbg to Wtfd (former
poss. of Enoch SCHOOLEY dec'd) adj Robert MOFFETT, Joshua
PUSEY; and 7a adj __ MASON, __ GASSAWAY.

3T:212   Date: 5 Aug 1829   RtCt: 8 Mar 1829 [30]
Curtis GRUBB & wife Harriet late HOUGH of Ldn to Jane HOUGH of
Ldn. B/S of 27a Lot #4 in div. of __ HOUGH, adj __ POSTON, Wm.
HOUGH. Wit: Geo. W. SHAWEN, Saml. HOUGH.

3T:214   Date: 24 Oct 1829   RtCt: 8 Mar 1830
Joseph L. CRAINE of Ldn to Peter GREGG of Ldn. B/S of 'Farmers
delight' beq. from land of Epaminondas M. LANE dec'd.

3T:215   Date: 15 Aug 1827   RtCt: 8 Mar 1830
Samuel PURCEL Jr. of Hllb to Valentine V. PURCEL of Ldn. B/S of
26a (less 2a meadow sold to Mahlon MORRIS) nr Hllb on N fork of
Kittocton Creek adj James COPELAND, William RUSSELL, __
LESLIE. Delv. to V. V. PURCEL 9 Jul 1834.

3T:217   Date: 11 Nov 1825   RtCt: 8 Mar 1830
John HOUGH & wife Pleasant, Thomas STEVENS & wife Nancy,
George PURCEL & wife Martha of Ldn to Valentine V. PURCEL of
Ldn. B/S of Lot #1 with grist mill nr Hllb in div. of Thomas PURCEL
dec'd allotted as widow's dower. Wit: Craven OSBURN, John
WHITE. Delv. to V. V. PURCEL 9 Jul 1834.

3T:220   Date: 23 Jan 1830   RtCt: 9 Mar 1830
Nimrod NEWLON of Ldn to Phebe POPKINS of Ldn. B/S of 1a with house at W end of Bloomfield adj Col. George MARKS.

3T:222   Date: 6 Mar 1830   RtCt: 8 Mar 1830
Rich'd. H. HENDERSON of Ldn and William JOHNSON of Ldn. Agreement – HENDERSON sold JOHNSON lot at end of Market St and must pay interest annually for 5 years then pay principal. Wit: Jno. J. MATHIAS. Delv. to HENDERSON 22 Jan 1833.

3T:222   Date: 1 Feb 1830   RtCt: 9 Mar 1830
Levi GIBSON & wife Mary and Humphrey B. POWELL of Ldn to Burr POWELL. B/S of interest in estate of Rebecca VERNON dec'd. Wit: Hamilton ROGERS, John SIMPSON.

3T:224   Date: 9 Mar 1830   RtCt: 9 Mar 1830
Robert COCKRAN of Ldn to James CROSS Jr. of Ldn. Trust for James CROSS as security to Peter OATYER, hire of black Smith to Ludwell LEE and bail in action by Saml. M. BOSS using ' Island Mills' grist and saw mill on Goose Creek & 40a, farm animals, household items.

3T:226   Date: 20 Feb 1830   RtCt: 9 Mar 1830
John P. STULL of WashDC and John ROSE of Ldn to William T. T. MASON of Ldn. B/S of 562½a 'Liberia' (from trust of Jun 1824 from Thomson MASON). Wit: Bob GETTY, Danl. BUSSARD.

3T:229   Date: 28 Oct 1829   RtCt: 10 Mar 1830
Hannah HATCHER to Amos HIBBS. B/S of 55a Lot #3 in div. of William REEDER dec'd. Abraham VICKERS, William RICHARDS Jr., John G. HUMPHREY and Anna VICKERS sold to HIBBS 55a Lot #2 in div. Delv. to HIBBS 3 Jun 1833.

3T:231   Date: 11 May 1830   RtCt: 10 Mar 1830
Sheriff Burr W. HARRISON & William Butler HARRISON. Release of trust on 300a 'Soldiers repose' and adj 317a on S side of Broadrun called 'Mahoneys tract' now occupied by Thomas GHEEN (DBk KKK:279). Delv. to HARRISON 12 Oct 1830.

3T:233   Date: __ Nov 1829   RtCt: 12 Apr 1830
Landon CARTER dec'd. Extract of division – allotted John A. G. CARTER 740a 'Loudoun tract' contiguous with Lsbg.

3T:233   Date: 25 Jun 1829   RtCt: 25 Jun 1829
W. A. BINNS of Ldn to John A. BINNS. Trust for debt to Charles BINNS 3rd, Benjamin SHREVE, Thomas ROGERS Admr. of Isaiah POTTS dec'd, Saml. CARR of Ldn using crops.

3T:234   Date: 8 Apr 1829   RtCt: 10 Apr 1830
Hugh SMITH & wife Elizabeth of Mdbg to James JOHNSON, Henry F. LUCKETT, Joseph EIDSON, Caleb N. GALLEHER and John P. DULANEY (trustees of Methodist Episcopal Church). B/S of lot adj Hugh SMITH on NE side of Jay St, to build church. Wit: Burr

POWELL, Abner GIBSON. Delv. to Edwin C. BROUN, Mdbg pr order 25 Oct 1860.

3T:237   Date: 23 Mar 1830   RtCt: 9 Apr 1830
Mary Ann SINGLETON of Ldn to Enoch GLASSCOCK of Ldn. B/S of dower rights to land of husband Samuel SINGLETON dec'd. Delv. to GLASSCOCK 5 May 1830.

3T:239   Date: 11 Mar 1830   RtCt: 13 Mar 1830
Richard H. HENDERSON of Lsbg to Henry CLAGGETT of Lsbg. B/S of house & lot at Market & Back Sts in Lsbg (from trust of Aug 1825 from Rich'd. H. LEE).

3T:240   Date: 13 Jan 1830   RtCt: 13 Mar 1830
Eli L. SCHOOLEY & wife Ann of Ldn to Josiah BROWN of Ldn. B/S of ½a Lot #1 & #2 in new addition to Wtfd of the last sold by David JANNEY dec'd. Wit: Saml. HOUGH, Noble S. BRADEN. Delv. to BROWN 6 Oct 1830.

3T:242   Date: 12 Feb 1830   RtCt: 15 Mar 1830
William McMULLEN & wife Elizabeth of Ldn to Joshua PANCOAST of Ldn. B/S of 84a (dev. from Alexander McMULLEN dec'd) on Beaverdam adj Jonathan CARTER, Joshua PANCOAST, Daniel HAINES. Wit: Burr POWELL, A. GIBSON. Delv. to PANCOAST 2 Jan 1832.

3T:243   Date: 28 Sep 1829   RtCt: 16 Mar 1830
George SHOVER (of Simon) & wife Susannah late SANDBOWER of Ldn to Adam CARN and Michael SANDBOWER of Ldn. B/S of 17a (Lot #7 in div. of John SANDBOWER dec'd); and 4a in German Settlement adj George SYFERD; and interest in dower land of widow Anna SANDBOWER. Wit: Samuel DAWSON, George W. SHAWEN.

3T:246   Date: 19 Mar 1830   RtCt: 19 Mar 1830
Jacob LYDER of Ldn to Joseph LODGE of Ldn. B/S of Lot #6 on upper farm and wood Lot #5 from div. of Lewis LYDER dec'd (DBk LLL:267). Delv. to LODGE 19 Mar 1839.

3T:247   Date: 17 Mar 1830   RtCt: 19 Mar 1830
Isaac PIGGOTT & wife Rebecca H. and William HATCHER of Ldn to Thomas HATCHER of Ldn. B/S of undivided 2/5th of 213a nr Goose Creek Meeting house from estate of Samuel HATCHER dec'd. Wit: Notley C. WILLIAMS, Thomas NICHOLS. Delv. to THOMAS 1 Mar 1834.

3T:249   Date: 19 Mar 1830   RtCt: 19 Mar 1830
Letitia LYDER of Ldn to Joseph LODGE of Ldn. LS of Lot #2 on upper farm with wood Lot #2 and Lot #5 on upper farm with wood Lot #4 from div. of Lewis LYDER dec'd. Delv. to LODGE 19 Mar 1839.

3T:251   Date: 17 Mar 1830   RtCt: 19 Mar 1830
Thomas HATCHER & wife Nancy L and William HATCHER of Ldn to Jonah HATCHER and Joshua HATCHER infants <21y of age and Isaac PIGGOTT of Ldn. B/S of 80a Lot #1 in div. of partnership of Samuel & Joseph HATCHER to heirs of Samuel HATCHER dec'd; Greenway branch of Beaverdam. Wit: Thomas NICHOLS, Notley C. WILLIAMS. Delv. pr order 16 Jul 1831.

3T:252   Date: 6 Mar 1830   RtCt: 19 Mar 1830
Noble S. BRADEN (Exor of Robert BRADEN) of Ldn to William WIRTZ Jr. of Ldn. B/S of 162a adj Saml. HOUGH, Curtis GRUBB, Wm. H. HOUGH, __ COOPER, __ COMPHER __ HIXSON. Delv. to Wm. WIRTS 4 Apr 1832.

3T:253   Date: 16 Mar 1830   RtCt: 19 Mar 1830
Thomas HATCHER to Isaac PIGGOTT. B/S of 61a (dev. by William REEDER to heirs of Sarah HATCHER dec'd, 1/3 of farm prch/o Thomas RUSSELL) adj __ LANE, __ DUNCAN. Delv. to Wm. PIGGOTT pr order 16 Jul 1831, filed DBk TTT:251.

3T:255   Date: 1 Oct 1829   RtCt: 19 Mar 1830
John YOUNG & wife Elizabeth of Nelson Co Ky to Stanley YOUNG of Nelson Co Ky. PoA. Delv. pr order 14 May 1830, DBk SSS:335.

3T:257   Date: 12 Nov 1829   RtCt: 19 Mar 1830
John YOUNG & wife Elizabeth late SINGLETON by attorney Stanley YOUNG of Nelson Co Ky to William FLETCHER of Ldn. B/S of Elizabeth's undivided 1/7th interest in 339a mainly in Ldn with mansion house in Fqr on Ashby's Gap turnpike road nr Goose Creek bridge, where Samuel SINGLETON dec'd resided, subject to widow's dower. Delv. pr order 14 May 1830, DBk SSS:333 [335].

3T:259   Date: 15 Feb 1830   RtCt: 19 Mar 1830
Benjamin SINGLETON & wife Mary of Hardin Co Ky to William FLETCHER of Ldn. B/S of undivided 1/7th interest in 339a mainly in Ldn with mansion house in Fqr on Ashby's Gap turnpike road nr Goose Creek bridge, where Samuel SINGLETON dec'd resided, subject to widow's dower. Delv. pr order filed 14 May 1830, DBk SSS:335.

3T:261   Date: 6 Dec 1829   RtCt: 19 Mar 1830
Benjamin SINGLETON of Hardin Co Ky to William FLETCHER of Ldn. B/S of undivided 1/7th interest in 339a mainly in Ldn with mansion house in Fqr on Ashby's Gap turnpike road nr Goose Creek bridge, where Samuel SINGLETON dec'd resided, subject to widow's dower. Delv. pr order 14 May 1830, DBk SSS:333 [335?].

3T:262   Date: 17 Mar 1830   RtCt: 19 Mar 1830
Thomas HATCHER & wife Nancy L. and Isaac PIGGOTT & wife Rebecca to William HATCHER. B/S of undivided 2/5th interest in 67a (dev. by Rebecca HATCHER dec'd to heirs of Samuel HATCHER

dec'd). Wit: Notley C. WILLIAMS, Tho. NICHOLS. Delv. to Wm.
HATCHER 1 Mar 1834.

3T:264   Date: 16 Mar 1830   RtCt: 20 Mar 1830
John WILLIAMS to & wife Elizabeth of Ldn to John BRADEN of Ldn.
Trust for debt to John WORSLEY of Ldn using 183a on Cotocton
Creek adj __ BAKER, __ RAMEY, __ WALTMAN. Wit: Geo. W.
SHAWEN, Noble S. BRADEN.

3T:267   Date: __ 1830   RtCt: 20 Mar 1830
Hono(u)r TILLETT of Ldn to John JACKSON. BoS for negro Milly.
Wit: John LAINBAUGH, James BROWN. Delv. to Mary JACKSON
15 Nov 1836.

3T:267   Date: 24 Mar 1830   RtCt: 24 Mar 1830
Samuel M. EDWARDS of Ldn to Pompey HAMPTON of Ldn. B/S of
land on road from Northfork meeting house to Coe's mill (from trust
of Stephen W. ROSZEL, dev. from his father).

3T:268   Date: 27 Jan 1830   RtCt: 27 Mar 1830
Mason MARKS & wife Hannah of Belmont Co Ohio to Hugh SMITH
of Ldn. B/S of 10a adj James HIXSON, Townshend D. PEYTON;
and 13a adj James HIXSON, William ALBRITTON (parts of estate of
Joseph DANIEL dec'd which fell to Hannah from father Joseph
DANIEL dec'd). Wit: Joshua LOYD, Robert PATTERSON. Delv. to
SMITH 2 Aug 1836.

3T:270   Date: 27 Mar 1830   RtCt: 30 Mar 1830
John TAYLOR & wife Susannah of Ldn to Jacob MOCK of Ldn. B/S
of 30a abt 2m N of Wtfd (inherited from father) adj Isaac STEER,
William PAXSON, Benj. HOUGH. Wit: S. HOUGH, N. S. BRADEN.
Delv. to MOCK 30 May 1830.

3T:273   Date: 28 Nov 1829   RtCt: 1 Apr 1830
William PAXSON & wife Jane of Ldn to Jacob G PAXSON of Ldn.
B/S of 108a (part of prch/o Exors of John HOUGH dec'd Apr 1806)
adj __ HOUGH, __ STEER, Saml. PAXSON, Wtfd road. Wit: Geo.
W. SHAWEN, Noble S. BRADEN. Delv. to Jacob 1 Oct 1830.

3T:275   Date: 1 Apr 1830   RtCt: 3 Apr 1830
Yoeman [yeoman] George KEENE & wife Nancy of Ldn to yeoman
Joshua PANCOAST of Ldn. Trust for debt to Gent. Joshua GREGG
using 100a, DBk DDD:392. Wit: Benjamin GRAYSON, John W.
GRAYSON.

3T:277   Date: 1 Apr 1830   RtCt: 3 Apr 1830
Yeoman Michael PLASTER & wife Jane of Ldn to Yeoman Joshua
PANCOAST. Trust for debt to Gent. Joshua GREGG using 116a
(cnvy/b father Henry PLASTER and Aaron BURSON) on
Beaverdam adj Isaac BROWN, James BURSON, Michael
PEDRICK, quaker road. Wit: Benjamin GRAYSON, John W.
GRAYSON.

3T:280   Date: 15 Mar 1830   RtCt: 3 Apr 1830
John WILLIAMS & wife Nancy and William WILLIAMS & wife
Elizabeth of Belmont Co Ohio by attorney Seth SMITH to Michael
PLASTER of Ldn. B/S of 2a (cnvy/b Jonathan BURSON to father
John WILLIAMS dec'd Aug 1815, DBk TT:C [006?]) adj John
WILKINSON, Isaac BROWN; and 1a (cnvy/b Jeremiah SANFORD
Sep 1810 to father John WILLIAMS dec'd, DBk MM:073) adj Jacob
HUMPHREY. Delv. to PLASTER 27 Sep 1831.

3T:282   Date: 18 Jun 1829   RtCt: 3 Apr 1830
John WILLIAMS & wife Nancy and William WILLIAMS & wife
Elizabeth of Belmont Co Ohio to Seth SMITH. PoA for sale of 4a
from shoemaker John WILLIAM dec'd of Ldn who left widow and
sons John and William. Delv. to Mich'l PLASTER 27 Sep 1831.

3T:284   Date: 6 Mar 1830   RtCt: 5 Apr 1830
Thomas C. DUVALL & wife Emma of PrG to David OGDEN of Lsbg.
B/S of lot at King & Cornwall Sts in Lsbg with 2 story brick house
(cnvy/b OGDEN Dec 1828, DBk SSS:375 [275]). Wit: Zadock
DUVALL, Joseph J. JONES.

3T:286   Date: 1 Apr 1830   RtCt: 7 Apr 1830
George RICKARD & wife Cevila/Sylvilla of Ldn to John CARR of
Ldn. Trust for debt to John WESLEY of Ldn using 153a adj Daniel
STONE, Benj. GRUBB, __ SHOEMAKER, __ COMPHER, __
STONE. Wit: Presley CORDELL, John J. MATHIAS. Delv. to
WORSLEY [WESLEY?] 30 Sep 1830.

3T:289   Date: 23 Jan 1830   RtCt: 8 Apr 1830
Aaron MILLER & wife Mary of Ldn to Peter COMPHOR of Ldn. B/S
of 66a adj Peter COMPHOR, Catherine COOPER wd/o Michael
COOPER dec'd. Catherine & Noah HIXSON. Wit: George W.
SHAWEN, Mortimer McILHANY. Delv. to COMPHER 24 Mar 1832.

3T:291   Date: 12 Apr 1830   RtCt: 12 Apr 1830
Philip WINCOOP of Ldn to John WINCOOP of Ldn. BoS for
household items, farm animals.

3T:292   Date: 30 Mar 1830   RtCt: 12 Apr 1830
Noble S. BRADEN (Exor of Robert BRADEN dec'd) to Evan EVANS
of Ldn. B/S of 96a William VIRTZ, Jonah THOMPSON, James
NIXON, __ MARTIN, __ McILHANY. Wit: John WRIGHT, James
COPELAND, Wm. Fen. BRADEN. Delv. to EVANS 6 Mar 1839.

3T:293   Date: 23 Aug 1828   RtCt: 12 Apr 1830
William NETTLE of Ldn to Noble S. BRADEN of Ldn. B/S of 21a
with saw mill (from trust of Sep 1825 from Mahlon JANNEY, dev. to
him by Mahlon JANNEY dec'd). Delv. to BRADEN 30 Jul 1835.

3T:295   Date: 27 Oct 1829   RtCt: 12 Apr 1830
Robert DARNE & wife Frances of Ldn to Robert HUNTER of Ffx.
B/S of 66a where William HUMMER was known to reside, on road
from Lsbg to Alex'a nr Ldn line, Broad run church road. Wit: Thomas

DARNE, Johnston CLEVELAND, Robt. RATCLIFFE. Delv. to HUNTER 11 Oct 1830.

3T:296   Date: 6 May 1826   RtCt: 12 Apr 1830
Burr POWELL to John UPP. Release of trust of Jun 1822 for debt to Admr. of James SEATON on house & lot in Mdbg.

3T:298   Date: 13 Apr 1830   RtCt: 13 Apr 1830
George GLASCOW now in Ldn to James GARRISON of Ldn. B/S of undivided 1/6th of house & lot in Lsbg of father Henry GLASCOW dec'd.

3T:299   Date: 9 Jan 1830   RtCt: 14 Apr 1830
Conrad BITZER & wife Catherine of Ldn to Jonathan CARTER of Ldn. B/S of 98a on Goose Creek where Edmund LOVETT now resides, adj CARTER, road to Coe's mill, Caleb GALLEHER. Wit: Tasker C. QUINLAN, Saml. M. EDWARDS. Delv. pr order 9 Apr 1846.

3T:301   Date: 15 Apr 1830   RtCt: 15 Apr 1830
Thomas R. SAUNDERS of Ldn to John THOMAS of Ldn. Trust for debt to Aaron HARLAN of Morgan Co Va using house & lot in Wtfd (prch/o Thos. R. MOTT).

3T:302   Date: 14 Apr 1830   RtCt: 15 Apr 1830
George COOPER and Adam COOPER & wife Susan of Ldn and John HEIS & wife Catherine late COOPER of PhilPa by attornies George & Adam COOPER to Charles GULLATT & Saml. M. EDWARDS of Ldn (as trustee of Ann SAUNDERS w/o Britton of Ldn). B/S of 52a adj Mrs. SAUNDERS allotment from div. of Casper EKART; and 13a adj heirs of __ FULTON, __ GREGG. Wit: Saml. DAWSON, John J. MATHIAS. Delv. to EDWARDS 6 Jul 1830.

3T:305   Date: __ Apr 1830   RtCt: 15 Apr 1830
George COOPER of Ldn to Adam COOPER of Ldn. B/S of 57a adj road to New Valley meeting house, Jno. UMBAUGH, Mrs. SAUNDERS, __ BROWN.

3T:307   Date: 30 Mar 1830   RtCt: 15 Apr 1830
Archibald McDANIEL of Ldn to Mahlon JANNEY of Ldn. B/S of 71a (cnvy/b John B. STEVENS Jan 1819 to Archibald & James McDANIEL) adj Cotocton Creek, Richard BROWN, Wm. SMITH. Delv. to JANNEY 8 Sep 1834.

3T:308   Date: 20 Apr 1830   RtCt: 22 Apr 1830
Thomas HALL & wife Elizabeth of Ldn to Abraham SKILLMAN of Ldn. B/S of 100a from div. of father William HALL dec'd, adj John BENEDUM, Peter COST, Mary HALL, Isaac HARRIS. Wit: Saml. M. EDWARDS, Presley CORDELL.

3T:310   Date: 21 Apr 1830   RtCt: 22 Apr 1830
Abraham SKILLMAN & wife Delila H. of Ldn to their dau. Elizabeth HALL w/o Thomas HALL. Gift of 100a (cnvy/b Hall 20 Apr 1830). Wit: Presley CORDELL, Saml. M. EDWARDS.

3T:311   Date: 24 Mar 1820 [30?]   RtCt: 29 Apr 1830
David YOUNG & wife Elizabeth of Ldn to John YOUNG of Ldn. B/S of 18a Lot #2 in div. of __ on NW fork of Goose Creek (mother Lois YOUNG gets profits thereof during her life). Wit: Thomas NICHOLS, John SIMPSON. Delv. to John YOUNG 9 Feb 1831.

3T:313   Date: 24 Mar 1830   RtCt: 29 Apr 1830
John BURKITT and Newton BURKITT (heirs of Elizabeth YOUNG, now dec'd, who m. a Henry BURKITT) of FredMd to John YOUNG, s/o John YOUNG dec'd, of Ldn. B/S of 18a Lot #4 in div.; on NW fork of Goose Creek. Delv. to Jno. YOUNG (s/o John) 8 Feb 1831.

3T:315   Date: 24 Mar 1830   RtCt: 29 Apr 1830
John BURKITT and Newton BURKITT (heirs of Elizabeth YOUNG, now dec'd, who m. a Henry BURKITT) of FredMd to William YOUNG of Ldn. B/S of 18a Lot #8 in div.; on NW fork of Goose Creek. Delv. to Wm. TATE pr order 8 Jun 1838.

3T:317   Date: 24 Mar 1830   RtCt: 29 Apr 1830
David YOUNG & wife Elizabeth of Ldn to William YOUNG of Ldn. B/S of 18a of Lot #7 in div.; on NW fork of Goose Creek. Wit: Thomas NICHOLS, John SIMPSON. Delv. to Wm. YOUNG 1 Mar 1844.

3T:319   Date: 13 Apr 1830   RtCt: 30 Apr 1830
Thomas WHITE of Ldn to Aaron MILLER of Ldn. B/S of 11a (part of prch/o John WHITE, John WRIGHT, Ebenezer GRUBB trustees of Nathaniel MANNING dec'd), adj __ BEANS, Joseph LEWIS, __ McARTOR. Delv. to MILLER 7 Jul 1831.

3T:320   Date: 16 Apr 1830   RtCt: 30 Apr 1830
Hannah MILLER of Ldn to Aaron MILLER of Ldn. B/S of 3a adj Jonah THOMPSON, Joseph LEWIS. Delv. 7 Jul 1831.

3T:321   Date: 24 Oct 1829   RtCt: 4 May 1830
Martha L. FRENCH, Alice T. TAYLOR, Simon T. TAYLOR and Thomas S. TAYLOR (heirs of William R. TAYLOR dec'd) to Mandley TAYLOR of FredMd. B/S of 17a Lot #2 in div. of Manly TAYLOR dec'd; and interest in widow's dower. Wit: Notley C. WILLIAMS, A. GIBSON.

3T:323   Date: 1 May 1830   RtCt: 4 May 1830
Richard H. HENDERSON of Ldn to Charles BINNS of Ldn. B/S of 130a (from trust from John HULL, man of colour), former prop. of Christopher GREENUP dec'd. Delv. to C. BINNS 9 Jun 1830.

3T:324   Date: 29 Dec 1829   RtCt: 5 May 1830
Frederick SLATES and John GEORGE of Ldn to Daniel POTTERFIELD of Ldn. B/S of 2a (prch/o Solomon VICKROY Sep 1822) adj __ ROARBAUGH. Delv. to POTTERFIELD 23 Mar 1832.

3T:326   Date: 28 Apr 1830   RtCt: 7 May 1830
George SANDERS & wife Elizabeth of Ldn to Thomas WHITE of Ldn. Trust for debt to Samuel NIXON using land (prch/o Abiel

JENNERS by John & George SANDERS) originally allotted to George at lower end of farm adj Absolom KALB, Simon SHOEMAKER Sr., __ WILDMAN, Andrew HILLMAN. Wit: Geo. W. SHAWEN, Mortimer McILHANY. Delv. to NIXON 6 Feb 1832.

3T:328 Date: 28 Apr 1830 RtCt: 7 May 1830
Andrew HILLMAN & wife Mary of Ldn to Thomas WHITE of Ldn. Trust for debt to George SAUNDERS using 112a (prch/o SAUNDERS) adj John SAUNDERS, __ MORRISON, __ PEACOCK, __ McKEMMEY, __ WILDMAN. Wit: Mortimere McILHANY, George W. SHAWEN. Delv. to Saml. NIXON 6 Feb 1832.

3T:331 Date: 1 May 1830 RtCt: 8 May 1830
Wilson C. SELDEN Jr. & wife Eliza A. late LEE to John M. HARRISON. Trust for debt to Commrs. Jennings BECKWITH, Burr W. HARRISON, Henry T. HARRISON and Edward L. BLACKBURNE using 742¾a (cnvy/b Ludwell LEE Dec 1825) on Broad run adj Levi WHALEY dec'd, __ MUSE, Coton Estate. Wit: James RUST, John J. MATHIAS.

3T:334 Date: 25 Nov 1829 RtCt: 8 May 1830
James R. GRAY of Todd Co Ky (s/o Agness GRAY dec'd late SINGLETON sister of Samuel dec'd) to William S. GRAY of Ldn. PoA for monies of Admr of Samuel SINGLETON dec'd.

3T:336 Date: 19 Nov 1829 RtCt: 8 May 1830
Benjamin P. GRAY, Washington SAMUEL and Nancy T. SAMUEL (son, son-in-law, and daughter of Agness GRAY dec'd late SINGLETON of Ldn heir of Samuel SINGLETON dec'd) of Gallatin Co Ky to William S. GRAY of Gallatin Co Ky. PoA for monies from estate of Samuel SINGLETON dec'd.

3T:338 Date: 3 May 1830 RtCt: 8 May 1830
William C. SELDON Jr. & wife Eliza A. of Ldn to Charles A. ALEXANDER of DC. Trust for debt for benefit of Eliza and any children using 742a (DBk MMM:025). Wit: John J. MATHIAS, James RUST.

3T:339 Date: 8 May 1830 RtCt: 8 May 1830
Sally Lacey MANNING to Samuel M. EDWARDS. Trust for debt to Jennings BECKWITH, Burr W. HARRISON, Henry T. HARRISON & Edward L. BLACKBURN (Commrs. for sale of T. ELLZEY dec'd estate) using 153a (L/L Dec 1789 by Wm. ELLZEY and Thomazin ELLZEY Exors. of Lewis ELLZEY dec'd to Robt TODD, cnvy to MANNING Nov 1829).

3T:342 Date: 9 Nov 1829 RtCt: 8 May 1830
Jennings BECKWITH, Burr W. HARRISON, Henry T. HARRISON & Edward L. BLACKBURN (Commrs. for sale of Thomazin ELLZEY dec'd estate) to Sally Lacey MANNING. B/S of 153a as above. BLACKBURN in Hamshire Co. Delv. to MANNING 18 Sep 1830.

3T:344 Date: 8 May 1830 RtCt: 8 May 1830
John H. MONROE of Lsbg to John JANNEY of Lsbg. Trust for
Samuel M. BOSS of Lsbg as endorser on bank notes using house &
lot on Loudoun St in Lsbg now occupied by MONROE; and brick
house and lot at Loudoun & Back Sts occupied by Michael
MORALLEE. Delv. to BOSS 6 Mar 1832.

3T:346 Date: 4 Nov 1829 RtCt: 8 May 1830
Presley GRAY, John H. SANDERS & wife Polly, John W. TAYLOR
& wife Jemima and Robert B. GRAY (husband, sons-in-law & ch/o
Agnes GRAY dec'd late SINGLETON, heir of Samuel SINGLETON
dec'd of Ldn) of Gallatin Co Ky to William S. GRAY of Gallatin Co
Ky. PoA. Wit: William GLEONNELL, Presley CHALFANT.

3T:349 Date: 8 Apr 1830 RtCt: 12 Apr 1830
William WILLIAMSON of Fqr and Burr POWELL of Ldn. Exchange
of land cnvy/b POWELL and 2a. Delv. pr order 29 Dec 1831.

3T:351 Date: 12 May 1830 RtCt: 12 May 1830
James GILMORE, B. SHREVE Jr., Asa PECK, James SINCLAIR
and Jno. SURGHNOR. Bond on GILMORE as constable.

3T:352 Date: 12 Apr 1830 RtCt: 10 May 1830
Joshua POTTS and Norval OSBURN & wife Elizabeth of Ldn to
Samuel D. LESLIE of Ldn. B/S of undivided 2/9th (POTTS' share)
and 6 shares (2/3, OSBURN's share, 1/9th share to LESLIE) 23½a of
Nathan POTTS dec'd. Wit: John WHITE, Craven OSBURN. Delv. to
LESLIE 13 Dec 1830.

3T:354 Date: 24 Feb 1830 RtCt: 10 May 1830
Joseph TAYLOR & wife Lydia of Ldn to William and James
THOMPSON of Ldn. B/S of 145a on Kittocton Creek adj William
HOUGH, __ PURSEL, Henry SMITH, Abdon DILLON, Israel
HOWELL. Wit: John WHITE, Craven OSBURN. Delv. to W. & J.
THOMPSON 13 Aug 1838.

3T:356 Date: 12 Jun 1829 RtCt: 10 May 1830
Benjamin PALMER & wife Ann of Belmont Co Ohio to Samuel
PALMER Jr. of Ldn. B/S of 9a (prch/o John THOMAS) adj PALMER,
Judith BOTTS; and 3a (prch/o John HUTCHISON) adj PALMER,
John WARFORD, Judith BOTTS, Phenehas THOMAS; and 36a
(prch/o of Samuel PALMER) adj John THOMAS, John WARFORD.
Wit: Thos. WHITACRE, Lott PALMER. Delv. to Samuel PALMER Jr.
29 Jun 1838.

3T:359 Date: 16 Jun 1830 RtCt: 16 Jun 1830
Commr Richard H. HENDERSON (case of John CRIDLER agst
Mary Eleanor MOTT and Armstead R. MOTT infant ch/o Thomas R.
MOTT dec'd) of Lsbg to John CRIDLER of Lsbg. B/S of ½a on
Market St in Lsbg adj heirs of James D. FRENCH dec'd, Christian
SERWICK. Delv. to CRIDLER 11 Jul 1837.

3T:360   Date: 22 Jan 1830   RtCt: 10 May 1830
George SULLIVAN & wife Winny of Ldn to Harrison CROSS of Ldn.
LS on 231a in CamP (LS from Portia HODGSON Oct 1828). Wit:
Burr POWELL, Abner GIBSON.

3T:363   Date: 5 Nov 1829   RtCt: 10 May 1829/10 May 1830
Joshua HUTCHISON, Charles LEWIS & William MERSHON
(Commrs. for sale of land of John DEBELL dec'd) to Harrison
CROSS. B/S of 168a adj Aris BUCKNER, Benjamin JAMES, __
HODGSON.

3T:364   Date: 9 Oct 1828   RtCt: 12 May 1829/10 May 1830
Thomas MARKS of Ldn to Isaac NICKOLS of Ldn. Trust for debt to
Valentine V. PURCEL of Ldn using Lot #16, #17, #18 & #19 in Hllb.
Wit: St[a]cy TAYLOR, Albert HEATON, Saml. PURSEL Jr. Delv. to
PURSELL 31 Jul 1830.

3T:366   Date: __ Apr 1830   RtCt: 11 May 1830
Nathaniel TYLER and John FITZHUGH & wife Marian of Ffx to John
J. COLEMAN. B/S of 300a ('Jackson's lott' with addition of 100a)
(from trust of FITZHUGH to TYLER May 1827) adj __ TIPPETT, __
STONESTREET. Wit: Wilson C. SELDEN Jr., Saml. M. EDWARDS.

3T:369   Date: 28 Oct 1829   RtCt: 11 May 1830
Joseph HOUGH& wife Rachel S. of Ldn to Frederick A. DAVISSON
of Ldn. B/S of lot in Hllb (cnvy/b Samuel CLENDENNING). Wit: John
WHITE, Mortimer McILHANY.

3T:371   Date: 24 Apr 1830   RtCt: 11 May 1830
John JANNEY and Nathan NEER of Ldn to Frederick A. DAVISON
of Ldn. Release of trust of Joseph HOUGH (sold to DAVISON).

3T:372   Date: 29 Mar 1830   RtCt: 12 May 1830
Edwin C. BROWN of Ldn to William F. LUCKETT of Ldn Release of
trust of Jan 1825 for debt to Noble BEVERIDGE.

3T:373   Date: 5 Feb 1830   RtCt: 13 May 1830
Rich'd H. HENDERSON and Hugh SMITH of Ldn to Enoch
FRANCIS of Ldn. B/S of 290a (from trust of James MOUNT for debt
to John PANCOAST).

3T:375   Date: 25 Sep 1829   RtCt: 17 May 1830
Thomas N. JONES & wife Hannah of Ldn to Henry PLASTER Jr. of
Ldn. B/S of ¼a lot in Union (cnvy/b Henry PLASTER Sr. in 1826) adj
Daniel LOVETT, Benedict PADGETT, PLASTER. Wit: Benj.
GRAYSON, John W. GRAYSON.

3T:377   Date: 12 Dec 1829   RtCt: 17 May 1830
Thomas H. GALLEHER & wife Patcy of Ldn to Henry PLASTER Sr.
of Ldn. B/S of 10a allotted in div. of farm of William GALLEHER
dec'd adj Union; and interest in dower of Mary GALLEHER. Wit:
Edward HALL, Francis W. LUCKETT. Sent to Exor at Union pr order
filed in 3P:420, 23 Dec 1852.

3T:379   Date: 10 May 1830   RtCt: 17 May 1830
John A. BINNS of Lsbg to William DODD of Lsbg. B/S of lot in Lsbg (from trust of Feb 1827 from Joshua RILEY).

3T:380   Date: 1 May 1830   RtCt: 18 May 1830
H. B. POWELL to Leonard JARVIS of BaltMd. B/S of lot in Mdbg (from trust of Jul 1828 from David SIMPSON, cnvy/b Felix TRIPLETT Sep 1826 to SIMPSON). Delv. to POWELL pr order 1 Jan 1845.

3T:382   Date: 18 May 1830   RtCt: 18 May 1830
Enoch SHRIGLEY of Ldn to George SMITH of Ldn. B/S of ½ of 1a SHRIGLEY and John HILL prch/o John BALL; adj schoolhouse lot, __ SHAVER, __ DAVIS. Delv. to SMITH 10 Feb 1831.

3T:383   Date: 26 Apr 1830   RtCt: 18 May 1830
Richard H. HENDERSON (Admr of William CLAYTON dec'd) of Ldn to Fielder BURCH of WashDC. B/S of ¼a in Snickersville now in possession of BURCH (prch/o Robert BRADEN) adj Wm. CLAYTON, Amos CLAYTON.

3T:384   Date: 24 Jun 1829   RtCt: 24 Jun 1831
John WILSON of Ldn to Levi G. GREGG [later gives as EWERS]. Trust for debt to Jane JOHNSON using land prch/o of Amos JOHNSON of Fqr on Ohio River in Mason Co; interest in a claim of JOHNSON's Admrs agt. DUNCAN's reps on ajudgment subject to William CHILTON's interest; household items. Delv. to EWERS 15 Jul 1830.

3T:386   Date: 19 May 1830   RtCt: 19 May 1830
Griffin TAYLOR & wife Susan A. R. of FredVa to George MARLOW of Ldn. B/S of 41a Lot #41 in div. of Thomas CHILTON dec'd, adj __ HENDERSON, __ SHREVE, __ DULIN, __ SMITH. Wit: Saml. M. EDWARDS, John J. MATHIAS. Delv. to MARLOW 11 Apr 1836.

3T:388   Date: 8 May 1830   RtCt: 20 May 1830
Mason CHAMBLIN & wife Dewanner of Ldn to Thirza RICE of Ldn. B/S of 27a adj RICE, Fenton VANDEVANTER; and 14a wood lot adj Joseph VANDEVANTER. Wit: James RUST, Presley CORDELL. Delv. to RICE 6 Jan 1831.

3T:390   Date: 8 May 1830   RtCt: 20 May 1830
James SINCLAIR & wife Leanna of Ldn to Thirza RICE of Ldn. B/S of 42a as Mason CHAMBLIN, RICE. Wit: James RUST, Presley CORDELL. Delv. to RICE 6 Jan 1831.

3T:392   Date: 20 Feb 1830   RtCt: 20 May 1830
Elizabeth LACEY of Ldn to Malcolm KIRK of Ldn. LS of 1a (western ¾ of Lot #6, original LS from James HEREFORD to Patrick CAVEN in 1798). Wit: Thomas BELTS, William McCLOUD. LACEY's acknowledgement from Muskingum Co Ohio.

3T:395 Date: 18 May 1830 RtCt: 21 May 1830
George W. HENRY of Ldn to James McILHANY of Ldn. Trust for debt to Rich'd. H. HENDERSON using negro girl Winny abt 8y old (prch/o Ishmael VANHORNE this day).

3T:396 Date: 18 May 1830 RtCt: 22 May 1830
John A. BINNS of Ldn to Mary HOUGH of Ldn. B/S of house & lot on Cornwall St in Lsbg now occupied by HOUGH (from trust of Nov 1825 from John SHEPHERD).

3T:397 Date: 4 May 1830 RtCt: 22 May 1830
Isaac EATON & wife Malinda of Mt. Gilead to James KITTLE of Mt. Gilead. B/S of Lot #30 & #31 (total 1a) in Mt. Gilead adj J. C. LICKEY. Wit: Amos GULICK, William M. BEALL, Burr POWELL, Abner GIBSON. Delv. to KITTLE 2 Feb 1835.

3T:399 Date: 4 Jan 1830 RtCt: 24 May 1830
Adam COULTER & wife Mary, Adam HIEGER and Daniel HIEGER of Coshocton Co Ohio to Daniel BOLAND of Ldn. B/S of undivided 3/8th of 21a of Charles CRIM dec'd, adj BOLAND. Wit: Charles BAKER, Naphtali LUWORK, Thomas McCLAIN. Delv. to BOLAND 22 May 1831.

3T:401 Date: 15 Mar 1830 RtCt: 2 Jun 1830
Henry RUSSELL & wife Matilda of Ldn to Archibald McDANIEL of Ldn. B/S of 172a (cnvy/b McDANIEL as Exor of Edward McDANIEL dec'd, Mar 1830) adj Joseph LEWIS, Thomas WHITE, Goose Creek. Wit: S. HOUGH, N. S. BRADEN. Delv. to McDANIEL (Exor of Edw'd McDANIEL) 2 Jun 1831.

3T:403 Date: 12 May 1830 RtCt: 27 May 1830
Commr George WISE (case of John STUMP and David RICKETTS vs. John T. NEWTON) to David RICKETTS of Ffx. B/S of 66a Lot #4 wood land on Lsbg turnpike; and 8a Lot #10 at Tuskarora Run at Goose Creek; and 3a Lot #12 on Tuscarora run.

3T:404 Date: __ May 1830 RtCt: 29 May 1830
John A. CARTER of Ldn to Charles SHREVE of Ldn. B/S of 700a from estate of father Landon CARTER of RichVa, adj __ LOVE, __ SWAN, __ WILDMAN, __ ELGIN. Delv pr order 28 Jan 1835.

3T:406 Date: 1 Mar 1830 RtCt: 2 Jun 1830
Archibald McDANIEL (Exor of Edward McDANIEL dec'd) of Ldn to Henry RUSSELL of Ldn. B/S of 172a adj Thomas WHITE, Joseph LEWIS.

3T:408 Date: 3 Mar 1830 RtCt: 2 Jun 1830
Mahlon JANNEY & wife __ of Ldn to John BRADEN of Ldn. Trust for debt to Archibald McDANIEL using 71a (cnvy/b by McDANIEL Mar 1830) adj Wm. SMITH, McDANIEL.

3T:411 Date: 8 Feb 1830 RtCt: 2 Jun 1830
Bernard GILPIN of MontMd to David CARR of Ldn. B/S of lot on W side of King St in Lsbg (cnvy/b Jacob FADELY) adj William

TAYLOR, Joseph BEARD, Thomas SAUNDERS. Wit: Wm. BROWN, Roger B. THOMAS.

3T:413 Date: 19 Jul 1830 RtCt: 10 Aug 1830
Report of Commr. Joshua HUTCHISON – court order dated 13 Aug 1829 in case of James ASHFORD & others vs. James GORE & others. Harrison CROSS purchased house & lot at $3.10/a.

3T:414 Date: 4 Feb 1829 RtCt: ___
William F. LUCKETT executed trust on 1 Jan 1825 on 17a for debt to Noble BEVERIDGE. Note was assigned to William RUST, then to John KINCHELOE. BEVERIDGE release his claim. See page 372 for deed where this belongs.

3U:001 Date: 7 Dec 1829 RtCt: 3 Jun 1830
William C. PALMER and Mason CHAMBLIN & wife Dewanner to Joseph FRED. B/S of 170a (5/9th interest cnvy/b John, Saml., James & William TORBERT & Joseph McDONALD, where Saml. TORBERT dec'd resided, prch/o Jinkin PHILIPS of Ky). Wit: James RUST, Presley CORDELL. Delv. pr order 29 Jan 1835.

3U:003 Date: 25 Jan 1830 RtCt: 3 Jun 1830
William C. PALMER and Mason CHAMBLIN & wife Dewanner of Ldn to Price JACOBS of Ldn. B/S of 52a (prch/o Thomas L. HUMPHREY) adj __ HATCHER, __ KEEN, Mrs. HUMPHREY, __ BALDWIN. Wit: James RUST, Presley CORDELL. Delv. to JACOBS 13 Sep 1830.

3U:004 Date: 11 Jan 1830 RtCt: 4 Jun 1830
Alfred GESLEN & wife Rebecca of Ldn to Abel MAHONY of Ldn. B/S of interest in 200a (from will of Patterson WRIGHT dec'd) on little Kittocton Creek adj Danl. WINE, Israel McGAVACK. Wit: Saml. HOUGH, Noble S. BRADEN. Delv. to MAHONEY 29 Aug 1838.

3U:006 Date: 11 Jan 1830 RtCt: 4 Jun 1830
Burr Washington McKIM & wife Catherine of Ldn to Abel MAHONY of Ldn. B/S of interest in 200a (from will of Patterson WRIGHT dec'd) on little Kittocton Creek adj Danl. WINE, Israel McGAVACK. Wit: Geo. W. SHAWEN, Noble S. BRADEN. Delv. to MAHONY 29 Aug 1838.

3U:008 Date: 26 Apr 1830 RtCt: 4 Jun 1830
Thomas C. DUVAL & wife Emma of PrG to Elizabeth CLAPHAM of Ldn. B/S of 169a with water, grist, merchant and saw mill (cnvy/b CLAPHAM Feb 1829, DBk SSS:304). Wit: Joseph J. JONES, John ANDERSON.

3U:011 Date: 6 Jun 1830 RtCt: 7 Jun 1830
William DODD & wife Mary of Ldn to John Alexander BINNS of Ldn. B/S of lot on Loudoun St in Lsbg (cnvy/b Joshua RILEY to BINNS for debt to Mary HUNT now DODD). Wit: John J. MATHIAS, Saml. M. EDWARDS. Delv. to BINNS 28 Jan 1834.

3U:013   Date: 8 Jun 1830   RtCt: 8 Jun 1830
Bani/Beni J. GREGG of Ldn to Sheriff William B. HARRISON. B/S of 300a & 150a in Preston Co Va and 100a in Allegany Co Md (judgments by Thomas GASSAWAY and James RUST). Gives small plat.

3U:014   Date: 28 May 1830   RtCt: 9 Jun 1830
Sarah R. POWELL of Ldn to Cuthbert POWELL of Ldn. B/S of 35a (part of 'Bellefield' prch/o James RUST Apr 1823) nr Blue Ridge adj RUST, C. POWELL, John RICHARD; and all dower rights in (1/3 of 'Bellefield' bequeathed to Burr G. POWELL by his grandfather). Delv. to C. POWELL 29 Nov 1836.

3U:016   Date: __ 1830   RtCt: 9 Jun 1830
Thomas L. HUMPHREY (trustee for benefit of William C. PALMER & Mason P. CHAMBLIN on mortgage by Thomas J. BENNETT, Jun 1828, DBk QQQ:381) and PALMER & CHAMBLIN to Thomas J. BENNETT. Release of mortgage.

3U:017   Date: 13 Feb 1830   RtCt: 10 Jun 1830
Isaac HARRIS & wife Sarah of Ldn to Benjamin SHREVE Jr. of Ldn. B/S of 3a (cnvy/b court decree and Joseph GILBERT) nr Lsbg adj James L. MARTIN, Tuskarora. Wit: Thomas SANDERS, John H. McCABE. Delv. to SHREVE 10 Feb 1832.

3U:019   Date: 6 May 1830   RtCt: 8 May 1830
Ludwell LEE of Ldn to dau Eliza A. SELDEN w/o Wilson C. SELDEN Jr. (as security on debt to Robert BENELEY). BoS for negro man Jesse a cooper now in WILSON's possession with negro Reuben blacksmith (also part of trust) still liable for any debt). Wit: James RUST, Jno. J. MATHIAS.

3U:019   Date: 11 Jun 1830   RtCt: 11 Jun 1830
Thornton WALKER to Rich'd H. HENDERSON. Assignment of proceeds from sale of land to Stephen W. ROSZEL dec'd and debts owed by Lewis FRENCH, Craven WALKER, estate of Jeremiah BRONAUGH dec'd, Benjamin MITCHELL, John McINTOSH. Delv. to HENDERSON 19 May 1831.

3U:020   Date: 11 Jun 1830   RtCt: 11 Jun 1830
Thornton WALKER to Sheriff William B. HARRISON. B/S of lot with house and 2-3a vacant lot in Union (writ against WALKER in name of Eli BEALL, John McPHERSON, James McPHERSON, John W. KEIRL, Matthew KEIRLE merchants.

3U:021   Date: 31 Jul 1829   RtCt: 14 Jun 1830
Jacob MILLER. Oath as Captain in 56th Reg. of Va Militia.

3U:021   Date: 5 Apr 1830   RtCt: 14 Jun 1830
Thomas HOUGH. Oath as 2nd Lt. in Troop of Cavalry, 2nd Reg, 2nd Div. of Va Militia. Delv. to HOUGH 24 May 1831.

3U:022 Date: 14 Jun 1830 RtCt: 14 Jun 1830
James CAYLOR, Lewis GRIGSBY & Wm. MERSHON. Bond on CAYLOR as constable.

3U:023 Date: 20 Jan 1830 RtCt: 15 Jun 1830
Samuel GREGG dec'd. Division - 31a Lot #1 & slave boy Alexander to Sarah Ann GREGG (<21y); 33a Lot #2 & slave boy Albert to Isaac NICHOLS Jr. for wife Mary; 34a Lot #3 & slave woman Phebe & infant child to Thos. Ellwood HATCHER for wife Elizabeth P.; 38a Lot #4 & slave girl Harriet to Nathan GREGG Jr. for wife Susan R. Divisors: John BRADEN, Noble S. BRADEN, Presley CORDELL. Gives plat.

3U:026 Date: 1 Jun 1830 RtCt: 16 Jun 1830
Gen. Hugh DOUGLAS dec'd. Division of land along the Potomac - 134a Lot #1, 50a Lot #2 & 33a Lot #3 (fee simple estate lots) and 100a Lot #4 & 22a Lot #5 (under lease from TEBBS) & slaves Ellick, Mary & Phyliss to Exor. Charles DOUGLAS; 134a Lot #6, 50a Lot #7 & 33a Lot #8 (deed lands) and 57a Lot #9 & 15a Lot #10 lease lands) and slaves Thompson, William, George, Rebecca & Harriet to Lewis DOUGLAS (of age 17 Nov 1827); 158a Lot #11, 50a Lot #12 & 33a Lot #13 (deed lands) and 121a Lot #14 & 39¾a Lot #15 (lease lands) and slaves Pamela & child Barney, Edward and Kitty to Archibald N. DOUGLAS. Divisors: Jno. BARROT, P. VIRTS, Aaron SCHOOLEY, H. BASSELL. Also dividends of the English fund derived through mother to Lewis F. and Archibald N. DOUGLAS (through brother Charles who is their Guardian) credited to estate. Divisors: Wm. T. T. MASON, Geo. M. CHICHESTER, Saml. DAWSON, Thos. GASSAWAY. Gives plat. Also plat of 'Mountain Farm' of 194¾a.

3U:036 Date: 12 Jun 1830 RtCt: 14 Jul 1830
Cyrus BURSON & wife Phebe of Ldn to Thomas FRED Jr. of Ldn. Trust for debt to George KEAN using 134a (cnvy/b Joseph BURSON). Wit: Notley C. WILLIAMS, Ben. GRAYSON. Delv. to FREDD 29 Jul 1831.

3U:038 Date: 22 Apr 1830 RtCt: 14 Jun 1830
Jacob COOPER & wife Mary of Ldn to George COOPER of Ldn. B/S of interest in 115a from Frederick COOPER dec'd. Wit: Mortimer McILHANEY, Geo. W. SHAWEN.

3U:039 Date: 14 Jun 1830 RtCt: 14 Jun 1830
Yeoman Joshua PANCOAST of Ldn to yeoman George KEENE of Ldn. Release of trust for debt to Joshua GREGG on 100a.

3U:040 Date: 14 Oct 1829 RtCt: 14 Jun 1830
Enoch FURR & wife Sarah of Ldn to Dr. Edward B. GRADY of Ldn. B/S of 78¼a where FURR now lives, adj Joshua FRED, Thomas A. HEREFORD. Wit: Ben. GRAYSON, John W. GRAYSON. Delv. to Jno. L. POWELL pr order of heirs filed 5T:58?, 4 Feb 1850.

3U:042 Date: 10 May 1830 RtCt: 14 Jun 1830
Eli TAVENNER & wife Nancy of Ldn to Charles B. HAMILTON of
Ldn. B/S of 2a. Wit: Jno. J. MATHIAS, Hamilton ROGERS. Delv. to
Nancy TAVENER pr order 4 Sep 1841.

3U:044 Date: 14 Jun 1830 RtCt: 14 Jun 1830
Sheriff Charles LEWIS to James CAYLOR. B/S of 184a (DBk
RRR:[309] from insolvent Thompson FOUCH from will of father
Thomas FOUCH dec'd) subject to lease of William LAFEVRE.

3U:046 Date: 25 Nov 1829 RtCt: 9 Mar 1830
William B. BRADFIELD of Belmont Co Ohio to Elwood B. JAMES of
Ldn. B/S of undivided 1/7th interest in estate of James BRADFIELD
dec'd. Wit: Timothy TAYLOR Jr., Charles TAYLOR, James H.
WEST.

3U:047 Date: 12 Jan 1830 RtCt: 14 Jun 1830
Jacob SUMMERS & wife Elizabeth of Ldn to Thomas W. LEE of
Ldn. B/S of 175a below Goose Creek on Elklick run (prch/o William
LYNE, assigned as dower to Martha ODEN since dec'd wd/o
Thomas ODEN dec'd). Wit: Charles LEWIS, John BAYLY. Delv. to
LEE 9 Jan 1835.

3U:049 Date: 22 Apr 1830 RtCt: 14 Jun 1830
George COOPER & wife Amelia of Ldn to Jacob COOPER of Ldn.
B/S of 40a (from father's estate) on Catoctin Mt. Wit: Mortimer
McILHANY, Geo. W. SHAWEN. Delv. to Jacob COOPER 3 Mar
1835.

3U:051 Date: 5 May 1830 RtCt: 11 Jun 1830
Isaac EATON & wife Malinda of Ldn to Stephen T. CUNARD (Admr.
of George A. McPHERSON dec'd for his heirs) of Ldn. B/S of ½a Lot
#29 in Mt. Gilead. Wit: Burr POWELL, Abner GIBSON. Delv. to
CONNARD 8 Aug 1831.

3U:053 Date: 22 Mar 1830 RtCt: 14 Jun 1830
William RICHARDS & wife Margaret of Ldn to William BENTON of
Ldn. B/S of 6a adj Sampson GUY, Wm. LEITH, Elijah ANDERSON,
BENTON; and 2a on N side of Goose Creek adj James PLASTER,
Millsville (except 1a to Jane ROLLS, ¼a to Thornton WALKER & ½a
to Robert POWELL). Wit: Edward HALL, Francis W. LUCKETT.

3U:056 Date: 20 Jan 1830 RtCt: 14 Jun 1830
Jesse McVEIGH & wife Elizabeth of Ldn to Mahlon FULTON of Ldn.
B/S of 4a (cnvy/b John RALPH) in Bloomfield adj James
JOHNSTON, John G. HUMPHREY, road to Ebenezer meeting
house. Wit: Burr POWELL, A. GIBSON.

3U:058 Date: 30 Dec 1829 RtCt: 14 Jun 1830
George SHEID. List of property sold at public auction on 4 Dec to
Capt. Washington HUMMER to pay for 3 years of taxes and balance
due to Garrison & Caylor executions agst SHEID. Property

transferred by HUMMER to William W. ELLZEY trustee of Lurena G. SHEID late DULIN for her benefit.

3U:059 Date: 15 Jun 1830 RtCt: 15 Jun 1830
Weaver Thomas F. MILLER of Ldn to yeoman Jacob SILCOTT of Ldn. BoS for household items.

3U:059 Date: 5 Jun 1830 RtCt: 16 Jun 1830
John WINSEL/VINSEL & wife Mary of Ldn to George DERRY of Ldn. B/S of 2a on S side of Short Hill adj Michael EVERHART. Wit: Samuel DAWSON, Geo. W. SHAWEN.

3U:062 Date: 5 Sep 1829 RtCt: 16 Jun 1830
Jacob LONG of Ldn to William and Sally LONG of Ldn. Gift of farm animals, farm and household items.

3U:063 Date: 20 Apr 1830 RtCt: 16 Jun 1830
Thomas SOBEBY/SOBEY and John HOCKING & wife Eleanor of Ldn to Lewis BERKELEY of Ldn. B/S of ½a Lot #85 & #86 in Aldie and 2a on Little River adj Col. Charles T. MERCER (all cnvy/b Gabriel GREEN). Wit: Burr POWELL, Robt. BAYLY. Delv. to BERKLEY 11 Sep 1834.

3U:065 Date: __ 1830 RtCt: 17 Jun 1830
Joseph WALTMAN of Ldn to Adam CARN and Michael SANBOWER of Ldn. B/S of 17a Lot #6 and 3a wood lot #6 in division and undivided ¼ interest in dower of Anna SANBOWER wd/o Jno. SANBOWER dec'd which Sarah SYPHERD late Sarah SANBOWER as child and heir is entitled (cnvy/b George SYPHERD & Sarah to WALTMAN).

3U:066 Date: 1 May 1830 RtCt: 17 Jun 1830
Joseph WALTMAN of Ldn to Adam CARN and Michael SANBOWER of Ldn. B/S of 21a (cnvy/b George SHOVER and wife Susannah late SANBOWER to Sheriff, then to WALTMAN, from div. of John SANBOWER dec'd).

3U:067 Date: 5 Apr 1830 RtCt: 17 Jun 1830
Ebenezer GRUBB & wife Leah of Ldn to George COOPER Jr. of Ldn. B/S of 42a Lot #6 and 14a Lot #15 from div. of Jacob WIRTS dec'd. Wit: Geo. W. SHAWEN, S. HOUGH. Delv. to Henry RUSE 12 Dec 1831.

3U:070 Date: 7 Jan 1830 RtCt: 17 Jun 1830
William FLETCHER & wife Harriet of Ldn to Thomas EACHES of Ldn. B/S of 165a (cnvy/b Amos HIBBS) on S fork of Beaverdam Creek adj Henry SMITH, George KEENE, M. & R. FULTON, Samuel RICHARDS. Wit: Burr POWELL, Abner GIBSON.

3U:072 Date: 4 Jan 1830 RtCt: 22 Jun 1830
John LOES & wife Catherine, Jacob HARRIER, Adam HARRIER, Jacob WAGGONER & wife Elizabeth and Daniel HARRIER of Coshoctan Co Ohio to Jacob CRIM of Ldn. B/S of 9a (5/8th of 15a Lot #15 in div. of Charles CRIM Sr. dec'd allotted to Martin HAGAR

and undivided by his children). Wit: Nathan DEAN, Adam CRIM. Delv. pr order 1 Feb 1832.

3U:075   Date: 24 May 1830   RtCt: 22 Jun 1830
Thomas ROGERS (as commr in suit for David JAMES & wife Charlotte late BRADFIELD, Amey W. BRADFIELD, Jefferson C. THOMAS & wife Mary late BRADFIELD and Elwood B. JAMES on behalf of William W. BRADFIELD and James P. BRADFIELD, heirs of James BRADFIELD) to David LOVETT. B/S of 86a (where James BRADFIELD lived at time of death) 3-4 miles W of Goose Creek Quaker meeting house adj LOVETT, David JAMES. Wit: Thomas NICHOLAS, Craven OSBURN. Delv. to LOVETT 2 May 1831.

3U:078   Date: 16 Jun 1830   RtCt: 21 Jun 1830
James L. MARTIN & wife Sarah of Ldn to Christopher FRYE of Ldn. Trust for debt to James PAYNTER using 13a 'Kirks Meadow' adj Lsbg (prch/o Isaac HARRIS).

3U:080   Date: 22 Jun 1830   RtCt: 23 Jun 1830
William F. LUCKETT & wife Harriet of Ldn to William HATCHER of Ldn. Trust for debt to Thomas HATCHER using 177a (cnvy/b Leven LUCKETT dec'd). Wit: Francis W. LUCKETT, Edward HALL.

3U:083   Date: 26 Jun 1830   RtCt: 26 Jun 1830
Burr W. HARRISON of Lsbg to John C. HANSBOROUGH of Culpeper Co Va. BoS for negro woman Delpha aged abt 35y, woman Pleasant abt 40y old and girl Mary abt 17y old (from trust of Samuel CARR for debt to John & James POGUE, Nov 1827).

3U:084   Date: 13 Jul 1830   RtCt: 5 Jul 1830
Burr W. HARRISON (as commr. in suit agst widow Rebecca SHAW, Eliza Ann SHAW, Sidney SHAW, Susan Bailey SHAW and John SHAW) to Simon SMALE. B/S of lot on Market St in Lsbg (leased from John SHAW who died 30 May 1822 with minor heirs). Delv. to SMALL 25 Dec 1830.

3U:086   Date: 3 Jul 1830   RtCt: 5 Jul 1830
John SHAW & wife Cynthia of Ldn to Commr. Burr W. HARRISON of Ldn. Trust for debt to Commr B. W. HARRISON with William H. JACOBS and John SHAW as securities for Rebecca SHAW using lot on Back St. in Lsbg (cnvy/b Simon SMALE Oct 1826) and adj lot (prch/o John W. WOOD Mar 1827). Wit: Tasker C. QUINLAN, Presley CORDELL.

3U:089   Date: 3 Jul 1830   RtCt: 5 Jul 1830
William H. JACOBS & wife Catherine of Ldn to Commr. Burr W. HARRISON of Ldn. Trust for debt to Commr B. W. HARRISON with William H. JACOBS and John SHAW as securities for Rebecca SHAW using Lot #57 at Loudoun & Liberty Sts. in Lsbg. Wit: Tasker C. QUINLAN, Presley CORDELL.

3U:092 Date: 6 Jul 1830 RtCt: 6 Jul 1830
Thomas SWANN now of WashDC to Mordicia THROCKMORTON of Ldn. Release of trust for debt of Thomas A. BROOKE to Bank of U.S. which was sold to THROCKMORTON.

3U:093 Date: 29 Sep 1829 RtCt: 6 Jul 1830
Elizabeth PADGET of Ldn to Timothy PADGET. Trust for debt to William THRIFT using 42a adj Andrew HEATH, Mary D. HAWLEY.

3U:095 Date: 6 Jul 1830 RtCt: 7 Jul 1830
Catherine S. HARDING of JeffVa to Alfred BELT of Ldn. B/S of 37½a Lot #10 in div. of John A. BINNS dec'd. Delv. to BELT 8 Jan 1830.

3U:097 Date: 12 May 1830 RtCt: 21 May 1830
Wilson C. SELDEN Jr. of Ldn to Edward E. COOKE of Ldn. Trust using mulatto girl Caroline now in possession of Wilson for benefit of Mrs. Eliza A. SELDEN w/o Wilson.

3U:098 Date: 12 Jul 1830 RtCt: 12 Jul 1830
Stephen McPHERSON, Jacob SILCOTT and Mason CHAMBLIN. Bond on McPHERSON as constable.

3U:098 Date: 7 Dec 1829 RtCt: 12 Jul 1830
William H. PEUGH of Morgan Co Ohio to Eli McVEIGH of Ldn. B/S of his 1/6th interest in 6a dower land of mother Mary PEUGH after her dec'd. Delv. to McVEIGH 20 July 1833.

3U:100 Date: 21 Jan 1830 RtCt: 12 Jul 1830
Hardage LANE & wife Ann(a) Rebecca Carroll LANE of St. Louis Mo to Newton KEENE of Ldn. B/S of undivided interest in 346 2/3a of 'Sisters tract' adj Benjamin BRIDGES, William HUMMER, William LANE's heirs (see DBk 3S:386). Wit: Tasker C. QUINLAN, Presley CORDELL. Delv. to KEENE 16 Mar 1844.

3U:102 Date: 21 Jan 1830 RtCt: 12 Jul 1830
Hardage LANE & wife Ann(a) Rebecca Carroll LANE of St. Louis Mo to Benjamin BRIDGES of Ldn. B/S of 215a (see DBk 3S:393). Wit: Tasker C. QUINLAN, Presley CORDELL.

3U:104 Date: 7 Aug 1830 RtCt: 12 Aug 1830
Otho R. BEATTY of Lsbg to Richard H. HENDERSON and Burr W. HARRISON of Lsbg. Trust to cover debts (to Christopher HEISKELL, Thos. B. BEATTY, Bank of the Valley, Jas. McILHANY, Geo. LEE, Eli BEATTY, Geo. CARTER, Samuel STERRET, John H. CANBY – some as his security) using all of his property (gives long schedule of notes). Wit: Chs. G. ESKRIDGE. Delv. to HARRISON 21 Jan 1831.

3U:110 Date: 18 Feb 1830 RtCt: 8 Mar/12 Jul 1830
Stacy TAYLOR & wife Ruth of Ldn to Valentine V. PURCELL of Ldn. B/S of 2a adj ___ SMITH. Wit: Richard MILTON, John WHITACRE, Saml. PURSEL Jr. Delv. to J. E. CARRUTHERS 8 Mar 1900.

3U:111 Date: 25 Dec 1829 RtCt: 12 Jul 1830
Mary PUGH/PEUGH of Morgan Co Ohio to Eli McVEIGH of Ldn. B/S of 6a (dower from husband Spencer PUGH dec'd) adj McVEIGH. Wit: George L. CORNER, John HARRIS. Delv. to McVEIGH 11 Mar 1834.

3U:112 Date: 10 Jul 1830 RtCt: 13 Jul 1830
Thomas PHILLIPS (Exor of James MOORE dec'd) to Joseph LEWIS. B/S of Lots #16, #17, #18 & #19 in new addition to Wtfd. Delv. to LEWIS 21 Jul 1831.

3U:114 Date: __ Feb 1830 RtCt: 7 Jul 1830
Edward B. GRADY to Charles RUSSELL. Release of trust for debt to Notley C. WILLIAMS using 167a. Wit: C. W. D. BINNS, Jas. L. HAMILTON, Jonah DRAIN.

3U:115 Date: 24 Jul 1830 RtCt: 24 Jul 1830
Loveless CONWELL & wife Elizabeth of Ldn to Isaac CONWELL of Ldn. B/S of 2a (prch/o Peter BENEDUM, DBk FFF:173). Wit: James RUST, Presley CORDELL.

3U:117 Date: 19 May 1830 RtCt: 26 Jul 1830
Enos POTTS (trustee of Jehu HOLLINGSWORTH of Aug 1816) of Ldn to Elizabeth WHITE, Rachel WHITE and Washington WHITE of Ldn. B/S of 136a (cnvy/b John HESKETT to HOLLINGSWORTH Nov 1815). Wit: Joshua OSBURN, Eli JANNEY, William HOGE. Delv pr order 1 Jun 1847.

3U:118 Date: 26 Jul 1830 RtCt: 27 Jul 1830
Robert ROBERTS & wife Nancy of Ldn to Christopher FRYE of Ldn. B/S of 8a (cnvy/b FRYE Jun 1828, DBk QQQ:374). Wit: John H. McCABE, Saml. M. EDWARDS. Delv. to FRYE 25 Jan 1831.

3U:120 Date: 26 Jul 1830 RtCt: 27 Jul 1830
Robert ROBERTS & wife Nancy of Ldn to James L. MARTIN of Ldn. Trust for debt to Christopher FRYE using 24a (prch/o James RUST) and 3a (cnvy/b John LICKEY, Benjamin THOMPKINS). Wit: John H. McCABE, Saml. M. EDWARDS. Delv. to FRYE 29 Jan 1831.

3U:123 Date: 20 Jul 1830 RtCt: 28 Jul 1830
John N. DAVIS of Ldn to Stephen BEARD of Ldn. BoS for farm animals, household items.

3U:124 Date: 20 Mar 1830 RtCt: 28 Jul 1830
George M. GRAYSON to Matthew CARPENTER. Release of trust of Oct 1825 for debt to Richard HALL on 84½a.

3U:125 Date: 20 Feb 1830 RtCt: 29 Jul 1830
James MONROE, George HAY & wife Eliza K. to Robert STANNARD. Trust for benefit of Hortensia Monroe ROGERS w/o Lloyd R. ROGERS of Md using 900a in Henrico Co Va and 15 slaves John Baker, Lewis Baker, John Richard, Joe Lumpkin, George Dabney, Jerry Dabney, Frank, Anne, (Anne's children) Fanny, Rebecca, William, Mary, Alice, Peggy, Rachel. Wit: Humph.

PEAKE, Joseph HAWKINS, Benj. M. BROCCHUS, Samuel C. ROSE, John RITACRE.

3U:129 Date: 27 Apr 1830 RtCt: 29 Jul 1830
John SMARR & wife Susan F. of Ldn to Caleb N. GALLEHER of Ldn. B/S of 33½a on Bear Branch of Goose Creek (prch/o James JOHNSON) adj Snicker's Gap turnpike, heirs of Dennis McCARTY dec'd, John JOHNSON dec'd. Wit: Burr POWELL, Abner GIBSON. Delv. to GALLEHER 1 Aug 1836.

3U:131 Date: __ 1830 RtCt: 29 Jul 1830
William VICKERS, William RICHARDS and Jacob SILCOTT of Ldn to Hiram SEATON of Ldn. B/S of 100a (trust of Jun 1826 from VICKERS to RICHARDS for debt to SILCOTT using 100a which SEATON thought was his, arbitrators found for VICKERS). Delv. to Henry YOUNG Exor of D. YOUNG 31 Jul 1851.

3U:133 Date: 29 Jul 1830 RtCt: 29 Jul 1830
Horace LUCKETT to Joshua PANCOAST. Trust for debt to David YOUNG using 190a (prch/o Alfred LUCKETT).

3U:135 Date: 29 Jul 1830 RtCt: 29 Jul 1830
John BAYLY of Ldn to Charles LEWIS of Ldn. B/S of 200a (from trust of Aug 1820 from Richard KEENE to BAYLY and James LEWIS Sr. since dec'd, DBk CCC:141). Delv. to LEWIS 24 Jun 1836.

3U:136 Date: 4 Jun 1830 RtCt: 24 Jun 1830
John A. BINNS and John GRAY (original purchaser at auction) of Ldn to Benjamin SHREVE Jr. of Ldn. B/S of 284a except ½a for burial ground (from trust of Wm. A. BINNS for debt to Cath. A. DURHAM, DBk 3N:53). Gives plat. Delv. to SHREVE 10 Feb 1832.

3U:139 Date: 27 Jul 1830 RtCt: 30 Jul 1830
Morris OSBURN & wife Jane of Ldn to Joel OSBURN Jr. of Ldn. B/S of 112a where Joel now lives, adj Elizabeth RUSSEL, __ HEATON, __ GREGG, __ BROWN. Wit: John WHITE, Craven OSBURN. Delv. to Joel OSBURN 29 Jan 1831.

3U:141 Date: 31 Oct 1829 RtCt: 2 Aug 1830
John ROBISON/ROBERTSON & wife Elizabeth and John RUSE & wife Sarah of Ldn to Stephen SANDS and William STOCKS of Ldn. B/S of 29 2/10a on W side of Catocton Mt. (cnvy/b Joseph SANDS to Jacob SANDS, at time thought to be 22a, 6/7th is ROBISON's, 1/7th is RUSE's). Wit: George W. SHAWEN, Saml. HOUGH.

3U:143 Date: 3 Apr 1830 RtCt: 3 Aug 1830
Robert RUSSELL of Ldn to John GRUBB of Ldn. Trust for George MILLER of Ldn (who purchased land of John WOLF Sr. dec'd which was allotted to RUSSELL & his children in case any minor children won't release title when they are of age) using 196a where RUSSELL now lives.

3U:145   Date: 3 Apr 1830   RtCt: 3 Aug 1830
John WOLF & wife Sarah, Robert RUSSELL, John JACOBS & wife Elizabeth, Christian MILLER, Catherine MILLER, Barbara MILLER and John MILLER & wife Catherine of Ldn to George MILLER of Ldn. B/S of 59a (Robert RUSSELL's wife's share from John WOLF Sr. dec'd). Wit: Ebenezer GRUBB, Mortimer McILHANY. Delv. to George MILLER 8 May 1843.

3U:148   Date: 4 Aug 1830   RtCt: 4 Aug 1830
John JACOBS of Ldn to Elizabeth JACOBS (m/o John) and George JACOBS (br/o John) of Ldn. B/S of interest in leased land now in possession of Elizabeth and George (possible interest in lease, suit in Sup Ct by Joseph D. LESLIE still pending).

3U:149   Date: 22 Apr 1830   RtCt: 16 Aug 1830
George COOPER & wife Amelia, Jacob COOPER & wife Mary, John COOPER & wife Magdalean and William COOPER & wife Elizabeth of Ldn to George SAUNDERS of Ldn. B/S of their 1/9th interest in land of grandfather Michael COOPER dec'd where his widow Catharine now resides. Wit: George W. SHAWEN, Mortimer McILHANY.

3U:151   Date: 13 Apr 1830   RtCt: 6 Aug 1830
Joshua PUSEY (Exor of James NIXON dec'd) of Ldn to George SAUNDERS of Ldn. B/S of 58½a Lot #10 (reserving 18a, from div. of James NIXON dec'd to children of his dau. Jane WHITE dec'd) on SE side of short hill.

3U:153   Date: 6 Aug 1830   RtCt: 7 Aug 1830
Amos HARVEY & wife Elizabeth of Ldn to William CLENDENING of Ldn. B/S of 100a (cnvy/b heirs of Ebenezer WILSON dec'd). Wit: George W. SHAWEN, John WHITE. Delv. pr order 21 Oct 1834.

3U:155   Date: 7 Dec 1829   RtCt: 10 Aug 1830
Harrison CROSS & wife Catherine of Ldn to Reuben HUTCHISON, Wickliff HUTCHISON and David JAMES. Trust for debt to Joshua HUTCHISON, Charles LEWIS and William MASON (as Commrs. in sale for John DEBELL dec'd of PrWm) using 168a purchased at sale. Wit: R. BAYLY, Ariss BUCKNER.

3U:158   Date: 9 Aug 1830   RtCt: 9 Aug 1830
Geo. H. ALDER, John H. BUTCHER, Joseph RICHARDSON and Enos BEST. Bond on ALDER as constable.

3U:159   Date: 12 Jun 1830   RtCt: 9 Aug 1830
James/Elijah VIOLETT Jr. of FredVa to Phebe VIOLETT of Ldn. Gift of all his real and personal estate, including negro Amanda, Sarah, Ralph & Eliza. [note: first half of document gives name as James, last half and signature as Elijah]

3U:160   Date: 11 Jun 1830   RtCt: 8 Sep 1830
Samuel McGWIGWIN & wife Nancy to Richard O. GRAYSON. Trust for debt to David GALLEHER using ¼a lot in Bloomfield, adj Joseph

BARTON, Richard CLARKE; and adj lot where McGWIGWIN lives (prch/o Col. George MARKS) and shop and household items, farm animals. Wit: Benjamin GRAYSON, John W. GRAYSON.

3U:164 Date: 16 Apr 1830 RtCt: 9 Aug 1830

Mahala BARR of Ldn to Evan WILKISON of Ldn. B/S of undivided interest in land of George NIXON the Elder dec'd on Beaverdam adj James DEWER, William CARR. Wit: Benj'n RUST Jr., Thomas C. GREGG, Wm. COHAGAN. Delv. to WILKISON 6 Dec 1834.

3U:165 Date: 3 Apr 1830 RtCt: 9 Aug 1830

George MILLER & wife Mary, John WOLF & wife Sarah, Robert RUSSELL and John MILLER & wife Catherine of Ldn to John JACOBS & wife Elizabeth, Christian MILLER, Catharine MILLER, Barbara MILLER, John MILLER, Mary MILLER, Sarah MILLER and Adam MILLER (heirs of Adam MILLER dec'd) of Ldn. B/S of 16½a and 3a between short hill and Blue ridge (land of John WOLF Sr. dec'd). Wit: Ebenezer GRUBB, M. McILHANY.

3U:168 Date: 3 Apr 1830 RtCt: 9 Aug 1830

John WOLF & wife Sarah, George MILLER & wife Mary, Robert RUSSELL, John JACOBS & wife Elizabeth, Christian MILLER, Catherine MILLER, Barbara MILLER, John MILLER (of Adam), Mary MILLER, Sarah MILLER and Adam MILLER of Ldn to John MILLER of Ldn (all legal heirs of John WOLF dec'd of Ldn). B/S of 28¾a. Wit: Ebenezer GRUBB, Mortimer McILHANY. Delv. to John MILLER 22 May 1844.

3U:171 Date: 9 Aug 1830 RtCt: 9 Aug 1830

Samuel NIXON of Ldn to Abraham SMITH of Ldn. B/S of undivided 1/3rd of 171a on S fork of Beaverdam (where James NIXON formerly resided) adj heirs of James WHITE, James William NIXON, Evan EVANS, John WRIGHT. Delv. to SMITH 2 Jul 1832.

3U:172 Date: 9 Aug 1830 RtCt: 9 Aug 1830

Samuel NIXON of Ldn to James William NIXON of Ldn. B/S of undivided 1/3rd of 169a on S fork of Beaverdam (where James NIXON formerly resided) adj heirs of James WHITE, __ THOMAS, __ HAMILTON, John WINE, Abraham SMITH. Delv. to Wm. NIXON 22 Sep 1835.

3U:174 Date: 8 Aug 1830 RtCt: 9 Aug 1830

Enoch SHRIGLEY of Ldn to James GRUBB of Ldn. B/S of undivided moiety of 12½a (prch/o Samuel HOUGH) on E side of short hill adj Peter WIRTZ, Robert BRADEN.

3U:175 Date: 3 Apr 1830 RtCt: 9 Aug 1830

George MILLER & wife Mary, Robert RUSSELL, John JACOBS & wife Elizabeth, Christian MILLER, Catharine MILLER, Barbara MILLER, John MILLER (of Adam), Mary MILLER, Sarah MILLER, Adam MILLER and John MILLER & wife Catharine of Ldn to John WOLF of Ldn. B/S of 27a (from John WOLF Sr. dec'd) between short hill and Blue ridge adj __ GRUBB, __ DERRY, heirs of Adam MILLER dec'd, John MILLER. Wit: Ebenezer GRUBB, Mortimer McILHANY.

3U:178 Date: 15 Jul 1830 RtCt: 11 Aug 1830
H. B. POWELL to Charles F. MERCER. B/S of 128a and 75a (from trust of Nov 1827 of Benjamin HAGERMAN).

3U:180 Date: 11 Aug 1830 RtCt: 12 Aug 1830
Catharine or Cate HULLS of Ldn. DoE for her child Mary MASON (cnvy/b Samuel DONAHOE to Cate) and her children John Henry, Charles William, Margaret Elizabeth. Wit: Burr W. HARRISON. Crossed out was a bill of sale from Samuel DONOHOE to Catharine – not being prov'd. can not be recorded, by mistake was put down]

3U:181 Date: 13 Jun 1830 RtCt: 13 Aug 1830
Samuel HAMMONTREE of Ldn to Craven VANHORN of Ldn. Trust for debt to Thomas FRED, John C. GREEN, Thomas MOUNT, Thornton F. OFFUTT, Sydnor BAILY using house and ¼a lot on S side of Main St in Union now occupied by HAMMONTREE, adj Mahlon BALDWIN, Mrs. ANDERSON.

3U:183 Date: 13 Aug 1830 RtCt: 14 Aug 1830
Richard H. LOVE to Presley SANDERS. Trust for debt to James L. MARTIN with Wilson C. SELDEN as security using household items.

3U:184 Date: 17 Aug 1830 RtCt: 18 Aug 1830
Solomon HOUSHOLDER of Ldn to Gideon HOUSHOLDER of Ldn. B/S of 24½a Lot #6 and 2a Lot #8 (allotted from Adam & Susannah HOUSEHOLDER dec'd). Delv. to Gideon 23 Jan 1832.

3U:185 Date: 20 Aug 1830 RtCt: 21 Aug 1830
Richard H. HENDERSON of Lsbg to Robert J. TAYLOR of AlexDC. B/S of 33a (from trust of Aug 1825 of Richard H. LEE) on W side of road from Lsbg to Aldie & Mdbg. Delv. to TAYLOR 1 Jun 1831.

3U:187 Date: 5 Aug 1830 RtCt: 23 Aug 1830
Daniel TRUNDLE of MontMD to John ROSE (Exor of Susan CHILTON dec'd) of Ldn. Trust for debt to ROSE using land purchased from estate. Delv. to John ROSE 4 Sep 1832.

3U:189 Date: 5 Aug 1830 RtCt: 23 Aug 1830
John ROSE (Exor of Susan CHILTON dec'd) of Ldn to Daniel TRUNDLE of MontMd. B/S of 325a adj estate of Samuel CLAPHAM dec'd, __ STEER, __ WILLIAMS. Delv. to Benj. SHREVE Jr. who m. Mary E. TRUNDLE to whom the premises were allotted in the div. of TRUNDLE's estate.

3U:191 Date: 23 Aug 1830 RtCt: 26 Aug 1830
Thomas SWANN of WashDC to John JANNEY of Lsbg. Assignment of mortgage from David JANNEY of 7 Apr 1811, DBk A:83. Delv. to JANNEY 4 Mar 1831.

3U:191   Date: 4 Sep 1830   RtCt: 4 Sep 1830
R. J. TAYLOR to Charles BINNS. Release of trust from John
LITTLEJOHN of 9 Jan 1805, land since sold to BINNS. Wit: Saml.
M. EDWARDS. Delv. 4 Oct 1836.

3U:192   Date: 13 Sep 1830   RtCt: 13 Sep 1830
Jesse McVEIGH and Townshend McVEIGH. Bond on Jesse as
Commissioner of Revenue in Second District.

3U:193   Date: 13 Sep 1830   RtCt: 13 Sep 1830
Jesse TIMMS and Robert MOFFETT. Bond on TIMMS as
Commissioner of Revenue in First District.

3U:193   Date: 10 Sep 1830   RtCt: 13 Sep 1830
Jesse TRIBBY. Oath as Lt. in 56th Reg, 6th Brig, 2nd Div of Va Militia.

3U:194   Date: 31 Aug 1830   RtCt: 13 Sep 1830
William RUSSELL. Qualified as Capt of Infantry in 56th Reg of Va
Militia.

3U:194   Date: 12 Feb 1830   RtCt: 13 Sep 1830
James GOVAN of Hanover Co to Joseph BLINCOE of Ldn. B/S of
500a adj Mrs. STONESTREET, __ COLEMAN. Delv. to BLINCOE
24 Feb 1841.

3U:196   Date: 15 Sep 1830   RtCt: 15 Sep 1830
George BUTLER & wife Betsey of Ldn to Elizabeth SULLIVAN of
Ldn. B/S of ¼a in Wtfd adj Mahlon JANNEY. Wit: John H. McCABE,
Presley CORDELL.

3U:197   Date: __ Sep 1830   RtCt: 15 Sep 1830
Joseph WOOD to George BUTLER. Release of trust of May 1826
for debt to John BUTLER using ¼a.

3U:198   Date: 22 Apr 1830   RtCt: 21 Sep 1830
George SAUNDERS & wife Elizabeth of Ldn to Andrew HILLMAN of
Ldn. B/S of 112a adj John SAUNDERS, __ MORRISON, __
PEACOCK, __ McKIMIE, __ WILDMAN; and 26a on E side of short
hill adj John WHITE, Thomas WHITE. Wit: George W. SHAWEN,
Mortimer McILHANY. Delv. to HILLMAN 7 Feb 1831.

3U:201   Date: 28 Nov 1829   RtCt: 22 Sep 1830
William PAXSON & wife Jane of Ldn to Sarah HOUGH of Ldn. B/S
of 20 perch lot in Wtfd adj Flemmon P. W. HIXSON, __ BRADEN.
Wit: Geo. W. SHAWEN, N. S. BRADEN. Delv. pr order ___.

3U:202   Date: 17 Sep 1830   RtCt: 22 Sep 1830
Amos JANNEY & wife Mary Ann of Ldn to Gideon HOUSEHOLDER.
Trust for debt to Adam HOUSHOLDER using 20a (cnvy/b Adam
HOUSEHOLDER, Sept. 1830). Wit: Ebenezer GRUBB, Geo. W.
SHAWEN. Delv. to Gideon HOUSEHOLDER 23 Jan 1832.

3U:205   Date: 17 Sep 1830   RtCt: 22 Sep 1830
Curtis GRUBB & wife Harriet of Ldn to Gideon HOUSEHOLDER of
Ldn. Trust for debt to Adam HOUSHOLDER using __a (cnvy/b

Adam HOUSEHOLDER, Sept 1830). Wit: Ebenezer GRUBB, Geo. W. SHAWEN. Delv. to Gideon HOUSEHOLDER 13 Mar 1833.

3U:208   Date: 9 Aug 1830   RtCt: 25 Sep 1830
David RICKETTS & wife Elizabeth of Ffx to Everett SAUNDERS of Ldn. B/S of 23a on Lsbg Turnpike road adj __ JENKINS, James F. NEWTON.

3U:210   Date: 26 Jun 1830   RtCt: 27 Sep 1830
Philip ALLENSWORTH & wife Elizabeth of Todd Co Ky to Enoch GLASSCOCK of Ldn. B/S of 339a on Ashbys Gap Turnpike road below the Goose Creek bridge (where Samuel SINGLETON dec'd resided, the mansion house in Fqr, but most of the land in Ldn). Wit: William PARHAM, Wm. M. TERNY.

3U:213   Date: 9 Aug 1830   RtCt: 27 Sep 1830
Charles Fenton MERCER of Lsbg to Usher SKINNER of Ldn. B/S of 100a (75a and 25a) on Bull Run Mt. on the Cool Spring where Benjamin HAGERMAN once lived. Delv. to SKINNER pr order 14 Mar 1831.

3U:215   Date: 16 Sep 1830   RtCt: 27 Sep 1830
Adam HOUSHOLDER & Sarah of Ldn to Curtis GRUBB of Ldn. B/S of 49a adj __ GRUBB, __ ALLDER, __ JANNEY. Wit: Ebenezer GRUBB, Geo. W. SHAWEN. Delv. to GRUBB 15 Feb 1830.

3U:217   Date: 27 Sep 1830   RtCt: 27 Sep 1830
Thomas JONES of Ldn to Abel JONES and Alfred JONES of Ldn. B/S of 5a where he now resides, adj Stephen McPHERSON, Joshua GREGG.

3U:218   Date: 9 Aug 1824   RtCt: 29 Sep 1830
Alexander M. BRISCOE & wife Matilda of PrWm to Enos WILDMAN of Lsbg. B/S of 1/6th of 1/7th interest in house & lot (belonged to John A. LACEY dec'd) at SE corner of King & Royal Sts in Lsbg

3U:220   Date: 9 Aug 1830   RtCt: 29 Sep 1830
Usher SKINNER & wife Rebecca of Ldn to Samuel M. BOSS and Michael MORALLEE of Ldn. Trust for debt to Samuel M. EDWARDS using 100a (prch/o Charles F. MERCER) on Bull Run. Wit: Robert BAYLY, Charles LEWIS. Delv. to EDWARDS 17 Aug 1837.

3U:222   Date: 28 May 1830   RtCt: 30 Sep 1830
Henson HUMPHREY of Guilford Co NC to Isaac ALBRIGHT of Guilford Co NC. PoA for interest in estate of Alexander WHITELY dec'd of Ldn.

3U:223   Date: 12 Aug 1830   RtCt: 1 Oct 1830
William GULICK & wife Mary of Ldn to Samuel M. EDWARDS of Lsbg. Trust for debt to George GULICK and Horace LUCKETT using 136a. Wit: Abner GIBSON, Burr POWELL.

3U:225   Date: 12 Aug 1830   RtCt: 1 Oct 1830
Charles Fenton MERCER of Lsbg to William GULICK of Ldn. B/S of 136a adj Joseph HAWKINS. Delv. to GULICK 15 Sep 1832.

3U:226   Date: 18 Mar 1830   RtCt: 1 Oct 1830
Price JACOBS & wife Catharine of Ldn to Samuel BEAVERS of Ldn.
B/S of 19½a (allotted to Reuben TRIPLETT from Reuben TRIPLETT
dec'd) adj BEAVERS, David GALLAHER. Wit: Francis W.
LUCKETT, N. C. WILLIAMS. Delv. to Thos. BEAVERS Exor of
Saml. BEAVERS 16 Mar 1839.

3U:228   Date: 17 Mar 1830   RtCt: 1 Oct 1830
Price JACOBS & wife Catharine of Ldn to Thomas M. HUMPHREY
of Ldn. B/S of 14¾a Lot #2 from div. of Jesse HUMPHREY dec'd
allotted to Rachael HUMPHREY. Wit: Francis W. LUCKETT, N. C.
WILLIAMS.

3U:229   Date: 13 Oct 1829   RtCt: 5 Oct 1830
George M. CHICHESTER & wife Mary of Ldn to John
RICHARDSON of Ldn. B/S of 2/14th interest in 40a 'Big Spring Mill'.
Wit: Fayette BALL, John H. McCABE.

3U:231   Date: 6 Oct 1830   RtCt: 6 Oct 1830
John LITTLEJOHN (agent of Michael BELL) to Benj'n WALKER,
John VANHORNE and Gabriel McGEATH. Release of trust of May
1809.

3U:232   Date: 20 Sep 1830   RtCt: 11 Oct 1830
Elam JACOBS. Oath as Capt. in 56th Reg, 6th Brig, 2nd Div of Va
Militia.

3U:232   Date: 11 Oct 1830   RtCt: 11 Oct 1830
Isaac NICHOLS (surviving trustee) and William HOGE, William
PIGGOTT & Thomas HATCHER (Exors of Samuel & Isaac
NICHOLS) of Ldn to David LOVETT of Ldn. Release of trust of Jun
1824 for Samuel & Isaac NICHOLS now dec'd and Swithen
NICHOLS.

3U:234   Date: 9 Aug 1830   RtCt: 11 Oct 1830
Isaac NICHOLS (surviving trustee) and William HOGE, William
PIGGOTT, & Thomas HATCHER (Exors of Samuel & Isaac
NICHOLS) of Ldn to John TAYLOR of Ldn. Release of trust of Feb
1822 for Samuel & Isaac NICHOLS

3U:236   Date: 11 Oct 1830   RtCt: 11 Oct 1830
George W. GIBSON & wife Mary (d/o Abigail GARRETT) of Ldn to
Joshua PUSEY of Ldn. B/S of 45a (except 10a, allotted to Abigail
GARRETT now dec'd from div. of father Joseph CAVANS dec'd) adj
PUSEY, Wm. HOLMES, Diadama PAXSON; and undivided interest
in 75a now in possession of Wm. P. FOX (allotted Ann CLEMENTS
formerly CAVENS the wd/o Joseph CAVENS dec'd as dower). Wit:
John H. McCABE, S. M. EDWARDS. Delv. to PUSEY 11 Aug 1851.

3U:237   Date: 16 Sep 1830   RtCt: 11 Oct 1830
Adam HOUSHOLDER & wife Sarah of Ldn to Amos JANNEY of
Ldn. B/S of 20a adj Catharine HIXON, Curtis GRUBB, __ RAMEY.

Wit: Ebenezer GRUBB, Geo. W. SHAWEN. Delv. to JANNEY 29 Jun 1833.

3U:239 Date: 28 Aug 1830 RtCt: 11 Oct 1830
Fleming HIXSON of Ldn to David MAGAHA of Ldn. B/S of 1/3 undivided interest in dower of 92a farm purchased by father Timothy HIXON of John HAMILTON. Delv. to MAGAHA 24 Apr 1832.

3U:240 Date: 11 Oct 1830 RtCt: 11 Oct 1830
Thomas M. SINCLAIR of Ldn to Sarah THORNTON called Sarah WATTERS and Mary THORNTON (heirs of Charles THORNTON dec'd) of Ldn. B/S of interest in estate of Saml. SINCLAIR dec'd except dower to widow. Delv. to Alfred BELT the Guardian of heirs 17 Jun 1831.

3U:242 Date: 28 Aug 1830 RtCt: 11 Oct 1830
David MAGAHA to David CONRAD. Trust for debt to Fleming HIXON using undivided interest in 92a (prch/o HIXON). Wit: D. ANNIN, Samuel C. DORMAN, Moses JANNEY.

3U:243 Date: 9 Jan 1827 RtCt: 11 Oct 1830
William P. FOX & wife Catharine E. of Ldn to Elizabeth SULLIVAN of Ldn. B/S of 12a Lot #6 and 63a Lot #1 (cnvy/b Joseph CAVENS Mar 1823, except rights of heirs of Ann CLEMMENTS at her death), and 10a lot adj Lot #1 (prch/o Zachariah DULANEY). Wit: Presley CORDELL, Noble S. BRADEN.

3U:245 Date: 17 Apr 1830 RtCt: 11 Oct 1830
Isaac NICHOLS Jr. (surviving trustee of Isaac & Samuel NICHOLS dec'd) to Nathan GREGG and Stephen GREGG (Exors of Thomas GREGG dec'd). Release of trust of Dec 1822.

3U:246 Date: 5 Jun 1830 RtCt: 12 Oct 1830
Noah HIX(S)ON & wife Cecelia of Ldn to Daniel COOPER of Ldn. B/S of 26a adj __ COMPHER, Catharine HIXSON. Wit: Geo. W. SHAWEN, Saml. HOUGH. Delv. pr order 6 Jun 1834.

3U:248 Date: 24 May 1830 RtCt: 14 Jun 1830
John McKNIGHT of Ldn to Charles CHAMBLIN of Ldn. B/S of 20a nr N fork of Goose Creek (formerly prop. of William McKNIGHT dec'd where John PANCOAST holds trust), adj McKNIGHT, Thomas JAMES, Charles McKNIGHT. Wit: S. B. T. CALDWELL, Enos NICHOLS, Nathan COCKRAN. Delv. pr order 5 Mar 1833.

3U:249 Date: 29 Aug 1828 RtCt: 18 Oct 1830
Mary SHAWEN wd/o Cornelius SHAWEN to Richard H. HENDERSON (agent for James EAKIN). Relinquishes rights to 193a which fell to Geo. W. SHAWEN in div. of Cornelius' estate.

3U:251 Date: 10 Sep 1830 RtCt: 19 Oct 1830
Robert A. LACEY & wife Maria of Florida to John P. SMART of Ldn. B/S of undivided ½ of 1/14th part (derived from Westward A. LACEY dec'd) of 40a 'Big Spring Mill' (see DBk UU:132 and UU:252). Wit:

Presley CORDELL, Saml. M. EDWARDS. Delv. to SMART 23 Jan 1832.

3U:253   Date: 8 Sep 1830   RtCt: 20 Oct 1830
Robert J. TAYLOR & wife Mary Elizabeth of AlexDC to William KING of Lsbg. B/S of lot on W side of King St in Lsbg. Wit: Newton KEENE, Adam LYNN.

3U:255   Date: 9 Sep 1830   RtCt: 20 Oct 1830
William KING & wife Susanna to Robert J. TAYLOR of AlexDC. Mortgage on above lot. Wit: Presley CORDELL, Saml. M. EDWARDS. Delv. to TAYLOR 10 Sep 1837.

3U:256   Date: 22 Mar 1830   RtCt: 22 Oct 1830
L. P. W. BALCH (surviving trustee) to James JOHNSON. B/S of 5a Lot #2 in div. of John HANDY dec'd (from trust of Dec 1822 of William H. HANDY, DBk FFF:162).

3U:258   Date: 30 Jul 1830   RtCt: 25 Oct 1830
Benjamin MOORE & wife Elizabeth, Nathan PRINCE & wife Mary, Henry FISHER & wife Margaret of Lewis Co Va and Mathias PRINCE & wife Magdalena, Mary SCOTT and John EVERHEART & wife Sarah Ann of Ldn to Nelson EVERHART of Ldn. B/S of 18a and 2a (from estate of Levi PRINCE dec'd). Wit: Ebenezer GRUBB, Geo. W. SHAWEN. Delv. to EVERHEART 11 Mar 1835.

3U:261   Date: 23 Oct 1829   RtCt: 25 Oct 1830
Thompson M. BENNETT of WashDC to William HOLMES of Ldn. B/S of undivided land inherited from brother Hamilton BENNETT (from estate of Charles BENNETT dec'd). Wit: Jno. CHALMERS, Henry WERTZ.

3U:263   Date: 19 Oct 1830   RtCt: 25 Oct 1830
John C. BAZZELL & wife Mary B. of Ldn to Thomas JAMES & wife Mary of Ldn. B/S of 24a on Valentine's branch nr Blue ridge and __ WARNER, __ TAYLOR, Alexander HARRISON. Wit: Craven OSBURN, Notley C. WILLIAMS. Delv. to JAMES 13 Apr 1831.

3U:265   Date: 1 Apr 1830   RtCt: 26 Oct 1830
James LOVE & wife Susanna of Ldn to Anna GOODIN of Ldn. B/S of interest in land allotted as dower to late Agness POULSON wd/o Jasper POULSON dec'd (4/10th of 2/5th of dower sold to LOVE by John TRIBBY & wife Lydia, Margaret SPENCER, William POULSON, Susanna PEIRCE). Wit: Samuel M. EDWARDS, Presley CORDELL.

3U:267   Date: 25 Oct 1830   RtCt: 28 Oct 1830
William DODD & wife Mary of Ldn to Samuel SUFFRON of Ldn. B/S of 2a (cnvy/b Miriam HOLE, Ann HOLE & Ruth HOLE to Major HUNT June 1810, DBk MM:138, which Major HUNT gave to Mary DODD late Mary HUNT wd/o of Major HUNT as life estate). Wit: Saml. M. EDWARDS, Presley CORDELL.

3U:269   Date: 13 Mar 1824   RtCt: 29 Oct 1830
James SAUNDERS & wife Prescilla of Berkeley Co Va, Presley SAUNDERS & wife Mary, Everitt SAUNDERS & wife Susan, Ramey G. SAUNDERS, Cyrus SAUNDERS, John SAUNDERS, Gunnell SAUNDERS and Editha SAUNDERS of Ldn and Henry SAUNDERS of the U.S. Army now in Ldn to Thomas SAUNDERS of Ldn (all ch/o Henry SAUNDERS dec'd). B/S of undivided shares in father's estate (widow Patience SAUNDERS rejected provisions of will, which also included son Crayton SAUNDERS and legacy to Anna AUSTIN, and debts still owed after sale of personal estate that Thomas will pay off). Wit: John SHAW, S. M. BOSS, John H. MONROE, Jas. H. HAMILTON, Saml. M. EDWARDS. Delv. to Thomas SAUNDERS 3 Dec 1834.

3U:272   Date: 27 Mar 1830   RtCt: 30 Oct 1830
Colin AULD of AlexDC to George COOPER of Ldn. B/S of 57a at foot of Cotocton Mt. adj heirs of Hugh FULTON, __ UMBAUGH, __ HIXSON. Wit: William PAGE, Newton KEENE, Adam LYNN.

3U:274   Date: 29 Oct 1830   RtCt: 30 Oct 1830
John SHAW of Ldn to Robert H. GOVER of Ldn. Trust for William H. JACOBS of Ldn as security on note to Jonathan ROBERTS using household items.

3U:275   Date: 4 Nov 1830   RtCt: 4 Nov 1830
Elizabeth MARTIN wd/o David MARTIN dec'd of Ldn to John WADE of Ldn. B/S of 20¼a (part of lot cnvy/b John CARR Jan 1809, DBk KK: 374).

3U:276   Date: 3 Nov 1830   RtCt: 4 Nov 1830
Edmund F. CARTER of Ldn to Samuel SMITH of Ldn. B/S of 5a adj Stacy TAYLOR, Samuel IDON; and 4a adj Samuel IDON.

3U:277   Date: 2 Aug 1830   RtCt: 4 Aug 1830
P. H. W. BRONAUGH to Francis W. LUCKETT & wife Sarah S. B/S of undivided 1/3 interest in land on Kanhawa River devised to Sarah from will of father William BRONAUGH dec'd (brother P. H. W. was a minor when other brother and sisters devised over her portion).

3U:279   Date: 4 Nov 1830   RtCt: 4 Nov 1830
Nathaniel GRIGSBY of Fqr to Mrs. Elizabeth KEEN & daus. Mary, Elizabeth & Martha KEEN of Ldn. Gift to mother Elizabeth of negro woman Letty abt 30y old, to Mary negro girl Eveline abt 12y old, to Elizabeth negro girl Roseanna abt 5y old, and to Martha negro boy John abt 12y old.

3U:280   Date: 19 Oct 1830   RtCt: 8 Nov 1830
George RICHARDS and John ROSE. Bond on RICHARDS as school treasurer.

3U:280   Date: 8 Nov 1830   RtCt: 8 Nov 1830
Jacob J. SHOVER and Philip HEATER. Bond on SHOVER as committee for estate of Susanna SHOVER a lunatic.

3U:281   Date: 8 Nov 1830   RtCt: 8 Nov 1830
Peter C. RUST, Uriel GLASSCOCK and James RUST. Bond on RUST as constable.

3U:281   Date: 8 Nov 1830   RtCt: 8 Nov 1830
Andrew S. ANDERSON, Elijah PEACOCK, Lewis COLE, Charles B. HARRISON. Bond on ANDERSON as constable.

3U:282   Date: 15 Dec 1828   RtCt: 10 Nov 1830
John CHAMBLIN dec'd. Division of slaves – negro Sarah, Bob, Eleanor & child and Chat to widow Mary CHAMBLIN; negro Cuff to Samuel COX; negro Stephen to Stephen CHAMBLIN; negro Ann to Albert CHAMBLIN; negro Clary to Leven CHAMBLIN; negro Armistead to Lee CHAMBLIN; negro Susan to Edith CHAMBLIN. Divisors: John G. HUMPHREY, William C. PALMER.

3U:283   Date: 5 Jan 1830   RtCt: 9 Nov 1830
Enos NICHOLAS. Oath as Lt. in troop of Cavelry in 2nd Reg, 2nd Div of Va Militia.

3U:284   Date: 8 Nov 1830   RtCt: 8 Nov 1830
Seth SMITH of Ldn to John WHITACRE of Ldn. Release of trust of May 1819, DBk YY:321, for Aaron BURSON.

3U:285   Date: 2 Sep 1819   RtCt: 15 Nov 1820/8 Nov 1830
Ferdinando FAIRFAX of WashDC to William SMALLWOOD of JeffVa. B/S of 21a (reserving mineral rights) in Shannondale on E side of Blue ridge mt. adj Ebenezer GRUBB, __ EVERHART, Peter DEMORY, Philip DERRY. Wit: Joseph PURSELL, Robert RUSSELL, Valentine JACOBS.

3U:287   Date: 1 Dec 1825   RtCt: 8 Nov 1830
Timothy TAYLOR of Ldn to Samuel B. T. CALDWELL of Ldn. B/S of 1a nr foot of Blue ridge adj __ HEATON, Marcus HUMPHREY, Thos. HUMPHREY.

3U:288   Date: 4 Nov 1830   RtCt: 8 Nov 1830
Henry G. SAMSELL of Ldn to Townshend McVEIGH of Ldn. Trust for debt to H. & J. H. McVEIGH using household items. Delv. to T. McVEIGH 24 Jan 1832.

3U:290   Date: 7 Jun 1830   RtCt: 8 Nov 1830
John BROWN of Ldn to brother James BROWN of Ldn. PoA for sale of land. Wit: Daniel HOFFMAN, Thos. DAUGHERTY. John BROWN acknowledged signature in Jackson Co Ohio.

3U:291   Date: 6 Nov 1830   RtCt: 8 Nov 1830
Jonah TAVEN(N)ER & wife Pleasant of Ldn to Joseph P. MAGEATH of Ldn. Trust for debt to James BROWN atty in fact for John BROWN of Ldn using land in Tavener's occupancy adj Eden CARTER, the Poor House establishment, Sarah HUMPHREY (cnvy/b James BROWN and Ann BROWN w/o John BROWN, Oct 1830). Wit: Benjamin GRAYSON, John W. GRAYSON. Delv. to R. H. HENDERSON Atty for creditor 19 Jan 1831.

3U:293 Date: 29 Oct 1830 RtCt: 8 Nov 1830
Jonas JANNEY Jr. & wife Pleasant of Ldn to James BROWN of Ldn.
B/S of ½a in Union (cnvy/b Isaac BROWN Jun 1824, DBk HHH:378)
adj Isaac BROWN, Samuel DUNKIN, Asa TRAHORN, __
GALLEHER. Wit: Thos. NICHOLS, Notley C. WILLIAMS.

3U:295 Date: 8 Nov 1830 RtCt: 8 Nov 1830
John ISH to Burr W. HARRISON. Trust for debt to Nathaniel
SEEVERS (Dpty Marshall of Sup Ct of Winchester) using 3a (see
DBk QQ:383) in Aldie on Little River subject to undivided dower of
widow of Aaron MARSTELLER dec'd.

3U:297 Date: 23 Oct 1830 RtCt: 8 Nov 1830
Eleanor DAMEWOOD formerly Eleanor MARSTELLER of Ldn to
John ISH of Ldn. B/S of dower interest in lands in Aldie of husband
Aaron MARSTELLER (she since widowed again since death of
husband Jacob DAMEWOOD). Delv. to ISH 1 May 1833.

3U:299 Date: 29 Oct 1830 RtCt: 8 Nov 1830
John WEST & wife Hannah of Ldn to Morris OSBURN of Ldn. B/S of
171a adj __ PANCOAST, __ PURSEL. Wit: Thomas NICHOLS,
Craven OSBURN. Delv. to OSBURN 17 Apr 1846.

3U:301 Date: 15 Oct 1830 RtCt: 8 Nov 1830
James BROWN atty in fact for John BROWN and Ann BROWN w/o
John of Ldn to Jonah TAVENER of Ldn. B/S of 110a adj Eden
CARTER, George BURSON, Sarah HUMPHREY, road from Union
to Snickers Gap, John WILLIAMS. Wit: John W. GRAYSON,
Benjamin GRAYSON. Delv. to B. W. HARRISON atty in suit of John
BROWN agst Jonah TAVENER, 17 Mar 1832.

3U:303 Date: 6 Nov 1830 RtCt: 8 Nov 1830
John SHAW & wife Cynthia of Ldn to William TORRISON of Ldn.
B/S of house and lot on Back St in Lsbg adj Simon SMALE, __
DONOHOE (prch/o Simon SMALE Oct 1826. Wit: Presley
CORDELL, John H. McCABE.

3U:305 Date: 8 Nov 1830 RtCt: 8 Nov 1830
Nathaniel SEEVERS (Dpty Marshall of Sup Ct Winchester) to John
ISH of Ldn. B/S of 3a in Aldie subject to undivided dower of widow
(from case of Jacob ISH agst Peter SKINNER Admr of Aaron
MARSTILLER dec'd and Burr MARSTILLER an heir, see DBk
QQ:383).

3U:306 Date: 1 Aug 1830 RtCt: 9 Nov 1830
Augustus P. F. LAURENS of Fqr to H. B. POWELL of Ldn. Trust for
debt to Townshend D. PEYTON using 21a with mills. Delv. to
POWELL pr order 4 Sep 1833.

3U:308 Date: 1 Aug 1830 RtCt: 9 Nov 1830
Townshend D. PEYTON & wife Sarah of Ldn to Augustus P. F.
LAURENS of Fqr. B/S of 21a with mills. Wit: Burr POWELL, A.

GIBSON. Delv. to Asa ROGERS who bought the property under a deed of trust, 22 Nov 1833.

3U:310   Date: 29 Oct 1830   RtCt: 11 Nov 1830

James TARLETON & wife Elizabeth of Ldn to Caleb N. GALLEHER of Ldn. B/S of 35a (allotted to Elizabeth from estate of John JOHNSON dec'd) where TARLTON now lives on Goose Creek adj Snickers Gap turnpike road, Mrs. GARRET, GALLEHER, __ LUCKETT. Wit: John SIMPSON, A. GIBSON. Delv. to GALLEHER 1 Aug 1836.

3U:312   Date: 19 Nov 1830   RtCt: 19 Nov 1830

Sydnor B. RUST of Ldn to Martha RUST wd/o Matthew RUST dec'd of Ldn. B/S of interest in 10a (leased by Sydnor of father Matthew) adj Lewis BERKELY, Benjamin HIXON, leased house where William K. ISH resides, ½ of garden & cornhouse, jail built by ISH; and rights to negro man George abt 25y old and man Peter abt 65y old.

3U:314   Date: 19 Nov 1830   RtCt: 19 Nov 1830

Sydnor B. RUST of Ldn to William K. ISH of Ldn. B/S of interest above house and lot, etc.

3U:315   Date: 18 Oct 1830   RtCt: 19 Nov 1830

Aaron S. GREGG & wife Elizabeth and Mahlon S. GREGG & wife Emily to Silas GARRETT. B/S of 22a (from estate of father Joseph GREGG dec'd). Wit: Notley C. WILLIAMS, David HANDLEY, Thomas EWERS, Thomas NICHOLS. Delv. 1 Feb 1834 pr order.

3U:317   Date: 20 Nov 1830   RtCt: 20 Nov 1830

Richard C. McCARTY and Dennis McCARTY of Ldn to Daniel JANNEY of Ldn. Trust for debt to William HOGUE of Ldn using interest in 350a on Goose Creek (from father Dennis McCARTY the elder dec'd). Delv. pr order 7 May 1833.

3U:318   Date: 4 Sep 1830   RtCt: 20 Nov 1830

Henry FRAZIER & wife Ann of FredMd to Thos. J. MARLOW of Ldn. B/S of 70a adj Adam SANBOWER, Jacob WALTMAN, MARLOW on main road from WALTMAN's to Berlin ferry. Delv. to MARLOW 9 Jul 1833.

3U:320   Date: 1 May 1830   RtCt: 30 Nov 1830

James R. COLEMAN & wife Jane of Ffx to Elizabeth TIPPETT of Ldn. B/S of 60a Lot #6 in 'Hill of Rocks' from div. of father's estate. Wit: Alex'r. WAUGH, Robt. RATCLIFFE, Wm. S. DARRELL.

3U:322   Date: 27 Nov 1830   RtCt: 30 Nov 1830

Samuel BOSS alias Samuel S. BOSS (son and only heir of Jacob BOSS dec'd a s/o Peter BOSS dec'd) & wife Catharine of BaltMd to Samuel M. BOSS of Lsbg. B/S of interest in lot with 2-story house at Loudoun & King Sts in Lsbg and lot adj Lsbg, Charles B. BALL, Saml. M. EDWARDS, Edward FRANCIS (from father Peter BOSS dec'd late of Lsbg who died leaving widow Mary BOSS, who has since departed, and heirs Peter BOSS, Saml. M. BOSS, Danl. C.

BOSS, Abraham J. BOSS, David BOSS, Mary MARTIN late Mary HAWKE and Wm. HAWKE ch/o Margaret HAWKE dec'd a dau.) Wit: Henry W. GRAY, N. G. BRYSON. Delv. to S. M. BOSS 20 Mar 1843.

3U:326   Date: 9 Oct 1830   RtCt: 1 Dec 1830
Jesse P. HATCH & wife Jane S. of Vermont to Hamilton ROGERS of Ldn. B/S of undivided 1/5th interest in 89a and 20a Lot #1 in div. of estate of William HAWLING s/o William dec'd (see DBk QQQ:249 & 250); and undivided interest in slaves Dick and James (dev. to William dec'd from estate of father Wm. dec'd). Wit: Wilson C. SELDEN, Presley CORDELL.

3U:328   Date: 27 Apr 1830   RtCt: 2 Dec 1830
John SMARR & wife Susan of Ldn to James SWART of Ldn. B/S of 6½a nr Goose Creek on Snickers Gap Turnpike road where SMARR now lives obtained from Dennis McCARTY dec'd. Wit: Burr POWELL, Abner GIBSON.

3U:329   Date: 15 Mar 1830   RtCt: 3 Dec 1830
Joel LINTHICUM & wife Jane H. of Hardy Co Va to John MARTIN of Ldn. B/S of house and lot on King St in Lsbg (except estate for life interest of Hen[r]y Moon DAVIS) now occupied by W. W. HAMMONTREE, adj Henry SAUNDERS, Jno. Nicholas KLINE, Enos WILDMAN. Delv. to MARTIN 20 Jul 8133.

3U:331   Date: 23 Jan 1830   RtCt: 4 Dec 1830
Timothy HIXSON & wife Leah of Bedford Co Pa to Andrew S. ANDERSON of Ldn. B/S of undivided interest in lands of Timothy HIXSON dec'd f/o Timothy and lands of Timothy's half brother Andrew HIXSON dec'd of Ldn.

3U:333   Date: 26 May 1830   RtCt: 6 Dec 1830
John H. MONROE and Samuel M. BOSS of Lsbg to Robert H. GOVER of Lsbg. LS (renewable forever) of lot on Royal St in Lsbg where GOVER now resides (see DBk FFF:126).

3U:335   Date: 26 May 1830   RtCt: 6 Dec 1830
Robert H. GOVER of Lsbg to Josiah L. DREAN of Lsbg. Trust for debt to Samuel M. BOSS using above lease. Delv. to Saml. M. BOSS 19 Jun 1839.

3U:336   Date: 13 May 1829   RtCt: 6 Dec 1830
David NEER & wife Susannah of Ldn to Richard HURDLE of Ldn. B/S of 4a on W side of short hill adj NEER, Hiram CARNEY. Wit: Jno. FITZSIMMONS, Saml. K. WHITE. Acknowledged by NEER in JeffVa. Delv. to HURDLE 24 Jun 1831.

3U:338   Date: 9 Dec 1830   RtCt: 9 Dec 1830
John LONG & wife Susan of Ldn to Peter STONEBURNER of Ldn. B/S of 11½a and 2a Lot #6 allotted in div. of D'l. STONEBURNER dec'd, DBk QQQ:488. Wit: Presley CORDELL, Thomas SAUNDERS.

3U:340   Date: 9 Mar 1830   RtCt: 10 Dec 1830
Joseph BARTON of Ldn to James JOHNSTON of Ldn. B/S of ¼a in Bloomfield adj William F. CLARK, Samuel McGWIGGIN.

3U:341   Date: 3 Apr 1830   RtCt: 10 Dec 1830
Isaac M. BROWN & wife Christina of Ldn to William BENTON of Ldn. Trust for George KILE and John KILE as security on debts to Hiram McVEIGH, Wm. R. SWART, H. & J. H. McVEIGH, Ludwell LUCKETT using Christina's interest in estate of father John KILE dec'd. Wit: Burr POWELL, A. GIBSON. Delv. pr order 21 Sep 1837.

3U:343   Date: 16 Oct 1830   RtCt: 16 Oct 1830
George GREGG of Ldn to A. S. ANDERSON of Ldn. PoA.

3U:344   Date: 13 Dec 1830   RtCt: 13 Dec 1830
Craven BROWN. Oath as 1st Lt. in a company of artillery, 2nd Reg, 2nd Div of Va Militia.

3U:344   Date: 7 Jun 1830   RtCt: 11 Dec 1830
John G. HILL to George VINCELL. Trust for debt to John WINE using ½ of 1a lot adj __ DAVIS, __ SHOVER. Wit: Geo. W. SHAWEN, S. HOUGH.

3U:347   Date: 3 Nov 1830   RtCt: 13 Dec 1830
Timothy CARRINGTON & wife Margaret of Ldn to Joshua OSBURN and Roger CHEW of Ldn. Trust for debt to John CHEW of Ldn using lot with house in Snickersville now occupied by CARRINGTON; woman Hannah abt 28y old, girl Emily abt 12y old, girl Frances abt 7y old, girl Sarah abt 5y old, boy Ellzey abt 3y old, girl Clarissa abt 5m old; and household items. Wit: Notley C. WILLIAMS, Craven OSBURN.

3U:350   Date: 30 Nov 1830   RtCt: 13 Dec 1830
Timothy PADGET & wife Elizabeth to James A. PADGET. Trust for debt to Wm. THRIFT and Walter A. SMITH ass'ee of Wm. MATTHEWS using 42a adj heirs of Andrew HEATH, James McKIM, Mary D. HAWLEY; with memo mentioning Baily PADGET. Wit: Charles LEWIS, Thomas DARNE.

3U:354   Date: 20 Jun 1829   RtCt: 13 Dec 1830
Robert WHITE & wife Mary of Franklin Co Indiana to Susannah POULSON and Mary POULSON of Ldn. B/S of interest in dower right of Agness POULSON dec'd. Wit: Nathaniel HAMMOND, Abraham JONES.

3U:356   Date: 1 Oct 1830   RtCt: 13 Dec 1830
Elizabeth JACOBS wd/o of Peter JACOBS dec'd, George JACOBS & wife Elizabeth, Christina JACOBS, Samuel COCKERELL & wife Elizabeth, Valentine JACOBS & wife Harriet, Peter JACOBS & wife Elizabeth, John JACOBS & wife Elizabeth, Rinard JACOBS, Adam JACOBS & wife Rachel of Ldn and Jesse PORTER & wife Mary of Indianna (heirs of Peter JACOBS) to Joseph LESLIE of Ldn. LS (during lives of Elizabeth & George JACOBS) of 60a adj Jno.

CONARD. Wit: Ebenezer GRUBB, Mortimer McILHANY. Delv. pr order 24 Mar 1835.

3U:359   Date: 30 Oct 1830   RtCt: 13 Dec 1830
Joseph HOUGH & wife Rachel of Ldn to Joseph LESLIE of Ldn. B/S of 55 pole lot in Hllb adj Samuel CLENDENING, heirs of Josiah WHITE, Frederick A. DAVISSON. Wit: Ebenezer GRUBB, Mortimer McILHANY. Delv. to LESLIE 1 Oct 1836.

3U:360   Date: 2 Aug 1830   RtCt: 14 Dec 1830
P. H. W. BRONAUGH of Ldn to Caldwell CARR. Trust for loan made to Francis W. LUCKETT in Oct 1829 as BRONAUGH's Guardian so he could graduate as a doctor or medicine from Daniel KERFORT (Guardian of Amanda CARR) of Fqr using 179a dev. by father William BRONAUGH dec'd. Delv. to CARR 11 Aug 1834.

3U:363   Date: 20 Dec 1830   RtCt: 20 Dec 1830
Rich'd H. HENDERSON (Exor of Thomas R. MOTT dec'd) to William JOHNSON of Lsbg. B/S of lot in Lsbg adj JOHNSON, James GARNER, turnpike road from Market St to AlexDC.

3U:364   Date: 18 Aug 1828   RtCt: 23 Dec 1830
Edward HALL & wife Louisa F. of Ldn to Charles GILL of Ldn. B/S of 5a adj HALL, William VICKERS, road from Cuthbert POWELL's to Mdbg. Wit: John C. GREEN, Thos. S. HALL, Mary FORREST, Francis W. LUCKETT, John W. GRAYSON.

3U:366   Date: 21 Dec 1830   RtCt: 24 Dec 1830
William MERCHANT of Ldn to John SURGHNOR. Trust for debt to William B. BURKE using horse. Wit: Presley CORDELL, Daniel LEWIS.

3U:367   Date: __ 183_   RtCt: 25 Dec 1830
Samuel M. EDWARDS and James McILHANY to Charles F. MERCER. Release of trust of Nov 1826, DBk NNN:393, for debt to Richard H. HENDERSON. MERCER has sold part of land to William GULICK.

3U:369   Date: 1 Dec 1830   RtCt: 28 Dec 1830
James PLASTER & wife Hannah of Ldn to Samuel RECTOR of Ldn. B/S of 167a on NW side of Goose Creek adj Wm. F. LUCKETT. Wit: Burr POWELL, A. GIBSON. Delv. to RECTOR 14 May 1833.

3U:371   Date: 30 Dec 1830   RtCt: 1 Jan 1831
John SCHOOLEY (Exor of William GREGG dec'd), George GREGG (heir & Exor of William GREGG dec'd), Nancy GREGG (w/o George Gregg) and Andrew S. ANDERSON (atty in fact for George GREGG) of Ldn to Robert MOFFETT of Ldn. B/S of interest in 247½a from William GREGG dec'd (½ to heirs of Aaron GREGG and ½ to Robert MOFFETT in right of this purchase). Wit: Saml. DAWSON, Saml. HOUGH. Delv. to MOFFETT 1 Feb 1832.

3U:375 Date: 29 Dec 1829 RtCt: 3 Jan 1831
Joshua B. OVERFIELD & wife Anna of Ldn to Joseph
RICHARDSON of Ldn. B/S of 17a on great road from Snickers gap
to Lsbg by Israel JANNEY; and interest in dower land of wd/o
Hudson OVERFIELD dec'd which lies between land of heirs of
Andrew HESSER dec'd and lot of Stephen CUNARD. Wit: Notley C.
WILLIAMS, Thomas NICHOLS.

3U:377 Date: 22 Sep 1830 RtCt: 3 Jan 1831
Charles TAYLOR & wife Nancy of Ldn to David HOWELL of Ldn.
B/S of 26a adj Hudson OVERFIELD's widow's dower, Joseph
RICHARDSON. Wit: Craven OSBURN, Thomas NICHOLS. Delv. to
HOWELL 9 Aug 1831.

3U:378 Date: 27 Dec 1830 RtCt: 3 Jan 1831
Joseph BOND & wife Elizabeth S. to Thomas PHILLIPS and Asa M.
BOND of Wtfd. B/S of 5a in Wtfd with tanyard (see DBk ZZ:97) adj
Jos. P. THOMAS, Robert BRADEN, William PAXSON, Fleming
PATTISON. Wit: Mortimer McILHANY, Saml. HOUGH. Delv. to
PHILLIPS 9 Jul 1832.

3U:380 Date: 13 Nov 1830 RtCt: 13 Nov 1830
Henrietta GASSAWAY, Samuel DAWSON and Charles
GASSAWAY to Gentlemen Justices John ROSE, Presley
CORDELL, Wilson C. SELDEN Jr. and Fayette BALL. Bond on
Henrietta to preserve estate of Thomas GASSAWAY dec'd during
contesting of will.

3U:381 Date: 27 Dec 1830 RtCt: 3 Jan 1831
Asa M. BOND of Wtfd to Thomas PHILLIPS of Wtfd. B/S of full rights
to ½ of water from spring at tanyard and can lay ditches and pipe.
Delv. to PHILLIPS 8 Jul 1832.

3U:382 Date: 1 Dec 1830 RtCt: 3 Jan 1831
Daniel LOVETT of Ldn to William CARR of Ldn. B/S of 150a adj
David FULTON, Charles B. ALEXANDER. Wit: Daniel C. LOVETT,
Isaac BRADFIELD, James P. LOVETT, Thomas A. LOVETT.

3U:384 Date: 8 Sep 1830 RtCt: 4 Jan 1831
Robert J. TAYLOR & wife Molly Elizabeth of AlexDC to John GRAY
of Lsbg. B/S of lot in Lsbg at King and Market St. Wit: Newton
KEENE & Adam LYNN in AlexDC.

3U:385 Date: 8 Sep 1830 RtCt: 4 Jan 1831
Robert J. TAYLOR & wife Molly Elizabeth of AlexDC to John GRAY
of Lsbg. B/S of lot on N side of Market St in Lsbg. Wit: Newton
KEENE & Adam LYNN in AlexDC.

3U:387 Date: 8 Sep 1830 RtCt: 4 Jan 1831
Robert J. TAYLOR & wife Molly Elizabeth of AlexDC to James
GARRISON of Lsbg. B/S of lot on N side of Market St in Lsbg. Wit:
Newton KEENE & Adam LYNN in AlexDC.

3U:389   Date: 8 Sep 1830   RtCt: 4 Jan 1831
Robert J. TAYLOR & wife Molly Elizabeth of AlexDC to Albert G. WATERMAN of Mdbg. B/S of lot on W side of King St in Lsbg adj James GARRISON. Wit: Newton KEENE & Adam LYNN in AlexDC.

3U:390   Date: 9 Sep 1830   RtCt: 4 Jan 1831
James GARRISON & wife Elizabeth to Robert J. TAYLOR of AlexDC. Mortgage on lot on N side of Market St. in Lsbg. Wit: Presley CORDELL, Saml. M. EDWARDS.

3U:392   Date: 30 Nov 1830   RtCt: 5 Jan 1831
Isaac S. CRAVEN & wife Sarah of WashDC and Eleanor V. CRAVEN of Ldn to Charles WILLIAMS of Ldn. B/S of 105a adj Mrs. CHILTON, __ CLAPHAM (from div. of Isaac STEER dec'd allotted to Joseph CRAVEN and Isaac S. and Eleanor V. heirs of Hannah CRAVEN dec'd a ch/o Isaac dec'd; Joseph CRAVEN is now dead, DBk III:33[32]). Delv. to WILLIAMS 24 Jun 1831.

3U:395   Date: 23 Dec 1830   RtCt: 6 Jan 1831
Anthony CUMMINGS & wife Maria of Tuscarawas Co Ohio to Joseph LAYCOCK of Ldn. B/S of 100a (cnvy/ John BENEDUM Feb 1824, except 1a sold to Thomas HALL Dec 1823) adj William A. BINNS. Wit: William CONWELL, James CONWELL. Delv. to LACOCK 30 Oct 1837.

3U:397   Date: 7 Jan 1831   RtCt: 7 Jan 1831
Mesheck LACEY (insolvent debtor in jail) to Sheriff William B. HARRISON. B/S of house & lot in Mdbg as his residence and house & lot in Mdbg used as Hatters shop (executions by George LOVE Admr of Wm. H. HAMPTON dec'd, Jonathan BUTCHER partner of Erroy Kinsey & Co, Joseph RICHARDSON, Hugh SMITH, John BETREE).

3U:398   Date: 1 Jul 1830   RtCt: 7 Jan 1831
William CUNNINGHAM & wife Nancy late CIMMINGS of Harrison Co Ohio to Richard H. HENDERSON of Ldn. B/S of land allotted Nancy in div. of father Thomas CIMMINGS dec'd of Ldn. Wit: Thomas DAY, Stephen CUNNINGHAM.

3U:400   Date: 20 Oct 1825   RtCt: 10 Jan 1831
Mahlon GREGG dec'd. Division of land on NW fork of Goose Creek nr Blue Ridge Mt. – court order dated 14 Jun 1825; 79a Lot #1 as dower to widow Sarah GREGG; 41a Lot #2 to Gilford G. GREGG; 41a Lot #3 to Nancy GREGG; 39a Lot #4 to Elizabeth GREGG; 37a Lot #5 to Edna GREGG now Edna NICHOLS w/o Enos NICHOLS; 47a Lot #6 to Adeline GREGG. Divisors: Joel OSBURN, Joshua OSBURN, James COCKRAN.

3U:403   Date: 28 Dec 1830   RtCt: 10 Jan 1831
William McKNIGHT. Qualified as 2nd Lt. in Company of Artillery in 2nd Reg, 2nd Div of Va Militia.

3U:403 Date: 1 Jun 1820 RtCt: 10 Jan 1831
Alexander CORDELL & wife Dianah/Dianna of Muskingum Co Ohio to John JANNEY of Ldn. B/S of 101a (dev. to Dianah by Sanford RAMEY dec'd) adj Margaret SAUNDERS, George W. SHAWEN. Delv. to JANNEY 21 Apr 1834.

3U:405 Date: 6 Jan 1831 RtCt: 10 Jan 1831
Jesse McVEIGH of Ldn to Thomas ROGERS of Ldn. B/S of 18a Lot #2 allotted to Samuel WHITE and 19a Lot #5 allotted to William WHITE (from trust to secure penal bills by Thomas BISCOE now dec'd to William WHITE, DBk AAA:219). Delv. to J. L. DREAN pr order ___.

3U:406 Date: 6 Jan 1831 RtCt: 12 Jan 1831
Alfred MOSHER of Troy, Rensselear Co NY (atty for Troy Thrashing Machine Co) to James McFarlan BOWMAN and Ira MOSTER of Troy. PoA to sell Deweys Patent Thrashing Machine (rights obtained Jan 29 1830 by Joel DEWEY Jr.) in Va.

3U:408 Date: 6 Dec 1830 RtCt: 24 Jan 1831
Jonah SANDS & wife Sarah of Ldn to Conrad R. DOWELL of Ldn. B/S of 28a adj John BROWN, Conrad BITZER. Wit: John SIMPSON, Thomas NICHOLS.

3U:410 Date: 16 Dec 1830 RtCt: 24 Jan 1831
George COOPER of Ldn to James GILMORE of Ldn. B/S of 2a on Clarke's run nr New Valley meeting house adj heirs of Hugh FULTON. Wit: W. H. CRAVEN, Geo. M. CHICHESTER, Asa PECK. Delv. to GILMORE 9 Sep 1831.

3U:411 Date: 24 Mar 1830 RtCt: 24 Jan 1830[31]
Rich'd. H. HENDERSON & wife Orra Moore of Lsbg to Jesse GOVER of Ldn. B/S of house & ½a lot in Wtfd recent prop. of Alexander HENDERSON dec'd s/o Rich'd. Wit: Thos. SAUNDERS, Saml. M. EDWARDS. Delv. to GOVER 19 Jul 1833.

3U:413 Date: 23 Dec 1829 RtCt: 24 Jan 1831
George W. HENRY & wife Dewana B. of Ldn to Jesse GOVER of Ldn. B/S of ½a lot in new addition to Wtfd adj R. H. HENDERSON, A. S. ANDERSON. Wit: Saml. DAWSON, John J. MATHIAS. Delv. to GOVER 19 Jul 1833.

3U:414 Date: 26 Jan 1831 RtCt: 26 Jan 1831
Thomas HATCHER & wife Nancy L. of Ldn to Guilford G. GREGG of Ldn. B/S of 41a Lot #3 (allotted Nancy L. in div. of father Mahlon GREGG dec'd) adj heirs of John BROWN, Morris OSBURN, James COCKRAN. Wit: Saml. M. EDWARDS, Presley CORDELL. Delv. to GREGG 12 Sep 1832.

3U:417 Date: 9 Sep 1830 RtCt: 26 Jan 1831
Chauncey BROOKS of BaltMD to Frederick BROOKS of Kanawha Co Va. B/S of land cnvy/b Abraham SKILLMAN to Thomas BROWN and land cnvy/b George NIXON to Thomas BROWN (cnvy/b by

trustee Samuel B. T. CALDWELL to BROOKS, DBk RRR:91). Wit: David B. FERGUSON, Wm. ASHMAN. Delv. to BROOKS 25 Mar 1832. (See DBk 3Y:72 rec'd dower also)

3U:419 Date: 27 Dec 1830 RtCt: 27 Jan 1831
William HOUGH (son of Garret) & wife Sarah Ann of Ldn to Joseph COX of Ldn. B/S of 6a adj Joseph JANNEY, Samuel B. HARRIS. Wit: Tasker C. QUINLAN, Presley CORDELL. Delv. to COX 22 Mar 1852.

3U:420 Date: 27 Jan 1831 RtCt: 28 Jan 1831
Garrett WALKER of Ldn to Joseph GORE of Ldn. Trust for Thomas GORE of Ldn as security on loan from John PANCOAST Jr. using 107a adj lot where WALKER lives. Delv. to Joseph GORE 18 Mar 1835.

3V:001 Date: 27 Jan 1831 RtCt: 28 Jan 1831
Elizabeth KITZMILLER (Exor of Martin KITZMILLER dec'd) of Ldn to Robert CAMPBELL of Ldn. LS of 3a Lot #21 & 3a #24 which Martin leased from __ CAVANS. Gives plat. Wit: Jno. A. BINNS, W. W. KITZMILLER. Delv. to CAMPBELL 9 Dec 1831.

3V:002 Date: 28 Jan 1831 RtCt: 29 Jan 1831
G(u)ilford GREGG of Ldn to Joel OSBURN of Ldn. B/S of 3a adj Issachar BROWN, Albert HEATON, OSBURN. Delv. to OSBURN 29 Sep 1831.

3V:003 Date: 27 Jan 1831 RtCt: 29 Jan 1831
Christopher FRYE & wife Margaret of Ldn to Robert CAMPBELL of Ldn. LS of 7a and 1a (from lease of James HERIFORD in Aug 1798 to Patrick CAVENS of 78 104/160a) adj KITZMILLER (see 3V:001 for plat). Wit: John H. McCABE, Presley CORDELL. Delv. to CAMPBELL 9 Dec 1831

3V:005 Date: 31 Jan 1831 RtCt: 31 Jan 1831
William B. BURKE of Ldn to George RICHARDS of Ldn. Trust for debt to Robert BENTLEY and John SURGHNOR of Ldn using 2 stage coaches, numerous horses, household items.

3V:007 Date: 23 Dec 1831 RtCt: 1 Feb 1831
Ebenezer GRUBB Sr. & wife Mary of Ldn to Edward DOWLING of Ldn. B/S of 177a on W side of Short hill adj John POTTS dec'd, __ GRUBB, DOWLING. Wit: Mortimer McILHANY, John WHITE. Delv. to DOWLING 18 May 1832.

3V:009 Date: 1 Feb 1831 RtCt: 2 Feb 1831
George RICKARD & wife Civilla of Ldn to Benjamin GRUBB of Ldn. B/S of 26a adj GRUBB, RICKARD. Wit: Mortimer McILHANY, Geo. W. SHAWEN.

3V:011 Date: 27 Jan 1831 RtCt: 3 Feb 1831
William CARR & wife Mary of Ldn to John H. MONROE, David CARR, Samuel M. BOSS, James HARRIS & Samuel SUFFRON (trustees of Methodist Episcopal Church, Lsbg Station in Baltimore

Conference). B/S of 10,000 feet of land to build house of worship, adj left of road to Nixon's Mill from Carr's house. Wit: Samuel CLARKE, Nelson HEAD, James HAMILTON.

3V:013 Date: 1 Feb 1831 RtCt: 5 Feb 1831
L. P. W. BALCH & wife Elizabeth E. W. of FredMd to Thomas CARLTON of FredMd. Trust for debt to Robert WILSON using 128a (prch/o Nicholas OSBURN Nov 1824, DBk III:146), adj Benjamin PALMER, Lewis LYDER.

3V:015 Date: 30 Dec 1830 RtCt: 23 Dec 1830/5 Feb 1831
John POPE (Exor of Christopher GREENUP dec'd late of Ky) to Walter ELGIN of Ldn. B/S of abt 100a (approx., can not dispute later) adj ELGIN, Charles BINNS, __ FULTON, George CARTER, Robt. ELGIN. Wit: James HAMILTON, Mordicai ELGIN, E. HAMMAT. Delv. to ELGIN 2 Jul 1831.

3V:017 Date: 25 Jan 1831 RtCt: 5 Feb 1831
William H. FOSTER of Ldn to Henry H. HAMILTON of Ldn. Trust for debt to Thomas W. DORMAN using household items.

3V:018 Date: 20 Nov 1830 RtCt: 8 Feb 1831
Burr W. HARRISON to merchants John & James POGUE. B/S of lot & house & store house on King St in Lsbg (from trust of Nov 1827 from Samuel CARR). (see end of book for advertisements referred to in this deed).

3V:020 Date: 24 Mar 1830 RtCt: 9 Feb 1831
John BURKITT and Newton BURKITT (heirs of Elizabeth YOUNG who m. Henry BURKITT now dec'd) of Fred Md to George YOUNG of Ldn. B/S of 18a Lot #10 (in div.) on NW fork of Goose Creek adj Griggsville tract. Delv. to Thos. YOUNG Exor of Geo. YOUNG 5 Sep 1853.

3V:022 Date: 29 Dec 1830 RtCt: 9 Feb 1831
William WILSON and Timothy TAYLOR Jr. to Charles TAYLOR. Release of trust of Apr 1821 for debt to Stephen WILSON using 42a.

3V:024 Date: 24 Mar 1830 RtCt: 9 Feb 1831
David YOUNG & wife Elizabeth of Ldn to George YOUNG of Ldn. B/S of 18a Lot #11 in Ct. div. on NW fork of Goose Creek adj Greggville tract. Wit: Thomas NICHOLS, John SIMPSON. Delv. to Thomas YOUNG Exor of George YOUNG 5 Sep 1853.

3V:026 Date: 13 Apr 1829 RtCt: 13 Apr 1829/11 Feb 1831
Narcissa GHEEN and Thomas GHEEN of Ldn to Richard H. HENDERSON of Ldn. Trust for debt to David YOUNG using 164a (Narcissa' life estate, 1/6th each shares of her children James and Leroy GHEEN, tract being the prop. of husband William GHEEN dec'd). Delv. pr order 9 Oct 1835.

3V:028 Date: 14 Feb 1831 RtCt: 16 Feb 1831
Elizabeth/Betsey MARTIN and James L. MARTIN of Ldn. DoE for slave Wilson abt 25y old. Wit: Joseph GASENER, Isaac HARRIE Jr.

3V:028   Date: 14 Feb 1831   RtCt: 14 Feb 1831
William BEVERIDGE, Hugh SMITH and Samuel CHINN. Bond on BEVERIDGE as constable.

3V:029   Date: 22 Jan 1831   RtCt: 14 Feb 1831
John ETHEL & wife Mary late MOUL, George W. MOUL and Daniel WILSON of Licking Co Ohio to Rowena ELGIN of Ldn. B/S of land of Philip MOUL dec'd (prch/o Anthony CONARD Mar 1812, DBk OO:319) left to widow Mary now ETHEL, Geo. W. MOUL and Rozanna H. MOUL who m. WILSON. Wit: Amelia JACKSON, Hannah HARTLY. Delv. to Tilghman GORE 5 May 1837.

3V:031   Date: 21 Jan 1831   RtCt: 14 Feb 1831
George W. MOUL and John ETHEL & wife Mary late MOUL of Licking Co Ohio (ch/o Philip MOUL dec'd) to David CONARD of Ldn. B/S of undivided 1/5th share of 28a of Philip MOUL from his father George MOUL dec'd (Philip MOUL now dec'd sold to Anthony CONARD f/o David on Mar 1812, DBk OO:318; Anthony sold to his son David; George W. now of age and two ch/o Philip dec'd died intestate). Wit: Daniel WILSON, Amelia JACKSON. Delv. pr order 18 Apr 1834.

3V:034   Date: 9 Apr 1830   RtCt: 11 Oct 1830/14 Feb 1831
Washington COCKE to Benjamin JAMES. B/S interest in 1/3 share of 2000a nr Gumspring (John SPENCER prch/o Washington COCKE in Apr 1805 COCKE's interest in 1/3 share of land granted to grandfather Catesby COCKE, who left children John C. COCKE, William COCKE (f/o Washington), and Elizabeth COCKE. Spencer left Ldn and died some where in western Va without paying any money to COCKE, which security Benjamin JAMES then paid). Wit: Thomas J. NOLAND, Wm. CHILTON, John HARRIS, Horace LUCKETT, William K. ISH.

3V:035   Date: 8 Dec 1830   RtCt: 12 Dec 1830/14 Feb 1831
Samuel O'BANNON & wife Frances to William MERSHON. Trust for debt to Thomas B. MERSHON (paid executions by John HUTCHISON Admr of Joseph B. MERSHON dec'd, Charles O'BANION, Hezekiah PERRY) using 93a on old Lsbg road adj Thos. B. MERSHON, Charles B. O'BANION. Wit: Thomas W. LEE, James MERSHON, Silas HUTCHISON.

3V:038   Date: 3 Feb 1831   RtCt: 15 Feb 1831
Townshend D. PEYTON of Ldn to dau. Emily A. HAMERSLEY w/o Thomas S. HAMERSLEY of Ffx. Gift of 123a on Little River adj Leven LUCKETT. Delv. to Townshend McVEIGH by order of Richard F. PEYTON? who bought land from HAMMERSLY 24 Jan 1832.

3V:039   Date: 25 Dec 1830   RtCt: 16 Feb 1831
Mandly TAYLOR & wife Catharine of FredVa to Bushrod RUST of Fqr. B/S of 83a (former prop. of Mandly TAYLOR dec'd), 231a

(prch/o Alfred H. POWELL, less 4a cnvy/t Cuthbert POWELL) and 2a (cnvy/b Cuthbert POWELL).

3V:041   Date: 15 Mar 1831   RtCt: 16 Feb 1831
Agnes TAYLOR to Mandly TAYLOR of FredVa. B/S of 17a) Lot #6 in div. of Mandly TAYLOR dec'd) and interest in dower of widow Agnes TAYLOR.

3V:043   Date: 15 Dec 1830   RtCt: 16 Feb 1831
Sarah TAYLOR to Mandly TAYLOR of FredVa. LS of 60a (allotted as dower to Sarah from husband Mandly TAYLOR dec'd) now in tenure of TAYLOR for life of Sarah. Wit: Alphonso ELGIN, Agnes TAYLOR.

3V:044   Date: 21 Jan 1831   RtCt: 16 Feb 1831
Bushrod RUST & wife Margaret to John L. POWELL. Trust for debt to Mandly TAYLOR using 3 lots containing 409a adj Daniel THOMAS, Joseph LEWIS, Cuthbert POWELL. CoE in Fqr.

3V:046   Date: 19 Aug 1820   RtCt: 19 Aug 1820/18 Feb 1831
George WAIGLEY & wife Mary of Ldn to William CARR of Ldn. A/L of ½a Lot #3 leased by James HEREFORD to Patrick CAVANS (transferred by John DORRELL to WAIGLEY). Wit: A. O. POWELL, John McCORMICK, Cornelius SHAWEN. Delv. to CARR 5 Nov 1831.

3V:048   Date: 19 Feb 1831   RtCt: 9 [19?] Feb 1831
Jesse TIMMS, Burr W. HARRISON and Charles G. ESKRIDGE to Lewis P. W. BALCH & wife Eliza E. W. Release of trust of Nov 1826 for debt to George CARTER.

3V:050   Date: 21 Feb 1831   RtCt: 21 Feb 1831
Philip GUTRIDGE & wife Ann of Ldn to James SINCLAIR of Ldn. Trust for debt to Joseph PEARSON of BaltMd using lot in Lsbg adj James L. SAMPSON on King St. Wit: Saml. M. EDWARDS, Presley CORDELL.

3V:051   Date: 11 Dec 1830   RtCt: 22 Feb 1831
Charles DRISH & wife Susanna of Tuskaloosa Co Alabama to William D. DRISH of Ldn. B/S of part of Lot #32 on W side of King St in Lsbg.

3V:054   Date: 1 Jan 1831   RtCt: 22 Feb 1831
William D. DRISH of Ldn to Henry CLAGETT of Ldn. Trust for debt to Charles DRISH of Tuskaloose Co Alabama using above lot. Delv. to CLAGETT 9 Jul 1835.

3V:056   Date: 24 Feb 1831   RtCt: 24 Feb 1831
Wm. B. BURKE to John A. BINNS and James SINCLAIR. PoA to sell land in trust to George RICHARDS for debt to Robert BENTLEY and John SURGHNOR; pay off trust, executions by John MARTIN, Edward HAMMAT, A. BRACKENRIDGE.

3V:057   Date: 24 Feb 1831   RtCt: 24 Feb 1831
William B. BURKE of Ldn to Geo. RICHARDS of Ldn. Trust for John A. BINNS, James SINCLAIR and John SURGHNOR of Ldn as securities using all household items and horses.

3V:058   Date: 14 Feb 1831   RtCt: 24 Feb 1831
William VANDEVANTER and Joseph D. VANDEVANTER of Ldn to David CARR of Ldn. B/S of 57¼a (Lot #4 in div. of dower allotted to Anna VANDEVANTER late MAINS) adj dower of Mary MAINS of William MAINS dec'd, John CARR. Delv. to CARR 13 Nov 1833.

3V:061   Date: 24 Feb 1831   RtCt: 24 Feb 1831
Simon W. RUST of Ldn to William K. ISH of Ldn. B/S of undivided interest in real estate of brother James T. RUST he received from father Mathew RUST; adj land of Lewis BERKELY. Wit: Burr WEEKS, Benjn. SMITH, John SMARR. Delv. to ISH 11 Jul 1832.

3V:062   Date: 23 Feb 1831   RtCt: 24 Feb 1831
Sydnor B. RUST, Simon William RUST and John RATRIE & wife Elizabeth of Ldn to Martha RUST of Ldn. B/S of 75a (given by Mathew RUST to son James T. RUST) adj reps of John CURRELS, James SWART, Lewis BERKLEY, Benjamin HIXON, estate of Mathew RUST dec'd. Wit: A. GIBSON, Jesse McVEIGH, H. SMITH.

3V:063   Date: 17 Jan 1828   RtCt: 25 Feb 1831
David SMITH of Ldn to Mary HOWELL of Ldn. B/S of 4a on NW fork of Goose Creek adj road from Snickers Gap to Lsbg (4 purchases from Stephen WILSON, Benjamin BRADFIELD, Levi WILLIAM and George JANNEY).

3V:065   Date: 26 Feb 1831   RtCt: 26 Feb 1831
James L. SAMPSON & wife Sally of Ldn to Charles G. ESKRIDGE of Ldn. Trust for debt to John GRAY of Ldn using interest in house and lot of Thomas JACOBS Sr. dec'd. Wit: Presley CORDELL, Saml. M. EDWARDS.

3V:067   Date: 26 Feb 1831   RtCt: 26 Feb 1831
John HITAFFER of Ldn to Francis H. PEYTON of Ldn. Trust for debt to Burr WEEKS & Co. using farm animals, household items. Delv. to Burr WEEKS 14 May 1832.

3V:068   Date: 1 Mar 1831   RtCt: 1 Mar 1831
Alexander BRACKENRIDGE & wife Elizabeth L. of Ldn to John J. MATHIAS of Ldn. Trust for debt to William JOHNSON of Ldn using 2 lots with houses in Lsbg. Wit: Presley CORDELL, John MATHIAS. Delv. to R. H. HENDERSON 30 Nov 1839.

3V:071   Date: 1 Mar 1831   RtCt: 1 Mar 1831
William JOHNSON & wife Margaret of Ldn to Alexander BRACKENRIDGE of Ldn. B/S of lot with blacksmith shop between Market and Lafayette Sts and lot with brickhouse opposite on S side of Lafayette St in Lsbg (both prch/o Isaac WRIGHT). Wit: Presley CORDELL, John J. MATHIAS.

3V:073 Date: 6 Aug 1829 RtCt: 2 Mar 1831
Henry M. DOWLING of Lsbg to James GARRISON of Lsbg. B/S of
½a lot on Market St. adj jail, Church, Edw'd HAINES. Wit: John W.
COE, M. PURSEL, Charles W. D. BINNS, Burr W. HARRISON.
Delv. to GARRISON 23 Jan 1834.

3V:074 Date: 3 Mar 1831 RtCt: 3 Mar 1831
William WILKISON. Receipt of funds from Narcissa GHEEN for
James GHEEN due on trust of Oct 1823 from Wm. GHEEN & wife
Narcissa and Jas. GHEEN to Charles TURNER. Delv. to Jas.
GHEEN 4 Sep 1833.

3V:075 Date: 3 Mar 1831 RtCt: 3 Mar 1831
William WILKISON. Receipt of funds from Mrs. Narcissa GHEEN for
Leroy GHEEN due on trust of Dec 1825 from Mrs. GHEEN and
Leroy GHEEN to Peyton POWELL. Delv. to Leroy GHEEN 4 Sep
1833.

3V:075 Date: 28 Feb 1831 RtCt: 4 Mar 1831
John HUTCHISON & wife Nancy of PrWm to Noble BEVERIDGE of
Ldn. B/S of 2 lots with houses in Mdbg lately owned and occupied
by Meshech LACEY as dwelling and hatters shop. Delv. to
BEVERIDGE Jun 1833.

3V:078 Date: 28 Feb 1831 RtCt: 4 Mar 1831
Meshech LACEY of Ldn to John HUTCHISON of PrWm. B/S of 2
lots with houses in Mdbg occupied by LACEY as dwelling and
hatters shop. Wit: H. H. HAMILTON, Geo. W. GIBBS, H. SMITH.
Delv. to N. BEVERIDGE Jun 1833.

3V:079 Date: 11 Oct 1830 RtCt: 5 Mar 1831
Peter RUST & wife Ann and Hiram SEATON & wife Nancy of Ldn to
William SEATON of Ldn. B/S of 190¼a on Goose Creek where
RUST now lives adj SEATON, heirs of Mrs. Joanna LEWIS. Wit:
Cuthbert POWELL, Francis W. LUCKETT. Delv. to grantee 20 Dec
1872.

3V:082 Date: 8 Mar 1831 RtCt: 9 Mar 1831
Samuel COX of Ldn to children Benjamin, Matilda, John, Thomas,
Samuel, Eliza Ann, George, Sarah Ann, Betsey, James & William
COX alias Newman [given or surname?]. Gift of 4a (prch/o William
AULT) adj late Aaron SAUNDERS, Basil NEWMAN, William ALT;
and farm animals and items, debt due from William MERCHANT,
interest in estate of brother James COX dec'd.

3V:083 Date: 7 Mar 1831 RtCt: 10 Mar 1831
James L. MARTIN & wife Sarah A. P. of Lsbg to Jesse TIMMS,
Richard H. HENDERSON, Burr W. HARRISON and Charles G.
ESKRIDGE of Ldn. Trust for debt to George CARTER using Lot #20
in Lsbg; and all moiety in lot cnvy/by Robert FULTON Mar 1828 to
James L. MARTIN and John H. MONROE; and part of adj Lot #8.
Wit: Presley CORDELL, John H. McCABE. Delv. to TIMMS ___.

3V:088 Date: 10 Mar 1831 RtCt: 10 Mar 1831
William COOPER & wife Elizabeth of Ldn to Charles GULLATT and Samuel M. EDWARDS of Ldn. Trust of 20a on E side of Catocton Mt. adj Frederick COOPER dec'd, __ FULTON, Jacob COOPER (paid by Britton SAUNDERS & wife Ann of Ldn) in trust for benefit of Ann SAUNDERS. Wit: John H. McCABE, John ROSE. Delv. to B. SAUNDERS 27 May 1837.

3V:090 Date: 10 Mar 1831 RtCt: 10 Mar 1831
Philip GOODRICH/GUTRIDGE to John MARTIN. Trust for debt to Samuel M. BOSS using household items.

3V:091 Date: 11 Mar 1831 RtCt: 11 Mar 1831
Elizabeth SULLIVAN of Ldn to Joshua PUSEY of Ldn. B/S of ½ of following lots - (SULLIVAN owns 2a Lot #6 and 63a Lot #1 allotted as dower to Ann CAVANS wd/o of Joseph CAVENS dec'd now Ann CLEMMENS, prch/o Wm. P. FOX Jan 1827, DBk WWW:241; and owns undivided 3/4th interest of Joseph CAVANS, John CAVANS, and John MARTIN & wife Sarah late CAVANS ch/o Joseph dec'd prch/o Wm. P. FOX Mar 1827, DBk OOO:132. PUSEY owns the remaining 1/4th interest in the 2 lots (prch/o George W. GIBSON & wife Mary late GARRETT d/o Abigal GARRETT d/o Jos. CAVANS dec'd). Wit: Saml. M. EDWARDS. Delv. to PUSEY 30 May 1833.

3V:094 Date: 14 Mar 1831 RtCt: 14 Mar 1831
Johnston CLEVELAND, Hugh SMITH, Thos. ROGERS, James ROGERS, Wm. MERSHON, Thos. B. MERSHON, Asa ROGERS, R. H. HENDERSON, Jas. McILHANY, Hamilton ROGERS, John J. COLEMAN and Aris BUCKNER. Bond on CLEVELAND as sheriff to collect levies and poor rate.

3V:095 Date: 14 Mar 1831 RtCt: 14 Mar 1831
Johnston CLEVELAND, Hugh SMITH, Thos. ROGERS, James ROGERS, Wm. MERSHON, Thos. B. MERSHON, Asa ROGERS, R. H. HENDERSON, Jas. McILHANY, Hamilton ROGERS, John J. COLEMAN and Aris BUCKNER. Bond on CLEVELAND as sheriff to collect Officers fees.

3V:097 Date: 14 Mar 1831 RtCt: 14 Mar 1831
Johnston CLEVELAND, Hugh SMITH, Thos. ROGERS, James ROGERS, Wm. MERSHON, Thos. B. MERSHON, Asa ROGERS, R. H. HENDERSON, Jas. McILHANY, Hamilton ROGERS, John J. COLEMAN and Aris BUCKNER. Bond on CLEVELAND as sheriff to collect and pay taxes.

3V:098 Date: 14 Mar 1831 RtCt: 14 Mar 1831
Joseph P. McGEATH. Qualified as 2nd Lt. of troop of cavalry in 2nd Reg, 2nd Div of Va Militia.

3V:098   Date: 5 Mar 1831   RtCt: 11 Mar 1831
John SOUDER of Ldn to Susannah SOUDER of Ldn. B/S of 4a Lot
#5 (in div. of Philip SOUDER dec'd) on Catocton Mt. adj __
FAWLEY.

3V:100   Date: 30 Jul 1830   RtCt: 14 Mar 1831
Mathias PRINCE & wife Magdalena and John EVERHART & wife
Sarah Ann of Ldn and Nathan PRINCE & wife Mary, Benjamin
MOORE & wife Elizabeth and Henry FISHER of Lewis Co Va to
Mary SCOTT of Ldn. B/S of 32a adj Levi WATERS, John CONARD,
__ DEMORY; and 4a on W side of Short hill adj __ ROPP; and 1/6th
interest in dower right (Nathan PRINCE's share) all from estate of
Levi PRINCE dec'd. Wit: Ebenezer GRUBB, Geo. W. SHAWEN.
Delv. to SCOTT 8 Jun 1835.

3V:103   Date: 10 Feb 1831   RtCt: 14 Mar 1831
Emmor GOURLEY of Montgomery Co Pa (s/o Samuel GOURLEY
dec'd who was br/o Joseph GOURLEY dec'd of Ldn) to Gourley
REEDER of Ldn. B/S of 1/7th of 1/6th interest in 103a on S fork of
Beaverdam (cnvy/b David LOVETT to Joseph who died without
issue, descended to brother Samuel who had 7 children).

3V:105   Date: 13 Nov 1830   RtCt: 14 Mar 1831
George MARKS & wife Mahala of Ldn to James JOHNSTON of Ldn.
B/S of 1 rood lot in Bloomfield adj Mahlon FULTON, Mrs. POPKINS,
JOHNSTON (DBk LLL:354). Wit: Notley C. WILLIAMS, Thomas
NICHOLS.

3V:107   Date: 12 Mar 1831   RtCt: 14 Mar 1831
Andrew HILLMAN & wife Mary of Ldn to George COOPER Sr. of
Ldn. B/S of 112a adj John SAUNDERS, __ MORRISON, __
PEACOCK, __ McKIMIE, __ WILDMAN, George SAUNDERS; and
26a on E side of Short hill adj John WHITE, Thomas WHITE. Wit:
George W. SHAWEN, Mortimer McILHANY. Delv. to George
COOPER __.

3V:109   Date: 1 Oct 1830   RtCt: 14 Mar 1831
Joseph LESLIE of Ldn to heirs of Peter JACOBS dec'd of Ldn. B/S
of 60a adj George SMITH, Ebenezer GRUBB, John CONARD. Delv.
to Jno. P. DERRY pr order 16 Oct 1867.

3V:111   Date: 14 Mar 1830 [31?]   RtCt: 14 Mar 1831
Joseph WOOD of Ldn to Jesse GOVER of Ldn. B/S of 2a in new
addition to Wtfd adj Andrew S. ANDERSON, GOVER. Delv. to
GOVER 19 Jul 1833.

3V:112   Date: 7 Feb 1831   RtCt: 14 Mar 1831
Lewis GRIGSBY to Aaron BURSON (or Michael PLASTER and
John WHITACRE). Release of trust of Sep 1817 by BURSON for
debt to Joshua PANCOAST on 100a.

3V:113   Date: 25 Oct 1830   RtCt: 14 Mar 1831
Commrs. Thomas J. MARLOW and Philip EVERHEART (case of
Samuel CROOKE vs. Nancy CROOKE wd/o Charles CROOKE
dec'd) to Peter DERRY. B/S of land (including dower rights,
descended from Charles CROOKE dec'd) in Lovettsville adj heirs of
Elias THRASHER dec'd, heirs of Philip BOGAR dec'd. Delv. to Peter
DERRY 22 Jul 1835.

3V:115   Date: 25 Oct 1830   RtCt: 14 Mar 1831
Peter DERRY & wife Eliza Ann to Samuel CROOK. Trust for debt to
Commrs. Thomas J. MARLOW and Philip EVERHEART using
above land. Wit: Craven OSBURN, Mortimer McILHANY.

3V:118   Date: 14 Mar 1831   RtCt: 14 Mar 1831
John JANNEY to Joseph TAVENNER. Assignment of mortgage
given by David JANNEY dec'd to Thomas SWANN in Apr 1811 on
prop. in Gap of Short hill formerly owned by Mahlon HOUGH, DBk
A:83, assigned to JANNEY in Aug 1830, DBk UUU:190 [191].

3V:119   Date: 9 Mar 1831   RtCt: 14 Mar 1831
Portia HODGSON of AlexDC to James HILL of Ldn. LS 275a. Delv.
to HILL 13 Oct 1834.

3V:121   Date: 20 Dec 1830   RtCt: 14 Mar 1831
Sheriff William B. HARRISON and Fanny WALKER (w/o Thornton
WALKER) to William GALLEHER. B/S of 2-3a adj Union (from
insolvent debtor Thornton WALKER, Jun 1830). Delv. to
GALLEHER 28 Mar 1834.

3V:123   Date: 11 Oct 1830   RtCt: 14 Mar 1831
Joseph LESLIE of Ldn to John CONARD Sr. of Ldn. B/S of 12½a on
road from Harper's Ferry to Hllb adj George JACOB, George
MILLER, CONARD. Delv. pr order 16 May 1833, see DBk 3X:167.

3V:124   Date: 30 Jul 1830   RtCt: 14 Mar 1831
Benjamin MOORE & wife Elizabeth, Henry FISHER & wife Margaret
and Nathan PRINCE & wife Mary of Lewis Co Va, and Mary SCOTT
and John EVERHART & wife Sarah Ann of Ldn to Mathias PRINCE
of Ldn. B/S of 10a (from Levi PRINCE dec'd) and 2a wood lot. Wit:
Ebenezer GRUBB, Geo. W. SHAWEN.

3V:127   Date: 23 Sep 1829   RtCt: 15 Mar 1831
Robert WICKLEFF & wife Agness late YOUNG, Moses WICKLEFF
& wife Nancy late YOUNG and Benjamin S. YOUNG & wife Nancy
late SINGLETON of Mecklenburg Co Ky (heirs of Sarah YOUNG
dec'd formerly SINGLETON and Nancy YOUNG d/o John
SINGLETON dec'd) to John S. B. ALLENSWORTH. PoA for
transactions with estate of Samuel SINGLETON dec'd – (Sarah
YOUNG was a sister and heir, also John SINGLETON was a brother
and heir of Samuel SINGLETON dec'd late of Ldn).

3V:129   Date: 21 May 1830   RtCt: 15 Mar 1831

Robert WICKLEFF & wife Agness late YOUNG & Moses WICKLEFF & wife Nancy late YOUNG of Mecklenburg Co Ky (wives are heirs of Sarah YOUNG dec'd late w/o William YOUNG and formerly SINGLETON who was a sister of Samuel SINCLAIR dec'd late of Ldn) to brother Benjamin S. YOUNG. PoA for transactions with estate of Samuel SINCLAIR dec'd.

3V:131   Date: 4 Apr 1830   RtCt: 15 Mar 1831

Coleman DUNCAN & wife Elizabeth late YOUNG of Logan Co Ky and James S. B. ALLENSWORTH & wife Catharine late YOUNG of Todd Co. Ky to Benjamin S. YOUNG of Mechlenburg Co Ky. PoA for transaction with estate of Samuel SINCLAIR dec'd who died intestate leaving land and negroes to wives who are children of Sarah YOUNG late SINGLETON his sister.

3V:133   Date: 11 Jan 1831   RtCt: 15 Mar 1831

William FLETCHER & wife Harriet of Ldn and Enoch GLASSCOCK of Ldn. Partition between FLETCHER and GLASCOCK of lands of Samuel SINGLETON dec'd – 74y to GLASSCOCK and 216a to FLETCHER. Acknowledgements and CoE in Fqr. Delv. to Robt. FLETCHER 14 Oct 1831.

3V:137   Date: 26 Jun 1830   RtCt: 15 Mar 1831

Robert WICKLEFF & wife Agnes late YOUNG, Moses WICKLEFF & wife Nancy late YOUNG by atty Benjamin S. YOUNG and Coleman DUNCAN & wife Elizabeth late YOUNG and James S. B. ALLENSWORTH & wife Catharine late YOUNG by atty Benjamin S. YOUNG and Benjamin S. YOUNG & wife Nancy late SINGLETON by her atty Robert SINGLETON of Fqr (residents of Ky and heirs of Samuel SINCLAIR dec'd) to William FLETCHER and Enoch GLASSCOCK of Ldn. B/S of interest in 339a on Ashbys Gap turnpike road below Goose Creek Bridge, the mansion house in Fqr and most of the land in Ldn. Delv. to Robt. FLETCHER pr order filed VVV:133, 14 Oct 1831.

3V:140   Date: 10 Mar 1831   RtCt: 15 Mar 1831

Ludwell LEE of Ldn to Bowles Armistead LEE (managed concerns of Ludwell for sometime past) of Ldn. BoS for slaves Peggy, Adam, Kingston & his wife Bridget, Boss & his wife Esther, Sampson, Robbin, Tom, Jenny & Milly and farm animals and plantation utensils.

3V:141   Date: 28 Apr 1830   RtCt: 15 Mar 1831

John M. RILEY & wife Mary R. late SINGLETON d/o William SINGLETON dec'd who was a br/o Samuel SINCLAIR (whose children are entitled to dist. of Samuel's estate) and Stanley SINGLETON (s/o William dec'd) & wife Mary of Breckenridge Co Ky to William FLETCHER of Ldn. B/S of 1/4th of 1/7th undivided interest in 339a, slaves, and personal estate of Samuel SINGLETON dec'd. Delv. to Robt. FLETCHER pr order filed VVV:133, 14 Oct 1831.

3V:143   Date: 15 Mar 1831   RtCt: 16 Mar 1831
William SMITH of Ldn to David BROWN of Ldn. B/S of 25a on Kittocton Creek (part of land prch/o __ HOUGH) adj John BROWN, Nathan GREGG, John PHILLIPS. Delv. to BROWN 2 Feb 1832.

3V:144   Date: 8 Sep 1829   RtCt: 16 Mar 1831
William SMITH of Ldn to John PHILIPS of Ldn. B/S of 25a on Kitticton adj John BROWN (part of land prch/o Thomas HOUGH Apr 1804, DBk EE:60). Wit: David REESE, David BROWN, Jonas SMITH.

3V:146   Date: 11 Nov 1829   RtCt: 16 Mar 1831
James COCKRAN & wife Rachel of Ldn to William SMITH of Ldn. B/S of 19a on NW fork of Goose Creek (part of land inherited by Rachel from father Jonathan BRADFIELD dec'd) adj heirs or Rebecca HATCHER, Stephen WILSON, Goose Creek meeting house. Wit: Thomas NICHOLAS, John WHITE. Delv. to SMITH 26 Sep 1834.

3V:148   Date: __ 1831   RtCt: 16 Mar 1831
Wilson C. SELDEN Jr. and Ludwell LEE of Ldn to Charles ESKRIDGE of Ldn. Trust using negro man Reuben a blacksmith by trade for benefit of Emily Justine LEE d/o Ludwell. Delv. to ESKRIDGE 29 Sep 1834.

3V:149   Date: 17 Mar 1831   RtCt: 17 Mar 1831
David LOVETT to Richard H. HENDERSON. Trust for debt to Deputy Marshall Nathaniel SEEVERS of Chancery Ct Winchester using 60a on branch of Goose Creek (see DBk WW:13).

3V:152   Date: 16 Mar 1831   RtCt: 17 Mar 1831
Jacob CRUSEN & wife Sarah of Ldn to James WHITE s/o Thomas of Ldn. Trust for debt to Thomas WHITE using 70-80a adj Samuel HOUGH, Charles B. HAMILTON, Absalom KALB (late Margaret SAUNDERS prch/o Dr. HOUGH, Jacob HOUSER & Peter COOPER and then bequeathed to CRUSEN and John RUSE). Wit: Mortimer McILHANY, John WHITE. Delv. to WHITE 20 May 1836.

3V:155   Date: 17 Mar 1831   RtCt: 17 Mar 1831
Dpty Marshall Nathaniel SEEVERS of Ct at Winchester to David LOVETT of Ldn. B/S of 60a (prch/o Thomas PRICE by Richard HIRST Jan 1818, DBk WW:13) (from case of Jesse HERST and James BRADFIELD vs. Elizabeth SINGER called Elizabeth HIRST, Martha HIRST (heirs of Richard HIRST dec'd).

3V:157   Date: 21 Mar 1821 [31]   RtCt: 21 Mar 1831
Commr George D. SMITH to Thomas J. MARLOW of Ldn. B/S of Lot #4 in div. of Adam SHOVER dec'd (from case of Henry WELLER & wife Catharine late SHOVER agst Barbara SHOVER, Aug 1829). Delv. to MARLOW 28 Jun 1836.

3V:158   Date: 29 Jan 1831   RtCt: 21 Mar 1831
Joseph L. VANDEVANTER of Ldn to Thirza RICE of Ldn. B/S of 19a adj John VANDEVANTER, reps of Jesse RICE, Thirza RICE, James SINCLAIR. Delv. to RICE 14 Apr 1833.

3V:160   Date: 1 May 1829   RtCt: 3 Jun 1830/24 Mar 1831
Richard Henry LEE to John CRIDLER. LS for 99y renewal forever of house and lot in Lsbg on Loudoun St formerly belonging to Mathew WEATHERBY dev. in trust to Lee for Episcopal congregation of St. James Church.

3V:161   Date: 26 Mar 1831   RtCt: 26 Mar 1831
Caleb C. SUTHERLAND of Ldn to Charles W. D. BINNS of Ldn. Trust for debt to Wilson J. DRISH of Ldn using interest in meadow lot and large adj lot on former road to Tuscarora which passed through lands of Benjn SHREVE but is now closed, ground rent on lot held by late Samuel CARR and prop. with blacksmith shop on Loudoun & King Sts in Lsbg (from father Alexander SUTHERLAND dec'd and his brothers John and Thomas SUTHERLAND dec'd).

3V:163   Date: 14 Mar 1831   RtCt: 26 Mar 1831
David CARR (trustee of Samuel CARR) of Ldn to John CARR of Ldn. B/S of 22a on Lsbg Turnpike road adj Benjamin SHREVE, William GILMORE; 11a adj James F. NEWTON; dower rights of Lucy D. CARR w/o Samuel to lot in Lsbg where Samuel CARR had stable built.

3V:165   Date: 19 Sep 1825   RtCt: 26 Mar 1831
Ann NEER (wd/o Conrad NEER dec'd), Christian MILLER & wife Sarah, Samuel NEER & wife Sarah, Nathan NEER & wife Eliza, Joseph RUSSELL & wife Ann and Martha NEER (heirs of Conrad NEER dec'd) of Ldn to Jesse NEER & Joseph NEER of Ldn. B/S of 135a on E side of Blue Ridge (cnvy/b Ferdinando FAIRFAX to Conrad Jul 1811) adj __ CLENDENING, __ GRUBB. Wit: John WHITE, Craven OSBURN, Ebenezer GRUBB, John WHITE.

3V:168   Date: 16 Oct 1830   RtCt: 26 Mar 1831
George MARLOW and Commr Samuel M. EDWARDS (case of Hanson MARLOW agst George MARLOW) of Ldn to Hanson MARLOW of FredMd. B/S of 98a (cnvy/b Exors of Conrad SHAFER dec'd to HANSON Mar 1821, DBk EEE:458).

3V:170   Date: 16 Mar 1831   RtCt: 28 Mar 1831
Thomas S. HAMERSLY & wife Emily A. of Ffx to Richard F. PEYTON of Ldn. B/S of 123a on Little River, Fqr road, adj Leven LUCKETT on N side of Ashby's Gap Turnpike. Delv. pr order filed in bundle containing folio 38, 24 Jan 1831.

3V:172   Date: 30 Mar 1831   RtCt: 30 Mar 1831
Thomas CARLTON and Robert WILSON of Fredericktown Md to L. P. W. BALCH of Fredericktown Md. Release of trust of Feb 1831 for

debt to Robert WILSON on 128a. Wit: Jno. McDONALD, Michl.
BALTZELL.

3V:174   Date: 28 Mar 1831   RtCt: 30 Mar 1831
L. P. W. BALCH & wife Eliza E. W. of FredMd to Jonah PURSELL of
Ldn. B/S of 128a adj Enos POTTS, Benjamin PALMER, Lewis
LYDER. Wit: Jno. McDONALD, Michl. BALTZELL. Delv. to
PURSELL 28 Aug 1832.

3V:177   Date: 31 Mar 1831   RtCt: 31 Mar 1831
James WEST, a man of colour of Ldn, former slave of John LYONS
Esqr. of Studley Hanover Co. but emancipated in Ldn. DoE for his
wife Judy he purchased from Frederick BELTZ dec'd. Wit: Rich'd H.
HENDERSON, Fenton M. HENDERSON.

3V:177   Date: 18 Aug 1830   RtCt: 18 Aug 1830/31 Aug 1831
Elizabeth HOLMES wd/o Joseph HOLMES dec'd, Samuel HOGE &
wife Mary, William HOLMES, Elijah HOLMES & wife Elizabeth, Isaac
HOLMES & wife Hannah, Thomas NICHOLS & wife Emily and Lot
HOMES & wife Sarah of Ldn (except Saml. HOGUE & wife) to Isaac
HUGHES of Ldn. B/S of 28a adj Joseph WHITE, William WHITE,
Howell DAVIS. Wit: Tasker C. QUINLAN, John H. McCABE, Presley
CORDELL. Delv. to HUGHES 12 Mar 1832.

3V:180   Date: 31 Mar 1830   RtCt: 1 Apr 1831
Thomas SANDS & wife Ruth late BIRDSALL, Anna GOODIN late
BIRDSALL, William BIRDSALL & wife Ruth, Andrew BIRDSALL &
wife Lydia, Hannah BIRDSALL and Benjamin BIRDSALL of Ldn
(except William & wife Ruth and Thomas SANDS & wife Ruth of
MontMd) to John BIRDSALL of Ldn. B/S of 150a (descended to all
parties and Betsey BIRDSALL heirs of Whitson BIRDSALL dec'd
who had prch/o Noah HATCHER Mar 1805) adj Mercer BROWN,
Mahlon & Stacy TAYLOR, Kittocton Run. Wit: Presley CORDELL,
Samuel M. EDWARDS, John SIMPSON, Thomas NICHOLS. Delv.
to Jno. BROWN 7 Nov 1832.

3V:184   Date: 30 Mar 1831   RtCt: 1 Apr 1831
George W. BRONAUGH of Ldn to Joshua PANCOAST of Ldn. Trust
for debt to Joshua GREGG of Ldn using 179a (1/4th of land of
William BRONAUGH allotted to George). Delv. to H. H. GREGG pr
order 19 Mar 1838.

3V:187   Date: 26 Mar 1831   RtCt: 2 Apr 1831
John LESLIE & wife Rachel of Ldn to Mortimer McILHANY of Ldn.
B/S of 70a (dev. to Rachel by father Archibald MORRISON dec'd)
adj John DAVIS, Frederick A. DAVISSON, Thomas WHITE,
McILHANY. Wit: John WHITE, Geo. W. SHAWEN.

3V:189   Date: 26 Mar 1831   RtCt: 2 Apr 1831
Mortimer McILHANY of Ldn to James WHITE of Ldn. Trust for debt
to John LESLIE using above 70a. Delv. to LESLIE 24 Apr 1832.

3V:192   Date: 6 Apr 1831   RtCt: 7 Apr 1831
Adam COOPER & wife Susanna of Ldn and John HEIS & wife
Catharine late COOPER of PhilPa by atty Adam COOPER to
Charles GULLATT & Samuel M. EDWARDS of Ldn. B/S of 52a
from div. of Casper EKART dec'd (with remainder of tract cnvy/t
Adam COOPER, DBk TTT:305) for benefit of Ann SAUNDERS w/o
Britton. Wit: W. C. SELDEN, Tasker C. QUINLAN. Delv. to B.
SAUNDERS 27 May 1837.

3V:195   Date: 5 Jun 1824   RtCt: 8 Apr 1831
James SAUNDERS of Ffx to William MINOR of AlexDC. Trust for
debt to Jane Sidney LEE of borough of Norfolk, Va (now residing in
Ffx), Samuel M. EDWARDS, Richard H. HENDERSON, Thomas R.
SAUNDERS, Samuel CARR, Samuel M. BOSS, Wm. D. DRISH
using slaves for life man Aaron, boy Charles, woman Sarah, farm
animals, farm and household items.

3V:199   Date: 19 Mar 1831   RtCt: 8 Apr 1831
Richard H. HENDERSON of Lsbg to Thomas BIRKBY of Lsbg. B/S
of lot with shop & stable on Back St. now occupied by BIRKBY, adj
__ SMALE, __ BENEDUM, __ STONESTREET, __ OATYER.

3V:200   Date: 19 Mar 1831   RtCt: 8 Apr 1831
Rich'd H. HENDERSON of Ldn to Caleb C. SUTHERLAND of Ldn.
B/S of lot on S side of Loudoun St (from trust of Joshua RILEY).

3V:201   Date: 12 Apr 1831   RtCt: 12 Apr 1831
Benjamin JACKSON and Stephen McPHERSON. Bond on
JACKSON as constable.

3V:202   Date: 19 Apr 1828   RtCt: 12 Apr 1831
William BRONAUGH dec'd. Division - court order dated 14 Jan
1828; 129a Lot #1with 50a wood Lot #1 to Patrick Henry William
BRONAUGH; 128a Lot #2 with 51a wood Lot #2 to Joseph William
BRONAUGH; 179a Lot #3 to trustee of Jeremiah W. BRONAUGH
dec'd; 179a Lot #4 to George William BRONAUGH; 18-20a Sulpher
Spring field. Divisors: George LOVE, Uriel GLASSCOCK, Price
JACOBS. Gives detailed plat.

3V:209   Date: ___   RtCt: 11 Apr 1831
A. S. ANDERSON. Receipt for payment from Israel WILLIAMS
towards trust of Jan 1829 on his farm in Cotoctin Mt. Wit: Wm.
FITZIMMONS, Geo. W. HENRY.

3V:209   Date: 31 Mar 1831   RtCt: 11 Apr 1831
Stacy LACEY & wife Mahala of Ldn to Presley SAUNDERS of Ldn.
B/S of 1¼a in Lsbg on E side of King St occupied by LACEY (cnvy/b
John HAMMERLY Nov 1828, DBk RRR:151). Wit: Saml. M.
EDWARDS, W. C. SELDEN Jr.

3V:211   Date: 11 Apr 1831   RtCt: 11 Apr 1831
John PHILLIPS (Admr dbn wwa of Israel PANCOAST dec'd) of Ldn
to Amey PHILLIPS of Ldn. B/S of 100½a (subject to 2a reduction for
a dam) adj Nathan GREGG, Samuel PIERPOINT, Amos JANNEY.

3V:212   Date: 11 Apr 1831   RtCt: 11 Apr 1831
Amey PHILIPS of Ldn to John PHILIPS of Ldn. B/S of 100a subject
to dam reduction of 2a (formerly owned by Israel PANCOAST dec'd)
adj Nathan GREGG, Samuel PIERPOINT.

3V:213   Date: 7 Apr 1831   RtCt: 11 Apr 1831
Abijah JANNEY of AlexDC (trustee for Ann HARPER late ELLICOTT
w/o Washington HARPER) to George WARNER. B/S of 146a
(cnvy/b Noble S. BRADEN Exor of Robert BRADEN) adj Wtfd road,
John BRADEN, __ PIERPOINT. Delv. to WARNER 1 May 1837.

3V:216   Date: 16 Oct 1830   RtCt: 14 Apr 1831
Samuel FITZGERALD & wife Sarah, John REED & wife Celia,
George MECE & wife Elizabeth and James STARR now of Ldn
(ch/o Mary STARR late BARR of NC) to Edward WILSON of Ldn.
B/S of undivided 3/4ths of 482a in Iredell Co NC on Fourth Creek adj
William STEEL (mortgaged by Christopher STARR to WILSON); and
5a in Ldn allotted to Mary STARR by her father George BARR dec'd.

3V:219   Date: 11 Apr 1831   RtCt: 11 Apr 1831
Yardley TAYLOR to Frederick A. DAVISSON. Release of trust of Oct
1827 for debt to William HOGE and Thomas HATCHER (Exors of
Isaac NICHOLS dec'd) and William GRAHAM, DBk PPP:118.

3V:221   Date: 20 Mar 1831   RtCt: 12 Apr 1831
Nathan GREGG Jr. & wife Susanna/ Susan R. of Ldn to Valentine V.
PURCEL of Ldn. Trust for debt to Thomas E. HATCHER using 34a
Lot #3 and 38a Lot #4 in div. of Samuel GREGG dec'd. Wit: John H.
McCABE, Presley CORDELL. Delv. to HATCHER 27 Mar 1834.

3V:223   Date: 20 Mar 1831   RtCt: 12 Apr 1831
Thomas E. HATCHER & wife Elizabeth of Ldn to Nathan GREGG
Jr. of Ldn. B/S of 34a Lot #3 from div. of Samuel GREGG dec'd. Wit:
John H. McCABE, Presley CORDELL. Delv. to GREGG 8 Dec 1831.

3V:225   Date: 12 Nov 1830   RtCt: 12 Apr 1831
Bennett COPELAND & wife Mary of Franklin Co Indianna to Andrew
COPELAND of Ldn. B/S of 1/3 interest in 202¾a (from father
Andrew COPELAND dec'd, who prch/o Ferdinando FAIRFAX Mar
1804) on NW side of Short hill adj __ NELSON, heirs of Charles
HUMPHREY, heirs of James WHITE, Richard GRUBB. Wit: James
OSBOU, Thomas THOMAS.

3V:227   Date: 13 Apr 1831   RtCt: 13 Apr 1831
John PHILLIPS & wife Priscilla of Ldn to Nicholas OSBURN of Ldn.
Trust for debt to John BRADEN of Ldn using 100a (cnvy/b Amy
PHILLIPS Apr 1831). Wit: Presley CORDELL, Samuel M.
EDWARDS. Delv. to BRADEN 21 Jan 1833.

3V:229 Date: 14 Apr 1831 RtCt: 14 Apr 1831
Edward WILSON of Ldn to Samuel FITZGERALD & wife Sarah, John REID & wife Lelia and George MECE & wife Elizabeth of NC and James STARR of Ldn (heirs of Christopher STARR dec'd). Release of mortgage of Sep 1815 on 482a in Iredel Co NC. Delv. 3 Dec 1821 [31].

3V:231 Date: 15 Apr 1831 RtCt: 15 Apr 1831
James RUST of Ldn to Uriel GLASCOCK of Ldn. Release of trust of Apr 1827 for debt to James VERNON of Ohio on 98a.

3V:232 Date: 16 Apr 1831 RtCt: 16 Apr 1831
John CRIDLER & wife Elizabeth of Ldn to William CARR of Ldn. B/S of lot in Lsbg on Air st at W end of town. Wit: Wilson C. SELDEN Jr., John H. McCABE.

3V:235 Date: 1 Jan 1831 RtCt: 19 Apr 1831
Daniel MAGINNIS of Ldn to James HAMILTON of Ldn. Trust for debt to James THOMAS of Ldn using farm animals, plough, bed. Wit: Josiah L. DREAN, E. HAMMATT.

3V:236 Date: 20 Apr 1831 RtCt: 20 Apr 1831
Samuel M. EDWARDS to Sally Lacy MANNING. Release of trust of May 1830 for Commrs. in div. of Thomazin ELLZEY dec'd, DBk TTT:339.

3V:237 Date: 12 Apr 1831 RtCt: 15 Apr 1831
John CRIDLER of Ldn to John A. BINNS and Josiah L. DREAN of Ldn. Trust for William W. KITZMILLER of Ldn as security on notes to Archibald MEANS, John MILLS, William APSEY, to Eli OFFUTT for hire of negro Isaac using lease on house & lot on Loudoun St in Lsbg from R. H. LEE as trustee of St. James Church, farm animals, household items. Wit: George TURNEY, George FOSTER. Delv. to DREAN 30 Apr 1830.

3V:239 Date: 25 Apr 1831 RtCt: 26 Apr 1831
William McCOY & wife Elizabeth of Ldn to Josiah L. DREAN of Ldn. Trust for debt to Caleb C. SUTHERLAND of Ldn using undivided interest in real estate of Martin CORDELL f/o Elizabeth. Wit: Jacob HULL, L. BEARD, Matthew GATES.

3V:240 Date: 22 Mar 1831 RtCt: 27 Apr 1831
Samuel MARKS of Ldn to Richard OSBURN of Ldn. B/S of 52¼a & 35a (Lot #2 & #3 in div. of Abel MARKS dec'd) on N fork of Goose Creek & blue ridge. Wit: Craven OSBURN, Isaiah B. BEANS, Joshua OSBURN. Delv. to OSBURN 5 Jun 1851.

3V:241 Date: 20 Jan 1831 RtCt: 29 Apr 1831
George RUST Jr. & wife Maria of JeffVa to George D. SMITH of Ldn. B/S of 318a (cnvy/b Joseph CALDWELL, s/o Moses dec'd and his mother Sarah Dec 1819, DBk ZZ:311) adj John WILLIAMS, __ MOFFETT, __ SCHOOLEY, __ CASSADY, __ MASON. Delv. to Admr __.

3V:243 Date: 29 Jan 1831 RtCt: 31 Jan/30 Apr 1831
Robert CAMPBELL & wife Jane to John H. McCABE. Trust for debt
to Christopher FRYE using 8a (3 lots cnvy/b FRYE Jan 1831) and
6a (prch/o heirs of Martin KITZMILLER dec'd Jan 1831). Wit: John J.
MATHIAS, Presley CORDELL. Delv. to FRYE 8 Mar 1832.

3V:246 Date: 30 Apr 1831 RtCt: 30 Apr 1831
Philip NELSON of Ldn to James GARNER of Ldn. Trust for debt to
John Nicholas KLINE of Ldn using house & lot on E side of King St
in Lsbg (cnvy/b KLINE). Wit: Saml. M. EDWARDS. Delv. to KLINE
29 Apr 1833.

3V:248 Date: 30 Apr 1831 RtCt: 30 Apr 1831
John Nicholas KLINE of Ldn to Philip NELSON of Ldn. B/S of house
& lot on E side of King St in Lsbg (cnvy/b John REIGER Feb 1814,
DBk RR:368) adj Jane R. DAVIS, heirs of Enos WILDMAN.

3V:249 Date: 5 Mar 1831 RtCt: 30 Apr 1831
John MANN & wife Mary of Ldn to John MANN Jr. of Ldn. B/S of 2a
(prch/o Joseph STUMP). [not signed by Mary] Delv. to John Jr. 22
Nov 1833.

3V:251 Date: 14 Apr 1831 RtCt: 30 Apr 1831
Jonathan POTTERFIELD & wife Sarah of Ldn to Adam COOPER of
Ldn. B/S of 12¾a adj __ WILLIAMS. Wit: Samuel DAWSON,
Samuel HOUGH. Delv. to Wm. STOCKS who have now released
the land, 27 Sep 1832.

3V:253 Date: 8 Dec 1830 RtCt: 2 May 1831
George GREGG & wife Nancy and Andrew S. ANDERSON atty for
George of Ldn to Robert MOFFETT of Ldn. B/S of 8a where
GREGG now lives on W side of Catocton Mt. (dev. from father
William GREGG dec'd). Wit: Samuel HOUGH, John J. MATHIAS.
Delv. to MOFFETT 1 Feb 1832.

3V:255 Date: 2 May 1831 RtCt: 2 May 1831
William JOHNSON & wife Margaret of Ldn to Samuel M. EDWARDS
of Ldn. Trust for debt to John WORSLEY using lot on E side of King
St in Lsbg. Wit: Wilson C. Selden Jr., Presley CORDELL.

3V:258 Date: 5 May 1831 RtCt: 5 May 1831
William THRIFT & wife Maria to William L. POWELL. Trust for debt
to Burr W. HARRISON (Commr. for sale of estate of Thomazin
ELLZEY dec'd) using 140a on Secolon Run abt 4m from Lsbg on
road from Lsbg to Gumspring (cnvy/b John T. BROOKE May 1825).
Wit: James RUST, Saml. M. EDWARDS.

3V:260 Date: 6 May 1831 RtCt: 6 May 1831
William W. KITZMILLER to John M. HARRISON. Trust for debt to
Burr W. HARRISON (Commr for sale of estate of Thomazin ELLZEY
dec'd) using lot and house on Loudoun St. in Lsbg where
KITZMILLER and mother Elizabeth live, including the tanyard (dev.
by father Martin KITZMILLER dec'd).

3V:263 Date: 6 May 1831 RtCt: 6 May 1831
John PHILLIPS & wife Priscilla of Ldn to David BROWN of Ldn. B/S of 7a on Kittocton Creek adj John BROWN, PHILLIPS. Wit: James RUST, John H. McCABE. Delv. to BROWN 2 Feb 1832.

3V:265 Date: 6 May 1831 RtCt: 6 May 1831
William McCOY (insolvent debtor) to Sheriff Johnston CLEVELAND. B/S of undivided interest in real estate of Martin CORDELL dec'd.

3V:265 Date: 25 Feb 1831 RtCt: 9 May 1831
Thomas FRANCIS. Oath as Cornet of a Troop of Cavalry in 2nd Reg, 2nd Div. of Va Militia.

3V:266 Date: 20 Jan 1831 RtCt: 9 May 1831
Capt. Stacy J. TAVENNER. Oath as Militia Officer including restricting dwelling in order that the same may be recorded in the Clerks Office in Loudoun.

3V:266 Date: 15 Apr 1831 RtCt: 9 May 1831
Widow Winefred HAMILTON, Charles B. HAMILTON Jr. & wife Sarah C., George W. SHAWEN & wife Jane, George W. HENRY & wife Dewanner and Mary HAMILTON (heirs of John HAMILTON dec'd) to Elijah JAMES of Ldn. B/S of 143a on great Catoctin Creek adj Jacob SPRING, __ SNUTZ; and 14a timber lot on SE side of Catoctin Creek. Wit: Saml. DAWSON, Samuel HOUGH. Delv. to JAMES 9 Apr 1832.

3V:269 Date: 9 May 1831 RtCt: 9 May 1831
Thomas GORE & wife Sarah of Ldn to Garrett WALKER of Ldn. B/S of 10a (prch/o Joseph WALKER, allotted WALKER from estate of father Benjamin WALKER dec'd) on Beaverdam Creek adj Samuel BEAVERS; and undivided share in a dower lot of Sarah VANHORNE dec'd wd/o John VANHORNE which belonged to estate of Benjamin WALKER dec'd, adj Samuel BEAVERS, dower of Sophia WALKER, James BROWN, Garrett WALKER. Wit: James RUST, John J. MATHIAS. Delv. to WALKER 23 Jul 1847.

3V:271 Date: 16 Apr 1831 RtCt: 9 May 1831
Exors of Isaac & Samuel NICHOLS dec'd to George KEENE of Ldn. Release of mortgage from William CARTER & wife Margaret to Isaac & Samuel NICHOLS Apr 1805, since cnvy/t KEENE.

3V:271 Date: 7 May 1831 RtCt: 9 May 1831
Michael SOUDER & wife Susan of Ldn to Casper SPRING of Ldn. B/S of 1a adj Margaret COOPER, SPRING. Wit: Samuel DAWSON, Geo. W. SHAWEN. Delv. to SPRING 5 Aug 1832.

3V:274 Date: 23 Apr 1831 RtCt: 9 May 1831
John LOGAN of Ldn to son Alfred LOGAN of Ldn. B/S of interest in estate of Isaac GIBSON of AlexDC who died intestate with large estate in Alex and Ldn leaving only a widow with dower rights and 6 reps. including sister Alice late GIBSON w/o John LOGAN. [not signed by Alice but does not list as dec'd]

3V:275   Date: 4 Apr 1831   RtCt: 9 May 1831
Christopher FRYE & wife Margaret of Ldn to Robert CAMPBELL of
Ldn. A/L (of Aug 1798 from James HERIFORD of Ffx) on 20a adj
John LITTLEJOHN, Saml. HOUGH. Wit: John H. McCABE, John J.
MATHIAS. Delv. to CAMPBELL 9 Dec 1831.

3V:278   Date: 16 Apr 1831   RtCt: 9 May 1831
William CARR of Ldn to Jonathan ROBERTS of Ldn. A/L of Lots #16
& #19 in survey (sold by Patrick CAVAN to George FEICHTER, then
to CARR, DBk PP:315). Wit: Josiah L. DREAN, John CRIDLER.
Delv. to ROBERTS 26 Aug 1832.

3V:279   Date: 9 May 1831   RtCt: 9 May 1831
Ferdinando STUCK and Peter STUCK to Adam KARN surv. Exor. of
Magdalena SHOVER dec'd. Bond on STUCK as Guardian of Julia
Ann SANBOWER a dist. of SHOVER dec'd (former Guardian was
Geo. SHOVER) (Geo. SHOVER cannot acct. for previous payments
to him so STUCK will sue to recover).

3V:280   Date: 9 May 1831   RtCt: 9 May 1831
Thomas GORE & wife Sarah of Ldn to James WELSH of Ldn. B/S of
20a Lot #3 in div. of Benjamin WALKER dec'd; and 15a allotted
Joseph WALKER from div. of Benjamin WALKER dec'd (cnvy/b
WALKER Mar 1825). Wit: James RUST, John J. MATHIAS. Delv. pr
order 27 Jul 1834.

3V:282   Date: 9 May 1831   RtCt: 9 May 1831
Presley CORDELL to Richard W. STONESTREET & wife Eleanor.
Release of trust of Jun 1829 for debt to Otho R. BEATTY using
house & lot in Lsbg.

3V:283   Date: 9 May 1831   RtCt: 9 May 1831
Nathan GREGG of Ldn to David CARR of Ldn. B/S of 46a adj David
BROWN, GREGG, __ BITZER, William BROWN, __ LOVE. Delv. to
CARR 31 Mar 1834.

3V:285   Date: 7 Apr 1831   RtCt: 9 May 1831
Gourley REEDER and Seth SMITH (Exors of John WILKINSON
dec'd) and daus. Mary WILKINSON, Hannah WILKINSON and Anna
WILKINSON of Ldn to George KEENE of Ldn. B/S of 90a adj
Samuel DUNKEN, heirs of Isaac COWGILL.

3V:287   Date: __ May 1831   RtCt: 9 May 1831
George RUST Jr. of JeffVa to Robert MOFFETT of Ldn. B/S of 2a
adj George SMITH (cnvy/b Jos. CALDWELL, DBk DDD:162). Delv.
to MOFFETT 16 May 1851.

3V:288   Date: 14 Apr 1831   RtCt: 9 May 1831
Israel WILLIAMS & wife Milly to George W. HENRY and Samuel
STOUTSENBERGER. Trust for debt to George BEAMER using
93¼a (from estate of Enos WILLIAMS dec'd) adj Joseph LEWIS,
Elizabeth CLAPHAM, heirs of Henry POTTERFIELD, Phenias

WILLIAMS, heirs of Moses DOWDLE, Sydnor WILLIAMS. Wit: Samuel DAWSON, Saml. HOUGH. Delv. to BEAMER 7 Jan 1834.

3V:290   Date: 7 Apr 1831   RtCt: 9 May 1831
Yeoman Daniel EACHES of Ldn to George KEENE assignee of John WILKINSON dec'd. Release of mortgage of 11 Feb 1811, DBk MM:401, for debt to Isaac & Samuel NICHOLS.

3V:292   Date: 11 Apr 1831   RtCt: 9 May 1831
Isaac NICHOLS (trustee of Isaac & Samuel NICHOLS dec'd) of Ldn to George W. BRONAUGH, Joseph W. BRONAUGH, P. H. W. BRONAUGH and reps. of Jeremiah W. BRONAUGH dec'd, heirs of William BRONAUGH dec'd of Ldn. Release of trust of May 1825 for debt to Samuel & Isaac NICHOLS using 250a.

3V:293   Date: 9 May 1831   RtCt: 9 May 1831
Charles T. MAGILL to Francis W. LUCKETT. Trust for Mrs. Mary D. MAGILL w/o Charles who will rel. rights to interest in 'Quarter Farm' dev. by father William BRONAUGH dec'd and interest in land cnvy/b brother Jeremiah W. BRONAUGH dec'd in trust to LUCKETT for her benefit and her dower interest in lot in Winchester dev. to Charles T. and brother John S. MAGILL by uncle A. MAGILL dec'd (part sold but not cnvy/t W. L. CLARKE) with agreement from Charles to let her keep slave woman Hariet & her child Margaret, woman Milly & her child Barkley and girl Louisa in trust to LUCKETT for her benefit.

3V:295   Date: 12 Apr 1831   RtCt: 9 May 1831
Joseph W. BRONAUGH & wife Ann S./Nancy S. and P. H. W. BRONAUGH of Ldn to Joshua NICHOLS and Burr W. HARRISON of Ldn. Trust for debt to Isaac NICHOLS of Ldn using 179a Joseph's share from estate of William BRONAUGH dec'd; and 179a P. H. W.'s share from estate of William BRONAUGH dec'd. Wit: F. W. LUCKETT, Presley CORDELL. Delv. to NICHOLS 25 Mar 1835.

3V:298   Date: 9 May 1831   RtCt: 9 May 1831
David CARR & wife Susannah of Ldn to John J. MATHIAS of Ldn. Trust for debt to Nathan GREGG of Ldn using 46a adj David BROWN, GREGG, __ BITZER, William BROWN, James LOVE. Delv. to GREGG 12 Nov 1832.

3V:301   Date: 30 Apr 1831   RtCt: 9 May 1831
Robert CAMPBELL & wife Jane of Ldn to John H. McCABE of Ldn. Trust for debt to Christopher FRYE of Ldn using 22a nr Lsbg adj John FEICHTER, Mrs. HUNT, __ CAMPBELL, __ THORNTON, __ HEREFORD. Wit: Presley CORDELL, John J. MATHIAS. Delv. to FRYE 8 Mar 1832.

3V:304   Date: 16 Aug 1830   RtCt: 10 May 1831
Martha CLAYTON and William CLAYTON of Snickersville to Perrin WASHINGTON of Ldn. B/S of ¼a on Snickers Gap Turnpike road nr Snickersville.

3V:305   Date: 19 Feb 1831   RtCt: 10 May 1831
George MARKS & wife Mahala of Ldn to David LOVETT, John
BRADEN, Sampson HUTCHISON, Horace LUCKETT, Benjamin
MITCHELL, James L. MARTIN, John J. COLEMAN, Thomas R.
SAUNDERS and George HANCOCK (Overseers of the Poor). B/S of
10a adj current Poor of the County land. Wit: Notley C. WILLIAMS,
Thomas NICHOLS.

3V:307   Date: 16 Aug 1830   RtCt: 10 May 1831
Martha CLAYTON of Snickersville to Perrin WASHINGTON of Ldn.
B/S of 1a on Snickers Gap Turnpike Road nr Snickersville.

3V:308   Date: 18 Oct 1830   RtCt: 10 May 1831
Hanson MARLOW & wife Louisa of FredMd to Jacob FAWLEY and
John HICKMAN of Ldn. B/S of 98a (from Conrad SHAFER dec'd)
adj Ferry road to Clapham's land, __ SHAFER, __ CORDELL, __
DAVIS, __ AMOND. Wit: Geo. W. SHAWEN, Samuel DAWSON.

3V:311   Date: 16 Mar 1831   RtCt: 10 May 1831
Perrin WASHINGTON & wife Hannah F. to Roger CHEW. Trust for
debt to John CHEW using 1a on Snickersgap Turnpike Rd and ¼a
on Turnpike Rd adj Thomas DRAKE. Wit: Notley C. WILLIAMS,
Craven OSBURN.

3V:314   Date: 10 May 1831   RtCt: 10 May 1831
James MONROE of Ldn to John A. BINNS of Ldn. Trust for debt to
Michael MORALLEE of Ldn using horses. Wit: J. L. DREAN.

3V:315   Date: 1 Jan 1831   RtCt: 11 May 1831
George CARTER of Oatlands to Daniel LOVETT of Ldn. B/S of 3a
(Sup Ct. order required CARTER to recover land from Apr 1823
deed, DBk KKK:97) adj CARTER, William CARR, Hogback Mt.

3V:316   Date: 11 May 1831   RtCt: 11 May 1831
Margaret H. D. TEBBS for herself and as Guardian of infant children
of Thomas F. TEBBS dec'd to Samuel J. TEBBS. Agreement –
Samuel agrees to rent from Margaret farm in Fqr where he now lives
for 3y certain, paying with cash, plaster, crops. Delv. to John H.
McCABE 6 Oct 1837 pr order.

3V:317   Date: 11 May 1831   RtCt: 11 May 1831
Ignatius ELGIN of Ldn to William A. POWELL of Ldn. B/S of ½a Lot
#4 on S. side of Cornwall St in Lsbg (cnvy/b Thomas BIRKBY, Apr
1824, DBk HHH:150). Delv. to POWELL 9 Apr 1835.

3V:319   Date: 13 May 1831   RtCt: 13 May 1831
Richard W. STONESTREET & wife Eleanor of Ldn to Josiah HALL
of Ldn. B/S of lot in Lsbg adj Martha BLINCOE, __ BAKER,
Sampson BLINCOE. Wit: Tasker C. QUINLAN, Thomas
SAUNDERS.

3V:321   Date: 28 Mar 1831   RtCt: 13 May 1831
Mary F. SPENCE of PrWm to Richard H. HENDERSON (trustee of
infant children of Thomas R. MOTT dec'd). B/S of 150a (Armistead

LONG recently dec'd Guardian of children and their grandfather had already made agreement with SPENCE) on Little River, SPENCE and her sister Mrs. Nancy DUVAL. Betsy TEBBS relinquished rights to the land.

3V:323   Date: 11 May 1831   RtCt: 11 May 1831
Richard H. HENDERSON and Jesse TIMMS of Ldn to Walter ELGIN Sr. & wife Diadema of Ldn. Release of trust of Jul 1822 for debt to George CARTER using 408a.

3V:325   Date: 13 May 1831   RtCt: 13 May 1831
Thomas J. MARLOW and Thomas ROGERS to Adam KARN (Exor. of Magdalena SHOVER dec'd). Bond – KARN paid MARLOW as Guardian of Mary Ann BAUCHMAN, John William BAUCHMAN, Charles BAUCHMAN and James Andrew BAUCHMAN infant ch/o Adam BAUCHMAN dec'd their share from estate of SHOVER dec'd. They are entitled to 1/12th of future distributions, but KARN wants MARLOW to now pay the children's share of any estate debts.

3V:326   Date: 13 May 1831   RtCt: 13 May 1831
Thomas J. MARLOW and Thomas ROGERS to Adam KARN (Exor of Magdalena SHOVER dec'd). Bond – KARN paid MARLOW as Guardian of infant children of Susan SHOVER late SANBOWER, w/o George SHOVER. They are entitled to 1/24th of future distributions, but KARN wants MARLOW to now pay the children's share of any estate debts.

3V:327   Date: 13 May 1831   RtCt: 13 May 1831
George SHOVER, Charlotte SHORTS and Thomas J. MARLOW to Adam KARN (Exor of Magdalena SHOVER dec'd). Bond – paid SHOVER and SHORTS late SHOVER. They will be entitled to 1/24th of future distributions, but KARN wants MARLOW to now pay the children's share of any estate debts.

3V:328   Date: 13 May 1831   RtCt: 13 May 1831
Catharine HEFNER and Thomas J. MARLOW to Adam KARN (Exor of Magdalena SHOVER dec'd). Bond – paid HEFNER. She will be entitled to 1/12th of future distributions, but KARN wants HEFNER to now pay the children's share of any estate debts. Wit: Adam HEFNER.

3V:328   Date: 13 May 1831   RtCt: 13 May 1831
Frederick ROLLER and John GEORGE to Adam KARN (Exor of Magdalena SHOVER dec'd). Bond – paid ROLLER as Guardian of Aaron ROLLER and Pricilla ROLLER infant children of Magdalena ROLLER late SANBOWER. They will be entitled to 1/18th of future distributions, but KARN wants ROLLER to now pay the children's share of any estate debts.

3V:329   Date: 20 Apr 1831   RtCt: 16 May 1831
John KELLY & wife Rebecca late MORRISON (dau. of James MORRISON dec'd of Butler Co Ohio) to John LESLIE of Ldn. B/S of

her interest in land dev. by Archibald MORRISON dec'd of Ldn to James MORRISON now dec'd of Butler Co Ohio. Wit: John K. WILSON, Isaac McKINNEY. Delv. to LESLIE 24 Apr 1832.

3V:331 Date: 14 Apr 1831 RtCt: 18 May 1831
Widow Winifred HAMILTON, George W. SHAWEN & wife Jane, Geo. W. HENRY & wife Dewannah, Charles B. HAMILTON Jr. & wife Sarah C. and Mary HAMILTON (heirs John HAMILTON dec'd) of Ldn to Joseph MEAD of Ldn. B/S of all their interest in 225a on Catoctin Creek adj Enos WILLIAMS, __ WATERMAN, __ ROBERSON. See DBK AAA:321 for relinquishment of Sarah HAMILTON. Wit: Saml. DAWSON, Saml. HOUGH. Delv. to Jos. MEAD 11 Feb 1832.

3V:335 Date: 27 Sep 1830 RtCt: 21 May 1831
Joseph CALDWELL & wife Eliza of Tuscaloosa Co Alabama to John CARR and David CARR of Ldn. B/S of house and lot in Lsbg at Market & Back Sts. Wit: Saml. M. EDWARDS, Presley CORDELL.

3V:337 Date: 21 May 1831 RtCt: 21 May 1831
Isaac NICHOLS (trustee of Isaac & Samuel NICHOLS dec'd) of Ldn to James BROWN of Ldn. B/S of 256¾a (from trust of Isaac BROWN Nov 1822) adj Eden CARTER, Michael PLAISTER, Henry PLAISTOR Jr.

3V:339 Date: 15 May 1821 RtCt: 1 Oct 1821 in Fqr/ 21 May 1831 in Ldn
Henry ADAMS of Fqr to Lewis EDMONDS of Fqr. Trust for debt to Thomas SHEARMAN and Josiah MURRAY of Fqr using negro woman Hellen & her child Francis, farm animals, household items.

3V:341 Date: 13 May 1831 RtCt: 23 May 1831
Robert RAY of NY to George RUST Jr. of JeffVA late of Ldn. Release of trust of May 1824 for debt to Nathaniel PRIME. Wit: Walter BOWNE, Jno. AHERN.

3V:342 Date: 7 May 1831 RtCt: 23 May 1831
Joseph H. CLOWES of Ldn to Theoderick LEITH of Ldn. Trust for debt to William C. PALMER of Ldn using household items.

3V:344 Date: 5 May 1831 RtCt: 24 May 1831
Joshua T. HOPE & wife Mercy of Ldn to William F. CLARK of Ldn. B/S of ½a lot in Bloomfield adj Thomas DRAKE, John G. HUMPHREY, John L. GILL. Wit: Notley C. WILLIAMS, John W. GRAYSON. Delv. to Jno. G. HUMPH[R]Y pr order 16 Jan 1832.

3V:346 Date: 29 Apr 1831 RtCt: 25 May 1831
William CARR & wife Mary of Ldn and William MAINS of Ross Co Ohio. Partition of 381½a on Kittocton Mt. purchased by CARR & William MAINS the elder since dec'd) from John C. HERBERT and Carlyle F. WHITING, Apr 1807, DBK BB:45. Partial division was done, but 9a were added during survey. MAINS is given 176a. Wit:

Presley CORDELL, Saml. M. EDWARDS. Delv. to Archibald MAINS agent for Wm. MAINS 18 Apr 1833.

3V:349   Date: 15 Feb 1831   RtCt: 28 May 1831
Elias JENKINS of Ldn to Everit SAUNDERS of Ldn. Trust for Wesley S. McPHERSON of Ldn as security for hire of slave Reuben from Ludwell LEE using 17¾a on turnpike from Lsbg to Goose Creek bridge adj Joseph T. NEWTON, Everit SAUNDERS. Wit: Eleazer THOMAS. Delv. to McPHERSON 12 Jan 1835.

3V:351   Date: 24 May 1831   RtCt: 13 Jun 1831
Jonathan ROBERTS. Qualified as 2nd Lt of a company of artillery in Va Militia.

3V:351   Date: 23 May 1831   RtCt: 13 Jun 1831
William FULTON. Oath as Ensign in 57th Reg Va Militia.

3V:351   Date: 23 May 1831   RtCt: 13 Jun 1831
Thomas CARR. Oath as Lt. of Infantry in 57th Reg, 6th Brig, 2nd Div. Va Militia.

3V:352   Date: 23 May 1831   RtCt: 13 Jun 1831
Saml. ELGIN. Oath as 3rd Lt. of Artillery, 2nd Reg, 2nd Div. of Va Militia.

3V:352   Date: 14 Jun 1831   RtCt: 14 Jun 1831
John MARTIN, Saml. M. BOSS and Edward HAMMAT. Bond on MARTIN as constable.

3V:353   Date: 14 May 1831   RtCt: 14 Jun 1831
Edw'd. HAMMAT, Saml. M. BOSS and John MARTIN. Bond on HAMMAT as constable.

3V:353   Date: 13 Jun 1831   RtCt: 13 Jun 1831
Sally BRONAUGH. Receipt for payment from Sampson HUTCHISON trustee in deed from Martin BRONAUGH since dec'd to HUTCHISON in trust for Sally's benefit dated Oct 1827. Released HUTCHSION as trustee. Wit: Saml. M. EDWARDS, George TURNER, John M. WILSON.

3V:354   Date: 21 Dec 1830   RtCt: 11 Apr 1831
Aaron SCHOOLEY & wife Elizabeth of Ldn to Mrs. Nancy NEILL of Ldn. Trust for benefit of wife using negro Harry P. DAWSON a carpenter by trade at present in service of SCHOOLEY; and interest in dower negroes in possession of Mrs. NEILL (from the demise of Elizabeth's father). Wit: Z. DULANEY, Samuel C. DORMAN, Saml. HOUGH, Joseph STEER, Wm. SUMMERS.

3V:356   Date: 21 Mar 1829   RtCt: 30 May 1831
Jesse TIMMS to John SIMPSON. Release of trust of Mar 1824 for debt to George CARTER on 194a.

3V:357 Date: 27 Sep 1828 RtCt: 24 Apr 1829/30 May 1831
Bennett MARKS of Ldn to Samuel MARKS of Ldn. B/S of 52¼a Lot #2 in div. of Abel MARKS dec'd. Wit: Mason MARKS, S. B. T. CALDWELL, Morris OSBURN.

3V:358 Date: 31 Dec 1830 RtCt: 30 May 1831
Thomas G. HUMPHREY of Ldn. DoE of slave George RIVERS.

3V:359 Date: 10 Feb 1831 RtCt: 30 May 1831
Susan E. LUCKETT of Jefferson Co Ky w/o Alfred LUCKETT of Ldn to Horace LUCKETT of Ldn. Releases dower rights and interest to land deeded to Horace by Alfred Feb 1830. Delv. to H. LUCKETT 11 Feb 1834.

3V:361 Date: 11 Feb 1831 RtCt: 30 May 1831
Ann SWIFT of __, William R. SWIFT & wife Mary D. of Washington Co NC, Jonathan T. PATTEN & wife Ann F. of NY City and Henry ALLISON & wife Mary S. of Linchburg Va but now residing __ Va to John J. MATHIAS and Hamilton R. MATHIAS of Ldn. B/S of 214a adj __ HAMILTON, Ludwell LEE (cnvy/b William SMITH in Jan 1807 to Jonathan SWIFT now dec'd). Acknowledgement for Ann SWIFT and Henry & Mary S. ALLISON in Madison Co. Va, for William R. & Mary D. SWIFT in Beaufort Co NC. Delv. to John J. MATHIAS 16 Apr 1832.

3V:366 Date: 1 Apr 1830 RtCt: 30 May 1831
James JOHNSTON & wife Mary of Ldn to James MOUNT of Ldn. B/S of 5a Lot #2 in div. of John HANDY dec'd, on Goose Creek. Wit: Benjamin GRAYSON, Notley C. WILLIAMS. Delv. to MOUNT 3 Sep 1835.

3V:369 Date: 29 Oct 1830 RtCt: 30 May 1831
Timothy CARRINGTON & wife Margaret and Roger CHEW of Ldn to James B. WILSON of Ldn. B/S of 2 tracts (20¼a) on Goose Creek (cnvy/b Dpty Sheriff Burr WEEKS Jun 1826). Delv. to WILSON 10 May 1838.

3V:370 Date: 15 Apr 1831 RtCt: 30 May 1831
Noble S. BRADEN (Exor of Robert BRADEN dec'd) of Ldn to Robert CAMPBELL of Ldn. B/S of 10a on Cotoctin Mt. adj Joshua PUSEY, Archibald MAINS, __ FOX, __ VERMILLION. Wit: Jos. A. BRADEN, Griffeth W. PAXSON, Fleming HIXON, J. L. POTTS, J. G. PAXSON.

3V:370 Date: 7 Feb 1831
B. W. SOWER Editor and publisher of Genius of Liberty published in Lsbg. Says annexed advertisements published in his paper 6 successive weeks from the day there are stated. [They evidently relate to the following]

Trustee Burr W. HARRISON. From trust by Samuel CARR of Nov 1827 for benefit of John and James POGUE. Public auction on 26 Jun next for valuable negro woman and negro girl. Also on that day from trust of Dec 1827 for benefit of John and James POGUE, selling a valuable carriage or coach. Dated May 22, 1830

Trustee B. W. HARRISON. From trust by Samuel CARR of Dec 1827 for benefit of John and James POGUE. Public auction on 9 Oct next of lot on King St. in Lsbg, also a carriage or coach and 3 horses. Dated 4 Sept 1830.

Trustee B. W. HARRISON. From trust of Samuel CARR of Dec 1827 for benefit of John and James POGUE. Public auction on 9 Oct next of lot on King St being the residence of CARR. Dated 4 Sep 1830.

Above sale is postponed until 20 Nov at Courthouse. Dated 16 Oct 1830.

Charles G. ESKRIDGE made oath that a copy of the advertisement dated 4 Sep 1830 was set on door of Court house on 1st day of Sept court and was still there next morning, copy of that dated 14 Oct 1830 was set up on a Court day in Nov previous to the Nov sale. Dated 8 Feb 1831. Signed Saml. M. EDWARDS.

INDEX

ADAIR
  Emily, 175
  Jeremiah, 175
ADAM
  Matthew, 13
  William F., 13
ADAMS
  Henry, 131, 241
  John R., 81
  Lucinda, 81
  Priscilla, 131
  Richard, 109
  William L., 15
ADLEY
  Thomas, 152
AHERN
  John, 241
ALBRIGHT
  Isaac, 205
ALBRITTIAN
  Mary, 172
  William, 172
ALBRITTON
  William, 183
ALDER
  George H., 201
  John, 87
ALDRIDGE &
  HIGDON, 61
ALEXANDER
  Charles A., 187
  Charles B., 91,
    97, 111, 216
  David, 170
  Fountaine, 123
  John, 111
  Penelope B., 111
  William, 53
ALLBAWGH
  George, 123
ALLDER
  ___, 205
  George H., 39,
    92, 94
ALLEN

David L., 40, 161
James, 40, 85,
  161
Martha, 40
S. C., 161
William, 157
ALLENSWORTH
  Catharine, 228
  Elizabeth, 178,
    205
  James B., 178
  James S. B., 228
  John S. B., 227
  Philip, 178, 205
ALLISON
  Henry, 243
  Mary S., 243
ALLISTON
  Susan, 109
  Wilfred, 109
ALT
  John, 28
  Mary, 28
  William, 28
AMBLER
  Lewis, 116, 178
  Sally, 178
AMOND
  ___, 239
  Anthony, 153
ANDERSON
  A. S., 214, 218,
    232
  Andrew, 162
  Andrew S., 64,
    66, 106, 130,
    132, 145, 162,
    163, 164, 210,
    213, 215, 226,
    235
  Elijah, 33, 42, 63,
    195
  John, 192
  Mrs., 203
ANKERS

John, 71
ANNIN
  D., 59, 207
  Daniel, 85, 95
  Helen C., 80, 100,
    138
  R., 54, 84
  Roberdeau, 6, 8,
    22, 26, 29, 33,
    41, 53, 59, 80,
    94, 100, 138
  William C., 59
ANSEL
  ___, 170
ANSELL
  Susannah, 11
APSEY
  William, 234
ARMSTEAD
  Fanny, 95
  John B., 73
ARNOLD
  ___, 74
ASBURY
  Henry, 127
ASHBY
  John, 19
ASHBY &
  STRIBLING, 29
ASHFORD
  James, 192
ASHMAN
  William, 219
ASHTON
  ___, 110
  Henry, 89
ATCHER
  Peter, 126
ATWELL
  Sythy, 6
AUBREY
  Francis, 81
AULD
  ___, 113

Colen, 40
Colin, 169, 209
Collin, 56, 172
AULT
___, 45
Betsey, 101
John, 60, 71
Mary, 60, 71
Rachel, 101
William, 60, 87, 224
AUSTIN
Anna, 209
William, 68
AWBREY
Thomas, 100
AWBURY
Francis, 172
AXLINE
Catherine, 17, 29, 58
Christena, 49
Christina, 4, 17, 52
Christinia, 156
David, 17, 49, 52, 75, 134
Henery, 17, 29
Henry, 4, 49, 58
John, 4, 17, 49, 52, 156

BACCHUS
Anna, 123, 169
BACKHOUSE
___, 162
BAGLEY
William, 53
BAILEY
George, 44
John, 80, 125
Sydnor, 70, 82, 83
BAILY
Ish, 76
John, 91
Robert, 127
Sydnor, 203

BAKER
___, 56, 147, 183, 239
Catherine, 164
Charles, 191
George, 178
Jacob, 164
John, 176, 199
Lewis, 199
W., 161
BALCH
Eliza E. W., 6, 222, 231
Elizabet E. W., 220
L. P. W., 6, 13, 36, 49, 53, 208, 220, 230, 231
Lewis P. W., 159, 222
BALDWIN
___, 192
John, 85
Mahlon, 149, 157, 175, 203
BALL
___, 67, 105
Charles, 69
Charles B., 212
Fayette, 3, 14, 26, 114, 143, 154, 157, 164, 206, 216
Horatio, 51
Isaac, 16
John, 9, 16, 142, 190
John B., 51
Mrs., 99
Pamelia, 75
Stephen, 5
William, 75
BALTZELL
Michael, 231
BANK OF ALEXANDRIA, 152

BANK OF THE VALLEY, 154, 156
BARCLAY
Frances, 166
Moses, 166
BARKER
Quintin, 155
BARR
George, 120, 233
Lott, 93, 119
Mahala, 202
Mary, 233
BARROT
John, 194
BARTEN
George, 56
BARTON
Benjamin, 84
Joseph, 162, 202, 214
BASFORD
Cassandra, 15
BASSELL
H., 194
BATTSON
Elizabeth, 120
James, 10, 120
John, 10, 156
Mahaly, 120
Nancy, 120
Thomas, 120
William, 10, 156
BAUCHMAN
Adam, 240
Charles, 240
James A., 240
John W., 240
Mary A., 240
BAUGHMAN
Andrew, 47
BAWCUTT
A. D., 127
BAWLDWIN
John, 77
BAYLEY
George, 3
Jesse, 22

John, 3, 59
Robert, 24, 61
BAYLY
  George, 126, 127
  J., 76, 161
  John, 18, 27, 40,
    44, 76, 82, 85,
    91, 138, 173,
    195, 200
  R., 201
  Robert, 27, 40,
    44, 55, 76, 82,
    91, 157, 196,
    205
  Samuel, 167
BAZZELL
  John C., 208
  Mary B., 208
BEACH
  John, 155
BEACHE
  Celinah, 155
BEAL
  Joseph, 52, 162
BEALE
  Amos, 15
BEALL
  David, 151
  David F., 128,
    129
  Eli, 193
  William M., 191
BEAMER
  Catherine, 128
  George, 78, 139,
    237
BEAN
  Samuel, 131
BEANS
  ___, 99, 141, 186
  Aaron, 121
  Absalom, 81
  Amos, 28, 29, 82,
    170
  Elizabeth, 156
  Isaiah B., 36, 100,
    113, 156, 234
  James, 19

Matthew, 121
Paxton, 29
Samuel, 36, 133
BEARD
  Jonathan, 46
  Joseph, 91, 192
  L., 61, 118, 234
  Lewis, 70, 91
  Orpah, 27
  Stephen, 27, 126,
    199
BEATTY
  Andrew, 95
  David, 14
  Eli, 198
  John, 14
  Josiah, 170
  Martha, 170
  O. R., 63
  Otho R., 40, 99,
    135, 147, 198,
    237
  Silas, 6, 13, 96
  Thomas B., 104,
    198
  William, 46, 154
BEATY
  Amanda, 14
  Andrew, 34
  Elizabeth, 84
  Elizabeth H., 14
  George, 34
  Josiah, 172
  Malvinia, 14
  Martha, 172
  Silas, 52
BEAVERS
  ___, 40
  James, 101
  Mahala, 101
  Samuel, 206, 236
  Thomas, 206
  William, 101, 157
BECKHAM
  Camp, 48
  Fontaine, 39
BECKWITH

Jennings, 167,
  187
BELL
  John D., 44
  Joseph D., 10,
    11, 100
  Michael, 206
BELT
  Alfred, 88, 102,
    109, 198, 207
BELTS
  Thomas, 190
BELTZ
  Frederick, 231
BENEDUM
  ___, 232
  Elizabeth, 179
  Henry, 179
  John, 185, 217
  Peter, 163, 199
BENELEY
  Robert, 193
BENNEDUM
  ___, 115
BENNETT
  Charles, 84, 93,
    96, 104, 126,
    136, 147, 168,
    208
  Hamilton, 208
  Henry A., 164
  James H., 104
  John H., 136
  Susan G., 157
  Thomas J., 96,
    167, 168, 172,
    193
  Thompson M.,
    157, 208
BENTLEY
  Robert, 40, 48,
    63, 92, 99, 151,
    219, 222
BENTLY
  Robert, 72
BENTON
  Sarah, 24

William, 8, 24, 63,
67, 72, 77, 83,
111, 195, 214
BERKELEY
Lewis, 196
BERKELY
Lewis, 212, 223
BERKLEY
George N., 20
John L., 32
Lewis, 12, 17,
223
Rufus, 59
BESICKS
Jesse, 71
BEST
Enos, 160, 201
James, 19
BETREE
John, 217
BETTON
Eliza, 81
Solomon, 127,
146
Turbert R., 20
Turbutt R., 81
BEVERIDGE
John, 37, 46, 101
Mary, 101
N., 224
Noble, 5, 39, 131,
133, 139, 172,
189, 192, 224
William, 84, 123,
221
BEVERLEY
Peter R., 103
Robert, 21
BEVERLY
Peter R., 21
BIGBY
Peter, 71
BINNS
Ann A., 104
C. W. D., 63, 199
Charles, 4, 6, 8,
21, 22, 23, 30,
53, 54, 74, 88,

97, 104, 154,
164, 169, 170,
180, 186, 204,
220
Charles D., 23
Charles W., 117,
143
Charles W. D.,
22, 23, 116,
141, 224, 230
Dewanner, 53,
153
John, 67
John A., 4, 7, 10,
13, 15, 19, 22,
36, 49, 50, 53,
56, 57, 60, 67,
68, 76, 97, 98,
125, 126, 133,
137, 146, 153,
164, 180, 190,
191, 192, 198,
200, 219, 222,
223, 234, 239
Mary A., 153
Mary M., 50
Nancy, 49
Sarah, 22, 153
Simon, 97
Simon A., 14, 21,
22, 53, 57, 96,
153, 169
W. A., 97, 180
William, 14, 104
William A., 4, 6,
49, 53, 57, 169,
200, 217
BIRDET
Sandford, 19
BIRDSALL
Andrew, 47, 50,
95, 231
Anna, 231
Benjamin, 50, 93,
97, 108, 120,
231
Betsey, 231
Hannah, 231

John, 231
Lydia, 47, 231
Ruth, 231
Whitson, 82, 231
William, 231
BIRKBY
Sarah, 68
Thomas, 63, 68,
98, 137, 146,
232, 239
BIRKLEY
Lewis, 138
BISCOE
Elizabeth, 96
J. B., 121, 122,
168
James B., 91, 123
Julia A., 96
Mary, 96
Susan, 96
Thomas, 17, 91,
96, 107, 174,
218
BISHOP
John, 165
BITTZER
Conrad, 52
John, 52
BITZER
___, 237, 238
Catherine, 60,
185
Conrad, 23, 60,
71, 88, 104,
126, 185, 218
George L., 47
HArmon, 157
BLACKBURN
Edward L., 167,
187
BLACKBURNE
Edward L., 187
BLAGROVE
Christopher, 7
BLEAKLEY
___, 161
BLEAKLY
___, 142

BLINCOE
  Joseph, 37, 204
  Martha, 99, 147,
    239
  Martha S., 8, 98
  Sampson, 8, 12,
    21, 88, 91, 97,
    104, 239
BODINE
  Maria, 167
BOGAR
  Philip, 227
BOGER
  ___, 145
  Catherine, 136
  David, 136
  Elizabeth, 152
  Hugh, 48
  John, 153
  John H., 52
  Margaret, 153
  Michael, 67, 83,
    105, 152
BOGESS
  Samuel, 25
BOGGESS
  Henley, 94
  Henly, 166
  Jane E., 94
  Mariah C., 94
  Nancy E., 94
  Rebecca, 94
  Samuel, 94
BOGGS
  H., 98
BOLAND
  ___, 78
  Daniel, 55, 156,
    159, 165, 191
  Patrick, 166
BOLEN
  Edward, 124
  Ezra, 12
  James, 19
  William, 124
BOLON
  William, 107
BONCE

Jacob, 26
BOND
  Asa M., 76, 216
  Elizabeth, 216
  Joseph, 28, 36,
    107, 125, 133,
    134, 148, 168,
    179, 216
BOOLIN
  Elizabeth, 113
BOOTH
  ___, 152
  Aaron, 19
  James, 19
  John, 7, 19, 42
BOOTHE
  John, 173
BOSS
  Abraham J., 213
  Catharine, 212
  Daniel C., 213
  David, 213
  Elizabeth F., 74
  Jacob, 212
  Mass, 212
  P., 87
  Peter, 96, 110,
    212
  S. M., 114, 209
  S. S., 85
  Samuel, 212
  Samuel C., 14
  Samuel M., 7, 10,
    21, 28, 32, 38,
    59, 60, 68, 69,
    74, 81, 85, 97,
    108, 116, 122,
    144, 151, 152,
    164, 180, 188,
    205, 212, 213,
    219, 225, 232,
    242
  Samuel S., 212
BOTTS
  Judith, 188
BOWLES
  James, 77
BOWMAN

James, 160
  James M., 218
  John, 160
BOWNE
  Walter, 241
BOYD
  Elizabeth, 14
  John, 14, 57, 116,
    172
BRACKENRIDGE
  A., 222
  A. P., 63
  Alexander, 223
  Elizabeth L., 223
BRADEN
  ___, 59, 82, 126,
    204
  Burr, 43, 72, 77,
    78, 102, 112,
    165
  Eliza, 61
  Elizabeth, 54, 72,
    77
  John, 42, 49, 56,
    72, 78, 88, 99,
    105, 127, 183,
    191, 194, 233,
    239
  Joseph, 72, 117
  Joseph A., 243
  Mary D., 77, 165
  N. S., 132, 164,
    183, 191, 204
  Noble S., 5, 9, 10,
    16, 28, 29, 36,
    37, 40, 41, 43,
    44, 48, 49, 51,
    54, 56, 57, 60,
    64, 70, 71, 72,
    76, 77, 90, 99,
    103, 104, 107,
    117, 118, 121,
    125, 126, 128,
    129, 130, 131,
    132, 133, 134,
    138, 139, 141,
    142, 147, 148,
    150, 151, 155,

159, 162, 163,
168, 169, 173,
176, 179, 181,
182, 183, 184,
192, 194, 207,
233, 243
R., 9
Robert, 2, 9, 16,
  17, 28, 29, 32,
  42, 46, 49, 51,
  54, 58, 61, 71,
  72, 77, 99, 112,
  132, 134, 147,
  150, 154, 159,
  162, 165, 182,
  184, 190, 202,
  216, 233, 243
William F., 184
BRADFIELD
____, 57, 111, 123
Amey W., 197
B., 37
Benjamin, 28, 49,
  50, 74, 161,
  223
Charlotte, 197
Elizabeth, 89, 151
Emily, 50
Isaac, 216
James, 49, 50,
  87, 111, 151,
  195, 197, 229
James P., 50, 87,
  89, 111, 151,
  197
John, 50, 105
Jonathan, 50, 86,
  229
Joseph, 105
Julian K., 105
Mary, 197
Rachael, 50
Rachel, 50, 161,
  229
Sarah, 50
William, 23, 75,
  105
William B., 195

William W., 197
BRADY
James, 13, 54,
  108
John, 100, 154
BRAGG
John, 178
Rebecca, 178
BRANTLY
W. S., 135
BRAWNER
James, 151
BREITENBAUGH
Samuel, 81
BRIDGES
Benjamin, 4, 106,
  117, 140, 158,
  178, 198
David, 106
Nancy, 106
BRIDGESS
David, 151
Nancy, 151
BRIEN
John, 108
BRISCOE
Alexander M.,
  205
Matilda, 205
BROCCHUS
Benjamin M., 200
BRONAUGH
____, 72
Ann C., 63
Ann S., 238
Elizabeth, 66
George W., 38,
  117, 231, 232,
  238
Jeremiah, 193
Jeremiah W., 7,
  63, 72, 130,
  177, 232, 238
John W., 177
Joseph W., 38,
  117, 232, 238
Martin, 51, 242
Mary C., 38

Nancy S., 238
P. H. W., 209,
  215, 238
Patrick H. W., 38,
  232
Sally, 51, 242
Sarah, 209
William, 7, 13, 33,
  38, 44, 51, 52,
  63, 66, 92, 117,
  177, 209, 215,
  231, 232, 238
William J., 38
BRONSON
Arthur, 100
BROOKBANK
Elizabeth, 40, 175
Hannah, 40, 175
John, 175
Thomas, 40, 175
BROOKE
Benjamin, 48,
  113, 163
E., 177
Hannah, 48, 163
James, 111
John T., 235
Thomas A., 198
BROOKS
Chauncey, 109,
  218
Frederick, 218
BROUN
Edwin C., 181
BROWN
____, 47, 175, 176,
  185, 200
Aaron, 33
Alice, 135, 149
Amanda C., 107
Ann, 144, 161,
  210, 211
Benjamin, 131
Betsey, 134, 135
Christina, 214
Clement, 169
Craven, 13, 214
Daniel, 37, 50

David, 50, 229, 236, 237, 238
David E., 135, 149, 167
David F., 107
Dawson, 17, 146
E. C., 119
Edwin C., 1, 2, 13, 120, 122, 137, 172, 189
Elizabeth, 2, 100
Ellen, 107
Fielding, 34, 131
George, 42
Hannah, 96, 100
Henery, 26
Hiram, 59, 101
Isaac, 81, 86, 96, 104, 114, 119, 144, 146, 183, 184, 211, 241
Isaac M., 147, 214
Isacher, 160
Issachar, 45, 84, 219
James, 3, 4, 18, 20, 50, 113, 183, 210, 211, 236, 241
John, 17, 18, 53, 58, 78, 116, 144, 146, 210, 211, 218, 229, 231, 236
John H., 161
Joseph, 14, 66
Josiah, 173, 181
Malinda, 100
Margaret, 58
Maria, 175
Mary, 3, 81, 173
Mason, 100
Mercer, 231
Moses, 81, 130
Nancy, 107, 130, 134

Nimrod, 53, 59, 62
Phebe, 107
Rachel, 37
Rebecca H., 107
Richard, 134, 185
Samuel, 96, 107, 134, 135, 144, 152
Sarah, 53, 59, 62, 66, 101, 146
Thomas, 109, 173, 218
Thomas T. D., 70
Uriah, 165
Vincent, 100
William, 29, 40, 69, 100, 134, 135, 161, 165, 170, 192, 237, 238
BRYAN
William H., 14, 55
BRYERLY
Samuel, 31
BRYSON
N. G., 213
BUCK
James, 117
Samuel, 68, 167
BUCKINGHAM
Thomas, 126
BUCKLEY
Joshua, 12
BUCKNER
Aris, 18, 35, 55, 80, 189, 225
Ariss, 24, 44, 201
Arriss, 18
BUCKNEY
Dennis, 21
BUMCROTS
John, 52
Permelia, 65
Willia, 65
BURCH
___, 190
Fielder, 25, 190

Sarah, 25
BURCKHARTT
Christopher, 84
BURGOYNE
Joseph, 152
Lewis, 152
BURKART
Valentine, 92
BURKE
William B., 215, 219, 222, 223
BURKIN
Elizabeth, 166
BURKITT
Elizabeth, 186
Henry, 186, 220
John, 186, 220
Newton, 186, 220
BURNHOUSE
Christopher, 29
BURR
Charles, 8
Mary, 115
Mary A., 8
BURRELL
Joseph, 72
BURSON
Aaron, 85, 183, 210, 226
Benjamin, 146
Cyrus, 10, 123, 124, 194
George, 211
James, 146, 183
Jesse, 12
Jonathan, 184
Joseph, 10, 194
Martha, 12
Mary, 10, 146
Phebe, 10, 123, 194
BUSSARD
Daniel, 180
J. R., 123
John R., 173
BUTCHER
___, 161
John, 166

John H., 166, 201
Jonathan, 166,
  217
Samuel, 88
BUTLER
  Betsey, 204
  George, 20, 204
  Henson, 135
  John, 204
  Moses, 16, 60
BYE
  William, 42
BYRNE
  John, 70

CALDWELL
  Eliza, 241
  Joseph, 121, 234,
    237, 241
  Mary E., 24
  Moses, 234
  S. B. T., 24, 53,
    92, 94, 110,
    114, 170, 207,
    243
  Samuel B. T., 31,
    77, 108, 109,
    120, 156, 168,
    210, 219
  Sarah, 234
CAMP
  Isaac, 70, 87, 145
CAMPBELL
  ___, 238
  Andrew, 26, 94,
    114
  Asa, 133
  James, 67, 106
  Jane, 26, 235,
    238
  Jean, 26
  John, 109
  Robert, 28, 219,
    235, 237, 238,
    243
  Robert B., 136

Samuel, 86, 100,
  108, 122, 172,
  175
CANBY
  John H., 14, 41,
    198
  Joseph, 125
CANDLER
  John, 107
CANVEY
  Charles, 81
CARLISLE
  Robert, 45, 160
CARLISLE &
  WHITING, 116
CARLTON
  Thomas, 220, 230
CARN
  Adam, 181, 196
CARNEY
  Hiram, 213
CARNICLE
  Jacob, 163
  Sarah, 163
CARPENTER
  Charles, 168
  Matthew, 199
CARR
  ___, 115, 129
  Amanda, 117,
    215
  Amanda M., 148
  Caldwell, 70, 82,
    94, 108, 117,
    148, 215
  David, 39, 55, 65,
    79, 94, 96, 108,
    114, 191, 219,
    223, 230, 237,
    238, 241
  James, 64
  Jane, 89
  John, 46, 65, 80,
    96, 116, 126,
    137, 184, 209,
    223, 230, 241

Joseph, 39, 70,
  82, 94, 108,
  127
Lucy, 96
Lucy D., 75, 230
Mary, 56, 94, 116,
  219, 241
Peter, 70, 94
Rebecca, 94
Samuel, 29, 32,
  36, 51, 52, 54,
  57, 61, 64, 65,
  66, 75, 76, 80,
  91, 96, 104,
  108, 111, 180,
  197, 220, 230,
  232, 243
Susannah, 238
Thomas, 120,
  126, 242
Washington M.,
  89
William, 4, 26, 40,
  45, 50, 56, 62,
  63, 64, 79, 91,
  94, 108, 116,
  126, 168, 202,
  216, 219, 222,
  234, 237, 239,
  241
CARRELL
  Abraham, 170
  Nancy, 170
CARRINGTON
  ___, 34
  Margaret, 214,
    243
  Timothy, 19, 75,
    77, 214, 243
CARROLL
  Charles, 98
  James, 146
CARRUTHERS
  J. E., 198
  James, 2
  Nancy, 2
CARSON
  James H., 63

CARTER
___, 129
Agnes, 25
Alfred G., 55
Catherine, 78
Charles, 57
David, 170
Delilah, 144
Eden, 144, 210, 211, 241
Edmond, 9
Edmund F., 169, 209
Edward, 35
Elizabeth, 2
Ephraim, 51
George, 6, 30, 48, 64, 73, 74, 78, 85, 90, 121, 173, 198, 220, 222, 224, 239, 240, 242
Hebe S. G., 55
Henry, 74
James, 2, 5, 48, 107, 134, 144
John, 78
John A., 191
John A. G., 180
Jonathan, 10, 25, 37, 73, 84, 92, 96, 170, 174, 181, 185
Landon, 180, 191
Landon F., 55
Levi, 2, 144
Margaret, 236
Nancy, 107
Peter, 51
Richard, 25, 40, 78
Robert, 113
Samuel, 21, 146
Sarah, 134
Thomas, 78
William, 45, 78, 146, 236
CARVER

Polly, 106
CASE
Christena, 84, 89
John, 84, 89
CASSADY
___, 234
CASTLEMAN
William, 101, 111
CATING
Edward, 111
Martha, 111
CATLETT
Charles J., 179
CAUGHOM
James, 9
CAVAN
Patrick, 237
CAVANS
___, 219
Abigail, 206
Ann, 225
John, 225
Joseph, 206
Patrick, 95, 222
Sarah, 225
CAVEN
Patrick, 190
CAVENS
Ann, 206
Joseph, 60, 161, 206, 207, 225
Patrick, 219
CAYLOR
James, 194, 195
CAZENOVE
A. C., 96
CHALFANT
Presley, 188
CHALMER
John, 80
CHALMERS
John, 111, 138, 170, 208
CHAMBLAIN
John, 77
CHAMBLIN
___, 176
Albert, 210

Asenath, 169
Charles, 19, 45, 54, 82, 100, 119, 165, 207
Dewanner, 89, 190, 192
Edith, 210
John, 82, 85, 155, 167, 168, 210
Lee, 210
Leven, 210
Lydia, 167
M. P., 149
Mary, 210
Mason, 89, 92, 190, 192, 198
Mason P., 193
Norval, 3, 4, 113, 131, 138
Sarah, 4, 131
Sarah W. T., 131, 138
Stephen, 210
William, 3, 81, 169, 170
CHAPMAN
Thomas, 63
CHAPPELL
James, 76
Thomas, 76
CHELTON
Sarah H., 85
CHEW
___, 17
John, 17, 23, 73, 214, 239
Mary, 161
Robert, 23
Roger, 75, 214, 239, 243
CHICHESTER
George M., 11, 14, 26, 27, 36, 41, 48, 91, 97, 114, 124, 143, 157, 158, 166, 194, 206, 218

Mary, 26, 27, 157, 206
CHILTON
  Mrs., 217
  Sarah, 27, 108
  Sarah H., 31
  Susan, 203
  Susanna, 157
  Thomas, 89, 157, 190
  William, 6, 16, 27, 76, 82, 108, 137, 190, 221
  William C., 31
CHINN
  Ann, 6
  Catherine, 6
  Charles E., 176
  Elias, 6
  Elias L., 119
  Elizabeth, 86
  Emily, 131
  Frances, 6
  Francis, 6
  Nancy, 6
  Patty, 6
  Rawleigh, 86
  Samuel, 86, 87, 130, 131, 221
  Thomas, 6, 100, 119, 133
CIMMINGS
  Nancy, 217
  Thomas, 217
CLAGET
  Henry, 91
CLAGETT
  Eveline, 173
  H., 53
  Henry, 54, 80, 116, 222
  Henry O., 173
CLAGETT & PAGE, 98
CLAGGETT
  ___, 27
  H., 92
  Henery, 15

Henry, 7, 181
CLAPHAM
  ___, 217
  Col., 153
  Elizabeth, 66, 71, 72, 100, 124, 166, 192, 237
  Josias, 66, 72, 100
  Samuel, 5, 66, 72, 100, 124, 136, 203
CLARK
  Addison H., 56
  Gidney, 79
  J. M., 70
  Richard, 162
  William F., 214, 241
CLARKE
  Addison H., 14
  Richard, 202
  Robert, 170
  Samuel, 220
  W. L., 238
  William F., 148
  William L., 102
CLATON
  Amos, 57
  William, 19
CLAYTON
  Amos, 75, 190
  Israel, 23
  Martha, 238, 239
  William, 19, 23, 190, 238
CLEGET
  Henry O., 104
CLEGETT
  Henry, 169
CLEGGETT
  ___, 135
  Henry, 169
  Thomas H., 168
CLEMENTS
  Ann, 206
CLEMMENS
  Ann, 225

CLEMMENTS
  Ann, 207
CLENDENING
  ___, 230
  Ruth, 55
  Samuel, 14, 37, 38, 45, 109, 135, 149, 150, 179, 215
  William, 7, 14, 38, 55, 143, 146, 201
CLENDENNING
  Samuel, 189
CLEVELAND
  J., 38, 106
  Johnson, 115
  Johnston, 27, 31, 35, 42, 81, 89, 115, 150, 157, 158, 178, 185, 225, 236
CLEWES
  ___, 109
  Joseph, 78, 93
  Thomas, 59
CLEWS
  Charles L., 146
  Joseph H., 146
CLIFFORD
  Betsey, 66
CLINE
  ___, 8
  Margaret, 51
  William, 51, 114, 151
CLOWES
  Ann, 56
  Charles L., 18, 149
  Joseph H., 241
  Thomas, 56, 125
COAD
  Barbary, 157
  William, 157
COCHRAN
  James, 28
  Rachael, 28

Richard, 152
COCHRANE
James, 18
COCKE
Catesby, 221
Elizabeth, 221
John C., 221
Washington, 221
William, 221
COCKEREL
D., 50
COCKERELL
D., 50
Elizabeth, 214
Samuel, 214
COCKERILL
Daniel, 19
R. H., 38
COCKERILLE
Daniel, 62
R. H., 115, 158
COCKRAN
___, 76
James, 44, 50,
59, 62, 68, 77,
86, 101, 217,
218, 229
John, 54
Nathan, 207
Rachel, 86, 229
Richard, 104, 122
Robert, 180
COCKRELL
Daniel, 49, 68,
101
COCKRILL
___, 50, 62
Daniel, 161
COE
Edward, 68
Edward M., 68
Elizabeth, 87
John W., 26, 41,
45, 47, 68, 224
Robert, 87
William, 68
William C., 173
COGSIL

Harvey, 100, 143
Mary, 100
COGSILL
Isaac, 23
COHAGAN
William, 202
COLE
Albert, 136
Catherine, 175
Joseph, 175
Lewis, 210
COLEMAN
___, 161, 204
James R., 212
Jane, 212
John J., 38, 115,
189, 225, 239
Johnston J., 118
COLLIER
Henry A., 107
COLLINS
John, 113
Levi, 97, 171
COMBS
Sarah, 129
William R., 129
COMFER
John, 6
COMPHER
___, 21, 182, 184,
207
Elizabeth, 60
Jacob, 133
John, 60, 66, 101,
138, 178
Peter, 48, 74, 97,
151
COMPHOR
Peter, 74, 153,
184
COMPHY
Betsey, 101
John, 101
CONARD
___, 65
Anthony, 136,
221
Barbara, 176

David, 112, 132,
153, 171, 221
Elizabeth, 171
John, 43, 49, 58,
112, 146, 154,
173, 174, 175,
176, 215, 226,
227
Jonathan, 146
Joseph, 146
CONNARD
John, 26
CONNER
Edward, 67, 105
Samuel, 67
CONRAD
Daniel P., 64
David, 207
John, 10, 35, 49,
58, 116
Mary Ann, 64
CONWELL
Elizabeth, 163,
199
Isaac, 199
James, 217
Loveless, 97,
163, 199
William, 217
COOK
Charles, 175
Samuel, 143
COOKE
Alexander, 143
Ann Maria, 143
Catherine E., 101
Edward E., 123,
145, 198
Elizabeth A., 143
Henry S., 145
John R., 101, 145
Maria P., 145
Stephen, 53, 101
William, 143
COOKSEY
Betsey, 142
Eleanor, 38
Elizabeth, 159

Levi, 159
Obed, 159
Susannah, 159
William, 142
COOPER
___, 21, 103, 159,
    182
Adam, 28, 73, 75,
    92, 185, 232,
    235
Amelia, 195, 201
Anna M., 90
Catharine, 73,
    201, 232
Catherine, 28, 92,
    184, 185
Daniel, 11, 22,
    34, 56, 106,
    157, 160, 207
Elizabeth, 22, 90,
    104, 145, 201,
    225
Eve, 11
Frederick, 90,
    104, 194, 225
George, 6, 28, 52,
    73, 74, 90, 92,
    93, 104, 126,
    131, 145, 158,
    178, 185, 194,
    195, 196, 201,
    209, 218, 226
Hannah, 128
Jacob, 6, 90, 104,
    114, 194, 195,
    201, 225
John, 6, 11, 34,
    90, 104, 201
Magdalean, 201
Magdalena, 6
Margaret, 236
Mary, 6, 90, 104,
    194, 201
Michael, 59, 90,
    128, 165, 184,
    201
Nathan, 116
Peter, 13, 229

Philip, 145, 158
Susan, 28, 185
Susanna, 92
Susannah, 73
Susannna, 232
William, 6, 90,
    104, 201, 225
COPELAND
___, 35
Andrew, 173, 233
Bennett, 233
David, 134
George, 65
James, 41, 102,
    173, 179, 184
John, 114, 118
Mary, 233
CORDELL
___, 239
Adam, 84
Alexander, 6, 21,
    24, 55, 57, 66,
    67, 70, 106,
    127, 176, 218
Amelia, 52, 172
Diana, 24, 70
Dianna, 218
Elizabeth, 234
Martin, 24, 234,
    236
Presley, 5, 6, 7,
    11, 24, 29, 32,
    41, 42, 43, 44,
    49, 50, 52, 54,
    56, 60, 61, 62,
    66, 75, 79, 81,
    86, 87, 88, 94,
    96, 97, 98, 105,
    109, 110, 111,
    113, 115, 116,
    118, 125, 127,
    132, 142, 151,
    152, 153, 155,
    157, 160, 161,
    164, 167, 169,
    170, 172, 178,
    184, 185, 190,
    192, 194, 197,

198, 199, 204,
    207, 208, 211,
    213, 215, 216,
    217, 218, 219,
    222, 223, 224,
    231, 233, 235,
    237, 238, 241,
    242
Susan, 84
CORNELL &
    NOSTRAND, 33
CORNER
George L., 199
CORNWELL
Loveless, 64
COST
___, 115
Jacob, 19, 54
John, 57
Jonathan, 143
Peter, 79, 185
Rachel, 57
COULTER
Adam, 191
Mary, 191
COWGIL
Isaac, 113
COWGILL
Isaac, 140, 155,
    237
Mary, 140
COX
Benjamin, 224
Betsey, 224
Eliza A., 224
George, 224
Hannah, 105
James, 224
John, 224
Joseph, 66, 105,
    219
Matilda, 224
Samuel, 28, 210,
    224
Sarah, 66
Sarah A., 224
Thomas, 224
William, 224

COXE
  ___, 72
CRAIG
  James, 169
CRAIN
  James, 37
CRAINE
  Henry, 34
  Joseph L., 179
CRAMPKIM
  Thomas, 27
CRANE
  Daniel, 136
  Elizabeth, 77
  John, 72
CRAVEN
  Abner, 16
  Eleanor V., 217
  Giles, 50, 68
  Hannah, 217
  Isaac S., 217
  Joel, 68
  Joseph, 66, 217
  Mahlon, 18, 19,
    20, 48, 93, 97,
    107, 134
  Samuel, 16, 138
  Sarah, 217
  W. H., 218
  William, 16
  William H., 158,
    166, 177
CRAWFORD
  ___, 114
  Henry, 119
  Nathaniel, 140,
    146, 165
CREBS
  Berry, 86
  Lucy J., 86
CRIDLER
  Elizabeth, 41, 234
  John, 41, 119,
    188, 230, 234,
    237
CRIM
  Adam, 123, 197
  Catherine, 123

Charles, 84, 89,
  105, 123, 156,
  165, 191, 196
Christiana, 123
Daniel, 105
Jacob, 84, 89,
  196
John, 90, 105,
  156, 158
Margaret, 156,
  158
Mary, 105
CROOK
  Charles, 96
  Samuel, 175, 227
CROOKE
  Charles, 227
  Nancy, 227
  Samuel, 227
CROOKS
  Samuel, 48
CROSS
  Betsey, 15
  Catherine, 201
  Elizabeth, 71
  Harrison, 55, 189,
    192, 201
  James, 180
CROUSE
  Catherine E., 156
  Eleanor, 156
  George, 156
  John W., 49
  Margaret, 49
CROWE
  Hiland, 14
CRUIT
  Hannah, 132
  William, 132
CRUMBAKER
  Catherine, 91
  David, 109
  John, 91
CRUSEN
  Jacob, 229
  Sarah, 229
CRUTHERS
  ___, 161

CUMMING
  John, 152
CUMMINGS
  Anthony, 79, 217
  John, 77
  Maria, 217
CUNARD
  Edward, 45, 94
  Stephen, 216
  Stephen T., 195
CUNNARD
  John, 39, 41
CUNNINGHAM
  Charles, 86
  Nancy, 217
  Stephen, 217
  William, 217
CURRELL
  James, 15
  John, 110
  John J., 15, 127,
    129, 156
  Pamela, 156
  Permealia, 129
CURRELS
  John, 223
CURRILL
  John J., 146
CURRY
  Robert, 37
CUSKING &
  JEWETT, 98

DABNEY
  George, 199
  Jerry, 199
DAGG
  James, 82
  John L., 82, 135
DAILEY
  Aaron, 26
  Ann, 21
  Grafton, 21
  Polly, 26
DAILY
  Aaron, 54
DAMEWOOD
  Eleanor, 211

Jacob, 7, 211
DANIEL
  Benjamin, 35, 109
  David, 19
  Hannah, 172, 183
  Hiram, 62
  Humphrey, 172
  Joseph, 90, 110,
    113, 120, 156,
    170, 172, 183
  Joseph H., 172
  Joshua, 118
  Martha, 172
  Mary, 172
  Sarah, 110, 113
  Tacey, 156, 172
  Tacy, 172
  Wallace, 170, 172
  William, 110
  William D., 92,
    113, 156, 172
DANIELS
  ___, 92
DARNALDSON
  Thomas, 70
DARNE
  Frances, 106, 184
  James, 27
  Robert, 106, 151,
    184
  Thomas, 20, 115,
    150, 158, 185,
    214
DARNELL
  Benedick, 69
DARRELL
  William S., 212
DAUGHERTY
  Thomas, 210
DAVIDSON
  Theodore, 93
  Theodore N., 140
DAVIS
  ___, 16, 67, 105,
    190, 214, 239
  Abel, 110
  Daniel, 70
  Elizabeth, 70, 86

Henry M., 5, 213
Howel, 43
Howell, 231
Jacob, 70
Jane H., 5
Jane R., 112, 235
John, 24, 70, 135,
  149, 231
John N., 199
John W., 86, 157
Joseph, 70, 71
Malinda, 70
Margaret, 70
Mary, 98
Mary A., 58
Samuel, 44
Sarah, 70, 71
Solomon, 58
Susannah, 70
Thomas, 67, 70,
  105
William, 44, 171
Zepheniah, 98
DAVISON
  Frederick A., 189
DAVISSON
  Frederick A., 22,
    56, 106, 149,
    189, 215, 231,
    233
DAWSON
  Elizabeth, 58
  Harry P., 242
  Richard, 167
  Samuel, 6, 11,
    26, 51, 56, 57,
    58, 89, 91, 94,
    102, 109, 113,
    121, 124, 131,
    139, 157, 166,
    171, 176, 179,
    181, 185, 194,
    196, 215, 216,
    218, 235, 236,
    238, 239, 241
DAY
  Henry, 116
  Thomas, 217

DAYMOOD
  Jacob, 7
DEAN
  Nathan, 197
DEBELL
  John, 189, 201
DEMORY
  ___, 26, 226
  Eve, 74
  John, 43, 74
  Mary, 175
  Peter, 29, 43,
    175, 176, 210
DENEALE
  J. E., 39
DENHAM
  Amos, 111
  Oliver, 121
DERRY
  ___, 74, 148, 203
  Barbara, 175
  Barbary, 19
  Eliza A., 227
  George, 196
  John P., 226
  Peter, 19, 41, 75,
    152, 227
  Philip, 19, 210
  William, 43, 57,
    175
DEWAR
  James, 173
DEWER
  James, 202
DEWEY
  Joel, 218
DIGGS
  John, 34, 39
  William D., 147,
    160
DILLON
  ___, 35
  Abden, 58
  Abdon, 9, 30, 31,
    35, 95, 160,
    188
  James, 29
DISHMAN

Samuel, 44
DIVINE
  Aaron, 116
  John L., 151
  William, 155
DIXON
  Simon, 111
DODD
  Mary, 192, 208
  William, 190, 192,
    208
DOLMAY
  George, 165
DONAHOE
  Samuel, 203
DONNEL
  Joseph, 52
DONOHOE
  ___, 211
  Sarah, 50, 70
  Stephen C., 9
DOOLEY
  William, 127
DORMAN
  M. R., 122
  Samuel C., 207,
    242
  Thomas W., 122,
    125, 220
DORMON
  T. W., 12
DORRELL
  James, 122
  John, 222
  Thomas, 122, 141
DORSETT
  Walter H., 37
DORSEY
  Dinah, 97, 99
  Edward, 60, 164
  Edwrad, 9
  George, 60
  H., 132
  Jonathan E., 114
  William H., 69,
    109
DOUGLAS
  ___, 170

Archibald N., 194
Charles, 194
Eveline B., 178
Evelyn B., 51
Hugh, 178, 194
J., 146
Lewis F., 194
Patrick, 178
Patrick H., 178
William B., 178
DOUGLASS
  Evelin B., 178
  Margaret, 113
DOWDELL
  Elizabeth E., 114
  Isaac S., 114
  Mary A., 114
  Moses, 114
  Thomas G., 114
DOWDLE
  Moses, 66, 238
DOWE
  ___, 7
DOWELL
  Conrad R., 71,
    218
DOWLING
  Catherine, 154
  Edward, 49, 134,
    143, 146, 219
  Henry M., 224
  Mrs., 74, 154
  Newton, 134
DRAIN
  John, 98
  Jonah, 199
DRAKE
  Jacob, 129
  Thomas, 12, 25,
    38, 88, 239,
    241
DREAN
  J. L., 55, 96, 218,
    239
  John, 108
  Josiah, 80
  Josiah L., 63, 75,
    76, 79, 104,

    111, 151, 213,
    234, 237
  Sarah S., 108
DRISH
  Barbara, 152
  Charles, 121, 222
  Eleanor, 51, 121,
    136, 161, 164
  Harriet, 152
  John, 15, 49, 51,
    61, 99, 113,
    121, 125, 136,
    161, 164
  John R., 121
  Martha, 164
  Nelly, 125
  Susanna, 222
  Susannah, 121
  W. D., 27
  William, 34
  William D., 14,
    15, 40, 58, 79,
    80, 136, 152,
    166, 222, 232
  Wilson J., 49,
    125, 164, 230
DULANEY
  John P., 180
  Z., 9, 42, 118,
    130, 161, 242
  Zachariah, 28, 67,
    70, 72, 105,
    117, 207
DULANY
  John P., 25, 111
  Mary E., 60
  Zachariah, 60,
    161, 165
DULIN
  ___, 190
  Edward, 135
  Francis, 69, 102
  John, 28, 130,
    140
  Lurena G., 196
  Margaret H., 69
  Rebecca, 140
DUNCAN

___, 182, 190
Abigal, 117
Charles, 4, 117
Coleman, 178, 228
Elizabeth, 178, 228
Polly, 92
Samuel, 12, 18, 23, 33, 42, 113, 146
DUNKEN
Samuel, 237
DUNKIN
Anna, 81
Charles, 46
James B., 83
John, 59
Samuel, 3, 29, 81, 121, 148, 211
DURHAM
Catharine A., 4
Catherine A., 200
Lee W., 142
DURYEE
Joseph, 33
DUVAL
A., 98
Ann F., 50
Emma, 192
John P., 50, 156
Nancy, 240
Thomas C., 192
DUVALL
Emma, 151, 184
Thomas C., 124, 151, 184
Zadock, 184
DYKES
___, 5

EACHES
Daniel, 18, 25, 29, 78, 148, 165, 238
Thomas, 196
William S., 157

EAKIN
James, 105, 207
EATON
Isaac, 12, 117, 191, 195
Malinda, 12, 191, 195
Matilda, 117
William P., 151
EBLIN
John, 142
ECKART
Ann, 75, 92
Cooper, 126
ECKHART
Ann, 28
Casper, 75
EDMONDS
Lewis, 241
EDWARDS
___, 45
Ann, 11, 17
Benjamin, 41, 99
Charles G., 34, 67, 97, 99, 132
John S., 16
Katherine, 16
Lidia D., 110
Rebecca, 110
S. M., 26, 206
Samuel M., 2, 8, 9, 11, 15, 17, 18, 21, 22, 26, 27, 28, 29, 30, 32, 34, 40, 46, 47, 48, 49, 50, 51, 52, 54, 55, 56, 59, 61, 63, 64, 67, 71, 73, 74, 75, 85, 86, 87, 88, 92, 96, 97, 98, 99, 101, 102, 104, 105, 109, 110, 111, 113, 115, 118, 121, 124, 125, 126, 131, 132, 133, 135, 141,

142, 147, 149, 151, 153, 155, 156, 157, 164, 166, 167, 169, 172, 176, 183, 185, 187, 189, 190, 192, 199, 204, 205, 208, 209, 212, 215, 217, 218, 222, 223, 225, 230, 231, 232, 233, 234, 235, 241, 242, 244
EIDSON
Elizabeth, 23
Joseph, 23, 93, 180
EIGH
Hiram, 214
EKART
Casper, 73, 185, 232
Mrs., 151
EKHART
Presly, 73
ELGIN
___, 191
Alphonso, 222
Charles, 28, 166
Diadema, 240
Gustavus, 22, 64, 154, 169
Ignatius, 6, 22, 110, 153, 169, 239
Jesse, 55, 76, 82, 91
Matthew, 120
Mordicai, 220
Robert, 169, 220
Rowena, 221
Samuel, 242
Sarah, 115
Walter, 79, 82, 115, 220, 240
William S., 119
ELLICOTT

Ann, 71, 233
ELLIOTT
  H., 39, 62, 82
  Henson, 19, 119
  John, 14
ELLIS
  Mary, 55
  Zachariah, 55
ELLZEY
  Anne E., 22
  Elizabeth, 110
  Frances W., 110
  Lewis, 1, 22, 58,
    187
  Mary, 110
  Mary C., 22
  Miss, 89
  Rosannah, 22
  Rosannah M., 22
  Sarah, 110
  T., 187
  Thomazin, 187,
    234, 235
  Tomazin, 167
  W., 51
  William, 18, 26,
    27, 46, 51, 52,
    73, 78, 80, 85,
    92, 110, 144,
    187
  William W., 196
ELZEY
  Lewis, 155
EMACK
  William, 159
EMARSON
  ___, 50
EMARY
  Jacob, 158
EMERSON
  ___, 62
  Thomas, 50
EMERY
  Jacob, 49, 52
Erroy KinseY & C,
  217
ESKRIDGE
  A. A., 49, 74

Alfred A., 8, 29,
  45, 62, 88, 101,
  104, 105, 112,
  122, 126, 130
Alfred G., 102
C. G., 53, 61
Charles, 92, 229
Charles G., 6, 7,
  8, 13, 21, 59,
  65, 73, 74, 93,
  97, 100, 101,
  104, 105, 108,
  114, 153, 198,
  222, 223, 224,
  244
ETHEL
  John, 221
  Mary, 221
  Thomas, 59
EVANS
  ___, 26, 30, 31,
    129
  Adam, 39, 41, 94
  Evan, 184, 202
  Henry, 82
  Jesse, 109
  John, 19, 150,
    158
  Mahlon, 20
  William, 82, 150
EVELAND
  D., 28
  Daniel, 87
  Joab, 87
EVERHART
  ___, 210
  Casper, 53, 129,
    156
  Jacob, 41, 42, 44,
    66, 75, 120,
    121, 128
  John, 128, 226,
    227
  Joseph, 128
  Mary, 129, 156
  Michael, 75, 129,
    156, 196
  Nelson, 208

Philip, 17, 49, 52,
  53
Sarah A., 226,
  227
Susannah, 75
William, 75
EVERHEART
  ___, 69
  Jacob, 63, 100
  John, 208
  Joseph, 173
  Michael, 90
  Philip, 58, 227
  Sarah A., 208
EWELL
  Bertrand, 111
EWER
  Ammon, 42
EWERS
  Ammon, 63
  Barton, 84, 141,
    148
  John, 43
  Jonathan, 5, 9,
    65, 76, 84
  Levi G., 169, 190
  Mary, 5
  Rachel, 84
  Thomas, 5, 65,
    212

FADELEY
  ___, 169
  Jacob, 80
  Polly, 80
FADELY
  Jacob, 79, 112,
    191
FADLEY
  Jacob, 63, 83,
    163
FAIRFAX
  Denny, 17
  Ferdinando, 21,
    48, 67, 90, 105,
    136, 148, 210,
    230, 233
FAIRHERST

George, 78
FAIRHIRST
Jeremiah, 110
FAIRHURST
George, 43, 110
FANT
E., 126
Edward L., 41,
88, 101, 108,
114, 122, 146
FARLING
James M., 40
FARR
Elijah, 124, 138,
160
Rachel, 124, 160
Sarah, 124, 160
William, 124, 160
FAW
A., 127
FAWLE
William, 108
FAWLEY
___, 152, 226
George, 164
Henry, 94, 163,
164
Jacob, 102, 109,
239
John, 70
Susannah, 163
FEAGAN
Charles, 14
FEICHSTER
___, 95
John, 56
FEICHTER
George, 237
John, 238
Peter, 29, 152
Susannah, 152
FEISTER
Peter, 163
FENTON
John, 42
FERGURSON
Amos, 101
Henery, 7

FERGUSON
David B., 219
FICHTER
Peter, 62
FIELDING
___, 12
FISHER
Charles, 98
Henry, 208, 226,
227
Margaret, 208,
227
FITZGERALD
Elizabeth, 65
Samuel, 233, 234
Sarah, 233, 234
FITZHUGH
Jn., 98
John, 31, 38, 189
Marian, 38, 189
Nathaniel, 38
William C., 32
FITZIMMONS
William, 232
FITZSIMMONS
John, 213
William, 145
FLEMING
Jesse, 76
R. J., 63
FLETCHER
Harriet, 154, 196,
228
Robert, 155, 228
William, 154, 155,
178, 182, 196,
228
FLOWERS
John, 56
Thomas, 63
FOLEY
Bailess S., 127
Bailys S., 127
Mrs., 15
Presley, 48, 114
S. J., 118
Sarah, 48
FORD

James W., 71, 72
FORREST
Mary, 215
FOSTER
George, 234
William H., 220
FOUCH
Thomas, 96, 125,
195
FOUCH
Thompson, 195
FOX
___, 59, 243
Abigail, 47
Amanda O., 52
Anne, 47
Catharine E., 207
Catherine E., 35
Elisha, 47
Frances, 58
George K., 63,
108
Joseph, 47
Joseph B., 52,
162
Mary, 9, 14, 29,
58, 121, 165
William, 43, 58,
76
William P., 35,
206, 207, 225
FRAME
John, 72
FRANCIS
Edward, 167, 212
Enoch, 4, 37, 68,
69, 107, 140,
150, 176, 189
John, 37, 69, 107
Thomas, 140, 236
FRANK
Luther, 25
Martin L., 25
Mary M., 25
FRAZIER
___, 69
Ann, 58, 212
Henry, 58, 212

FRED
  Joseph, 78, 192
  Joshua, 194
  Thomas, 25, 194,
    203
FRENCH
  Burgess, 176
  Garrison B., 48,
    154
  George W., 48,
    154
  James, 81
  James D., 119,
    188
  Lewis, 193
  Martha L., 98, 99,
    186
  Mason, 35
FREY
  John, 107
  Philip, 131
FRITIPAUGH
  Conrad, 68
FRY
  ___, 152
  Elizabeth, 73
  Hannah, 140
  Isaac, 140
  John, 67, 73, 145,
    172
  Peter, 91, 139,
    153
  Philip, 67, 73, 93,
    131, 145
FRYE
  Christopher, 95,
    197, 199, 219,
    235, 237, 238
  Elizabeth, 102
  Margaret, 95,
    219, 237
  Michael, 102,
    103, 131
  Philip, 44, 102,
    103
FULTON
  ___, 67, 84, 105,
    185, 220, 225

Abraham M., 65
David, 64, 83,
  216
George, 67, 106
Hugh, 114, 153,
  209, 218
M., 155, 196
Mahlon, 129, 162,
  195, 226
R., 155, 196
Rachel, 114
Robert, 35, 64,
  83, 224
William, 83, 153,
  242
FURGERSON
  Amos, 98
FURGUSON
  Amos, 157
FURR
  Enoch, 166, 194
  Miner, 111
  Newton, 166
  Sarah, 194

GABBY
  William, 33, 80,
    83
GAINER
  Charles L., 46
GALLAHER
  David, 23, 206
  John S., 35
  William, 12
GALLEHER
  ___, 211
  Caleb, 185
  Caleb N., 180,
    200, 212
  Daniel, 107
  David, 44, 201
  Eli C., 73
  Elizabeth, 107
  Margery, 13
  Mary, 189
  Patcy, 189
  Susan, 73
  Thomas H., 189

William, 13, 44,
  81, 83, 86, 107,
  189, 227
GALLIHER
  Caleb M., 29
  David, 29
  Eli C., 29, 30
  John, 29
  Mary, 29
  Samuel, 29
  Thomas, 29
  William, 29, 73
GARDNER
  Charles L., 126
  Elizabeth, 126
  Joseph, 139
GARNER
  Arthur, 10
  James, 33, 53,
    102, 215, 235
GARRET
  Abigail, 54
  Enos, 156
  Mrs., 212
  Samuel, 54
GARRETT
  ___, 94
  Abigail, 206
  Abigal, 225
  Enos, 126
  George C., 113
  Joseph, 20, 30,
    43, 93, 97
  Mary, 206, 225
  Silas, 212
  Stephen, 17, 34,
    62
GARRISON
  Elizabeth, 80,
    153, 217
  French, 104
  James, 40, 80,
    136, 143, 153,
    155, 161, 185,
    216, 217, 224
  Garrison & Caylor,
    195
GARROTT

Enos, 127, 160
Nelly, 127
GARRY
  Michael, 81
GASENER
  Joseph, 220
GASSAWAY
  ___, 1, 179
  Charles, 216
  Henerietta, 11
  Henrietta, 216
  Thomas, 11, 13,
    26, 57, 58, 141,
    157, 193, 194,
    216
GATES
  Matthew, 234
GEORGE
  John, 75, 76, 171,
    173, 186, 240
  Thomas, 72, 100
GESLEN
  Alfred, 192
  Rebecca, 192
GETTY
  Bob, 180
GETTYS
  James, 115
GHEEN
  James, 105, 220,
    224
  Leroy, 105, 220,
    224
  Narcissa, 91, 105,
    220, 224
  Thomas, 76, 140,
    180, 220
  William, 105, 220,
    224
GHEENE
  Thomas, 82
GIBBS
  Edward A., 142
  George W., 224
GIBSON
  ___, 129, 163
  A., 1, 2, 6, 10, 13,
    14, 19, 20, 24,

37, 38, 39, 54,
  61, 64, 84, 94,
  100, 103, 107,
  109, 110, 129,
  131, 134, 159,
  170, 173, 174,
  176, 181, 186,
  195, 212, 214,
  215, 223
Abner, 10, 13, 23,
  34, 60, 64, 84,
  98, 104, 116,
  117, 120, 121,
  128, 133, 139,
  140, 157, 165,
  171, 175, 181,
  189, 191, 195,
  196, 200, 205,
  213
Alice, 135, 149,
  236
Amos, 26, 139
David, 34, 38, 64
Eli, 34, 64
Elizabeth, 135,
  149, 165, 171
Emsey F., 148
George W., 206,
  225
Isaac, 236
James, 163
John, 48, 79, 135,
  149, 163, 165
Joseph, 48
Levi, 34, 63, 64,
  180
Mahlon, 165
Mary, 180, 206,
  225
Mirian, 48
Moses, 163
Rebecca, 149
Solimon, 113
Thomas W., 84,
  137
William, 132
GILBERT
  Joseph, 193

GILL
  Charles, 215
  John L., 25, 162,
    241
GILLMORE
  William, 4
GILMORE
  ___, 135, 169
  James, 45, 55,
    188, 218
  William, 4, 46, 65,
    69, 112, 167,
    230
GILPIN
  Bernard, 191
  Rachel, 107
  Samuel, 63, 75,
    107
GLASCOCK
  Enoch, 176
  French, 73
  Uriel, 234
GLASCOW
  George, 185
  Henry, 185
GLASSCOCK
  ___, 157
  Daniel, 77
  Elijah, 127
  Enoch, 102, 178,
    181, 205, 228
  Nancy, 23
  Uriel, 23, 35, 84,
    177, 210, 232
GLASSGOW
  ___, 121, 170
  George W., 155
  Henry, 155
GLEONNELL
  William, 188
GOARE
  Elizabeth, 153
GOLD
  Daniel, 86, 91,
    145, 154
  Phebe, 86, 91,
    154
GOODHART

Elizabeth, 139
Henry, 102, 139
GOODHEART
Elizabeth, 132
Henry, 132, 139,
158
GOODIN
Anna, 208, 231
David, 81
GOODRICH
Philip, 225
GORDON
Bazil, 71
GORE
Elizabeth, 142
James, 192
Joseph, 43, 78,
101, 111, 148,
160, 165, 219
Joshua, 19, 88,
125, 155
Sarah, 236, 237
Thomas, 219,
236, 237
Tilghman, 221
Truman, 48, 166
William, 99
GOUPHENOR
Jacob, 61
GOURLEY
Emmor, 226
Joseph, 23, 113,
226
Samuel, 226
GOVAN
James, 204
GOVER
Hannah J., 8
Jesse, 36, 51,
107, 134, 168,
218, 226
Robert H., 209,
213
Samuel, 126
GOWER
Mrs., 11
GRADY

Edward B., 12,
56, 58, 96, 142,
166, 194, 199
GRAHAM
Hugh, 106
John, 20, 76
William, 29, 233
GRANT
Esther, 48
GRAVES
John, 117
Nancy, 139
GRAY
___, 166
Agnes, 176, 178,
188
Agness, 187
Benjamin P., 187
French S., 101
Harriet, 161
Henry W., 137,
213
James R., 176,
187
Jemima, 176
John, 6, 7, 8, 40,
51, 59, 64, 114,
121, 125, 130,
161, 200, 216,
223
Polly, 176
Presley, 176, 178,
188
Robert B., 176,
188
William H., 130
William S., 176,
187, 188
GRAYHAM
Tamar, 42
William, 42
GRAYSON
___, 35, 161
Benjamin, 17, 38,
59, 72, 79, 84,
87, 90, 123,
124, 125, 142,
144, 145, 148,

154, 155, 160,
161, 162, 183,
189, 194, 202,
210, 211, 243
George M., 199
John W., 17, 23,
25, 34, 35, 57,
59, 69, 72, 79,
81, 83, 87, 90,
121, 123, 124,
142, 148, 149,
154, 155, 160,
183, 189, 194,
202, 210, 211,
215, 241
Richard O., 66,
201
William, 27
GREEN
Ann L., 154
Charles T., 154
Eliza J., 154
Gabriel, 196
George, 154
Hugh, 154
James W., 154
Jane, 154
John C., 110,
203, 215
Mary, 154
Nelson, 152
Rawleigh, 5
Sarah A., 154
GREENLEASE
James, 127
GREENUP
Christopher, 176,
186, 220
GREENWALL
Daniel, 7
GREGG
___, 185, 200
Aaron, 215
Aaron S., 212
Adeline, 217
Beni J., 193
Edna, 217

Elizabeth, 212, 217
Emily, 212
George, 166, 214, 215, 235
Gilford G., 217
Guilford, 219
Guilford G., 218
H. H., 231
Henly H., 33
John, 30, 38, 84, 88, 95, 139
Joseph, 141, 148, 212
Joshua, 30, 33, 84, 109, 123, 141, 169, 183, 194, 205, 231
Josiah, 71, 109, 141
Mahlon, 217, 218
Mahlon S., 212
Nancy, 215, 217, 235
Nathan, 32, 72, 79, 115, 132, 134, 135, 194, 207, 229, 233, 237, 238
Peter, 71, 95, 114, 179
Samuel, 32, 47, 194, 233
Sarah, 217
Sarah A., 194
Smith, 75, 77
Stephen, 75, 77, 79, 115, 132, 135, 207
Susan, 75, 77
Susan R., 194, 233
Thomas, 15, 35, 50, 79, 82, 132, 141, 155, 207
Thomas C., 202

William, 15, 56, 64, 163, 166, 215, 235
GREGG
Levi G., 190
GREY
John, 59
GRIFFIN
Henry, 80
GRIFFITH
Israel T., 4, 113, 126, 131, 132, 137
J. T., 48, 145
GRIGGSBY
Lewis, 46
GRIGSBY
Lewis, 24, 68, 93, 194, 226
Nathaniel, 209
GRIMES
___, 78
George, 5, 78, 110, 132
GROVE
Eve, 57
Philip, 57
GROVER
Christian, 29
GRUBB
___, 145, 203, 219, 230
Benjamin, 84, 134, 148, 153, 184, 219
Curtis, 179, 182, 204, 205, 206
E., 41, 174
Ebenezer, 8, 10, 17, 21, 22, 28, 29, 43, 49, 52, 59, 90, 112, 129, 134, 146, 148, 153, 156, 171, 174, 175, 176, 186, 196, 201, 202, 203, 204, 205, 207,

208, 210, 215, 219, 226, 227, 230
Elizabeth, 78
Harriet, 179, 204
J., 52
James, 159, 174, 202
John, 56, 78, 107, 145, 158, 200
Leah, 171, 196
Mary, 175, 176, 219
Richard, 175, 176, 233
William, 58, 175, 176
GULATT
Charles, 28
GULICK
Amos, 46, 143, 151, 191
George, 149, 205
Martha, 149
Mary, 205
Moses, 95, 149, 174
William, 37, 95, 174, 205, 215
GULLATT
Charles, 48, 73, 74, 92, 185, 225, 232
GUTRIDGE
Ann, 222
Philip, 222, 225
GUY
Sampson, 195
Samson, 25

HACY
William, 81
HAGAR
Martin, 196
HAGERMAN
Benjamin, 26, 37, 46, 60, 203, 205

Verlinda, 60
HAINES
    Daniel, 181
    Edward, 62, 224
    Elizabeth, 22, 141
    Stacey, 22
    Stacy, 141
HAINS
    Joseph, 1, 142
HALL
    Edward, 3, 12,
        23, 25, 33, 35,
        38, 46, 63, 72,
        102, 107, 130,
        131, 132, 139,
        149, 156, 163,
        189, 195, 197,
        215
    Elizabeth, 79, 185
    Jonathan, 82
    Josiah, 137, 239
    Josias, 170
    Louisa F., 215
    Mary, 185
    Richard, 199
    Samuel, 97
    Thomas, 59, 79,
        97, 185, 217
    Thomas S., 215
    William, 82, 163,
        185
HALLEY
    James H., 12
    John H., 35
HALLY
    John H., 44
    Samuel, 44
HAMERLY
    John, 34
HAMERSLEY
    Emily A., 221
    Thomas S., 221
HAMERSLY
    Emily A., 230
    Thomas S., 230
HAMILTON
    ___, 25, 115, 141,
        202, 243

Ann B., 32
Ann W., 85
Anna, 73
Cassandra, 21
Charles B., 3, 24,
    32, 66, 81, 112,
    130, 134, 136,
    147, 170, 174,
    195, 229, 236,
    241
Charles H., 2
Dewanner B., 129
E. G., 121
Erasmus G., 21,
    169
H. H., 27, 224
Harvey, 128, 129
Henry H., 220
James, 21, 32,
    47, 122, 136,
    161, 220, 234
James H., 36,
    125, 154, 209
James L., 85, 88,
    131, 168, 199
Jane, 32
John, 4, 17, 24,
    27, 32, 35, 57,
    71, 76, 78, 89,
    90, 112, 122,
    126, 129, 130,
    133, 147, 167,
    170, 174, 207,
    236, 241
Lucina, 129
Mary, 236, 241
Mathew, 85
Nancy, 24
Samuel, 53, 54
Samuel G., 73,
    85, 138
Sarah C., 236,
    241
William, 114, 140
Winefred, 147,
    236
Winifred, 57, 174,
    241

HAMMAT
    E., 121, 220
    Edward, 222, 242
    Giles, 103
HAMMATT
    E., 234
    Edward, 11, 32,
        41, 144, 177
    Samuel, 9, 32,
        144
HAMMERLEY
    H., 99
HAMMERLY
    Jane, 113
    John, 39, 113,
        232
    William, 91
HAMMET
    E., 91
    Edward, 46
HAMMETT
    ___, 164
    Edward, 63, 75
    George, 81
    George W., 45,
        56
    Samuel, 45, 47,
        51, 63, 70, 96,
        124
    William, 81
HAMMILTON
    Erasmus G., 140
    John, 56
HAMMOND
    George, 131
    J., 136
    John L., 65
    Mary, 131
    Nathaniel, 214
HAMMONTREE
    Samuel, 203
    W. W., 213
    William W., 63,
        112
HAMPTON
    Pompey, 183
    William H., 217
HANCOCK

Catharine, 47
Fenton M., 59
G., 178
George, 55, 103, 239
HANDLEY
David, 161, 212
HANDSLEY
Frederick, 148
HANDY
Given, 37, 176
John, 208, 243
John C., 172
W., 151
William, 117
William H., 142, 170, 208
HANES
Edward, 163
John W., 117
HANLEY
William J., 114, 168
HANLY
___, 72
HANN
John, 25, 77, 85
HANNA
Vicy, 159
William, 159
HANNAH
Vicy, 110
William, 84, 110
HANSBOROUGH
John, 36, 96
John C., 197
HARDEN
Elizabeth, 17, 62
William, 62
HARDING
Catherine S., 198
Charles B., 106
E., 176
Elizabeth A. B., 67, 106
John H., 80

John J., 48, 53, 58, 63, 135, 153
Susan P. B., 67, 105
William H., 48, 67, 105
HARDON
William, 17
HARDY
Charles, 99, 149, 163
HARELEN
Samuel, 65
HARLAN
Aaron, 117, 185
Elizabeth, 117
HARLEN
Elizabeth, 64
HARLES
James, 18
HARLOW
Elizabeth, 34
HARPER
Ann, 71, 72, 99, 233
Enoch, 34
Margaret, 113
Samuel, 168
Thomas J., 56, 113
Washington, 233
Washington T., 72
HARRIE
Isaac, 220
HARRIER
Adam, 196
Daniel, 196
Jacob, 196
HARRIS
___, 27
George, 36
Isaac, 115, 185, 193, 197
James, 219
John, 199, 221
Richard L., 150

Samuel, 105, 115
Samuel B., 89, 219
Sarah, 115, 193
Sarah A., 36
William P., 115
HARRISON
Alexander, 45, 208
Ann, 31
B. W., 6, 12, 93, 197, 211
Burr W., 29, 30, 64, 65, 73, 74, 85, 108, 113, 114, 122, 140, 141, 144, 167, 173, 180, 187, 197, 198, 203, 211, 220, 222, 224, 235, 238, 243
Catherine, 110
Charles B., 210
Elizabeth T., 31
Frances, 31
Henry T., 85, 108, 167, 187
John M., 125, 167, 187, 235
Mathew, 157
Matthew, 125, 126
Moses, 88
Rebecca T., 125
Thomas, 31
Thomas J., 125
William B., 55, 59, 61, 89, 116, 124, 132, 138, 140, 158, 176, 177, 180, 193, 217, 227
HARTLY
Hannah, 221
HARTMAN
Martin, 81
HARVEY

Amos, 37, 55,
   109, 201
Elizabeth, 55,
   109, 201
HATCH
Jane, 88, 129
Jane S., 213
Jesse P., 88, 129,
   213
HATCHER
___, 192
Amanda M., 148
Anna V., 148
Edith, 30, 31, 47,
   95, 132
Elizabeth, 233
Elizabeth P., 194
Emsey F., 148
Gourley R., 148
Hannah, 18, 42,
   148, 180
James, 78, 132
Joan, 148
Jonah, 159, 182
Joseph, 18, 72,
   148, 182
Joshua, 148, 159,
   182
Mary A., 148
Nancy, 159
Nancy L., 182,
   218
Nicholas, 29
Noah, 70, 82,
   160, 231
Rachel, 82
Rebecca, 75, 95,
   148, 182, 229
Samuel, 18, 74,
   132, 148, 159,
   181, 182
Sarah, 42, 182
Thomas, 30, 47,
   75, 86, 148,
   159, 181, 182,
   197, 206, 218,
   233

Thomas E., 194,
   233
William, 148, 159,
   181, 182, 183,
   197
HATCHERS
Thomas, 142
HAW
___, 123
HAWKE
Margaret, 213
Mary, 213
William, 213
HAWKINS
John, 7
Joseph, 76, 177,
   200, 205
HAWLEY
Mary D., 198, 214
Samuel, 100
HAWLING
Isaac, 169
Isaac W., 6
Jane, 88
John, 88
Joseph L., 88
Martha, 88
Mary, 88
William, 22, 88,
   129, 166, 169,
   213
HAY
Eliza K., 199
George, 32, 199
Maria A., 32
HAYMAN
William, 116
HAYNES
Anthony, 100
HAYS
Charles, 176
James, 164
John T., 176
Nancy, 164
Sarah, 176
William, 176
HEAD
George, 7, 8

Nelson, 220
HEATER
Philip, 15, 39, 49,
   109, 118, 170,
   209
HEATH
Andrew, 198, 214
HEATON
___, 200, 210
Albert, 189, 219
Dr., 29
James, 27, 122
Jonathan, 19, 82,
   99, 122, 135,
   155
Jonothan, 82
Lydia, 122
Townsend, 133
HEATOR
Philip, 166
HEFNER
Adam, 47, 240
Catharine, 240
HEIR
Jane, 33
Thomas, 22, 33
HEIRS
Catherine, 28
John, 28
HEIS
Catharine, 73,
   232
Catherine, 74, 92,
   185
John, 73, 92, 185,
   232
HEISKELL
Christopher, 198
HEISKILL
John, 145
HELM
Mary A., 126, 127
Strother M., 126,
   127
HENDERSON
___, 190
A. S., 162

Alexander, 40,
70, 218
Fenton M., 231
Orra M., 29, 34,
70, 74, 85, 87,
109, 136, 218
R., 162
R. H., 39, 40, 42,
65, 69, 93, 130,
166, 171, 210,
218, 223, 225
Richard, 69
Richard H., 2, 3,
8, 9, 11, 12, 15,
16, 18, 26, 29,
30, 32, 33, 34,
36, 46, 47, 48,
49, 54, 55, 60,
63, 65, 66, 68,
70, 73, 74, 80,
85, 87, 89, 90,
91, 96, 102,
103, 104, 105,
108, 109, 114,
118, 119, 122,
126, 131, 135,
136, 138, 142,
145, 146, 150,
151, 153, 154,
164, 166, 176,
180, 181, 186,
188, 189, 190,
191, 193, 198,
203, 207, 215,
217, 218, 220,
224, 229, 231,
232, 239, 240
HENDSLY
Frederick, 58
HENRY
Dewana B., 218
Dewaner B., 121
Dewanna B., 130
Dewannah, 241
Dewanner, 236
Dewanner B.,
129, 130
G. W., 129, 177

George, 82
George W., 8, 15,
26, 39, 56, 67,
73, 81, 102,
112, 121, 130,
132, 171, 191,
218, 232, 236,
237, 241
HERBERT
John C., 241
HEREFORD
___, 238
James, 190, 222
Thomas A., 194
HERIFORD
___, 77
James, 219, 237
HERREFORD
Eliza, 25
Theoderick M., 25
Thomas A., 25
HERRIFORD
Ann C., 5
Francis, 5
James, 95
John B., 5
Margaret A., 5
Mary A. B., 5
Thomas A., 166
HERST
Jesse, 229
HESKETT
John, 199
HESSAR
Andrew, 86
John, 86
Mary, 86
HESSER
Andrew, 5, 65,
155, 169, 216
Daniel, 155
David, 155
John, 89, 155,
169, 170
Lydia, 170
Margaret, 169
Mary, 65
Sarah, 155

HIBBS
Amos, 23, 113,
154, 155, 180,
196
Valentine, 5
HICKMAN
___, 159
Catherine, 128
Henry, 153
John, 239
Mary, 145
Michael, 128
Peter, 78, 128,
134
William, 48
HIEGER
Adam, 191
Daniel, 191
Jacob, 165
Martin, 165
HILL
James, 48, 227
John, 190
John G., 16, 214
Hill SeminarY, 85
HILLIARD
Ann Eliza, 30
Joseph, 30, 96,
111, 151
HILLIEARD
Joseph, 40
HILLMAN
Andrew, 187,
204, 226
Mary, 187, 226
HIRST
Elizabeth, 229
Heston, 165
Jesse, 129, 132
Jonathan, 50
Martha, 229
Richard, 229
HITAFFER
John, 79, 223
HIXON
Benjamin, 26,
212, 223
Catharine, 206

F. W. P., 117, 145
Fleming, 207, 243
Fleming W. P.,
  145
James, 29
Nancy, 34
Noah, 12, 150
Rebeckah, 34
Timothy, 207
HIXSON
___, 182, 209
Andrew, 213
Benjamin, 94
Catharine, 207
Catherine, 116,
  159, 184
Cecelia, 207
Celia, 159
David, 46
F., 162
Fleming, 207
Fleming G. W. P.,
  51
Fleming W. P.,
  161
Flemmon P. W.,
  204
James, 54, 94,
  138, 156, 170,
  183
Jane, 159
Leah, 213
Margaret, 132
Mary, 116, 159
Noah, 68, 159,
  184, 207
Rebecca, 64, 66
Reuben, 116, 159
Ruth, 64, 162
Samuel, 64, 66,
  130, 162, 163
Stephen, 142
Stephenson, 68,
  159
Tacey, 94
Timothy, 65, 66,
  161, 162, 213
William, 129

HOCKING
Eleanor, 196
John, 196
Joseph, 167
HOCKINGS
Joseph, 34, 62
HOCKITY
Samuel, 37
HODGSON
___, 189
Mrs., 55
Portia, 46, 189,
  227
HOEY
James, 118, 131,
  156
William, 131, 156
HOFFMAN
Daniel, 210
Philip, 81
HOGE
Elizabeth, 144
Isaac, 56, 144
James, 10, 12,
  40, 47, 54, 78,
  117, 139, 142,
  151, 174
Jesse, 12, 25, 37,
  43, 86, 144,
  161
Jonathan, 117
Mary, 93, 231
Phebe, 144
Rachel, 144
Samuel, 93, 231
W., 87
William, 1, 12, 30,
  31, 32, 43, 44,
  47, 50, 54, 63,
  95, 117, 121,
  142, 144, 199,
  206, 233
HOGUE
James, 18, 125
Jesse, 50
Mary, 1, 103
Miller, 10, 128

Samuel, 4, 103,
  231
Tacy, 128
William, 1, 4, 18,
  20, 50, 107,
  131, 212
HOLE
Ann, 208
Miriam, 208
Ruth, 208
HOLLAND
Francis, 100
HOLLINGSWORTH
Jehu, 15, 155,
  164, 170, 199
Jehue, 82
Senior, 82, 155,
  164
HOLLOWAY
Aaron, 140
Rachel, 140
HOLMES
Elijah, 93, 103,
  231
Elizabeth, 93,
  103, 231
Hannah, 93, 103,
  231
Isaac, 93, 103,
  231
John, 5, 48, 78,
  129, 144, 154,
  165, 169
Joseph, 66, 93,
  98, 103, 231
Lot, 103, 172
Lott, 93
William, 2, 33, 78,
  93, 103, 167,
  168, 172, 206,
  208, 231
HOMES
Lot, 231
Sarah, 231
HOOF
John, 104
HOOPER
James, 166

HOPE
Christian, 25
Joshua T., 25,
241
Mercy, 241
HORN
Daniel, 164
Mary, 164
HORSEMAN
James, 27
Jemmima, 27
William, 27, 31
HORSMAN
Esaias, 31
HOSKINSON
Andrew T., 55
Ann W., 55
HOUGH
___, 52, 162, 229
Amasa, 28, 150
Barnet, 97, 135
Barnett, 108
Barret, 219
Benjamin, 161,
183
Bernard, 15, 61,
64, 69, 91
Edward S., 96,
111
Elizabeth, 95
George W., 9
Hanson, 164
Harriet, 179
Isaac, 16, 90,
128, 138, 150
Jane, 164, 174,
179
Jane G., 150
John, 7, 23, 38,
95, 125, 129,
136, 138, 174,
179, 183
Joseph, 15, 61,
64, 96, 109,
135, 149, 150,
151, 152, 160,
169, 189, 215
Lucy, 135

Lucy C., 15, 64
Lydia, 59
Mahlon, 7, 227
Mary, 191
Mary A., 162
Mary Ann, 28
Mrs., 165
Peyton, 107
Pleasant, 179
Rachel, 215
Rachel S., 151,
189
Rebecca, 95, 174
Robert R., 9, 28,
34, 38, 75, 87,
96, 110, 111,
150
S., 9, 21, 51, 118,
129, 130, 132,
183, 191, 196,
214
Samuel, 7, 11,
25, 27, 28, 33,
36, 37, 51, 57,
59, 60, 71, 77,
84, 90, 91, 94,
101, 103, 105,
107, 121, 124,
125, 128, 130,
131, 132, 133,
134, 138, 144,
150, 151, 159,
160, 162, 164,
165, 169, 173,
174, 179, 181,
182, 192, 200,
202, 207, 215,
216, 229, 235,
236, 237, 238,
241, 242
Sarah, 204
Sarah A., 219
Sarah C., 87, 110
Thomas, 109,
193, 229
William, 7, 48, 59,
105, 136, 153,

160, 179, 188,
219
William H., 11,
23, 28, 34, 43,
130, 136, 138,
139, 153, 160,
162, 167, 174,
182
HOUSEHOLDER
Adam, 56, 66, 70,
71, 116, 178,
203
Daniel, 173
Gideon, 204
Mary, 21
Ruth, 21
Solomon, 145
Susannah, 203
HOUSER
Abigail, 25
Jacob, 25, 27,
229
HOUSHOLDER
Adam, 21, 204,
205, 206
Gideon, 203
Sarah, 21, 205,
206
Solomon, 203
HOWARD
John B., 100
HOWEL
Timothy, 44
HOWELL
___, 50
David, 216
Israel, 160, 188
Jesse, 52
Lewellen, 165
Mary, 50, 62, 77,
160, 223
Timothy, 38
HOWSER
Jacob, 141
Philip, 51
HUFF
Elizabeth, 136
George, 136

HUFFMAN
___, 17
HUGHES
___, 170
Constantine, 125
Edward, 63, 159
Elisha, 40, 175
Elizabeth, 40
Fanny, 40
Hannah, 40
Hugh, 52
Isaac, 21, 25,
161, 231
Jane, 40
John, 40, 52
Lydia, 40
Maria, 40
Martha, 74
Mary, 40, 93, 125
Matthew, 40
Ruth, 40
Samuel, 40, 175
Sarah, 40, 52, 61
Thomas, 40, 61,
74, 93, 110,
125, 130, 175
HUGHS
Thomas, 52
HULL
Jacob, 234
John, 186
HULLS
Catharine, 203
John, 6
HUMMER
___, 150
Frances, 106
Levi, 106, 141
Martena B., 142
Martha, 141
Nancy, 106, 151
Polly, 106
Washington, 106,
141, 142, 150,
158, 195
William, 106, 141,
151, 184, 198
HUMMERS

William, 158
HUMPHREY
___, 170
Abner, 58, 128
Abner G., 58, 99,
100
Charles, 173, 233
Henson, 205
Jacob, 184
Jane, 84
Jesse, 9, 66, 111,
123, 124, 138,
146, 160, 206
John G., 25, 58,
84, 99, 100,
128, 180, 195,
210, 241
Joseph, 81
Marcus, 24, 210
Margaret, 20, 89,
173
Mary, 111, 123,
124, 146
Mary A., 66, 173
Mary M., 20
Morris, 66, 138
Moses, 89
Mrs., 192
Rachael, 206
Rachel, 124, 138,
160
Sarah, 210, 211
Thomas, 24, 58,
66, 99, 100,
154, 210
Thomas G., 15,
243
Thomas L., 96,
114, 171, 192,
193
Thomas M., 111,
123, 124, 138,
146, 206
Uree, 173
HUMPHREYS
___, 76
HUMPHRY
John G., 148, 241

HUNT
John, 45
Major, 45, 208
Mary, 19, 192,
208
Mrs., 238
HUNTER
Andrew, 26, 35,
39, 41
Robert, 184
HUNTON
Charles, 11
Eppa, 11
HUNTT
Gerard L. W., 168
HURDLE
Nancy, 154
Richard, 213
HUTCHESON
Henry, 72, 143
John, 76, 81
Reuben, 76, 91
Susan, 72
HUTCHISON
Andrew, 178
Bersheba, 178
Betsy, 178
Elijah, 93
George, 115
Henery, 30
Henry, 93, 137
Henry H., 121
Jeremiah, 110
John, 115, 177,
188, 221, 224
Joshua, 20, 115,
178, 189, 192,
201
Keron, 177
Lewellen, 4, 117
Lydia, 148
Mary, 178
Nancy, 224
Reuben, 3, 201
Sampson, 3, 19,
44, 51, 239,
242
Samuel, 115

Silas, 178, 221
Susan, 121
Wesley, 177
Wickliff, 201
William, 178
HYDE
Daniel, 72

IDEN
Samuel, 159
IDEN
James, 21
IDON
Samuel, 74, 209
IREY
John, 66, 78, 98
Samuel, 117
Sarah, 78
IRVIN
John, 70
ISH
Jacob, 19, 23, 33,
 73, 81, 120,
 211
John, 19, 23, 81,
 211
Lucinda, 81
William K., 106,
 123, 212, 221,
 223

J. & J. Douglas, 105
J. & J. Pogue, 98
JACKSON
Amelia, 221
Asa, 160
Benjamin, 30,
 123, 232
David, 66, 130
Elisha W., 62, 79
James, 165
John, 34, 131,
 183
John W., 43, 138,
 139
Lavinia, 126
Mary, 138, 183
Rebecca, 62

Robert, 38
Samuel, 107, 126
Samuel A., 119
Sarah, 119
JACOB
George, 227
Mrs., 41
JACOBS
Adam, 214
Catharine, 206
Catherine, 33, 81,
 197
Christina, 214
Elam, 206
Elizabeth, 72,
 109, 201, 202,
 214
George, 201, 214
Harriet, 214
Jacob, 83
John, 201, 202,
 214
Maria, 81
Peter, 214, 226
Price, 4, 13, 30,
 33, 81, 130,
 131, 160, 192,
 206, 232
Rachel, 214
Rinard, 214
Ryland, 143
Ryland P., 160
Thomas, 74, 223
Valentine, 210,
 214
William, 3, 81
William A., 152
William H., 197,
 209
JAMES
Abigail, 47, 59,
 127
Anne, 47
Benjamin, 189,
 221
Charlotte, 197
Daniel, 36

David, 175, 197,
 201
Dean, 54, 59, 127
Elias, 36
Elijah, 40, 52, 61,
 65, 109, 130,
 133, 178, 236
Elwood B., 89,
 111, 195, 197
Jacob, 47
John, 127
Jonathan, 36
Margaret, 169
Mary, 208
Nancy, 127
Sarah, 61, 133
Smith, 47, 127
Thomas, 39, 45,
 76, 77, 82, 119,
 142, 160, 161,
 162, 169, 207,
 208
William, 47, 127
JAMESON
Andrew, 50
JANNEY
___, 58, 59, 131,
 205
Abel, 30, 31, 35,
 95, 129, 131,
 151
Abijah, 71, 72, 99,
 233
Amos, 131, 153,
 204, 206, 233
Blackstone, 43
Daniel, 19, 38,
 131, 144, 168,
 172, 179, 212
David, 164, 181,
 203, 227
Eli, 66, 78, 93,
 110, 199
Elisha, 35, 36, 46
George, 35, 36,
 97, 223
Hannah, 24

Israel, 43, 144,
216
Jane, 144
Jesse, 50, 62,
119
John, 8, 21, 27,
60, 64, 70, 73,
85, 89, 92, 104,
108, 122, 126,
127, 129, 131,
135, 150, 157,
188, 189, 203,
218, 227
Jonas, 95, 211
Jonathan, 144
Joseph, 22, 66,
75, 105, 131,
166, 219
Lydia, 129
Lydia S., 36
M., 2
Mahlon, 5, 20, 70,
110, 148, 168,
170, 184, 185,
191, 204
Mary Ann, 204
Moses, 107, 207
Pheneas, 91
Phineas, 144
Pleasant, 144,
211
Stacey, 17
Stephen, 39, 84
Susannah, 36
Thomas, 166
JANNY
John, 166
JARVIS
Leonard, 190
Washington, 56
Jarvis & Brown, 98
JAVIS
Washington, 163
JENKINS
___, 205
Elias, 88, 242
Henry, 88
Job, 49

Mary, 49
William, 49
JENNERS
Abiel, 21, 121,
128, 154, 187
G. W., 50
William M., 9, 49,
50, 61, 81, 88,
98, 130
JENNINGS
Edmond, 147
Edmund, 29
Edward, 134
JOHNSON
___, 20, 157, 174
A., 63
Amos, 190
Ann J., 6
Benjamin, 19, 113
Casper, 19, 73
Charles, 30
George H., 166
James, 58, 99,
100, 180, 200,
208
Jane, 169, 190
John, 200, 212
Margaret, 6, 223,
235
Martha, 19
Mrs., 66
Rebecca, 6, 112
Thomas, 86, 112
Thomas J., 6
William, 53, 180,
215, 223, 235
JOHNSTON
Hugh, 130
James, 99, 113,
130, 195, 214,
226, 243
Mary, 243
JONES
___, 72, 118, 161
Abel, 205
Abraham, 214
Alfred, 205
Alice, 138

Cagby, 152
Hannah, 86, 189
James, 138
John, 21, 57, 73,
115
Joseph J., 184,
192
Philip, 21
Philip C., 65
Richard, 29
Richard S., 21, 57
Sarah, 21, 29, 94,
138
Thomas, 13, 21,
29, 57, 84, 138,
205
Thomas N., 86,
189
William, 29
William J., 8, 13,
22, 26, 29
JONSON
Benjamin, 26

KALB
Absalom, 141,
229
Absolom, 187
John, 61, 141,
147
Samuel, 25, 27,
61, 90, 141,
147
Susannah, 27,
141, 147
KARN
Adam, 237, 240
KEAN
George, 194
KEEN
___, 192
Elizabeth, 209
Martha, 209
Mary, 209
KEENE
Elizabeth, 150

George, 114, 155,
183, 194, 196,
236, 237, 238
N., 81
Nancy, 183
Newton, 71, 150,
158, 198, 208,
209, 216, 217
Richard, 80, 200
KEENER
Christian, 110
David, 110
Samuel, 110
KEERFORT
Daniel, 117
KEIRL
John W., 193
KEIRLE
Matthew, 193
KEITH
J. M., 58
KELLY
John, 240
Rebecca, 240
KENT
Benjamin, 139
Elijah, 34, 75, 168
Elizabeth, 34, 168
KENWORTHY
Rebecca, 43
William, 37, 43
KEPHART
David, 57
KERFOOT
Daniel S., 148
KERFORT
Daniel, 215
Kerr & Fitzhugh,
108
KERRICK
Walter, 74, 159
KERSEY
Jesse, 117
Keyser & Shaffer,
98
KIDWELL
___, 65
Elizabeth, 59, 148

Thomas, 27, 59,
148
KILE
Christina, 214
George, 214
John, 8, 24, 61,
214
Winefred, 24
KILGORE
George, 59
Thomas J., 107
KILGOUR
Charles J., 119
KIMBLER
Bayley, 67
Daniel, 67, 103
John, 67
KINCHELOE
James, 109
John, 192
KING
Susanna, 208
William, 13, 36,
51, 116, 137,
208
KINGSMARK
George, 85
KIRBY
Sarah, 106
Thomas H., 1
KIRK
James, 115
Malcolm, 190
Robert, 115
KITCHEN
Elijah, 158
Elisha, 27, 158
Susan, 158
KITTLE
James, 191
KITZMILLER
___, 95
Elizabeth, 219,
235
Martin, 219, 235
W. W., 137, 219
William W., 133,
234, 235

KLEIN
Lewis, 7, 9, 142
KLINE
John, 16
John N., 63, 213,
235
Katherine, 16
Nicholas, 62
KNOX
Jannet, 54
Joseph, 53, 54,
138
William P., 63
KOONCE
Elizabeth, 72
Nicholas, 72

LACEY
Benjamin R., 5,
12, 38, 39
David, 96
Elias, 12
Elizabeth, 190
Huldah, 4, 27
Israel, 2, 3
John, 3, 4
John A., 205
Joseph, 12, 27
Julia A., 38
Mahala, 232
Maria, 207
Meshack, 12
Meshech, 224
Mesheck, 39, 87,
125, 130, 217
Mrs., 35
Naomi, 27
Neoima, 4
Patience, 9
Piaty, 9
Rachael, 9
Robert A., 4, 207
Ruanna, 9
Ruth, 4, 27
Stacey, 48
Stacy, 45, 113,
232
Tacey, 4, 27

Thomas, 9, 96
Westward A., 207
Westwood A., 2, 3
LACY
Mahala, 45
LAFEVRE
William, 195
LAFFERTY
Anna, 123, 169
George, 123
LAINBAUGH
John, 183
LAMBAUGH
John, 63
LANE
___, 182
Abby, 81
Ann R. C., 198
B. M., 20
B. R., 35
Catherine, 77
Eliza, 81
Elizabeth, 44
Epaminondas M., 77, 179
Flavious J., 72
Flavius J., 77
Hardage, 158, 198
Joseph, 44
Philoporman R., 44
William, 20, 44, 81, 106, 150, 158, 198
LANGLEY
___, 34
Susanna, 17, 34, 57
Walter, 17, 34, 57
LANHAM
Walter, 76
LAROWE
Isaac, 101, 172
LASLIE
Amanda, 52
B., 38

Samuel D., 38
Thomas, 52
LATIMER
James, 158
LATIMORE
Thomas, 80
LAURENS
Augustus P. F., 211
LAWRENCE
Alexander, 33, 80, 83
LAYCOCK
Emily, 142
Joseph, 142, 217
LEATH
James, 75
Martha, 75
William, 46
LEE
___, 81, 110
Alexander, 138
Alexander D., 173
Alice, 138
Bowles A., 228
Edmond J., 56
Edmund J., 22, 27, 96
Eliza A., 92, 93, 187, 193
Emily J., 229
Fanny, 72, 92, 93
George, 51, 69, 112, 153, 178, 198
Jane S., 232
Joshua, 85, 173
Ludwell, 4, 14, 16, 19, 22, 65, 92, 93, 98, 117, 118, 123, 136, 139, 173, 180, 187, 193, 228, 229, 242, 243
Matthew P., 161
R. H., 234

Richard H., 63, 69, 92, 93, 117, 181, 203, 230
Thomas L., 51, 72, 92
Thomas W., 20, 141, 195, 221
William, 46
William L., 46
LEETH
James, 22
Martha, 22
LEFEVER
William, 51
LEITH
James, 33
Martha, 42
Mary, 25
Theoderick, 241
William, 33, 195
LESLIE
___, 179
Amanda O., 162
Benjamin, 46, 151
John, 149, 231, 240
Joseph, 214, 215, 226, 227
Joseph D., 201
Rachel, 149, 231
Samuel D., 188
Thomas, 162
LEWIS
___, 75
Betty, 5
Catherine, 69
Charles, 18, 27, 32, 34, 39, 41, 43, 46, 51, 53, 54, 55, 61, 68, 69, 71, 80, 85, 87, 89, 92, 95, 100, 110, 114, 115, 116, 119, 125, 127, 136, 144, 157, 173, 177, 178, 189,

195, 200, 201,
205, 214
Daniel, 215
Elizabeth O., 90
George, 79, 126
James, 80, 100,
200
Joanna, 69, 224
John, 5
John H., 65
Joseph, 76, 83,
90, 99, 118,
131, 148, 156,
161, 170, 177,
186, 191, 199,
222, 237
Rebecca, 5
Samuel, 37
Stephen, 69
William D., 34
LICKEY
J. C., 151, 191
John, 199
John C., 117
LILLY
Ann, 8, 24
LINTHECUM
Otho M., 87
LINTHICUM
Jane H., 213
Joel, 213
LINTON
John, 11
Sally, 11
LITTLE
George, 74
LITTLEJOHN
John, 13, 25, 60,
204, 206, 237
LITTLETON
Charles, 140
Elizabeth, 51
Feilding, 122, 124
Fielding, 176, 177
John, 126
John K., 17, 79,
103
Richard K., 17

Thomas, 140,
155, 165
William, 51
William K., 17
LIVINGSTON
John, 3
LLOYD
Evan, 64
John, 36, 149
LOCK
Jane, 48
LOCKARD
John, 117
LOCKHART
Josiah, 99
LODGE
Abner, 119, 162
Catherine, 165
John, 165
Jonathan, 48
Joseph, 177, 181
Laban, 170
Samuel, 39, 76
Tamzen, 119, 162
Tamzer, 118
William, 47
LOES
Catherine, 196
John, 196
LOGAN
Alfred, 236
Alice, 236
David, 40
John, 236
Maria, 40
LONG
Armistead, 240
Armstead, 122
Benjamin, 21
Catherine, 7
Conrad, 175
D., 35
Durett, 21, 112
Jacob, 196
John, 7, 102, 139,
213
Joshua, 21
Sally, 196

Susan, 102, 213
William, 196
LOVE
___, 135, 169,
191, 237
Augustine, 170
E. A., 106
ELI A., 116
Eliza M., 67
Elizabeth, 71
George, 217, 232
J. P., 106
James, 29, 32,
40, 41, 44, 81,
131, 133, 208,
238
John, 19, 38, 41,
44, 116
John P., 79, 87,
116, 145
Leah, 115
Richard H., 45,
67, 143, 203
Samuel, 41
Susanna, 32, 41,
44, 208
Thomas, 106,
116, 141
Thomas B., 38,
44, 115, 116
LOVETT
D., 38, 45
Daniel, 86, 189,
216, 239
Daniel C., 216
David, 9, 25, 29,
49, 54, 55, 62,
84, 101, 111,
127, 154, 156,
179, 197, 206,
226, 229, 239
Edmond, 120
Edmund, 185
Elizabeth, 120
Hannah, 83, 139
James P., 216
John, 83, 139
Jonas, 83, 139

Jonathan, 10, 61,
83, 139
Joseph, 83, 139
Matilda, 61, 83,
139
Nancy, 83, 139
Naomi, 83, 139
Thomas A., 216
LOYD
Joshua, 183
LUCAS
Barton, 101
Delilah, 149
Isaiah, 149
Nancy, 149
LUCKET
Leven, 174
LUCKETT
___, 212
Alfred, 174, 200,
243
Ann C., 63
Anna, 38
F. W., 238
Frances W., 163
Francis W., 7, 10,
12, 13, 19, 20,
25, 33, 37, 38,
46, 63, 72, 81,
83, 84, 91, 100,
102, 104, 107,
111, 116, 117,
121, 131, 132,
140, 144, 171,
189, 195, 197,
206, 209, 215,
224, 238
Harriet, 197
Henry F., 5, 137,
180
Horace, 65, 91,
95, 120, 122,
123, 124, 174,
176, 177, 200,
205, 221, 239,
243
Horrace, 14

Leven, 13, 39, 95,
197, 221, 230
Ludwell, 38, 63,
91, 107, 117,
214
Philip H., 108
Samuel, 14
Sarah S., 38, 117,
209
Susan E., 243
Thomas H., 5
William F., 189,
192, 197, 215
LUFBOROUGH
Nathan, 145
LUKE
Elizabeth, 125
John, 17
Joseph, 125
LUMM
Samuel, 56
LUMPKIN
Joe, 199
LUWORK
Naphtali, 191
LYDER
Cornelia, 177
Jacob, 181
Letitia, 177, 181
Lewis, 155, 170,
177, 181, 220,
231
Lydia, 177
Mahala, 155
Mary, 160
LYNE
Margaret, 61
Thomas, 59
William, 61, 91,
116, 130, 173,
195
LYNN
___, 12
Adam, 81, 135,
208, 209, 216,
217
Fielding, 73
LYON

John, 5
John C., 63, 67,
110
LYONS
John, 27, 31, 231

MADDISON
Rachel, 114
MAGAHA
David, 207
MAGEATH
Joseph P., 210
MAGILL
A., 238
Charles T., 38,
238
John S., 143, 238
Mary D., 38, 238
MAGINNIS
Daniel, 133, 234
MAHON
Alexander, 92
J. D., 92
MAHONY
Abel, 192
MAINES
Archibald, 116
William, 116
MAINS
A., 53
Anna, 223
Archibald, 88, 89,
115, 133, 242,
243
Mary, 88, 223
William, 88, 89,
115, 223, 241
MAN
John, 100
Mandeville &
Lamour, 153
MANLEY
John S., 63
MANN
Bernard, 116
George, 21, 96
Jacob, 109, 110,
116, 152

John, 96, 120,
235
Mary, 96, 235
Sarah, 109, 116
MANNING
Euphamia, 28
Euphemia, 28
Nathaniel, 28, 72,
78, 112, 132,
186
Sally L., 187, 234
MANSFIELD
John, 24, 176
MANTZ
Casper, 58
MARKS
Abel, 20, 76, 77,
80, 85, 86, 89,
92, 108, 170,
234, 243
Bennett, 31, 85,
243
Elizabeth, 85
George, 11, 13,
30, 56, 59, 84,
123, 180, 202,
226, 239
George S., 157
Hannah, 76, 120,
172, 183
Isaiah, 12
John, 12, 70, 84
Keziah, 70, 87,
108
Lydia, 12, 170
Mahala, 59, 123,
226, 239
Mary, 20, 31, 77,
86, 89, 107
Mason, 20, 76,
85, 89, 99, 113,
120, 172, 183,
243
Samuel, 89, 92,
107, 108, 168,
234, 243
Thomas, 9, 31,
70, 77, 79, 85,

87, 89, 92, 108,
189
Watts, 89
MARLOW
Edward, 153, 164
George, 153, 164,
190, 230
Hanson, 230, 239
Louisa, 239
M., 26
Thomas, 133
Thomas J., 48,
84, 117, 120,
143, 145, 164,
212, 227, 229,
240
MARLOWE
Thomas J., 9
MARMADUKE
John, 14
John A., 14, 116
Silas, 14
MARSH
James, 35, 84
MARSHALL
Eleanor, 73
Jacob, 12
Ruel, 23, 57, 73
MARSTELLER
Aaron, 211
Eleanor, 211
Elenor, 7
MARSTILLER
Aaron, 211
Burr, 211
MARTEN
James L., 83
MARTIN
___, 184
Andrew, 67, 77,
111
Caleb, 77, 111
David, 126, 209
Edward, 67, 111
Elizabeth, 77,
209, 220
Jacob, 28
James, 79

James L., 45, 51,
53, 56, 61, 115,
144, 168, 193,
197, 199, 203,
220, 224, 239
John, 10, 38, 59,
60, 63, 67, 69,
79, 83, 91, 93,
97, 108, 111,
137, 144, 152,
156, 213, 222,
225, 242
Margaret, 33
Mary, 213
Sarah, 197, 225
Sarah A. P., 224
Sophia, 28
William, 8
MASON
___, 1, 179, 234
Ann, 179
Charles W., 203
Enoch, 160
John, 177
John H., 203
John T., 13
Margaret E., 203
Mary, 13, 203
Richard B., 14
Stevens T., 13
Temple, 55
Thompson, 57
Thompson F., 47
Thompson T., 66
Thomson, 14, 16,
179, 180
Thomson F., 16,
176
Westwood T., 14
William, 201
William T. T., 13,
14, 27, 37, 41,
54, 61, 64, 67,
179, 180, 194
MASSUTH
Aaron, 95
MATHIAS
Caroline F., 172

Hamilton R., 243
John, 27, 129, 223
John J., 2, 6, 11, 20, 26, 27, 42, 43, 47, 48, 49, 53, 54, 63, 64, 66, 70, 73, 74, 75, 79, 80, 89, 92, 99, 102, 105, 120, 134, 138, 142, 144, 155, 157, 161, 164, 166, 171, 172, 175, 178, 180, 184, 185, 187, 190, 192, 193, 195, 218, 223, 235, 236, 237, 238, 243

MATTHEWS
William, 214

MAULSBY
Benjamin, 29, 62, 63, 163

MAUND
Thomas, 26, 46

MAYNE
William, 99

McARTOR
___, 186

McBRIDE
Hiram, 27, 148
James, 27
William, 27, 148

McCABE
___, 11, 57, 157
Henry, 53, 54, 154
Jane, 154
John, 115
John F., 22
John H., 11, 15, 17, 21, 30, 32, 34, 39, 40, 43, 52, 54, 63, 68, 80, 81, 85, 87, 94, 99, 113,

114, 115, 116, 126, 127, 135, 151, 152, 154, 164, 193, 199, 204, 206, 211, 219, 224, 225, 231, 233, 234, 235, 236, 237, 238, 239
John J., 64
Mary, 99, 154, 164

McCARTY
___, 77
Billington, 174
Dennis, 10, 94, 95, 103, 128, 200, 212, 213
Dennis T., 174
Emily, 13, 27
Emily R., 97
G. W., 95, 103, 174
George, 95
Jonathan, 148
Margaret, 103, 174
Margret, 103
Richard C., 103, 174, 212
Stephen, 174
Thaddeus, 103
Thadeous, 103
Washington, 103
William M., 13, 26, 27, 97
William R., 24
William T., 103

McCLAIN
James, 49
Thomas, 191

McCLOSKY
William, 155

McCLOUD
William, 190

McCORMICK
___, 74

Helen C., 33, 53, 54, 80, 83, 138
Hugh, 33, 80
John, 6, 16, 27, 29, 30, 33, 39, 40, 43, 46, 49, 53, 54, 80, 83, 101, 136, 138, 153, 170, 222
Mary, 54, 80, 136, 138, 170

McCOY
Elizabeth, 234
William, 133, 234, 236

McCRADY
A., 100
Anthony, 12

McCRAY
James, 39

McDANIEL
___, 82
Ann, 1, 120, 122, 165, 175
Anne, 121
Archibald, 29, 151, 155, 164, 185, 191
Edward, 48, 155, 165, 191
James, 1, 2, 13, 108, 116, 120, 121, 122, 130, 146, 151, 152, 155, 172, 175, 185
Mary A., 151, 165
William, 122

McDONALD
Edward, 148
John, 231
Joseph, 149, 192

McDOWELL
John, 38

McFADEN
Mary, 55
Timothy, 55

McFARLAN

James, 24
McFARLAND
James, 85, 116
McGARRICK
___, 2
McGARVICK
___, 152
Amelia, 42
Henry, 42
Isaac, 106
James, 42
John, 42
Patrick, 42
Pleasant, 42
Tamar, 42
William, 42
McGAVACK
Israel, 192
P., 132
Patrick, 165
McGAVICK
James, 29
Pattrick, 29
McGEATH
___, 9, 23
Gabriel, 206
Joseph, 165
Joseph P., 225
McGEE
Arthur, 66
McGETH
___, 35
John, 172
McGRAW
___, 59
McGUIRE
Edward, 57, 101
Hugh, 37
McGWIGGIN
Samuel, 214
McGWIGWIN
Nancy, 201
Samuel, 161, 201
McILHANEY
Mortimer, 73, 194
McILHANY
Cecelia, 48

James, 39, 41,
45, 48, 49, 50,
54, 64, 198,
215, 225
M., 202
Margaret, 36
Mortimer, 33, 52,
56, 57, 195,
201, 202, 203,
204, 215, 216,
219, 226, 227,
229
Mortimere, 158,
187
Mortimore, 29
McILHANY
___, 74, 133, 184
Cecelia, 123
James, 3, 8, 15,
26, 71, 84, 87,
91, 99, 111,
116, 118, 122,
123, 126, 131,
132, 133, 135,
141, 166, 191
Margaret, 111,
141, 166
Mortimer, 22, 65,
76, 78, 84, 90,
100, 107, 128,
140, 141, 145,
147, 149, 151,
155, 156, 159,
161, 162, 184,
187, 189, 231
Mortimore, 2, 5,
19, 22, 23
Rosannah, 22
McINTOSH
John, 193
McINTYRE
C. C., 36, 61, 155
Christopher C.,
26, 70
P., 72
Patrick, 70, 136
Pattrick, 26
McKEMIE

Francis, 60
McKEMMEY
___, 187
McKEMMIE
Francis, 89
McKENNA
James L., 117
McKENNEY
Leah, 29
McKIM
Burr W., 125, 192
Catherine, 192
James, 214
McKIMIE
___, 204, 226
McKIMMIE
Mary, 131
Wayne, 131
McKINNEY
Isaac, 241
McKNAB
William, 91
McKNIGHT
Alley, 45
Ally, 160
Charles, 166, 207
Deborah, 45, 82,
160
Eli, 9, 45, 160
John, 82, 207
William, 45, 68,
207, 217
McMORMICK
M., 84
McMULLEN
___, 12, 23, 35
A. B., 92
Alexander, 170,
181
Andrew, 39, 170
Andrew B., 174
Barbara, 1
Daniel, 1
David, 1
Elizabeth, 181
George, 132
Nancy, 174

William, 73, 170,
181
McMULLEN
Alexander, 1
McMULLIN
A. B., 96
Andrew B., 37
Daniel, 152
Nancy, 37
McNAB
William, 55, 76
McNABB
William, 82
McPHERSON
___, 123
Benjamin, 176
George, 72, 132,
195
Henry, 127
James, 140, 193
John, 36, 82, 108,
193
Kezia, 140
Mary, 36, 93
Priscilla, 132
Rebecca, 36
Samuel, 36
Sarah, 20, 93
Stephen, 4, 20,
30, 41, 48, 84,
93, 97, 113,
120, 142, 198,
205, 232
Wesley S., 69,
242
McVEIGH
Eli, 77, 85, 198,
199
Elizabeth, 195
H., 210, 214
Hiram, 79, 107,
122, 162
J. H., 210, 214
James H., 4, 84,
124
Jesse, 13, 17, 29,
34, 53, 76,
106, 148, 149,

154, 172, 178,
195, 204, 218,
223
Keron, 10
T., 119
Townsend, 6, 19,
50, 52, 79, 80,
82, 156, 162,
172
Townshend, 1,
10, 17, 95, 120,
204, 210, 221
MEAD
Aquila, 43
Aquilla, 33
Hiram N., 66
Joseph, 88, 145,
147, 241
MEANS
Archibald, 54, 234
MECE
Elizabeth, 233,
234
George, 233, 234
MELLON
Jane, 82
Joseph, 82
MENDENHALL
Jacob, 3
MERCER
___, 60
Charles F., 9, 26,
37, 60, 76, 81,
113, 203, 205,
215
Charles T., 196
Col., 66
MERCHANT
James, 11, 22,
34, 56
Mary, 34
William, 114, 215,
224
MERRICK
William D., 93
MERSHON
James, 221
Joseph B., 221

Thomas B., 18,
115, 124, 127,
177, 178, 221,
225
William, 32, 65,
106, 123, 124,
151, 177, 189,
194, 221, 225
METCALF
Thomas, 41
Methodist Episcopal
Church, 180
MIDDLEBURG
John, 19, 139
MIDDLETON
___, 113
Robert W., 35
MILHOLLIN
Patrick B., 48
MILLAN
A., 10, 11
MILLER
___, 148
Aaron, 5, 65, 78,
159, 184, 186
Adam, 41, 93,
101, 202, 203
Barbara, 201, 202
Catharine, 202
Catherine, 93,
201, 202
Christian, 201,
202, 230
Daniel, 143, 159
David, 127
Elizabeth, 93,
101, 131, 144
Emily J., 159
George, 10, 131,
144, 174, 200,
201, 202, 227
Hannah, 186
Hellen, 178
Jacob, 193
James, 22, 104
Jesse, 93, 101
John, 201, 202,
203

Joseph, 134
Lucinda, 148
Maru, 159
Mary, 5, 78, 159,
184, 202
Mary C., 159
Peter, 78, 93, 101
Rachel, 159
Rebecca, 93
Robert H., 98
Sarah, 202, 230
Thomas F., 148,
196
William, 85, 95
MILLS
John, 234
Lewis, 167
MILTON
Henry, 110
Richard, 58, 198
MINES
John, 150, 154
MINOR
Nathan, 153
William, 232
MISKELL
William, 10
MISKILL
William, 60
MITCHEL
Carter, 114
Robert, 114
MITCHELL
Benjamin, 13, 30,
41, 42, 71, 72,
77, 102, 123,
137, 193, 239
Martha C., 72
MOCK
Jacob, 75, 183
MOFFETT
___, 234
Benjamin, 26
Elizabeth, 126
Josiah, 126
Robert, 5, 8, 14,
18, 21, 39, 55,
61, 64, 73, 80,

97, 121, 124,
126, 136, 171,
173, 177, 179,
204, 215, 235,
237
MOLER
George W., 57
MONEY
Nicholas, 166
MONROE
A. G., 6
Bithiny, 6
James, 113, 137,
156, 199, 239
John H., 32, 83,
98, 108, 188,
209, 213, 219,
224
MONTHIETH
___, 140
MOON
Henry, 114
Isaac W., 114
MOOR
Daniel, 66
MOORE
___, 11, 60
Ann, 36
Asa, 26, 36, 68,
125, 133, 148
Benjamin, 208,
226, 227
Elizabeth, 208,
226, 227
James, 41, 105,
134, 149, 168,
199
James G., 119
John, 44, 119,
120, 173, 177
Joseph, 119
Samuel, 169
Sarah A., 36
MORALEE
Michael, 137
MORALLEE
Mary, 119

Michael, 33, 69,
97, 108, 133,
155, 168, 188,
205, 239
Thomas, 41, 51,
108, 119, 137
MORAN
Gustavus A., 110,
156
John, 120
Lydia, 110
William, 32, 156
MORGAN
David, 17
Eleanor, 118
Eliza, 57
Jesse, 79, 146
Philip, 57
MORRALLEE
Michael, 22
Thomas, 63
MORRIS
Catherine, 55
Elizabeth, 100
John H., 36
Mahlon, 1, 22, 55,
111, 179
Nancy, 155
Robert W., 111
Thomas, 82, 133,
155
MORRISON
___, 67, 94, 175,
187, 204, 226
Archibald, 5, 22,
89, 145, 231,
241
Edward, 73, 78,
107, 145
Flora, 107
James, 240
Jane, 107, 145
Joseph, 2, 60, 89
Rachael, 56
Rachel, 231
Rebecca, 240
MORROW
___, 70

Jane, 9
John, 9
William, 9
MOSHER
Alfred, 218
MOSS
John, 163
Thomas, 67
MOSTER
Ira, 218
MOTT
Armstead, 154
Armstead R., 188
Mary E., 154, 188
Thomas R., 3, 27,
46, 104, 122,
125, 126, 151,
185, 188, 215,
239
MOUL
George, 221
George W., 221
Mary, 221
Philip, 221
Rozanna H., 221
MOUNT
Ezekiel, 168
Hannah, 176
James, 37, 107,
176, 189, 243
John, 42
Stephen R., 148,
162
Thomas, 203
MOXLEY
William, 83
MULL
___, 58, 76
Abigail, 11
Catherine, 7
David, 171
George, 11
John, 7
Mary, 15
MULLEN
S., 121
Samuel, 51
MULLIKIN

William, 89
MULLIN
Samuel, 41
MURDOCK
A., 98
William F., 98
MURRAY
James B., 100,
136, 137
Josiah, 127, 241
Mary A., 22, 53,
153
Ralph, 18
Reuben, 77
Samuel, 14, 22,
49, 53, 169
MURRY
___, 27
MURSHON
Thomas B., 127
MUSE
___, 187
MYERS
Sarah, 133
Sarah C., 100

NAYLOR
James, 127
NEAR
David, 35
Eve, 35
James, 57
Jesse, 141
John, 35
Nathan, 122
Samuel, 29
Susannah, 35
NEER
Ann, 230
Conrad, 230
David, 174, 213
Eliza, 123, 161,
230
Jesse, 10, 230
Joseph, 230
Martha, 230

Nathan, 123, 150,
161, 162, 189,
230
Samuel, 10, 230
Sarah, 230
Susannah, 213
Negro (slaves)
Aaron, 232
Abraham, 97
Adam, 9, 97, 228
Adeline, 142
Albert, 17, 194
Alce, 178
Alexander, 194
Alfred, 95
Alice, 51, 199
Alle, 51
Ally, 104
Amanda, 15, 73,
106, 109, 178,
201
Amos, 142
Ann, 9, 34, 67,
95, 97, 106,
109, 147, 169,
210
Anna, 10, 98, 112
Anne, 199
Annice, 31
Anthony, 11
Armistead, 210
Armstead, 142
Austin, 67, 106
Barkley, 238
Barnett, 167
Barney, 194
Belcher, 16
Bennet, 31
Betsey, 115, 117
Betsy, 117
Bill, 14, 67, 106,
122, 169
Bob, 67, 106, 210
Boss, 228
Bossy, 93, 136
Bridget, 228
Burr, 67
Burwell, 93

Butler, 34, 39
Byas, 130
Caleb, 33
Caroline, 31, 178, 198
Carter, 31
Catherine, 178
Chana, 68
Charles, 9, 58, 178, 232
Charles W., 203
Charlott, 67
Charlotte, 9, 17, 31, 88, 106, 130, 165
Chat, 210
Clarissa, 34
Clary, 210
Cliarissa, 214
Cloe, 167
Cordelia, 69, 117
Corline, 178
Cornelia, 98
Cuff, 210
Cyrus, 95, 165
Dan, 122
Daniel, 67, 98, 106, 178
Daniel Rivers, 168
Daphney, 31
Davy, 69
Delia, 58
Delpha, 65, 197
Delsa, 119
Dennis Buckney, 21
Dick, 67, 106, 115, 213
Dinah, 31
Edmond, 31
Edmund, 15, 73
Edney, 178
Edward, 194
Eleanor, 97, 210
Eliza, 31, 67, 106, 201
Eliza Rivers, 168

Eliza Stott, 23
Elizabeth, 169
Ellen, 67
Ellen Esther, 117
Ellick, 194
Ellzey, 147, 214
Emily, 20, 67, 88, 106, 130, 147, 214
Emma, 130
Esther, 37, 98, 228
Evelina, 15, 73
Eveline, 209
Fanny, 199
Fenton, 67, 104, 106
Fich, 67
Forester, 130
Frances, 178, 214
Francis, 88, 130, 241
Frank, 5, 31, 33, 45, 57, 93, 117, 199
Freelove, 31
Geoffrey, 32
George, 9, 13, 31, 42, 67, 68, 106, 142, 194, 212
George Dabney, 199
George Rivers, 243
Grace, 42
Gus, 67, 106
Gustine, 67, 106
Hannah, 16, 31, 69, 98, 167, 214
Hariet, 238
Harriet, 9, 53, 122, 130, 142, 194
Harriett, 147
Harrison, 142
Harry, 93, 156

Harry P. Dawson, 242
Hary, 136
Helen, 9, 130
Hellen, 241
Henery, 31
Henny, 142
Henry, 67, 69, 106, 130, 137
Henson, 42, 112
Hester, 142
Horrace, 31
Humphrey, 31, 98
Ibby Ann, 42
Isaac, 9, 67, 69, 98, 106, 234
Isabella, 178
Jack, 33, 67, 69, 106
Jackson, 73, 95
Jacob, 121
James, 31, 38, 69, 76, 89, 110, 115, 178, 213
Jane, 61, 62, 69, 104, 117
Jeffrey, 31
Jennings, 12
Jenny, 228
Jerry, 14
Jerry Dabney, 199
Jess, 15
Jesse, 31, 36, 92, 98, 193
Jim, 5, 9, 31, 76, 93, 136
Joe, 109, 142
Joe Lumpkin, 199
John, 93, 97, 160, 178, 209
John Baker, 199
John Bowman, 160
John Diggs, 34, 39
John H., 203

John Richard,
199
Johnson, 58
Joseph, 31, 95,
113
Judah, 67, 106
Judy, 231
Kendal, 15
Kingston, 93, 228
Kit, 97
Kitty, 13, 67, 106,
115, 130, 194
Lana, 9
Landon, 78
Laurinda, 178
Leah, 98
Leonard, 69
Let, 58, 95
Letitia, 67, 106
Letty, 115, 209
Lewis, 31
Lewis Baker, 199
Lewis Mills, 167
Lige, 11
Limas, 67, 106
Lizzy, 31
Lloyd, 58
London, 118
Louisa, 34, 39,
238
Lucinda, 31, 98
Lucy, 31, 38
Luke, 95
Madison, 31
Mahlon, 31
Malinda, 169
Mandeville, 14
Manervy, 178
Mareah, 178
Margaret, 9, 95,
104, 130, 238
Margaret E., 203
Maria, 57, 67, 69,
95, 106, 142,
147, 165, 178
Mariah, 58, 109
Martha, 169, 178

Mary, 9, 31, 34,
37, 42, 57, 65,
112, 117, 176,
178, 194, 197,
199
Mary Jane, 97
Mary Mason, 203
Massey, 31
Matilda, 17, 31,
34, 57, 67, 106
Melvida, 16
Menervy, 178
Mereah, 178
Mesheck, 178
Mille, 93
Milley, 67
Milly, 9, 67, 97,
106, 119, 183,
228, 238
Mima, 95
Minca, 178
Monica, 34, 39
Moses, 16, 58,
69, 89
Moses Butler, 16
Moses Harrison,
88
Moses Williams,
71
Nace, 67, 106
Nan, 67, 106
Nancy, 31, 39,
67, 97, 106
Nat, 58
Neale, 24
Ned, 112
Nelson, 58, 67,
106
Nicholas, 32
Oscar, 17
Pamela, 194
Peg, 9, 67, 106
Peggy, 9, 199,
228
Peter, 6, 11, 88,
130, 212
Peter Bigby, 71
Phebe, 194

Phil, 117, 156
Phyliss, 194
Pinkey, 106
Pinky, 67
Pleasant, 65, 67,
106, 197
Presley, 112
Quitinia, 16
Rachael, 33
Rachel, 45, 67,
88, 98, 106,
130, 199
Ralph, 31
Randal, 98
Rebecca, 128,
194, 199
Resin Williams,
99
Reuben, 92, 193,
229, 242
Richard, 117
Richard Henry,
115
Rippin, 93
Robbin, 228
Robin, 117, 165
Robinson, 31
Rodney, 67, 106
Rosanna, 31
Rose, 95, 112,
122
Roseanna, 209
Rosetta, 5
Ross, 67, 106
Rubin, 178
Sabra, 178
Sabro, 178
Sally, 32, 67, 68,
169
Sam, 67, 106
Sampson, 93,
104, 136, 169,
228
Samuel, 13
Samuel Hockity,
37

Sarah, 69, 141,
  201, 210, 214,
  232
Sarah Ann, 5
Sarah Rivers, 168
Saray, 5
Sidney, 122
Sim, 61
Simon, 16
Smith, 31, 180
Solomon, 98
Sophy, 31
Squire, 31
Stephen, 3, 20,
  93, 115, 210
Sucky, 109
Sukey, 57
Susan, 51, 69,
  95, 104, 210
Sylve, 142
Tasker, 169
Tenor, 67, 106
Tereny, 31
Thompson, 194
Tilda, 106
Tildy, 38
Tim, 69
Tish, 67, 106
Tom, 33, 93, 109,
  228
Travis, 37
Truman, 6
Uriah, 122
Voll, 9
Wallace, 17
Washington, 95
Wesley, 31
Whorton, 24
William, 9, 14, 17,
  39, 58, 194,
  199
Wilson, 220
Winefred, 67, 106
Winney, 128
Winny, 112, 117,
  165, 191
NEILL
Nancy, 242

NELSON
___, 233
Philip, 235
NETTLE
William, 114, 132,
  184
NEWLON
Nimrod, 84, 180
NEWMAN
Basil, 224
Bazzill, 28
William, 224
NEWTON
Enos W., 39, 162
Harriet, 154
James F., 45, 65,
  205, 230
John, 63, 154
John T., 104, 191
Joseph T., 56, 65,
  80, 96, 105,
  242
Nelley S., 56
Sarah, 39
NICEWANGER
___, 35, 175
Catherine, 43,
  174
Henry, 174
John, 43, 174
NICEWANNER
Henry, 81
NICHOLAS
Enos, 210
Thomas, 35, 197,
  229
NICHOLLS
Isaac, 140
Lydia, 150
William J., 114
NICHOLS
Ann, 119
Barbaray, 119
Dolphin, 119, 162
Edna, 162, 217
Emily, 93, 103,
  119, 231

Enos, 118, 119,
  124, 162, 207,
  217
George, 107, 119
Hannor, 118
Harman, 119, 162
Isaac, 5, 9, 16,
  18, 26, 30, 31,
  32, 47, 50, 54,
  63, 64, 65, 82,
  86, 95, 97, 125,
  128, 129, 142,
  144, 150, 168,
  172, 194, 206,
  207, 233, 236,
  238, 241
Isaiah, 82
Jacob, 58
James, 118, 119,
  162
Joel, 118, 119,
  162
John, 43, 93, 97
Joshua, 238
Mary, 64, 194
Nathan, 92, 94,
  162
Nathaniel, 39,
  118, 119
Pleasant, 118,
  119
Rachel, 119, 162
Samuel, 16, 18,
  26, 30, 31, 32,
  47, 95, 125,
  142, 151, 172,
  206, 207, 236,
  238, 241
Sarah, 94, 118,
  119, 162
Swithen, 84, 206
Swithin, 132
Tamzen, 119
Thomas, 5, 24,
  30, 37, 49, 50,
  62, 65, 74, 75,
  84, 89, 93, 103,
  119, 120, 123,

128, 129, 144,
151, 155, 159,
160, 169, 170,
179, 181, 182,
183, 186, 211,
212, 216, 218,
220, 226, 231,
239
Thomas S., 132
Thomas T., 89
William, 71, 132,
172
NICKLIN
John, 77, 152
NICKOLS
Amor, 161
Amor S., 82
Dolphin, 161
Hannah, 82
Isaac, 43, 44, 47,
48, 56, 82, 117,
139, 142, 151,
159, 160, 179,
189
Jacob, 151
James, 161
John, 43
Joshua, 159
Mary, 48
Nathan, 76, 94
Samuel, 43, 44,
82, 139
Sarah, 82
Stacy, 82
Swithen, 101, 148
Thomas, 45, 160
Thomas T., 151
William, 78, 82,
159, 179
NISESWANER
John, 43
NIXON
____, 161
George, 109, 173,
202, 218
James, 11, 29,
34, 49, 128,
184, 201, 202

James W., 128,
202
John, 6, 78
Mary, 128
Samuel, 128,
186, 187, 202
Sarah, 7, 29, 94,
128
William, 202
NIXSON
James, 72
Joel, 71, 82
John, 79
NOBLE
George, 74, 145,
166
NOLAND
Catherine, 13, 43
E., 19
Elizabeth, 5
Elizabeth M., 133
Lloyd, 5, 13, 16,
108, 120, 122,
125, 133, 178
Pierce, 25
Sarah, 133
Thomas J., 1, 13,
17, 133, 221
William, 1, 13, 24,
26, 43, 58, 72
NORIS
Abby W., 35
Seaton W., 35
NORRIS
Abbey W., 20
George H., 147
Seton W., 20
William, 65, 98
NORTON
Barbara, 10, 16,
61
Elvira, 61
Hiram, 61
Nathaniel, 10, 61
NORWOOD
George, 40
Nostrand & White,
54

NYSWANGER
Catherine, 42
Christian, 42, 74
Henry, 42
John, 42
Mary, 42
OATYER
____, 232
Peter, 61, 125,
180
OAYTER
Peter, 126
O'BANION
Charles, 221
Charles B., 221
Francis, 86
O'BANNON
Frances, 221
Samuel, 221
ODEN
Alexander, 142
Betsey, 142
Elias, 116
Hezekiah, 142
John, 141
Lewis, 142
Martha, 142, 195
Nathaniel S., 24,
59
Richard, 141
Sarah, 116
Thomas, 116,
130, 141, 142,
195
OFFUTT
Charles, 150, 168
Eli, 121, 157, 234
Thornton F., 203
OGDEN
Andrew, 29, 40,
64, 126, 131
Benjamin, 40, 79
Daniel, 40
David, 51, 53,
151, 153, 184
Eliza, 151
Elizabeth, 40, 64

Hezekiah, 40
Lydia, 40
Robert, 29, 40
OGDON
Benjamin F., 63
David, 63
Robert, 141
O'NEAL
Thomas, 48
ONEALE
Thomas, 20
ORRISON
Annanias, 75
Arthur, 24, 127
Betsey, 24
Matthew, 46, 69
OSBOU
James, 233
OSBURN
Addison, 107
Albert, 107, 113
Balaam, 34
Craven, 35, 37,
  38, 45, 52, 55,
  58, 62, 65, 70,
  73, 74, 75, 76,
  81, 82, 87, 94,
  96, 99, 101,
  108, 109, 110,
  115, 116, 119,
  120, 123, 149,
  151, 154, 156,
  157, 160, 161,
  162, 164, 167,
  173, 175, 176,
  179, 188, 197,
  200, 208, 211,
  214, 216, 227,
  230, 234, 239
Elizabeth, 188
Enos, 162
Herod, 1, 99
Jane, 200
Joab, 99
Joel, 99, 119,
  122, 200, 217,
  219
Jonah, 107

Joshua, 39, 43,
  52, 58, 77, 89,
  94, 99, 105,
  161, 162, 199,
  214, 217, 234
Lawson, 97
Mason, 113, 122
Morris, 59, 85, 89,
  92, 99, 101,
  107, 108, 122,
  161, 162, 168,
  200, 211, 218,
  243
N., 102
Nicholas, 77, 80,
  122, 220, 233
Norval, 188
Pleasant, 99
Richard, 99, 154,
  234
Thomas, 52
OSBURNE
Craven, 1, 22, 24,
  25
Jane, 25
Joshua, 1, 15, 19,
  20, 21, 22, 24,
  29, 31
Morris, 25, 29
Nicholas, 6
Norval, 1, 14, 23
Richard, 25
Turner, 15
OTTERBACK
Philip, 61
OVERFIELD
Anna, 97, 169,
  216
Benjamin, 146,
  149
Elizabeth, 97
Hudson, 216
Joshua, 39
Joshua B., 47, 49,
  96, 97, 169,
  216
Martin, 39, 97
OWENS

Cuthbert, 12
OWSLEY
Thomas, 177
OXLEY
Aaron, 166
Cynthia, 166
Elizabeth, 166
Enoch, 166
Frances, 166
Henry, 166
Jamima, 166
Jesse, 142
John, 166
Lewis, 166
Mary, 166
OYTCHER
Peter, 125

PADGET
Baily, 214
Elizabeth, 198,
  214
James A., 47, 214
Timothy, 198, 214
PADGETT
Benedict, 131,
  132, 189
Eleanor, 131
PAGE
Eliza, 55
Peyton R., 14, 55
William, 209
PAGIT
Timothy, 59
PAINTER
Jonathan, 72
PALMER
Abel, 77
Able, 85
Ann, 188
Benjamin, 188,
  220, 231
Lott, 188
Milburn, 143
Philip, 116
Samuel, 73, 188

William C., 168, 171, 192, 193, 210, 241
Palmer & Chamlin, 96
PANCOAST
___, 211
Israel, 134, 135, 233
John, 12, 30, 31, 59, 62, 88, 95, 169, 189, 207, 219
Joshua, 30, 31, 62, 65, 87, 95, 109, 123, 141, 181, 183, 194, 200, 226, 231
PANCUST
John, 107
PARHAM
William, 205
PARKER
Hannah, 46, 151
Mrs., 133
Thornton, 86
PARMER
John E., 34
PARMES
John E., 26
PARROTT
John, 63
Paton & Butcher, 166
PATTEN
Ann F., 243
Jonathan T., 243
PATTERSON
John B., 61, 98, 129
Mahala, 61
Robert, 183
PATTISON
Fleming, 216
PAXON
___, 9
Jacob G., 177
Jane, 7

William, 7, 16, 24
PAXSON
Anne, 68
Diadama, 206
Diademia, 54
Griffeth W., 243
J. G., 243
Jacob G., 183
Jane, 118, 129, 131, 164, 183, 204
John, 40, 68
John G., 134
Mahalah, 134
Matthew, 129
Samuel, 68, 183
William, 118, 129, 131, 164, 183, 204, 216
PAYNTER
James, 197
PAYTON
Craven, 115
Richard F., 44
Townsand D., 44
PEACH
Rebecca, 135, 149
Samuel, 135, 149
PEACOCK
___, 187, 204, 226
Cassandria, 113
Elijah, 3, 32, 56, 60, 78, 95, 131, 138, 161, 210
PEAKE
Humphrey, 44, 45, 104, 105, 200
PEARCE
Jane, 46, 137
John S., 137
John T., 46
PEARSON
Joseph, 222
PECK

Asa, 15, 69, 97, 108, 188, 218
John C., 114
PEDRICK
Michael, 183
PEERS
Ann H., 93, 126
Eleanor, 7, 34, 39, 40, 93, 126
Henry, 7, 34, 39, 63
PEIRCE
Susanna, 208
PELTER
Catherine, 12
George, 12
PENCE
Jacob, 136
PERDEM
Arey, 65
PERKINS
Alfred, 176
PERREY
Mary, 52
PERRY
Benjamin W., 63, 121
Hezekiah, 221
PEUGH
Elisha, 89
Elisha M., 80
Mary, 123, 124, 198, 199
Samuel, 10, 20, 123, 124
William H., 198
PEUSEY
___, 2
Joshua, 2, 3, 5, 15
PEYTON
Francis H., 223
Henry, 66
Mrs., 89
Richard F., 54, 221, 230
Sarah, 211
Townsend D., 95

Townshend D.,
170, 183, 211,
221
PHILIPS
___, 118
Amey, 233
Jenkin, 149
Jinkin, 192
John, 229, 233
Rachel, 125, 133
Thomas, 23, 36,
76, 125, 133,
148, 179
PHILLIPS
___, 166
Amey, 233
Amy, 233
John, 229, 233,
236
Priscilla, 233, 236
Rachel, 148
Thomas, 28, 29,
36, 107, 134,
148, 149, 168,
171, 199, 216
Phillips & Bond, 168
PIERPOINT
___, 233
Eli, 38, 41, 106
Hannah, 38
Samuel, 233
PIGGOT
William, 95, 142
PIGGOTT
Isaac, 159, 181,
182
Mary, 159
Rebecca, 182
Rebecca H., 148,
181
Rebeccah, 159
William, 18, 30,
31, 32, 43, 44,
47, 74, 150,
159, 182, 206
PILES
J., 113
PLAISTER

___, 86
Henry, 4, 72, 139
Michael, 241
Nancy, 72, 139
Susan, 72
PLAISTOR
Henry, 241
PLASTER
Hannah, 215
Henry, 73, 146,
183, 189
James, 33, 195,
215
Janel, 183
Michael, 72, 183,
184, 226
POGUE
James, 61, 64,
65, 92, 197,
220, 243
John, 61, 64, 65,
92, 197, 220,
243
POLEN
William, 24
POLIN
Elizabeth, 44, 55
Nathaniel, 127
William, 44, 55
POLSON
Jesper, 108
William, 108
POMEROY
Dade, 46
POOL
Elias, 36, 51, 57,
102, 168
Margaret, 51
POPE
John, 176, 220
POPKINS
Mrs., 226
Phebe, 180
PORTER
Jesse, 214
Mary, 214
POSTON
___, 179

Jacob G., 32
Joseph, 28, 59,
76
Leonard R., 17,
79, 103
Mary E., 79
Mary E., 17
Wilsey, 17
POTTERFIELD
___, 53, 61, 148
Catherine, 163
D., 100
Daniel, 30, 51,
163, 186
Elizabeth, 51, 163
Henry, 51, 145,
163, 237
Israel, 163
Jonah, 163
Jonathan, 90,
163, 235
Joseph, 163
Mary, 163
Sarah, 163, 235
POTTS
___, 52, 66, 162,
175, 176
David, 29, 49,
123, 134, 169
Edward, 123
Eliza, 123
Elizabeth, 62
Enos, 15, 47, 50,
87, 199, 231
Ezekiel, 123, 154
Isaiah, 25, 62,
180
J. L., 145, 243
Jane, 52, 123,
169
Jared, 23
John, 134, 219
Jonas, 5, 49, 62,
123, 134, 169
Joseph L., 49,
134
Joshua, 188
Lusinda, 23

Nathan, 1, 23, 188

William, 123, 169

POULSON

___, 131, 133

Agnes, 36

Agness, 79, 208, 214

Elizabeth, 79

Jasper, 36, 79, 81, 146, 208

Mary, 36, 214

Susannah, 214

Thomas, 79, 146

William, 79, 208

POULTON

Alfred, 177

Lucinda, 86

Lydia, 177

Thomas, 86, 133, 169

POWELL

___, 167

A. H., 122

A. O., 142, 222

Alfred H., 31, 53, 85, 101, 106, 108, 120, 122, 147, 153, 222

Ann, 8, 24

Burr, 1, 2, 6, 10, 13, 14, 16, 19, 20, 23, 24, 31, 35, 37, 39, 47, 53, 54, 60, 61, 63, 64, 74, 84, 85, 94, 98, 100, 107, 108, 109, 110, 116, 117, 120, 122, 129, 130, 131, 133, 134, 139, 140, 152, 157, 159, 165, 170, 173, 174, 175, 176, 180, 181, 185, 188, 189, 191, 195, 196, 200,

205, 211, 213, 214, 215

Burr G., 193

C., 53

Catherine, 19, 84

Charles, 80

Charles L., 127

Cuthbert, 17, 31, 32, 53, 84, 85, 108, 113, 127, 140, 171, 193, 215, 222, 224

Dr., 69

Elisha, 8, 24, 25, 33, 46

Elizabeth, 106, 171

George C., 84, 122, 135

H. B., 14, 17, 57, 65, 78, 79, 87, 98, 110, 120, 121, 131, 146, 154, 162, 172, 175, 190, 203, 211

Humphrey, 90

Humphrey B., 12, 20, 31, 37, 39, 60, 63, 64, 73, 84, 85, 95, 110, 129, 140, 165, 172, 180

James, 24

James L., 25

John L., 53, 85, 157, 166, 194, 222

Leven, 16, 31, 53, 85, 106, 140, 153, 171

Ludwell E., 8, 24

Major, 5

Mary, 24, 171

Mary C., 171

Mary E., 171

Peyton, 4, 20, 112, 224

Robert, 8, 24, 195

Robert M., 33, 46

Sarah R., 193

T. W., 74

William, 24, 25, 106

William A., 53, 106, 145, 171, 239

William L., 29, 152, 235

PRICE

Thomas, 229

PRIME

Nathaniel, 241

PRIMM

John, 156

Sophia M., 156

PRINCE

Levi, 208, 226, 227

Magdalena, 208, 226

Mary, 208, 226, 227

Mathias, 43, 208, 226, 227

Matthias, 175

Nathan, 208, 226, 227

PRIOR

Emily, 119

Samuel, 119

Prison Bounds, 71

PROBASCO

Jacob, 58

PROVIN

Clark, 117

PRYOR

Emily, 118, 162

Samuel T., 162

PUESEY

Joshua, 64

PUGH

___, 59

Mary, 77, 85

Spencer, 77, 85, 199

PURCEL
___, 74
George, 179
John, 167
Jonah, 162
Martha, 179
Mary, 167
Samuel, 38, 79, 179
Thomas, 167, 179
Valentine V., 133, 167, 169, 175, 179, 189, 233
PURCELL
M., 29
Valentine, 29, 118
Valentine V., 198
Volentine V., 9
PURDEM
Jeremiah, 65
Permelia, 65
PURDIM
Mary, 65
PURSEL
___, 188, 211
Burnard, 155
Edwin, 155
Enos, 155
George, 87
M., 224
Samuel, 45, 160, 169, 175, 189, 198
PURSELL
Enos, 155
Jonah, 231
Joseph, 210
Samuel, 82
PUSEY
___, 35
James, 54
Joshua, 32, 34, 37, 43, 44, 48, 49, 60, 67, 72, 121, 128, 135, 152, 165, 169, 171, 179, 201, 206, 225, 243

Mary, 43, 44, 169
PYKE
Abraham, 98
PYOTT
James, 109
John, 75

QUINLAN
Hugh, 114
T. C., 167
Tasker C., 66, 101, 103, 108, 113, 114, 120, 121, 122, 128, 138, 140, 145, 152, 160, 163, 170, 172, 173, 185, 197, 198, 219, 231, 232, 239

RACE
John W., 57
RAHN
Philip, 51
RALPH
John, 129, 195
RAMBO
Elizabeth, 164
John, 164
RAMEY
___, 183, 206
Jacob, 105
Lydia, 67, 70, 105, 118, 176
Sandford, 2, 8, 24
Sandford J., 9
Sanford, 67, 70, 105, 116, 118, 152, 176, 218
Sanford J., 68, 105, 111, 118, 165, 176
RAMSAY
John, 169
RAMSEY
John, 122
William, 70

RAMY
___, 56
RATCLIFFE
Robert, 185, 212
RATICOE
James, 39
RATLIFF
Joshua, 171
Nancy, 171
RATRIE
John, 223
Ratrie, 223
RAWLINGS
Stephen, 110, 153, 157, 171
RAY
Robert, 241
RAZOR
Dorcas, 48, 166
George, 48, 166
Jacob, 48, 166
Mary, 48
READER
Martha, 42
Zenus, 42
RECTOR
Caleb, 18
Mary A., 18, 148
Samuel, 215
REDENOWER
Christopher, 112
REDMAN
Mrs., 127
REECE
David, 109, 170
REED
A., 58
Andrew, 141
Celia, 233
James, 3, 81, 86
John, 233
Joshua, 77, 87, 145
Mary, 81
Miner, 57
Minor, 75
William, 12, 50
REEDER

Gourley, 30, 83, 95, 154, 226, 237
Israel, 22
Martha, 22, 75
William, 42, 180, 182
Zeneas, 22
REESE
David, 229
REID
John, 234
Lelia, 234
REIGER
John, 235
REIGOR
John, 112
REILEY
Joshua, 62
RHEA
Robert, 146
RHODES
George, 11, 27, 176
William, 42, 116
RICE
Jesse, 230
Thirza, 190, 230
RICHARD
John, 193
RICHARDS
Eleanor, 165
George, 4, 7, 14, 16, 53, 54, 60, 63, 68, 69, 74, 81, 85, 97, 99, 108, 110, 112, 151, 152, 209, 219, 222, 223
Humphrey, 70
Jesse, 163, 165
John, 74, 143, 171
Margaret, 46, 195
Sampson, 171
Samuel, 83, 155, 196

William, 46, 180, 195, 200
RICHARDSON
George, 39
John, 143, 206
Joseph, 47, 96, 159, 201, 216, 217
Mary, 100
Susanna, 159
RICKARD
Cevila, 184
Civilla, 219
George, 184, 219
RICKETTS
David, 104, 191, 205
Elizabeth, 205
Ricketts & Newton, 45
RIGOR
John, 121
RILEY
Ann, 19, 68
John M., 228
Joshua, 11, 17, 19, 68, 81, 105, 146, 190, 192, 232
Mary R., 228
Nancy, 81
RIMER
John, 43
RINGER
David, 123
RINGGOLD
Gen., 32
Maria A., 32
RINKS
Lorrence, 43
RITACRE
John, 200
RITCHIE
Isaac, 83
RITE
Charles, 50
RIVERS
Daniel, 168

Eliza, 168
George, 243
Sarah, 168
ROARBAUGH
___, 186
ROBERDEAU
Daniel, 85
Gen., 85
Jane, 33
ROBERSON
___, 241
ROBERTS
George E., 117
Jonathan, 102, 209, 237, 242
Nancy, 199
Robert, 95, 96, 199
ROBERTSON
Elizabeth, 200
John, 16, 118, 145, 200
ROBINSON
Thomas, 46
ROGERS
___, 94
Asa, 18, 37, 38, 39, 80, 84, 95, 96, 100, 101, 123, 124, 133, 143, 159, 172, 177, 212, 225
Elizabeth, 54
Hamilton, 24, 27, 28, 41, 66, 68, 74, 88, 98, 102, 103, 110, 123, 129, 141, 179, 180, 195, 213, 225
Hortensia M., 199
Hugh, 10, 13, 19, 20, 84, 94, 124, 149, 159, 172, 178
James, 172, 176, 177, 225
Lloyd R., 199

Mary, 10, 13, 88
Nancy, 64
Polly, 20
Sanford, 172
Thomas, 1, 2, 3,
12, 19, 24, 33,
43, 71, 79, 107,
120, 123, 127,
139, 144, 165,
168, 172, 176,
177, 180, 197,
218, 225, 240
William, 54
ROLLER
____, 94
Aaron, 240
Conrad, 33, 144
Daniel, 144
Frederick, 17, 240
John, 33, 144
Magdalena, 240
Margaret, 144
Pricilla, 240
ROLLS
Jane, 195
ROMINE
John, 97
Rebecca, 97
Susan, 97
ROMINES
Peter, 149
ROOF
John, 11, 90
ROPP
____, 226
Nicholas, 175
ROSE
Anna, 8
Charlotte, 97
Christopher, 62,
113
John, 4, 6, 8, 11,
16, 28, 39, 51,
54, 62, 97, 112,
166, 170, 180,
203, 209, 216,
225
John W., 61, 62

Robert, 17
Samuel C., 200
William, 42, 157,
161, 171
ROSS
Richard, 145
ROSSELL
____, 7
ROSZEL
Anna, 147
Stephen, 50, 147
Stephen W., 183,
193
ROSZELL
Kitty, 147
Mrs., 67
Nancy, 70
Phebe, 70
Sarah, 70, 92
Stephen, 70, 92
Stephen C., 70,
92, 147
Stephen G., 70
Stephen W., 70,
92, 104, 147
ROULSTON
Samuel, 100
ROW
George, 133
ROWAND
Thomas, 114
ROWLES
George W., 81
ROZEL
Sarah, 107
ROZELL
Anne, 54
George, 30
Stephen, 54
Stephen C., 25
Stephen G., 31
ROZZELL
Sarah, 9
RUSE
Christian, 83
Frederick, 83
Henry, 83, 196
Jacob, 11

John, 150, 200,
229
Peter C., 82
Sarah, 150, 200
Solomon, 66, 78,
98
Tabitha, 66
RUSH
T. M., 92
RUSK
James, 71
RUSSEL
Aaron, 151
Benjamin C., 62
Elizabeth, 200
Ethelus, 62
Henry, 131
John, 128
Mahlon, 151
Mary, 55
Nancy, 55
Robert, 55
Thomas, 55
William, 55
RUSSELL
____, 74, 110
Aaron, 46
Ann, 230
Catherine, 179
Charle A., 142
Charles, 142,
161, 199
Eliza, 142
Elizabeth, 142
Elizabeth J., 142
Henry, 75, 129,
151, 155, 191
James, 42
James H., 46
Joseph, 230
Margaret, 142,
161
Matilda, 151, 191
Robert, 41, 142,
153, 164, 200,
201, 202, 210
Sarah Ann, 142

Thomas, 8, 34,
49, 55, 182
William, 41, 46,
151, 172, 177,
179, 204
RUST
___, 27, 94
Alfred, 127
Ann, 224
Benjamin, 129,
202
Benjamin F., 69
Bushrod, 70, 94,
108, 221, 222
Elizabeth F., 69
George, 11, 17,
27, 37, 74, 79,
102, 145, 166,
234, 237, 241
James, 9, 11, 15,
23, 32, 34, 44,
54, 74, 84, 88,
97, 160, 187,
190, 192, 193,
199, 210, 234,
235, 236, 237
James T., 223
Mandley T., 121
Manly T., 89, 157
Margaret, 222
Maria, 234
Martha, 212, 223
Mathew, 106, 223
Matthew, 212
Peter, 69, 87, 224
Peter C., 4, 112,
210
Peter H., 87
Sally, 32, 74, 121
Sarah, 89
Simon W., 106,
223
Sydnor B., 212,
223
William, 88, 108,
127, 160, 192
RYAN
John, 133

SACHMON
Charles, 4
SACKMAN
Charles, 17, 33
Sarah, 33
SACKMON
Samuel, 43
SAFFER
B. F., 178
William, 80
SAGAR
George W., 2
SAGARS
George, 5
SAGER
Delilah, 144
Eve, 109
George, 89, 143
George W., 134,
144
Henry, 117
SAGERS
Delila, 87
George, 87, 89
John, 91
SAGLE
Henry, 59
Michael, 65
SAMPSON
James L., 222,
223
Sally, 223
SAMSELL
Henry G., 210
SAMUEL
Nancy T., 187
Washington, 187
SANBOWER
Adam, 78, 100,
134, 139, 145,
212
Ann, 109
Anna, 196
Christenah, 78
Christian, 139
Christiana, 134

John, 46, 53, 101,
124, 139, 196
Julia A., 237
Magdalena, 240
Michael, 124, 196
Sarah, 100, 196
Susan, 240
Susannah, 53,
196
SANDBOWER
Anna, 181
John, 46, 181
Michael, 181
Susannah, 181
SANDERS
___, 87, 115
Aaron, 114
Ann, 48, 75
Britton, 75
Crayton, 91
Edward, 14
Elizabeth, 186
George, 186, 187
Henry, 91, 116
John, 91, 187
John H., 176, 188
Mrs., 73
Patience, 91
Peter, 128
Polly, 176, 188
Presley, 170, 203
Susanna, 114
Thomas, 11, 17,
75, 87, 91, 116,
117, 161, 193
SANDFORD
___, 2
SANDS
Jacob, 16, 65,
200
Jonah, 30, 71,
218
Joseph, 200
Ruth, 231
Sarah, 218
Stephen, 9, 16,
24, 90, 114,
142, 200

Thomas, 231
SANFORD
A. M., 171
Augustine, 45
Augustine M., 33,
  39, 45, 71, 147
Jeremiah, 114,
  184
Lydia, 45
Mahala, 45
Robert, 33, 39,
  45, 71, 171
Sarah, 45
SAUNDERS
___, 45, 151, 157
Aaron, 224
Ann, 28, 73, 92,
  185, 225, 232
Britton, 28, 73,
  92, 185, 225,
  232
Crayton, 91, 209
Cyrus, 209
Editha, 209
Elizabeth, 2, 19,
  204
Everett, 11, 56,
  62, 104, 105,
  205
Everit, 55, 242
Everitt, 6, 11, 55,
  209
Evritt, 107, 155
George, 2, 19,
  187, 201, 204,
  226
Gunnell, 36, 155,
  209
Henry, 5, 56, 209,
  213
J., 155
James, 209, 232
John, 2, 22, 56,
  89, 95, 107,
  187, 204, 209,
  226

Margaret, 25, 59,
  95, 141, 218,
  229
Mary, 209
Mary B., 56
Mrs., 151, 185
P., 55
Patience, 22, 56,
  209
Peter, 150
Prescilla, 209
Presley, 11, 63,
  67, 69, 93, 102,
  147, 156, 170,
  209, 232
R. G., 34, 55, 63
Ramey G., 41,
  102, 209
Susan, 209
Thomas, 6, 56,
  69, 73, 114,
  192, 209, 213,
  218, 239
Thomas R., 142,
  185, 232, 239
William, 36
SAWYER
Samuel, 159
SCHOLFIELD
Samuel C., 164
SCHOOLEY
___, 164, 234
Aaron, 194, 242
Ann, 181
Daniel, 1, 2, 179
Eli L., 1, 2, 66,
  173, 179, 181
Elizabeth, 168,
  242
Enoch, 1, 2, 179
Ephraim, 1, 2, 3,
  179
John, 1, 2, 9, 129,
  131, 153, 163,
  166, 179, 215
Jonas P., 133

Mahlon, 1, 2, 3,
  12, 66, 167,
  168, 173, 179
Reuben, 1, 2, 3,
  173
Thomas, 1, 2, 179
SCOTT
Charles, 70
Elizabeth, 70
James, 150, 154
Mary, 208, 226,
  227
Phebe, 86, 150,
  154
Robert, 133, 140
SEATON
Alley, 77
Hiram, 25, 33, 46,
  69, 75, 77, 87,
  111, 200, 224
James, 185
Nancy, 33, 224
William, 87, 224
SEEDERS
Sarah S., 108
William, 8, 63,
  108
SEEVERS
George W., 86,
  89, 91, 135,
  154
Nathaniel, 211,
  229
SELDEN
Dr., 99, 164, 173
Eliza A., 187,
  193, 198
Miles, 32
W. C., 117, 131,
  133, 163, 167,
  232
Wilson C., 74, 86,
  88, 114, 125,
  153, 187, 189,
  193, 198, 203,
  213, 216, 229,
  234, 235
SELDON

Dr., 54
Eliza A., 187
W. C., 6
William C., 187
Wilson C., 78, 92, 93, 123
SEMPLE
  John, 100
SERVICK
  Elizabeth, 75
SERWICK
  Christian, 75, 188
SETTLE
  Daniel, 59
  Jane, 59
  Margaret, 162
  Newman, 59
  William, 38, 162
SHAFER
  ___, 239
  Conrad, 230, 239
  Jacob, 166
SHAFFER
  Henery, 32
  John, 43, 44
SHAVER
  ___, 190
  Conrad, 153
SHAW
  Cynthia, 197, 211
  Eliza A., 197
  John, 10, 22, 29, 56, 62, 133, 153, 163, 197, 209, 211
  Rebecca, 62, 163, 197
  Sidney, 197
  Susan B., 62, 197
Shaw Tiffany & Co, 98
SHAWEN
  ___, 16
  Anne, 68
  Catherine, 68
  Cornelious, 70
  Cornelius, 68, 207, 222

D., 9, 66, 130
David, 12, 40, 43, 51, 58, 68, 87
George M., 68
George W., 2, 4, 5, 6, 7, 8, 11, 16, 17, 19, 20, 21, 23, 25, 27, 40, 42, 48, 49, 51, 52, 56, 57, 60, 61, 64, 66, 70, 71, 73, 78, 80, 84, 90, 91, 94, 100, 101, 104, 105, 113, 124, 126, 128, 131, 139, 145, 147, 148, 150, 153, 156, 158, 159, 163, 164, 166, 176, 179, 181, 183, 184, 187, 192, 194, 195, 196, 200, 201, 204, 205, 207, 208, 214, 218, 219, 226, 227, 231, 236, 239, 241
Jane, 236, 241
Mary, 68, 207
SHEAD
  George, 56
SHEARMAN
  Thomas, 241
SHEID
  George, 59, 156, 195
  Lurena G., 196
  Martena B., 142
  William, 142
SHELTON
  John C., 71
SHEPHERD
  Catherine, 101, 111
  Charles, 104, 110
  Elizabeth, 110

Humphrey, 101, 111
John, 191
SHIELDS
  Alfred, 134
  James H., 15
SHIPMAN
  Susana, 62
SHIRLY
  James, 29
SHOEMAKER
  ___, 184
  Daniel, 57
  Jacob, 44
  Josiah, 57
  Maria, 57
  Prescilla, 65, 163
  Priscilla, 57
  Simon, 2, 13, 25, 34, 65, 78, 90, 107, 141, 145, 187
SHOEMATE
  M. C., 85
SHORTRIDGE
  George D., 121
SHORTS
  Charlotte, 39, 240
  John, 67
SHOVER
  ___, 214
  Adam, 39, 46, 53, 84, 117, 229
  Adam E., 46
  Barbara, 229
  Catharine, 229
  Charlotte, 240
  George, 46, 53, 84, 181, 196, 237, 240
  Henry, 53, 117
  Jacob J., 209
  Magdalena, 237, 240
  Rosannah, 117
  Simon, 53, 181
  Susan, 240
  Susanna, 209

Susannah, 53,
181, 196
Valentine F., 84
SHOWATER
J., 29
SHREVE
___, 190
B., 188
Benjamin, 54, 63,
124, 166, 180,
193, 200, 203,
230
Charles, 191
William, 71, 120
SHRIEVE
B., 176, 177
Benjamin, 16, 21,
27, 62, 65
SHRIGLEY
Enoch, 16, 150,
159, 174, 190,
202
SHRIVER
John, 10
SHUMAKER
Daniel, 158
Jacob, 128
SHUMATE
M. C., 161
SHUTT
Jacob, 109
SIDEBOTTOM
John, 44
SILCOT
Craven, 113
SILCOTT
Abraham, 50
Craven, 81, 104,
113
Jacob, 23, 30,
104, 113, 137,
140, 148, 196,
198, 200
Jesse, 23, 87,
145
Lee, 50
Lucinda, 148
Peyton, 86

SIMMS
James, 72
SIMPSON
___, 60
David, 71, 95, 98,
114, 190
Elizabeth, 23, 98
French, 23, 78
Henson, 24, 38
James, 38
John, 1, 2, 4, 12,
19, 23, 29, 44,
55, 66, 73, 74,
76, 82, 87, 91,
93, 98, 103,
115, 117, 144,
177, 180, 186,
212, 218, 220,
231, 242
Joseph, 3
Martin, 98
Mary, 33
Matilda, 76, 82,
91
Samuel, 33
William L., 126
Simpson & Gregg,
71
SINCLAIR
Amos, 166
Eleanor, 166
George, 166
James, 47, 61,
67, 89, 123,
188, 190, 222,
223, 230
John, 10, 18, 25,
29, 42, 55, 76,
91, 138, 139,
140, 170
Leanah, 89
Leanna, 190
Samuel, 12, 166,
178, 207, 228
Samuel C., 109,
138
Thomas M., 207
SINGER

Elizabeth, 229
SINGLETON
Agnes, 176, 188
Agness, 178, 187
Allen, 140
Allin, 178
Benjamin, 178,
182
Elizabeth, 182
Hellen, 178
John, 227
John F., 160
Joshua, 133, 178
Lucinda, 160
Mary, 182, 228
Mary A., 181
Mary R., 228
Nancy, 227, 228
Nancy W., 133
Robert, 133, 140,
178, 228
Samuel, 133,
160, 176, 181,
182, 187, 188,
205, 227, 228
Sarah, 227, 228
Stanley, 228
vincent, 178
Vincent, 178
W. G., 129
William, 160, 228
SKILLMAN
Abraham, 109,
185, 218
Abram, 144
Delila H., 185
Elizabeth, 185
John, 46
SKINNER
Amos, 24, 103,
177
Gabriel, 171
Margaret, 103
Peter, 95, 211
Phebe, 131
Rebecca, 205
Usher, 205
SLATER

Christena, 23
Jacob, 23, 84
John, 23
William, 23, 60,
  71, 84, 138
SLATES
  Frederick, 186
SMALE
  ___, 232
  Simon, 63, 81,
    197, 211
SMALLEY
  Cynthia, 166
  James, 166
SMALLWOOD
  ___, 113
  William, 210
SMALLY
  David, 40
SMARR
  John, 13, 200,
    213, 223
  Susan, 213
  Susan F., 200
  William, 13
SMART
  John P., 207
SMITH
  ___, 190, 198
  Abraham, 7, 94,
    128, 202
  Amos, 140
  Ann, 68, 149
  Benjamin, 130,
    135, 223
  Burr, 10
  Charles, 68, 104
  David, 19, 50, 71,
    101, 106, 111,
    144, 161, 223
  Delia, 24
  Edward J., 111
  Eleanor, 49
  Elizabeth, 29, 49,
    94, 140, 180
  Esther, 48
  Fleet, 57

George, 6, 24, 41,
  190, 226, 237
George D., 229,
  234
H., 19, 65, 79, 80,
  223, 224
Henry, 38, 44,
  155, 188, 196
Hugh, 10, 18, 21,
  29, 44, 53, 64,
  67, 73, 85, 87,
  94, 95, 106,
  119, 130, 131,
  146, 156, 170,
  178, 180, 183,
  189, 217, 221,
  225
Jacob, 75, 139,
  165, 174
John, 48, 77, 140
John T., 175
Jonas, 229
Knight G., 98
Lewis M., 46
Margaret, 49
Martha, 165
Mary, 128, 140
Mrs., 121
Perenah, 156
Rachel, 140
Rebecca, 140
Richard, 177
Robert, 146
Samuel, 140,
  146, 165, 175,
  209
Sarah, 38
Seth, 12, 13, 30,
  70, 107, 121,
  138, 140, 148,
  175, 184, 210,
  237
Susanna, 173
T. W., 82
Thomas, 174
Thomas W., 135,
  149, 163
Treadwell, 147

Walter A., 214
Weadon, 177
William, 48, 50,
  62, 75, 77, 82,
  93, 101, 119,
  121, 146, 161,
  168, 177, 185,
  191, 229, 243
SMITLEY
  Catherine, 164
  John, 164
Snickers Gap
  Turnpike Co, 168
SNOUFFER
  George, 86
  Young, 86
SNUTZ
  ___, 236
SOBEY
  Thomas, 196
SORBOUGH
  John, 58
SOUDER
  Anthony, 6
  John, 57, 226
  Margaret, 23
  Michael, 23, 236
  Philip, 23, 57, 226
  Susan, 236
  Susannah, 226
SOUDERS
  ___, 91
SOWER
  B. W., 137, 243
SPENCE
  Betty, 59
  James, 65
  John, 10, 50, 63
  Mary F., 50, 239
  Nancy, 65
SPENCER
  John, 37, 177,
    221
  Margaret, 146,
    208
  William, 177
SPRING
  Adam, 139

Andrew, 71, 94,
163, 164
Casper, 23, 236
David, 94
Elizabeth, 94, 164
George, 164
Jacob, 164, 236
John, 94
Joseph, 94
Martha, 94
Mary, 94, 164
Michael, 34, 94,
101
Rachel, 34, 94,
101
Sarah, 164
Susannah, 164
STALKS
William, 145
STANNARD
Robert, 199
STARR
Christopher, 233,
234
James, 233, 234
Mary, 233
STATLER
John, 22, 56
Samuel, 166
STEADMAN
E., 99
STEAR
Isaac E., 127
STEARNS
Calvin, 166
Mary, 166
STEEL
William, 233
STEER
___, 183, 203
Benjamin, 5, 136
Elizabeth, 138
Isaac, 28, 183,
217
Isaac E., 12, 128,
165
Joseph, 36, 242

William, 23, 27,
125, 138, 139
William B., 36
William E., 35
STEPHENS
Henery, 8
Isaac, 146, 165
John B., 82
Thomas, 25
Thomas D., 48
Thomas H., 156
STEPHENSON
John, 51, 125,
169
STERRET
Samuel, 198
STERRETT
Samuel, 28, 61,
80
STEVENS
Henry, 155
John B., 185
Nancy, 179
Thomas, 179
STIDMAN
James, 49, 63,
156
STOCKS
Elizabeth, 16
Nathan, 24
William, 16, 24,
114, 200, 235
STOCKTON
L. W., 14
STONE
___, 184
Anthony, 50
Daniel, 64, 71,
76, 107, 153,
163, 184
James, 104
Peter, 102
T. S., 92
William H., 126
STONEBURNER
Catherine, 46,
102, 139
Christian, 102

Christiana, 152
Christina, 139
Daniel, 102, 132,
139, 158, 213
Elizabeth, 139
Henry, 102, 132,
139, 158
Jacob, 12, 109,
152
Margaret, 102,
139
Mary, 139
Peter, 102, 139,
213
Sarah, 102, 139
Susannah, 152
STONESTREET
___, 189, 232
Augustus, 37
Basil, 37
Bazil, 168
Benjamin A., 37
Eleanor, 39, 237,
239
Elizabeth S., 37
Gustavus, 168
Hester, 168
James E., 98
Mrs., 204
Richard, 40
Richard W., 39,
147, 237, 239
STOTT
Eliza, 23
STOUTSEN-
BERGER
Jacob, 133
John, 133
Samuel, 133, 237
STREAM
Pleasant, 154
William, 154
STRIBLING
Cecelia, 48, 123
Erasmus, 92
Francis, 48, 58,
123
Taliaferro, 48

STUBBLEFIELD
___, 129
___, 156
George, 35
James, 26, 35,
39, 58
Mary, 26
STUCK
___, 152
Ferdinando, 237
Peter, 94, 164,
237
STULL
John P., 180
STUMP
John, 104, 191
Joseph, 235
SUDDITH
___, 47
William, 91, 105
SUFFRON
Samuel, 208, 219
SULIVAN
Elizabeth, 74
Elizabeth B., 74
SULLIVAN
Catherine, 127
Eliza, 127, 146
Elizabeth, 35,
204, 207, 225
George, 189
James B., 146
John C., 127, 146
Luther O., 127,
129, 146
M., 5
Mary, 146
Matilda R., 146
Owen, 127, 129,
146
Wade, 146
Warner, 146
Winny, 189
SUMMERS
Albina, 52
C., 116
Edward, 57

Elizabeth, 173,
195
Jacob, 80, 85, 93,
100, 130, 173,
195
William, 52, 129,
155, 242
SURGHENOR
___, 7
SURGHNOR
John, 8, 10, 116,
137, 188, 215,
219, 222, 223
SUTHERLAND
Alexander, 230
Caleb C., 230,
232, 234
John, 230
Thomas, 230
SWAN
___, 191
SWANK
___, 152
SWANN
John, 56
Thomas, 36, 53,
54, 55, 91, 160,
198, 203, 227
SWART
Adrian, 44
Adrian L., 44
Alexander, 55,
76, 82, 91
Barnet, 55
Benjamin, 82
Bernard, 55, 76,
82
Bernard., 91
Elizabeth, 104
James, 44, 46,
76, 82, 91, 171,
213, 223
Martin H., 44
Matilda, 76, 82,
91
Polly, 82
Stella, 76, 82
William, 19

William R., 37,
100, 104, 178,
214
SWARTS
James, 121
SWAYNE
Thomas, 12, 40,
68
SWICK
Priscilla, 3
Thomas, 3
SWIFT
Ann, 243
Jonathan, 243
Mary D., 243
William R., 243
SYFERD
George, 181
SYPHARD
George, 100
Sarah, 100
SYPHERD
George, 41, 123,
196
Sarah, 123, 196

TALBOT
Joseph, 5
TALBOTT
___, 5
TALBURT
John, 85
TARLETON
Elizabeth, 212
James, 212
TATE
Levi, 30, 43, 47
Prescilla, 47
William, 47, 186
TAVENER
Eli, 24
George, 12, 78
John, 32
Jonah, 4, 30, 31,
76, 78, 104,
211
Joseph, 78
Miriam, 32

Nancy, 24
Stacey, 30
Stacy, 30, 47
TAVENNER
Eli, 113, 195
Elizabeth, 119
Johnathan, 119
Jonah, 48, 113,
119, 175, 210
Jonathan, 175
Joseph, 66, 227
Nancy, 195
Pleasant, 210
Stacy J., 236
TAVENOR
Richard, 127
TAVENTER
Jonah, 95
TAWPERMAN
John, 120
Peter, 120
TAWPERMON
Peter, 120
TAYLOR
___, 50, 208
Agnes, 222
Alice S., 98
Alice T., 98, 99,
186
B. F., 1
Benjamin, 50
Benjamin F., 125
Bernard, 9, 11,
38, 50, 58, 62,
74, 75, 77, 86,
129, 159
Catharine, 221
Charles, 102,
175, 195, 216,
220
David, 18
Griffin, 89, 190
Hannah, 128
Harriet, 171
Henry, 71, 130,
171
Henry G., 50
Henry S., 88, 135

Jemima, 176, 188
John, 116, 183,
206
John W., 176,
188
Joseph, 40, 82,
130, 133, 160,
188
Joseph D., 79
Lydia, 130, 188
Mahlon, 231
Mandley, 186
Mandly, 221, 222
Mary, 62, 130
Mary E., 208
Molly E., 216, 217
Nancy, 216
R. J., 204
Robert J., 46, 93,
103, 104, 116,
203, 208, 216,
217
Ruth, 198
Samuel E., 34
Sarah, 75, 171,
222
Simon T., 98, 99,
186
Stacey, 69
Stacy, 36, 52, 69,
81, 82, 109,
155, 164, 170,
175, 189, 198,
209, 231
Susan, 89
Susan A. R., 190
Susannah, 183
Thomas, 68
Thomas G., 99
Thomas S., 98,
186
Timothy, 24, 31,
50, 102, 111,
124, 175, 195,
210, 220
William, 29, 142,
192
William R., 186

Yardley, 11, 30,
35, 44, 47, 49,
50, 56, 75, 95,
97, 128, 134,
135, 144, 233
TEBBETTS
A. G., 73
TEBBS
___, 194
Betsey, 40, 50, 63
Betsy, 240
Charles B., 113
Elizabeth, 44
Foushee, 10, 11,
40, 44, 50, 63,
108
Foushee C., 63
Foushee F., 11
Hannah S., 50
M. H. D., 168
Margaret, 40, 44
Margaret H. D.,
113, 239
Samuel J., 50,
239
Thomas, 33
Thomas F., 50,
54, 113, 239
William W., 113
Willoughby W.,
10, 50, 63
TEMPLETON
John, 40
TERNY
William M., 205
THARP
David, 129
THATCHER
Calvin, 19
Richard, 19, 38,
84
THOMAS
___, 202
Daniel, 222
Eleazer, 242
Elizabeth U., 76
George, 89
Herod, 166

James, 33, 45,
63, 87, 96, 110,
144, 234
Jefferson C., 76,
197
John, 27, 63, 66,
121, 146, 185,
188
Joseph, 75, 76,
94
Joseph P., 216
Leonard, 75
Mary, 197
Phenehas, 188
Philip, 76, 94
Phinehas, 75
Roger B., 192
Thomas, 233
Thomas George &
Thomas, 68
THOMPKINS
Benjamin, 199
THOMPSON
___, 52, 162
Andrew, 132
Daniel, 127
Edward C., 145
James, 25, 37,
52, 62, 75, 109,
161, 162, 173,
188
Jonah, 77, 127,
184, 186
Lee, 50, 155
Nancy, 161
Reed, 32
Samuel, 58, 136,
148, 156
William, 37, 38,
63, 109, 143,
173, 188
THORNTON
___, 238
Benjamin, 83
Charles, 102,
109, 167, 207
Levi, 165
Mary, 207

Sarah, 207
THRASHER
Archibald, 143
Elias, 143, 227
John, 143
Malinda, 143
Sarah, 143
Thomas, 143
THRELKELD
William, 33
THRIFT
Maria, 167, 235
William, 6, 18, 22,
32, 47, 65, 80,
91, 98, 112,
114, 121, 141,
145, 167, 198,
214, 235
THROCKMORTON
Mordecai, 166
Mordicia, 198
TIDBALL
Alexander S., 123
TILLETT
Erasmus G., 98,
138, 157
Giles, 34, 39
Honor, 36, 51,
183
James, 85, 86,
88, 130, 145,
146, 173
Margaret, 36
Samuel, 36, 66,
67, 98, 113
Samuel A., 113
Uree, 173
TIMMS
Jesse, 6, 30, 48,
74, 90, 106,
113, 140, 154,
167, 173, 177,
204, 222, 224,
240, 242
William L., 130
TIPPET
Elizabeth, 115
John C., 115

TIPPETT
___, 189
Cartwright, 8, 115
Charles B., 160
Elizabeth, 8, 212
James, 155
John C., 27, 31
Mary A., 8
TITUS
Jeremiah, 57
Tunis, 65
TODD
Robert, 187
TOLBOTT
___, 164
TOMLINSON
Caroline, 4
William, 4
TORBERT
James, 192
John, 88, 192
Nancy, 88
Samuel, 88, 149,
192
William, 192
TORBET
John, 25
TORREYSON
John, 67, 111
Lewis, 111
Lydia, 148
Samuel, 148
TORRISON
William, 211
TOWNER
Jacob, 98
TOWPERMAN
Peter, 157
TRACEY
Everett, 119
Everitt, 119
Tamar, 119
Tamer, 119
TRAHORN
Asa, 211
TRAVENS
Joseph K., 117
TRAYHERN

Ruth, 20, 59
Thomas, 20, 59, 85
TRAYHORN
Thomas, 77
TRIBBE
___, 40
TRIBBY
Deborah, 81
Ephraim, 166
Jesse, 103, 204
John, 79, 208
Lydia, 79, 208
Mary, 170
Thomas, 81, 109, 170
TRIPLETT
___, 140
Enoch, 102, 133
Felix, 98, 190
J. S. L., 35
John C., 37
Margaret C., 50
Polly, 102
Reuben, 23, 146, 206
Reubin, 167
Thomas, 133
TRUNDLE
Daniel, 203
Mary E., 203
TUCKER
Nicholas, 154
William D., 120, 137
TULEY
Joseph, 14
TUNIS
Richard, 76
TURBERVILLE
___, 35
John, 20
TURLEY
James, 126
TURNER
Amanda M., 74
Charles, 11, 224
George, 242

Jonah, 9
Matilda, 11
Samuel, 55, 74
TURNEY
George, 234
TURNIPSEED
Henry, 39
TUSTIN
Samuel, 146
TUSTON
Septimus, 7
TUTT
Charles P., 36, 41, 111
TYLER
A., 38
Edmund, 34, 46, 62, 82, 119
Henry B., 11
John W., 11, 63
Nathaniel, 38, 160, 166, 189
William B., 51
TYLOR
Sarah, 51
TYTUS
Francis J., 149
Jane, 149
Tuenies, 149

UMBAUGH
___, 114, 209
Catherine, 56, 170
John, 15, 56, 113, 161, 170, 185
UNDERWOOD
John, 6, 86, 98
Margaret, 89
Samuel, 98
UPDIKE
Rufus, 49, 79, 111, 175
UPP
John, 100, 104, 185
Sarah, 100
URTON

___, 17, 57
UTTERBACK
William, 86

VANDENHEVEAL
J. C., 43
VANDENVENTER
Mary, 29
VANDEVANTER
___, 94
Anna, 89, 223
Elizabeth, 89
Fenton, 190
Gabriel, 46, 137
Gabril, 120
J., 53
John, 230
Joseph, 190
Joseph D., 223
Joseph L., 230
Sarah, 3, 138
William, 223
VANDEVENTER
Charles, 89
Isaac, 62
John, 89
Joseph, 89
William, 89
VANDEVORT
Jonathan, 166
VANHORN
Ann, 3
Craven, 203
Everline, 156
Ishmael, 100, 147, 156, 177
VANHORNE
Ishmael, 25, 191
John, 3, 206, 236
Sarah, 236
VANPELT
Richard, 76
VANSICKLE
Philip, 147
VANSICKLER
Philip, 144, 147
VANVACTER
Absalom, 35, 74

VANVACTOR
  Absalon, 57
VARNES
  John, 109
VERMILLION
  ___, 243
  Leven, 175
VERNON
  ___, 129
  Abner, 76
  Abraham, 34, 64
  Daniel, 9, 34, 64,
    76
  James, 23, 35,
    234
  John, 34, 64, 76,
    84
  Nancy, 35
  Phebe, 84
  Rebecca, 64, 180
  Rebeckah, 34
VERTS
  ___, 33
  Michael, 65
  Peter, 145
  William, 43
VERTZ
  ___, 165
VICKERS
  Abraham, 146,
    180
  Anna, 42, 180
  Archibald, 162
  Mary, 146
  Pleasant, 162
  Thomas, 146
  William, 25, 33,
    35, 42, 46, 146,
    200, 215
VICKROY
  Solomon, 186
VINCEL
  John, 109
VINCELL
  ___, 148
  George, 92, 214
  John, 92
  Philip, 92

VINSEL
  John, 196
  Mary, 196
VINSELL
  George, 6
VIOLET
  James, 42
  John, 42
VIOLETT
  Elijah, 8, 111, 201
  James, 201
  Jemima, 42
  John, 22, 69
  Phebe, 201
VIRTS
  Jacob, 17
  Michael, 57
  P., 194
VIRTZ
  Adam, 48
  Jacob, 17, 75,
    173
  Peter, 174
  Phebe, 103
  William, 103, 128,
    184
VOILET
  John, 75

WADE
  John, 126, 209
  Robert, 126
WAGGONER
  Elizabeth, 165,
    196
  Jacob, 165, 196
WAIGLEY
  George, 222
  Mary, 222
WAITE
  Obid, 129
  W. W., 137
WALDRON
  Celia, 76
WALKER
  Alice, 12
  Benjamin, 206,
    236, 237

Craven, 12, 13,
    132, 148, 175,
    193
  Fanny, 132, 227
  Garrett, 41, 48,
    219, 236
  Isaac, 9, 29, 36,
    68, 129, 134
  John, 9
  Joseph, 236, 237
  Letititia, 9
  Lewis, 12, 68, 87
  Sophia, 236
  Thornton, 86,
    131, 132, 147,
    167, 193, 195,
    227
WALLACE
  David M., 63
WALTERS
  Jacob, 66
WALTMAN
  ___, 58, 183
  David, 121, 128,
    147
  Elias, 42, 63, 70,
    135, 174
  Emanuel, 21, 42,
    49, 57, 63, 69,
    128, 135, 145,
    157, 174
  Jacob, 21, 42, 49,
    57, 63, 66, 69,
    118, 121, 122,
    128, 135, 141,
    157, 174, 178,
    212
  John, 44, 121,
    144, 147
  Joseph, 42, 46,
    53, 123, 126,
    128, 141, 145,
    174, 196
  Margaret, 42
  Maria, 44, 147
  Martha, 69, 141
  Mary, 178
  Mary Ann, 42

Rachael, 42
Samuel, 21, 118
Susannah, 42
WAR
John, 172
WARD
Samuel, 43
WARFORD
___, 40, 161
Abraham, 157
Betsey, 108
Elizabeth, 85, 92, 157
James, 85, 89, 92
John, 188
William, 157
WARNER
___, 208
George, 134, 135, 233
Peter, 25
WARR
John, 166
WASHINGTON
Hannah, 239
Perrin, 238, 239
WATERMAN
___, 241
A. G., 62, 104, 108, 121, 122, 125, 146, 172
Albert G., 175, 217
Waterman & Camp, 62
WATERS
Benjamin, 110
Jacob, 26, 39, 41, 44, 49, 94, 121, 145, 147, 157, 171, 177
Levi, 226
WATKINS
Bernard, 95
WATT
Dewanner, 153
Dewanner G., 147

Duanna, 39, 40
Gill, 174
John G., 9, 39, 40, 110
WATTERS
Sarah, 207
WATTSON
Thomas, 135
WAUGH
Alexander, 20, 212
Beverly, 29
WEADON
John, 30, 137, 168
WEATHERBY
Jane, 37
Mathew, 230
WEATHERLY
Peter, 67
WEATHEROW
John, 113
WEBB
John, 169
William, 84
WEEK
Burr, 147
WEEKS
Burr, 62, 79, 95, 120, 122, 125, 146, 176, 223, 243
James, 109, 110
WELLER
Catharine, 229
Henry, 229
WELLS
Asa, 19
WELSH
James, 237
WELTY
Elizabeth, 102, 103
WENNER
Daniel, 134
Elizabeth, 21
George, 20

John, 20, 21, 124, 134, 171, 173
Jonathan, 42, 126, 132, 141, 145
Mary, 20
Susanna, 42
William, 20, 21, 134
WERG
Anna, 29
WERTS
John, 171
WERTZ
Henry, 115, 159, 208
William, 129, 156
WESLEY
John, 96, 184
WEST
Erasmus, 58
Hannah, 211
James, 231
James H., 195
John, 169, 211
WHALEY
James, 118
Levi, 187
WHARTON
C. H. W., 111
Charles W., 80
WHEELER
Thomas, 102
WHEERY
Mrs., 2
WHITACRE
Alice, 123
Amos, 48, 50
John, 50, 198, 210, 226
Thomas, 188
WHITE
___, 126
B., 134
B. W., 65
Beniah, 18
Benjamin, 15, 71
Daniel, 142

Elizabeth, 79,
    115, 199
Garret, 70
James, 202, 229,
    231, 233
Jane, 201
John, 10, 25, 28,
    35, 36, 38, 52,
    55, 58, 59, 70,
    74, 76, 81, 82,
    87, 96, 99, 101,
    106, 108, 109,
    110, 112, 115,
    119, 123, 129,
    142, 148, 149,
    151, 154, 155,
    156, 161, 162,
    167, 173, 175,
    176, 179, 186,
    188, 189, 200,
    201, 204, 219,
    226, 229, 230,
    231
Josabed, 35
Joseph, 142, 179,
    231
Joshua, 58
Josiah, 28, 41,
    58, 115, 141,
    149, 150, 173,
    215
Jozabed, 8, 60,
    73, 81, 115,
    121
Leah, 115
Levi, 2, 25, 142,
    161
Mary, 36, 214
Mrs., 165
Rachel, 115, 199
Richard, 79
Robert, 36, 58,
    154, 214
Samuel, 218
Samuel K., 213
Thomas, 2, 5, 7,
    13, 32, 58, 64,
    67, 77, 78, 89,

102, 103, 107,
    112, 128, 145,
    151, 158, 174,
    186, 187, 191,
    204, 226, 229,
    231
Washington, 79,
    115, 199
William, 25, 115,
    142, 161, 218,
    231
White &
    Clendening, 29
WHITELY
    Alexander, 205
WHITING
    Carlyle F., 241
    George B., 82, 91
WHITMAN
    Michael, 14
WHITTLE
    Thomas, 114
WHORTON
    C. H. W., 138
WICKLEFF
    Agnes, 228
    Agness, 227, 228
    Moses, 227, 228
    Nancy, 227, 228
    Robert, 227, 228
WICKLIFFE
    Agness, 178
    Moses, 178
    Nancy, 178
    Robert, 178
WIGGINGTON
    Presley, 10
    Sarah Ann, 10
WILDMAN
    ___, 11, 187, 191,
    204, 226
    Bennett H., 152,
    158
    Charles B., 152
    Charles J. B., 158
    Eleanor, 6, 83
    Eleanor A., 158

Elizabeth A., 152,
    158
Ellen A., 152
Enos, 22, 32, 57,
    61, 63, 104,
    105, 146, 152,
    157, 158, 205,
    213, 235
Jane, 32, 57, 147,
    174
Jane D., 158
John, 6, 54, 83
John H., 152
John W., 158
Martin, 97
William, 48
WILKERSON
    John, 4
WILKINS
    A., 156
WILKINSON
    ___, 23, 26, 94
    A. C., 66
    Anna, 237
    Elizabeth, 81
    Evan, 112, 114
    Hannah, 237
    John, 114, 146,
    184, 237, 238
    Mary, 237
    William, 1, 20, 50,
    93, 97, 149
WILKISON
    Evan, 173, 202
    William, 224
WILKS
    John, 93
WILLIAM
    John, 184
    Levi, 223
    Notley C., 19
WILLIAMS
    ___, 21, 90, 203,
    235
    Alse, 118
    Charles, 217
    Daniel, 7
    Eliza, 7, 56

Elizabeth, 183, 184
Ellis, 7
Eneas, 16, 24
Enos, 56, 79, 164, 237, 241
Henrietta, 167
Israel, 30, 145, 161, 163, 232, 237
James, 176
Jane, 159
John, 3, 7, 10, 11, 36, 42, 48, 56, 79, 114, 128, 163, 165, 178, 183, 184, 211, 234
John W., 30, 66
Joseph, 7
Martha, 7
Mary, 7
Milly, 237
Moses, 71
N. C., 10, 64, 151, 160, 168, 206
Nancy, 52, 162, 184
Notley C., 5, 15, 17, 25, 33, 34, 57, 59, 64, 65, 73, 75, 84, 89, 123, 128, 129, 130, 139, 141, 142, 159, 162, 169, 170, 181, 182, 183, 186, 194, 199, 208, 211, 212, 214, 216, 226, 239, 241, 243
Phenias, 238
Phineas, 163
Presley, 159
Resin, 99
Richard, 118
Samuel, 157, 160

Sidnor, 79
Sydnah, 56
Sydney, 163
Sydnor, 238
William, 184
WILLIAMSON
William, 188
WILLIS
Carver, 29
WILLSON
John, 19
Sarah, 19
WILSON
___, 169
Charlotte, 97
Daniel, 221
Ebenezer, 109, 201
Edward, 37, 120, 233, 234
Elizabeth, 35, 86, 131
Hannah, 35, 37, 160
Hannah P., 62
Isaac, 97
J., 117
J. L., 50
James B., 10, 94, 128, 243
John, 125, 169, 190
John K., 241
John M., 69, 71, 88, 242
John T., 93, 97
Moses, 10, 128
Robert, 220, 230, 231
Sarah, 169
Stephen, 35, 37, 49, 50, 58, 62, 74, 75, 86, 159, 160, 161, 220, 223, 229
Tamar, 10
William, 35, 58, 220

WILTER
Catherine, 158
Jacob, 158
WINCEL
___, 52
George, 43
WINCOOP
John, 184
Philip, 184
WINE
Catherine, 136
Daniel, 130, 136, 192
Elizabeth, 136
George, 136
Jacob, 28, 136
John, 133, 202, 214
Margaret, 136
WINEGARDNER
Adam, 15, 79
WINN
___, 142
John, 4
WINSEL
George, 114, 145
John, 91
WIRE
David, 71, 91
WIRTS
Elizabeth, 171
Henry, 171
Jacob, 49, 171, 196
Leah, 171
Loucinda, 171
Mary A., 171
Peter, 52, 171
Susannah, 171
William, 171
WIRTZ
Peter, 29, 202
William, 182
WISE
George, 45, 104, 105, 191
WOLF

John, 200, 201,
   202
Sarah, 201, 202
WOLFORD
   John, 23, 95, 133
   William, 25, 141
WOOD
   Eliza, 127, 146
   J. J., 39
   James, 121, 153
   John W., 22, 179,
      197
   Joseph, 5, 20, 66,
      162, 167, 168,
      204, 226
   Lydia, 5, 20
   Thomas, 127, 146
WOODFORD
   ___, 45, 100
WOODS
   James, 11, 157
WOODY
   Elizabeth, 61, 62
   Mrs., 56
   William, 68
WOODYARD
   Walter, 29
WOOSTER
   Boston, 33
WORSLEY
   John, 56, 67, 127,
      167, 183, 235
WRIGHT
   ___, 74
   Aaron, 103
   Alfred, 137
   Ann, 28
   Anthony, 7, 67,
      105, 154

Christianna, 154
Isaac, 27, 54, 223
John, 28, 29, 50,
   72, 77, 102,
   112, 154, 184,
   186, 202
Joseph H., 103,
   132, 137
Jotham, 11, 157
Lewis, 154
Mary, 132
Nancy, 103, 132,
   137
Patterson, 7, 103,
   132, 136, 137,
   192
R. L., 102
Samuel, 154
Sarah, 154
William, 75, 103,
   121, 122, 132,
   136, 137
WYCOFF
   James, 162
WYNKOOP
   Gerrard, 76
WYNN
   John, 1, 93, 97,
      107, 142
WYSELL
   Frederick, 100

YAKEY
   Simon, 97
YEAKEY
   ___, 153
YEAKY
   Simon, 112
YOUNG

Agnes, 228
Agness, 227, 228
Alexander, 8
Archibald, 119
Benjamin, 228
Benjamin S., 178,
   227, 228
Catharine, 228
David, 30, 31, 47,
   59, 62, 95, 132,
   139, 186, 200,
   220
Elizabeth, 178,
   182, 186, 220,
   228
George, 220
Henry, 200
Isaac, 100
John, 178, 182,
   186
Lois, 186
Manderick, 88
Margaret, 100
Masekeh, 46
Nancy, 178, 227,
   228
Sarah, 227, 228
Stanley, 182
Thomas, 8, 220
Thomas H., 119
William, 47, 151,
   186, 228

ZIMMERMAN
   ___, 28, 44, 62,
      161, 168
   Adam, 38
   Eliza, 38
   Henry, 38

Loudoun County, Virginia Will Book Abstracts, Books A-Z, Dec. 1757-Jun. 1841

Loudoun County, Virginia Will Book Abstracts, Books 2A-3C, Jun. 1841-Dec. 1879 and Superior Court Books A and B, 1810-1888

Loudoun County, Virginia Will Book Index, 1757-1946

Genealogical Abstracts from The Brunswick Herald, *Brunswick, Maryland: Mar. 6 1891-Dec. 28 1894*

Genealogical Abstracts from The Brunswick Herald, *Brunswick, Maryland: Jan. 4 1895-Dec. 30 1898*

Genealogical Abstracts from The Brunswick Herald, *Brunswick, Maryland: Jan. 6 1899-Dec. 26 1902*

Genealogical Abstracts from The Brunswick Herald, *Brunswick, Maryland: Jan. 2 1903-June 29 1906*

Genealogical Abstracts from The Brunswick Herald, *Brunswick, Maryland: July 6 1906-Feb. 25 1910*

CD: *Loudoun County, Virginia Personal Property Tax List, 1782-1850*

323333